Teaching Students With High-Incidence Disabilities

This book is dedicated to Herman B. and Barbara M. Prater

SAGE was founded in 1965 by Sara Miller McCune to support the dissemination of usable knowledge by publishing innovative and high-quality research and teaching content. Today, we publish over 900 journals, including those of more than 400 learned societies, more than 800 new books per year, and a growing range of library products including archives, data, case studies, reports, and video. SAGE remains majority-owned by our founder, and after Sara's lifetime will become owned by a charitable trust that secures our continued independence.

Los Angeles | London | New Delhi | Singapore | Washington DC | Melbourne

Teaching Students With High-Incidence Disabilities

Strategies for Diverse Classrooms

Mary Anne Prater
Brigham Young University

SAGE

Los Angeles | London | New Delhi
Singapore | Washington DC | Melbourne

FOR INFORMATION:

SAGE Publications, Inc.
2455 Teller Road
Thousand Oaks, California 91320
E-mail: order@sagepub.com

SAGE Publications Ltd.
1 Oliver's Yard
55 City Road
London, EC1Y 1SP
United Kingdom

SAGE Publications India Pvt. Ltd.
B 1/I 1 Mohan Cooperative Industrial Area
Mathura Road, New Delhi 110 044
India

SAGE Publications Asia-Pacific Pte. Ltd.
3 Church Street
#10-04 Samsung Hub
Singapore 049483

Acquisitions Editor: Terri Accomazzo
Editorial Assistant: Erik Helton
eLearning Assistant: Chelsey Postal
Production Editor: Bennie Clark Allen
Copy Editor: Diane DiMura
Typesetter: C&M Digitals (P) Ltd.
Proofreader: Sue Schon
Indexer: Jean Casalegno
Cover Designer: Candice Harman
Marketing Manager: Kara Kindstrom

Printed in the United States of America

Library of Congress Cataloging-in-Publication Data

ISBN: 978-1-4833-9059-8

This book is printed on acid-free paper.

SUSTAINABLE FORESTRY INITIATIVE

Certified Chain of Custody
Promoting Sustainable Forestry
www.sfiprogram.org
SFI-01268

SFI label applies to text stock

17 18 19 20 21 10 9 8 7 6 5 4 3 2 1

Brief Contents

Contents

1   Learner Characteristics and Special Education Laws   2

5   Assessment for Instruction   178

6   Teacher-Directed Instruction   218

7   Supporting Students in General Education   258

8 Student-Mediated Instruction 304

9 Strategies for Learning 334

Preface

Two early life events started me on my current career path. At age seven, I started writing a book. At the time I had no idea of the magnitude of such an endeavor. And at age 14, I was teaching children in a church-sponsored setting. I adored the opportunity to touch the lives of those not much younger than I. The book I started to write at age 7 was never finished, but I have never stopped teaching.

One of my passions is ensuring students who don't learn easily receive quality instruction. As a former special educator and one who has taught special education methods of instruction at the university level for years, I have not been satisfied with the textbooks available on this topic. So it made perfect sense to take the information I did teach and write one. *Teaching Students With High-Incidence Disabilities* was written for use in undergraduate and graduate courses preparing future special educators to teach students with learning disabilities, emotional behavioral disorders, intellectual disabilities, attention deficit hyperactivity, and high functioning autism. This book can also serve as a reference for those who have already received formal preparation in how to teach special needs students.

The book begins with a description of the characteristics of students for whom these methods of instruction are effective followed by a description of the legal basis on which special education is defined in the United States. Chapter 1, then, provides the context for the rest of the book. Chapters 2, 3, 4, and 5 address skills ancillary to, but necessary for, effective instruction to take place in the classroom. Chapter 2 provides an overview of the collaborative process and related skills necessary for special educators. Behavior management and organizational skills, also critical for the success of students, are presented in Chapter 3. Chapter 4 addresses using technology with individual students and in classroom instruction, and Chapter 5 explores the role of assessment for learning.

Chapters 6, 7, 8, and 9 comprise the core of instructional methods. Chapter 6 begins this section by outlining effective teaching practices that are teacher directed through explicit instruction. Focusing on access to the general education curriculum, Chapter 7 describes how to differentiate instruction and provide accommodation for students with high-incidence disabilities. Chapter 8 focuses on teaching students to mediate their own instruction through cooperative learning and peer tutoring. General strategies necessary for learning, including attention, mnemonic, organizing, study, test-taking, and notetaking strategies, are addressed in Chapter 9. Strategies presented in these four chapters are effective across all content areas.

Chapter 10 through 14 address specific curricular areas, including reading and writing (Chapter 10), mathematics (Chapter 11), science and social studies (Chapter 12), social and emotional learning (Chapter 13), and life skills (Chapter 14). Where appropriate, each chapter discusses difficulties that students with high-incidence disabilities may encounter in the particular curricular area, content-based standards promoted for all students including students with disabilities, and specific strategies for teaching students with high-incidence disabilities these content areas. Chapter 14 also focuses on transition from secondary to postsecondary life, including learning, working, living, and playing.

Several helpful features are included in each chapter. For example, each chapter begins with a list of key ideas and learning objectives. Interspersed throughout each chapter are boxed features:

- **Technology Spotlights** provide additional information on how technology can be applied to the topics discussed. Within these spotlights are descriptions of websites, assistive technology devices, teacher tools, and so forth.

- **Short Case Studies** provide real-life examples of students and teachers applying the skills to be addressed.

- **Teacher Tips** give teachers concrete ideas to apply related to chapter content.

Each chapter addresses implications for students from culturally and/or linguistically diverse populations; and each ends with a summary, review questions and activities, and the Council for Exceptional Children standards covered within the chapter. Also, seven sample lesson plans in the Appendix offer clear and specific examples of teacher-directed instruction for teaching students with high-incidence disabilities.

In writing this book, I have focused on scientifically or evidence-based practices. The methods described here have been validated through experimental research. In several cases, however, I mention that the research is limited and the topic warrants further study. Some current practices that have not been empirically validated were deliberately excluded. Most of the material is based on the behavioral model of learning, with additional attention given to constructivism.

As with all projects of this magnitude, more people than I could begin to mention influenced and supported me in this endeavor. I am appreciative of my colleagues who influenced a previous version of this book—namely, Rhonda Black, Nari Carter, Dave Edyburn, Gordon Gibb, Cecily Ornelles, and Garnett Smith; and to my friend and colleague, Tom Sileo with whom I have written much and learned more than I could measure. I also thank Ellie Young for her willingness to share her incredible expertise in social emotional learning and coauthoring Chapter 13. And I could not have completed this book without the support of my current office compadres, Tina Dyches, Lynnette Erickson, Al Merkley, and Jeanna Nichols. They cheered me on and celebrated with me through all stages of this process. Members of the editorial team at Sage are also to be thanked and credited here for the contributions they made to help me see this project come to fruition. I also wish to thank the reviewers who provided invaluable feedback and suggestions and who are listed separately.

This book is dedicated to my parents, Herman Bates and Barbara Mathis Prater, who thought I should study business or law, but who always supported my decision to become a special educator and who never doubted, ever since I was seven years old, that I would someday write a book.

Mary Anne Prater

Digital Resources

SAGE edge offers a robust online environment you can access anytime, anywhere, and features an impressive array of free tools and resources to keep you on the cutting edge of your learning experience. Visit the open-access SAGE edge website at **edge.sagepub.com/prater**.

SAGE edge for Instructors supports your teaching by making it easy to integrate quality content and create a rich learning environment for students.

- **Test banks** provide a diverse range of pre-written options as well as the opportunity to edit any question and/or insert your own personalized questions to effectively assess students' progress and understanding.

- Editable, chapter-specific **PowerPoint® slides** offer complete flexibility for creating a multimedia presentation for your course.

- EXCLUSIVE! Access to full-text **SAGE journal articles** that have been carefully selected to support and expand on the concepts presented in each chapter.

- **Multimedia content** appeals to students with different learning styles.

- **Lecture notes** summarize key concepts by chapter to help you prepare for lectures and class discussions.

SAGE edge for Students provides a personalized approach to help you accomplish your coursework goals in an easy-to-use learning environment.

- Mobile-friendly **eFlashcards** strengthen your understanding of key terms and concepts.

- Mobile-friendly practice **quizzes** allow you to independently assess your mastery of course material.

- An online **action plan** allows you to track your progress through the course and materials and to individualize your learning experience.

- **Learning objectives** reinforce the most important material.

- **Multimedia** web links make it easy to mine internet resources and further explore topics.

- EXCLUSIVE! Access to full-text **SAGE journal articles** that have been carefully chosen to support and expand on the concepts presented in each chapter.

Acknowledgments

SAGE Publishing gratefully acknowledges the following reviewers for their kind assistance:

Beverly Barkon, *Carlow University*

John Beach, *Curry College*

Patricia A. Becker, *Cardinal Stritch University*

Kathleen R. Biddle, *Juniata College*

Sally Brannan, *Wittenberg University*

Donald D. Deshler, *University of Kansas*

Nicole Dobbins, *University of North Carolina, Greensboro*

Maryann Dudzinski, *Valparaiso University*

Sara Flanagan, *University of Kentucky*

Heather Garrison, *East Stroudsburg University of Pennsylvania*

Bruce A. Golmic, *Robert Morris University*

Judy Harris-Looby, *Barry University*

Veda Jairrels, *Clark Atlanta University*

Endia J. Lindo, *University of North Texas*

Steven LoCascio, *New Jersey City University/Saint Peter's University*

Marie C. McGrath, *Immaculata University*

Diane D. Painter, *Shenandoah University*

Misty Vetter Parsley, *Lipscomb University*

Belinda Conrad Richardson, *Bellarmine University*

Eric Shyman, *St. Joseph's College, New York*

Jane M. Sileo, *State University of New York at New Paltz*

Carol Strax, *Dominican College*

Stathene Varvisotis, *University of Nebraska, Kearney*

Kim Viel-Ruma, *University of Georgia*

Roberta Lois Wohle, *Fairleigh Dickinson University*

Clara Wolman, *Barry University*

Ruth Zealand, *The College of New Rochelle*

Ruth Zealand, *The College of New Rochelle*

About the Author

Mary Anne Prater

Mary Anne Prater is dean of the David O. McKay School of Education and a professor and former chair of the Department of Counseling Psychology and Special Education at Brigham Young University. She earned her PhD at Utah State University and was a Post-doctoral Fellow at the University of Kentucky in 1997.

Prior to joining the faculty at BYU in 2001, Dr. Prater was professor, department chair, and associate dean at the University of Hawaii at Manoa (11 years); assistant professor at Southern Illinois University at Carbondale (3 years); and adjunct professor at the University of Alaska at Anchorage.

She has authored or coauthored eight books and over 70 refereed articles. One book was translated into Korean and another into Arabic. Dr. Prater has presented or co-presented over 100 professional presentations nationally and internationally. In addition, she has worked in various professional leadership positions, including serving as the president of the Teacher Education Division (TED) of the international Council for Exceptional Children (CEC) in 2015.

About the Contributor

Ellie Young

Ellie Young is an associate professor of school psychology at Brigham Young University. She worked as a school psychologist in Kansas and Missouri for 9 years prior to earning her PhD from the University of South Florida. She has been employed by BYU since 2001. In addition to her numerous journal publications and professional presentations, Dr. Young is coauthor of the book, *Positive Behavior Support in Secondary Schools: A Practical Guide* (Guilford Press, 2012).

©iStockphoto.com/Steve Debenport

Learner Characteristics and Special Education Laws

Definitions and Prevalence Rates

There are at least three reasons why a methods-of-instruction textbook includes a large section on characteristics of students with **high-incidence disabilities (HID)**. First, the number of students with diverse learning needs is increasing dramatically within the United States. Students with specialized needs represent those not only with confirmed disabilities, but those considered at risk for school failure due to familial or environmental factors as well as those who are English learners (EL). Teachers need to be prepared to work with all types of learners with special needs.

Second, in order for teachers to be familiar with their students, they must have a broad understanding of their students' distinctiveness. Students who receive specialized services qualify for these services because they were not succeeding in the general education system. In this chapter, how students with HID differ from their nondisabled counterparts is explained. As with all similar discussions, there is risk in making statements that are assumed to apply to all individuals within the group. Keep in mind at all times that the statements made in this book are generalizations. Students are individuals with their own unique needs and characteristics. Teachers should become acquainted with each student as an individual.

Third, understanding learner characteristics provides background information on why particular methods of instruction and strategies are effective for this population. Knowing that students with HID often have memory difficulties, for example, helps teachers understand why mnemonic strategies are important to use, particularly for students with HID.

Chapter 1 is divided into two sections. In the first section, definitions of HID are discussed including prevalence rates and specific learner characteristics that impact instruction. An overview of laws and reform efforts that have impacted the field of special education for over 50 years comprise the second section. In the United States, such legislation defines what special education is and who qualifies for these services. Thus, educators must have a solid understanding of the laws that ground their profession.

Before discussing definitions and characteristics, **person-first language** used throughout the book must be introduced. Rather than referring to students with disabilities as intellectually disabled, emotionally disturbed, learning disabled, or autistic, this population should be referred to as students with intellectual disabilities, emotional disturbance, learning disabilities, or autism. When referring to students in this way, person-first language is being used. Language can be a powerful tool. The words people use reflect their attitudes, perceptions, beliefs, and assumptions. Person-first language goes beyond political correctness; it places the focus on the individual, rather than on the disability. The use of person-first language helps us remember that all people are unique and that certain abilities or disabilities are attributes but do not define who these students are.

Learning Objectives

- Compare and contrast the learning characteristics among students with learning disabilities, emotional/behavior disabilities, intellectual disabilities, high-functioning autism, and attention-deficit/hyperactivity disorder.

- Discuss the implications of increased diversity in the student population on the field of special education. Include examples of linguistic, cultural, and socioeconomic diversity, as well as changing family structures.

- Describe the major tenants of the Individuals with Disabilities Education Act, Section 504 of the Rehabilitation Act, and The Elementary and Secondary Education Act and how they impact special education services in the United States.

- Outline the IEP process. Include the requirements to be included on all IEP documents as well as who attends IEP meetings and what role they each play.

Before receiving special education services in the United States, students must qualify under the criteria provided through the **Individuals with Disabilities Education Act (IDEA).** First passed in 1975, reauthorized by the U.S. Congress in 1997 and again most recently in 2004, the Act defines who qualifies for special education services. Although researchers continue to study the characteristics of students with disabilities, in practice, the U.S. federal government defines what those characteristics must be in order to qualify for special education services. Hopefully the laws mandating and defining special education reflect best practice identified by researchers. Educators preparing to teach students with HID must have an understanding not only of research-based learner characteristics, but they must understand the legal criteria and definitions of the populations they are teaching.

Categorical Versus Cross-Categorical Disabilities

IDEA states that between ages 3 and 9 students can be identified as developmentally delayed in one or more of the following areas: physical, cognitive, communication, social/emotional, or adaptive development (U.S. Department of Education [USDOE], 2014). After age 9, students qualify for special education if they have been diagnosed with one or more of the following; this is considered the categorical approach to identification:

- specific learning disabilities,

- speech or language impairments,

- intellectual disabilities,

- emotional disturbance,

- multiple disabilities,

- hearing impairments,

- orthopedic impairments,

- other health impairments,

- visual impairment,

- autism,

- deaf-blindness, or

- traumatic brain injury.

Historically, the **categorical approach** to identifying students for special education services became the foundation for the services provided. In other words, students identified with different disabilities under IDEA were not mixed within classrooms. For example, students with learning disabilities were not educated in the same classroom as children with emotional disturbance. The diagnosis of the student was assumed to imply the type of services and instruction needed (Benner, 1998). Teacher certification or licensure was also based on disabling conditions. For example, students with learning disabilities (LD) were educated in LD classrooms by LD certified teachers.

Over time, educators and advocates recognized that students with HID have more in common with each other than they have differences. Schools began to educate students with various disabilities within the same classroom and states began to collapse areas of teacher licensure. The labels mild, moderate, or severe disabilities were thought to better reflect the instructional needs of students (Benner, 1998). These labels also focused attention away from the type of disability. Special educators often refer to this as a **cross-categorical approach**. Conversely, grouping students by their disability category (e.g., learning disabilities or intellectual disabilities) was considered a categorical approach to special education. Teacher licensure also followed the pattern away from categorical toward cross-categorical preparation. Rather than becoming a licensed LD or ED (**emotional disturbance**) teacher, for example, teachers were prepared and licensed to educate students with mild to moderate disabilities. Teachers with mild to moderate certification were qualified to teach students with mild to moderate LD, ID and ED. In most states the delivery of services and teacher licensure does not follow the strict categorical distinctions. However, IDEA still includes these categories for identifying students for special education services, and research supports some distinct differences.

Technically, HID are defined as those that occur in more than 100,000 people in the United States. For the purposes of this book, HID refers to students with learning disabilities (LD), emotional/behavioral disorders (EBD), mild to moderate intellectual disabilities (ID), high-functioning autism (HFA) and attention–deficit/hyperactivity disorder (ADHD). Four of the five are included in IDEA as disabling conditions; ADHD is not included in IDEA. However, many students with ADHD are identified as having other health impairment (OHI) as their disabling condition under IDEA. Given that OHI encompasses more than students with ADHD, the label ADHD will be used throughout the book. In addition, students with ADHD have several learning needs similar to other HID and so ADHD is included in this book.

For years, LD, EBD, mild to moderate ID, and ADHD were grouped together and labeled mild to moderate disabilities. With the increased number of students being identified with high-functioning autism, they are now often included in this group. Research documents that students with HID, including HFA, perform similarly on school tasks with the exception of behavioral performance of students with EBD (Gage, Lierheimer, & Goran, 2012). However, such global statements about similarities have been challenged. For example, Emily Bouck and Rajiv Satsangi (2015) analyzed data from over a million students and reported that students with mild ID demonstrated achievement levels significantly lower to that of other students with HID. Achievement level differences resulted in students with mild ID receiving different educational programming than their peers (e.g., curriculum, accommodations, instructional environments). Bouck and Satsangi argue that students with mild ID are quantitatively and qualitatively different than other students with HID.

Generally speaking, students with HFA and students with HID can participate in typical school curriculum with additional learning and support. Although the term *curriculum* is used to mean many things, within the context of this book, **curriculum** is defined as an interrelated set of instructional plans and activities based on specified content that when implemented lead to student learning outcomes. Depending upon the state, special educators who educate and support students with HID might be licensed as cross-categorical, high-incidence, or mild/moderate special educators.

The percentage of the student population who are 6 to 21 years of age served under IDEA in four of the disabling conditions (excluding ADHD) during 2003 and 2012 appear in Table 1.1. (ADHD is not included because students with ADHD are not served under IDEA unless categorized as OHI.) Clearly, prevalence rates have changed during that time period. This may have occurred for at least two reasons. The definitions and the manner in which educators are identifying students have varied over time. Also, unlike most low incidence disabilities, HID are not medically defined. No physical markers substantiate the diagnosis, so professional judgment is often necessary. This has contributed to the changes in prevalence rates over time.

TABLE 1.1   Percentage of Student Population Ages 6–21 Served Under IDEA

Disability	2003	2012
Learning Disability	4.3	3.4
Intellectual Disability	0.9	0.6
Emotional/Behavior Disorder	0.7	0.5
Autism	0.2	0.7

Source: U.S. Department of Education (2014).

Students may be diagnosed with more than one disability. Students with ADHD, for example, frequently exhibit characteristics of other disabling conditions. Identifying students as ADHD is particularly difficult given their learning and behavioral profiles are similar to students with LD and/or EBD (Salend & Rohena, 2003). In fact, this was a major argument to not include ADHD as a separate disabling condition in the reauthorization of IDEA in 1997. One study found that a learning disability was present in 70% of the children identified as ADHD (Mayes, Calhoun, & Crowell, 2000). Another national study found that 4% of children between the ages of 6 and 11 years of age were diagnosed as having both ADHD and LD (Pastor & Reuben, 2002). Researchers have also estimated that between 9% and 19% of school-age students with intellectual disabilities meet criteria for an ADHD diagnosis (Handen, Janosky, & McAuliffe, 1997). These are only examples of the percentage of learners who may qualify for special education services under more than one disabling condition.

In the next section, a brief discussion of the definitions for each of the categories of HID is presented. Definitions have changed in the past and will change again in the future as professionals continue to learn more about these conditions.

IDEA High-Incidence Disabilities

As stated earlier, four of the five high-incidence disabling conditions addressed in this book are included in IDEA. They include LD, EBD, ID, and autism. The fifth condition, ADHD is not included in IDEA although students with ADHD can receive special education services through IDEA if identified as having an OHI.

Learning Disabilities

Sandie is a fourth-grade student who lives in a metropolitan U.S. suburb with her mother and younger brother, Sam. Although she's small for her age, her physical and emotional development are typical. When asked, she says her favorite activities are riding her bike, playing board games with Sam, and baking cookies with her mother.

In school, Sandie's favorite subject is art. Her least favorite subject is reading. She has a lot of friends and is characterized by both her teacher and her peers as being a leader. Sandie's third-grade teacher, Mrs. Morris, became concerned when Sandie wasn't keeping up with her peers in reading. Mrs. Morris talked to Sandie's mother and with her consent referred Sandie for testing. According to the school's diagnostic team, Sandie scored above average on the intelligence test, average in math, and more than 2 years below her grade level in reading and written language skills. Sandie qualified for special education services as having a learning disability in reading and written language.

Except when Sandie attends the resource room for 1-hour a day to work on her reading and writing skills, she remains in her general fourth-grade class. Although she is making progress, her disabilities impact performance in subject areas that require independent reading and writing. Sandie's special education teacher, Ms. Underwood, and her fourth-grade teacher, Mr. Quinn, have worked together to modify some of the general education requirements so Sandie can gain the information without needing to independently read material. In addition, when agreed upon by her teacher, Sandie demonstrates her content knowledge orally rather than through written responses.

Learning disabilities (LD) is the most prevalent disability in the United States. In the most recent count, LD represented between 3% and 4% of the total population and about 41% of all students with disabilities served under IDEA (USDOE, 2014). The IDEA definition for specific learning disabilities follows:

Specific learning disability is defined as follows:

(A) In general.—The term 'specific learning disability' means a disorder in 1 or more of the basic psychological processes involved in understanding or in using language, spoken or written, which disorder may manifest itself in the imperfect ability to listen, think, speak, read, write, spell, or do mathematical calculations.

(B) Disorders included.—Such term includes such conditions as perceptual disabilities, brain injury, minimal brain dysfunction, dyslexia, and developmental aphasia.

(C) Disorders not included.—Such term does not include a learning problem that is primarily the result of visual, hearing, or motor disabilities, of [intellectual disabilities], of emotional disturbance, or of environmental, cultural, or economic disadvantage. (IDEA, 2004, Sec. 602[30])

Historically, the most common method for identifying learning disabilities has involved both an aptitude-achievement discrepancy and exclusionary criteria (Buttner & Hasselhorn, 2011). Aptitude is represented by general intelligence or performance on an IQ test, and achievement is represented by specific performance on academic achievement tests. Students with LD are expected to achieve better academically than they do. The exclusionary criteria involves ruling out poor achievement due to socioeconomic factors, cultural differences, inadequate instruction, and other disabling conditions. When students achieve below a level predicted by their IQ score and their poor achievement cannot be explained by the exclusionary factors, they are assumed to have a learning disability.

Over time researchers and practitioners have argued that the discrepancy model does not accurately identify learning disabilities for at least three reasons. First, it doesn't truly differentiate between low achievers and those with LD. Second, using a discrepancy criterion makes it very difficult to identify children in the early elementary grades as having a learning disability (Hallahan & Mercer, 2002). And third, the discrepancy approach provides teachers no information about forms of effective interventions for the student (Buttner & Hasselhorn, 2011).

The most recent reauthorization of IDEA indicates that to identify students with LD, schools no longer need to consider whether the student has a severe discrepancy between achievement and intellectual ability. Instead, students' evaluations may be based on whether they respond to scientific, research-based intervention. This is referred to as response to intervention (RTI). Response to intervention is defined as a change in behavior or performance attributable to appropriate intervention. Students could be identified as having LD only if they do not improve satisfactorily after receiving intensive instruction.

Although there are advantages to including a response to instruction criterion, there are concerns as well. According to some authors, it will impact not only the identification and service of students with LD, but it will change how the field conceptualizes learning disabilities (e.g., Scanlon, 2003). The current view of LD is a presumed cognitive processing disorder when other possible explanations for below expected learning are excluded. It has been argued that including a response to intervention component may redefine LD as being low school achievement (e.g., Scanlon, 2003). More details regarding response to intervention are presented in Chapter 7.

Emotional/Behavioral Disabilities

Benjamin is in seventh grade and lives in a small rural community with his parents and older brother. His stature is large for his age and his favorite subject in school is physical education. He does well with the physical requirements of most sports, although he gets into arguments and fights when playing team sports. He has few friends and is often found playing by himself at home, school, and around the town. His favorite activities are to play video games and basketball. He would like to play on the school's basketball team, but given his negative history with team sports, the coach will not consider it.

Benjamin has an older brother, Mitchell, who excels in everything. When Benjamin was in fifth grade, his parents became particularly concerned about Benjamin's lack of achievement, particularly because he wasn't excelling like his older brother did at that age. They knew he was very bright and capable of work equivalent to his brother's. After his parents referred him for testing at the school, the school's diagnostic team concluded that he had an emotional/behavioral disability that warranted special attention. Since that time Benjamin has attended a small-group counseling session with the school psychologist on a weekly basis. During these sessions, Benjamin is learning appropriate social skills. In addition, the school psychologist developed a self-managed work completion checklist which Benjamin routes through his general education teachers weekly and returns the report to the school psychologist. His social skills and work completion rates are improving.

Students with **emotional/behavioral disabilities (EBD)** represent 6.4% of the total number of students with disabilities served in the United States, which equals about 0.5% of the total school population (USDOE, 2014). Prevalence rates, however, are estimated to be much higher. For example, some researchers and government agencies report that 10% to 20% of all school-age children exhibit emotional distress or impairment (Hanchan & Allen, 2013). Many professionals believe EBD stands as the most underrepresented of all the disability categories. They attribute the low identification rates to the federal law's vague and poorly written definition, which has in turn led to variations in definitions and criteria used across states (Hanchan & Allen, 2013).

When the **Education for All Handicapped Children Act (EAHCA)** passed in 1975, the label, *seriously emotionally disturbed (SED)* was used to describe this population of students. The SED label and corresponding definition raised questions in the minds of educators and parents. Of particular concern were the following: (a) including the qualifier, *seriously* in the label, (b) excluding socially maladjusted students in the definition, and (c) not providing a more precise definition (Council for Children with Behavioral Disorders [CCBD], 1987). Autism was included in the original 1975 definition of SED, but has been subsequently removed and created as a separate category of disabling conditions covered under IDEA.

In response to the SED label, professionals created their own labels to best represent their views of this population. A group of representatives from 30 professional organizations created a coalition and proposed a new label, *emotional or behavioral disorder* (EBD), and an accompanying definition. This proposed definition included the following elements:

- EBD is characterized by behavioral or emotional responses in school so different from appropriate age, cultural, or ethnic norms that they adversely affect educational performance (i.e., academic, social, vocational, and personal skills).

- EBD is

  - more than a temporary, expected response to stressful events in the environment,
  - consistently exhibited in 2 different settings, at least one of which is school-related, and
  - unresponsive to direct intervention in general education or the condition is such that general education interventions would be insufficient.

- EBD can co-exist with other disabilities.

- EBD includes those with schizophrenic disorders, affective disorders, anxiety disorders, or other sustained disorders of conduct or adjustment when they adversely affect educational performance. (McIntyre & Forness, 1996)

Although this proposed label and definition enjoyed widespread support, others opposed the change fearful that large numbers of students not previously served would now qualify for special education services and place additional burdens on school district budgets. In the 1997 reauthorization of IDEA, only one change was made—the qualifier, seriously, was dropped from the label. No additional changes were made in the 2004 reauthorization. Thus the current IDEA definition reads:

Emotional disturbance is defined as follows:

(i) The term means a condition exhibiting one or more of the following characteristics over a longer period of time and to a marked degree that adversely affects a child's educational performance:

  (A) An inability to learn that cannot be explained by intellectual, sensory, or health factors.
  (B) An inability to build or maintain satisfactory interpersonal relationships with peers and teachers.
  (C) Inappropriate types of behavior or feelings under normal circumstances.
  (D) A general pervasive mood of unhappiness or depression.
  (E) A tendency to develop physical symptoms or fears associated with personal or school problems.

(ii) The term includes schizophrenia. The term does not apply to children who are socially maladjusted, unless it is determined that they have an emotional disturbance. (USDOE, 1999, p. 12422)

The future of the federal definition of ED remains unclear. The current definition has been criticized for being based on outdated concepts with little or no empirical support (Forness & Kavale, 2000). Yet, there has been reluctance by legislators to make the necessary changes. Given its universal support, the label *EBD*, not ED, is used throughout this book.

Intellectual Disabilities

Janeese is 15 years old and lives with her grandmother and two younger sisters. When her parents divorced 10 years ago, Janeese's grandmother gained sole custody. Janeese's favorite subject in school is reading. She likes to read all kinds of children's literature. She also enjoys helping around the house with chores and playing with her younger sisters.

When Janeese started school at age 6, her teacher, Ms. Knudsen, was concerned about the slow progress she was making. After several months, Ms. Knudsen met with Janeese's grandmother about these concerns and they decided to refer Janeese for testing. Janeese scored below average on both the intelligence test and the adaptive behavior scale. A district test used to assess readiness for school also scored Janeese below average across all areas. The diagnostic team, along with Ms. Knudsen, the principal, and Janeese's grandmother decided that Janeese had intellectual disabilities and qualified for special education. They also concluded that she would be better educated in a full-day special education kindergarten. Since then, Janeese has received some form of special education which has varied year to year according to Janeese's needs. Most recently her special education goals focus on developing life skills.

Of the students with disabilities served under IDEA, 7.4% are identified as having **intellectual disabilities (ID)** (USDOE, 2014). This represents 0.6% of the total school population. Studies have shown the prevalence to be about 1% percent of the total U.S. and world populations (Maulik, Mascarenhas, Mathers, Dua, & Saxena, 2011).

Intellectual disabilities has been a difficult construct to define. The American Association on Intellectual and Developmental Disabilities (AAIDD), formerly the American Association for Mental Retardation (AAMR), has led the field in trying to define ID. In 1959, they conceptualized ID as having three criteria: (a) subaverage general intelligence, (b) adaptive behavior impairment, and (c) having occurred during the developmental period (before age 18). That basic definition remains today, although how it is operationalized has changed. Back then, general intelligence was defined as one standard deviation below the mean or average on an intelligence test. Using this cut-off score, statistically about 16% of the population would be diagnosed as having ID (Smith, 1997).

In 1973, a substantial change was made by revising the IQ cut-off score from one to two standard deviations below the mean (score of 70 or below) which would statistically reduce the number of individuals identified as having intellectual disabilities to approximately 2.25% (Smith, 1997). The new 1973 definition placed more emphasis on adaptive behaviors. *Adaptive behavior* is defined as the collection of conceptual, social, and practical skills that people have learned so they can function in their everyday lives.

Then in 1992, substantial changes were made by moving away from historical reliance on levels of deficit identified by performance on an IQ test and toward a system of supports. Severity of disability was replaced by a system classifying the intensities and patterns of support required by the individual. They included intermittent needs, limited needs, extensive needs, and pervasive needs.

The IDEA definition of intellectual disabilities used in the schools is similar to the 1973 AAIDD definition. It reads: *"Intellectual disabilities* means significantly subaverage general intellectual functioning, existing concurrently with deficits in adaptive behavior and manifested during the developmental period, that adversely affects a child's educational performance" (USDOE, 1999, p. 12422).

Another significant change occurred in 2010 when the federal government recognized the inappropriateness of the label mental retardation. In that year, the U.S. Congress passed Rosa's Law, an Act that replaced the term *mental retardation* with intellectual disabilities in special education and other laws. The Act is named after Rosa Marcellion, a girl with Down syndrome whose family was instrumental in getting a similar law passed in Maryland.

As with LD and EBD, what the future holds for the field of intellectual disabilities remains unclear. As research develops and the political climate changes, the definition will continue to evolve.

High-Functioning Autism

Most people who know Dylan characterize him as a 15-year-old adolescent who is tall for his age, loves puzzles and math, and keeps to himself. Batman is his favorite fictional character and he can tell you anything you want to know about the Batman comic books, TV series, or movies. Dylan will interact with his peers if they initiate it, but otherwise he prefers to be by himself. He was diagnosed with autism when he was 2 years old. In his early schooling, Dylan attended special education classes, but now he participates in all general education classes in the high school. He is also a member of a small-group social skills and language class that consists of three other students with disabilities and four peers without disabilities. They meet daily with the special education teacher to learn and practice social and conversational skills. Dylan's overall goal is to learn to become a pilot. His parents are concerned that he will have difficulty achieving that goal and are uncertain about his adult future.

As with the previously discussed disabling conditions, the definition and prevalence of **autism** has changed over the years. While the percentage of students served as LD, ID, and EBD has decreased in the last decade, autism rates have grown immensely. In the most recent national data available, students with autism comprise 7% of all students receiving special education services, which represents 0.7% of the school population, an increase of 0.5% in less than 10 years (USDOE, 2014).

Two studies examined the prevalence rates of autism of school-age students between 2002 and 2008. In the state of Utah, the prevalence increased 100%. By 2008, 1 in 77 eight-year-olds were identified with autism (Pinborough-Zimmerman et al., 2012). In Wisconsin, the overall prevalence increased 84% with approximately 1 in 110 students identified with autism (Maenner & Durkin, 2010). Nationally, estimates based on 11 communities indicated that 1 in 68 eight-year-old children fell within the autism spectrum (Centers for Disease Control and Prevention, 2014). Increased prevalence of autism have occurred for several reasons including increased awareness, changes in the diagnostic criteria, and the inclusion of autism as a separate disabling condition in IDEA (Pinborough-Zimmerman et al.; Volker, 2012).

When IDEA first passed in 1975, autism was included in the definition of EBD, but became a separate disabling condition in 1990 (Hallahan, Kauffman, & Pullen, 2014). IDEA defines *autism* as a

> developmental disability significantly affecting verbal and nonverbal communication and social interaction, usually evident before age 3 that adversely affects a child's educational performance. Other characteristics often associated with ASD are engagement in repetitive activities and stereotyped movements, resistance to environmental change or change in daily routines, and unusual responses to sensory experiences. . . . Autism does not apply if a child's educational performance is adversely affected because the child has an emotional disturbance . . . (34 C.F.R. 300.8[c][1])

Typically a highly qualified professional, such as a psychiatrist, clinical psychologist, or pediatrician, makes the diagnosis.

Autism is a complex condition with varying characteristics and is considered a spectrum disorder or a group of disorders with similar characteristics which can range from mild to severe. Often professionals refer to autism as autism spectrum disorder or ASD. The focus in this book is on students with **high-functioning autism (HFA).** Although autism prevalence rates have increased, data are difficult to ascertain for the higher-functioning end of the autism spectrum because most studies do not report the prevalence at different functional levels (Volker, 2012).

Students with HFA demonstrate significant social interaction difficulties and unusual patterns of behavior or interests. Intellectually, they function average to above average which supports their ability to succeed in general education classes. However, their social skills can hamper their ability to relate and interact appropriately with others in classes and elsewhere. They have difficulty adjusting their behavior to the setting and to judging what others are thinking. Their behavior could range from being aloof and withdrawn to overly enthusiastic to a degree that is inappropriate. Students with HFA can become fixated on a topic and talk about it incessantly and not understand why those around them are not as passionate as they are on this topic. They also have a need for consistency and sameness not wanting routines, settings, or environmental elements to change (Sansosti & Sansosti, 2012; Volker, 2012).

Attention-Deficit/Hyperactivity Disorder

Eric attends elementary school as a fifth grader and looks like a typical 10-year-old boy. He lives in a large U.S. city with his parents and paternal grandfather. He is an only child. When asked, he says art and physical education are his favorite subjects. He likes school and has many friends. His favorite activities at home are video games and skateboarding.

Eric was diagnosed by his pediatrician as having attention-deficit disorder with hyperactivity

(Continued)

(Continued)

when he was 8 years old. His doctor prescribed medication that helps him concentrate, particularly during school hours. His general education teacher provides minimal accommodations to help Eric keep focused. When Eric was first diagnosed, his teacher was particularly concerned about his lack of work completion and difficulty attending during large-group instruction or independent work time. Eric was found to qualify for special education services through another health impaired diagnosis. Mr. Riley, Eric's special education teacher, is teaching Eric self-management procedures so he can focus himself and complete his work to a greater degree than before.

Attention-deficit/hyperactivity disorder (ADHD) is NOT an identified disability under the IDEA but is included in this text because many students receive special education services under other health impairment (OHI). ADHD affects between 5.9% and 7.1% of students (Willcutt, 2012). About three times as many boys are identified with ADHD than girls (Pastor & Reuben, 2002). ADHD does not appear in IDEA as a separate disability category, but has been defined as a disorder by the American Psychiatric Association (APA) in 2013. They define ADHD as persistent patterns of inattention and/or hyperactivity-impulsivity that interfere with functioning or development, as characterized by inattention and/or hyperactivity and impulsivity. The APA definition lists characteristics that a student must demonstrate. All of these characteristics must occur often, have lasted for at least 6 months, be inconsistent with developmental level, and negatively impact social, academic, and/or occupational activities. In addition, at least several of the characteristics must have occurred before age 12, be present in two or more settings, and not caused by other disorders.

In order to demonstrate inattention, students must demonstrate six or more of the following characteristics. The student must be having difficulty (a) paying close attention to details, (b) sustaining attention, (c) listening when spoken to directly, (d) following through on instructions or task, and/or (e) organizing tasks and activities. Other criteria include (a) avoiding, disliking, or being reluctant to sustain mental effort; (b) losing things needed for tasks or activities; (c) being easily distracted by extraneous stimuli; and/or (d) being forgetful in daily tasks.

Hyperactivity and impulsivity are demonstrated by six or more of the following characteristics: (a) fidgets with or taps hands or feet or squirms in seat, (b) leaves seat when inappropriate, (c) runs or climbs when inappropriate, (d) unable to play quietly, (e) "on the go" as if "driven by a motor," (f) talks excessively, (g) blurts out an answer before the question has been fully asked, (h) difficulty waiting turns, and/or (i) interrupts or intrudes on others.

During the 1997 IDEA reauthorization process, Congress seriously considered including ADHD as a separate disability category. In fact, the Congressional passage of the reauthorization was delayed by serious debate about whether or not ADHD should be included in the law as another disability category. Proponents argued that including ADHD would help serve a large proportion of students currently unidentified or inappropriately labeled under another disability, particularly LD or EBD. Opponents asserted that the definition and accompanying identification practices for ADHD were seriously questionable (Ysseldyke, Algozzine, & Thurlow, 2000). The compromise was to add ADHD to the list of conditions that render a student eligible for services as **other health impaired (OHI)**.

The IDEA definition of OHI reads as follows:

> *Other health impairment* means having limited strength, vitality or alertness, including a heightened alertness to environmental stimuli, that results in limited alertness with respect to the educational environment, that—
>
> (i) Is due to chronic or acute health problems such as asthma, attention-deficit disorder or attention-deficit/hyperactivity disorders, diabetes, epilepsy, a heart condition, hemophilia, lead poisoning, leukemia, nephritis, rheumatic fever, and sickle cell anemia; and
>
> (ii) Adversely affects a child's educational performance. (USDOE, 1999, p. 12422)

Myths about ADHD abound in the field. Even parents and teachers who have experience with children and adolescents with ADHD have common misunderstandings (Pancheri & Prater, 1999). Most of the controversies and misunderstandings surround the use of stimulant medication to treat students with ADHD. Although stimulant medication is an effective intervention for most individuals with ADHD, medication should not be used to the exclusion of instructional and behavior management interventions.

TEACHER TIP #1.1

MYTHS AND FACTS ABOUT ADHD

Myths about ADHD often permeate the media. Below are some myths and facts about ADHD that can be shared with parents or other educators.

Myth	Fact
ADHD is not a medical condition.	ADHD is a medical disorder, not the student choosing to misbehave.
Medicine for ADHD will make a student feel drugged.	Medicine in the proper dosage helps the student focus and control behavior.
Students with ADHD are learning to use the condition as an excuse for their behavior.	ADHD is a disability. Students with this condition have to learn to cope with their symptoms of inattention, impulsivity, and hyperactivity.

(Continued)

(Continued)

Myth	Fact
Having ADHD means the student is lazy or dumb.	ADHD has nothing to do with motivation or intelligence.
Students with ADHD just need good discipline.	Behavior management techniques can be helpful for students with ADHD, but only if the students are physically capable of engaging in the appropriate behaviors (e.g., paying attention). Most students with ADHD need both medicine and behavior management techniques.

Source: Adapted from *ADHD Myths and Facts—Topic Overview*, WebMD, http://www.webmd.com/add-adhd/childhood-adhd/tc/adhd-myths-and-facts-topic-overview.

Technology Spotlight #1.1

Web Resources for Learning About Disabilities

Teachers will undoubtedly interact with parents and other educators who are not as well informed about disabilities, and who will want to become better informed about their child's or students' disabilities. Web resources are useful starting places for learning more about disabilities.

Autism and Autism Spectrum Disorder

Autism Speaks: https://www.autismspeaks.org/

National Autism Association: http://nationalautismassociation.org/

National Institute of Mental Health: http://www.nimh.nih.gov/health/topics/autism-spectrum-disorders-asd/index.shtml

Comprehensive Disability Resources

The Cornucopia of Disability Information: http://codi.buffalo.edu/

Disability Resources on the Internet: http://www.disabilityresources.org/

Special Education Resources on the Internet: http://seriweb.com/

Attention-Deficit/Hyperactivity Disorder

Attention Deficit Disorder Association: http://www.add.org/

Children and Adults with Attention-Deficit/Hyperactivity Disorder: http://www.chadd.org/

National Institute of Mental Health: http://www.nimh.nih.gov/health/topics/attention-deficit-hyperactivity-disorder-adhd/index.shtml

Emotional/Behavioral Disorders

The Behavior Home Page, Kentucky: http://www.state.ky.us/agencies/behave/homepage.html

The Council for Children with Behavior Disorders: http://www.ccbd.net/

You Can Handle Them All: http://www.disciplinehelp.com/

Learning Disabilities

Learning Disabilities Association of America: http://ldaamerica.org/support/new-to-ld/

LD Online: http://www.ldonline.org/

LD Resources: http://www
.ldresources.com/

**Intellectual Disabilities
and Developmental Disabilities**

The Arc: http://thearc.org/

The American Association on
Intellectual and Developmental
Disabilities: http://www.aaidd.org/

The National Down Syndrome
Society: http://www.ndss.org/

For Parents

National Parent Information Network:
http://www.npin.org/

Our-Kids: http://www.our-kids.org/

PACER Center: http://www.pacer.org/

Parents Helping Parents: http://www
.php.com/

Characteristics That Impact Instruction

As discussed previously, students with HID demonstrate some similar characteristics. At the same time, distinctive features across disabling conditions are also evident. Within this section categorical similarities and differences are discussed in the areas of cognitive, academic, social competence, and motivational characteristics that impact instruction.

Cognitive Characteristics

Cognition is defined as the act or process of knowing including both awareness and judgment. Generally speaking, students with HID differ from their typical peers in various cognitive ways. Three are addressed briefly—attention, memory, and concept formation.

Attention

Attention is the ability to concentrate on a particular stimulus. Students with attention problems have difficulty sustaining attention, focusing attention, and dividing attention. A specific type of attention is selective attention. Students with poor selective attention have difficulty filtering out distractions so they can focus on what is relevant. Students may also have difficulty with voluntary attention. Voluntary attention requires energy and practice, but can become automatic over time. When individuals first learn to drive a car they devote full attention to thinking about the operations. With experience, they no longer need to devote full attention and can drive while listening to the radio or talking to passengers in the car.

Students with HID, as well as other low achieving learners, frequently exhibit problems with attention. The coexistence of LD and ADHD, as well as ID and ADHD in many students documents that attention and learning problems are interrelated and often coexist (Mayes et al., 2000; Neece, Baker, Blacher, & Crnic, 2011). Seventy years ago, attention was proposed to be the core deficit in autism and researchers continue to demonstrate attention deficits in this population (Caterino, 2014). Teachers must design their classroom environment as well as instruction to accommodate the needs of learners with attention difficulties. In Chapter 9, instructional and classroom environmental strategies to compensate for learner attention deficits are detailed.

Memory

Students with HID may have difficulty with memory tasks. After being exposed to information, **memory** is the ability to encode, process, and retrieve that information. Memory problems can be the result of difficulty encoding, processing, and/or retrieving information. Working memory is a limited capacity system that allows temporary storage and manipulation of information for complex cognitive tasks (e.g., comprehension, reasoning). In contrast, long-term memory is thought to be limitless and involves the permanent storage of information. Since memory cannot be separated distinctly from learning, it makes sense that a student's performance in academic and cognitive areas is directly linked to memory.

Many students with HID have difficulties with memory. For example, weaknesses in working memory have been documented for students with reading disabilities (e.g., Swanson, Kehler, & Jerman, 2010) and ADHD (e.g., Andersen, Egeland, & Øie, 2012). In addition, research indicates that students with learning disabilities and mild intellectual disabilities lack appropriate strategies to help them recall information (Maehler & Schuchardt, 2009). **Strategies** are deliberate, consciously applied procedures that help learners store and retrieve information and solve problems. For example, effective learners catch themselves not paying attention while reading. They go back and reread more deliberately to gain comprehension of what they are reading. They may even stop at the end of every paragraph and restate in their mind what they just read. These would be examples of strategies for reading comprehension.

Typical learners develop general strategic knowledge and recognize that strategy use improves their performance on memory tasks. Students with HID may not develop and use these strategies as a typical learner does. They may not know useful strategies or know how to apply them for a specific task. They may fail to plan or monitor their work, or they may have strategies but use them ineffectively. Without the use of strategies, performance is hampered. But when taught appropriate strategies, students can enhance their memory skills (Mastropieri & Scruggs, 2000). Consequently, one role of education is to assist students to develop and to use mnemonic strategies. In Chapter 9, how teachers can teach and use mnemonic strategies to help their students acquire, retain, and recall information is discussed.

Concept Formation

"**Concepts** are the fundamental structure for thought throughout a human being's lifetime" (Prater, 1998, p. 417). Years ago, David P. Ausubel (1968) stated,

> Anyone who pauses long enough to give the problem some serious thought cannot escape the conclusion that man lives in a world of concepts rather than a world of objects, events, and situations . . . Reality, figuratively speaking, is experienced through a conceptual or categorical filter. (p. 505)

Typical students learn concepts through observation, experience, and schooling. A young child learns to differentiate between a dog and a cat by someone shaping their understanding. A toddler calls a cat a dog for the first time and is corrected by his parents who also explain why the cat is not a dog. The young child begins to understand the differences between cats and dogs and when exposed to other domestic animals such as cows and horses, he adds them to his conceptual framework of animals. Then upon a visit to the zoo and exposure to monkeys, lions, and elephants, the child begins to expand his conceptual understanding of animals. This is a fundamental way in which children develop conceptual knowledge.

Students with HID may demonstrate limited knowledge of concepts. Social or perceptual problems may inhibit their ability to accurately learn concepts through observation and experience of the world around them. Learners with intellectual disabilities, in particular, often do not learn in informal or naturally occurring situations. Research documents, for example, that young children with mild intellectual disabilities have significant deficits in understanding and using basic directional (e.g., left, right) and positional (e.g., on, under) concepts (Prater, 1998). Learning language and developing concepts are an interrelated process because concepts represent word meanings. Abstract concepts in particular can be difficult for students with HID. Students with autism, for example, use and understand language literally and thus have difficulty understanding sarcasm, irony, and other abstract uses of language.

All students benefit from explicit concept instruction. However, given that students with HID (a) often fail to learn concepts through experience, (b) demonstrate language difficulties, and (c) have particular difficulties learning abstract concepts, concept instruction for this population is particularly vital (Prater, 1998).

TEACHER TIP #1.2
TEACHING CONCEPTS

When teaching new concepts, apply the following strategies:

- Directly teach new concepts. Do not assume students will acquire this knowledge without being taught explicitly.

- Teach new concepts by beginning with concrete examples (e.g., role-playing sharing), then move to semi-concrete examples (e.g., pictures of children sharing) and then abstract examples (e.g., reading passages about children sharing).

- Relate new concepts to the students' relevant experiences.

- Provide students graphic organizers that visually illustrate new concepts (see Chapter 9).

Source: Carter, Prater, & Dyches, 2009.

Academic Skills

By definition, students with LD, ID, EBD, ADHD, and HFA all demonstrate **academic difficulties**. Students with LD must achieve poorly in one or more academic areas, students with ID generally achieve below average in all academic areas, while learners with EBD, ADHD or HFA cannot receive special education services unless their difficulties hamper their educational experience. Thus teachers may assume that all learners identified with high-incidence disabilities have academic deficits. Students representing the five disability categories addressed in this book often demonstrate achievement patterns (see Table 1.2). Although these patterns exist, teachers must be very careful not to overgeneralize and assume the pattern will be the same for all students with a particular disability. Teachers must always consider the patterns of individuals.

Social Competence

All students live within social structures. Being socially competent or having the skills necessary to be accepted and fulfilled socially, particularly demonstrating appropriate interpersonal skills are important for success in school and beyond. Many students with HID have not developed age-appropriate **social competence**. Students identified with EBD, for example, demonstrate internalizing (e.g., social withdrawal, anxiety) and externalizing (e.g., aggression, acting out) behaviors that impact relationships with others (Kern et al., 2015). Other students, including those with LD have difficulty picking up on social cues (e.g., facial expressions, body language) (Most & Greenbank, 2000). Students with attention problems such as difficulty waiting their turn or blurting out answers may be viewed by their peers and others as rude and insensitive to others (Csoti, 2001).

TABLE 1.2 **Achievement Patterns for Students With High-Incidence Disabilities**

Disability	Achievement Patterns	Example
Learning Disability	Peaks and valleys indicating areas of both strengths and deficit	Above average math skills but below average reading skills
Intellectual Disability	Generally flat line below average in all areas	Below average in math, reading, and other subject areas
Emotional/Behavioral Disorder	Pattern is not typical except that difficulties need to impact education so you would expect some low areas. May also demonstrate very high performance.	Inconsistent performance in math although testing indicates very high ability. Reading is average.
Attention-Deficit/Hyperactivity Disorder	Pattern is not typical except that difficulties need to impact education so you would expect some low areas. May also demonstrate very high performance.	Inconsistent performance in all academic areas although tests indicate high ability in all areas
High-Functioning Autism	Pattern is not typical except that difficulties need to impact education so you would expect some low areas. May also demonstrate very high performance.	Inconsistent performance in all academic areas although may demonstrate very high performance in areas of student's interest.

Students with high-functioning autism typically misunderstand or ignore social cues given by others, such as trying to change the subject of conversation which can lead to their peers viewing them as strange, impolite, or offensive (Volker, 2012). Even if students demonstrate appropriate social skills in one setting, they may not generalize or transfer their skills to other situations.

The social competence needs of students with HID often go ignored. In fact, in some cases the social dimensions of life present greater problems for this population than their specific academic deficits. Students with HID often require direct and deliberate instruction in social skills that lead to social competence. Chapter 13 is devoted to this topic.

Motivation and Attribution

Even though students may have the ability or skills they need to succeed in school, they may fail if they are not motivated to succeed. **Motivation** is the need or desire that causes someone to act or behave. A learner is **intrinsically motivated** if she acts, participates, or behaves because of her curiosity or desire to succeed, contribute, or participate. An extrinsically motivated student participates to receive an external consequence, often some form of tangible reward.

Motivation affects the learning process. Without motivation, students are unlikely to learn. However, the converse is not necessarily true. Motivated students cannot learn if they don't have the appropriate prerequisite skills. Motivation only works in encouraging students to persist in doing something if they are capable of doing it. Students with HID may be more prone to discouragement, particularly given their history of poor academic achievement. This can lead to low motivation for learning. One study, for example, found that students with ADHD in comparison to students without disabilities preferred easier work, enjoyed learning less, had less persistence, and relied more on external rather than internal standards to judge their performance (Carlson, Booth, Shin, & Canu, 2002).

TEACHER TIP #1.3

MOTIVATING STUDENTS

Teachers can help motivate students by

- designing classrooms to be positive and supportive environments,
- teaching at the students' appropriate levels of understanding,
- engaging students in their own learning,
- making school fun and interesting,
- designing for errorless learning,

- using natural consequences that lead to failure as an opportunity to teach,
- teaching self-management and self-determination skills so students become responsible for their own learning and behavior, and
- connecting effort and knowledge or skills to outcomes.

Another important related concept is **attribution** style. People attribute their successes and failures to internal/external, stable/unstable, and global/specific factors. Students who explain their successes to causes that are within themselves ("I worked really hard."), stable ("I will always be like this.") and global ("This will always influence what happens to me.") demonstrate a positive attributional style. On the other hand, students who explain their successes to causes outside of their control ("My horoscope was good today."), unstable ("It won't last.") and specific ("It only happened this one time.") demonstrate a negative attributional style (Tabassam & Grainger, 2002).

Generally speaking, students with HID, particularly students with LD attribute their failure to stable internal causes and their successes to external factors (Tabassam & Grainger, 2002). A student may believe she passed a test because "the teacher likes me" or "it was my lucky day." On the other hand, a failed test is attributed to "because I am stupid." Teachers can help students connect knowledge, effort, and achievement by linking task success or failure to effort and application of skills and strategies (Kozminsky & Kozminsky, 2002).

Diverse Populations

In addition to students with disabilities, schools are serving more students with other specialized needs. This is due in part to the United States becoming an increasingly diverse society. Our country has seen large numbers of immigrants from non-English speaking countries and an increased number of births within diverse populations in recent years. This diversity impacts schools more than any other aspect of society because the average age of groups representing diverse populations is younger than what has traditionally been called the majority population (Yates & Ortiz, 2004). Within this context, the word *diversity* is used in place of the word *minority*. Changing terminology is important for two reasons. First, what has been called the minority population is becoming the majority. In fact, ethnically and linguistically diverse learners already represent the majority student population in many school districts. Second, the word minority somewhat disenfranchises this population from the citizenry of the United States.

Race and Ethnicity

Diversity in our population can be defined across many different characteristics including race and ethnicity. Traditionally **race** is based on biological factors and includes these categories: White or Caucasian, Black or African American, American Indian, Alaska Native, Asian, Native Hawaiian, and Other Pacific Islander. People who identify their origin as Hispanic, Latino, or Spanish may be any race, thus Hispanic or Latino are considered an ethnic group. **Ethnicity** relates to sociological or cultural factors, such as nationality, religion, socioeconomic class, or linguistic origin. In Table 1.3, the U.S. population by percentage of race/ethnicity in 2000 and 2010 is presented. Review of these numbers indicates percentage growths in the Asian and Hispanic or Latino, with declines in the White population.

English Learners

Directly related to the increase of racial and ethnic diversity within the United States, is the dramatic rise in the number of students whose native language is not English.

TABLE 1.3   **U.S. Population by Race/Ethnicity in 2000 and 2010**

Race/Ethnicity	2000 Percentage of Total	2010 Percentage of Total
White only	75.1	63.7
Black or African American only	12.3	12.6
American Indian and Alaska Native only	0.9	0.9
Asian only	3.6	4.8
Native Hawaiian and Other Pacific Islander only	0.1	0.2
Hispanic or Latino	12.5	16.3
Two or more races	2.4	2.9

Source: U.S. Census Bureau (2000b, 2010b).

Data from the 1990, 2000, and 2010 censuses listed in Table 1.4 document the number of individuals who spoke other languages. Both the total number of individuals, as well as the top 10 ranked languages for all three years, are provided.

Spanish is the most predominantly spoken second language in the United States. Other Western European-based languages have decreased while Asian languages are gaining in prominence. Chinese, for example, ranked fifth in 1990 but second in 2000 and 2010. Tagalog (Philippine Islands) rose from sixth to fifth to third and Vietnamese from ninth to sixth to fourth within the same time period.

TABLE 1.4   **U.S. Census Data Regarding Language Spoken at Home and Ability to Speak English for Persons 5 years and Over: Top 10 Non-English Languages Identified for 1990, 2000, and 2010**

Language Other Than English	1990 Rank	1990 Total in Millions	2000 Rank	2000 Total in Millions	2010 Rank	2010 Total in Millions
Spanish	1	17.3	1	28.1	1	37.6
French*	2	1.7	3	1.6	5	1.3
German	3	1.5	4	1.4	7	1.1
Italian	4	1.3	7	1.0	11	0.7
Chinese	5	1.3	2	2.0	2	2.9
Tagalog	6	0.8	5	1.2	3	1.6

(Continued)

TABLE 1.4 **(Continued)**

Language Other Than English	1990		2000		2010	
	Rank	Total in Millions	Rank	Total in Millions	Rank	Total in Millions
Polish	7	0.7	10	0.7	15	0.6
Korean	8	0.6	8	0.9	6	1.1
Vietnamese	9	0.5	6	1.0	4	1.4
Portuguese	10	0.4	12	0.6	17	0.7
Arabic	13	0.3	11	0.6	8	0.9
Russian	15	0.2	9	0.7	9	0.9
African Languages	NA	NA`	NA	NA	10	0.9

Source: U.S. Census Bureau (1990, 2000a, 2010a).

Note: `Includes Cajun

NA = not available

English learners (ELs) are defined as "those who have such limited English skills that they cannot profit from general education instruction without support" (Yates & Ortiz, 2004, p. 45). Educators use a number of terms when referring to this population including *English language learners* (ELLs), *limited English proficient students*, *non-native English speakers* and so forth. For the purpose of this book, students with limited proficiency in English will be referred to as English learners (ELs).

The 2010 U.S. census reported that 21% of the population 5 to 17 years of age spoke languages other than English in their homes. Of those, 22% did not speak English well or at all. The percentage of students receiving limited English support in the schools is approximately 9.1% nationally. The states providing EL services to the highest percentage of students include California (23.2%), Nevada (19.6%), New Mexico (16.1%), Texas (14.9%) and Hawaii (13.5%). The states providing EL services to the lowest percentage of students include West Virginia (0.7%), Mississippi (1.3%), Vermont (1.5%), Louisiana (1.9%), and New Hampshire (2.0%) (National Center for Education Statistics, 2013).

Socioeconomic Status and Family Structures

The United States is also becoming more socioeconomically diverse. **Socioeconomic status** refers to an individual's or family's social and economic status in relation to others. In 2002, 17% of the nation's children were members of families living below the poverty level. That percentage rose to 19.5% in 2013 (National Center for Education Statistics, 2013). The household family structure in which children live also varies. While the majority of children lived with two parents in 2013 (69%), approximately one fourth lived with only their mother (24%) and 4% lived with only their father. Another 4% lived in households with neither parent present with most being raised by grandparents. A never-married parent is becoming more common. Of the single parent households, the proportion of children living with a parent who has never married increased from 7% in 1970 to 45% in 2013 (U.S. Census Bureau, 2014).

Disabilities

Changing demographics in the United States have particularly challenged the special education field. Many students with disabilities come from **culturally and/or linguistically diverse (CLD)** populations. A major controversy for over 40 years has centered on the proportion of students from CLD populations identified with disabilities. Generally speaking, more or fewer CLD students are identified with disabilities than should be identified given the proportion of CLD students in the population. Researchers indicate that factors contributing to these disproportionate representations include racially biased tests, racially biased professionals, and inadequate community resources, among other factors (Hallahan & Mercer, 2002; Harry & Klingner, 2006). As stated by Donna Y. Ford (2012),

> Cultural differences among students, families, and teachers have been offered as a major explanation for overreferrals and, thus, overrepresentation . . . Specifically, differences in values, beliefs, attitudes, customs, and traditions between White teachers and their [CLD] students contribute to low expectations and deficit thinking on the one hand . . . and cultural misunderstandings and cultural clashes on the other. (pp. 392–393)

The percentages of students served through IDEA by race/ethnicity in the categories described in this chapter appear in Table 1.5. Based on these data, a higher percentage of Native Hawaiian/Pacific Islander, Hispanic/Latino, American Indian/Alaska Native,

TABLE 1.5   Percentage of Total Number of Students Identified With Disabilities by Race/Ethnicity in 2012

	American Indian/ Alaska Native	Asian	Black or African American	Hispanic/ Latino	Native Hawaiian Pacific Islander	White	Two or More Races
Learning Disabilities	46.4	26.7	41.8	49.0	52.9	36.0	35.6
Emotional Behavior Disorders	6.3	2.5	8.8	3.9	4.8	6.4	8.5
Intellectual Disabilities	6.8	7.6	10.5	6.8	5.9	6.4	6.0
Autism	4.2	18.0	5.5	5.8	5.1	8.9	8.6
Total of 4 Disabling Conditions	63.7	54.8	66.6	65.5	67.7	57.7	58.7

Source: Adapted from Office of Special Education and Rehabilitative Services (2014).

and African American students were identified with LD than White or Asian students. Other differences noted in the data include African American students being identified with emotional/behavior disorders and intellectual disabilities in higher proportions than the other racial/ethnic groups; and White and Asian students are identified in higher percentages with autism.

Much has been written about the disproportion of students from ethnically diverse populations identified as having disabilities. Lloyd M. Dunn (1968) is often credited as the first to mention the overrepresentation of minority students in special classes for students with mild intellectual disabilities. Since that time, national and local studies have examined this issue. A few recent findings follow:

- African American and Hispanic students are disproportionately identified as LD in some states (Hallahan & Mock, 2003).

- Whites are twice as likely to be identified with autism as Hispanic and American Indian/Alaska Native students (Travers, Tincani, & Krezmien, 2011).

- African Americans and Native Americans are overrepresented in special education and Latino students were somewhat more likely than White students to be identified as having ID (Sullivan, 2011).

- English learners are disproportionately underrepresented in EBD identification when compared with students identified as LD (Gage, Gersten, Sugai, & Newman-Gonchar, 2013).

- White non-Hispanic students are more often diagnosed with ADHD than African American or Hispanic students (Pastor & Reuben, 2002).

- African American secondary-age students are overrepresented in the category of mild intellectual disabilities (Jasper & Bouck, 2013).

Given changes in our populations including the increased numbers of students from CLD populations, all teachers need to be grounded in sensitivity toward and appropriate instruction for diverse learners. Additional information and specific ideas focused on these populations are integrated throughout the book.

TEACHER TIP #1.4

CONSIDERATIONS WHEN EVALUATING AN ENGLISH LEARNER FOR A LEARNING DISABILITY

- Do not wait to assess until the student is fully proficient in English.

- Ensure the student is struggling in first language as well as English.

- Determine the student is receiving adequate opportunities to learn.

- Ensure the student is participating in instructional practices that are research-based and valid for English learners.

- Evaluate how the student is doing as compared with peers of the same-language, same-age and same similar background experiences.

- Start the assessment with the assumption that the student's learning difficulties are based on external factors. Keep that assumption unless data suggest otherwise.

Source: Klingner & Eppolito (2014).

Key Legislation

Federal legislation has impacted the field of special education for over 50 years. In fact, in the United States such legislation defines what special education is and who qualifies for these services. Initial legislation was driven by historic movements toward deinstitutionalization and normalization, advocacy on behalf of those with disabilities, and the civil rights movement. In lieu of discussing every legislative act and court case that lead to our current time, only three legislative acts that have the greatest impact on special educators today are presented. They include the Individuals with Disabilities Education Act, Section 504 of the Rehabilitation Act, and The Elementary and Secondary Education Act.

Individuals with Disabilities Education Act

The Individuals with Disabilities Education Act or IDEA was originally passed and signed into law as The Education for All Handicapped Children Act (EAHCA) or Public Law 94–142 in November 1975. When the EAHCA was reauthorized in 1990, the title of the law was changed to IDEA. It was again reauthorized in 1997 and in 2004.

Under the U.S. Constitution education is the responsibility of the states. When EAHCA (now IDEA) was first passed, it required states to provide services to all children and adolescents regardless of their disabilities. The Act also provided federal funds to support states that now had increased educational responsibility for serving these students. Thus, IDEA is considered a bill of rights for children and a federally funded mandate for the schools. However, the federal government has yet to fully fund the amounts committed to the states through IDEA. Schools are currently responsible for implementing the mandates of IDEA without enough accompanying federal funds to support these requirements.

In addition to providing services to school-age students, children with disabilities between ages 3 and 5 who are experiencing developmental delays may also receive these services. States must define developmental delays and ensure the delays are measured by appropriate diagnostic instruments and procedures in one or more of the following developmental areas: physical, cognitive, communication, social or emotional, or adaptive.

Most all of the rules and regulations defining how IDEA operates are guided by six major principles (Murdick, Gartin, & Crabtree, 2002):

- **Zero Reject** has been defined as the "theoretical nucleus of the Act" (p. 23). Zero reject is based on the principle that all children can learn and can be taught, regardless of the severity or nature of their disabilities. Thus, schools must educate all children. No child may be excluded from public education. This principle is affirmed through the Act's inclusion of guaranteeing a **free, appropriate public education**, sometimes called by the acronym FAPE. All children must be afforded the opportunity to attend school and that schooling must be provided at public expense.

- **Nondiscriminatory assessment** refers to using evaluation methods that are nonbiased and multifaceted when diagnosing the child's disability and providing appropriate program plans and educational placements. Tests and evaluation materials must not be racially or culturally discriminatory. All tests must be administered in the student's native language or other appropriate mode of communication, valid for the purpose for which they are being used, and administered by qualified personnel. In addition, no single test or procedure can provide the basis for identification or placement decisions.

- **Procedural due process** is guaranteed to all parties involved in the education of students with disabilities. Due process protects the rights of parents and the school district when disagreements arise related to identification and placement decisions for students with disabilities. If parents disagree with the results of the school's evaluation, for example, they can obtain an independent evaluation at public expense. If the school or the parents disagree with the identification, evaluation, placement, or special education related services for the student, either party can request a due process hearing. States must also offer the opportunity to resolve these disagreements through mediation by a third party before holding a hearing.

- **Parental participation** is interrelated with the procedural due process principle. Parent is defined in the Act and provisions are outlined for appointing surrogate parents, when necessary. IDEA requires that parents participate as members of the multidisciplinary team that makes decisions about the child's education. Parental responsibilities include:

  ○ providing written consent for testing and evaluation,
  ○ participating in determining whether their child is eligible for services,
  ○ assisting in the development of the child's individualized education program (IEP),
  ○ reviewing the child's progress at least annually, and
  ○ advocating for their child.

- **Least Restrictive Environment (LRE)** means that students with disabilities are to be educated with students without disabilities to the maximum extent possible. That is, their education should take place in the same environment as most typical students, but where the student with a disability can succeed (as measured by the students' IEP goals). The Act states that students with disabilities can only be removed from the general educational environment when the nature or severity of the disabilities does not allow satisfactory participation even with supplementary aids and services.

- **Individualized Education Programs (IEPs)** are central to ensuring an appropriate education is provided to students with disabilities. The IEP is a written document developed collaboratively between parents and school personnel. In essence, the IEP is the student's individualized program plan that details services and goals related specifically to the student's educational needs. Although six principles guide IDEA, the IEP is considered the cornerstone of special education because it directs and provides a means of monitoring all aspects of a student's educational program. In fact, the IEP formalizes the free, appropriate public education for students with disabilities (Drasgow, Yell, & Robinson, 2001).

Several amendments were added to IDEA when it was reauthorized in 1997 and 2004. These amendments have the greatest impact on teachers.

- **Changing the IEP team composition and written document.** Amendments added an increased emphasis on general education by requiring general education teacher participation on IEP teams. Also, additional required elements were added to the IEP document. Further information on IEP teams and the IEP document follows in the section under *IEP Process.*

- **Access to the general curriculum.** IDEA requires that students with disabilities have access to the general curriculum, that is, the same curriculum as that provided to students without disabilities. Access is the opportunity to meaningfully interact with the curriculum in order to learn (Nolet & McLaughlin, 2000). Some conditions, such as physical, sensory, or cognitive disabilities create barriers to access of typical general education curriculum. These barriers must be removed by providing an array of supports to the student. However, removing such barriers is not sufficient. To have full access, students need to be actively engaged with the curricular materials.

- **Universal design for learning.** Universal design refers to elements or features that make a system more likely to be compatible for large or universal audiences. Universal design for learning (UDL) involves designing and using instructional materials that allow the instructional goals to be achieved by a wide range of students regardless of their abilities to "see, hear, move, read, write and understand English, attend, organize, engage, and remember" (Orkwis & McLane, 1998, p. 90). The concept of UDL is incorporated throughout the 2004 authorization of IDEA including to the extent possible using UDL principles in the development of standards, assessments, curriculum, and instructional methods. A further discussion of UDL appears in Chapter 7.

- **Including students with disabilities in State or district wide assessment.** States and districts use large-scale assessment instruments to document the academic achievement of all students for the purpose of accountability. These assessments establish whether students have met district or State standards. IDEA now requires that schools include all students with disabilities in all assessment programs with accommodations when necessary. States must also develop alternative assessments for students who cannot participate in high-stakes tests.

- **Adding disciplinary provisions to the Act.** A section was added on discipline. If a student with disabilities has behavior problems, the IEP team must consider strategies to address these problems. A proactive behavior management plan, based on functional behavioral assessment should be included. Regulations regarding a student's suspension or placement change based on behavior were clarified.

School personnel, parents, and students are all greatly impacted by IDEA. Most of what occurs in special education in the United States is defined by this Act. Special educators need to know, understand, and apply the mandates of IDEA in identifying and evaluating students, writing individual program plans, working collaboratively with parents and other professionals, and delivering services to students with disabilities.

Section 504 of the Rehabilitation Act

In 1973, the U.S. Congress passed the Rehabilitation Act which authorized federal support for rehabilitating and training individuals with mental and physical disabilities. Section 504 of this Act is a nondiscriminatory regulation impacting all recipients of federal funds, including public schools (Smith, 2002). Section 504 states

> No otherwise qualified individual with a disability . . . shall solely by reason of her or his disability, be excluded from the participation in, be denied the benefits of, or be subjected to discrimination under any program or activity receiving federal financial assistance. (29 U.S.C. Section 794)

If a student with disabilities is denied services, it may be considered discrimination only if the student was otherwise qualified. Tom Smith (2002) describes this concept with the following example:

> He or she must be qualified *to do something* before the presence of a disability can be a factor in discrimination. If the student wants to participate in some activity that he or she is not otherwise qualified

to do, not allowing him or her to participate would not be considered discrimination. For example, a 16-year-old boy with attention-deficit/hyperactivity disorder (ADHD) tries out for the basketball team but cannot dribble, shoot, or pass. The coach therefore does not allow the boy to play on the team. This is not discrimination under Section 504 because the boy was not otherwise qualified to be on the team. (p. 260)

Unlike IDEA, Section 504 does not provide any federal dollars to support students with disabilities. However, if schools are found to be in noncompliance with Section 504, they may lose their other federal financing.

Eligibility for protection and services under Section 504 are different than those provided under IDEA. IDEA uses a categorical approach to identifying students who qualify for services. Section 504 uses a functional, noncategorical approach. A person is considered to have a disability if she or he "(i) has a physical or mental impairment which substantially limits one or more of such person's major life activities, (ii) has a record of such an impairment, or (iii) is regarded as having such an impairment" [29 U.S.C. Section 706(8)].

A *physical or mental impairment* is defined as

- any physiological disorder or condition, cosmetic disfigurement, or anatomical loss affecting one or more of the following body systems: neurological; musculoskeletal; special sense organs; respiratory, including speech organs; cardiovascular; reproductive; digestive; genitourinary; hemic and lymphatic; skin; and endocrine;

- any mental or psychological disorder, such as mental retardation, organic brain syndrome, emotional or mental illness, and specific learning disabilities.

The physical or mental impairment must also have an impact on a major life activity. Major life activities are identified in the Act as walking, talking, seeing, hearing, speaking, breathing, learning, working, and performing manual tasks. Most children and adolescents who receive Section 504 services in public schools receive such services because their disability impacts their learning. Students may, however, qualify for protections and services under Section 504 due to other major life activities.

Section 504 does not require formal IEPs. The Act does require, however, that schools develop a Section 504 plan for each qualifying student. Students who are identified for Section 504 services may be those with ADHD, medical conditions or communicable diseases (e.g., HIV/AIDS, cardiac problems, cancer), as well as those who are ineligible or no longer qualify for IDEA services (e.g., students with a low IQ score but not low enough to qualify as having intellectual disabilities).

The Elementary and Secondary Education Act

The third piece of legislation that has impacted public schools and teachers most recently is the **Elementary and Secondary Education Act (ESEA).** ESEA was reauthorized and labeled the **No Child Left Behind Act (NCLB)** of 2001. Similar to the manner in which IDEA defines the operation of special education in public schools, the ESEA 2001 reauthorization moved the federal government into being a major player in shaping general education instruction. The ESEA underwent revisions again in 2015 and was relabeled, **Every Student Succeeds Act (ESSA)**. The ESSA modified NCLB and provided more flexibility to states' accountability for achievement of all students. The Act still requires that states implement a statewide accountability system including test scores of all students in every public school. Students are tested in reading and math in Grades 3 through 8 and once in high school, as well as in science three times between Grades 3 and 12. Test results must be reported by subgroups including students with disabilities. One percent of the total student population (estimated to be less than 10% of all students with disabilities) may take alternative assessments based on alternative academic achievement standards. These alternative standards must align with academic content standards, promote access to the general education core, and be designated in the IEP. Under ESSA, the high-stakes nature of these tests is greatly reduced from the requirements in NCLB because tests scores alone are not the only way schools are evaluated. ESSA requires that states eliminate unnecessary or redundant tests.

Common Core and Standards

Although the **Common Core State Standards** were not developed by nor mandated by the federal government, these standards have received national attention and have impacted the field of special education. The Common Core defines what students should be able to know and do at certain benchmarks of their schooling experience. In other words, the Core represents a set of standards. The development of the Common Core began with 48 state governors and state education commissioners recognizing the need for a set of clear college- and career-ready standards for kindergarten through 12th grade in language arts/literacy and mathematics. Teams of teachers, principals, researchers, and leading experts developed these standards. Currently, 43 states have voluntarily adopted and are working to implement the standards.

The primary purposes of standards are to focus on a core of important information and to ensure that all students receive instruction in the same content. The reasoning behind the Common Core is not new; professional organizations and states have been developing standards for many years. For example, standards in science and social studies adopted by professional organizations may be found in Chapter 12.

The field of special education has been impacted by the Common Core and other educational standards. In general, the impact of standards-based education on students with disabilities has been both criticized and embraced. Historically, educators have tended to lower standards for students with learning and behavior problems. Proponents see standards-based education as a means toward reversing this trend (Hoover & Patton, 2004). They want to ensure students with disabilities are given the opportunity to achieve the same standards as their nondisabled peers. Opponents, on the other hand, view standards as challenging the rights to individualization, so important and prominent in the field of special education (McDonnell, McLaughlin, & Morrison, 1997).

As discussed previously, students with disabilities must have access to the general education curriculum. One way to define that is to indicate they must have meaningful opportunities to achieve the same standards, the Common Core or other standards, as those without disabilities. Special educators need to identify means for meeting both standards and individualization in the education of students with disabilities.

The Individualized Education Program (IEP) Process

The **IEP process** under IDEA drives educational services provided for students with disabilities. IDEA outlines a set of procedures that govern how school districts are to provide these services.

Enosa, a fourth-grade Pacific Islander American, is having difficulty keeping up with his peers in math skills. He is well liked and considered a leader in the classroom. His third-grade teacher expressed concern about his math skills as he began to lag behind his peers at the end of the school year. She shared this information with Enosa's fourth-grade teacher, Mrs. Williams, who tried several individual interventions at the beginning of the school year. For example, she set up a peer tutoring system for additional practice, provided him with graph paper to better line up his numbers, and let him tape a number line to his desk. Mrs. Williams collected data before and during each of these interventions. Enosa's math skills improved but he still lagged behind the other students. She spoke with his parents about her concerns and obtained their verbal, then written permission, to refer him for an individualized evaluation.

Referral Process

The first step of the IEP process is the referral of a student who is suspected to have a disability. Referrals may be made by teachers, parents and family members, or other professionals. Typically the referral goes to a **multidisciplinary team** who coordinates the evaluation process. Once data on a specific student are collected the team determines (a) whether the student qualifies for services under IDEA and needs special education and related services, and (b) the student's educational needs. If the student is eligible and needs services provided under IDEA, the **IEP team** then convenes to develop the Individualized Education Program. The multidisciplinary team and the IEP team may or may not consist of the same members. If they do, once the child is determined to be eligible, the same group of individuals usually continue the meeting to develop the IEP and then determine how best to deliver special education services to the student.

IEP Team Members

IEP team members include the student's parents, school professionals, and others at the discretion of the parents or the school. The team develops and reviews the IEP at least annually and makes revisions as needed. IDEA requires specifically that the IEP team consist of the following:

- **The student's parents**;
- **At least one general education teacher** if the student will or may be participating in a general education environment;

- **At least one special educator**, preferably the service provider for the student;

- **A representative from the local education agency (LEA)**. The **LEA** is usually the equivalent of the school district. This person must be qualified to provide or supervise the delivery of specially designed instruction for students with disabilities, as well as be knowledgeable about the general curriculum and availability of LEA resources;

- **An individual who can interpret the instructional implications of test results**;

- At the discretion of the parents or the school, **other individuals,** who are knowledgeable about the student, **including related services personnel** as appropriate; and

- When appropriate, **the student**.

An IEP team member need not attend the meeting, in whole or in part, if the parent and the local education agency agree that the member's attendance is not necessary because her area of curriculum or related services is not being discussed or modified in the meeting. When the meeting does involve a modification to or discussion of the member's area of curriculum or related services, the team member may be excused if the parent and local education agency consent and the member provides input into the development of the IEP in writing prior to the meeting. Parental consent to these two conditions must be in writing.

Parent Participation

Meaningful parental involvement is a fundamental principle underlying IDEA. When the Act was first passed in 1975, "for the first time in public school educational history, parents of students with disabilities attained formal educational planning status equal to that of teachers and administrators" (Martin, Marshall, & Sale, 2004, p. 285). Allowing or encouraging parental participation does not, however, guarantee parents will be involved as active and collaborative members of the team. Team attitudes and practices can greatly impact how welcomed and comfortable parents feel. Team attitudes are demonstrated in ways such as

- whether or how well the parents are prepared by the school prior to the meeting,

- where and when the meeting is held,

- who conducts the meeting and how they ask for team member participation, and

- how influential the parents' perspective is in the decision-making process.

Lack of parental involvement, even when it is encouraged, can be misinterpreted by professionals. Sometimes parents feel frustrated because they don't see themselves as being treated as equal members of the team or they are unfamiliar with IEP procedures and special education jargon. Professionals should not assume that parents' nonparticipation is due to apathy or lack of appreciation. Cultural or linguistic differences can also be barriers to understanding one another and working productively together. A thorough discussion of collaborating across diverse cultures, including working with parents and family members may be found in Chapter 2.

TEACHER TIP #1.5

INCREASING PARENT PARTICIPATION IN THE IEP PROCESS

Ideas for increasing parent participation include the following:

- Ask if they would like to talk to other parents about special education before the first meeting.

- Provide them information about parent support groups and national organizations and agencies.

- Invite them to visit classrooms before the meeting.

- Invite them directly to speak up, not just if they want to speak.

- Ask them specific questions to engage them in the discussion and decisions.

- Sit beside them at the meeting which can remove both physical and psychological barriers.

- Visit the parents in their home.

- Offer to videotape the student during school and then share with parents.

- Ask parents the best time to call or contact them.

- Encourage parents to bring a parent liaison with similar cultural background to the meeting.

- Provide positive feedback by contacting parents when the student is *being good*, not just when there are problems.

- Try to avoid educational jargon.

Source: Dabkowski, 2004; Lytle & Bordin, 2001.

General Educator Participation

General educators are required members of the IEP team if the student will or may be participating in the general education environment. If the student has more than one general education teacher, they do not all need to attend the meeting. Only one is required. However, if participation of more than one would be beneficial to the student's success, then it would be appropriate for them to attend.

General education teacher participation may not be needed in all IEP meetings or during the entire meetings. For example, general educators should participate in discussions and decisions about how best to adapt the general education curriculum for the student. But if the teacher is not responsible for implementing a related service (e.g., physical or occupational therapy), then he or she need not be involved in discussions and decisions about this service.

TEACHER TIP #1.6

ASSISTING GENERAL EDUCATION
TEACHERS' PARTICIPATION IN THE IEP PROCESS

To help alleviate general educators' concerns about feeling disconnected to the IEP process and resenting the amount of time required to attend IEP meetings, try some of these strategies:

- Personally invite general educators to attend meetings and be involved in the IEP process.

- Control the time needed for meetings by being organized and coming prepared.

- Consider general education teacher's schedules when arranging meetings.

- Conduct the meeting in the general education teacher's classroom.

- Share special education paraeducators to handle routine paperwork and to cover classes for meetings.

- Use an agenda to organize meetings.

- Inform general educators ahead of time what will be discussed and what helpful information they can provide.

- Encourage general educators to initiate IEP goals including classroom accommodations.

- Give general educators a copy of the IEP. (Menlove, Hudson, & Suter, 2001)

Student Participation

No later than when students turn 16 years old, they must be invited to attend their IEP meetings. In addition, discussions and decisions made in the meeting must reflect student interests and preferences and their postsecondary aspirations should provide direction to the plan of study and needed transition services (Martin et al., 2004). More specific information about transition services is located in Chapter 14.

Recent reports indicate that although students should be part of their IEP meetings many educators fail to invite them and when they do attend, they are not prepared with the necessary self-determination and self-advocacy skills needed to be a contributing team member. James Martin, Laura Huber Marshall, and Paul Sale (2004) surveyed over 1,600 IEP team members and discovered significant differences between the responses of when students did and did not attend the meeting. When students were present, parents understood better the reason for the meeting, felt more comfortable sharing their thoughts, and understood more of what was said. In addition, administrators talked more about the student's interests, needs, and strengths. General educators also felt more comfortable sharing their thoughts and better about the meeting.

Research indicates that direct instruction using published curricula or person-centered planning prior to the meeting coupled with an IEP meeting facilitator appear instrumental in improving student involvement. The facilitator's role in the meeting is to direct questions to the student, avoid jargon, and use language and vocabulary familiar to the student (Test et al., 2004). A sample list of published materials to help prepare students for IEP meeting participation appears in Table 1.6.

TABLE 1.6 **Sample List of Published Curricula for Teaching IEP Involvement**

Curriculum	Authors (Year)	Accessible Through
Getting the Most Out of IEPs: An Educator's Guide to the Student-Directed Approach	Thoma & Wehman (2010)	Paul H. Brookes Publishing www.brookspublishing.com
Next S. T. E. P.: Student Transition and Educational Planning	Halpern, Herr, Doren, & Wolf (2000)	Pro-Ed Publishing www.proedinc.com
Student-Led IEPs: A Guide for Student Involvement	McGahee, Mason, Wallace, & Jones (2001)	eric.ed.gov/?id=ED455623
Whose Future Is It Anyway? A Student-Directed Transition Planning Process (2nd ed.)	Wehmeyer, Lawrence, Garner, Soukup, & Palmer (2004)	www.ou.edu/education/centers-and-partnerships/zarrow/trasition-education-materials/whos-future-is-it-anyway.html

TEACHER TIP #1.7

PREPARING STUDENTS FOR IEP PARTICIPATION

Incorporate this information within daily instruction to help prepare students for active IEP meeting participation:

- Teach the purposes of the IEP and the IEP process.

- Identify members of the student's IEP team and their roles and responsibilities.

- Teach vocabulary terms that may arise during the meeting.

- Acquaint students with their current IEPs.

- Teach students appropriate social interaction skills such as listening and feedback.

- Discuss with students their interests and potential transition goal.

- Role-play an IEP meeting. (Snyder & Shapiro, 1997)

The IEP team's responsibility is to design the student's program of special education and related services. The team documents their decisions on the written IEP. They then determine where services can best be provided to this student based on the decisions made and documented on the IEP. The development of the IEP document must precede the service delivery or placement decision.

Enosa has received special education services for three years. Although he is only just now turning 14, he's been invited and attended his IEP meeting each year. The first year he was a passive participant, but now that he has learned some specific self-determination and social skills, each year he comes to the meeting more prepared to make a contribution.

The IEP Document

IDEA specifies that the IEP document include the following:

- **A statement of the student's present levels of academic achievement and functional performance** which includes how the student's disability impacts his or her involvement and progress in the general curriculum.

- **A statement of measurable annual goals including academic and functional goals.** These statements must be related to meeting the student's needs to help him or her be involved in and progress in the general curriculum as well as meet other educational needs related to the disability.

- **A description of how progress toward meeting the annual goals will be measured and when periodic reports on the progress will be made.** The Act suggests, for example, that quarterly or other periodic reports concurrent with report cards would be appropriate.

- **Benchmarks or short-term objectives** must be included if the student will take alternate assessments aligned to alternate achievement standards.

- **Statements of the special education and related services to be provided** and **program modifications or supports for school personnel** that will be provided for the student to (a) advance toward attaining the annual goals, (b) be involved and progress in the general curriculum, (c) participate in extracurricular and other nonacademic activities, and (d) be educated and participate with other students with and without disabilities. These services must be based on peer-reviewed research to the extent practicable.

- **An explanation of the extent, if any, to which the student will not participate with children without disabilities in the general class.**

- **A statement of any individual modifications in the administration of State or districtwide assessments** in order for the student to participate in such assessment. If the IEP team determines that the student will not participate, the IEP must include a statement of why that assessment is inappropriate for the student and how the student will be assessed.

- **The projected date services will be initiated,** as well as the anticipated frequency, location, and duration of those services.

- **Beginning at least by age 16 appropriate measurable postsecondary goals related to training, education, employment, and where appropriate, independent living skills and the transition services needed to reach those goals.** By at least one year before the student reaches the age of majority under State law, a statement must be included that the student has been informed of his or her rights that will transfer at age of majority (see Chapter 14 for more information).

Present Levels of Academic Achievement and Functional Performance

Present levels are listed as the first element required on the IEP document because it is the beginning point from which the plan is developed. Present levels refer to the student's current academic and functional strengths and limitations and the skills that need to be improved. This information is derived from the student's most recent formal and informal assessment as well as information contributed by the parents.

The present levels should contain a statement of how the disability impacts the student's involvement and progress in the general education curriculum and a description of the student's performance in skill areas affected by the disability. These statements should be written so they are helpful for writing annual goals and benchmarks or short-term objectives, if appropriate (Gibb & Dyches, 2016). (See Figure 1.1 for present level samples.)

| FIGURE 1.1 | **Examples of Present Levels of Academic Achievement and Functional Performance** |

Joey, a fourth-grade student, has difficulty reading which impacts his ability to read core curriculum materials in his general education classroom. Joey's reading fluency scores indicate he orally reads on a 1.0 grade level, reading passages at an average rate of 58 words a minute 100% accurately. His attention to decoding words interferes with his fluency. On three different trials, Joey answered 3 out of 5 reading comprehension questions correctly on the material he orally read (1.0 reading level), but answered all questions correctly on material read to him up to a 4.0 reading level.

Telly is a 12th-grade student whose mathematical skills limit his success in a general education math class. He can count coins to a dollar and dollar bills to $20. In addition, he can write and type dollar and cent amounts accurately with decimals. He is highly interested in learning to use an electronic checking account.

Annual Goals, Benchmarks, and Short-Term Objectives

The heart of the IEP document is measurable annual goals and short-term objectives or benchmarks. Annual goals represent the IEP team's projections or their best estimate of what the student can accomplish during one school year. Students who require alternative assessment aligned to alternate achievement standards must also include benchmarks or short-term objectives. If required, each annual goal is divided into about three to five short-term objectives or benchmarks, which describe meaningful intermediate and measurable outcomes between the student's current levels of performance and the annual goal. Short-term objectives should be used when the annual goal can be divided into discrete skill components. Benchmarks can be used when the annual goal does not divide into discrete parts. Benchmarks indicate the amount of progress toward a goal that a student is expected to make within specified segments of a school year. If a student achieves all the benchmarks or short-term objectives, he should be capable of achieving the annual goal. Examples of annual goals, benchmarks, and short-term objectives for Joey and Telly introduced in Figure 1.1 may be found in Figure 1.2. Additional information regarding writing measurable goals, objectives and benchmarks is addressed in Chapter 6.

FIGURE 1.2   Examples of Annual Goals With Short-Term Objectives and Benchmarks

Annual Goal: Given a second-grade reading passage, Joey will increase his oral reading fluency to 100 words per minute with 98% accuracy on 2 consecutive timings.

- Benchmark 1: Given a 1.0 grade reading passage, Joey will orally read the passage to 100 words per minute with 98% accuracy on 2 consecutive timings.

- Benchmark 2: Given a 1.5 grade reading passage, Joey will orally read the passage to 100 words per minute with 98% accuracy on 2 consecutive timings.

- Benchmark 3: Given a 2.0 grade reading passage, Joey will orally read the passage to 100 words per minute with 98% accuracy on 2 consecutive timings.

- Benchmark 4: Given a 2.5 grade reading passage, Joey will orally read the passage to 100 words per minute with 98% accuracy on 2 consecutive timings.

Annual Goal: Using a pseudo computerized bank account with preprogrammed company names and an account balance, Telly will send 10 checks to the correct companies with correct amounts at 100% accuracy.

- Objective 1: Given a company name, Telly will select the correct company by clicking on the name 10 out of 10 trials.

- Objective 2: Given 10 dollar and cent amounts, Telly will type the correct amount in the appropriate boxes 10 out of 10 trials.

- Objective 3: Given a company name and a dollar and cent amount, Telly will select the correct company and type in the correct amount in the appropriate boxes 10 out of 10 trials.

Special Education and Related Services

The IEP must include a statement of the special education and related services to be provided to the student. **Special education** is defined by IDEA as specially designed instruction to meet the unique needs of a student with a disability. It includes instruction conducted in classrooms, homes, hospitals, institutions, and other settings, as well as instruction in physical education.

IDEA defines **related services** as developmental, corrective, and other supportive services needed to assist a student with a disability to benefit from special education. Specific services listed in IDEA include transportation, speech-language pathology and audiology, psychological services, physical and occupational therapy, recreation, therapeutic recreation, social work services, counseling services, rehabilitation counseling, orientation and mobility services, medical services (for diagnostic and evaluation purposes only), and early identification and assessment of disabling conditions.

The IEP team determines the type(s) of special education and related services required by the student in order to meet the goals established. Once the type of services has been identified, the team determines where (i.e., service delivery or placement) the student can best receive these services to accomplish the goals.

Service Delivery

Continuum of Services

One of IDEA's principles is the *least restrictive environment*, defined as providing students with disabilities educational services with their non-disabled peers to the greatest degree possible. Even though the least restrictive environment for most students with HID may be the general education classroom, school districts must also provide a variety of placement options, or a **continuum of services**. Across this continuum, the general education classroom is viewed as the most typical setting with home and hospital as the most restrictive settings. One would expect the greatest number of students with disabilities served in the general education classroom and the fewest in homes and hospitals.

Figure 1.3 provides a visual representation of the continuum of services. Each level moving upward represents a progressively more restrictive environment serving fewer numbers of students. At the bottom level students or their teacher may receive support delivered in the general education classroom. Students are not *pulled out* for specialized instruction at this level. They are, however, pulled out for resource room support at the next level. Students receiving resource room support attend their general education classroom for all but 1 or 2 hours a day, during which time, they spend in the resource room where special education services are delivered. Moving up the continuum, students in part-time general and special class would spend approximately half of the school day in both types of classroom. The next level, full-time special classes in general schools are just that, self-contained classrooms for students with disabilities housed within a school for all children. Those in special schools live at home, but attend a segregated school designed for students with disabilities, while students educated in a residential school live in dormitories as part of the schooling experience. The most restrictive forms of service delivery are home and hospital.

FIGURE 1.3 | **Continuum of Services**

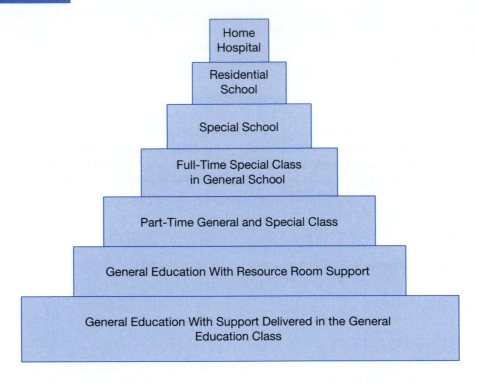

Home
Hospital

Residential
School

Special School

Full-Time Special Class
in General School

Part-Time General and Special Class

General Education With Resource Room Support

General Education With Support Delivered in the General
Education Class

Inclusive Education

Although a continuum of services must be provided for students with disabilities, many professionals and parents have questioned the assumption that students who need more intensive services need to be segregated from their typical peers to receive those services. These individuals believe that if students cannot meet traditional academic expectations in the general classroom, then the expectations should change, not the setting. They support the concept of **inclusion**. "Inclusion represents the belief or philosophy that students with disabilities should be fully integrated into general education classrooms and schools and that their instruction should be based on their abilities, not their disabilities" (Friend & Bursuck, 2002, p. 4).

How schools implement inclusion varies. Some schools designate specific general education classrooms as the inclusion classrooms. Other schools distribute students with disabilities across all classrooms to better represent the proportion of those with disabilities found in the general population. In most inclusion classrooms, teachers continue to implement the general curriculum with accommodations provided to those with special needs. Sometimes general educators and special educators co-teach in the inclusive general education classrooms. Specialized services, such as speech therapy may be delivered in the general education classroom. Different inclusion models can be seen across schools and districts. No one size fits all. Educators who adopt inclusion need to find the model that best fits their students' needs.

Technology Spotlight #1.2

Computer Programs Simplify the Task of Writing IEPs

While key components of the IEP must be present, there is little uniformity in IEP forms between schools, districts, and states. Since the mandate of IEPs in the mid-1970s, the most common technology utilized for IEPs involved preprinted NCR (no carbon required) forms on which teachers would write the IEP by hand during the IEP meeting and then separate the color-coded pages to distribute to the parent, school, and special education teacher. The task of preparing the IEP was time consuming and the documents did not look professional.

As technology became more sophisticated, schools began adopting commercially developed IEP software products. Such software has been used district- or statewide to ensure consistency within the district or state and compliance with federal mandates. Significant efforts were devoted to customizing the software to meet local requirements and preferences.

In recent years, IEP software developers have migrated their products from software-based tools to web-based systems. Thus, an IEP can be accessed via the web (with appropriate passwords, of course) so that it can be modified during a meeting or updated from the teacher's home computer. This advancement has been an important step in the development of making IEPs more professional, accurate, and responsive to the original mandates of documenting the expectations and accomplishments of each student with a disability.

To learn more about various computerized IEP products, visit the following:

e-IEP PRO: http://e-ieppro.com/products.html

Excent: http://www.excent.com

GoalView: http://www.ltools.com/GOALVIEW/index.asp

OnCourse: Special Education and IEP Suite: http://www.oncourse systems.com

IEP Review and Revision

IDEA requires that the IEP be reviewed and, if necessary, revised at least annually. This requirement ensures that the schools treat the IEP as a work in progress that constantly changes and evolves in response to an individual student's needs. When reviewing the IEP, the team must consider the following:

- any lack of progress toward the annual goals and in the general education curriculum (if appropriate),
- results of any reevaluation,
- information about the student provided by the parents,

- student's anticipated needs, and

- other considerations as needed. (Drasgow et al., 2001)

Although the IEP specifies goals for a student, the IEP is not the curriculum. The IEP goals supplement and support the curriculum; they do not replace it. Special educators need a working understanding of curriculum, particularly given the requirement that students with disabilities have access to the general curriculum. They also need to understand the role of standards in the education of students with disabilities. The relationship between curriculum, standards, and IEPs can be complicated. Prior to discussing this relationship, curriculum and standards are discussed in more general terms.

Aligning Curriculum, Standards, and IEPs

When it comes to curriculum, standards, and IEPs, recent legislation appears contradictory. IDEA clearly states that students with disabilities must have meaningful access to the same curriculum as their nondisabled peers. Yet the basic premise of individualization based on individual student's needs also permeates IDEA. IDEA also states that all students with disabilities participate in all assessments, with accommodations and alternate assessments as indicated on the IEP (see Chapter 7 for a discussion of testing

FIGURE 1.4   Flowchart for Aligning Standards, IEPs, and Assessments

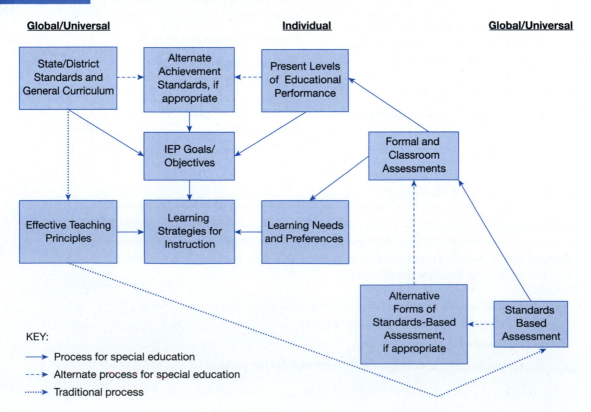

accommodations). ESEA requires students with disabilities to be accountable for the same standard achievement as their peers without disabilities and that only 1% of the student population may be assessed using alternative achievement standards.

Mary Anne Prater and Cecily Ornelles (2002) developed a model describing how teachers can integrate these seemingly conflicting mandates. A visual representation of this model may be found in Figure 1.4. On the left and right sides of the model are universal aspects of the process that apply to all students. All students (a) have access to the general curriculum, (b) are expected to achieve prespecified standards, (c) benefit from effective teaching methods, (d) are held accountable for achieving standards, and (e) participate in both formal and classroom assessment processes. The IEP process must overlay these steps for students with disabilities. In the middle of the model, IEP process steps impacted by the universal requirements are listed.

This model suggests that IEP goals and objectives should be determined by the general curriculum and the Common Core or other state standards, as well as present levels of educational performance. For the 1% of students being assessed using alternative achievement standards, these standards can be used along with the present level of performance to determine IEP goals and objectives. As reflected in Figure 1.4, once the IEP has been developed and service delivery options determined, the student should be taught using effective teaching principles and learning strategies for instruction.

SUMMARY

Students with high-incidence disabilities (HID) include those with learning disabilities (LD), emotional behavioral disorders (EBD), mild to moderate intellectual disabilities (ID), attention-deficit/hyperactivity disorder (ADHD) and high-functioning autism (HFA). All of these disabilities with the exception of ADHD are defined in the Individuals with Disabilities Education Act (IDEA). ADHD is addressed in this book given that students with ADHD have many common learning characteristics with those in other HID categories.

The definitions of these disability conditions have changed over the years and will continue to evolve as the field gains greater understanding of the conditions. Definitions and other factors influence prevalence rates. Approximately 3% to 4% of all students ages 6 to 21 are identified as having LD. Students with ID, EBD, and HFA are each represented by less than 1% of the total school population. Given that ADHD is not listed in IDEA, only estimates are available and indicate that approximately 6% to 7% of all students have ADHD.

Students with HID typically demonstrate difficulties in their cognitive functioning, which includes attention, memory, and concept formation. By definition, students with HID demonstrate academic difficulties and many have social deficits. Difficulties with motivation and attribution also impact students with HID.

The increased racial, ethnic, socioeconomic, and linguistic diversity in the United States has influenced the education field, including special education. Care must be taken when identifying diverse students with a disability by ensuring learning difficulties are not based on experiential, cultural, or linguistic differences. Proportionately more American Indian/Alaska Native, Black, Hispanic/Latino, and Native Hawaiian/Pacific Islanders are being identified with HID than White and Asian students.

Three federal laws, the Individuals with Disabilities Education Act (IDEA), Section 504 of the Rehabilitation Act, and the Elementary and Secondary Education Act (ESEA), impact special education services in the United

States. IDEA is the most directly aligned with special education because it defines the operation of special education in schools, including who is eligible for services as well as what and where services are provided. IDEA is based on six major principles: zero reject, nondiscriminatory assessment, procedural due process, parental participation, least restrictive environment, and Individualized Education Programs (IEPs).

Students with disabilities can also receive school services through Section 504 under a 504 plan (instead of an IEP), and applies primarily to students with ADHD. The most recent reauthorization of ESEA mandates that each state implement accountability systems that include test scores of all students. One percent of the total student population (or about 10% of all students with disabilities) may take alternative assessments based on alternative achievement standards.

The IEP process under IDEA drives educational services provided for students with disabilities. Specific procedures are outlined for identifying students as having a disability, as well as planning, implementing, and evaluating IEPs. Parents or family members are key players in all of the steps of the IEP process. Students, when appropriate, should also be involved, particularly by participating in their IEP meetings. The IEP document must contain specific content including present levels of performance, goals and objectives, and special education and related services needed, among other elements.

One of IDEA's principles is the least restrictive environment, or providing students with disabilities education services with their nondisabled peers to the greatest degree possible. Although a continuum of services must be provided, most students with HID attend general education classes with support which is often referred to as an inclusive education.

REVIEW QUESTIONS

1. Describe general characteristics of the five categorical high incidence disabilities (HID). Compare and contrast these characteristics.

2. Historically, what have been the challenges defining the five HID?

3. Discuss three ways students with HID differ from their peers in cognition. Explain each and describe school-related tasks that would be difficult for students with deficits in each of these areas and why they would be difficult.

4. Describe the changing cultural, linguistic, and socioeconomic diversity in the United States. Provide examples in each area and describe how they have impacted the field of special education.

5. What are the six major principles of IDEA? Why are these principles important for protecting the educational interests of students with disabilities?

6. Describe when a student might qualify for services under Section 504 but not qualify under IDEA.

7. How has the Elementary and Secondary Education Act impacted the field of special education? Be specific.

8. Why is it important for parents, general educators, and students to participate in the IEP process? What can special educators do to encourage active participation of these members?

9. Define and describe the connections among the following: present levels of performance, IEP annual goals, access to general curriculum, universal design, and state/district standards. Provide an example based on a hypothetical student.

10. Provide two examples of aligning curriculum, standards, and IEPs, including the Common Core.

ACTIVITIES

1. Select one disabling condition described in the chapter and write about your personal experience interacting with an individual or individuals with the condition. Compare and contrast the characteristics described in the text with your experience.

2. Using the websites provided in Technology Spotlight #1.1, create a one-page summary of characteristics of each of the high incidence disabilities addressed in this chapter. Make the summaries suitable to share with parents and general education teachers.

3. Access your state's rules and regulations for special education. Write a paper on how your state defines LD, EBD, ID, and autism. Include ADHD if the state addresses this condition.

4. Go to the Council for Exceptional Children's website (www.cec.sped.org). Identify the information available about laws pertaining to special education. Write a summary of information available at this site.

Council for Exceptional Children (CEC) Standards

The Council for Exceptional Children (CEC) is a premiere national professional organization comprised of special educators, paraeducators, relative service personnel, parents, and others interested in individuals with disabilities and/or those with gifts and talents. This organization has generated 10 standards for the preparation of special educators. These standards are listed in each chapter as they relate to the content within the chapter. The standards that apply to Chapter 1 are Standards #1, #2, and #6.

CEC Initial Preparation Standard #1: Learner Development and Individual Learning Difference

Beginning special education professionals understand how exceptionalities may interact with development and learning and use this knowledge to provide meaningful and challenging learning experiences for individuals with exceptionalities.

1.1 Beginning special education professionals understand how language, culture, and family background influence the learning of individuals with exceptionalities.

1.2 Beginning special education professionals use understanding of development and individual differences to respond to the needs of individuals with exceptionalities.

CEC Initial Preparation Standard #2: Learning Environments (partial)

Beginning special education professionals create safe, inclusive, culturally responsive learning environments so that individuals with exceptionalities become active and effective learners and develop emotional well-being, positive social interactions, and self-determination.

2.1 Beginning special education professionals through collaboration with general educators and other colleagues create safe, inclusive, culturally responsive learning environments to engage individuals with exceptionalities in meaningful learning activities and social interactions.

CEC Initial Preparation Standard #6: Professional Learning and Ethical Practice (partial)

6.2 Beginning special education professionals understand how foundational knowledge and current issues influence professional practice.

6.3 Beginning special education professionals understand that diversity is a part of families, cultures, and schools, and that complex human issues can interact with the delivery of special education services.

REFERENCES

American Psychiatric Association. (2013). *Diagnostic and statistical manual of mental disorders* (5th ed.). Washington, DC: Author.

Andersen, P. N., Egeland, J., & Øie, M. (2012). Learning and memory impairments in children and adolescents with attention-deficit/hyperactivity disorder. *Journal of Learning Disabilities, 46*(5), 453–460.

Ausubel, D. P. (1968). *Education psychology: A cognitive view*. New York, NY: Holt, Rinehart & Winston.

Benner, S. M. (1998). *Special education issues within the context of American society*. Belmont, CA: Wadsworth.

Bouck, E. C., & Satsangi, R. (2015). Is there really a difference? Distinguishing mild intellectual disability from similar disability categories. *Education and Training in Autism and Developmental Disabilities, 50*(2), 186–198.

Buttner, G., & Hasselhorn, M. (2011). Learning disabilities: Debates on definitions, causes, subtypes, and responses. *International Journal of Disability, Development, and Education, 58*(1), 75–87.

Carlson, C. L., Booth, J. E., Shin, M., & Canu, W. H. (2002). Parent-, teacher-, and self-rated motivational styles in ADHD subtypes. *Journal of Learning Disabilities, 35*, 104–113.

Carter, N., Prater, M. A., & Dyches, T. T. (2009). *Making accommodations and adaptations for students with mild to moderate disabilities*. Upper Saddle River, NJ: Pearson.

Caterino, L. C. (2014). Cognitive, neuropsychological, academic, and adaptive functioning. In L. A. Wilkinson (Ed.), *Autism spectrum disorder in children and adolescents: Evidence-based assessment and intervention in schools* (pp. 75–99). Washington, DC: American Psychological Association.

Centers for Disease Control and Prevention. (2014). *Prevalence of autism spectrum disorder among children aged 8 years*. Retrieved from http://www.cdc.gov/mmwr/preview/mmwrhtml/ss6302a1.htm?s_cid=ss6302a1_wTop of Form

Council for Children with Behavioral Disorders. (1987). Position paper on definition and identification of students with behavior disorders. *Behavioral Disorders, 13*, 9–19.

Csoti, M. (2001). *Social awareness skills for children*. London, England: Jessica Kingsley.

Dabkowski, D. M. (2004). Encouraging active parent participation in IEP team meetings. *TEACHING Exceptional Children, 36*(3), 34–39.

Drasgow, E., Yell, M. L., & Robinson, T. R. (2001). Developing legally correct and educationally appropriate IEPs. *Remedial and Special Education, 22*, 359–373.

Dunn, L. M. (1968). Special education for the mildly retarded. Is much of it justifiable? *Exceptional Children, 35*, 229–237.

Ford, D. Y. (2012). Culturally different students in special education: Looking backward to move forward. *Exceptional Children, 79*(4), 391–405.

Forness, S. R., & Kavale, K. A. (2000). Emotional or behavioral disorders: Background and current status of the E/BD terminology and definition. *Behavioral Disorders, 25*, 264–269.

Friend, M., & Bursuck, W. D. (2002). *Including students with special needs: A practical guide for classroom teachers*. Boston, MA: Allyn & Bacon.

Gage, N. A., Gersten, R., Sugai, G., & Newman-Gonchar, R. (2013). Disproportionality of English learners with emotional and/or behavioral disorders: A comparative meta-analysis with English learners with learning disabilities. *Behavioral Disorders, 38*(3), 123–136.

Gage, N. A., Lierheimer, K. S., & Goran, L. G. (2012). Characteristics of students with high-incidence disabilities broadly defined. *Journal of Disability Policy Studies, 23*(3), 168–178.

Gibb, G. S., & Dyches, T. T. (2016). *Writing quality Individualized Education Programs* (3rd ed.). Boston, MA: Pearson.

Hallahan, D. P., Kauffman, J. M., & Pullen, P. C. (2014). *Exceptional learners: An introduction to special education* (13th ed.).: Boston, MA: Pearson.

Hallahan, D. P., & Mercer, C. D. (2002). Learning disabilities: Historical perspective. In R. Bradley, L. Danielson, & D. P. Hallahan (Eds). *Identification of learning disabilities: Research to practice* (pp. 1–67). Mahwah, NJ: Erlbaum.

Hallahan, D. P., & Mock, D. R. (2003). A brief history of the field of learning disabilities. In H. L. Swanson, K. R. Harris, & S. Graham (Eds.), *The handbook of learning disabilities* (pp. 16–29). New York, NY: Guilford Press.

Hanchan, T. A., & Allen, R. A. (2013). Identifying students with emotional disturbance: School psychologists' practices and perceptions. *Psychology in the Schools, 50*(2), 193–208.

Handen, B. L., Janosky, J., & McAuliffe, S. (1997). Long-term follow-up of children with mental retardation/borderline intellectual functioning and ADHD. *Journal of Abnormal Child Psychology, 23,* 287–295.

Harry, B., & Klingner, J. (2006). *Why are so many minority students in special education?* New York, NY: Teachers College Press.

Hoover, J. J., & Patton, J. R. (2004). Differentiating standards-based education for students with diverse needs. *Remedial and Special Education, 25,* 74–78.

Jasper, A. D., & Bouck, E. C. (2013). Disproportionality among African American students at the secondary level: Examining the MID disability category. *Education and Training in Autism and Developmental Disabilities, 48*(1), 31–40.

Kern, L., Evans, S. W., Lewis, T. J., State, T. M., Weist, M. D., & Wills, H. P. (2015). CARS comprehension intervention for secondary students with emotional and behavioral problems: Conceptualization and development. *Journal of Emotional and Behavioral Disorders, 23*(4), 195–205.

Klingner, J., & Eppolito, A. M. (2014). *English language learners: Differentiating between language acquisition and learning disabilities.* Arlington, VA: Council for Exceptional Children.

Kozminsky, E., & Kozminsky, L. (2002). The dialogue page: Teacher and student dialogues to improve learning motivation. *Intervention in School and Clinic, 38,* 88–95.

Lytle, R. K., & Bordin, J. (2001). Enhancing the IEP team: Strategies for parents and professionals. *TEACHING Exceptional Children, 33*(5), 40–44.

Maehler, C., & Schuchardt, L. (2009). Working memory functioning in children with learning disabilities: Does IQ make a difference? *Journal of Intellectual Disabilities Research, 53,* 3–10.

Maenner, M. J., & Durkin, M. S. (2010). Trends in the prevalence of autism on the basis of special education data. *Pediatrics, 126*(5), 1018–1019.

Martin, J. E., Marshall, L. H., & Sale, P. (2004). A 3-year study of middle, junior high, and high school IEP meetings. *Exceptional Children, 70,* 285–297.

Mastropieri, M. A., & Scruggs, T. E. (2000). *The inclusive classroom: Strategies for effective instruction.* Upper Saddle River, NJ: Merrill/Prentice Hall.

Maulik, P. K., Mascarenhas, M. N., Mathers, C. D., Dua, T., & Saxena, S. (2011). Prevalence of intellectual disability: A meta-analysis of population-based studies. *Research in Developmental Disabilities, 32,* 419–436.

Mayes, S. D., Calhoun, S. L., & Crowell, E. W. (2000). Learning disabilities and ADHD: Overlapping spectrum disorders. *Journal of Learning Disabilities, 33,* 417–424.

McDonnell, L. M., McLaughlin, M. J., & Morrison, P. (1997). *Educating one and all: Students with disabilities and standards-based reform.* Washington, DC: National Academic Press.

McIntyre, T., & Forness, S. R. (1996). Is there a new definition yet or are our kids still seriously emotionally disturbed? *Beyond Behavior, 7*(3), 4–9.

Menlove, R. R., Hudson, P. J., & Suter, D. (2001). A field of IEP dreams: Increasing general education teacher participation in the IEP development process. *TEACHING Exceptional Children, 33*(5), 28–33.

Most, T., & Greenbank, A. (2000). Auditory, visual, and auditory-visual perception of emotions by adolescents with and without learning disabilities, and their relationship to social skills. *Learning Disabilities Research, 15,* 171–178.

Murdick, N., Gartin, B., & Crabtree, T. (2002). *Special education law.* Upper Saddle River, NJ: Merrill/Prentice Hall.

National Center for Education Statistics. (2012). *Children living in poverty.* Washington, DC: Author. Retrieved from https://nces.ed.gov/programs/coe/pdf/coe_cce.pdf

National Center for Education Statistics. (2013). *Digest of education statistics: Elementary and secondary education.* Washington, DC: Author. Retrieved from http://nces.ed.gov/programs/digest/d13/tables/dt13_204.20.asp

Neece, C. L., Baker, B. L., Blacher, J., & Crnic, K. A. (2011). Attention-deficit/hyperactivity disorder among children with and without intellectual disability: An examination across time. *Journal of Intellectual Disability Research, 55,* 623–635.

Nolet, V., & McLaughlin, M. J. (2000). *Accessing the general curriculum: Including students with disabilities in standards-based reform.* Thousands Oak, CA: Corwin.

Orkwis, R., & McLane, K. (1998). *A curriculum every student can use: Design principles for student access.* Reston, VA: The ERIC Clearinghouse on Disabilities and Gifted Education.

Pancheri, C., & Prater, M. A. (1999). What teachers and parents should know about Ritalin. *TEACHING Exceptional Children, 31*(4), 20–26.

Pastor, P. N., & Reuben, C. A. (2002). *Attention deficit disorder and learning disability: United States, 1997–1998* (Vital and Health Statistics Series 10, No. 206). Washington, DC: U.S. Government Printing Office.

Pinborough-Zimmerman, J., Bakian, A. V., Fombonne, E., Bilder, D., Taylor, J., & McMahon, W. M. (2012). Changes in the administrative prevalence of autism spectrum disorders: Contributions of special education and health

from 2002–2008, *Journal of Autism and Developmental Disabilities, 42,* 521–530.

Prater, M. A. (1998). Teaching concepts: Procedures for the design and delivery of instruction. In E. L. Meyen, G. A. Vergason, & R. J. Whelan (Eds.), *Educating students with mild disabilities: Strategies and methods* (2nd ed., pp. 417–435). Denver, CO: Love.

Prater, M. A., & Ornelles, C. (2002, April). *Aligning statewide and curricular assessment with educational practices: Examples from the field.* Paper presented at the annual meeting of the Council for Exceptional Children, New York.

Salend, S. J., & Rohena, E. (2003). Students with attention deficit disorders: An overview. *Intervention in School and Clinic, 38,* 259–266.

Sansosti, J. M., & Sansosti, F. J. (2012). Inclusion for students with high-functioning autism spectrum disorders: Definitions and decision making. *Psychology in the Schools, 49*(10), 917–931.

Scanlon, D. (2003, August). Changing LD eligibility—Proceed with caution. *CEC Today, 10*(2), 12.

Smith, J. D. (1997). Mental retardation as an educational construct: Time for a new shared view? *Education and Training in Mental Retardation and Developmental Disabilities, 32,* 167–173.

Smith, T. E. C. (2002). Section 504: What teachers need to know. *Intervention in School and Clinic, 37,* 259–266.

Snyder, E. P., & Shapiro, E. S. (1997). Teaching students with emotional/behavioral disorders the skills to participate in the development of their own IEPs. *Behavioral Disorders, 22,* 246–259.

Sullivan, A. L. (2011). Disproportionality in special education identification and placement of English language learners. *Exceptional Children, 77*(3), 317–334.

Swanson, H. L., Kehler, P., & Jerman, O. (2010). Working memory, strategy knowledge, and strategy instruction in children with reading disabilities. *Journal of Learning Disabilities, 43*(1), 24–47.

Tabassam, W., & Grainger, J. (2002). Self-concept, attributional style and self-efficacy beliefs of students with learning disabilities with and without attention deficit hyperactivity disorder. *Learning Disability Quarterly, 25*, 141–151.

Test, D. W., Mason, C., Hughes, C., Konrad, M., Neale, M., & Wood, W. (2004). Student involvement in Individualized Education Program meetings. *Exceptional Children, 70*, 391–412.

Travers, J. C., Tincani, M., & Krezmien, M. P. (2011). A multiyear national profile of racial disparity in autism identification. *The Journal of Special Education, 47*(1), 41–49.

U.S. Census Bureau. (1990). *Language spoken at home: 1990*. Washington, DC: Author. Retrieved from http://www.census.gov/prod/cen1990/cqc/cqc16.pdf

U.S. Census Bureau. (2000a). *Language use and English-speaking ability: 2000*. Washington, DC: Author. Retrieved from http://www.census.gov/prod/2003pubs/c2kbr-29.pdf

U.S. Census Bureau. (2000b). *Overview of race and Hispanic origin: 2000*. Washington, DC: Author. Retrieved from http://www.census.gov/prod/2001pubs/c2kbr01-1.pdf

U.S. Census Bureau. (2010a). *Language use in the United States: 2010*. Washington, DC: Author. Retrieved from https://www.census.gov/prod/2013pubs/acs-22.pdf

U.S. Census Bureau. (2010b). *Overview of race and Hispanic origin: 2010*. Washington, DC: Author.

Retrieved from http://www.census.gov/prod/cen2010/briefs/c2010br-02.pdf

U.S. Census Bureau. (2014). *Household relationship and family status of children/1 under 18, by age and sex: 2014*. Washington, DC: Author. Retrieved from http://www.census.gov/hhes/families/files/cps2013/tabC1-all.xls

U.S. Department of Education. (1999, March 12). Assistance to states for the education of children with disabilities and the early intervention program for infants and toddlers with disabilities: Final regulations. *Federal Register, 64*, 12406–12672.

U.S. Department of Education. (2014). *Thirty-sixth annual report to Congress on the implementation of the Individuals with Disabilities Act*. Washington, DC: Author. Retrieved from http://www2.ed.gov/about/reports/annual/osep/2014/parts-b-c/36th-idea-arc.pdf

Volker, M. A. (2012). Introduction to the special issue: High-functioning autism spectrum disorders in the school. *Psychology in the Schools, 49*(10), 911–916.

Willcutt, E. G. (2012). The prevalence of DSM-IV attention-deficit/hyperactivity disorder: A meta-analytic review. *Neurotherapeutics, 9*, 490–499.

Yates, J. R., & Ortiz, A. A. (2004). Classification issues in special education for English Language Learners. In A. M. Sorrells, H. J. Rieth, & P. T. Sindelar, *Critical issues in special education: Access, diversity, and accountability* (pp. 38–56). Boston, MA: Allyn & Bacon.

Ysseldyke, J. E., Algozzine, B., & Thurlow, M. L. (2000). *Critical issues in special education* (3rd ed.). Boston, MA: Houghton Mifflin.

$\circledS$SAGE edge™ · ●

Review ➡ Practice ➡ Improve

Get the tools you need to sharpen your study skills. Access videos, practice quizzes, eFlashcards and more at **edge.sagepub.com/prater.**

Educational Collaboration

Key Topics

Models of Working Together

Special educators do not work in isolation. To ensure quality education for students with disabilities, special educators work with students' families, paraeducators, other school personnel, and staff from government agencies or private industry. This chapter is devoted to discussing the skills and processes needed to work together to ensure that all students are given the best education possible.

Collaboration is an interactive style that may be applied regardless of the model individuals have adopted for working with others. Before discussing collaboration in detail, four models used by special educators are presented: consulting, co-teaching, coaching, and mentoring. Special educators consult and co-teach when working with others to improve student performance. They participate in coaching and mentoring when the focus is on improving their own teaching performance.

Learning Objectives

- Define, compare and contrast, and create case studies of the four models of working together.

- Define the critical elements of collaboration and describe the role of interactive communication, problem-solving, and conflict resolution in effective collaboration. Create examples of when collaboration did and did not work and explain why.

- Describe and provide examples of best practices when working with paraeducators and students' family members.

- Describe how cultural differences impact the manner in which individuals collaborate. Provide examples of strategies teachers can use to engage family members across cultures.

Working to Improve Student Performance

Consultation

Camille, a seventh-grade student with a learning disability, attends all general education classes. She works on grade level in all subjects except math. Camille's special education teacher, Mr. Herring, meets with Camille's math teacher, Mr. Ernest, for 5 to 10 minutes weekly to review Camille's progress. Mr. Herring never directly teaches Camille. Mr. Ernest brings work samples, weekly test results, and a form similar to the one found in Figure 2.1 to each of their meetings. Mr. Herring recommends modifications in instructional procedures, the classroom environment, assignments, and tests to help Camille succeed. For example, Camille understands most math concepts but often makes computational errors. Mr. Herring suggests she be allowed to use a calculator to check her work. She sometimes misaligns place values so now at Mr. Herring's suggestion, she uses a grid to line up numbers accurately. Mr. Herring has also recommended Camille be given more time to complete timed tests and that she be seated in a less distractible place in the classroom. Mr. Ernest has been willing and successful in making these modifications on his own.

Although teachers and other individuals work together for the benefit of students, the models under which they operate vary greatly. Mr. Herring, Camille's special education teacher, meets weekly with Camille's general education math teacher, Mr. Ernest. During this time Mr. Herring provides him suggestions to facilitate Camille's success in his classroom. This represents the consulting model, a fundamental process used in applied professions such as education, psychology, and business.

Marilyn Friend and Lynne Cook (2013) define school **consultation** as "a voluntary process in which one professional assists another to address a problem concerning a third party" (p. 191). Others extend this definition to include increasing the capacity of

FIGURE 2.1   **Discussion Guide for Special Education Consultation**

General Education Teacher_____   Date_____

Special Education Teacher_____

Evaluation of Last Week's Work

Student's Name	Evaluation (check one)			Comments
	Better	Same	Worse	

Planning

Topics to be covered next week _____

Instructional procedures to be used _____

Assignments or tests to be given _____

Criteria for evaluation to be used _____

Student's Name	Problems Student May Encounter	Recommended Modifications

Additional concerns or comments:

the person receiving the consulting to handle similar situations in the future (Erchul & Martens, 2010). In education, most consultation is case based with a consultant (e.g., Mr. Herring) working through a teacher (e.g., Mr. Ernest) to serve a student (e.g., Camille). The consultant may be a special educator, school psychologist, speech therapist, or other school professional. For some educational professionals, consultation is expected as part of their job requirements. For example, school psychologists typically spend about 20% of their time consulting with others in the schools (Erchul & Martens, 2010). The person receiving the consultation, the consultee, is usually a teacher, although sometimes a parent or even a student. Generally speaking, the consultee, or teacher, is responsible for identifying the problem, seeking out the consultant, and implementing any recommendations given by the consultant. Communication is considered one way because the expert is providing the advice; and ownership of the problem and solution is on the individual seeking and/or receiving the advice. Historically, consultation in special education has been used to address a variety of needs such as prereferral interventions, general education supports, and integration of special education interventions in the general education setting (Eisenman, Pleet, Wandry, & McGinley, 2011).

Mr. Herring and Mr. Ernest use a guide similar to the one in Figure 2.1 to facilitate their weekly discussions. Mr. Ernest completes the form prior to the meeting with the exception of the sections entitled *problems student may encounter* and *recommended modifications*. This information is provided by Mr. Herring during the meeting.

All teacher consultation models have two major goals: first, to provide services to remediate immediate problems, and second, to increase consultees' skills to prevent or respond more effectively to similar problems in the future. A growing amount of literature supports consultation as an effective model for solving immediate problems. However, limited research exists that teachers generalize skills learned through consultation to new, but similar problems, without additional training (Riley-Tillman & Eckert, 2001).

Some general and special educators do not like the consultation model because it assumes one party is the expert and the other is the novice. For example, in a general and special educator relationship, both are experts, although that expertise differs. A general educator is the expert with the content being taught and typical large-group instructional methods; whereas, the special educator has disability characteristics and strategies expertise. Thus, many teachers prefer the co-teaching or collaborative models for general and special educators working together.

Co-Teaching

Students identified with high-incidence disabilities who attend Riverdale High School enroll in core general education classes (i.e., English, math, history, science). Mr. Norry and Mrs. Lu are certified special educators but co-teach with the general education teachers in core classes. Mr. Norry co-teaches with general educators in English and history classes and Mrs. Lu co-teaches in the general education math and science classes. Each meets weekly with their respective general educators to evaluate effectiveness of past instruction and plan future lessons. Although they take turns teaching the class, the general education teachers are primarily responsible for the content and the special educators are primarily responsible for ensuring that the instruction, assignments, tests, and classroom environment are appropriate for all students in the classroom.

Special educators, Mr. Norry and Mrs. Lu, implement the second model of working together, they co-teach with their general education colleagues. Friend and Cook (2013) define **co-teaching** as involving "at least two appropriately credentialed professionals" (p. 163). Co-teaching can take place with two teachers, or a teacher with another school professional (e.g., speech therapist). The purpose is to deliver instruction jointly to a diverse group of students in the general education setting (Friend, Cook, Hurley-Chamberlain, & Shamberger, 2010). General educators may co-teach with an English language learner, gifted and talented, or other school specialist. In this chapter, co-teaching refers to a general educator co-teaching with a special educator. In an effectively co-taught classroom, both teachers plan, instruct, evaluate, and implement behavior management. Together they develop a differentiated curriculum and promote an appropriate learning environment that meets the needs of a diverse group of students.

Developing the skills to become effective co-teachers takes time and experience. When teachers start co-teaching, they may feel uncomfortable sharing classrooms, materials, and teaching responsibilities. They may be guarded and defensive about *their* content, pedagogy, or students. As the relationship develops, teachers begin to compromise by becoming more open and willing to work together as a coordinated pair. The ultimate goal is to reach a level of collaboration.

Susan Gately and Frank Gately (2001) outline eight elements of a co-teaching relationship and describe three developmental stages of each element (see Table 2.1). Some co-teachers will move through these stages in a few weeks. Others will require several months or as much as a year or more; and some may never reach the collaborative stage. Collaboration requires willingness to change, flexibility, commitment to the co-teaching relationship, and strong interpersonal and communication skills (Friend & Cook, 2013).

TABLE 2.1   The Eight Components of Co-Teaching Relationships Across Developmental States

	Beginning	Compromising	Collaborating
Interpersonal Communication	Teachers are guarded, overly polite, and may have possible communication style clash and lack of openness; they may have some level of dissatisfaction, difficulty interpreting verbal and nonverbal messages.	Teachers are more open, interactive, and have an increased amount of communication, better understanding and appreciation for one another's styles.	Nonverbal communication increases; teachers become models of effective communication for students.
Physical Arrangement	Physical space may be separated; students with disabilities sit together, and sense an "invisible wall." Special educator feels no ownership for classroom materials and asks permission to use them.	There is more shared space and materials, less territorial feelings; special educator moves freely around the room but rarely takes center stage.	Teachers intentionally intersperse students in seating arrangement; all students participate in cooperative learning groups; teachers move through classroom fluidly and in balance with one another.
Familiarity with Curriculum	Special educator is unfamiliar with content and/or general education teacher's methodology; both teachers may lack confidence in one another.	Increased confidence in other's expertise. General education teacher becomes more willing to modify curriculum and share planning and teaching.	Both teachers appreciate each other's expertise; both are familiar with the curriculum.
Curriculum Goals and Modifications	Program is driven by textbook and standards; accommodations are driven by IEPs. Special educator serves as a "helper" in the classroom; there is little interaction regarding curriculum modifications.	General educator views modifications as "watering down" the curriculum but willing to try them.	Both teachers differentiate concepts that all students must know from those that most should know, which supports modifications of content, assignments, test, and so forth.

	Beginning	Compromising	Collaborating
Instructional Planning	There may be distinct and separate content being taught to individuals or small groups. Special educator may assume the role of an instructional aid as general education teacher instructs.	Teachers begin to share responsibility for planning instruction.	Teachers continually plan together; mutual planning and sharing of ideas becomes the norm.
Instructional Presentations	Teachers often present separate lessons either simultaneously to the different groups or sequentially to the whole class.	Both teachers direct some of the activities. Special educator may present "mini-lessons" to clarify or instruct strategies to assist students.	Both teachers participate in presenting the lesson, providing instruction and structuring lesson activities. Students discuss concerns and ask questions of both teachers.
Classroom Management	Either teacher may assume the sole role of the behavior manager while the other teaches.	Mutual development of rules and routines begins usually within context of needs of the whole class; there may be some resistance to individualization of behavioral expectations.	Both teachers are involved in planning and implementing classroom management; individual behavior plans are more prominent; community- and relationship-building activities are common.
Assessment	There are two separate grading systems or one system maintained by the general educator; evaluation tends to focus on knowledge of content.	Teachers begin to explore alternative assessment possibilities; there is increased concern for evaluation tools that capture student progress.	Both teachers appreciate and implement alternative assessment when appropriate; both consider ways to integrate IEP goals and evaluation tools into daily instruction.

Source: Adapted from Gately, S. E., & Gately, F. J. (2001).

Because Mr. Norry and Mrs. Lu and their respective general educators take distinct responsibility for different aspects of the classroom, they are co-teaching, but not yet truly collaborating.

When two teachers are assigned to simultaneously teach the same group of students, they may adopt one or more ways of working together. Friend and Cook (2013) describe six co-teaching approaches:

- **One Teaching, One Observing.** One teaching, one observing is appropriate when the educator observing has a specific goal. The goal usually is to observe one student, a small group of students, or the whole class for behaviors of concern. Major problems arise if this approach is used indiscriminately or exclusively because it can result in one teacher, usually the special educator, being consigned to the role of assistant. Teachers can use this approach effectively, however, by using it sparingly and by exchanging roles periodically.

- **One Teaching, One Drifting.** One teaching, one drifting is similar to the previous approach with the exception that the second teacher supports instruction by walking around the room and assisting those needing help. Two specific drawbacks are the drifting educator being viewed as an assistant or being a distraction to students. In addition, this approach can encourage students to become dependent learners by waiting for the drifting teacher to help rather than trying on their own.

- **Station Teaching.** Co-teachers implementing **station teaching** divide the instructional content and take responsibility for teaching it simultaneously to smaller groups within the larger classroom. Benefits include lower student–teacher ratio and integration of students with disabilities into smaller groups rather than being singled out. Disadvantages include distracting noise and movement, as well as taking time to transition from one group to the next.

- **Parallel Teaching.** In **parallel teaching**, the teachers jointly plan, but they deliver instruction separately to a heterogeneous group of one half of the whole classroom. The teachers do not exchange groups as they would in station teaching. This approach is not appropriate for initial instruction unless both educators can proficiently teach the material. It is often used for drill-and-practice, test reviews or projects requiring a lot of teacher supervision. Advantages and disadvantages of parallel teaching are similar to those for station teaching.

- **Alternative Teaching.** **Alternative teaching** is used when it is appropriate to select a small group of students to be instructed in a way that is somehow different from the large group. Alternative teaching occurs within the general education classroom and should be rotated among teachers. This approach may be used when adaptations or modifications are provided or when preteaching, reviewing, or reteaching are necessary. It may also be used when a few students have serious behavior problems and would benefit from working in a small group. Disadvantages include possible stigmatization of students being selected repeatedly for small-group work.

- **Team Teaching.** In **team teaching**, both teachers share planning for and instruction of all students. They usually instruct together, such as one explaining a concept and the other demonstrating the concept. Both circulate among students while they are working on independent work or in cooperative learning groups. They may intersperse the other approaches when needed, but they always alternate roles in a fluid manner. Team teaching requires mutual trust and commitment as well as teaching styles that mesh well together.

All of these models of co-teaching assume that both teachers remain in the classroom through the lesson. Generally, however, not enough special educators are hired to teach in each general classroom. This often necessitates students with disabilities being disproportionately assigned to general education classrooms, a less than ideal situation. In response to this concern, James Walsh and Barbara Jones (2004) present four co-teaching schedules:

- Special educator splits time between two different classes in one or more periods of the school day.

- Special educator divides teaching time between two different classes on different days of the week.

- Special educator's schedule has a flexible schedule depending upon the planned activities for each class.

- Paraeducators represent the special educator in co-taught general education classes as directed by the special educator.

Working in a co-taught classroom is far from easy. In particular, breaking down barriers can be difficult. For example, one study discovered that in co-taught secondary classrooms, general educators presented content information during 30% of the classroom time, whereas the special educator did so less than 1% of the time (Harbort et al., 2007). Other barriers include co-teacher differences in personalities, as well as communication and conflict styles (Pratt, 2014).

Thomas Scruggs, Margo Mastropieri, and Kimberly McDuffie (2007) conducted an analysis of 32 studies of co-teaching in inclusive classrooms and concluded that co-teachers prominently use the "one teach, one assist" practice, with the general educators providing most of the instruction and the special educators assisting individual students. Other studies have found similar results, particularly at the secondary level (e.g., Moin, Magiera, & Zigmond, 2009). Care must be taken that the special educator does not become an instructional aide in the general education classroom.

Special and general educators co-teaching at the secondary level (i.e., middle and high schools) can be particularly challenging for several reasons. First, general education teachers emphasize more complex curricular content. Second, the gap between the skills of students with disabilities and their peers is greater than in elementary classrooms. Third, secondary teachers tend to rely more on didactic instruction. And fourth, secondary teachers are educated as content specialists and often have significant autonomy (Cole & McLeskey, 1997). Additionally, secondary schools often rely on computer-generated student class schedules. Relying on computer-generated schedules does not work for co-taught classes because care must be taken in selecting the student composition of these classrooms. For example, the number of students with learning difficulties in a classroom should be proportional to the number of similar students in the schools (Nierengarten, 2013).

Although not easy, co-teaching can be an effective model for including students with disabilities in the general classroom. Lisa A. Dieker (2001) observed successfully co-taught secondary classrooms and discovered they all had the following in common:

- The classroom climate was positive with both teachers and class members accepting all students.

- Teachers and students viewed co-teaching as a positive experience.

- Students were engaged in high levels of active learning.

- Both teachers had high expectations for behavior and academic performance.

- Both teachers were committed to planning time.

- Multiple methods were used to evaluate student progress.

TABLE 2.2   Strategies for Co-Teaching at the Secondary Level

Preparing to Co-Teach

- Assess the current situation.
- Involve an administrator.
- Become acquainted with your teaching partner.
- Create a workable schedule.

Planning to Co-Teach

- Seek support for a common planning period or for other means of support for planning (e.g., substitute teachers).
- Ask general educator to provide an overview of the courses' content, curriculum, and standards.
- Discuss what will be taught and how it will be taught.

Co-Teaching

- Expand your knowledge about co-teaching models.
- Discuss teaching style differences.
- Create unobtrusive signals for moving on, assistance needed, or teacher sidebar required.
- Use consistent attention and transition signals with students.
- Post a structured class agenda.

Assessing

- Discuss grading procedures in advance.
- Consider a variety of assessment options.
- Create rubrics for grading.
- Share the grading load.

Source: Adapted from Murawski & Dieker (2004).

TEACHER TIP #2.1
USING CO-PLANNING TIME EFFICIENTLY

Time to co-plan can be sparse. Teachers can be more efficient by adhering to guidelines such as the following:

- Establish and keep a regularly scheduled time to collaborate.
- Find a quiet place without distractions.
- Keep to the topic of planning.

- Create and use an agenda.
- Identify roles and responsibilities early on and stick to them.
- Divide up the work while maintaining parity.
- Save discussions of individual students to the end.

- Consistently build in time for assessment and feedback.

- Keep copies of your plans for future reference.

- Use a *What/How/Who* approach by asking what needs to be taught, how will the lesson be taught, and who may need additional attention (Murawski, 2012).

Research examining co-teaching is limited and has received mixed results. Studies have primarily examined professionals' or students' perceptions of the effectiveness of co-teaching and observations and/or interviews of students' and/or teachers' involvement in co-teaching. Generally, studies have found that school personnel and students perceive co-teaching to be beneficial to both general education and special education students in terms of improving social and academic performance (Scruggs, Mastropieri, & McDuffie, 2007). As one example of a research study, Gloria Wilson and Craig Michaels (2006) surveyed 127 students with disabilities and 219 students without disabilities about being co-taught. Students favored co-teaching, expressed interest in being co-taught again, and reported they received better grades in co-taught classes. Studies also support that educators perceive co-teaching to contribute to their professional development (Scruggs et al., 2007). For example, teachers who had successfully co-taught attributed this experience to their increased energy, creativity, trust of others, and use of humor (Murawski & Spencer, 2011). In addition, some studies have documented improved learning by students in co-taught classes (e.g., Rea, McLaughlin, & Walther-Thomas, 2002), while others found no difference (e.g., Idol, 2006). Clearly, additional research is needed to verify co-teaching as an effective instructional model for the benefit of students with and without disabilities.

Working to Improve Teacher Performance

Coaching

Miss Huntington, a new special educator who is struggling with classroom management, seeks help from Mrs. Garcia, a behavior specialist in the school district. After observing Miss Huntington's class and meeting with her to set goals, Mrs. Garcia visits Miss Huntington's classroom during which time she models effective classroom management strategies. As the classroom climate improves, Mrs. Garcia gradually withdraws her participation and becomes an observer. They continue their relationship throughout the school year.

Mrs. Nevers and Mr. Hoopai are the special educators in Roosevelt Elementary School. Both have taught for several years and have just returned from a professional development workshop on improving reading fluency. They decide to help each other implement the new strategies learned. As they discuss this idea, they realize they will need to observe in each other's classroom and ask the principal for support for their plan. He agrees to allow them to use volunteers in their classrooms during short periods of the day so they can watch each other teach. They also plan to meet during lunch or after school to receive feedback from one another.

Coaches are not just used by athletes to improve individual or group performance. Coaching is often used in education. In fact, peer coaching has been found to be one of the more powerful training models for teachers (Cornett & Knight, 2009). **Peer coaching** is a process through which two or more professional colleagues work together reflecting on current practice, building or refining new skills, sharing ideas, conducting action research, teaching one another, and/or problem-solving. Although some individuals equate mentoring with coaching, peer coaching is designed specifically to foster the acquisition and development of new classroom instructional practices (Kohler, Crilley, Shearer, & Good, 2001).

Two coaching models, expert and reciprocal, can be used together or separately. Expert peer coaching consists of a specially trained teacher observing, lending support, giving feedback, and making suggestions to a less skilled teacher. For example, many schools use literacy coaches, behavior coaches, or instructional coaches. Miss Huntington and Mrs. Garcia are engaged in the expert coaching model. Mrs. Garcia is using her expertise in behavior management to coach Miss Huntington. In contrast, Mrs. Nevers and Mr. Hoopai are implementing the reciprocal model which consists of a pair or small group of teachers observing and providing feedback to one another to jointly improve skills and reflect on best practice (Donegan, Ostrosky, & Fowler, 2000). Reciprocal coaching can also be called peer coaching (Gudwin & Salazar-Wallace, 2010).

Coaching in education has many advantages including the following:

- Improving teachers' skills and attitudes

- Assisting teachers in transferring knowledge learned in professional development workshops to the classroom

- Reducing the feeling of isolation of teachers who work independently

- Promoting collegiality and trusting relationships among teachers

- Encouraging reflective practice

- Increasing feelings of teacher effectiveness

- Improving student achievement (Donegan et al., 2000; Cornett & Knight, 2009)

Research supports the effectiveness of coaching across types and experience levels of professionals involved, the settings in which they teach, and the type of coaching provided. For example, in one study, teachers successfully taught novice teachers two reading strategies they had learned the previous year. Teacher interviews discovered that most of the teachers valued working with a partner, preferred this method to traditional in-service presentations, and perceived themselves as successful (Vaughn & Coleman, 2004). In another study, teachers participated in a five-day workshop on sociocultural instructional practices followed by seven individual coaching sessions. Results indicated that this model resulted in significant and positive change in teachers' teaching skills and classroom organization (Teemant, Wink, & Tyra, 2011).

Coaches are not just for the weaker teachers (Knight, 2007). Professional athletes and performing artists, for example, continue to improve their performance through coaching. Similarly, all teachers could benefit from coaching. Jim Knight recommends that coaches focus on the "big four" by providing instructional coaching in the areas of managing behavior, enhancing content knowledge, improving direct instruction, and implementing formative assessment.

   Not all good teachers are good coaches. Successful coaching requires coaches to be disposed toward the work, understand the process of change, and have the capability of prioritizing areas of change (Herll & O'Drobinak, 2004). Additionally, successful coaches demonstrate appropriate interpersonal skills, have a deep understanding of the subject matter and how children learn, are familiar with the curriculum, understand the concept of adult learning, and know how to build trust, provide feedback, access resources, and provide appropriate support. Awareness of coaching resources and knowledge of the practice of coaching are also necessary (Feger, Woleck, & Hickman, 2004). As in any collaborative working relationship, coaches must build and maintain trust with the teachers with whom they are working.

TEACHER TIP #2.2

QUESTIONING TECHNIQUES FOR PEER COACHES

Successful coaching requires effective questioning techniques. Below are some tips:

- Be sensitive to the type, number of, and timing of questions raised.
- Use genuine questions that require reflection rather than a single correct answer.
- Allow the teacher to reflect before responding.
- Keep questions focused on curriculum and student needs.

Technology Spotlight #2.1

Technology Tools for Collaboration and Coaching

Many technology tools have been developed in recent years that can be used to collaborate with others without needing to be face to face. The following website lists 27 tools that are free to use:

http://www.educatorstechnology.com/2012/08/the-top-27-free-tools-to-collaborate.html

As one example of the 27 tools, wiggio.com allows groups or pairs to create a shared calendar, upload files, meet through a chatroom or conference call, poll members, send text, e-mail and voice messages, and paste links. Google docs can also be used to share information electronically by storing documents online and accessing them from any computer.

(Continued)

(Continued)

When teachers coach one another, there is little time for providing feedback. A coach may observe a lesson being taught, take notes about what is occurring, and then need to find time to meet. Bug-in-Ear (BIE) is a technological approach that allows feedback in real time without being obtrusive. The teacher being coached wears an ear bud audio receiver, while the coach provides immediate feedback through a microphone. Advanced BIE can be done virtually through Skype, a free software program that allows audio and visual connections (Rock, Zigmond, Gregg, & Gable, 2011). Thus, the coach could be in a different building while watching and providing feedback to the teacher. Studies have shown this technology to be effective in coaching preservice teachers as well as with current teachers (Rock, Schumacker, Gregg, Howard, Gable, & Zigmond, 2014; Scheeler, Congdon, & Stansbery, 2010).

Mentoring

Mr. Behar, a special educator with 20 years of experience has been selected by Mrs. Wilkes, a new special educator in the school, to be her mentor. They meet weekly during which time Mr. Behar gives Mrs. Wilkes some tips on improving her teaching and relating to the students and parents in the school. At first, Mrs. Wilkes had difficulty understanding school requirements such as how to obtain curricular materials or the expectations regarding bus duty. Mr. Behar explained these specific procedures and expectations. Mrs. Wilkes has also asked Mr. Behar questions about individual students, such as how to make a particular testing accommodation or how to approach a student's parents about a problem. As Mrs. Wilkes's first year as a teacher progresses, she is feeling more confident and is relying less on Mr. Behar's support. The district mentoring program has been designed, however, that they will remain in this relationship for 3 years. Knowing Mr. Behar will be her mentor for 2 more years is comforting to Mrs. Wilkes.

Mr. Behar and Mrs. Wilkes represent the **mentoring** model in which an expert provides trusted guidance to a mentee, someone who is a novice in that particular situation. The mentoring model originated and was recorded in ancient Greek literature. A mentor was considered "part 'parent' and part peer model, guide on the side, expert, diagnostician, appraiser and advocate" (Dettmer, Knackendoffel, & Thurston, 2013, p. 403). Within the context of education, the purpose of mentoring is to provide new teachers the technical and emotional support they need to successfully begin and continue their careers. Mentors help mentees develop expertise and facilitate their induction into the culture of teaching and into the specific local context, like the school or community (Hobson, Ashby, Malderez, & Tomlinson, 2009). Effective mentors can be idea givers and materials suppliers as well as confidants and consultants. Teachers, like students, need to feel a part of a community of learners and have a support network in place. Effective mentoring provides teachers these kinds of supports.

Given the challenges of first year teachers, mentoring and induction programs have received increased attention in the field of special education and in education in general. Well-designed mentoring programs benefit both the mentee and the mentor. Such programs increase retention rates for new teachers by improving their effectiveness, attitudes, and skills. In addition, mentoring programs provide veteran teachers with challenges that help them feel stimulated and useful (Darling-Hammond, 2003). Mentoring also provides mentors an opportunity to self-reflect on their own practice, something they may not do otherwise. Some studies suggest that mentoring programs may be the most effective support beginning teachers can receive (Hobson et al., 2009).

Although having sufficient knowledge and expertise of teaching and content being taught are necessary prerequisites to being a good mentor, not all good teachers are good mentors. Mentors should also demonstrate these attributes:

- Commitment to the role of mentoring

- Positive, supportive, approachable, nonjudgmental, and trustworthy demeanor

- Empathetic and a good listener

- Acceptance of beginning teachers

- Considered an expert by their peers

- Skilled at providing instructional support

- Effective in different interpersonal contexts

- Record of improving their own teaching

- Communicator of hope and optimism (Hobson et al., 2009)

Recommended practice in the use of mentors includes the following:

- Both mentors and mentees should volunteer for mentoring.

- Ideally, mentors and new teachers are in the same building but minimally they should be teaching the same type of students and the same subjects.

- Mentors need to undergo training on topics such as their role, ways to establish rapport and trust, and appropriate strategies to provide feedback and work with adult peers.

- Mentors must remember that their role is as a facilitator, not an evaluator. This sets the correct tone for their relationship.

- Observing one another's classrooms several times for half a day, particularly during the first months of the teaching can be particularly helpful.

- Mentors should hold regular meetings with their mentees as well as be available for informal interactions as needed.

- Mentors must provide both work-based and psychosocial support.

- Mentors should make certain their mentees are sufficiently challenged and engage in deeper levels of thinking and reflection about teaching and learning. (Griffin, Wohlstetter, & Bharadwaja, 2001; Lloyd, Wood, & Moreno, 2000)

Research has documented that mentoring helps beginning teachers become more effective and stay longer in the field, particularly if the mentor provides a lot of guidance and the pair meet frequently (Darling-Hammond, 2003). For example, one study examined mentees' and mentors' perceptions of the benefits of mentoring. Mentees found they increased their knowledge of classroom, school, and district assessment practices, while mentors reported the greatest benefit to be the opportunity to reflect about their own practice (Mathur, Gehrke, & Kim, 2012). Schools that provide mentors with released time to work with beginning teachers reduce attrition rates by more than two thirds. In addition, these new teachers not only stay in the profession longer, but they become competent more quickly (Darling-Hammond, 2003).

TEACHER TIP #2.3
PROCEDURES FOR EFFECTIVE MENTORING

Once the mentor and mentee have been matched, follow through with these activities.

- Outline a plan including observations, formal conferencing, and informal meetings.

- Schedule as many opportunities as possible for the mentor to observe the mentee teaching.

- Determine prior to the observation what will be observed. The mentee, in particular, should identify what he or she would like the mentor to observe.

- Follow up each observation with a conference immediately following the observation. The mentor should remember he or she is a facilitator, not an evaluator.

- Set up opportunities for the mentee to observe the mentor teaching, also followed by a conference.

- Include informal meetings during which questions can be raised outside the realm of classroom teaching (e.g., "What resources are available to me through the school district?").

Collaboration as a Process

Mr. Clark and Ms. Ferrara co-teach a fourth-grade classroom with 28 students, five of whom qualify for special education services. Mr. Clark is a special educator and Ms. Ferrara is an elementary education teacher. They are now in their second year of co-teaching and feel as though they work together in a fluid manner. When they teach, they alternate roles and both feel comfortable interjecting comments or clarifications as needed. They spend about 30 minutes a day reviewing the events of the day and planning for future instruction. All students in the classroom treat both teachers equally, approaching either one with comments or questions. Both teachers state they have learned a lot from this experience. Mr. Clark has gained a greater appreciation of the demands of elementary teachers and Ms. Ferrara has learned more about making accommodations for diverse learners.

Collaboration may be manifested across a variety of school contexts, whether working in a team or co-teaching. **Collaboration** is not an act, but "a style for direct interaction between at least two coequal parties voluntarily engaged in shared decision making as they work toward a common goal" (Friend & Cook, 2013, p. 6). Mr. Clark and Ms. Ferrara are collaborating because they serve as experts in their particular domain (i.e., coequal parties); and they work together to plan and implement (i.e., shared decision making) quality instruction for their students (i.e., a common goal). Both teachers work together almost as one.

To further explain collaboration, Friend and Cook (2013) provide seven defining characteristics:

- **Collaboration is voluntary**. Inasmuch as collaboration is an interactive style, it cannot be forced upon people. "States may pass legislation, school districts may adopt policy, and site administrators may implement programs, but unless school professionals and their colleagues choose to collaborate, they will not do so" (p. 6).

- **Collaboration requires parity among all participants**. Parity is the quality or state of being equal or equivalent. Each person's contribution to the group must be equally valued and each person must have equal power in decision making. Parity must exist when engaged in collaborative activities although one team member may hold power over another member in a different context (e.g., a principal and a teacher).

- **Collaboration is based on mutual goals**. Although individuals may have differing opinions and goals across many areas, each must agree that the specific goal toward which they are working in this collaborative relationship is mutually valued and agreed upon.

- **Collaboration depends on shared responsibility for participation and decision making**. All members of the collaborative team have joint or shared responsibility. Shared responsibility does not imply equal responsibility of completing tasks. More often than not, there is inequity in this regard. For example, Mr. Clark may assume more responsibility for the classroom management planning and implementation and Ms. Ferrara assumes primary responsibility for lesson planning. That does not preclude the team from sharing responsibility for participation and decision making.

- **Individuals who collaborate share resources**. Resources may include expertise, time, availability, or materials. Individual members will have different resources available to them. Sharing resources can be difficult, particularly when resources are scarce. Nonetheless, true collaborators work together in taking advantage of pooled resources. Mr. Clark and Ms. Ferrara have pooled their materials together sharing them as needed by either teacher.

- **Individuals who collaborate share accountability for outcomes**. Shared accountability for outcomes is an outgrowth of shared responsibility. Mr. Clark and Ms. Ferrara equally share the responsibility and accountability for their students' academic and social outcomes.

- **A sense of community evolves from collaboration**. As educators collaborate individuals' strengths can be maximized and individuals' weaknesses minimized and the group as a whole becomes stronger. What follows is a sense of community, not unlike a school club or sports team, who are working together toward a common goal.

Christine Walther-Thomas, Lori Korinek, and Virginia McLaughlin (1999) add other defining attributes of collaboration:

- **Collaboration is not synonymous with inclusion.** With the move toward including more students with disabilities in the general education classroom, some teachers have concluded that inclusion implies collaboration. Collaboration is a vehicle through which inclusion may be successful, but inclusion can occur in other ways, such as through the consulting model. And similarly, teachers can collaborate without adopting an inclusion model in their classrooms.

- **Friendship is not a prerequisite for successful collaboration.** Those who collaborate must demonstrate appropriate interpersonal and communication skills with one another. This is not equivalent to friendship. Ms. Ferrara and Mr. Clark work very well together and are viewed by their district as a model of collaboration. They appreciate and enjoy one another, but they do not socialize outside of the classroom except at work-related functions.

- **Effective collaboration isn't easy or quickly achieved.** As demonstrated in Table 2.1, collaboration is an evolving process and can be initially very labor intensive. After one year of hard work, Mr. Clark and Ms. Ferrara finally feel as though they are truly collaborating.

- **Individuals new to collaboration might overwork the process unintentionally.** Collaboration is not appropriate for every decision school personnel need to make. Shared decision making is important when dealing with fundamental issues, but it may not be necessary or desirable to address specific day-to-day responsibilities collaboratively.

Individuals who collaborate effectively demonstrate appropriate personal characteristics and interactive communication skills. Effective collaboration relies heavily on individuals getting along and interacting in an appropriate fashion. Similar to the characteristics of effective mentors described earlier, effective collaborators have the ability to show they are caring, respectful, and empathetic. They develop and maintain a positive rapport with all team members. They communicate appropriately with other team members and know how to accept and give feedback. Appropriate communication is the beginning and in many ways the substance of effective collaboration.

Interactive Communication

Communication is the means by which information is conveyed from one person to another. The message is composed of both ideas and thought and is transmitted through verbal and nonverbal forms of communication. Communication can be hampered by noise, defined as those factors that interfere with or distort the ability to send or receive messages. Noise includes physical (e.g., loud voices, hot room), as well as psychological factors (e.g., daydreaming).

Listening. Listening is a critical element of communication and collaboration. Not only does listening promote understanding, it also helps establish rapport. Several obstacles can interfere with effective listening. Research indicates, in fact, that over 75% of what is heard is ignored, misunderstood, or quickly forgotten (Thomas, Correa, & Morsink, 2001).

While someone else is speaking teachers may be guilty of formulating a response or reviewing notes preparing for their report instead of listening. Teachers may find themselves daydreaming or reacting to a "hot" topic (e.g., Common Core standards) which sends thoughts away from the speaker's message. At other times, individuals might "tune out," particularly when listening to information already known. Physical, verbal, gestural, or environmental distracters can all interfere with effective listening.

Very few people are truly good listeners. But individuals can become better listeners by mentally preparing for listening by deliberately shutting out distractions; mentally rehearsing and categorizing the main ideas heard; making notes of important details; attending to nonverbal behavior; seeking to connect inferences, facts, and opinions; and listening to what is not being said (Friend & Cook, 2013).

Nonverbal communication. Messages are conveyed through more than the use of words. In fact, as much as 90% of the content of a message is transmitted through vocal inflections and nonverbal behaviors (Thomas et al., 2001). Nonverbal modes of communication include using space, touch, and time to communicate. Others include bodily movements and physical appearance (Finnegan, 2002). Nonverbal messages can confirm, deny, confuse, emphasize, or control verbal messages. Teachers need to be sensitive to the nonverbal messages they may be giving and those being sent by others.

Nonverbal behaviors are learned within context of one's culture. Thus, cultural norms determine how people interpret nonverbal behavior. For example, an individual who is attending to another in the traditional European American culture would be

- facing the speaker squarely or at a slight angle;
- having an open posture (not crossing arms or legs);

- leaning toward the speaker at times;

- maintaining eye contact; and

- appearing relaxed and interested, not fidgety or watching the clock. (Thomas et al., 2001)

Yet in some cultures, too much eye contact, for example, is a sign of disrespect. Smiling may represent embarrassment. Cultural differences can be found in areas such as space, touch, appearance, voice tone, and body language (Dettmer et al., 2013). Teachers must be aware of and sensitive to the cultural context in which they learned nonverbal behaviors and the cultural context of others with whom they are interacting.

Speaking. When individuals speak they generally use statements to provide, share or guide information. Statements can also be used to seek information ("Please provide the actual test scores."), clarify information ("I'm not certain I understand what you mean by that."), and summarize ("It looks like we've decided to move forward with our previous decision.").

Like nonverbal communication, verbal signals and skills also contribute to accurate communication. The rate, pitch, volume, and quality of the voice affect interpretation of what is being said. Intonation is another important contributor. For example, the phrase, "Please work with Zach on preparing for the test" would be interpreted differently if different words are emphasized (see Table 2.3).

Providing and accepting feedback. When working with others, providing feedback can be a critical aspect of effective communication. Feedback is providing information to others about their performance or behavior. Feedback is most effective when it is concise, specific, direct, and delivered immediately or as soon after the event occurred as possible. Effective feedback is also not evaluative but descriptive and focused on a changeable behavior or situation. Feedback should be checked to ensure that it was received as intended (Friend & Cook, 2013; Thomas et al., 2001).

TEACHER TIP #2.4

PROVIDING FEEDBACK

Additional tips for giving feedback include the following:

- Ensure you have all the facts first.

- Don't assign blame or appear judgmental.

- Be thoughtful, not impulsive, in providing feedback.

- Provide the feedback in private.

- Ensure your nonverbal communication isn't contradicting your words.

Accepting feedback is also a critical skill for collaborators. When receiving feedback, many individuals focus on the negative aspects of the message. Most people don't like to

TABLE 2.3   **An Example of Intonation Influencing Meaning**

Phrase	Word Emphasized	Potential Meaning
Please work with Zach on preparing for the test.	Zach	Focus on only helping Zach.
	Test	Focus only on test preparation.
	Please	Frustration

hear they have weaknesses or areas to improve, particularly if they feel confident and competent. Individuals may also react with real concern about how the feedback could harm them.

TEACHER TIP #2.5
RECEIVING FEEDBACK

When feedback is given to you, keep in mind that this is an opportunity to learn. Consider the following tips regarding receiving feedback:

- Willingly listen without interrupting, objecting, or denying what is being said.
- Listen carefully and try to understand the speaker.
- Express respect for the speaker's point of view.
- Ask for clarification if needed.
- Show genuine interest in receiving feedback and willingness to make personal changes if necessary.

Problem-Solving Process

Although effective communication is in many ways the substance of collaboration, collaborators also need to be skilled at problem-solving. Teaching alone may be considered an ongoing process of problem-solving (Snell & Janney, 2000). Teachers solve countless problems throughout each day. In fact, nearly all of teachers' tasks and activities can be conceptualized as some type of problem to be solved (Friend & Cook, 2013).

Teachers make many sole decisions every day. Increasingly, however, teachers and other school professionals are sharing responsibility for problem-solving in collaborative teams. Problem-solving involves at least four major stages. Each is described below.

Identifying the problem. The first step in problem-solving is identifying and pinpointing the problem. When dealing with student-focused problems, these might include student goals and abilities, student participation, and classroom community (Snell & Janney, 2000). This step may seem obvious; however, accurately identifying the problem is the most critical step in problem-solving. In fact, the potential success of solving the problem rests on delineating the problem accurately. "A problem well stated is a problem half solved" (Melamed & Reiman, 2000, p. 18).

Friend and Cook (2013) suggest that well-identified problems have these characteristics:

- All participants agree that the problem exists.

- The discrepancy between the current and desired situations is identifiable and participants agree on the factors that indicate the discrepancy.

- The problem statement is broad enough to invite many kinds of solutions.

Generating and selecting possible solutions. Once the problem has been determined, the next step is brainstorming potential solutions, during which time each member of the group spontaneously contributes ideas without criticism or evaluation. Then criteria by which the potential solutions will be judged are generated and applied to the list of ideas. Positives and negatives of each potential solution are also delineated. Then a final solution is selected. Minimal criteria should include knowledge about the students and their learning, as well as the classroom situation. Additional criteria may include the potential intrusiveness and feasibility of the solution.

Planning and implementing a solution. Effective planning involves not only what will be done, but who will do it and by when. Figure 2.2 represents a sample form on which planning information may be specified. When collaborators design specific and detailed plans, they are more likely to be successful in implementing the solution.

Another aspect of this step in the problem-solving process involves identifying criteria that will be used to evaluate success. No "correct" criteria exist; however, the criteria should be understood and agreed upon by all participants (Friend & Cook, 2013).

Evaluating outcomes. Evaluating outcomes involves both success of goal completion as well as satisfaction of those involved. Three possible outcomes exist. First, the solution solved the problem and the goal was met. If this is the case, then the problem-solving process is complete, at least for now. Second, the solution was partially successful. If the team has been thoughtful in the analysis of the problem and selection and implementation of the solution, at least partial success should be achieved. If partial success is achieved, rather than beginning from scratch, repeat the necessary problem-solving stage(s). The problem may need to be redefined or the solution adapted or refined. The third potential outcome is no success. If the solution did not work, evaluate why success was not achieved and similar to the action taken with the second outcome, repeat the problem-solving process as needed. Unlike achieving partial success, however, no success may involve starting from the beginning.

Conflict Resolution

Teams deal not only with student-centered problems, but team-centered problems as well. Difficulties can arise such as not reaching consensus on problem identification or selection of the solution. In addition, communication barriers and logistical and role constraints may create conflict (Snell & Janney, 2000). Conflict occurs within school-based teams when individuals perceive that others are interfering with their goal

FIGURE 2.2 **Planning Guide for Implementing Potential Solutions**

Student's Name _____ Date _____ Team Members _____

Problem _____ _____

Potential Solution _____ _____

Criteria for Evaluating Success _____

Task/Activity	Person Responsible	Date to Be Accomplished	Outcome/ Results	Evaluation Based on Criteria

Overall outcome _____

Next step _____

attainment or when any participant views the current relationship or system as not working (Friend & Cook, 2013; Melamed & Reiman, 2000).

When humans interact, conflict is inevitable. In fact, conflict is neither good nor bad. Conflict can result in seeking for new solutions and making improvements. Conflict can also result in hostility and destructiveness (Thomas et al., 2001). What matters is how people respond to conflict.

Some individuals respond to conflict by getting into a power struggle. They appear unwilling to bend on their point of view. Others avoid conflict by pretending it doesn't exist. Some people automatically accommodate others by giving in to their decisions or by expressing willingness to compromise. Knowing their personal style can help teachers be better prepared for conflict when it arises. Those who often get into power struggles need to consciously examine whether the issue is worth taking such a strong stand. In some instances, it may be (e.g., ethical decisions). But in most cases, it probably is not. Avoidance of the conflict will also not solve the problem, neither will accommodating others without discussion. Compromise is probably used most often in school-based decisions. The negative aspect of compromise is that some team members with strong opinions may feel dissatisfied creating additional conflict later. No particular style is better than another. All have positive and negative aspects; and all may be appropriate in different contexts (Friend & Cook, 2013).

Sometimes individuals creating conflict appear to be deliberately sabotaging the collaborative effort. Often the individual engaging in these behaviors is not aware that he or she is creating conflict. Specific examples of types of interpersonal conflict with sample potential solutions appear in Table 2.4.

Jim Melamed and John Reiman (2000) recommend applying the following principles for resolving school-based conflict:

- Allow participants to share their perspectives. Ensure each is heard by the other.

- Consider the common ground. Everyone has overlapping interests. Look for easy points of agreement.

- Deal with emotional or relational issues appropriately. Help participants separate past difficulties with current and future issues.

- Decide in advance what the decision-making standard will be. For example, must all agree or does majority rule?

- Set ground rules for discussion. If someone violates these expectations, remind everyone of the ground rules.

TABLE 2.4   Types and Examples of Interpersonal Conflict and Potential Solutions

Type of Conflict	Definition	Potential Solutions
Consensus Blocking	An individual tries to stop the group from reaching consensus by introducing extreme or irrelevant information.	Identify the information as extreme or irrelevant. If extreme emotion is displayed, bring the meeting to an end and discuss in private.
Power Seeking	An individual seeks control of the group.	Clear role definitions help avoid this problem. If not done in advance, use this opportunity to clarify roles. It may help to ask opinions of power seeker to diffuse need to take control.
Recognition Seeking or Time Dominating	An individual draws attention to himself or herself by making inappropriate statements or displaying inappropriate behavior. An individual monopolizes the communication.	Set limits on the amount of time each team member can speak. Speak to the person outside of the meeting. If willing to change, employ a subtle signal the next time it begins to occur.
Clowning	An individual uses jokes as a way to handle nervousness. Small amounts of joking can relieve tension, but too much can be distracting and demeans the work trying to be accomplished.	Examine the commitment of workers. If appropriate, speak with the person privately.

Source: Adapted from Pugach & Johnson (2002).

Sometimes negotiating may be necessary to resolve conflict. Negotiation is a conflict management technique using a give-and-take process among participators. It may be used either formally or informally and generally follows these steps:

- Understand your motivation and the motivation of others.

- Clarify the issues.

- Identify expectations and goals.

- Discuss each specific issue.

- Make and respond to offers.

- Monitor for ethics and integrity. (Friend & Cook, 2013)

As school personnel continue to collaborate together and with others, conflict is inevitable; however, it need not be a destructive factor. In fact, conflict can be constructive and very helpful. Individual team members should always remember the overall goal for teamwork is to ensure quality education for students with disabilities.

Working With Specific Groups

In addition to working with other professionals, special educators collaborate with paraeducators and parents and family members of their students. All of the principles of effective collaboration, such as interpersonal communication skills and the problem-solving process, apply regardless of the group or individuals working together. Specific guidelines related to working with paraeducators and families, however, warrant particular attention.

Paraeducators

Mrs. Quincy, a newly licensed special educator, accepted a teaching position one month ago. She will work with two paraeducators, Ms. Allen and Mr. Huang. Ms. Allen has been employed by the school for over 10 years, but this is Mr. Huang's first year as a paraeducator. Mrs. Quincy was asked by the principal to participate in interviewing paraeducators. Mr. Huang was hired specifically to help one of the students, Opal, transition from special and general education classrooms throughout the day. Ms. Allen has typically stayed in the special education classroom assisting the teacher with various assigned tasks. Mrs. Quincy is somewhat nervous about needing to train a new paraeducator. But she is also worried about working with Ms. Allen who has worked in the school for such a long time. Mrs. Quincy is afraid Ms. Allen will expect the classroom to be run like the previous teacher expected.

Most special educators work with one or more paraeducators on a daily basis. They generally have primary responsibility for providing paraeducator training, supervising them, and formally evaluating their work. In the past, paraeducators were called *paraprofessionals*, *instructional aids*, or *educational assistants*. *Paraeducators* is used today because it mirrors *paramedics* and *paralegals* as someone who works alongside a professional (Ashbaker & Morgan, 2013).

Paraeducators are defined as employees who, following appropriate training, perform tasks as prescribed and supervised by the teacher or other licensed school professional. The teacher, however, always maintains responsibility for assessing the student and family needs, as well as planning, evaluating, and modifying programs (IDEA Partnership, 2001). Although Ms. Allen has more experience as a paraeducator than Mrs. Quincy has as a new special educator, Mrs. Quincy is ultimately responsible for what occurs in her classroom.

Recent legislation has impacted the preparation and role of the paraeducator. The Individuals with Disabilities Education Act (IDEA) and the No Child Left Behind Act (NCLB) (reauthorized and renamed the Every Student Succeeds Act) define paraeducators and require that schools train, limit roles, and supervise them (Ashbaker & Morgan, 2013). Paraeducators must have met one of the following requirements:

- Met a rigorous standard of quality that demonstrates specific knowledge related to instruction, reading, writing, and mathematics

- Completed at least 2 years of study at an institution of higher education

- Obtained an associate's or higher degree (Trautman, 2004)

Special educators like Mrs. Quincy often participate in the hiring of paraeducators. Characteristics to look for in hiring potential paraeducators include the following:

- Qualified according to current legal requirements

- Previous work experience, particularly in schools

- Appropriate skills for the position

- Positive attitude toward children and adolescents

- Interest in self-improvement

- Quality interpersonal skills

- Quality communication skills

- Ability to follow directions, written and oral

- Good organizational skills

- Positive outlook on life (Trautman, 2004)

Much more emphasis is being placed on preparing paraeducators for their roles. Training should occur both as a preservice experience and as professional development. Preservice training occurs before the paraeducator begins working, usually during the summer months or minimally a few days before school starts. Preservice training should involve a general school orientation including a presentation of school policies that impact paraeducators (e.g., confidentiality). Additional important topics to be taught include procedures relating to home–school communication, behavioral management, and emergency situations. Characteristics of the students with whom they will be working, Individualized Education Plans (IEPs), instructional methods, and general roles and responsibilities should also be addressed (Trautman, 2004). Betty Ashbaker and Jill Morgan (2013) suggest teachers should participate in or at least be informed about the training that paraeducators receive and that all activities related to paraeducator training and supervision be well documented.

Professional development occurs while the paraeducator is working in the school and can take several forms. Paraeducators may enroll in credit courses at local colleges, attend workshops sponsored by the school district, or be coached on the job in a manner similar to the coaching model described previously in this chapter. The coaching model must be used cautiously, however, when the person acting as the coach for a paraeducator is the special educator because the roles of coach and evaluator can conflict.

New special educators like Mrs. Quincy might participate in the hiring and training of new paraeducators. Or they may encounter paraeducators who are long-term school employees. New teachers may experience paraeducators who are much older than themselves, act as though they are the teacher and know more than the students and teacher, and are intimidating. New teachers need to recognize their own professional training and exude confidence using assertive language and acting in charge. At the same time, new teachers need to respect and vocalize appreciation for the paraeducators' knowledge and experience (McGrath, Johns, & Mathur, 2010).

Regardless of the experience level of the paraeducator and the teacher, there are several stages through which both must travel together. The first stage includes getting to know one another and each other's working styles. Some paraeducators, for example, may prefer to work in a structured, highly supervised situation. Others may thrive with less structure and desire more independence. Some teachers prefer paraeducators who are self-starters, whereas others may want to direct most of their paraeducators' work. When style differences vary, discussion and solutions can be planned prior to potential problems arising (Trautman, 2004).

Once the teacher and the paraeducator know one another, the next step is to clarify roles and responsibilities. Although paraeducators will be involved in both instructional and noninstructional activities, they need to recognize that the teacher is the person responsible for the instruction of each student in the classroom. Once specific responsibilities have been determined, they should create a daily schedule together. Each daily classroom activity should be listed with who is responsible for each. Recess, lunchtime, and other breaks should be included. As the year progresses, evaluate the schedule to determine whether it needs to be changed or readjusted.

Most paraeducators in special education devote a large portion of their time to instruction. For example, one study found that special education paraeducators typically spend 85% to 90% of their time preparing for instruction and engaged with students in instructional activities. These activities include tutoring small groups or individual students under the direction of the special educator, collecting data, and implementing teacher-created behavior management plans (ERIC/OSEP, 2003). Another study discovered that 97% of the paraeducators surveyed provide one-on-one instruction on a daily or weekly basis (Carter, O'Rourke, Sisco, & Pelsue, 2009). And in a third study, the top two primary responsibilities as reported by paraeducators were providing behavioral and social support (53%) and implementing teacher-planned instruction (48%) (Fisher & Pleasants, 2012). In addition to instructing, paraeducators perform clerical and housekeeping tasks such as preparing, gathering, and organizing materials; correcting papers; or straightening up the classroom. Duties and responsibilities should be delineated into written job descriptions.

Schools are hiring more and more paraeducators assigned to either classrooms or to individual students with disabilities, which has resulted in paraeducators providing a significant amount of instructional and support services to conservatively hundreds of thousands of students nationwide (Giangreco, 2010). In fact, "states that include a higher percentage of their students with disabilities in general education classes . . . tend to have service delivery systems that have more paraprofessionals than special educators" (Giangreco, p. 2). Such a proliferation of paraeducators concerns many professionals. Their concerns center on the fact that the least trained and prepared person (i.e., paraeducator) is working with the most severe cases (i.e., students with more severe disabilities). Research does not support that this model works.

The responsibility for deciding whether a student needs individual paraeducator support, particularly to be successful in the general education environment, rests on the IEP team. Research suggests that too much paraeducator support can have the following negative impacts:

- The paraeducator may become overprotective of the student inhibiting other social interactions.

- The classroom teacher may not assume ownership for the student.

- Parents may view the paraeducator as the student's teacher.

- The number and quality of peer interactions may decrease.

- The student may be embarrassed and be teased or bullied.

- Some students' undesirable behavior may increase because of dislike of paraeducator support.

- The student's ability to become an independent learner may be hampered. (Giangreco, 2010; Mueller & Murphy, 2001)

Paraeducators, however, should be viewed as valuable members of the school community and should be assigned to students based on the need as specified by the IEP team. Patricia Mueller and Francis Murphy (2001) designed a process by which the IEP team can systematically determine the need and role of a paraeducator. The IEP team should answer questions such as these:

- Is there a safety concern for self or others?

- Does the student require continual teacher prompts during instruction?

- Does the student require continual teacher prompts during other times?

- Do other students include the student in classroom activities?

- Is the student receptive to peer tutoring and cooperative group learning?

If the team determines that a student needs paraeducator support, they need to carefully plan by analyzing the student's entire school day and breaking the day into periods or times of the day. They should then systematically review each time period focusing on what the student can or cannot do, the extent to which he or she needs assistance, areas that could be used to promote social acceptance, how peers could be used, and areas that could be targeted for independence. A plan for paraeducator assistance can focus on where, when, and how the paraeducator will provide the support and how all involved in the education of the student, including peers, will be used to promote social interactions and independence (Mueller & Murphy, 2001).

Care must be taken so that students with disabilities do not develop overdependence on paraeducators, particularly those who are assigned to provide them general education support. Overdependence on paraeducators can adversely affect the social and academic growth of students with disabilities (Giangreco, 2010). Students with disabilities may feel stigmatized because they are the only ones singled out for paraeducator support. Ways of reducing overdependence include seating students with disabilities with their peers, encouraging interaction with their classmates and teacher, avoiding unnecessary close proximity to the paraeducator, assigning the paraeducator to other duties to free up the teacher to interact with the student, and using student-mediated strategies (e.g., cooperative learning, peer tutoring) as described in Chapter 8.

Managing, supervising, and evaluating paraeducators are additional roles for special educators. Teachers should meet with their paraeducators on a regular basis. Some teachers prefer to schedule a specific time each week. Others meet daily during lunch, or before or after school. Written meeting agendas help ensure that all issues needing attention are addressed. Recording the results of the meeting can keep everyone on track (Trautman, 2004).

Most school districts require an annual evaluation of paraeducators. Teachers should, however, conduct evaluations more frequently. Several formal evaluations may be scheduled throughout the year and the regularly scheduled meeting times can be used as an opportunity for informal evaluation. Creating a form for a specific paraeducator can be helpful in ensuring that the evaluation of the paraeducator is in concert with the job description.

TEACHER TIP #2.6

GUIDING EVALUATION QUESTIONS

Before and after observing the paraeducator teach, do and ask these questions:

- Describe what you are teaching and a correct response.

- Describe your lesson plan.

- Tell me about the materials you need and how you will keep them organized.

- How will you respond when the student responds correctly/incorrectly?

- How will you handle inappropriate behaviors?

- What might be distracting to the students during your lesson?

Source: Adapted from Carnahan, Williamson, Clarke, & Sorensen (2009).

Legislation places demands on the qualifications and use of paraeducators, which impacts both paraeducators and special educators. Special educators need to demonstrate specific competencies in management, supervision, and evaluation of paraeducators. One study surveyed administrators, special educators, and paraeducators to identify teacher competencies needed to work with paraeducators. Seven major categories emerged: communicating with paraeducators, planning and scheduling, providing instructional support, modeling for paraeducators, conducting public relations, training paraeducators, and managing paraeducators (Wallace, Shin, Bartholomay, & Stahl, 2001). Participants were also asked to identify the extent to which they observed teachers' demonstration of these competencies. Unfortunately, respondents considered the competencies as very important, but the competencies were not observed frequently.

TEACHER TIP #2.7

TOP 10 THINGS PARAEDUCATORS WANT TEACHERS TO KNOW

Cathryn G. Riggs (2004) suggests the following are the top 10 things paraeducators want teachers to know and do:

1. Know your paraeducators' names, backgrounds, and interests.

2. Be familiar with district policy regarding paraeducators.

3. Consider paraeducators as team members.

4. Explain your classroom expectations to paraeducators.

5. Define specific roles and responsibilities for yourself and paraeducators.

6. Direct and supervise paraeducators.

7. Communicate and provide feedback to paraeducators.

8. Recognize the experience and knowledge paraeducators can share.

9. Take ownership for all students.

10. Respect paraeducators.

Related Service Personnel

Many students with high-incidence disabilities receive related services. As described in Chapter 1, *related services* are defined as developmental, corrective, and other supportive services needed to assist a student with a disability to benefit from special education. These services may include speech–language pathology and audiology, psychological services and counseling services, and physical or occupational therapy, among other services. Special educators often work closely with related service providers. Sometimes related service personnel provide their service within the general education classrooms. More frequently, students are pulled out of their classroom to receive related services. For example, a school psychologist may work in the classroom with a small group of students who need social skill development or a student may receive one-on-one speech–language therapy by a speech pathologist in a separate therapy room.

Regardless of the setting in which students receive related services or whether such interventions are integrated into the general education curriculum, special educators work collaboratively with related service personnel usually on a daily basis. Collaboration may require co-planning and co-teaching together or more typically collaboration requires making mutually agreed upon schedules for delivering services to the students who need them.

TEACHER TIP #2.8
COLLABORATING WITH RELATED SERVICE PERSONNEL

When students receive related services, their teachers should

- find time to meet with the related service provider (RSP) at the beginning and throughout the year to discuss the student's goals and progress.

- agree on intervention goals and the student's therapy schedule.

- ask questions about the student's therapy, interventions, and progress.

- if asked, be willing to implement interventions that will support the student's related services goals in your classroom.

- invite the RSP into your classroom for therapy integration.

- always treat the RSP as a professional.

- use the RSP as a resource.

- be honest in providing feedback about the therapy schedule, therapy integration in your classroom, the student's progress, and so forth.

Source: Adapted from Bauer, Iyer, Boon, & Fore (2010).

Parents and Other Family Members

In addition to paraeducators and other professionals, special educators also collaborate with parents and other family members of the students they teach. Parents advocating on behalf of their children with disabilities were the catalyst for the adoption of the original laws mandating special education services (Turnbull & Turnbull, 2015). Thus, parent and family involvement was an original tenet of IDEA with their roles expanding with each reauthorization of the law.

As discussed in Chapter 1, parents have the rights and responsibility to participate as active members of decision-making teams on behalf of their children with disabilities. Yet, professionals should strive to move beyond the minimal compliance requirements of IDEA in order to establish true collaboration for several reasons. First, parents know their child better than the professionals. Family members can provide invaluable information and support to the child's education. Second, research demonstrates that family participation in the child's education coincides with positive academic achievement (Brown & Brandon, 2009). And third, families want what is best for the child and most want to support the school in any way they can. Educators should view family members as an asset and solicit their support in whatever ways they can.

Developing collaborative relationships with parents and other family members is similar to developing other collaborative relationships. That is, those skills and competencies for effective collaboration addressed thus far apply to working with parents and family members. In fact, when working with family members, the role of communication and interpersonal skills cannot be overstated. One group of researchers interviewed adult family members of children with and without disabilities, service providers, and administrators. Based on this information, they generated indicators of professional behavior that facilitate collaborative partnerships between families and professionals. The researchers organized the indicators into six broad themes: communication, commitment, equality, skills, trust, and respect. Attributes and examples of each theme are presented in Table 2.5. The researchers concluded, "The results of this study underscore the point that common sense and ordinary human decency are at the heart of positive partnerships between families and professionals serving children with disabilities" (Blue-Banning, Summers, Frankland, Nelson, & Beegle, 2004, p. 179).

The demographics of families have altered dramatically in the last 50 years. For example,

> families are more diverse in structure and style, spend less time together, are poorer, need more schooling than ever in history, are more likely to be single, and have shifted their value base to be more protective of their children. (Knopf & Swick, 2008, p. 420)

Teachers will communicate and collaborate more effectively with the students' families if teachers understand general changes in family dynamics and the impact these dynamics have on family function. Just as each student has unique characteristics, so does each family. Educators will work with a broad spectrum of families. While they shouldn't probe for information, teachers should provide opportunities for family members to share information about their background, socioeconomic status, special circumstances (such as caring for an elderly relative in the home), and how they define their family unit, among other helpful pieces of information (Dyches, Carter, & Prater, 2012).

Also unique to each family is how members are coping with having a child with a disability in their family. Generally speaking, the type and severity of the child's disability, the family's circumstances, the formal and informal supports available, and the personalities of family members influence the degree to which the family unit feels stress (Sileo & Prater, 2012). Some families have effective coping strategies, while others do not. Parenting styles can also vary dramatically across families which influence the behavioral patterns of their children. Another difference across families is family members' perceptions about disabilities and special educational services. Some parents may be in denial that their child has a disability or that special services are needed. Some welcome the extra services while others are not interested in their child receiving them. Recognizing all of these differences in family characteristics and attitudes contributes to the overall need for special educators to become acquainted with the family of each of their students. While doing so, parents need to be recognized as the true experts on their children.

TABLE 2.5 **Collaborative Family–Professional Partnerships Themes and Indicators**

Themes	Attributes	Examples of Indicators
Communication	Quality: positive, understandable, respectful of all members Quantity: enables efficient and effective coordination and understanding of all members	Being clear, honest, tactful, and open Listening Sharing resources Communicating frequently Coordinating information
Commitment	Members share assurance of each other's (a) devotion and loyalty to student and family and (b) belief in importance of goals being pursued.	Being consistent, accessible, sensitive, and flexible Regarding work as *more than a job* and the student and family as *more than a case*.
Equality	Members feel equity in decision making and service implementation and work to help others feel equally empowered.	Being willing to explore all options Fostering harmony Avoiding *turfism* Allowing reciprocity Validating others Advocating for student or family with other professionals
Skills	Members perceive others as competent in fulfilling their roles.	Being willing to learn Expecting student progress Taking action Considering the whole student or family
Trust	Members view others members as reliable and dependable.	Following through on commitments Being discreet Keeping the student safe
Respect	Members regard each other with esteem and demonstrate that esteem through communication and actions.	Being nonjudgmental and courteous Valuing the student Exercising nondiscrimination Avoiding intrusion

Source: Adapted from Blue-Banning et al. (2004).

Although general interpersonal and communication skills are important, additional strategies for collaborating specifically with parents and family members are also necessary. Sample strategies follow:

- **If possible, build rapport with parents before school begins.** Contact them by telephone and invite them to attend school events or to meet personally.

- **Ask parents who they would like to communicate with, how often, and through what means.** Identifying a major contact person for the school can be helpful, particularly if several teachers and/or specialists work with the student. Some parents prefer phone calls, e-mail messages, or notes sent home. Others may wish face-to-face meetings. Most will benefit from a combination of all three means of communication.

- **Clearly and consistently express your concern and interest in the child as an individual.** Make it a point to recognize and celebrate the child's capabilities and strengths. Family members need to know specifically that teachers value the student and their perspective regarding his or her needs. Once genuine interest in the child is demonstrated, parents are more likely to talk honestly.

- **Put yourself in the shoes of the parents.** Parents appreciate professionals who understand their frustration and concern. They may feel overwhelmed and struggle with the realities of everyday life. Examining the parent's point of view helps professionals be less judgmental.

- **Do not make assumptions about the families of your students; avoid stereotyping.** Some parents believe professionals make assumptions about their families and their parenting skills simply because they have a child with a disability.

- **Use everyday language.** "Parents want information that is free from technical jargon, is provided by a credible source, and focuses on their questions and concerns" (Martin & Hagan-Burke, 2002, p. 63). Parents can feel alienated and excluded if they don't understand the language being used. Even phrases that use ordinary words can be confusing to those who are not familiar with them (e.g., "30 minutes three times a week," "access to the general education curriculum," "high stakes testing").

- **Make yourself available to parents and other family members.** Sometimes parents don't know who to turn to with questions about their child and his or her disability. If they receive most of their information from the popular media, it may be inaccurate information. Establish yourself as someone who can be trusted and who is willing to help them learn more.

Sometimes teachers make assumptions about parents who don't appear to be involved in their child's education. For example, parents may not attend an IEP meeting although they had agreed to do so. Teachers must be very cautious in making assumptions about parents and family members. A. Lin Goodwin and Sabrina King (2002) generated the following list of common misconceptions about parent involvement:

- **Parents who don't visit school don't care about their child's education.** Parents may not visit the school for various reasons. Some parents feel intimidated by school personnel whom they consider to be authority figures. Parents may be working more than one job or reluctant to hear once again that their child is in trouble. Perhaps the parents had negative school experiences as students and continue to feel uncomfortable in that setting.

- **Good parent involvement looks the same**. Many expectations of parental involvement, such as reading to children every night, are embedded in middle-class norms. "Parents who do not conform to these implicit rules become easy targets for parent bashing" (p. 10).

- **All parents respond to the same strategies.** Typical parent involvement such as parent–teacher conferences, open houses, and active Parent Teacher Association participation does not work for everyone and may, in fact, exclude some parents.

- **Financial struggles of parents inhibit school support**. Parents can provide support in other ways. Schools need to be creative in finding ways beyond financial or large amounts of time that parents can contribute to their child's school.

- **All parents have the same goals for their children**. Teachers cannot assume they know the parents' aspirations for their child. Careful dialogue among all members of the school team making these decisions is critical.

Technology Spotlight #2.2

Communicating With Parents and Family Members

Using technology when communicating with parents and other family members can be very effective. However, nothing is more frustrating than an Internet site that is out of date. Online gradebooks, for example, can be helpful in organizing and communicating individual student grades, but if a teacher has not entered current assignment grades, parents could believe their child is performing lower than he or she truly is, and then come to not trust the gradebook or the teacher.

When designing a classroom website, wiki, or blog teachers need to make certain the information is accurate and current and they should follow copyright and student privacy policies. Photos of students should not be posted without first obtaining permission from parents. Once permission is obtained, do not use names or other identifiers of students in the images. Consider the possible limited access for parents and their children due to disabilities or language. Use Internet tools that test the accessibility of the online materials (e.g., www.disabled-world.com/disability/accessibility/websitedesign/; www.bobby-approved.com/).

(Continued)

(Continued)

Make the reading level appropriate for those who are going to access the site and consider translating the text to the home languages of your students (Dyches et al., 2012). Information that would be appropriate for a class website or blog includes teacher contact information, descriptions of courses or curriculum, calendar of events, announcements, classroom policies, homework information, electronic materials, and grading rubrics (Dyches et al., 2012).

E-mail, texts, and apps can be used to communicate with parents, if they are agreeable and have provided their e-mail address or text number. Standard professional etiquette should be used whether handwriting or typing a message. Teachers should always remember that using technology to communicate should supplement rather than replace in-person communication. Keep the messages concise and stick to the purpose for the communication.

Be certain that information is not sent to multiple people if that was not the intent (Dyches et al., 2012).

Apps can also be used to communicate with families. Some are focused primarily on communication (e.g., Edmodo), while others embed functions such as grade books and attendance (e.g., Infinite Campus). Several of the apps are designed for schoolwide communication tools rather than for a single classroom (e.g., PowerSchool, SchoolReach) (Prater & Sileo, 2015).

Families can be directed to Internet sources to support their and their child's needs. A few include Discovery Education (www.discoveryeducation .com/parent/), Family Education (www.familyeducation.com), National Education Association (www.nea.org/ parents/), National Parent Teacher Association (www.pta.org/), Parents Helping Parents (www.php.com/).

Collaborating Across Diverse Cultures

Four Cultural Dimensions

Cultures vary across many dimensions. Educators working with others from differing cultural backgrounds need to develop sensitivity to these dimensions, recognizing the impact they have on their interactions with others, and responding accordingly. A discussion of four cultural dimensions, efficiency, independence, equity, and communication styles, follows. Within this section and throughout the book, the characteristics of any specific group are stated as generalizations. No two families from the same cultural group will exhibit the same beliefs or behaviors. Teachers should avoid stereotyping and become acquainted with each student and his or her family. These generalizations are provided only to demonstrate the contrast among cultural groups.

Efficiency. The focus on efficiency is tied directly to cultural perceptions of time. European-based cultures place a great deal of emphasis on using time wisely (e.g., "Time is money."). Other cultures, such as American Indians, Alaska Natives, and Pacific Islanders, are less time conscience. For example, it is customary in Hawaii to "talk story" before any formal discussion takes place. "Talking story" allows participants to get to know one another or get caught up on each other's lives (Sileo & Prater, 2012).

In contrast, in Alaska Native populations, it is polite to sit in silence for minutes (even up to a half hour) while gathering thoughts prior to speaking. In one study, an American Indian parent support group always started at least 30 minutes after the parents arrived. The European American facilitator perceived and characterized the meeting as always starting late. The American Indian mothers, however, did not believe the meetings started late because they perceived the time spent before the meeting interacting informally as part of the meeting (Kalyanpur, 1998).

Independence. European Americans value independence and individual autonomy. Other cultures rely on group processes, particularly surrounding the family. In fact, many ethnic communities have cultural roots in a collectivist orientation. Such groups emphasize interdependence and cooperative behaviors to attain common goals and group welfare. The focus is on the needs of the group in contrast to individual needs (Sileo & Prater, 2012).

Hispanic families are typically patriarchal and have a collective orientation. Children are taught to be dependent on their parents and to seek their approval. On the other hand, American Indian children are encouraged to develop independence and make personal choices at an early age. In the Chinese culture, if a family member is successful, the whole family receives credit, although accomplishments are downplayed in order to avoid appearing proud and arrogant. Many special education regulations have been based on an assumption that independence is an important outcome. Transition services as prescribed in IDEA, for example, are based on a European American culture which may not be compatible with the values of other cultures (e.g., Latin American) (Kalyanpur & Harry, 1999).

Equity. The value placed on equity and lines of authority vary across cultures. In some cultures, young people rely on major decisions being made by their "elders." For example, students of traditional Asian American cultures may defer to their parents' wishes when it comes to important life decisions such as marriage and careers. This has great implications for collaborating with families from culturally diverse backgrounds. For example, families may view professionals as the experts and believe they have nothing to contribute to team efforts. Other cultures, such as Puerto Ricans, extend their family units to include not only traditional extended family (e.g., grandparents, aunts, uncles, cousins), but to godparents, close friends, and neighbors (Correa & Jones, 2000).

Communication styles. Communication skills are learned within the context of culture. As with all collaborative relationships, communication between professionals and family members is critical. Even if the parents are English proficient, different communication styles can still be a barrier. In general, European Americans focus on verbal communication that is precise and logical. Other cultures, such as Asian, American Indian, Arab, Latino, and African American, tend to rely on "situational cues, established hierarchies and non-confrontational responses" while communicating with others (Turnbull, Blue-Banning, Turbiville. & Park, 1999, p. 169). In some cultures, such as Chinese, Japanese, Arabian, and Latin American, verbal contracts are binding. Agreements usually are not written down but "understood."

Nonverbal communication such as use of personal space, eye contact, touch, and silence can create miscommunication if not placed within the correct cultural context. Pacific Islanders rely on an uplifted nod of the head or raised eyebrows to agree or to recognize someone's presence. Southeast Asians tend to smile even when they are sad or being reprimanded. The smile should not be interpreted as a challenge or as disrespect. Interpreting nonverbal communication accurately is critical to collaborating with families.

Working With Others From Culturally Diverse Populations

Although most school programs are based on European American and middle-class values, personnel working within those schools, particularly paraeducators, may represent other cultures. Creating effective collaboration can be a difficult process when team members come from different cultural backgrounds. Teachers can work effectively with others of differing cultural backgrounds if they adhere to at least three principles. First, they should be aware of and sensitive to their own cultural backgrounds and how it impacts their role as a teacher. Second, teachers need to be knowledgeable about and sensitive to the cultures of students and others with whom they work. And third, they should respect the students' cultures and draw upon cultural experiences of students and their families to provide authentic cultural perspectives in teaching procedures, the curriculum, and collaborative efforts. A discussion of the first two principles follows. The third principle, providing culturally responsive practices in teaching, will be discussed throughout subsequent chapters.

Understand your culture. The four dimensions discussed previously can provide a framework for understanding an individual's culture. Teachers should ask themselves questions such as "How do I value time?" "How do I value money?" "What is more important, the finished product or the process of working toward a finished product?" "How do I best communicate?" "How do I prefer others communicate with me?" "Do I prefer to work independently or with others?"

The next step is recognizing how your culture relates to other team members' cultures. "Recognizing one's culture and how it influences behavior is necessary, but not sufficient, for working effectively in a multicultural society. Collaborators must also be able to assess how their perspective differs from that of those with whom they are working" (Harris, 1996, p. 356).

School professionals should take this step further by questioning *taken-for-granted* beliefs imbedded in current professional practice. For example, Maya Kalyanpur (1998) studied American Indian mothers' participation in a parent support group on their reservation and identified four *puzzlements* that arose from interacting across cultures. First, the professionals saw themselves coming to the reservation as beneficial to the community. The American Indian response was, "We look after our own." American Indians tend to assist each other and work in a caring and cooperative manner. Second, the professionals measured the children's skills against mainstream culture and concluded that their culture wasn't providing them the necessary skills and thus wasn't helpful for the children. Third, the professionals conceptualized the support group as an opportunity to teach parenting skills not recognizing that imbedded in that belief is the assumption that the mothers' parenting skills were insufficient, poor, or wrong, not just different from their cultural beliefs about child-rearing. And fourth, the professionals assumed that the structure and expectations of a parent support group was appropriate when in fact it was incompatible with the norms and values of the American Indian culture.

Naturally occurring group events are more likely to generate the needed infrastructure for support groups than a meeting contrived by an outsider for this purpose.

Be knowledgeable about and sensitive to others' culture. Learning about other cultures may seem overwhelming, particularly if a variety of cultures are represented in the school community. Nonetheless, teachers should seek out an understanding of other cultures represented, particularly if they will be developing collaborative relationships with individuals representing those cultures. Learn about their culture through activities such as reading, observing, asking questions, participating in activities, and visiting homes and communities.

Teachers also need to recognize that regardless of all the work they put into learning about other cultures, they will not fully understand the intricacies of that culture. One strategy that can help is to solicit support from paraeducators to bridge the gap between themselves and students' families. Paraeducators, who often come from the same cultural groups as the students and their families, can assist teachers in interacting with and involving them in culturally responsive ways.

Strategies for Working With Diverse Families

Although IDEA requires that families be involved in their child's education, cultural and linguistic differences can create barriers to parent participation in the IEP processes (Harry, 2008). When significant cultural differences exist between school personnel and students' families, the likelihood of miscommunication and misunderstanding significantly increases, which can negatively impact parents' ability to meaningfully contribute to their child's education (Araujo, 2009).

Culturally and/or linguistically diverse (CLD) families are often underrepresented in school involvement. This may be due to (a) lack of time or energy, (b) inadequate linguistic abilities, (c) inadequate schooling experiences, (d) perceived lack of welcome, and (e) school personnel's assumptions regarding parents' interest or ability (Brown & Brandon, 2009). Educators must recognize these barriers and put into place strategies to help overcome them. Small interventions, such as placing welcome banners in various languages in the school office or sending school–home notes in the family's language, can go a long way to making families feel welcome and want to participate.

One cultural perception that specifically impacts special educators working with diverse families involves differences in how disability is perceived. Differences in functioning that are perceived as disabling in one culture may not necessarily be perceived the same way in another (Harry, 2008). Within a social context, a "disability" exists only when it inhibits the functioning of an individual in an area that is highly regarded by a particular society. Moreover, when individuals' learning, behavioral, or physical characteristics do not meet a cultural group's expectations, they may be considered in a variety of ways—as distinct, diverse, different, deviant, or disabled.

Special educators need to understand and account for these cultural differences and nuances to effectively serve students with disabilities and to effectively collaborate with their family members. For example, how parents of students with disabilities perceive their child's condition or disability can impact how they will respond to all steps of the IEP process. For instance, in a review of studies, Evangeline Danseco (1997) discovered that parents who believe that disabilities are caused by an evil spirit often seek folk remedies; and parents who believe their child's disability is punishment for the parent's past transgression seek to change their offending behavior. Parents' beliefs about the nature and cause of childhood disability impact directly on how those with disabilities are treated in the home and the decisions parents make about interventions at school.

Strategies to involve parents and family members representing diverse cultures are listed in Table 2.6. These ideas provide a starting point for developing cultural sensitivity. In order to collaborate effectively with others from diverse cultures, however, more specific strategies are needed. Using Table 2.7 as a template, first identify your cultural perspective across the four dimensions discussed earlier. Next, do the same for the other individual's or family's perspective. And last, where differences exist, create strategies to bridge those differences.

TABLE 2.6   Strategies to Engage Parents/Family Members Across Cultures

- Learn about the families in the school's community.

- Work with cultural mediators representing the families' cultures.

- Make a concerted effort to reach out to families. They may rely more heavily on being invited to participate rather than take the initiative themselves.

- Understand family structure and lines of authority.

- Learn and use words and greetings in families' languages.

- Clearly express commitment to meaningful and culturally responsive family involvement.

- Recognize that some families may be surprised by the amount of participation expected of them in the United States.

- Be aware that some families perceive schools in the United States very differently from reality.

- Use trained interpreters when interacting with linguistically diverse parents, especially during IEP meetings.

- Provide parent education on topics such as what is and what causes disabilities, as well as how to help their child at home.

- Use as few written forms as possible for non-English speaking/reading parents and provide translation in their native language.

- Translate classroom-based materials (e.g., school–home notes, newsletters) into families' native languages.

- Recognize the potential barriers to getting families involved in school programs.

- Survey family members regarding home language, cultural practices, needs, concerns, perspectives, and ideas.

- Plan and implement family–school collaborative activities based on the survey findings.

- Assign a family liaison to oversee family–school activities.

- Create a school cultural resource binder.

- Create space within the school for families to gather even during school hours.

- Generate multiple ways to involve families in and inform them about school.

Sources: Correa & Jones (2000); Dyches et al. (2012); Goodwin & King (2002); Rodriguez, Blatz, & Elbaum (2014); Sileo & Prater (2012)

TABLE 2.7   **Sample Worksheet for Developing Strategies Sensitive to Diverse Cultures**

Dimension	My Culture	The Other Person's Culture	Strategies
Efficiency	Time is very important.	Efficient use of time is not important.	Avoid scheduling meetings too close together.
Efficiency	Direct approach, get right to the task.	Indirect approach: discuss personal issues first.	Respect quality of the interaction.
Independence	Prefer to keep feelings private.	Open sharing of personal feelings.	Respect others sharing personal feelings.
Independence	Parents have responsibility for raising children.	Extended family share responsibility for raising children.	Allow parents time to take decisions to others.
Equity	All members of the team are equal participants.	Hierarchy of authority is important even in team work.	Ensure clarity about role responsibilities among all members.
Equity	Prefer active family involvement.	Accept teachers' opinions.	Involve parents across all levels of program.
Communication Styles	All formal decisions are done in writing.	Verbal agreement is binding.	Ensure verbal commitments are not made unless they are final decisions.
Communication Styles	Individuals speak one at a time.	One individual talking over another person's talking is acceptable and common.	Develop awareness that talking over is not meant to be intrusive or rude.

Other Considerations

Teachers need to be aware of other considerations when working with parents and families. First, a significant number of families from diverse cultures are immigrants. Some have acquired entry into the United States legally and others are undocumented. Teachers working with immigrant populations must realize the complexity and possible mixed status of their students' families. For example, the adults may be citizens, permanent residents, or undocumented immigrants. At the same time, the children could be native-born citizens or immigrants, like the adults (Olivos, 2009).

Complications may arise when trying to collaborate with immigrant families. Recent pressure from policymakers has resulted in increased immigration enforcement. Family members may avoid doing anything to call attention to themselves, including participating in their child's education. They may choose not to visit the school, talk to their children's teachers, or fill out paperwork with parental information. School professionals need to make them feel comfortable and if necessary ensure them that their involvement in activities such as their child's IEP meeting will not unduly expose them (Olivos, 2009).

Teachers also need to be aware of a second issue, that is, the number of students coming from linguistically diverse families is increasing. Teachers need to be prepared to work with translators as they interact with family members. First and foremost, the student should not serve as the translator. A third party who knows the appropriate translation for educational terms, who knows other aspects of the culture, such as nonverbal communication, and who does not have a vested interest in the outcome of decisions, is always the best choice. Some schools and school districts hire translators for this purpose. When working with a translator use the following strategies:

- Speak directly to the parents and other family members, not to the translator.

- Check for understanding with both the family and the translator.

- Avoid jargon and oversimplification of educational information.

- Be aware of nonverbal communication of both the family and the translator.

- Ask the family members to share back their understanding of the key points of the meeting. (More, Hart, & Cheatham, 2013)

Developing cross-cultural collaboration across home and school can be a challenging task. All involved, however, have the same outcome in mind—quality education for students with disabilities. Welcoming families and other school personnel from outside the majority school culture, encouraging them to collaborate, and providing them with the supports they need, can be a powerful package for schools, families, and students with disabilities.

TABLE 2.8   Myths About Collaborating Across Cultures

1. Individuals sharing membership in a cultural group are by virtue of that membership able to work with other members of that cultural group in a culturally competent way.

2. Members of culturally diverse groups always represent their communities.

3. One member of the culturally diverse group can represent the whole.

4. Districts and schools should choose a representative from a diverse group to represent that group's interests.

5. Given the number of ethnic communities, it is not feasible or cost-effective to collaborate with them all.

6. The Anglo-American culture is the U.S. culture.

7. Key differences in culture are visible evidences such as language, lifestyle, and food.

8. Cultural competence is developed simply by working with others from a different culture.

9. Collecting information from a community isn't relationship based, but task based.

10. Written information is more reliable, valid, and substantial than verbal information.

Source: Adapted from Elliott, C., Adams, R. J., & Sockalingam, S. (2010). *Ten myths that prevent collaboration* (www. awesomeli brary.org/multiculturaltoolkit-myths.html).

SUMMARY

To be successful, special educators must work effectively with others. Collaboration, consulting, coaching, and mentoring are four models of working together used in the schools. Consulting and co-teaching are used to improve student performance. Coaching and mentoring are used to improve a teacher's own teaching performance.

School consultation usually involves a consultant working through a teacher to serve a student. Some argue consultation between general and special educators is not the best model because it implies one teacher has more knowledge than the other which can create resentment. In contrast, collaboration requires parity among participants. Collaboration is a style or process of interaction in which all parties are engaged in shared decision making working toward a common goal. Effective collaboration requires appropriate interactive communication skills, knowledge and application of problem-solving processes, and conflict resolution skills.

Special and general educators who co-teach share equal teaching responsibilities for all students assigned to that class. Becoming a skilled or collaborative co-teacher takes time and experience. Six co-teaching approaches can be applied in the classroom: one teaching, one observing; one teaching, one drifting; station teaching; parallel teaching; alternative teaching, and team teaching. Each has advantages and disadvantages. Co-teaching at the secondary level has unique challenges, including the increased gap in achievement between students with high-incidence disabilities and their nondisabled peers and the increased complexity of the subject matter being studied.

Not only do teachers work together to improve student learning, they do so to improve their own teaching. The purpose of peer coaching is to share ideas or build or refine skills of teacher colleagues working together; and the purpose of teacher mentoring is to provide new teachers technical skills and emotional support for success.

Special educators also work closely with paraeducators, related service personnel, administrators, and students' family members. Paraeducators are unique in this list given that special educators are responsible for managing, supervising, and evaluating them. Paraeducators should never have exclusive responsibility for students; that is the special educator's responsibility. Collaborating with parents and other family members of students is not only required by IDEA, but an important strategy to support student success.

Schools in the United States generally reflect European American culture. However, many students come from diverse cultures which often vary across dimensions such as efficiency, independence, equity, and communication styles. Special educators need to develop sensitivity to their own and others' cultural values and the impact they have on collaborative efforts. Based on this information, educators need to generate and apply strategies for working across cultures.

REVIEW QUESTIONS

1. Define *consultation* and explain the benefits and challenges of consulting with others. Why might consultation not be the best model for teachers? Provide several examples.

2. Compare and contrast the six approaches to co-teaching. In doing so, address advantages and disadvantages of each approach and provide examples of when you would use each.

3. Create two case studies each of when coaching or mentoring would be appropriate. Explain why one model would be better in each of the four case studies.

4. Define *collaboration* and provide at least two experiences in which you have or have not been in a collaborative relationship. Defend your categorization based on the characteristics of collaboration.

5. Discuss why interactive communication skills and effective problem-solving processes are important for effective collaboration.

6. What are some strategies special educators can use when they encounter conflict when working in school-based teams?

7. What are special educators' responsibilities when working with paraeducators? Be specific.

8. Why are interpersonal communication skills particularly important when working with parents and families?

9. Define the four dimensions by which cultures vary. Compare and contrast your cultural background with one that differs from yours across these four dimensions.

10. Which strategies for collaborating with parents and family members from diverse cultures do you think are the most pertinent?

ACTIVITIES

1. Interview a special education teacher, a general education teacher, a paraeducator, or a parent with a child with disabilities. Use the following questions to guide your interview. Write a paper describing the interviewee's responses.

   a. In what ways do you collaborate with others on behalf of your child or children with disabilities?

   b. In general, how collaborative are the teachers and staff at your school?

   c. What challenges and rewards have you experienced in collaborating with others?

   d. What suggestions and advice do you have for new special educators about collaborating with others?

2. With another student, write a two-page paper in which you compare and contrast different models of collaboration. Include in your paper a discussion about your collaborative experience, including who did what, how you divided up responsibilities, whether or not both contributed equally to the process, and so forth.

3. Ask a friend, colleague, or other associate to give you feedback on your communication style. Specifically address your listening habits, nonverbal cues, speaking style, and how you accept and give feedback. Write a summary of what you learned.

4. Search your library's electronic database for articles on co-teaching. Read two articles and write summaries of the key points.

Council for Exceptional Children (CEC) Standards

The Council for Exceptional Children (CEC) is a premiere national professional organization comprised of special educators, paraeducators, related service personnel, parents, and others interested in individuals with disabilities and/or those with gifts and talents. This organization has generated 10 standards for the preparation of special educators. These standards are listed in each chapter as they relate to the content within the chapter. The standards that apply to Chapter 2 are Standards #2 and #7.

CEC Initial Preparation Standard #2: Learning Environments (partial)

Beginning special education professionals create safe, inclusive, culturally responsive learning environments so that individuals with exceptionalities become active and effective learners and develop emotional well-being, positive social interactions, and self-determination. Beginning special education professionals:

2.1 Through collaboration with general educators and other colleagues create safe, inclusive, culturally responsive learning environments to engage individuals with exceptionalities in meaningful learning activities and social interactions.

CEC Initial Preparation Standard #7: Collaboration

Beginning special education professionals collaborate with families, other educators, related service providers, individuals with exceptionalities, and personnel from community agencies in culturally responsive ways to address the needs of individuals with exceptionalities across a range of learning experiences. Beginning special education professionals:

7.1 Use the theory and elements of effective collaboration.

7.2 Serve as a collaborative resource to colleagues.

7.3 Use collaboration to promote the well-being of individuals with exceptionalities across a wide range of settings and collaborators.

REFERENCES

Araujo, B. E. (2009). Best practices in working with linguistically diverse families. *Intervention in School and Clinic, 45,* 116–123.

Ashbaker, B. Y., & Morgan, J. (2013). *Paraprofessional in the classroom: A survival guide* (2nd ed.). Boston, MA: Pearson.

Bauer, K. L., Iyer, S. N., Boon, R. T., & Fore, C., III (2010). 20 ways for classroom teachers to collaborate with speech-language pathologists, *Intervention in School and Clinic, 45*(5), 333–337.

Blue-Banning, M., Summers, J. A., Frankland, H. C., Nelson, L. L., & Beegle, G. (2004). Dimensions of family and professional partnerships: Constructive guidelines for collaboration. *Exceptional Children, 70,* 167–184.

Brown, M. R., & Brandon, R. R. (2009). Working with culturally and linguistically diverse families. *Intervention in School and Clinic, 45*(2), 83–84.

Carnahan, C. R., Williamson, P., Clarke, L., & Sorensen, R. (2009). A systematic approach for supporting paraeducators in educational settings: A guide for teachers. *TEACHING Exceptional Children, 41*(5), 34–43.

Carter, E., O'Rourke, L., Sisco, L. G., & Pelsue, D. (2009). Knowledge, responsibilities, and training needs of paraprofessionals in elementary and secondary schools. *Remedial and Special Education, 30*(6), 344–359.

Cole, C. M., & McLeskey, J. (1997). Secondary inclusion programs for students with mild disabilities. *Focus on Exceptional Children, 29*(6), 1–15.

Cornett, J., & Knight, J. (2009). Research on coaching. In J. Knight (Ed.). *Coaching: Approaches and perspectives* (pp. 192–216). Thousand Oaks, CA: Corwin.

Correa, V. I., & Jones, H. (2000). Multicultural issues related to families of children with disabilities. In M. J. Fine & R. L. Simpson (Eds.), *Collaboration with parents and families of children and youth with exceptionalities* (pp. 133–154). Austin, TX: Pro-Ed.

Danseco, E. R. (1997). Parental beliefs on childhood disability: Insights on culture, child development and intervention. *International Journal of Disability, Development, and Education, 44*(1), 41–52.

Darling-Hammond, L. (2003). Keeping good teachers: Why it matters, what leaders can do? *Educational Leadership, 60*(8), 6–13.

Dettmer, P., Knackendoffel, A. P., & Thurston, L. P. (2013). *Collaboration, consultation, and teamwork for students with special needs* (7th ed.). Boston, MA: Pearson.

Dieker, L. A. (2001). What are the characteristics of "effective" middle and high school co-taught teams for students with disabilities? *Preventing School Failure, 46*, 14–23.

Donegan, M. M., Ostrosky, M. M., & Fowler, S. A. (2000). Peer coaching: Teachers supporting teachers. *Young Exceptional Children, 3*(3), 9–16.

Dyches, T. T., Carter, N. J., & Prater, M. A. (2012). *A teacher's guide to communicating with parents: Practical strategies for developing successful relationships*. Boston, MA: Pearson.

Eisenmann, L. T., Pleet, A. M., Wandry, D., & McGinley, V. (2011). Voices of special education teachers in an inclusive high school: Redefining responsibilities. *Remedial and Special Education, 32*(2), 91–104.

Erchul, W. P., & Martens, B. K. (2010). *School consultation: Conceptual and empirical bases of practice* (3rd ed.). New York, NY: Springer.

ERIC/OSEP Special Project. (Spring 2003). Paraeducators: Providing support to students with disabilities and their teachers. *Research Connections in Special Education* (No. 12). Arlington, VA: The ERIC Clearinghouse on Disabilities and Gifted Education.

Feger, S., Woleck, K., & Hickman, P. (2004). How to develop a coaching eye. *Journal of Staff Development, 25*(2), 14–18.

Finnegan, R. (2002). *Communicating: The multiple modes of human interconnection*. London, England: Routledge.

Fisher, M., & Pleasants, S. L. (2012). Roles, responsibilities, and concerns of paraeducators: Findings from a statewide survey. *Remedial and Special Education, 33*(5), 287–297.

Friend, M., & Cook, L. (2013). *Interactions: Collaboration skills for school professionals* (7th ed.). Boston, MA: Pearson.

Friend, M., Cook, L., Hurley-Chamberlain, D., & Shamberger, C. (2010). Co-teaching: An illustration of the complexity of collaboration in special education. *Journal of Educational and Psychological Consultation, 20*, 9–27.

Gately, S. E., & Gately, F. J., Jr. (2001). Understanding coteaching components. *TEACHING Exceptional Children, 33*(4), 40–47.

Giangreco, M. F. (2010). One-to-one paraprofessionals for students with disabilities in inclusive classrooms: Is conventional wisdom wrong? *Intellectual and Developmental Disabilities, 48*(1), 1–13.

Goodwin, A. L., & King, S. H. (2002). *Culturally responsive parental involvement: Concrete understandings and basic strategies*. Washington, DC: American Association of Colleges for Teacher Education.

Griffin, N. C., Wohlstetter, P., & Bharadwaja, L. C. (2001). Teacher coaching: A tool for retention. *The School Administrator, 58*(1), 38–40.

Gudwin, D. M., & Salazar-Wallace, M. D. (Eds.). (2010). *Mentoring and coaching: A lifeline for teachers in a multicultural setting*. Thousand Oaks, CA: Corwin.

Harbort, G., Gunter, P. L., Hull, K., Brown, Q., Venn, M. L., Wiley, L. P., & Wiley, E. W. (2007). Behaviors of teachers in co-taught classes in a secondary school. *Teacher Education and Special Education, 30*(1), 13–23.

Harris, K. C. (1996). Collaboration within a multicultural society: Issues for consideration. *Remedial and Special Education, 17*, 355–362.

Harry, B. (2008). Collaboration with culturally and linguistically diverse families: Ideal versus reality. *Exceptional Children, 74*(3), 372–388.

Herll, S., & O'Drobinak, B. (2004). Role of the coach: Dream keeper, supporter, friend. *Journal of Staff Development, 25*(2), 42–45.

Hobson, A. J., Ashby, P., Malderez, A., & Tomlinson, P. D. (2009). Mentoring beginning teachers: What we know and what we don't. *Teaching and Teacher Education, 25,* 207–216.

IDEA Partnership. (2001). Retrieved from http://www .nasdse.org/Projects/IDEAPartnership/tabid/413/Default .aspx

Idol, L. (2006). Toward inclusion of special education students in general education: A program evaluation of eight schools. *Remedial and Special Education, 27*(2), 77–94.

Kalyanpur, M. (1998). The challenge of cultural blindness: Implications for family-focused service delivery. *Journal of Child and Family Studies, 7,* 317–332.

Kalyanpur, M., & Harry, B. (1999). *Culture in special education: Building reciprocal family-professional relationships.* Baltimore, MD: Paul H. Brooks.

Knight, J. (2007). *Instructional coaching: A partnership approach to improving instruction.* Thousand Oaks, CA: Corwin.

Knopf, H. T., & Swick, K. J. (2008). Using our understanding of families to strengthen family involvement. *Early Childhood Education Journal, 35,* 419–427.

Kohler, F. W., Crilley, K. M., Shearer, D. D., & Good, G. (2001). Effects of peer coaching on teacher and student outcomes. *The Journal of Educational Research, 90,* 240–250.

Lloyd, S. R., Wood, T. A., & Moreno, G. (2000). What's a mentor to do? *TEACHING Exceptional Children, 33*(6), 4–13.

Martin, E. J., & Hagan-Burke, S. (2002). Establishing a home-school connection: Strengthening the partnership between families and schools. *Preventing School Failure, 46*(2), 62–65.

Mathur, S. R., Gehrke, R., & Kim, S. H. (2012). Impact of a teacher mentorship program on mentors' and mentees' perceptions of classroom practices and the mentoring experience. *Assessment for Effective Intervention, 38*(3), 154–162.

McGrath, M. Z., Johns, B. H., & Mathur, S. R. (2010). Empowered or overpowered? Strategies for working effectively with paraprofessionals. *Beyond Behavior, 19*(2), 2–6.

Melamed, J. C., & Reiman, J. W. (2000). Collaboration and conflict resolution in education. *The High School Magazine, 7*(7), 16–20.

Moin, L. J., Magiera, K., & Zigmond, N. (2009). Instructional activities and group work in the US inclusive high school co-taught science class. *International Journal of Science and Mathematics Education, 7,* 677–697.

More, C. M., Hart, J. E., & Cheatham, G. A. (2013). Language interpretation for diverse families: Considerations for special education teachers. *Intervention in School and Clinic, 49*(2), 113–120.

Mueller, P. H., & Murphy, P. V. (2001). Determining when a student requires paraeducators support. *TEACHING Exceptional Children, 33*(6), 22–27.

Murawski, W. W. (2012). 10 tips for co-planning more efficiently. *Teaching Exceptional Children, 44*(4), 8–15.

Murawski, W. W., & Dieker, L. A. (2004). Tips and strategies for co-teaching at the secondary level. *TEACHING Exceptional Children, 36*(5), 52–58.

Murawski, W. W., & Spencer, S. A. (2011). *Collaborate, communicate, and differentiate! How to increase student learning in today's diverse schools.* Thousand Oaks, CA: Corwin.

Nierengarten, G. (2013). Supporting co-teaching teams in high schools: Twenty research-based practices. *American Secondary Education, 42*(1), 73–83.

Olivos, E. M. (2009). Collaboration with Latino families: A critical perspective of home-school interactions. *Intervention in School and Clinic, 45*(2), 109–115.

Prater, M. A., & Sileo N. M. (2015). What really works in education: Collaborating with families. In W. W. Murawski & K. L. Scott (Eds.), *What really works in secondary education* (pp. 322–334). Thousand Oaks, CA: Corwin.

Pratt, S. (2014). Achieving symbiosis: Working through challenges found in co-teaching to achieve effective co-teaching relationships. *Teaching and Teacher Education, 41,* 1–12.

Pugach, M. C., & Johnson, L. J. (2002). *Collaborative practitioners: Collaborative schools* (2nd ed.). Denver, CO: Love Publishing.

Rea, P. J., McLaughlin, V. L., & Walther-Thomas, C. S. (2002). Outcomes for students with learning disabilities in inclusive and pullout programs. *Exceptional Children, 68,* 203–222.

Riggs, C. G. (2004). Top 10 list: To teachers: What paraeducators want you to know. *TEACHING Exceptional Children, 36*(5), 8–12.

Riley-Tillman, T. C., & Eckert, T. L. (2001). Generalization programming and school-based consultation: An examination of consultees' generalization of consultation-related skills. *Journal of Educational and Psychological Consultation, 12,* 217–241.

Rock, M. L., Schumacker, R. E., Gregg, M., Howard, P. W., Gable, R. A., & Zigmond, N. P. (2014). How are they now? Longer term effects of eCoaching through online bug-in-ear technology. *Teacher Education and Special Education, 37*(2), 161–181.

Rock, M. L., Zigmond, N. P., Gregg, M., & Gable, R. A. (2011). The power of virtual coaching. *Educational Leadership, 69*(2), 42–47.

Rodriguez, R. J., Blatz, E. T., & Elbaum, B. (2014). Strategies to involve families of Latino students with disabilities: When parent initiative is not enough. *Intervention in School and Clinic, 49*(5), 263–270. doi: 10.1177/105345123513956

Scheeler, M. C., Congdon, M., & Stansbery, S. (2010). Providing immediate feedback to co-teachers through bug-in-ear technology: An effective method of peer coaching in inclusion classrooms. *Teacher Education and Special Education, 33*(1), 83–96.

Scruggs, T. E., Mastropieri, M. A., & McDuffie, K. A. (2007). Co-teaching in inclusive classrooms: A metasynthesis of qualitative research. *Exceptional Children, 73*(4), 392–416.

Sileo, T. W., Sileo, A. P., & Prater, M. A. (1996). Parents and professional partnerships in special education: Reflections on cultural diversity. *Intervention in School and Clinic, 31,* 145–153.

Sileo, N. M., & Prater, M. A. (2012). *Working with families of children with special needs: Families and professional partnerships and roles.* Boston, MA: Pearson.

Snell, M. E., & Janney, R. E. (2000). Teachers' problem-solving about children with moderate and severe disabilities in elementary classrooms. *Exceptional Children, 66,* 472–490.

Teemant, A., Wink, J., & Tyra, S. (2011). Effects of coaching on teacher use of sociocultural instructional practices. *Teaching and Teacher Education, 27,* 683–693.

Thomas, C. C., Correa, V. I., & Morsink, C. V. (2001). *Interactive teaming: Enhancing programs for students with special needs.* Upper Saddle River, NJ: Prentice Hall.

Trautman, M. L. (2004). Preparing and managing paraprofessionals. *Intervention in School and Clinic, 39,* 131–138.

Turnbull, A. P., Blue-Banning, M., Turbiville, V., & Park, J. (1999). From parent education to partnership education: A call for a transformed focus. *Topics in Early Childhood Special Education, 19,* 164–172.

Turnbull, R., & Turnbull, A. P. (2015). Looking backward and framing the future for parents' aspirations for their children with disabilities. *Remedial and Special Education, 36*(1), 52–57.

Vaughn, S., & Coleman, M. (2004). The role of mentoring in promoting use of research-based practices in reading. *Remedial and Special Education, 25*, 25–38.

Wallace, T., Shin, J., Bartholomay, T., & Stahl, B. J. (2001). Knowledge and skills for teachers supervising the work of paraeducators. *Exceptional Children, 67*, 520–533.

Walsh, J. M., & Jones, B. (2004). New models of cooperative teaching. *TEACHING Exceptional Children, 36*(5), 14–20.

Walther-Thomas, C., Korinek, L., & McLaughlin, V. L. (1999). Collaboration to support student success. *Focus on Exceptional Children, 32*(3), 1–18.

Wilson, G. L., & Michaels, C. A. (2006). General and special education students' perceptions of co-teaching: Implications for secondary-level literacy instruction. *Reading & Writing Quarterly, 22*, 205–225.

$SAGE edge™ ••

Review ➡ Practice ➡ Improve

Get the tools you need to sharpen your study skills. Access videos, practice quizzes, eFlashcards and more at **edge.sagepub.com/prater.**

©iStockphoto.com/Christopher Futcher

CHAPTER

3

Behavior and Classroom Management and Organization

Behavioral Model

Ms. Orgill is starting her first year as a special education teacher. She will be teaching students with varying disabilities in a half-day self-contained classroom. The rest of the day she will be team teaching with one of the general education teachers. She is excited but nervous about starting her first year. Her cooperating teacher for student teaching was exceptional and provided her a great model in classroom organization and behavior management. But now, Ms. Orgill is on her own. She'll need to physically arrange her classroom and design a behavior management program for her students. This will be more difficult than learning to implement someone else's plan. She's not certain where to begin.

Learning Objectives

- Explain the importance of classroom management including the elements of physical classroom arrangement, time management, classroom scheduling, and classroom rules. Create case studies depicting examples and nonexamples of each.

- Define and provide examples of the following terms: *Premack principle, reinforcement* (positive, negative), *aversive stimulus, schedules of reinforcement* (continuous, intermittent, ratio, fixed, variable), *punishment, extinction, time-out, response cost, overcorrection, token economy, contingency contracts*, and *differential reinforcement of incompatible behaviors*.

- Explain the five factors teachers should consider when it appears positive reinforcement is not working.

- Define positive behavioral interventions and supports and provide examples of interventions in each tier.

- Describe and provide examples of how cultural background influences views of appropriate behavior and disciplinary procedures.

The manner in which teachers organize and manage their classroom greatly impacts student learning. In fact, learning may be defined as a change of behavior or performance over time as a result of the learner's experience and interaction with the world (Driscoll, 2005). Teachers can enhance student performance and behavior through effective classroom management and organization.

Learning theory can generally be classified in one of the following categories: behavioral, developmental, cognitive, or constructivist (Driscoll, 2005). Special education as a field has connections to each of these learning theories. The most prominent in special education, however, is the behavioral model, which is based on the following five general assumptions. First, the focus is on the observable, what the student does, rather than speculation about unconscious motives. Second, behavior is learned. Other factors, such as neurological and physiological factors, may impact behavior, but behavior is generally still the result of learning. Third, the only way to know that learning has occurred is to observe a change in behavior. Fourth, changes in behavior are governed by laws of effect. And, fifth, behaviors are also governed by the contexts in which they occur.

Teachers consistently identify classroom discipline as a major concern, yet discipline receives little attention in the general education literature. Elizabeth Hardman and Stephen Smith (2003) analyzed 13 major elementary education journals across a 10-year period and found that only .01% of the articles addressed classroom discipline. They argue that although educators insist on rigorous research when discussing methods of teaching reading, math, science, and social studies, the results of their study indicate that educators rarely conduct research on methods of classroom discipline. Of the articles that addressed teacher intervention for dealing with behavior problems, the most frequent suggestion was to talk to students and ask them to reflect on their behavior. Although this may work with some students, in today's classrooms many students need more substantive procedures.

Before school started, Ms. Orgill attended a statewide professional development conference in which several different programs related to discipline and behavior management were described. Many of them seemed to be based on similar techniques and principles she had learned in her teacher preparation program. She heard about many different programs for the first time and was surprised there were so many. She wondered how effective they were and whether she should even consider using any of these techniques.

Many classroom management programs are available for teachers to select. In choosing the best programs, Edward Kame'enui and Craig Darch (1995) suggest they should be evaluated in terms of the following five standards: effectiveness, usefulness, adaptability, alignment with instruction, and proactivity. In Kame'enui and Darch's examination of four current classroom management approaches—behavior management, assertive discipline (Canter & Canter, 2001), teacher effectiveness training (Gordon, 2003), and cooperative discipline (Albert, 1996)—the behavioral approach was the only one that fully or partially met all five criteria.

Although behavioral approaches to classroom management have an empirical basis, behavior management, sometimes called behavior modification, has been criticized for several reasons such as forcing compliance, treating the symptoms not the causes, generating short-term benefits with limited transfer value, and devaluing self-discipline (e.g., Kohn, 1999). Overall, however, behavior management, when applied appropriately, has been documented many times over as a powerful tool for creating a supportive learning environment (e.g., de Bruin, Deppeler, Moore, & Diamond, 2013; DuPaul, Eckert, & Vilardo, 2012; Goh & Bambara, 2012).

In the first section of this chapter, classroom management including environmental considerations and time management issues that contribute to overall successful management and organization in the classroom are discussed. The rest of the chapter is devoted to behavioral principles and applications. These principles apply when working with one student or with a whole classroom of students, as well as when working with students with high-incidence disabilities or those identified as at risk for school failure.

Classroom Management

Teachers with effective classroom management skills know how to physically arrange the room and how to create an ambiance that impacts student learning favorably. They also know how to effectively schedule student activities throughout the day and how to use their time wisely. Lastly, effective teachers create and consistently apply classroom rules, not to demand compliance, but to ensure the safety and well-being of their students and others.

Physical Classroom

Immediately after she was hired, Ms. Orgill visited her new classroom. She noticed that it was somewhat small, although she knew she would only be teaching eight to 10 students half-day. One side of the classroom had three windows which looked out on the playground. Another side was covered in bulletin boards. What looked like the front of the classroom was a large chalkboard. The back of the classroom had cubby holes and a coat rack along with a sink and a small cupboard. She had 12 student desks and chairs, one teacher desk and chair, two small bookcases and one 4-drawer filing cabinet. A small kidney-shaped table was also in the room.

Teachers generally have little control over the physical environment they have been assigned. Effective teachers, however, maximize their resources and creatively enhance the environment to make it as conducive to learning as possible. The goal is to ensure that all elements of the environment are facilitators, not detractors, of learning. Robert DiGiulio (2007) suggests that designing the physical environments requires that teachers focus on furniture, materials, the human factor (or how the materials will be used), and the ambiance or feeling of the room.

Furniture, Materials, and the Human Factor

The size and needs of the students' bodies determine classroom furniture and arrangement. All desks, tables, and chairs should fit the size of the students and should be arranged to ensure appropriate distance between students. Displays such as bulletin boards should be at the students' eye level when possible. Other furniture, such as freestanding bookcases and shelves that are higher than the students, should be placed against outside walls. Furniture should be arranged to allow students to move around the room. In general, each passageway should allow two children to pass each other comfortably. The number of pathways should depend on the size of the room, as well as the number of students in the classroom and their age. If the total classroom space does not allow for various seating configurations, students can be taught to move desks, chairs, and tables in an efficient and appropriate manner (Clayton & Forton, 2001).

Teachers need to limit the amount of furniture and materials. Too much furniture can crowd students and be hazardous. Too many materials can create an overly stimulating environment. All pieces of furniture should have at least one clear purpose and be actively used for at least part of the day. Furniture not in regular use should be removed. Also all materials should have a clear purpose based on students' needs, and teachers should control storage space so it is neat, safe, and easily accessible (Clayton & Forton, 2001).

Students with specific physical and learning needs should be considered in the design of the classroom space. For example, a student in a wheelchair may need additional space to join a group or to maneuver around the classroom. Easily distractible students may need a study carrel in which to do seatwork.

The physical aspects of a classroom can reveal the teacher's approach to learning. Classrooms with desks separated and spread across the room usually indicate that students are expected to work independently. If the desks are clustered, the teacher probably favors cooperative or small-group learning. If all the desks are facing a main wall with a chalkboard, then the teacher probably delivers large-group instruction. When work stations are part of the classroom, perhaps with study carrels, computers, and/or a silent reading area, the arrangement indicates that students are at least sometimes working independently or in pairs. Regardless of the configuration of the furniture, it should always be arranged so the teacher can see all students at all times. Ideas for creating various workspaces are outlined in Table 3.1.

Teachers need to ensure that each student has some personal space, a place to work, and somewhere to store materials. The availability of personal space and ownership can be critical for some students. For example, students who have experienced homelessness may be very protective of personal space, and the place which they are assigned in school may be the only place they can call their own.

Ms. Orgill decides she will start the school year with the desks separated from one another in rows. Once she has established classroom rules and students have become accustomed to the rules, she anticipates grouping students together which will necessitate moving desks into clusters. She decides to keep two extra student desks and place them away from the instructional area. She's anticipating she will receive a computer and will use the extra desks for that purpose. She arranges another corner of the room with the kidney shaped table for small-group work. She will request additional chairs for the table so that students don't need to bring their chairs for group work. Cubby holes will be labeled with students' names in which they may keep personal items not kept in their personal desk.

TABLE 3.1   Ideas for Creating Workspace

Type of Student Work	Ideas for Workspace in the Classroom
Cooperative Learning	• Set up a permanent area for small-group work. If not enough room exists for each group to work simultaneously, rotate them through the small-group work area. • Use round tables or chairs arranged in circles in different areas of the room. • Group desks into clusters of three to five.
Peer Tutoring	• Group desks into pairs. • Set up computer stations that allow partners to work together.
Individual Work	• Provide clipboards for work that can be taken anywhere in the room. • Create a rug area for sitting or stretching legs. • Provide additional chairs throughout the room where students can take their individual work.

Source: Adapted from Clayton & Forton (2001).

Classroom Ambiance

Classroom ambiance impacts how well students learn. Teachers should strive to create an environment that is pleasing to most students most of the time by making the classroom welcoming, comfortable, and engaging (Clayton & Forton, 2001).

The environmental factors impacting each of the five senses should be considered. For example, teachers should be aware of the room temperature, lighting, noise levels, odors, and other sensory variables that affect student learning. These environmental variables are particularly important for students who are easily distracted. Students easily distracted by visual movement, for example, should not directly face doors or windows. Teachers may consider adding a table or floor lamp to areas dimly lit. Some students may prefer to work in natural light, which should be allowed within reason. To reduce general noise level, teachers should separate quiet and noisy spaces as much as possible. Headphones or earmuffs can be used by individual students who prefer a quieter atmosphere.

Although each individual may have learning preferences, some educators advocate the use of learning style inventories to determine the optimal learning environment for each student (e.g., Brand, Dunn, & Greb, 2002; Lovelace, 2005); the validity of such inventories and using results to design or modify instruction and the learning environments have been questioned (e.g., Kavale & LeFever, 2007; Wilson, 2012). Joel Stellwagen (2001) conducted a review of research on learning styles and concluded the following:

> Clearly, teachers who manage their classrooms around learning style instruction are engaging in a practice of debatable value. Substantive issues exist, such as the lack of supportive research, the questionable reliability and validity of the learning style inventories, and basic misunderstandings about the theoretical basis and use of learning style instruction. (p. 267)

Catherine Scott (2010) goes further by stating that using learning styles as a guide for instructional practice "promotes damaging stereotypes about individuals and interferes with the development of evidence-based best practice" (p. 14).

Given the lack of research supporting the validity of learning style assessment and instruction, the author does not support their use. However, students can be given some choices within reason and allowed to work in the environmental situation in which they feel most comfortable without formal learning style assessment or intervention. Teachers could allow, for example, students to decide where in the classroom they want to read independently. They may wish to sit at a chair by the window with natural light or use a study carrel with a lamp and/or earmuffs. Some children like to read in a beanbag chair or by sitting on the floor. Allowing some flexibility in student choices can be extremely beneficial to both the students and their teacher.

Ms. Orgill is concerned about the large windows in her classroom and that the movement on the playground will distract her students. She decides to request the type of blinds that can be lowered from the top or from the bottom. If lowered from the top, natural light will be allowed to enter the room, but students will not be distracted by the activities on the playground. If she is not successful in acquiring such blinds, she anticipates putting up poster board that can be easily removed across the bottom of the windows.

Effective Time Management

Teachers must be effective managers of their and their students' time. In Chapter 6, the effective use of student time to facilitate learning will be discussed. Teachers' use of time is also important. The most prevalent activity that hampers teachers' use of time is paperwork. There are several ways to reduce the time needed to deal with paperwork. Where possible, teachers can create forms for recording conference notes, sending messages home, taking meeting minutes, observations, and so forth. Teachers then need only to check a box or write a small note in a box in lieu of writing an entire message or anecdotal record. Teachers often find it helpful to set aside a few minutes each day to handle paperwork so that it doesn't build up and become overwhelming. To help with grading, teachers can create an answer key and use other individuals, such as student assistant, classroom volunteer, or paraeducator, as graders. Students can also be instructed in how to correct their own papers.

Technology Spotlight #3.1

Managing Your Student's Time With a Hall Pass Timer

Not only is it challenging for teachers to manage their time, managing students who are out of the classroom can be particularly challenging. Students leave the classroom all the time and it is quite common for teachers to lose track of how long a student has been gone. Some students seem to have a particular problem returning to the classroom in a timely manner. The Hall Pass Timer is an outstanding example of a technology product that teachers never knew they needed, but everyone will want one!

The Hall Pass Timer consists of two parts: The Teacher Monitor and the Hall Pass. Teachers use the Teacher Monitor to set an allotted time for a student to be out of the class (e.g., 1 to 5 minutes). When a student leaves the room, the Hall Pass has a countdown timer illustrating how much time is left. The time is synchronized and displayed on the Teacher Monitor. Warning lights (green, yellow, red) and a time's up alarm on both the Hall Pass and Teacher Monitor remind both the teacher and the student of the time status. A memory time feature in the Teacher Monitor provides the time for the last three uses of the Hall Pass (www.stokespublishing .com/timers.html).

Classroom Scheduling

Ms. Orgill sets up a daily and weekly schedule for herself and her paraeducator. Although she's not certain at the beginning of the year how much time it will take, she builds in 40 minutes a day for herself and her paraeducator to complete paperwork and plan for the next day. She's not certain exactly how much time they will need, so she's prepared to adjust her time schedule as they become more accustomed to the routine.

Weekly and daily schedules among special educators vary. Their schedules are influenced primarily by service delivery model (e.g., resource room, self-contained classroom, itinerant teacher, inclusion) and grade level (e.g., elementary or secondary school). All special educators, regardless of the service delivery model or grade level they teach, need to schedule their time wisely. They need time to meet with others, including general educators, parents, and other professionals. Also time should be allocated to periodically observe their students in other classrooms. In some situations, special educators are responsible for conducting formal assessment for students referred for special education services. Teachers need sufficient time to fulfill these obligations and should work collaboratively with their direct supervisor, usually the school principal, to ensure that enough time has been slotted for obligations beyond teaching students.

Teachers must use instructional time wisely. They should create and post a daily and weekly schedule and adhere to the schedule. At the same time, teachers need to be flexible and willing to change when situations arise that require such flexibility. Within the school day, teachers should schedule the most difficult subjects when students are alert. Teachers can make more preferred activities (e.g., recess, art, physical education) contingent on less preferred activities (e.g., math, reading). This strategy, referred to as the **Premack principle** (Premack, 1965) states that a behavior that has a high probability of occurring may be used as a reinforcer of an activity that has a low frequency of occurrence. The Premack principle has been demonstrated to be an effective technique in the classroom (Wheeler & Richey, 2014). More information on reinforcers is presented later in this chapter.

Elementary resource rooms are designed as **pull-out programs**. Students remain in the general education classroom except for a portion of the day (usually 30 to 90 minutes). At the beginning of the school year, special and general educators must work collaboratively to determine the best time for students to attend the resource room. Typically, general educators prefer that students with disabilities receive special education instruction at the same time their general education peers are receiving instruction on the same content. For example, if the fourth-grade teachers instruct math from 11:00 to 11:45, they would like the students receiving special education math instruction to attend the resource room during the same time period. This preference becomes problematic when general education teachers in several grades teach the same content at the same time. Yet, if resource room services are scheduled at other times of the day, students may be pulled out of their general education classroom and miss other essential content and/or fun activities. These concerns are inherent in *any* pull-out program.

Special educators teaching in self-contained classrooms have more flexibility in their daily and weekly schedules. They must ensure, however, that all the needs of the students are being addressed within the classroom schedule. As discussed in Chapter 1, self-contained special education classrooms are not, however, the most ideal placement for instruction particularly when considering the least restrictive environment and access to general education curriculum provisions in IDEA.

The schedule for secondary special education classrooms is often based on the master schedule used by the school. Block scheduling for secondary school has become more popular in recent years. Instead of the traditional six- or seven-period schedule, the number of classes offered during the school day is reduced, thus increasing the length of time for each (e.g., 90 to 120 minutes). Several variations of the block schedule have emerged.

Some districts hold four classes per day that end after one semester. Others continue with eight classes, four of which are held on alternating days (e.g., A/B day schedule) which continues throughout the academic year.

Although educators have suggested that block scheduling holds promise for students receiving special education services, little research has been conducted in this area. In fact, there exists a paucity of research in the effectiveness of block scheduling in general (Zepeda & Mayers, 2006). In one study, special educators indicated they preferred block scheduling over the traditional schedule (Santos & Rettig, 1999). They liked, for example, the flexibility block scheduling allows for resource scheduling. "In one school it was easier for students to come to the resource room for part of the block to receive assistance after the general education teacher presented the main lesson" (p. 55). Additional advantages included, among others, (a) teachers being *forced* to modify their teaching methods to include more varied and active learning strategies, (b) more time for individualized instruction, and (c) general improvements in student behavior. Disadvantages were also found, including, among others, (a) longer gaps between sessions negatively affecting student retention of material, (b) confusion among students about where they should be, and (c) an increase in students coming to class unprepared.

In another study, Donald Weller and James McLeskey (2000) examined the impact of block scheduling in a Midwestern inclusive high school in which the general education and special education teachers team taught. They discovered benefits in that block scheduling (a) facilitated team teaching and inclusion; (b) allowed for more student-centered learning activities; and (c) benefited all students, especially those from less traditional backgrounds. They also found that block scheduling (a) increased the need for both teachers and students to be more organized, (b) increased the number of absences, and (c) was difficult to adjust to for some students.

Classroom Rules

All classrooms need rules. These rules should be valued similarly to our society's set of laws. The rules are designed not to force students to be compliant but for the safety and well-being of all who inhabit the classroom. Using the word, *expectations*, instead of rules may be more appropriate for secondary students. To adolescents the term, *rules*, may seem coercive (Young, Caldarella, Richardson, & Young, 2012). A set of suggestions for designing and implementing classroom rules or expectations follows.

1. **Develop rules at the beginning of the school year.** Classroom rules should be established the first day of school and should be discussed with the students periodically throughout the year.

2. **If appropriate, involve students in developing the rules.** Depending on their age and sophistication, students should participate in developing the rules. Teachers may find that the students' rules are stricter than those the teacher would have set. Students who have participated in creating rules are more likely to willingly adhere to them than students who have rules imposed.

3. **The behavior in the rule should be observable and measurable.** Rules are similar to behavioral objectives in that the behavior described should be capable of being observed and measured. Thus rules such as *Students will respect one another's property* should be avoided. Instead this rule may be stated as *Students will ask other students for permission to use their materials.*

4. **Rules should be stated in positive terms.** A rule such as *Students will not hit other students* should be written as *Students will keep their hands and feet to themselves.* Stating the rule in positive terms provides students with a list of behaviors they should exhibit rather than behaviors they should not.

5. **The number of rules should not exceed five.** A photograph has circulated among educators of a playground surrounded by a wall on which nearly 100 rules were written. Those who use the playground don't have the time or inclination to read all of the rules, let alone remember and apply them. Teachers should keep the number of rules to a minimum because they will be easier for the students to remember and easier for the teacher to enforce.

6. **Demonstrate examples and nonexamples of the rules**. Many students, particularly those with disabilities, need explicit examples and nonexamples of how the behavior stated in the rule looks and sounds like in various contexts. The teacher can begin by modeling and then asking the students to demonstrate examples and nonexamples of the rules.

7. **Rules should be posted in the classroom.** Posting the rules serves as a reminder to students and the teacher. In addition, the teacher can refer to the rule chart easily when reminding the students about the rules or reviewing them for potential revision.

8. **The consequences for keeping or breaking rules should be well defined and understood by each student.** Identifying and communicating to students the consequences of rule breaking and rule keeping is critical, but often ignored by teachers. Consequences are discussed in detail later in this chapter.

9. **Teachers must deliver consequences consistently for keeping or breaking the rules.** Many teachers develop and post well-written rules, but never require students keep them. For example, a rule found commonly in classrooms reads *Students will raise their hand to talk.* Yet few teachers actually require students to raise their hand every time they have something to say. Having such a rule, therefore, is not only useless, but failure to enforce it teaches students that the classroom rules are unimportant. Assuming that the rules are appropriate and that students are generally compliant, a basic rule of thumb is to consistently apply consequences

(i.e., punishment) for breaking rules, but occasionally reinforce students for keeping them. In the development stage, teachers need to consider how they are going to consistently deliver the consequences for breaking the rules. This consideration can help shape the rules.

10. **Rules should be reviewed and if necessary revised throughout the school year.** Reasons to revise the rules may include observation that a rule is ambiguous, unnecessary, or difficult to enforce. Also, as the year progresses, incidents may occur that could have been avoided if a rule had been instigated earlier. The introduction of new students to the classroom or the maturation of the students also influences the need to revise rules. If appropriate, students should be involved in these revisions.

The first day of class, Ms. Orgill discussed classroom rules with her students. Although she had some ideas of what she wanted as rules, she allowed the students to help select them. She made certain that they were written in positive terms and few in number. She wrote them on a large poster board and posted them on the bulletin board. They read: *Students will be in the classroom when the bell rings. Students will keep hands and feet to themselves. Students will follow Ms. Orgill on the first request. Students will replace all materials to their proper place. Students will walk quietly in the halls between class periods.* Ms. Orgill devised consequences for keeping and breaking the rules, as well as a method of administering consequences.

Behavior Management Techniques

Not only do teachers need effective classroom management skills, they also need to understand and apply principles of behavior management to individuals or groups of students. Within this section behavior management is discussed including ways to increase, maintain, decrease, or eliminate behaviors. Given that cultural expectations influence behavior, a section focused on implications for culturally diverse students is also presented. All of the principles discussed have been shown to be effective across a wide range of individuals, although continual research refining the application of the principles will always remain.

Twila is a fourth-grade student who has been identified as having emotional/behavioral disorders. She claims to hate school and does not get along with any of her peers primarily because she starts verbal and physical fights. She attends Ms. Rains's general fourth-grade classroom all day. The special educator, Mr. Rodriguez, consults with Ms. Rains twice a week. At the first of the year, Twila was constantly getting into trouble both in the classroom and on the playground. Mr. Rodriquez observed Twila and her classmates and in doing so he identified what occurs prior to and following Twila's fighting with her peers.

The overriding principle of the behavioral approach to learning is that behavior is controlled by the **consequences** or the events that follow the occurrence of a behavior. These consequences may serve to strengthen, maintain, weaken, or eliminate a behavior. In addition, an **antecedent** or event that precedes behavior may impact the occurrence of a specific behavior. When the antecedents and/or consequences change(s), so does the behavior.

Increasing and Maintaining Behaviors

Mr. Rodriguez observed Twila for 1 hour. During that time, Twila initiated a fight with a peer three times. Each time, Mr. Rodriguez observed that before she started a fight, she was either being ignored by the teacher and her peers or she was being asked to do something academically or physically challenging. What happened after in each instance was a lot of attention from both the teacher and her peers.

By definition, **reinforcement** is a change in a stimulus or event after the occurrence of a behavior that increases the future probability of that behavior; therefore, a **reinforcer** is a consequence that increases or maintains the previous response or behavior. The behavior or response increased or maintained is not necessarily a positive or desired behavior. "Reinforcement is an ethically neutral scientific principle applicable to any behavior, desirable or not" (Justen & Howerton, 1993, p. 37). In Twila's case, attention from her teacher and classmates appears to be reinforcing her starting fights, an undesirable behavior. A teacher who yells at a student for being out of his seat could be reinforcing the student's undesirable out-of-seat behavior. Also, a teacher who praises a student for completing her work on time could be reinforcing her desirable work-completion behavior. Teachers can only determine whether the consequence (yelling or praising) is a reinforcer by examining future occurrences of the behavior (initiating fights, out of seat, or completing work on time). If the behavior maintains or increases, then the consequence is reinforcing.

Positive Reinforcement

A positive reinforcer, like all reinforcers, maintains or increases a behavior when it is delivered contingent upon the occurrence of that behavior. Positive reinforcers increase or maintain both desired and undesired behaviors. In the previous examples, the teacher's yelling and verbal praise were positive reinforcers. One increased an undesired behavior and the other a desired behavior. The attention Twila gets appears to be reinforcing her starting fights. So the teacher's and peers' attention (consequence) is a positive reinforcer reinforcing Twila's negative behavior (fighting).

A positive reinforcer can be anything from a piece of paper to extra free time. Teachers cannot make assumptions about what will reinforce their students. The only way to determine if something is reinforcing to a student is to provide the reinforcer and observe its effect on the behavior. The true test comes in future behavior. If a reinforcer is administered following the occurrence of a behavior and the behavior increases or is maintained, the consequence is reinforcing the student. For additional examples of this principle, see Table 3.2.

TABLE 3.2   Examples of Positive Reinforcement

Antecedent	Behavior	Consequence	Future Event
Kim's teacher reminds the class to write their name on their math assignment.	Kim writes her name on her math assignment for the first time.	Kim's teacher places a star on her math paper next to her name.	Kim continues to write her name on her math assignment. (desired behavior)
James and Billy see each other in the hall.	Billy calls James a name.	James cries.	Billy continues to call James names. (undesired behavior)
Tyron's teacher explains that test grades will determine final class grades.	Tyron receives 85% and 82% on his mid-term and final history exam.	Tyron obtains a grade of B in history.	Tyron continues to study for exams. (desired behavior)
Nathaniel is given a watercolor set for his birthday.	Nathaniel paints his first watercolor painting.	Nathaniel receives verbal praise from his parents and friends.	Nathaniel continues to paint with watercolors. (desired behavior)
Martha's classmates talk among themselves leaving her out of the conversation.	Martha cracks jokes in class during inappropriate times.	Martha's peers laugh at her jokes.	Martha continues to crack jokes at inappropriate times. (undesired behavior)

Teachers must keep in mind that what may reinforce one student may not reinforce another student. So how do teachers decide what reinforcers to use? First, consider the student's age, gender, interests, and backgrounds. For example, what reinforces a high school senior is much different than what reinforces a six-year-old. Second, consider the behavior the student is supposed to exhibit. Even though the item or activity would generally reinforce the student, the length of time it would take the student to complete the task may not be worth it to the individual. Few adults, for example, would work extra hours for a 10-cents-an-hour pay raise. Third, when possible, use natural reinforcers or those that are naturally available in a situation. For example, enterprising teachers often use classroom privileges, such as the opportunity to lead the student line or erase the chalkboard, as reinforcers. Natural reinforcers are advantageous because they are low cost to the teacher and more likely to be available to the student after the behavior has been established.

Another way to determine what is reinforcing is to directly ask the student. This is sometimes accomplished through a formal reinforcement inventory, given in a personal interview or in written form. Some inventories are open-ended questions, such as "If I had free time in school, I would spend it . . ." Other inventories provide students with choices: "If I had free time in school, I would spend it (a) listening to music, (b) playing a board game, (c) working on the computer, (d) playing outside, or (e) completing a puzzle." Depending on the age, attitude, and cognitive ability of the students, it is often better to provide choices because students may otherwise not know what to write or say.

In addition, providing students choices ensures that the reinforcers selected are within control of the teacher. Figure 3.1 provides an example of a reinforcement survey.

Other strategies for determining reinforcers include asking other teachers who have worked with the student, asking the student's family members, and observing what the student selects when given choices. Young children, for example, can be observed during free play to determine what activities and toys they select.

FIGURE 3.1 Example of a Reinforcer Survey

Reinforcer Survey

Name_____   Date_____

✓ **Put a check mark in front of your favorite activities and things.**

My Favorite Activities	My Favorite Things
☐ 5 Extra Minutes of P.E.	☐ Board Game
☐ 5 Minutes in the Library	☐ Card Game
☐ 5 Minutes Free Time	☐ Chalk
☐ Color	☐ Comic Book
☐ Computer Time	☐ Crayons
☐ Draw a Picture	☐ Eraser
☐ Errand to the Office	☐ Free Time Tickets
☐ Extra Recess	☐ Grab Bag Toy
☐ Help the Teacher	☐ Jacks
☐ Help the Classroom Aide	☐ Jump Rope
☐ Listen to Music	☐ Key Chain
☐ Pass Out Papers	☐ Marble
☐ Pass Out Supplies	☐ Marker
☐ Play a Game	☐ Note Home
☐ P.E. Time	☐ Pen
☐ Play With the Class Pet	☐ Pencil
☐ Read a Magazine	☐ Play Money
☐ Read in the Reading Corner	☐ Puzzle
☐ Read to a Friend	☐ School Supplies
☐ Sharpen Pencils	☐ Stamps
☐ Share and Tell	☐ Stickers

Twila's fighting behavior appears to be reinforced by the attention she receives. Mr. Rodriguez and Ms. Rains brainstorm other reinforcers that could be used with Twila to give her more attention when she behaves appropriately. Ms. Rains talks to Twila's mother and learns that Twila likes to read stories to her little brother and sister each night. Ms. Rains knows she is an exceptional reader and so she invites Twila to read aloud a few of the pages of the book she is reading to the class after lunch each day. She agrees. Although this should give Twila attention for an appropriate behavior, they decide she will also need to be taught appropriate social skills for interacting with her peers.

TEACHER TIP #3.1

USING PRAISE NOTES

Both verbal and written praise can be positively reinforcing to students. Praise notes can be used as a school-, grade-, or classwide intervention to improve student behavior. For example, one school identified habitual tardiness as problematic. Teachers identified those students in their classes with moderate to severe tardiness. Parents received a newsletter explaining the program. Then teachers wrote a praise note with a specific comment to being on time whenever the targeted student arrived on time. Teachers also gave as little attention as possible to the student when he was tardy. The intervention improved the students' on-time behavior and was relatively easy to administer (Caldarella, Christensen, Young, & Densley, 2011).

Technology Spotlight #3.2

Reinforcing and Providing Feedback Electronically

Technology can simplify the administration of positive reinforcement and feedback in the classroom. ClassDojo (www.classdojo.com) is an example of an electronic real-time classroom tool to help manage student behavior. It's quick to set up and use and is completely free.

With ClassDojo, teachers can assign points to individual students for specific behaviors, learning habits, and accomplishments in class such as participating, helping others, and staying on task. Awarding points can be done remotely with any smartphone, tablet, or iPod touch. Teachers can display student progress in the classroom using an interactive whiteboard or computer and projector.

Each student has an assigned avatar that can be individualized by the teacher or the student. Students can be given access so they can track their own progress. Teachers can follow both individual and classwide performance trends in real time without any extra data entry. Parents can also be kept in the loop with instant messaging and reports.

Negative Reinforcement

> Laramie, an eighth grader with learning disabilities, has a history of not completing his work. When he does complete it, it's sloppy and hard to read. Mr. Jennings, his math teacher, conferences monthly with each student to review his or her work. He's noticed that Laramie is always absent on the day his conference is scheduled. Given Mr. Jennings's tight schedule, he doesn't have time to conference with a student if he or she is absent the day it is scheduled. They have, therefore, never held a conference together.

All reinforcers maintain or increase behavior. Negative reinforcers, therefore, maintain or increase behavior; but in this instance the behavior is being maintained or increased to avoid or terminate an aversive stimulus. An **aversive stimulus** typically results in pain or discomfort and may produce escape or avoidance behavior. Every day examples of responding to negative reinforcement in our lives include buckling a seat belt to avoid the warning noise created by the car, closing the window blinds to avoid a glare in the room, or driving the speed limit to avoid getting a traffic ticket. The increased/maintained behaviors are buckling the seat belt, closing the window blinds, and driving the speed limit. The aversive stimuli are the car's warning noise, the sun's glare, and the traffic ticket.

Negative reinforcement occurs in classrooms as well. Many teachers use negative reinforcement unknowingly because many students complete their school work not because of the positive reinforcement that follows, but to avoid being embarrassed or singled out by the teacher for unacceptable work. Although typically present, negative reinforcement should not be promoted in classrooms because of the avoidance or escape behavior it may create. For example, a student might not attend class to avoid being penalized. Laramie appears to be missing class on the day of the conference to avoid having to be told he is doing poorly. Table 3.3 contains examples of negative reinforcement in classrooms.

TABLE 3.3   **Examples of Negative Reinforcement**

Antecedent	Behavior	Consequence	Future Event
Joe threatens to hit Eric if he doesn't give him his lunch money.	Eric gives his lunch money to Joe.	Joe doesn't hit Eric.	Eric continues to give his lunch money to Joe. (undesired behavior)
Classroom rules are that you come to class on time or you get a detention slip.	Shauna comes to class on time.	Shauna's teacher doesn't give her a detention slip.	Shauna continues to come to class on time. (desired behavior)
The teacher announces it's time for reading.	Billy has a tantrum.	Billy avoids participating in reading activities.	Billy continues to have tantrums before reading. (undesired behavior)

(Continued)

TABLE 3.3   (Continued)

Antecedent	Behavior	Consequence	Future Event
Vince is sent to the principal's office for breaking the computer.	Vince lies to the principal about breaking the computer.	Vince's parents are not called.	Vince continues to lie about his actions. (undesired behavior)
Molly's parents threaten to ground her if she doesn't pass all of her courses.	Molly passes all of her first semester courses.	Molly's parents don't ground her.	Molly works toward passing her second semester courses. (desired behavior)

Primary and secondary reinforcers

Reinforcers may be defined as primary or secondary. **Primary reinforcers** are those that are biologically important to an individual (Alberto & Troutman, 2012). Food and liquids, for example, are primary reinforcers. Primary reinforcers should be reserved for young children and students with severe disabilities. **Secondary reinforcers** are those that have acquired their reinforcing effect through pairing with a primary reinforcer. Grades, verbal praise, stickers, and activities are examples of secondary reinforcers used typically in schools. Other reinforcers are listed in Table 3.4. Teachers should use low cost reinforcers (in terms of time, effort and money) whenever possible.

Schedules of Positive Reinforcement

Mr. Jennings decides to randomly schedule his conferences with students so Laramie cannot avoid conferencing with him by being absent. He also decides that Laramie needs additional incentives to complete his work neatly and on time. During their first conference, they discuss his need to improve submitting work neatly and on-time. They decide that each day Laramie submits his work on time, he will be granted 2 minutes of free time. An additional 2 minutes will be added for each assignment submitted neatly written. Laramie may use his accumulated free time each Friday to work on the computer, play a math game with a classmate, or work on a jigsaw puzzle.

The frequency with which positive reinforcement is delivered is called the **schedule of reinforcement**. Teachers can apply a **continuous schedule of reinforcement,** meaning the student is reinforced for every occurrence of the behavior. Continuous schedules are most useful when students are in the acquisition stage of learning (i.e., learning a new behavior). Mr. Jennings will be reinforcing Laramie on a continuous schedule of reinforcement. In contrast, with **intermittent schedules of reinforcement**, positive reinforcement follows some, but not all correct responses or occurrences of the behavior. Intermittent schedules (a) keep students from becoming satiated on the reinforcers, (b) teach students to work for longer periods of time, and (c) teach students to delay gratification and to work for longer periods of time. A teacher may choose ratio, interval, or response-duration schedules (Alberto & Troutman, 2012). In addition, each of these

TABLE 3.4   Possible Secondary Reinforcers

Examples of Secondary Reinforcers			
Tangible	**Activities**	**Privileges**	**Social**
Stickers and stars	Free time	Be line leader	High five
School supplies (e.g., pencils, erasers)	Listen to music	Erase the chalkboard	Handshake
Small toys	Work on the computer	No homework for the day	Verbal praise
Books and magazines	Play a game	Be excused from a test	A note to the student
Fast food coupons	Complete a puzzle	Go to the gym	A note to parents
	Watch a movie	Eat lunch with the teacher	A phone call to parents
	Class party	Select where to sit for the day	
	Field trips	Decorate a bulletin board	
		Become a tutor	

types of schedules can be fixed or variable (e.g., fixed ratio, variable response-duration). Teachers often move from a continuous to an intermittent schedule of reinforcement.

In a **ratio schedule of reinforcement,** a student is reinforced after exhibiting the behavior a specific number of times. Ratio schedules may be fixed or variable. Within a **fixed ratio schedule**, the student is reinforced after a specified number of correct responses. A **variable ratio schedule** is one in which the student receives the positive reinforcement after an average of a specified number of correct responses. An **interval schedule of reinforcement** involves the passage of time. A student must exhibit at least one correct response during the specified interval of time. As with fixed ratio schedules, the fixed interval schedule requires that the interval of time remains constant, while in a variable interval schedule the intervals are of varying length. The third major category is the **response-duration schedule of reinforcement**. Within this type of schedule, a student must exhibit a behavior for the duration of a chosen time interval. As with the other schedules, response-duration schedules can be fixed or variable. (Table 3.5 lists examples).

TABLE 3.5   Examples of Schedules of Reinforcement

	Ratio	**Interval**	**Response-Duration**
Fixed	Hal earns 1 minute of free time for every seventh math problem answered correctly.	Nancy receives a star if she toilets during the hour.	Mike's teacher delivers verbal praise every 5 minutes that he works at his desk during independent study time.
Variable	Marcy receives 1 point for an average of every third table she wipes clean.	Melissa earns 5 cents toward an ice cream cone if she contributes to the small-group discussion at least once during an average of every 10 minutes.	Charles earns a "good buck" for an average of every 10 minutes he stays at his work station.

When Positive Reinforcement Appears Not to Be Working

Ms. Orgill, the new special educator introduced at the beginning of the chapter, set up a positive reinforcement system in her classroom. She learned the basic principles of behavior management and reinforcement and believed she had thought of everything before her students arrived the first day. After the first week of teaching, she was frustrated. One of her students, Julian, didn't respond at all to the reinforcement system. Ms. Orgill had tried several different reinforcers, none of which seemed to work. She was uncertain what to do next.

It is not uncommon for a teacher to proclaim that "nothing reinforces this student." When positive reinforcement does not seem to be working, teachers should consider the following five points.

First, teachers need to ask whether the behavior or task is within the student's repertoire. That is, can the student do the task or behave in the manner desired? The author once offered a free trip to Hawai'i to any of her colleagues who could solve her computer problem. She was safe in making such a promise because, although the consequence was extremely reinforcing for those involved, she was certain no one would be able to solve the problem (and they weren't). Teachers need to examine whether they are setting up their students for such failure. Positive reinforcement is not effective if the student is incapable of performing the task or exhibiting the behavior that will result in the reinforcing consequence. Positive reinforcement cannot take the place of effective instruction.

Second, teachers should analyze whether the consequence is actually reinforcing to the student. The teacher may have selected the reinforcer based on careful observation, or even asked the student directly, but if the desired effect is not occurring, the object, activity, or social interaction is not reinforcing the student and needs to be reexamined.

Third, the amount of time that elapses between the occurrence of the behavior and the administration of the reinforcer needs to be evaluated. That is, the reinforcer must be delivered as soon after the behavior occurs as possible in order for it to be paired with the behavior and thus be effective.

The fourth consideration is similar. Teachers need to examine the schedule of reinforcement, specifically the frequency with which the positive reinforcement is being delivered. If reinforcers are administered too frequently, students can experience satiation. On the other hand, if reinforcers are administered too infrequently, they aren't powerful enough to act as reinforcers.

Schedules of reinforcement should be thinned. For example, when students are learning a new skill, they may need to be reinforced for each accurate or appropriate response. If teaching students to identify whether numeric values are greater than, less than, or equal to each other, the teacher could start with a continuous schedule by reinforcing students for every problem completed accurately, then move to a fixed ratio (every fifth problem completed accurately), then move to a variable ratio (an average of every 10th problem completed accurately), and eventually fade the reinforcement all together.

Fifth, it is possible that what reinforces the student may not be under the control of the teacher. Involvement of parents and other family members can help in this instance. Parents can make events or privileges at home contingent on social or academic behavior at school. For example, students may earn television-watching time or outings with other family members.

In order for reinforcement to work properly, the following rules should be applied:

- Reinforcement will not work if the student is unable to perform or has not been taught the requested behavior.

- One can tell whether reinforcement works only by trying it and observing its effect on the behavior.

- What reinforces one student may not reinforce another student.

- Reinforcers should be applied during or immediately following the desired behavior.

- The reinforcer must be applied only when the desired behavior occurs.

- New behaviors should be reinforced frequently. Once they are established, the behavior should be maintained with reinforcement that is administered less frequently.

After consulting with her mentor teacher, Ms. Orgill recognized that she needed to reexamine several of her assumptions about the reinforcement system and why it wasn't working for Julian. Ms. Orgill concluded that the time delay between keeping the classroom rules and when the reinforcer was administered was working for all the students but Julian. She had originally designed the system so that students were reinforced at the end of each day for keeping classroom rules. Julian needed more immediate reinforcement. Therefore, Ms. Orgill modified her system for Julian. She developed a checklist with three different time periods and taped it to his desk. She told Julian that if he received a checkmark next to each time period, he would receive the reinforcer at the end of the day. Then, at the end of each time period, she marked the checklist simultaneously praising him for keeping the rules. She found that this was much more effective for Julian.

Decreasing and Eliminating Behaviors

As consequences, reinforcers increase or maintain associated behavior. When consequences decrease or eliminate behaviors, the process is referred to as punishment. Extinction is another behavioral technique that also decreases or eliminates behaviors.

Hank, a preschooler with a developmental disability, has a history of tantrum behavior at home. As Hank begins school, his mother shares this information with his teacher, Ms. King. Then Hank has a tantrum once a day at school during the first week. Ms. King notices that it occurs after he has not gotten his way with an adult (e.g., teacher, paraeducator, parent volunteer). She asks the adults to ignore his tantrum behavior. Over time, Hank stops having tantrums in school.

Extinction

When a reinforcer that has been maintaining a behavior is withheld and the rate of occurrence decreases or is eliminated, the procedure is referred to as **extinction**. Extinction will be effective only if the reinforcer that is maintaining the behavior has been identified and is under the control of the teacher. For example, a student who makes funny noises in class may be reinforced by the teacher's reprimands and peers' laughter. The teacher can withhold the reprimands but cannot control the peer laughter. Thus extinction would not be effective unless the peers' laughter could also be withheld. Extinction would not work with Twila as she initiates fights for several reasons including the fact that the teacher cannot control her classmates' reactions.

Once a behavior is reinforced after a period of being withheld, the schedule of reinforcement becomes intermittent, which is a powerful schedule of maintaining or increasing behavior. Thus, extinction is usually slow to take effect. Once the reinforcer is withheld, the behavior usually continues and often increases before significant reduction occurs. Extinction, therefore, should not be used to decrease and eliminate behaviors that are potentially dangerous to the student, to others, or to the environment, such as physical fighting or physical destruction of property. This is another reason extinction is not a good choice for managing Twila's fight-initiating behavior.

Extinction often takes the form of planned ignoring. For example, what has maintained Hank's tantrum behavior is the adult attention he gets. Over time, he no longer receives reinforcement for his tantrums and he eventually stops them. Other examples of the use of extinction may be found in Table 3.6.

TEACHER TIP #3.2

IMPLEMENTING EXTINCTION

The following guidelines may be implemented with extinction:

- Define the problem behavior(s).
- Record **baseline data** and continue to collect data while implementing the program.
- Set a goal for the target behavior.
- Determine the planned ignoring procedure that will be used.

- Decide when you will begin using the procedure.
- Provide positive reinforcement for desirable behaviors.
- Anticipate potential problems and have a back-up plan.
- Using the data collected, evaluate the effectiveness of the procedure. Make changes, if needed.

Punishment

In order to know if a consequence is a reinforcer, one needs to know the effect it has on the behavior. The same is true of punishment. By definition, **punishment** is any consequential event that decreases or eliminates the behavior. Examples appear in

TABLE 3.6   **Examples of Extinction**

Antecedent	Behavior	Past Consequences	Current Consequences	Future Event
Zachary's teacher asks a question.	Zachary yells out the answer without raising his hand.	Zachary's teacher reminds him to raise his hand. Teacher attention has maintained Zachary's behavior.	Zachary's teacher consistently ignores Zachary.	Zachary eventually stops yelling out the answer.
Emily and Matthew see each other on the school bus.	Emily makes faces at Matthew.	Matthew makes faces back at Emily which has maintained Emily's behavior.	Matthew does not look at Emily, nor make faces at her.	Emily eventually stops making faces at Matthew.
Mia misses the art activity because of a dentist appointment.	Mia draws inappropriate pictures on her math homework assignments.	Mia's teacher speaks to her in private about the pictures. This attention has maintained Mia's behavior.	Mia's teacher ignores her pictures.	Mia stops drawing pictures on her homework assignments.

Table 3.7. Although a discussion of punishment follows, teachers should use forms of punishment in very limited degree. An overabundance of punishment techniques can negatively impact school climate and the learning environment. Specific punishment techniques include time-out, response cost, and overcorrection. Each is discussed below.

Time-out. **Time-out** is defined as denying a student access to the opportunity for reinforcement contingent upon the occurrence of a particular behavior for a fixed short amount of time. The label *time-out* is actually a shortened form of the term "time-out for positive reinforcement" (Alberto & Troutman, 2012). Time-out may or may not

TABLE 3.7   **Examples of Punishment**

Antecedent	Behavior	Consequence	Future Event
During silent reading, Kelly has difficulty decoding some words in her self-selected book.	Kelly begins reading out loud.	The other students in Kelly's classroom laugh at her.	Kelly stops reading out loud during silent reading time.
Juan's classmates don't answer the question he asks while standing in the lunch line.	Juan pushes the other students in the lunch line.	The cafeteria worker makes Juan go to the end of the line.	Juan does not push during lunch line again.
Natalie's teacher asks Natalie to stop tapping her pencil on the desk.	Natalie uses her pencil to write on her desk top.	Natalie's teacher makes her scrub her desk top clean.	Natalie does not write on her desk top again.

involve isolation. In fact, different levels of time-out may be characterized as follows: (a) contingent observation time-out, where the student is required to observe the other students behaving appropriately; (b) exclusion time-out, where the student is placed where she cannot observe the other students, nor can they observe her; and (c) seclusion time-out, where the student is placed alone in a safe and secure room.

Not all students are appropriate candidates for time-out. Students who engage in self-stimulating or self-harming behavior, for example, should not be placed in exclusion or seclusion time-out (Kerr & Nelson, 2009). It is also important to remember that time-out periods should be short. One rule of thumb is 1 minute of time-out for either the age or the grade level of the student. So an appropriate time-out period for a first-grade student would be from 1 to 6 minutes, while a middle school student's time-out period would be within the range of 6 to 14 minutes. Once out of time-out, students need to be reinforced for appropriate behavior and correct responses as soon and frequently as appropriate.

Time-out can be a relatively easy procedure, except when the student resists. Teachers should be prepared to add time to time-out if the student refuses to physically move. They must remain calm and not raise their voices. If teachers find themselves becoming angry, they should walk away and after calming down return to the student, adding minutes to time-out or taking away a privilege.

TEACHER TIP #3.3

IMPLEMENTING TIME-OUT

Use the following guidelines when implementing time-out:

- Identify appropriate students for implementing time-out.
- Define the problem behavior(s).
- Record baseline and continue to collect data while implementing the program.
- Determine a goal for the target behavior.
- Decide where time-out will occur. Ensure that the place is safe, free from reinforcers, well lighted, easily monitored, and close enough to place the student with minimal distraction.
- Ensure that non-time-out environment is rewarding.
- Determine how long the time-out period will last.
- Explain time-out to the student in advance.
- Implement time-out when needed.
- Using the data collected, evaluate the effectiveness of the procedure. Make changes if needed.

Response cost. *Response cost* is defined as the removal of specific amounts of positive reinforcement contingent upon the occurrence of a particular behavior. The reinforcer that is removed may have been earned contingently (e.g., earned free time, points) or simply given unearned (e.g., recess time, unearned allowance). Teachers need to be careful not to withdraw through response cost more reinforcers than the student has or could possibly earn so that the student does not get *in the hole* without an opportunity to earn any positive reinforcers (Kerr & Nelson, 2009). This circumstance may result in aggressive or avoidance behavior. Otherwise, few side effects have been reported regarding the use of response cost procedures. Response cost is easy to implement and is an acceptable mild aversive consequence to undesirable behavior.

TEACHER TIP #3.4

IMPLEMENTING RESPONSE COST

The following may be used as guidelines for implementing response cost:

- Define the problem behavior(s).

- Record baseline data and continue to collect data while implementing the program.

- Identify reinforcers the student can earn.

- Specify the amount or level of reinforcement that will be removed.

- Implement the response cost procedures.

- Using the data collected, evaluate the effectiveness of the procedure. Make changes if needed.

- Maintain the change making certain intermittent positive reinforcement for appropriate alternative behavior is being implemented.

Overcorrection. With **overcorrection** the student is taught the correct behavior through an "exaggeration of experience" (Alberto & Troutman, 2012). Overcorrection differs from typical correction procedures in which the error or inappropriate behavior is simply corrected. There are two forms of overcorrection: restitutional and positive-practice. In **restitutional overcorrection**, the student must not only restore a disturbance he has caused in the environment, but improve upon it. In **positive-practice overcorrection**, the student must exhibit an exaggerated practice of the appropriate behavior. Applying overcorrection procedures requires one-to-one instruction and consequently a lot of teacher time. It can also be aversive to both students and teachers (Kerr & Nelson, 2009). Table 3.8 lists examples of time-out, response cost, and overcorrection.

Two questions should be answered appropriately before selecting overcorrection as the response to misbehavior. First, is the problem deliberate, frequent, severe, or very annoying? If the response is *yes*, overcorrection may be an appropriate procedure. Second, is the procedure that needs to be corrected complex or simple? Overcorrection may be more appropriate for simple procedures because the student is more likely to perform it accurately (Gable, Arllen, & Rutherford, 1994).

TABLE 3.8   Examples of Time-Out, Response Cost, and Overcorrection

Behavior	Consequence	Technique
Mark, a high school student, plays too roughly in his physical education class.	Mark is sent to the sidelines to "cool off" before returning to play. He is there about 10 minutes.	Time-out (contingent observation)
Ursula cries when she is asked to share crayons.	The teacher asks Ursula to sit in a chair set off from the group. After 1 minute, Ursula, if she has stopped crying, may return to the group.	Time-out (exclusion)
Jerry breaks all the pencils on the table.	Jerry is sent to the time-out room for 8 minutes.	Time-out (seclusion)
Katelyn is playing with something she brought from home and doesn't finish her work.	Katelyn must stay in during recess to finish her work.	Response cost
Jenny does not complete her homework.	Jenny, her teacher, and her parents agreed previously that she would lose 25 cents of her weekly allowance for every day she did not complete her homework.	Response cost
Sean wrote graffiti on the bathroom walls.	Sean must clean not only his graffiti, but the entire bathroom walls.	Overcorrection (restitutional)
Eddie runs down the hall.	The hall monitor has Eddie walk down the hall the correct way three times.	Overcorrection (positive-practice)

TEACHER TIP #3.5

IMPLEMENTING OVERCORRECTION

Use the following guidelines when implementing overcorrection:

- Define the problem behavior(s).

- Record baseline data and continue to collect data while implementing the program.

- Select a verbal cue to use when the student engages in the problem behavior(s).

- Select a restitution activity relevant to the problem behavior.

    OR

- Select a positive practice overcorrection activity that is long and extensive enough to have an impact on the student's behavior.

- Decide when the intervention will be in effect.

- When the student engages in the problem behavior, give the verbal cue and proceed with the intervention.

- Avoid unnecessary physical contact and conversation during the overcorrection activity.

- If the student reengages in the problem behavior during the overcorrection procedures, restart the sequence.

- Never use the verbal cue with the overcorrection procedure until the problem behavior has been reduced.

- Always provide ample opportunities for positive reinforcement for appropriate behavior.

- Using the data collected, evaluate the effectiveness of the procedure. Make changes if needed (Gable et al., 1994).

Comparing the Impact of Consequences

To illustrate how the impact of the consequence on future occurrences of the behavior determines whether the consequence is a reinforcer or punishment, examples are provided in Table 3.9. A brief discussion of each example follows.

In the first example, Julie hits a student and is sent to the principal's office. If she continues to hit students, then it is possible that being sent to the principal's office is positively reinforcing and/or avoiding her own classroom is negatively reinforcing.

TABLE 3.9 Comparison of Types of Reinforcement and Punishment

Behavior	Consequence	Future Event	Defining Principles and Techniques
Julie hits another student in class.	Julie's teacher sends her to the principal's office.	Julie continues to hit students in class.	Going to the principal's office is positively reinforcing.
Same	Same	Same	Going to the principal's office allows Julie to avoid the classroom, which is negatively reinforcing.
Same	Same	Julie stops hitting students in class.	Going to the principal's office is punishing.
Patrick completes his math worksheet accurately for the first time.	Patrick's teacher congratulates him in front of the class.	Patrick continues to complete his math worksheet accurately.	Receiving public praise positively reinforces Patrick.
Same	Same	Patrick discontinues doing well on his math worksheets.	Receiving public praise acts as a punisher for Patrick.
Harry acts out in class.	Harry's teacher sends him to the time-out room.	Harry stops acting out.	Going to the time-out room was punishing for Harry.
Same	Same	Harry continues to act out.	Going to the time-out room allows Harry to avoid the classroom, which is negatively reinforcing.

If, however, Julie stops hitting students in class, then being sent to the principal's office has functioned as punishment.

Patrick, in the second example, receives public praise for doing well on his math worksheet. This may be positively reinforcing or punishing. Public praise is a good example of something teachers assume is positively reinforcing which may not be positively reinforcing for many students, particularly those from diverse cultural backgrounds.

In the third example, the time-out room, considered punishment by the teacher, can be negatively reinforcing. When Harry is sent to the time-out room for acting out in class, if he stops acting out, the time-out room is punishing. If he continues to act out, the time-out room may be an opportunity to avoid doing work in the classroom and thus be negative reinforcement.

Making these comparisons is critical to the appropriate application of behavior management techniques. Professionals often naively continue programs, such as time-out, without examining the effect the program has on the student's behavior. Then when the student's behavior does not decrease, the teacher may assume that "time-out doesn't work."

Although punishment can effectively reduce undesirable behavior, Erik Drasgow (1997) suggests punishment is generally not an effective consequence for several reasons. First, teachers may be tempted to select punishment as their first "line of defense" because it is quick and easy to use. This may lead to an overuse of unnecessary punishment. Second, in addition to reducing undesirable behavior, punishment may cause students to strike back, withdraw, or develop escape or avoidance behaviors. Third, as teachers are models of adult behavior for students, teachers who rely on punishment are, in effect, demonstrating how adults should react to undesirable behavior. Fourth, the effects of punishment may not be maintained or generalized unless it is applied in multiple settings and administered by multiple individuals. And fifth, punishment does not teach students new skills. Undesirable behavior may be reduced, but students do not learn acceptable forms of behavior.

Other Behavior Management Procedures

Token Economy

Mr. Hubbard teaches eight elementary students with emotional/behavioral disabilities in a self-contained classroom and uses a behavior management system whereby students can earn "bucks" for keeping classroom rules. At the beginning of the school year, they collectively decide what the rules should be. After explaining how the program will work, he invites students to design the "bucks" which they photocopy on varying colors to help discriminate the 1, 5, 10, and 20 "buck" denominations. They also create a menu of reinforcers from which they may spend their earned "bucks." Mr. Hubbard determines the system whereby he will disseminate the bucks for keeping the class rules and when the students may spend them.

Token economy is one of the most commonly used behavior management systems in special education and includes three components: the tokens; the rewards or backup reinforcers; and a set of rules describing what behaviors earn tokens, how many tokens are earned, and the cost of the backup reinforcers (Kazdin, 2000). Students earn tokens for exhibiting certain behaviors, and later, these tokens can be exchanged for back-up reinforcers.

The first step in setting up a token economy is to select the target behaviors. These target behaviors may involve academic work (e.g., work completion, accuracy, rate) and/ or social behaviors (e.g., attendance, talking out, sitting in seat). Next, the tokens should be selected. A **token** is an object or symbol that has little to no reinforcing value alone, but takes on value when paired with a positive reinforcer. Tokens can be anything from poker chips to paper clips to points or check marks. Token selection must consider durability, ease of administration, and protection from duplication and loss. Teachers also need to determine how tokens will be stored and/or recorded, since the tokens will be exchanged at a later time for back-up reinforcers. Mr. Hubbard likes using "bucks" as his tokens because it represents something similar to money and the principles of saving and spending can be emphasized. Teachers may wish to conduct reinforcement inventories in order to determine effective reinforcers (see Figure 3.1). Teachers should keep in mind that the back-up reinforcers need to be changed periodically to avoid satiation.

Token economies do not need to be complex to be effective. In fact, simplicity increases sustainability. In addition, involving students in the operation of the system can save teacher time and teach students responsibility. Mr. Hubbard wanted his students to have a vested interest in the token economy system. Thus, he set up a contest among the students for designing the "bucks."

In order to be effective, specific rules for earning and losing tokens must be set and communicated to the students through discussion, modeling, and public posting. The ratio of tokens to each target behavior and the exchange rate of tokens for back-up reinforcers must be specific and posted. Teachers can develop a rules chart that lists the target behaviors and the number of tokens that may be earned for each, along with a menu chart listing the back-up reinforcers and the token exchange rate for each. Figure 3.2 is an example of a rules chart and Figure 3.3 is a menu chart.

Teachers must also determine the procedures for exchanging the tokens. Usually tokens are exchanged at the end of a time period (e.g., end of the class period, end of the day, once a week). The exchange time period varies, depending on the students' needs.

FIGURE 3.2   **Example of a Rules Chart**

Class Rules	
Be in the classroom when the tardy bell rings.	1 token
Bring books, pencils, and paper to class.	2 tokens
Turn in homework at the beginning of class.	2 tokens
Follow the teacher's directions immediately.	1 token
Raise your hand when you need help.	1 token

FIGURE 3.3   Example of a Menu Chart

Token Economy Reinforcer Menu

Correct Papers	15 Tokens	Eraser	10 Tokens
Sit in the Teacher's Chair	15 Tokens	Ball	15 Tokens
Feed the Fish	20 Tokens	Book Mark	15 Tokens
Be Lunch Line Leader	20 Tokens	Grab Bag Toy	15 Tokens
Work on a Puzzle	20 Tokens	Card Game	20 Tokens
Listen to Music	30 Tokens	Pencil	20 Tokens
Homework Pass	50 Points	Pen	30 Tokens
5 Extra Credit Points	50 Points	Comic Book	40 Tokens

Prior to implementation, teachers need to discuss and model, not only the target behaviors but the token delivery and exchange procedures as well. Once the program is under way, tokens should be administered immediately after the desired behavior. Responsible teachers evaluate the effectiveness of the program, particularly the back-up reinforcers. Students often become satiated on the back-up reinforcers; thus teachers need to change the reinforcers periodically. Teachers also need to combine verbal praise with the delivery of the tokens.

Teachers should work toward fading the token economy system when the students' academic and social behaviors have improved to acceptable levels. Fading may be accomplished by increasing the behavioral expectation for a given number of tokens, decreasing the number of tokens given for specific behaviors, or both. The rate of verbal praise should remain the same (Naughton & McLaughlin, 1995).

If problems occur within a token economy, teachers need to ask themselves several questions. First, are the tokens being administered immediately following the desired behavior? The principles described under positive reinforcement apply to token economy as well. Second, is the reinforcement menu being adjusted periodically? Change is necessary in order to control satiation or boredom. Third, has the number of tokens required to earn reinforcers been altered as needed? If the number of tokens required to obtain the reinforcer is too low, students may earn the reinforcer and then give up. If the number is too high, the student may become discouraged and also give up. Fourth, do some students choose not to participate? Students are more likely to participate if they are involved in the development of the system. In addition, once they earn a reinforcer, they are more likely to desire to participate in the future. Fifth, is the system too costly in terms of time and effort? The more simple the system, the more likely it will be sustainable. Sixth, have the social reinforcers been combined with the delivery of tokens, and has the token system been faded gradually? The goal is to fade the use of the tokens to more natural consequences, such as praise and attention (Kazdin, 2000).

TEACHER TIP #3.6

IMPLEMENTING A TOKEN ECONOMY

Use the following steps to set up a token economy:

- Define the problem behavior(s).

- Record baseline data and continue to collect data while implementing the program.

- Select the tokens considering durability, ease of administration, and protection from duplication and loss. If necessary, make materials (e.g., point cards).

- Determine how earned tokens will be stored and/or recorded.

- Select the back-up reinforcers. Conduct a reinforcement inventory if necessary.

- Determine the exchange rate of tokens for back-up reinforcers (e.g., 10 chips = 1 pencil, 25 chips = 30 minutes of free time).

- Create a rules chart that includes the target behaviors and the number of tokens earned for each.

- Create a menu chart that includes the back-up reinforcers and the exchange rate for each.

- Determine procedures for exchanging tokens for back-up reinforcers including how often exchanges may occur (e.g., every day, every Friday).

- Discuss and model the target behaviors for students.

- Discuss the implementation procedures and post the rules and menu charts.

- Implement the token economy system, coupling verbal praise with delivery of tokens.

- Periodically review the effectiveness of the program, particularly the back-up reinforcers. Make changes as needed.

- When appropriate, fade the token economy system.

TEACHER TIP #3.7

IMPLEMENTING THE GOOD BEHAVIOR GAME

The **Good Behavior Game (GBG)** incorporates many behavior principles discussed thus far. Classroom rules are set and consequences are applied for keeping or breaking the rules. GBG uses a form of token economy given that students are awarded points or points are taken away and the points can be exchanged later for a desired reinforcer.

Although individuals receive the consequences, students are competing in teams to earn the greatest number of points at the end of the day or week. The team with the highest number of points earns the reward. Although GBG has been shown to be an effective intervention to improve challenging behaviors in the classroom (Flower, McKenna, Bunuan,

(Continued)

(Continued)

Muething, & Vega, 2014), Renée Lastrapes (2013) suggests having the class compete against the teacher, particularly when there are students who would find it reinforcing to have the other team win.

Use the following guidelines for implementing the Good Behavior Game:

- Discuss the game's procedures with the students.

- Jointly create the classroom rules. Determine the points lost or earned for each.

- Determine the overall reinforcers for the team with the most points and when they will be awarded.

- Post the rules and the consequences (e.g., how many points lost or earned).

- Teach the students how to respond to their classmate who earns points and how to give nonverbal signs to show disapproval (e.g., head shake, frown).

- Divide the class into at least two equal teams or have the class compete against the teacher.

- Begin implementing with short time periods and at times of the day when students are likely to be most attentive. Later move to other times of the day.

- Award or remove points from individual students based on their behavior.

- Use prompts, particularly when just beginning the game (e.g., "I see someone doing something that could take a point away unless it's corrected in the next 5 seconds.")

- If a student refuses to play, verbalize to the class that this student is not part of the game and the points lost will not go against his or her team, but that the student will also not receive the reward. Allow the student to reenter the game when ready.

- At the end of the predetermined award period, provide the reinforcers to the team with the most points (or the whole class if competing against the teacher).

Contingency Contracting

In addition to teaching the eight students in his classroom, Mr. Hubbard is also responsible for monitoring Mario, a sixth-grade student who is fully included in general education. Mario's academic abilities are very strong, but he is noncompliant. That is, he is capable of completing work assigned; he just doesn't do it. Mr. Hubbard has developed a personal relationship with Mario by meeting with him on several occasions.

Mr. Hubbard suggests that a contingency contract be developed between himself, Mario, and his grade teacher, Mrs. Zimmerman. The three of them meet and decide that if Mario will complete and turn in his work on time every day for two weeks, Mr. Hubbard will play basketball with him after school. They write this agreement and all sign it indicating they agree to comply with their portion of the contract.

Like token economies, contingency contracting is a procedure often applied by special educators. There are some notable differences, however. Token economies are usually developed and implemented for groups of students. Contracts are more often used with individual students, although they could be used with groups. A **contingency contract** is a written document indicating the contingencies for reinforcement (if-by-then statements). The "if" portion is the target behavior, the "by" is a date for accomplishing the target behavior, and the "then" portion is the reinforcer. A contract should be agreed on and signed by all parties involved (e.g., student, teacher, parents). Good contracts ensure success because they are negotiated and fair to all parties and allow for renegotiation if needed (Kerr & Nelson, 2009). Two examples of contingency contracts appear in Figures 3.4 and 3.5.

FIGURE 3.4   One Example of a Contingency Contract

Work Completion Contract

Behavior: At the beginning of the math period, Alicia will turn in her math homework.

Criteria: If Alicia turns in her math homework 4 out of 5 days,

| 1 | 2 | 3 | 4 | 5 |

Reinforcement: then Alicia will earn a gel pen.

Contract Period: March 24 to March 28

Signed _____ Mrs. Thompson

_____ Alicia

FIGURE 3.5   Another Example of a Contingency Contract

Walking in the Hall With Hands and Feet to Self

Anton will walk in the hall and keep his hands and feet to himself during

Recess Time ☐

Lunch Time ☐

P.E. Time ☐

Dismissal Time ☐

For each day that Anton walks, keeping hands and feet to himself, he will earn a **coupon for 5 minutes of computer time.** The coupon may be redeemed the next day at school.

This contract is in effect from October 15 to October 29.

Signed _____ Mr. Johnson

_____ Anton Stravouski

TEACHER TIP #3.8
IMPLEMENTING CONTINGENCY CONTRACTS

Use the following steps for implementing contingency contracts:

- Meet with all persons involved. Discuss what behavior(s) need to be improved.

- Based on the list, select one or two important educational and/or social targeted behaviors.

- List available reinforcers that are meaningful and fair.

- Write the contract using positive terms with specific language regarding behavior

and consequences. Include a definite beginning and ending for the contract to be in effect.

- Sign the contract.

- Provide praise for progress toward fulfilling the contract.

- Keep a record of performance.

- Fade written contracts after new behaviors have been established.

Differential Reinforcement of Other Behaviors

> Kelly, one of Mr. Hubbard's students, likes to play with his pencil, pretending it's an airplane or trying to bounce it off his desk using the eraser tip. Mr. Hubbard ignores Kelly's pencil play. But when Kelly begins to use the pencil to write, Mr. Hubbard reinforces him with praise such as, "Kelly, you are getting your work done. Terrific job!"

Differential reinforcement of other behavior refers to the replacement of an inappropriate or challenging behavior by reinforcing an incompatible behavior and ignoring the inappropriate behavior. Kelly's inappropriate behavior is playing with his pencil, which his teacher ignores. The incompatible but appropriate behavior is using his pencil to write. The inappropriate behavior is being placed on extinction, whereas a behavior that the student could not do at the same time as the inappropriate behavior is being reinforced. Kelly would not be able to play with his pencil and write at the same time. Differential reinforcement of other behavior provides a positive alternative to punishment and may be described as a seesaw effect, whereby the teacher drives up the rate of the appropriate behavior through reinforcement, while driving down the other end of the seesaw (the inappropriate behavior) through extinction (Scott, Anderson, & Alter, 2012).

Sometimes the appropriate behavior identified for replacing the challenging behavior needs to be explicitly taught. If Kelly, for example, did not know how to properly hold his pencil and write, Mr. Hubbard would have needed to instruct him on how to do so. As previously discussed, reinforcement will not work if the behavior being reinforced has yet to be learned.

TEACHER TIP #3.9

IMPLEMENTING DIFFERENTIAL REINFORCEMENT OF OTHER BEHAVIORS

Use the following steps to implement differential reinforcement of other behaviors:

- Identify an inappropriate or challenging behavior to be targeted.

- Identify an appropriate behavior that is incompatible (cannot be done at the same time) as the challenging behavior.

- Determine whether the student needs to be taught the appropriate behavior. If so, teach the appropriate behavior.

- Ignore the student when exhibiting the challenging behavior.

- Provide reinforcement when the student is exhibiting the incompatible appropriate behavior.

Record-Keeping and Decision-Making Procedures

School systems keep a multitude of records on their students, including personal information (e.g., parents' names, address, phone number), academic performance (e.g., standardized test scores, class grades), and medical records (e.g., immunization reports). Additional file information, such as Individualized Education Programs (IEPs), individual test results, and related service reports, is kept on students receiving special education services. In addition to all of these important documents, effective teachers keep records regarding students' progress toward accomplishing IEP goals, their progress mastering the curriculum, and their progress toward demonstrating specific target behaviors.

Effective teachers gather student performance and progress data and use that data to determine effectiveness of the intervention. In terms of targeted behaviors, the interventions are those that have been described in this chapter. Prior to intervening to change student behavior, however, an Antecedent-Behavior-Consequent (ABC) assessment is conducted and a hypothesis formulated, then that hypothesis is tested. Remember Twila, the fourth-grade student who started fights? Mr. Rodriguez, the special educator, observed Twila and hypothesized that before she started a fight, she was either being ignored or she was being asked to do something challenging. Mr. Rodriguez, in essence, conducted an ABC assessment. The ABC assessment will be described in further detail in Chapter 5.

Once the hypothesis is generated, the next step is the collection of baseline data. (Specific data collection procedures are outlined in Chapter 5.) During baseline, data are collected on the student's behavior prior to intervention. Baseline data give teachers a picture of the behavior analogous to a pretest. The hypothesized pattern behavior, antecedents, and consequences should be considered prior to collecting baseline data.

Following the collection of baseline data, an intervention is applied. The intervention also relates directly to the hypothesized pattern between behavior, antecedents, and consequences as outlined in the ABC assessment. Since Mr. Rodriguez thought the attention Twila was receiving for initiating fights was reinforcing that behavior, another intervention to give her appropriate attention, reading aloud to her class, was tried.

Applied behavior analysis (ABA) is the "process of applying sometimes tentative principles of behavior to the improvement of specific behaviors, and simultaneously evaluating whether or not any changes noted are indeed attributed to the process of application" (Baer, Wolf, & Risley, 1968, p. 91). Therefore, applied behavior analysis is more rigorous than what is commonly called behavior modification or behavior management. ABA includes both application of the principles of behavior and verification of these principles through systematic record-keeping and decision-making procedures. All of the principles and techniques described thus far fit under the heading of ABA.

ABA is used to test functional relationships between behavior patterns and intervention. This tool is vital in advancing behavioral science. The same principles are used by teachers to ensure the effectiveness of interventions used in the classroom. Merely collecting data, however, is insufficient. Teachers should chart the data and use this information to make decisions regarding whether implementation should be continuous or whether changes are warranted. The charting and decision-making procedures will be discussed in Chapter 5.

Positive Behavioral Interventions and Supports (PBIS)

Positive behavioral interventions and supports (PBIS) is a framework or approach for helping school personnel adopt and organize evidence-based behavioral interventions into an integrated continuum. The goal of PBIS is to enhance social and emotional behavior outcomes for all students. PBIS is not a curriculum or a single intervention; instead, it is a framework that incorporates a multitiered system of support. The model focuses on preventing behavior problems from occurring and to intervene quickly when they do. PBIS is typically implemented schoolwide.

Like the response to intervention (RTI) model described in Chapter 7, PBIS is usually comprised of three tiers. RTI and PBIS have additional similarities. Both focus on (a) making data-based decisions about students and the effectiveness of the system, (b) providing a continuum of services and interventions that are based on students' needs, and (c) taking a team approach (Young et al., 2012). The models are very similar with the exception that PBIS targets student behavior and emotional needs, whereas RTI targets student academic difficulties. Both PBIS and RTI are considered multitiered systems of support (see Chapters 7 and 13).

Tiered Approach

Tier 1 or the first tier of PBIS is sometimes referred to as the universal or primary tier. All students are involved in Tier 1 interventions and support. Rules and expectations with positive consequences are implemented for all students. All of the previous discussion regarding creating, demonstrating, and posting rules applies here. Providing verbal and written praise as reinforcers for demonstrating the expectations is a critical element of Tier 1. Some schools elect to include other reinforcers or implement a schoolwide token economy system.

Another component of Tier 1 is teaching social skills to all students. "Social skills are interactions between two or more persons; the skills involve action; and the interactions are positive, effective, and valued by society" (Young et al., 2012, p. 64). Social skills instruction is addressed in detail in Chapter 13.

Just as a teacher would collect performance data on an individual student to determine whether the intervention was effective, schoolwide data are taken to assess the effectiveness of the school's PBIS. Appropriate data may include students' attendance and tardy records, number of referrals to the office, students' academic performance, and so forth. These data help identify students who need more intensive supports at Tier 2.

Screening instruments can also serve as a tool for identifying targeted students, not for referral to special education, but to implement strategies in the general classroom as a form of early intervention. About 20% of secondary-age students have a mental health or behavior/emotional disability, yet only about 1% are served in special education (Young et al., 2012). Thus, a large portion is not receiving specialized services. Screening helps identify those students so they can receive the supports they need.

Tier 2, secondary or targeted interventions, is designed for at-risk students who did not respond to Tier 1 strategies, which represents 5% to 10% of the student body. Tier 2 interventions are targeted to the needs of the individual students through an ABC assessment (see Chapter 5). Based on the ABC assessment, specific behavioral interventions discussed in this chapter can be identified and implemented. Also, individual students may need additional social skills instruction tailored to their specific needs. Self-management instruction may also be helpful to these students. Self-management encompasses many procedures in which students manage their own behavior and learning, by moving away from external or teacher control of monitoring and reinforcing behavior and academic performance, to requiring students take responsibility for their own learning and behavior. Self-management is discussed in detail in Chapter 9. Although specific behaviors are targeted for individual students, interventions are often delivered in groups. For example, three students in one grade level may receive social skills instruction in a small group or a specialized token economy could be implemented for five students who have similar behavioral needs.

Similar interventions to those provided in Tier 2 are also applied in **Tier 3**, referred to as tertiary, prevention, or intensive intervention. The differences between Tier 2 and Tier 3 lie in the intensity, dosage, and individualization provided. Approximately 1% to 8% of the student body will not respond to the previous Tiers and require Tier 3 interventions. All of the principles described in this chapter are applied: conducting an ABC assessment, identifying appropriate interventions, collecting data on student performance, and making decisions about the efficacy of the intervention. Students who do not respond to Tier 3 interventions are frequently referred for special education services.

PBIS Framework

The PBIS framework emphases three elements: school climate, proactive strategies, and systematic, systemwide practices (Farrell, Collier-Meek, & Pons, 2013). First, schools that have a healthy school climate generally feel safe, calm, and nurturing. In such schools, teachers foster positive personal relationships with each other and their students. They rely on positive classroom management procedures (e.g., high rates of praise) while reducing unnecessary criticism and punishment. The second element of the PBIS model, proactive strategies, involves creating positively stated expectations or rules, systematically teaching the rules, and reinforcing students for meeting the expectations. Through data collection, teachers track where and when problems occur and implement proactive prevention strategies. The third element, systemwide practices, means that all faculty and staff understand and apply the PBIS model. This implies that all faculty and staff receive professional development to prepare them to apply the proactive strategies. For example, the bus driver can praise students who follow the bus riding rules and the lunch worker can give high fives to students who bus their dishes. Students who seriously violate the rules would be referred for instruction (e.g., social skills instruction) and/or receive additional support. Because PBIS is a framework, not a specific curriculum or intervention, the application of PBIS varies from school to school.

Much work goes into preparing to become a positive behavior support school. Planning involves such activities as developing a common language to discuss behavior issues among teachers, students, and family members; creating proactive strategies for reinforcing positive behavior; providing professional development for all school employees; and instructing students and family members on how the model will be implemented. Planning can easily take one full year before the model is fully implemented (Young et al., 2012).

TEACHER TIP #3.10

SETTING UP A SCHOOLWIDE PBIS

1. Establish a schoolwide leadership team to guide and direct the process. Members of the team should include an administrator, grade-level representatives, support staff, and parents.

2. Secure administrator agreement of active support and participation and commitment from at least 80% of the staff.

3. Conduct a self-assessment of the current schoolwide discipline system.

4. Create a data-based decision-making implementation action plan.

5. Establish a means to collect data on a regular basis to evaluate the effectiveness of schoolwide PBIS efforts.

Source: PBIS, U.S. Department of Education Office of Special Education Programs Technical Center (www.pbis.org/).

Implications for Culturally and/or Linguistically Diverse Students

The Relationship Between Behavior and Culture

Behavior is learned as a result of students' experiences and interactions with the world. Styles of behavior are shaped through daily encounters with significant others (Neal, McCray, Webb-Johnson, & Bridgest, 2003). Cultural variance impacts how children are disciplined in their homes as well as what behaviors are viewed as acceptable.

Within this section characteristics of cultural groups are presented and should be considered generalizations based on research and reports in the professional literature. Care must be taken, however, to ensure that cultural groups are not stereotyped. In addition, teachers must always remember that variance occurs not only across groups, but within cultural groups as well.

Cultural groups vary in terms of acceptable disciplinary actions. The dominant middle-class European American culture is one of few that promotes positive reinforcement and limits punishment (McIntyre & Silva, 1992). Physical punishment, such as hitting, spanking, or scolding children, is well accepted in many cultural groups and is often an integral part of the culture. For example, according to Paulette Hines and Nancy Boyd-Franklin (2005),

> many African American parents believe that our society allows African American youth a very narrow "window for error." The principle "Spare the rod, spoil the child" is a common rule of thumb, and physical punishment is often an accepted mode of discipline. (p. 97)

Other cultures also use punishment as a predominant way of disciplining children. The disciplinarian may be designated as the father, the mother, or both. For example, Iranian fathers often maintain discipline in the family by scolding or slapping children (Jalali, 2005), while Jamaican women are responsible for disciplining their children through spankings and tongue-lashings (Brice-Baker, 2005). Deprivation of privileges as a form of punishment is also used by various cultural groups (Kalyanpur & Harry, 1999).

Several examples of disciplinary actions accepted in cultural groups could be viewed as not only inappropriate, but abusive by the dominant culture. For example, traditional Vietnamese families may tie a misbehaving child's ear to a doorknob as punishment. And a common disciplinary procedure among low-income Hispanic families from the Caribbean Islands is to make children kneel on uncooked rice when they misbehave (McIntyre & Silva, 1992). Teachers should familiarize themselves with culturally accepted disciplinary practices, keep an open mind, and self-examine their own beliefs about discipline and abuse. At the same time, school personnel must be knowledgeable about definitions of abuse used in their school district and report suspected cases of such abuse.

Several studies have documented that African American students receive office referrals and harsh punishment at a significantly higher rate than European American students; yet studies have not demonstrated that African American students have higher rates of misbehavior. This pattern of disproportionality has been referred to as the discipline gap (Monroe, 2006) and is attributed at least partially to implicit classroom management decisions teachers make unconsciously (Milner & Tenore, 2010).

Not only do disciplinary procedures vary across cultures, perceptions of appropriate and inappropriate behavior are impacted by culture as well. For example, many cultures promote collaborative and group processes. This orientation impacts students' concepts of giving and sharing with others. Hispanic children, for example, are often taught to share their belongings with others. As a result, some children may not believe *helping themselves* to someone else's belongings is wrong (Grossman, 1995). American Indian children are taught to work for a meaningful goal for the benefit of a group, not for individual recognition (Hammond, Dupoux, & Ingalls, 2004). Although teachers need to examine their own cultural biases and develop sensitivity to the perspective of students from various cultural backgrounds, they also need to promote a sense of personal and professional responsibility.

English learners can be susceptible to having behavioral and social difficulties. Their lack of English proficiency acts as a stressor that can make them at risk for externalizing behaviors (e.g., fighting, demonstrating aggression, talking out) and internalizing behaviors (e.g., withdrawal, depression) (Dawson & Williams, 2008). In fact, a large body of research supports an association between language delays and subsequent behavior/emotional problems (Dobbins & Rodriguez, 2013).

Culturally Responsive Behavior Management

Given the increasingly diverse student population, all teachers need to be prepared to create and implement behavior management procedures that are culturally sensitive. This begins with understanding one's own culture, as well as being knowledgeable and sensitive to the culture of their students (see Chapter 2). Teachers must remember they are viewing their students' behaviors through their own cultural lens and may misperceive their students' culturally specific behaviors. Teachers must also remember that the reverse is also true. The students and parents view the school's culture and behavioral expectations through their cultural lens (Cartledge, Singh, & Gibson, 2008). Differences in expectations, procedures, and consequences have the potential to create confusion and ineffectiveness. For example, a teacher has designed the classes' token economy system such that students earn their back-up reinforcers once a week. The delayed reward would not be effective for students from American Indian cultures that believe in "living for the day" (Hammond et al., 2004).

Classroom management begins with the classroom environment. Teachers can use the classroom "strategically to communicate respect for diversity, to reaffirm connectedness and community, and to avoid marginalizing and disparaging students" (Weinstein, Curran, & Tomlinson-Clarke, 2003, p. 271). If the students represent a wide range of international countries, a world map could be displayed with students' pictures displayed across their country of origin. For students who have a long lineage in the United States, an ancestor's country could be identified and the same thing accomplished. Representation within the curriculum, such as books written by or about diverse individuals should be available. Music representing various cultures could be played during free time. Greetings and other expressions written in the representative languages could be displayed. Ideas for reflecting a variety of cultural groups within the classroom environment are endless and only require some creativity. Teachers are cautioned, however, to avoid stereotypical portrayals or demeaning aspects of the culture being represented.

Teachers need to hold discussions with students about rules and why and how the rules are important. Such discussions should occur with all students, but become particularly important with culturally and/or linguistically diverse students. The procedures outlined earlier in this chapter such as establishing rules, demonstrating examples and nonexamples, and reviewing the rules are critical steps when working with these students to avoid confusion or misunderstanding.

As discussed in Chapter 2, working with diverse families members requires a collaborative relationship. Such relationships are even more critical when establishing behavioral expectations, procedures, and consequences. Teachers should educate parents about the classroom expectations and any behavior management program that has been designed, whether it be for one individual child, a small group, or the whole classroom of students.

If necessary, teachers can work with parents to reach compromises to ensure the effectiveness, yet cultural responsiveness, of the classroom management program.

Maya Kalyanpur and Beth Harry (1999) developed an approach they call "a posture of cultural reciprocity." They suggest applying this approach while engaging in "explicit discussions with families regarding differential cultural values and practices" (p. 118). This approach, which is appropriate when examining student behavior in context of cultural values, includes the following steps:

1. **Identify the cultural values embedded in the teacher's interpretation of a student's misbehavior.** For example, Anna is constantly interrupting Ms. Keyes with questions or statements at what Ms. Keyes believes are inappropriate times. From the context of her European American cultural values, Ms. Keyes views this type of behavior as rude.

2. **Discover whether the student's culture recognizes the same values and assumptions as the teacher.** Ms. Keyes discusses this behavior with Mrs. Martinez who is familiar with Anna's culture. Mrs. Martinez explains that in Anna's culture, several individuals talking at the same time is very common. Within that context, Anna's behavior is not considered rude, but perfectly acceptable.

3. **Acknowledge and respect any cultural differences.** Ms. Keyes explains to Anna and her family how their assumptions and beliefs differ from her own.

4. **Collaboratively determine the most effective way of accommodating both belief systems.** Ms. Keyes works out a solution acceptable to her and to Anna and her family. Ms. Keyes explains that there are times when constant questions and statements interrupt the flow of instruction. All agree that it is important that Anna learn that in the dominant culture interruptions are considered rude. Therefore, Ms. Keyes will teach Anna to not interrupt and will use positive reinforcement to assist her in learning this important interpersonal communication skill.

SUMMARY

Teachers' classroom environment and use of time contribute to overall successful management and organization in the classroom. Effective teachers maximize their resources and creatively enhance the classroom to make it as conducive to learning as possible.

For example, they place the furniture and materials in the classroom to maximize the space ensuring that each student has some personal space. In addition, effective teachers use their time wisely by establishing, posting, and adhering to a daily and weekly schedule.

Effective teachers also establish classroom rules at the beginning of the school year involving, if appropriate, the students. They limit the number of rules, state them positively, and consistently administer consequences for obeying and breaking the rules. They also review the rules periodically with the students and revise them if needed.

Understanding the principles of behavior can help teachers in implementing individual and group behavior management. Reinforcement (positive and negative) and punishment refer to consequent events that follow a response or behavior. Reinforcers increase or maintain the behavior, while punishers decrease or eliminate the behavior. Negative reinforcement is often confused with punishment. Negative reinforcement maintains or increases behavior; the behavior is being maintained or increased to avoid or terminate an aversive stimulus. Punishment decreases the future occurrence of the behavior. Teachers should always combine punishment with reinforcement. Examples of punishment include extinction, time-out, overcorrection, and response cost. Token economies, contingency contracts, and differential reinforcement of other behaviors are other effective tools for managing behavior in the classroom.

In the vast majority of cases, students respond to positive reinforcement. When it appears reinforcement is not working, teachers should consider whether the behavior or task is within the student's repertoire or whether the consequence is actually reinforcing to the student.

In addition, reinforcement should be delivered as soon after the behavior occurs as possible. It is possible that too much time has elapsed between the occurrence of the behavior and receipt of the reinforcer. Similarly, the reinforcer could be administered too frequently creating satiation or not frequently enough. A fifth possibility is that what reinforces the student is not under the control of the teacher.

Positive behavioral interventions and supports (PBIS) is a framework adopted by many schools designed to help school personnel organize and implement evidence-based behavioral interventions into an integrated continuum. The framework focuses on school climate, proactive strategies, and systematic, systemwide practices. The goal of PBIS is to enhance social and emotional behavioral outcomes for all students using a tiered approach.

Behaviors are shaped by cultural influences such as how children are disciplined at home and what behaviors are viewed as acceptable by a particular culture. Teachers need to be sensitive to how students' cultural backgrounds influence their behavior. They need to hold discussions with students about rules and why and how classroom rules are important. Teachers should also educate parents about classroom expectations and any behavior management program that has been designed. Even though cultures also vary in their use of consequences, teachers should use positive procedures whenever possible.

REVIEW QUESTIONS

1. What time management issues do special education teachers face? How can teachers effectively address these issues?

2. Why is establishing and teaching classroom rules considered a proactive strategy for addressing challenging behavior? What should teachers consider in establishing classroom rules?

3. Explain the behavioral approach to learning. How do consequences impact behavior?

4. Explain the difference between positive and negative reinforcement. What is the effect of positive and negative reinforcement on behavior?

5. When a teacher selects reinforcement for student behavior, what criteria should be used to select specific reinforcements? In addition to asking students about their preferences and using checklists, how else can teachers determine appropriate reinforcers for their students?

6. What five points should a teacher consider in the event that reinforcement does not appear to be working? How do these points illustrate basic principles regarding reinforcement?

7. Any time a teacher implements interventions to change behavior, what basic guidelines should be followed?

8. Define *punishment*. What are specific punishment techniques? Explain each. Is it possible for punishment to be reinforcing? Explain. How does punishment differ from negative reinforcement?

9. What basic elements must be in place for a token system to be effective? As a teacher, how would you assess the effectiveness of your token economy system?

10. Why is it important to understand the cultural background of students? How can a teacher address cultural differences in a constructive manner?

ACTIVITIES

1. With prior permission, observe a friend or family member and select a behavior to evaluate. For 5 days, record antecedents and consequences that impact the specific behavior.

2. Review your state's guidelines for behavior interventions. Write a summary of how various interventions are classified. Give examples of interventions from each category.

3. Arrange to visit a general education classroom. Keep a log of how the teacher reinforces behavior. Track the number of times the teacher uses positive means to reinforce behavior during a half-hour time period.

4. Select three private or public locations (e.g., movie theater, classroom, library). Make a list of explicit rules stated at the location and also list implicit rules that you believe are expected to be followed when visiting the location.

Council for Exceptional Children (CEC) Standards

The Council for Exceptional Children (CEC) is a premiere national professional organization comprised of special educators, paraeducators, related service personnel, parents, and others interested in individuals with disabilities and/or those with gifts and talents. This organization has generated 10 standards for the preparation of special educators. These standards are listed in each chapter as they relate to the content within the chapter. The standards that apply to Chapter 3 are Standards #2, #5, and #6:

CEC Initial Preparation Standard 2: Learning Environments (partial)

Beginning special education professionals create safe, inclusive, culturally responsive learning environments so that individuals with exceptionalities become active and effective learners and develop emotional well-being, positive social interactions, and self-determination. Beginning special education professionals:

2.1 Through collaboration with general educators and other colleagues create safe, inclusive, culturally responsive learning environments to engage individuals with exceptionalities in meaningful learning activities and social interactions.

CEC Initial Preparation Standard 5: Instructional Planning and Strategies (partial)

Beginning special education professionals select, adapt, and use a repertoire of evidence-based instructional strategies to advance learning of individuals with exceptionalities. Beginning special education professionals:

5.1 Consider an individual's abilities, interests, learning environments, and cultural and linguistic factors in the selection, development, and adaptation of learning experiences for individuals with exceptionalities.

CEC Initial Preparation Standard 6: Professional Learning and Ethical Practice (partial)

Beginning special education professionals use foundational knowledge of the field and their professional ethical principles and practice standards to inform special education practice, to engage in lifelong learning, and to advance the profession:

6.1 Beginning special education professionals understand that diversity is a part of families, cultures, and schools, and that complex human issues can interact with the delivery of special education services.

REFERENCES

Albert, L. (1996). *Cooperative discipline.* Circle Pines, MN: American Guidance Service.

Alberto, P. A., & Troutman, A. C. (2012). *Applied behavior analysis for teachers* (9th ed.). Boston, MA: Pearson.

Baer, D. M., Wolf, M. M., & Risley, T. R. (1968). Some current dimensions of applied behavior analysis. *Journal of Applied Behavior Analysis, 1*(1), 91–97.

Brand, S., Dunn, T., & Greb, F. (2002). Learning styles of students with attention deficit hyperactivity disorder: Who are they and how can we teach them? *Clearing House, 75,* 268–273.

Brice-Baker, J. (2005). British West Indian families. In M. McGoldrick, J. Giordano, & N. Garcia-Preto (Eds.), *Ethnicity and family therapy* (3rd ed. pp. 117–126). New York, NY: Guilford Press.

Caldarella, P., Christensen, L., Young, K. R., & Densley, C. (2011). Decreasing tardiness in elementary school students using teacher-written praise notes. *Intervention in School and Clinic, 47*(2), 104–112.

Canter, L., & Canter, M. (2001). *Assertive discipline: Positive behavior management for today's classroom* (3rd ed.). Los Angeles, CA: Canter & Associates.

Cartledge, G., Singh, A., & Gibson, L. (2008). Practical behavior-management techniques to close the accessibility gap for students who are culturally and linguistically diverse. *Preventing School Failure, 52*(3), 29–38.

Clayton, M. K., & Forton, M. B. (2001). *Classroom spaces that work.* Greenfield, MA: Northeast Foundation for Children.

Dawson, B. A., & Williams, S. A. (2008). The impact of language status as an acculturative stressor on internalizing and externalizing behaviors among Latino/a children: A longitudinal analysis from school entry through third grade. *Journal of Youth and Adolescence, 37*, 399–401.

de Bruin, C. L., Deppeler, J. M., Moore, D. W., & Diamond, N. T. (2013). Public school-based interventions for adolescents and young adults with autism spectrum disorder: A meta-analysis. *Review of Educational Research, 83*(4), 521–550.

DiGiulio, R. (2007). *Positive classroom management* (3rd ed.). Thousand Oaks, CA: Corwin.

Dobbins, N., & Rodriguez, C. D. (2013). Providing support for English language learners with behavioral needs. *Intervention in School and Clinic, 48*(3), 152–158.

Drasgow, E. (1997). Positive approaches to reducing undesirable behavior: Is punishment effective? *Beyond Behavior, 8*(2), 10–13.

Driscoll, M. P. (2005). *Psychology of learning for instruction* (3rd ed.). Boston, MA: Pearson.

DuPaul, G. J., Eckert, T. L., Vilardo, B. (2012). The effects of school-based interventions for attention deficit hyperactivity disorder: A meta-analysis 1996–2010. *School Psychology Review, 41*(4), 387–412.

Farrell, A. F., Collier-Meek, M. A., & Pons, S. R. (2013). Embedding positive behavior interventions and supports in afterschool programs. *Beyond Behavior, 23*(1), 38–45.

Flower, A., McKenna, J. W., Bunuan, R. L., Muething, C. S., & Vega, R. (2014). Effects of the Good Behavior Game on challenging behaviors in school settings. *Review of Educational Research, 84*(4), 546–571.

Gable, R. A., Arllen, N. L., & Rutherford, R. B., Jr. (1994). A note on the use of overcorrection. *Beyond Behavior, 5*(3), 19–21.

Goh, A. E., & Bambara, L. M. (2012). Individualized positive behavior support in school settings: A meta-analysis. *Remedial and Special Education, 33*(5), 271–286.

Gordon, T. (2003). *Teacher effectiveness training.* Three Rivers, MI: Three Rivers Press.

Grossman, H. (1995). *Educating Hispanic students: Implications for instruction, classroom management, counseling, and assessment.* Springfield, IL: Charles C Thomas.

Hammond, H., Dupoux, E., & Ingalls, L. (2004). Culturally relevant classroom management strategies for American Indian students. *Rural Special Education Quarterly, 23*(4), 3–9.

Hardman, E. L., & Smith, S. W. (2003). Analysis of classroom discipline-related content in elementary education journals. *Behavioral Disorders, 28*, 173–186.

Hines, P. M., & Boyd-Franklin, N. (2005). African American families. In M. McGoldrick, J. Giordano, & N. Garcia-Preto (Eds.), *Ethnicity and family therapy* (3rd ed., pp. 87–100). New York, NY: Guilford Press.

Jalali, B. (2005). Iranian families. In M. McGoldrick, J. Giordano, & N. Garcia-Preto (Eds.), *Ethnicity and family therapy* (3rd ed., pp. 451–467). New York, NY: Guilford Press.

Justen, J. E., & Howerton, D. L. (1993). Clarifying behavior management terminology. *Intervention in School and Clinic, 29*, 36–40.

Kalyanpur, M., & Harry, B. (1999). *Culture in special education.* Baltimore, MD: Paul H. Brookes.

Kame'enui, E. J., & Darch, C. B. (1995). *Instructional classroom management: A proactive approach to behavior management.* White Plains, NY: Longman.

Kavale, K. A., & LeFever, G. B. (2007). Dunn and Dunn model of learning-style preferences: Critique of Lovelace meta-analysis. *The Journal of Educational Research, 101*(2), 94–97.

Kazdin, A. E. (2000). Token economy. In A. E. Kazdin, *Encyclopedia of psychology* (vol. 8, pp. 90–92). Washington, DC: American Psychological Association.

Kerr, M. M., & Nelson, C. M. (2009). *Strategies for addressing behavior problems in the classroom* (6th ed.). Boston, MA: Pearson.

Kohn, A. (1999). *Punished by rewards: The trouble with gold stars, incentive plans, A's, praise, and other bribes.* Boston, MA: Houghton Mifflin.

Lastrapes, R. E. (2013). Using the Good Behavior Game in an inclusive classroom. *Intervention in School and Clinic, 49*(4), 225–229.

Lovelace, M. K. (2005). Meta-analysis of experimental research based on the Dunn and Dunn model. *The Journal of Educational Research, 98*(3), 176–183.

McIntyre, T., & Silva, P. (1992). Culturally diverse childrearing practices: Abusive or just different? *Beyond Behavior, 4*(1), 8–12.

Milner, H. R., & Tenore, F. B. (2010). Classroom management in diverse classrooms. *Urban Education, 45*(5), 560–603.

Monroe, C. R. (2006). Misbehavior or misinterpretation: Closing the discipline gap through cultural synchronization. *Kappa Delta Pi Record. 42,* 161–165.

Naughton, C. C., & McLaughlin, T. F. (1995). The use of a token economy system for students with behavioral disorders. *B.C. Journal of Special Education, 19*(2/3), 29–38.

Neal, L. I., McCray, A. D., Webb-Johnson, G., & Bridgest, S. T. (2003). The effects of African American movement styles on teachers' perceptions and reactions. *The Journal of Special Education, 37*(1), 49–57.

Premack, D. (1965). Reinforcement theory. In D. Levine (Ed.), *Nebraska symposium on motivation* (pp. 123–188). Lincoln: University of Nebraska Press.

Santos, K. E., & Rettig, M. D. (1999). Going on the block: Meeting the needs of students with disabilities in high schools with block scheduling. *TEACHING Exceptional Children, 31*(3), 54–59.

Scott, C. (2010). The enduring appeal of 'learning styles.' *Australian Journal of Education, 54*(1), 5–17.

Scott, T. M., Anderson, C. M., & Alter, P. (2012). *Managing classroom behavior using positive behavior supports.* Boston, MA: Pearson.

Stellwagen, J. B. (2001). A challenge to the learning style advocates. *Clearing House, 74,* 265–268.

Weinstein, C., Curran, M., & Tomlinson-Clarke, S. (2003). Culturally responsive classroom management: Awareness into action. *Theory into Practice, 42*(4), 269–276.

Weller, D. R., & McLeskey, J. (2000). Block scheduling and inclusion in a high school: Teacher perceptions of the benefits and challenges. *Remedial and Special Education, 21,* 209–218.

Wheeler, J. J., & Richey, D. D. (2014). *Behavior management: Principles and practices of positive behavior supports* (3rd ed.). Boston, MA: Pearson.

Wilson, M. L. (2012). Learning styles, instructional strategies, and the question of matching: A literature review. *International Journal of Education, 4*(3), 67–87.

Young, E. L., Caldarella, P., Richardson, M. J., & Young, K. R. (2012). *Positive behavior support in secondary schools.* New York, NY: Guilford Press.

Zepeda, S. J., & Mayers, R. S. (2006). An analysis of research on block scheduling. *Review of Educational Research, 76*(1), 137–170.

$SAGE edge™ • ●

Review ➡ Practice ➡ Improve

Get the tools you need to sharpen your study skills. Access videos, practice quizzes, eFlashcards and more at **edge.sagepub.com/prater.**

Integrating Technological Applications

To most people, the term *technology* conjures up images of smart phones, computers, mobile tablets, or even robots. Today individuals and communities have become more and more dependent on technology to function. Technology brings both positive and negative aspects to our lives. A computer glitch or hacker can create havoc and shut down services harming individuals and communities alike. At the same time, the proliferation of technology has created conveniences and made information more readily available to those who have access to technology, including students with high-incidence disabilities (HID).

The use of technology in special education has grown within the last three decades in conjunction with the widespread availability of such tools. However, the use of technology for educational purposes goes back to the 1800s. In fact, a new technology introduced in the 1840s was predicted to revolutionize education—namely, the blackboard (Bouck, 2010). Even though the blackboard was a convenient tool, it did not change the way students were educated in schools. The same can be said today about most technology used in schools. Technology has yet to totally revolutionize education as some predicted; nevertheless, the marketplace has showcased a rich palette of devices and interventions which can be used by individuals with HID to enhance communication, independence, and learning. "For most of us, technology makes things easier. For a person with a disability, it makes things possible" (Edyburn, Higgins, & Boone, 2005, p. xiii).

The purpose of this chapter is to introduce classroom applications of assistive and instructional technology for students with HID. In particular, the chapter focuses on assistive technology, integrating appropriate technology to support and enhance instruction, and online learning. Specific tools and applications, as well as implications for culturally and/or linguistically diverse students are also discussed.

Learning Objectives

- Define *assistive technology* (AT), describe the SETT framework, and explain the technology integration process. Provide examples for each.

- Discuss the importance of family participation with AT selection and implementation. Include specific implications for culturally and/or linguistically diverse (CLD) students.

- Compare and contrast assistive technology, video modeling, computer-assisted instruction, online learning, and blended learning. Include advantages and disadvantages of each for students with high-incidence disabilities.

Assistive Technology

Dylan is a fourth-grade student who has been diagnosed with learning disabilities in reading and writing. He can verbalize his thoughts well but has difficulty getting them on paper. His Individualized Education Plan (IEP) lists goals in the area of written expression including spelling, penmanship, and sentence/paragraph structure. Dylan remains in the general education classroom all day. The special educator, Mrs. Zabriski, consults with his fourth-grade teacher, Mr. Twitty. During the most recent parent teacher conference, Dylan's mom tells Mr. Twitty that he has learned to use their home computer but is not proficient in word processing. She would like to see Dylan taught to word process and allowed to type his written work, rather than handwrite all of it. Mr. Twitty isn't certain what to tell Dylan's mom, but he assures her he will get back to her after consulting with Mrs. Zabriski.

Mr. Rodriquez is concerned about Walter, one of his eighth-grade students with emotional/behavior disorders (EBD). Walter's independent reading skills are not adequate for the reading demands made in his science class. He knows Walter could have access to assistive technology, but he doesn't know where to start. He decides to consult with the district assistive technology (AT) specialist for help.

The discipline of special education technology has evolved primarily as a result of legal and policy mandates as opposed to growth based on a research knowledge base. Given this perspective, some people consider the roots of the special education technology to be anchored in principles of advocacy. In fact, federal policy has played a critical role in expanding the use of technology for persons with disabilities for over a century. For example, in 1879, Congress allocated funds to the American Print House for the Blind to produce Braille materials. Twenty-five years later, Congress passed a law to promote the circulation of reading matter among the blind. In 1958, federal funds were allocated for the purchase of captioned films and to distribute the films through schools for the deaf. These few examples illustrate the role Congress has played in creating national policy to foster wide-spread change through the acquisition and use of emerging technologies for individuals with disabilities.

One of the first comprehensive U.S. federal legislative acts was the Technology Related Assistance for Individuals Act, passed in 1988 (Yell, 2016). The Tech Act provided funding to establish a birth-to-death system of assistive technology service delivery in each state. This comprehensive birth-to-death mandate typically left little attention on school-age children and youth. However, this changed with the 1997 reauthorization of the Individuals with Disabilities Education Act (IDEA). The reauthorization specifically required that Individualized Education Program (IEP) teams consider assistive technology when planning the educational program of each student with a disability (Yell, 2016).

Assistive technology devices are defined in IDEA as follows: "Assistive technology device means any item, piece of equipment, or product system, whether acquired commercially off the shelf, modified, or customized, that is used to increase, maintain, or improve the functional capabilities of a child with a disability." Many people believe assistive technology (AT) applies only to computers, but in reality, assistive technology devices (e.g., adaptive feeding instruments, wheel chairs, vision aids) have a long history in the field of special education and rehabilitation. At the same time, some have argued that including the word, *any*, in the definition broadens the definition to include *anything*. Other observers have noted that the definition simply reflects the fact that assistive technology solutions may involve (a) no technology, (b) low technology, or (c) high technology.

The success of AT for students with disabilities is dependent not only on having access to a device, but also on factors involving selection, acquisition, and use of a tool. These ideas are codified in the following federal definition of **assistive technology services**:

> Assistive technology service means any service that directly assists a
> child with a disability in the selection, acquisition, or use of an assistive

technology device. The term includes (a) the evaluation of the needs of a child with a disability, including a functional evaluation of the child in the child's customary environment; (b) purchasing, leasing, or otherwise providing for the acquisition of assistive technology devices by children with disabilities; (c) selecting, designing, fitting, customizing, adapting, applying, maintaining, repairing, or replacing assistive technology devices; (d) coordinating and using other therapies, interventions, or services with assistive technology devices, such as those associated with existing education and rehabilitation plans and programs; (e) training or technical assistance for a child with a disability or, if appropriate, that child's family; and (f) training or technical assistance for professionals (including individuals providing education or rehabilitation services), employers, or other individuals who provide services to, employ, or are otherwise substantially involved in the major life functions of that child.

IDEA requires schools to provide AT if it is needed for a student to (a) receive a free appropriate public education (FAPE) or (b) be supported in the least restrictive environment (Yell, 2016). FAPE can include a variety of services such as special education, related services, supplementary aids and services, program modifications or support for school personnel. AT, just like other components of FAPE, must be provided at no cost to parents. However, in the 2004 reauthorization of IDEA, a section was added specifying that schools did not need to provide or maintain surgically implanted devices, such as cochlear implants, given the medical nature of such devices (Yell).

Research generally supports the value of AT for students with HID. For example, Beata Batorowicz, Cheryl Missiuna, and Nancy Pollock (2012) reviewed studies examining the impact of technology on the written productivity of students with learning disabilities and concluded the following. Providing word processors without instruction did not impact writing skills. However, when instruction was provided, revision amount and quality improved. Similarly, students who received training on strategies using spell-checkers improved. Not surprising, spell-checkers particularly helped students with severe spelling problems. Word prediction software received mixed results with variability among individual students. Speech recognition, on the other hand, improved the quality of writing over handwriting, but it does not perform as well as dictation to humans. Students who used software for concept mapping or organizing strategies increased the quality and length of their papers over those written by hand using printed organizers. Multimedia software (e.g., text, graphics, animation, audio) had a positive impact on students' motivation and attitudes toward writing and the text was judged to be of better quality with fewer errors than those handwritten and word processed.

Emily Bouck (2016) discovered that the most common forms of AT stated on the IEPs of students with HID were calculators (37.1%), computers (10.5%), books on tape (8.7%), and computer software (7.6%). Calculators have been a common accommodation to support students with math disabilities. However, based on these data, little AT is being provided for students with reading or writing disabilities. In another study using the same data set, only 7.8% of the students with HID reported using AT in their secondary school during the past year. Students with ADHD reported the highest use (40.9%), followed by students with LD (6.8%), mild ID (2.4%) and EBD (0.1%) (Bouck, Maeda & Flanagan, 2012). These percentages stand in contrast to Diane Golden's (1999) estimation of the percentage of students with HID who would benefit from AT (i.e., 25%–35% of the students with LD, 25%–35% for students with ID, 10%–20% for students with EBD).

SETT Framework

IDEA requires that IEP teams determine the AT needs of individual students. To help facilitate AT consideration by team members, Joy Zabala (2005) created the **SETT Framework**, which focuses the attention of IEP teams on the Student, the Environment, the Tasks required for active participation in the activities of the environment, and then the Tools needed for the student to address the tasks. SETT was designed to facilitate gathering and organizing data to enhance assistive technology decision-making. This model has been widely adopted and implemented due to the intuitive nature of the four core areas, its ease of use in assessment and decision-making, and the fact that the student is the initial and primary focus. In addition, this model illustrates how changes in the environment, or the task, can fundamentally alter the need for tools which is the final consideration (see Table 4.1).

One of the unintended consequences of the consideration mandate is the consideration paradox (Edyburn, 2000). That is, how can IEP teams consider assistive technology if they don't know what possibilities to consider? The assistive technology consideration paradox currently paralyzes many school-based teams because they don't have the knowledge and resources to fulfill the consideration mandate. As a result, they may meet procedural compliance by checking the box on the IEP that indicates they considered assistive technology but they fail to meet the intent of the mandate by actively exploring relevant technologies for enhancing the student's academic performance and documenting such efforts.

Technology Integration Process

While technology can be a valuable resource for improving instruction, the process of integrating technology into the curriculum is not easily or quickly accomplished. The difficulties that one will encounter are well documented and include lack of teacher time; limited access to hardware, software, and support; insufficient leadership and lack of a common vision or rationale for technology use; limited training and support; and the impact of current assessment practices on defining what teachers must teach and what students must learn with technology may not be readily measured on standardized tests (Office of Technology Assessment, 1995).

The goal of integrating technology into the curriculum is to link software, media, Internet, and technology tools with specific instructional objectives in ways that facilitate teaching and learning. This view is commonly referred to as *curriculum correspondence*. Applying the principle of curriculum correspondence results in focused, purposeful, and manageable technology use. In addition, students are better able to master specific instructional objectives.

Despite the clearly stated commitment to technology integration and recognition of the common barriers, the literature generally overlooks an essential component of the integration process—namely, what does technology integration look like and how is it

TABLE 4.1	Key Questions Associated With Zabala's SETT Model

Areas	Key Questions
Student	1. What does the student need to do?
	2. What are the student's special needs?
	3. What are the student's current abilities?
Environment	4. What materials and equipment are currently available in the environment?
	5. What is the physical arrangement? Are there special concerns?
	6. What is the instructional arrangement? Are there likely to be changes?
	7. What supports are available to the student?
	8. What resources are available to the people supporting the student?
	9. What are the attitudes and expectations of family, staff, and others?
Tasks	10. What activities take place in the environment?
	11. What activities support the student's curriculum?
	12. What are the critical elements of the activities?
	13. How might the activities be modified to accommodate the student's special needs?
	14. How might technology support the student's active participation in those activities?
	15. What tasks occur in natural environments that enable progress or mastery toward IEP goals?
	16. What tasks are required for active involvement in identified environments?
Tools	17. What strategies might be used to invite increased student performance? What no-tech, low-tech, and high-tech options should be considered when developing a system for a student with these needs and abilities doing these tasks in these environments?
	18. How might these tools be tried out with the student in the customary environments in which they will be used?

Source: Zabala (2005).

achieved? Without models, principles, and strategies, the challenge of integrating technology into the curriculum can be an overwhelming task with unpredictable results.

In order to use technology in the classroom, Dave Edyburn (1998) suggested teachers implement a four-step process. This model of the integration process was developed to (1) describe the various tasks involved in integrating software into the curriculum, (2) provide a planning guide for individuals interested in technology integration, (3) serve as a tool for discussing the process among the major stakeholders, and (4) assist in the identification of methods and resources for facilitating the process. The technology integration process describes the major tasks involved in selecting, acquiring, implementing, and integrating instructional technologies into the curriculum.

TABLE 4.2   **Edyburn's Model of the Technology Integration Process**

Phase 1: SELECTION	Phase 2: ACQUISITION	Phase 3: IMPLEMENTATION	Phase 4: INTEGRATION
Planning	Previewing	Organizing	Linking
Locating	Evaluating	Teacher Training	Managing
Reviewing	Purchasing	Student Training	Assessing
Deciding			Extending

Source: Edyburn (1998).

The process appears generic in the sense that the process is the same regardless of ability level, subject matter, or type of technology. The process is divided into four phases and each phase is comprised of three or four tasks which must be completed in working through the activities of a given phase (These steps are displayed in Table 4.2). The process is recursive. That is, while phase one results in a comprehensive list of products which address a specific instructional objective, phases two, three, and four must be repeated with each new product. Thus, it becomes readily apparent that this process involves a significant commitment of time and effort. As a reasonable goal, it is suggested that special educators initially work through this process until they have found three to 10 products which will support the varied needs of their students.

Selection

Selection focuses on planning for the use of technology, media, and materials to enhance teaching and learning. These tasks can be completed cooperatively with other colleagues in the context of program planning or they can be completed by an individual teacher. Upon completion of phase one, educators will have a comprehensive, prioritized listing of products that support the teaching and learning of a specific instructional objective.

1. Planning involves identifying the needs of students, including specific barriers of content instruction that may be remedied through technology. Although research supports the efficacy of AT for students with disabilities, the key is to match the individual student's needs and the target standard or goal with the appropriate tool. Educators should consider both general and content-specific supports needed (Israel, Marino, Delisio, & Serianni, 2014).

2. Locating consists of the search for appropriate technologies, media, and materials to support the specified objective. An exhaustive search should be conducted to identify any products that purportedly could be used to enhance instruction for the objective and, from that search, a comprehensive list created. Useful resources to assist in the task of locating appropriate instructional media include the following:

   - Center on Technology and Disability: http://ctdinstitute.org/
   - Closing the Gap Solutions: http://www.closingthegap.com/solutions/

- Disability.gov's Guide to Assistive and Accessible Technologies: https://www.disability.gov/resource/disability-govs
- National Center on Accessible Educational Materials: http://aem.cast.org
- Understood for Learning and Attention Issues: https://www.understood.org
- Wisconsin Assistive Technology Initiative: http://wati.org

3. During the underline reviewing step, rank the lists of items generated in the previous step. This can be accomplished by examining various reviews and consulting other evaluative tools to determine what others have found effective. Useful resources to assist in the task of reviewing include:

- Children's Software Revue: http://childrenssoftware.com/
- ConnSENSE Report: http://connsensereport.com/

4. The task of underline deciding involves determining what to do with the list of products that has been assembled. For example, decisions must be made regarding how many products will be reviewed.

Ms. Katz returns from a conference in which she was introduced to the technology integration process. She decides to implement the model by searching for new tools to help her students develop reading skills. First, she determines that many students' IEPs have objectives related to reading words associated with functional vocabulary. She conducts an Internet search and locates commercial vendors. With these resources, she locates several possible products, including apps, and creates a list. Ms. Katz decides that, having limited time, she will start by looking at the first five products on her list.

TEACHER TIP #4.1

SELECTING SOFTWARE

Use these questions to help guide your selection of computer software including apps for students:

1. How easily will my students be able to read the screens?

2. How consistent is the placement of menus and objects on the screen?

3. How intuitive are the features? That is, how clear and obvious are the options represented?

(Continued)

(Continued)

4. Are the choices presented to the student labeled with logical and understandable names?

5. Can the software program be adjusted by attributes such as difficulty level, vocabulary, sound, speed, amount of graphics, and so forth?

6. Do the graphics encourage interaction or convey important information? Do the graphics provide access to students who have difficulty reading text?

7. Does the software come with easy-to-follow documentation (e.g., a manual)?

8. Does the software provide on-screen instruction (e.g., help menus or balloons)?

9. Does the software provide auditory cues through synthetic (computer-generated) or digitized (recorded) speech, sounds, or music? If so, do I have the appropriate equipment to support these cues?

10. Does the software provide visual prompts to help students understand the task?

11. Does the software come with built-in alternative access methods such as switches, alternate keyboard, or touch screen?

12. What built-in utilities, such as a spell-checker, dictionary, or thesaurus are included?

13. Can the student use alternatives to a mouse (e.g., joystick, keyboard)?

14. Can the cursor be changed (e.g., larger arrow, a hand, a pointed finger, a pencil)?

15. Does the software allow creation of a customized program that allows you to enter, for example, a specific word list or set of math problems? (Alliance for Technology Access, 2005)

Acquisition

The tasks involved in the **acquisition** phase focus on personally reviewing products for the purpose of assessing whether or not a program will meet the needs and expectations of the teacher, family members, and students. Subsequently, successful evaluation results in a decision to purchase a product. At the end of this phase, the school will own a product that can be used to enhance teaching and learning.

1. Previewing requires making the necessary arrangements to personally review a product. Often this means downloading a demo copy from the Web or contacting a company for a trial use. Personally reviewing each product prior to purchase is a critical step in selecting the appropriate tool.

2. Evaluating consists of assessing whether or not a program will meet the needs and expectations of the teacher, family members, and students. (More discussion on family involvement follows the technology integration section.) While evaluation forms may be helpful, a comparison of three or more similar products usually results in a decision about which product is most suitable for a given classroom or individual student. The cycle of previewing and evaluating may

continue down the entire list generated in the locating task. While evaluating, consider whether the technology will help the student blend in with other peers (King-Sears & Evmenova, 2007). Only after the evaluation results in a decision to select a specific product does the integration process move to the next step.

3. Purchasing involves the administrative details associated with acquiring sufficient copies of a given product. Usually this means someone will need to determine where to purchase the product, at the best price, and make arrangements for payment and delivery.

Ms. Katz proceeds through the acquisition phase by previewing and evaluating products until she finds two products that she thinks will be valuable for her students. She selects Survival Signs and Symbols (www.attainmentcompany.com) and the Talking Symbols Notepad (www.horizonhealthandsafety.com). She works with her technology specialist to order the products.

Implementation

Phase three, the implementation phase, focuses on examining factors involved in "making it work." At the end of this phase, a new product will be assimilated into the school's technology system and teachers, students, and if necessary family members, will have been trained to use it.

1. Organizing involves inventorying and installing or downloading a newly purchased product. If it is a piece of software, decisions about whether to install a product on an individual machine or on a network need to be made.

2. The task of teacher training requires that teachers be provided with the necessary training to fully implement a product. Typically, training is simply "teach yourself" since only a single copy of the product was purchased. Teachers need to acquire the skills and knowledge to operate the program, conduct basic troubleshooting, and be introduced to methods and ideas for using the product in the classroom.

3. Student training involves teaching students how to access it, why they would use it, and how to navigate through it. This task ensures that students are prepared to interact with the product when it is subsequently introduced in the curriculum. Sometimes family members also need training so they can support student implementation outside of the classroom.

Integration

The integration of technology is the last phase of implementation. The tasks involved in this phase focus directly on using products in the classroom and, if appropriate, at home, to enhance teaching and learning. Considerable time and effort have been expended to reach this phase. Yet those efforts will greatly increase the likelihood of integration success.

1. The <u>linking</u> step involves examining the curriculum and determining when a product should be used, how the program can best be used to facilitate learning, and what activities would be useful both prior and subsequent to a product's use by students. Curriculum frameworks and calendars are important tools for this task. Obviously, technology tools are of greatest value when they are available at the appropriate time rather than being discovered several weeks after a unit is completed.

2. <u>Managing</u> consists of providing time for students to use a product and ensuring that all students are successfully achieving the objectives. Fortunately, access to hardware for students has increased. However, not all classrooms have access for every student simultaneously. Creative strategies must be used for managing limited computer and tablet access in the classroom. In addition, teachers should have plans for the occasional malfunction (see Technology Spotlight #4.1).

3. <u>Assessing</u> involves evaluating the results of instruction and determining whether any changes should be made now or in the future. Often in special education, a program may be revisited during the school year to provide opportunities for maintenance of previously learned skills.

4. Finally, the task of <u>extending</u> recognizes that unless additional instructional applications for a new tool are created, the tool may be returned to the shelf for storage until sometime in the future. Identify ways of extending the value of the product and then continue the technology integration process at the <u>linking</u> task in this last phase, rather than starting the entire process over again.

In the final phase of integration, Ms. Katz makes a plan for when each student will use each new product as she prepares her weekly lesson plans and reviews each students' IEP objectives. She also considers the management plan of rotating students through using the three iPads and one laptop in her classroom. She is interested in whether students are learning and making progress, so she prepares periodic academic probes to assess each student's mastery of the functional vocabulary. She also attends professional development workshops and reads professional journals for new ideas to extend the power of the tools she has recently acquired.

Technology Spotlight #4.1

Training Students to Troubleshoot and Problem Solve

In addition to training students how to use technology, Tamarah Ashton and K. S. Hall (2000) have noted that it is important for teachers to model a problem-solving process for students when trying to repair the inevitable glitches that arise with routine technology use. They propose the following steps for inspiring self-confidence in troubleshooting and problem-solving.

Step 1: Keep It Simple

- Try to isolate the problem to determine if it is the computer, the software, or one of the peripherals like the mouse, keyboard, monitor, or printer.

- Check to be certain each cable is securely connected for the power, monitor, projection device, printer, and keyboard.

- If it appears the computer has locked up, learn the key combinations that allow you to quit the program without having to restart the computer. If necessary, reboot the computer by turning off the power, waiting several seconds, and then restarting.

Step 2: Be Persistent

- Some peripheral problems are caused by not turning on devices in the correct sequence.

- If you did not discover a problem with the cable connections, consider swapping the peripheral device with another identical one. For example, if the monitor appears to not be working, try connecting the computer to a different monitor. If it works, you've found your solution; if not, the culprit must lie elsewhere so keep problem-solving.

- Software difficulties can be just as difficult to detect, if not more so, than hardware problems. Rebooting the computer is often necessary to resolve a software problem. If that doesn't work, carefully note any error messages you receive so that you can seek technical assistance.

Step 3: Narrow Down the Problem

- Throughout the troubleshooting process, continue to narrow down the problem and localize it to one or more subcomponents. Although the problem may persist, completing these basic troubleshooting steps will allow you to more effectively communicate your technological dilemma to technical support staff.

When Troubleshooting Isn't Enough

The next challenge that awaits you is what to do in the event that the technical support staff is unavailable and/or the above troubleshooting steps have confirmed that the problem is beyond your technical prowess. An obvious option is to have another computer available to use in class. If software is being used or demonstrated, keep backup copies or original disks in the classroom to be reloaded.

Besides having back-up copies, it is also important to think about alternatives. For example, if you were planning to show students information via the Internet, you may want to prepare PowerPoint slides, just in case you have difficulty accessing the Internet.

Source: Adapted from Ashton & Hall (2000).

Family Participation

Each federal mandate for students with disabilities has emphasized enhanced family participation in their child's special education. Family involvement in AT decision-making is now not only mandated but has been considered best practice for some time (Parette, VanBiervliet, & Hourcade, 2000). Yet barriers may inhibit culturally diverse family involvement in the AT decision-making processes. Crystal Kemp and Howard P. Parette (2000) suggest these barriers include (a) prejudice and discrimination, (b) the perception that AT-related advantages are not beneficial to themselves or their child, and (c) a disconnect between the values of European American professionals and the values of non-European American families.

Professionals should consider at least four issues when engaged in collaborative AT decision-making with families (Parette et al., 2000). First is the importance of family values. When values of the professionals differ from values held by families, dissonance occurs. Values in this case are similar to the four cultural dimensions of efficiency, independence, equity, and communication styles addressed in Chapter 2.

The second issue involves the impact of AT on shifting family roles. Providing AT for students with disabilities may require more of parents and other family members. Professionals often do not consider the demands placed on families when AT recommendations are made. These demands may include learning to use, maintain, and repair a specific device. The inclusion of an AT device can contribute to or reduce caregiving demands or stressors on families (Parette, 1999).

The third family value impacting AT decisions is the potential for abandonment. Lack of family involvement in meaningful ways during AT planning may result in the abandonment of devices (Parette et al., 2000). Abandonment wastes limited resources available to school systems and is detrimental to the students. Professionals need to consider the likelihood that families will simply discard and not use the prescribed AT device.

The fourth consideration is family acceptance of AT. Acceptance is impacted by the availability of information and training that is user friendly and accessible, as well as follow-up support available to families. Family members need information. How that information is provided remains as important as what is provided (Hourcade, Parette, & Huer, 1997). For example, parents can (a) receive didactic instruction on how to use a specific device, (b) watch as a professional shows them how to use it, and/or (c) watch another student actually implement the device. Digital recordings in which the device is being used in real-life settings can be particularly powerful.

Special considerations need to be made when working with students and their families from diverse cultures. A discussion about this topic may be found in the Implications for Culturally and/or Linguistically Diverse Students section of this chapter.

Dylan's fourth-grade teacher, Mr. Twitty, shared with his special education teacher, Mrs. Zabriski, that Dylan's parents wanted him to be taught word processing and allowed to submit his written papers and projects typed. She called Dylan's parents and convened an IEP meeting to discuss this issue as a team. During the meeting, Mrs. Zabriski introduced the SETT framework which they used to make their decision to include a word processing goal on his IEP. Mr. Twitty could check out a laptop computer from the school district for Dylan's use in his classroom throughout the remainder of the year. Mrs. Zabriski would design a schedule so that Dylan could be taught basic word processing using an instructional aide and peer tutors supervised by Mrs. Zabriski. Mr. Twitty agreed that he could turn in his written work typed.

Mr. Rodriquez's district technology specialist introduces him to the SETT model. Using the model, together they engage Walter's IEP team in a discussion about his potential need for AT. As a result, the team decides that peer support will be useful for the science class's reading demands. In addition, Mr. Rodriquez will use presentation tools like BrainPop (www.brainpop.com) and interactive websites to illustrate key concepts that some students find difficult to understand by reading about them.

Finally, the team discusses the need to provide Walter with digital alternatives to the textbooks, such as e-books, companion textbook websites, or text-to-speech software, so that he can gain the necessary information by listening rather than reading. The assistive technology specialist then follows up with additional product information and obtains selected products on a trial basis to use with Walter in the classroom and at home to determine the next steps.

Technology Integration Across the Curriculum

In addition to implementing AT devices with individual students, teachers can deliberately integrate technology across the curriculum. The goal is not to use technology to improve, increase, or maintain the functional capability of a student with a disability. Rather, the goal is to teach students to use technology in ways that enhance their knowledge of content. For example, Internet resources have increased immediate access to current information. Appropriate Internet links can be invaluable tools for students researching a topic. Word processing, spreadsheets, presentation software, and so forth have improved the creation and production of written products. Simulations and other computerized tools allow students to visualize cause and effect in ways that have not been available until recently. The list could go on and on.

Sometimes teachers decide they want to use technology for reasons that are less than ideal. For example, they may wish to implement technology because the tools are available, other teachers are using them, the principal likes technology, or technology is part of the school culture (Roblyer, 2003). The best reason to use technology in the classroom is that it provides clear benefits over other methods. Potential beneficial applications of technology to the teaching process are outlined in Table 4.3.

Specific Technology Tools

Tools for Cognitive and Academic Difficulties

Both complex and simple technology tools can support students with HID in many ways. Sometimes, educators and family members desire the devices and tools with "bells and whistles" when in reality a less complex and resource-demanding tool would suffice. Examples of other low-technology tools are listed in Teacher Tip #4.2.

TABLE 4.3   Examples of Integrating Technology Across the Curriculum

Curriculum Unit	Standard	Related Technology Goal
Earth Surface	Students will demonstrate their understanding that volcanoes, earthquakes, uplift, weathering, and erosion reshape the Earth's surface.	Students will (1) access information through the Internet regarding the Earth's surface, and (2) simulate the impact of an earthquake in the local area using computer software.
Writing	Students will (1) prepare to write by gathering and organizing information and ideas, (2) compose a written draft, (3) revise the draft by elaborating and clarifying, and (4) edit the draft for conventional usage.	To accomplish the standards, students will use the following software, corresponding to the step in the writing process: (1) Internet resources, Kidspiration/Inspiration; (2–4) word-for-word processing; and (4) spelling and grammar checkers.
Weather	Students will (1) observe, measure, and record the basic elements of weather; (2) interpret recorded weather data for simple patterns; and (3) evaluate weather predictions based on observational data.	Students will (1) access the Internet to acquire current weather conditions, (2) collect daily data and place it on an Excel spreadsheet, and (3) use video equipment to broadcast weather reports.

TEACHER TIP #4.2
LOWER TECHNOLOGY SUPPORTS

Not all assistive technology needs to be "high technology." Below is a list of "lower technology" supports for students with high-incidence disabilities:

- Pencil grips
- Highlighting pens or tape
- Post-it notes
- Picture or written schedule
- Reading pens

- Cellophane tape or Velcro to hold materials in place
- Slant boards
- Specialty or adapted paper (e.g., carbonless or larger size paper)
- Book holders
- Calculators
- Digital recorders
- Closed-caption televisions

Mason, an 11th-grade student with ADHD has difficulty attending while reading. His parents think using a highlight pen will help him select relevant information as he reads his textbooks. They recognize, however, that he isn't supposed to write in his textbooks. When they present this problem to one of his teachers, Mr. Hopkins, he suggests Mason use highlight tape, an alternative to pens. The tape comes in a dispenser similar to scotch tape but the highlight tape can be easily removed without leaving a mark in the book.

Students with HID typically do not have problems with physical access to technology. Rather, the critical issues tend to involve cognitive skills like organization, memory, and attention. They also need support in subject areas such as reading, writing, mathematics, and social/emotional skills. Tables 4.4 and 4.5 present examples of technological tools including software, apps, e-books, physical tools, and so forth that may be used with this population. Those listed are simply examples. Additional tools may be readily identified through internet searches.

TEACHER TIP #4.3
CAUTIONS WHEN USING SPELL-CHECKERS

Students often rely on spell-checkers when they word process documents. Be aware of these factors:

1. Consider the needs of the student when selecting word processing programs with spell-checkers. They may provide one of the following:

   i. the correctly spelled word

   ii. a list of words from which to choose

   iii. a complete dictionary and thesaurus

   iv. speech synthesized recitation of the words

2. The larger the size of the spell-checker's word database means the program will recognize more misspellings and provide alternative spellings.

3. Spell-checkers that allow the user to add words also allow users to add misspelled words.

4. Homonyms are words that sound alike but are spelled differently (e.g. they're, their, there). Spell-checkers may not correct homonyms if they are spelled correctly (e.g., Their going home.)

5. Students often spell words phonetically (e.g., fonix). Spell-checkers may not recognize such words to provide alternative spellings.

6. If the first two to three letters are spelled correctly, the more likely the spell-checker will recognize it and provide alternatives. (Schwab Learning, 2003)

TABLE 4.4   **Examples of Technological Tools Aiding Students With High-Incidence Disabilities**

Challenges	General Tool Description	Specific Examples
Accessibility	Internet access	• WebAim: webaim.org • Endeavor Desktop Environment: www.ablelinktech.net
Prompts/Cues	Electronic auditory or visual prompts	• Visual Assistant: www.ablelinktech.com • WayFinder: www.ablelinktech.com

(Continued)

TABLE 4.4   (Continued)

Time Management and Organization	Electronic reminders, calendars, schedules, to-do lists	• My Video Schedule: itunes.apple.com • Quarter Hour Watch: www.toby-churchill.com • Remember the Milk: www.rememberthemilk.com • TextMinder: itunes.apple.com • Time Timer: www.timetimer.com • Timer and Touch HD: itunes.apple.com • Timers4Me: play.google.com • Watchminder: www.watchminder.com • Week Planner for Kids: itunes.apple.com
Study Skills	Electronic encyclopedias, software support for studying	• Yahooligans!: squirrelnet.com • WYNN: www.freedomscientific.com

TABLE 4.5   Examples of Technological Tools for Curricular Support

Challenges	General Technology	Specific Examples
Mathematics	Calculators, "talking" tools, manipulatives	• Let's Do the Math: www.amazon.com • Marble Math Junior: itunes.apple.com • Mathmateer: itunes.apple.com • Peter Pig's Money Counter: www.amazon.com • StepPad: www.attainmentcompany.com • Talking Scientific Calculator: www.activeforever.com • Talking Tape Measure: www.independentliving.com • Telling Time Quiz: itunes.apple.com • WebMATH: webmath.com
Reading	Digitized speech output, electronic books, apps for reading support	• Bookshare: www.bookshare.org • ChooseIt! Literacy: itunes.apple.com • e-books: www.free-ebooks.net • Hideout: itunes.apple.com • Kurzweil 3000-firefly: www.kurzweiledu.com • Language Therapy: itunes.apple.com • My Word Wall: itunes.apple.com • Start-to-Finish Books: start-to-finish.com • ReadingPen: wizcomtech.com

Challenges	General Technology	Specific Examples
Social/Emotional	Apps for social/emotional support	• Calm Counter: itunes.apple.com • Conversation Builder: itunes.apple.com • Conversation Social Stories: itunes.apple.com • IPrompts XL: itunes.apple.com
Writing	Spell checkers, concept mapping, apps for writing support	• Clicker Docs: itunes.apple.com • Clicker Books: itunes.apple.com • Co:Writer: donjohnston.com • Kidspiration, Inspiration: www.inspiration.com

TEACHER TIP #4.4

SELECTING APPS

In today's mobile technology, apps are abundant. Selecting appropriate apps for the classroom, however, can become a daunting task. When costs are involved, teachers need to be particularly careful in selecting apps that will be most effective. Use these steps when selecting apps:

1. Identify the learning objectives.

2. Conduct a search using "Best New Apps," "Top Free Apps," or "Top Paid Apps."

3. Select five to 10 apps to investigate.

4. Solicit other educators' opinions through blogs or websites (e.g., www.freetech 4teachers.com).

5. Select standards and align with the app or identify where it has already been done (e.g., illuminations.nctm .org).

6. Match students' limitations to essential features of the app.

7. Gather additional data and select an app.

8. Prepare the student to use an iPad.

9. Prepare the iPad such as discontinuing all the preloaded apps. (Powell, 2014)

Video Modeling

Video modeling (VM) is defined as instruction delivered through video clips in which an adult, a peer, or self as model demonstrates a behavior being taught. Although some commercially prepared videos are available, many teachers create their own videos to address the specific needs of their students. Advantages of VM include decreased reliance on adults to instruct and assist students while increasing student independence. In addition, students can view videos repeatedly and modeling of the skill does not vary.

The biggest disadvantage to VM is the lack of teacher knowledge, equipment, support, and/or time to create the videos (Weng, Savage, & Bouck, 2014).

Modeling has been known for many years to be an effective instructional tool, particularly for students with disabilities (See Chapter 6). Video modeling has been shown to be effective with a wide range of students with varying abilities and across a range of curricular content (Carnahan, Basham, Christman, & Hollingshead, 2012). For example, VM has been shown to be effective in teaching vocational skills (e.g., Allen, Wallace, Renes, Bowen, & Burke, 2010), social behaviors (e.g., Charlop, Dennis, Carpenter, & Greenberg, 2010), mathematics (e.g., Burton, Anderson, Prater, & Dyches, 2013), and reading fluency and comprehension (e.g., Hitchcock, Prater, & Dowrick, 2004).

In a review of the VM literature, particularly focusing on students with autism, Christopher Rayner, Carey Denholm, and Jeff Sigafoos (2009) concluded that VM can be an effective instructional tool, leading to improved student performance. However, a number of studies resulted in mixed results among participants indicating that VM may not be effective for all. In addition, the verdict on who should be the model has not been resolved. There are some indications that peers and self are more effective models than adults. Also unclear at this time is whether first-person or third-person video view is more effective. A first-person view would show only the hands of the model from the participant's perspective, while the third-person video would take the perspective of a person watching the model.

Video self-modeling (VSM), a subset of video modeling, has received increased attention over recent years. Thomas Creer and Donald Miklich (1970) introduced VSM to the field. They videotaped a boy hospitalized with asthma role-playing effective social skills and discovered that the role-plays had no effect on improving behavior, but viewing the videotapes did.

VSM has been used in two ways—namely positive self-review and feedforward (Prater, Carter, Hitchcock, & Dowrick, 2011). Positive self-review involves capturing the student demonstrating the skills accurately or appropriately, editing the video retaining the best examples of the targeted behavior, and then showing the positive examples to the student. The goal is to develop more consistent performance. For example, a student athlete may be video recorded and then shown his best form in throwing or hitting a ball. The skills in positive self-review recordings are already available in the person's repertoire. On the other hand, feedforward captures the student demonstrating successes they haven't yet demonstrated fluently. In this case, the recordings are edited so that the student is successfully engaged in the desired behavior. For example, a student may be recorded during seatwork and any inappropriate behaviors are edited out. Or a student may be recorded reading orally and all of the hesitations, sounding out, or teacher prompts are removed from the recording. The use of feedforward is appropriate for behaviors the student is capable of achieving but has not yet demonstrated fluently or independently (Boisvert & Rao, 2015).

In one study, Cami E. Burton, Darlene H. Anderson, Mary Anne Prater, and Tina T. Dyches (2013) recorded students with autism or intellectual disabilities completing five story problems using a script of seven steps. When needed, the teacher provided prompts to ensure the student answered the problems correctly. The prompts were then removed from the videos and students watched themselves using the steps independently to answer the story problems correctly. They then completed the same problems live.

Each student could pause the video, fast-forward or rewind as needed. Fading procedures were implemented including completion of novel problems. All students quickly learned and maintained the new skills through VSM.

TEACHER TIP #4.5
CREATING VIDEO-BASED INSTRUCTION VIDEOS

Use the following steps when creating videos for video-based instruction:

1. Decide if one video for the whole task will be sufficient or if multiple videos will be needed.

2. Task analyze by breaking the skill into small teachable steps.

3. Select the model (i.e., self, peer, adult).

4. Decide on the video's perspective (i.e., from the model's or an observer's point of view).

5. Select where the video will be recorded. Control environmental distractions.

6. Prepare for filming (e.g., obtain permissions, prepare equipment).

7. Film the video using stabilizing equipment.

8. Edit the video using an app (e.g., Video, iMovie).

9. Save the video for playback on an app.

10. Pilot the video with someone not involved and make adjustments as needed. (Weng et al., 2014)

Computer-Assisted Instruction

Computer-assisted instruction (CAI) refers to instructional materials that are delivered by the means of computer technology. CAI may involve presenting new knowledge in a tutoring-like session, providing drill-and-practice opportunities, or simulation activities. The use of computers in schools began in the 1960s. Developers sought to create a means for individualized instruction that allowed students to receive immediate feedback and correct their responses (Molnar, 1997). Since the creation of the microcomputer in the 1970s, computer use in the schools has become widespread. Initially, CAI was delivered through desktop and then laptop computers; but recent developments of mobile tablet computers have resulted in education entering a new era (Weng, Maeda, & Bouck, 2014). Perceived advantages of tablets include easier access through multitouch screens and cost-effective educational applications, as well as ease in mobility allowing greater flexibility (Weng et al., 2014). Application of multimedia has also enhanced the quality of instruction that is possible if the instruction incorporates evidence-based practice and provides appropriate scaffolding opportunities (Kennedy & Deshler, 2010).

Although CAI has been advocated for all students, some professionals believe that CAI is particularly promising for students with HID. For example, it has been argued that CAI is beneficial for students with autism because it allows them to bypass the social complexities of learning and presents monotone, limited-affect computer-generated speech, among other advantages (Pennington, 2010). Similarly, others have suggested that CAI can be a powerful tool for students with learning disabilities because it provides multiple practice opportunities, can be individualized, and delivers immediate feedback (Seo & Woo, 2010).

Not only have professionals advocated the use of CAI for students with disabilities, some research has documented CAI as having promise to improve their achievement. CAI and other technologies should not, however, be considered a panacea. Reviews of research demonstrate mixed results. For example, in a review of research using technology to teach students with autism academic skills, Victoria Knight, Bethany McKissick and Alicia Saunders (2013) concluded that only a limited amount of high-quality research has been conducted, thus using technology to teach academics to students with autism should be used with caution. The authors also concluded that there exists more evidence of teaching English language arts versus other content using technology, and that technology is most effective in teaching discrete skills.

Specific tools can be used to facilitate student learning through CAI. Two specific examples include supported eText and speech-to-text recognition:

1. **Supported eText** refers to electronic text that is modified or enhanced to increase reading comprehension or enhancing students' ability to learn from text (Anderson-Inman, 2009). Written text that is available to read in an electronic format is more dynamic, flexible, and malleable than printed text. For example, electronic text can be modified in the following ways:

   - Font type, size, and color can be changed, as well as the background to the text.
   - Text materials can be read out loud.
   - Concepts can be defined and explained.
   - Multiple illustrations can appear simultaneously.
   - Links can lead to supportive information.
   - Documents can be accessed from different computers in different geographic locations. Supported eText holds promise for promoting access to content for students with HID (Anderson-Inman & Horney, 2007).

2. **Speech-to-text recognition** technology synchronously transcribes text from speech input and displays the text on a whiteboard or computer screen (Shadiev, Hwang, Chen, & Huang, 2014). This technology can be used to create text from the students' oral speech or to create text from teacher instruction. Research has shown speech-to-text recognition technology to have the following distinct advantages:

- helps students better understand lecture content;
- allows students to confirm missed or misheard parts of oral instruction; and
- can be used to take notes, complete homework or prepare for exams. (Shadiev et al., 2014)

TEACHER TIP #4.6

eTEXT SUPPORTS

Book Builder, available through the Center for Applied Special Technology (bookbuilder. cast.org), provides a template that allows users to create e-books including eText supports (e.g., text to speech, hyperlinks to an online glossary). Once books are created, they may be shared with others who have an account. Many books already exist on the website (Knight, Wood, Spooner, Browder, & O'Brien, 2015).

Online and Blended Learning

Online Learning

The opportunities for online learning are increasing for all students including those with disabilities. **Distance learning**, or delivery of instruction to an individual student who is not present in a traditional classroom, began in the late 1800s. At that time, distance education was delivered through correspondence courses. This evolved in the mid-1900s to televised instruction, "teaching machines," and authoring tools to develop coursework on stand-alone machines. All of these efforts progressed to delivering instruction through computer networks or **online learning**. The first private fully online school was introduced in 1991, which followed with the first public online school starting 5 years later. In 2010, the number of K–12 students enrolled in online courses in the United States was estimated at one and one-half million students with the most growth occurring in full-time online learning (Tonks, Weston, Wiley, & Barbour, 2013).

Online educational opportunities, including cyber or online schools, are growing at a rapid pace. In fact, most states offer statewide full-time virtual schools (Hashey & Stahl, 2014) and research shows that about 7.2% of those enrolled in online programs are students with disabilities (Molnar et al., 2013). This percentage is nearly one half of the number of students with disabilities served in brick-and-mortar schools. The disproportionate number may be a reflection of lack of access for students with disabilities. It is also possible that some students enrolled in online instruction have not been identified as having a disability but would be if they were enrolled in brick-and-mortar schools.

An estimated 90% of all K–12 online education curricula were developed by for-profit companies with school districts purchasing access to these materials (Patrick,

Kennedy, & Powell, 2013). Although any published curricular materials need careful evaluation prior to schools adopting them, selecting online materials must be done with more caution and care because the online product is primarily delivering instruction, making assignments, and administering assessments with the students' teacher taking a secondary role (Greer, Rowland, & Smith, 2014).

Online learning has many advantages, one of which is the ability to present information in multiple ways, an important principle of universal design for learning (UDL) (Hashey & Stahl, 2014). In fact, the application of UDL is often found in technologically supported instruction. The principle behind UDL is to design and use instructional materials that allow the instructional goals to be achieved by a wide range of students regardless of their abilities. (For a complete discussion of UDL, see Chapter 7.)

If UDL is considered when online programs are initially designed, the results can be powerful. Yet, this is generally not the case, making access for students with disabilities troublesome.

The following tools are available to assist educators in evaluating the accessibility of products or digital materials used in online learning (Hashey & Stahl, 2014):

- The Center on Online Learning and Students with Disabilities identified the extent to which product developers or publishers used in K–12 instructional materials offer easy to locate information about product accessibility (centerononlinelearning.org/resources/vpat/).

- Web.AIM.org has created a web accessibility tool to evaluate websites' accessibility strengths and areas in need of improvement (wave.webaim.org/).

Although there exists a proliferation of online course offerings and schools, relatively little research has been done on the efficacy of this instructional format, particularly with students with disabilities. Diana Greer, Mary Rice, and Bryan Dykman (2014) reviewed research that examined the impact of online learning on students with disabilities. They concluded that carefully designed online curriculum does have the potential to help students with disabilities learn content and meet educational standards.

TABLE 4.6 **Advantages and Disadvantages of Online Learning Environments for Students With Disabilities**

Advantages	Disadvantages
• Ability to present information in multiple ways (e.g., audio, video, text)	• Current programs are not accessible to students with disabilities (e.g., level is inappropriate or equipment not accessible).
• Ability for students to demonstrate understanding in multiple ways	• Students have difficulty navigating and completing tasks independently.
• Can customize instruction to the needs of individual students (e.g., pace, focus)	• Parents need to structure student time or modify/enhance content.

Sources: Greer, Rowland et al. (2014); Hashey & Stahl (2014).

They also concluded that students with disabilities did not achieve academically at the same rate as their nondisabled peers in this environment, and that parents and students were generally satisfied with their online experience.

Blended Learning

Online learning takes place independent of a brick-and-mortar school building; students receive their complete education through the internet. In contrast, **blended learning** delivers a portion of instruction through online learning, the latter of which has some element of student control in terms of when and where it will be delivered. Although there are several models of blended learning, the most common is the **flipped class-room** model (Smith & Basham, 2014). In this model, students receive teacher-directed instruction online as homework and then engage in practice and application during class time. That is, the traditional model of receiving instruction in the classroom and then completing application exercises as homework is "flipped."

Blended learning can be implemented using online resources available, or teachers can create their own instructional videos and burn them on DVDs or download them onto the Internet. All of the cautions addressed for online learning apply when using currently available Internet resources.

TABLE 4.7   Examples of Tools and Resources to Support Online and Blended Learning

Product	Content	Description
BrainPOP (www.brainpop.com) BrainPOP Jr. (K–3) BrainPOP Español BrainPOP ESL	Science, social studies, English, math, engineering and technology, health, arts, and music	Animated characters introduce and illustrate concepts. Good for flipped classrooms. Quizzes, game play, and activities are included.
Gizmos (www.explorelearning.com)	Science and math	Provides a collection of virtual manipulatives allowing students to view and interact with science and math principles.
Khan Academy (www.khanacademy.org)	Science and math	YouTube-hosted videos with pictures and diagrams to teach science and math concepts.
OER Commons (www.oercommons.org)	Language arts, math, science, social studies, and art	Identifies varied and multiple online resources that align with the Common Core.
Study Island (www.studyisland.com/web/index)	Reading and math	Lessons align to Common Core standards, so it can be used as a tool to prepare students for state assessments or to study a particular area of concern.

Source: Greer, Rowland, & Smith (2014b); Smith & Basham (2014)

Flipped classrooms have at least two advantages. First, the video recorded instructional component can be viewed multiple times and made available to those who are absent from class. Second, the teacher can provide guidance while students are practicing the skills in the classroom, allowing for quick error correction and reteaching when necessary. Disadvantages include (a) resources that are needed to create video recorded instruction (e.g., teacher time, equipment), and (b) students who need access to equipment (e.g., DVD player, Internet) outside of the school.

Implications for Culturally and/or Linguistically Diverse Students

Technological tools are not culture-free in that they are "human creations and as such reflect the culture of the individuals who create them" (Chen, 2007, p. 1114). For example, computer software demonstrates cultural preferences in analytic and logical thinking and organization of information. Given the increased numbers of diverse students being served in public schools, many of whom have been identified as having a disability, the implications of cultural and linguistic differences related to assistive technology and other technological tools must be considered.

As mandated in IDEA, AT needs must be considered by IEP teams for all students with disabilities. Yet, an overriding assumption with and reason for AT is that it helps facilitate independence, a value which many cultures do not promote, at least to the degree that European American culture does.

Some research has documented differences in perspective of AT with diverse populations. For example, researchers discovered that African American families express preference to not use some forms of AT because of the attention and stigma attached to the student. Other researchers found that Asian American families preferred that AT technical training and assistance be provided by community members, rather than school personnel (Parette, Huer, & Scherer, 2004). Although there exist limited studies investigating cultural diversity dimensions of AT, practitioners need to be willing to "cross diverse boundaries and to become sensitive and responsive to building and maintaining support networks that increase the likelihood of embracing technology and decreasing abandonment" for this population (Jeffs & Morrison, 2005, p. 24).

Family cultural values must be considered carefully in the promotion and selection of AT devices as well as training of family members to use the devices. Families from varying cultures might perceive and desire technology very differently. Sensitivity to family and cultural factors early in the AT decision-making process significantly increases the likelihood of success (Parette et al., 2000). Table 4.8 lists important questions to ask families when engaged in AT decision-making, particularly if the family comes from a culturally diverse population.

More information in the areas of AT devices and services, training, and funding options may be especially important for culturally diverse families, particularly those from lower socioeconomic backgrounds. When technology devices are provided, a typical question is who actually owns the device. If the school system purchased the device, families must understand that the school owns the device, even if it is used in the home. Schools should have policy related to responsibility for theft and damage when the device is used off school grounds. If teachers help parents access devices through

TABLE 4.8 **Questions to Ask Family Members About AT Application**

General Categories	Specific Questions
Expectations for Independence	Do you want your child to perform daily tasks for himself or herself? Will you use AT in community settings outside the home? If so, what commitment outside the home is needed for successful application?
Home	Are there reasons not to use the device at home? How will AT affect your child and your home environment? How will AT affect other members of the family?
Outside the Home	Are there reasons not to use AT outside the home? Will AT make you or your child self-conscious or cause undue attention if used in public settings? Outside of the home, how will others feel if AT is used in their presence?
Benefits and Support	How will you and your child use the device? How often will your child use the device? What do you think AT will do for your child? How quickly do you expect to receive benefits? What training is needed? How will you pay for the device? If your child needs assistance, who will provide it?

Source: Adapted from Parette & McMahan (2002).

funding mechanisms outside the schools, the actual ownership should be determined in advance and understood by all (Hourcade et al., 1997).

The following criteria can help IEP teams determine whether a proposed AT change is positive or negative for the family:

- family member's receptiveness to the AT device;
- family member's willingness and/or ability to implement the AT;
- the availability of support resources for the family; and
- compatibility of the AT with the overall family system. (Parette et al., 2000)

Delivery and structure of online courses reflect explicit styles of instruction and interaction expectations which may differ from diverse cultural preferences and styles. For example, in one study of adult learners, Korean and Chinese students preferred asynchronous or delayed communication tools such as discussion boards and e-mails over synchronous (e.g., live chat, video conferencing) tools. The researcher concluded that the Asian cultural communication styles of thinking before you speak were reflected in these results (Wang, 2007).

A few studies have examined the impact of technology on K–12 CLD students. For example, video self-modeling (VSM) has been shown to increase reading fluency and comprehension with Hawaiian and nonstandard English speaking young students (Hitchcock et al., 2004), as well as improve high school English learners' (ELs') reading fluency (Boisvert & Rao, 2015). Using culturally responsive instruction and culturally relevant materials enhance the learning process. For example, Précille Boisvert and Kavita Rao used cultural stories that the students had learned when younger for their reading passages. In addition, preliminary results indicate that VSM is as effective for EL as it is for non-EL (Ortiz, Burlingame, Onuegbulem, Yoshikawa, & Rojas, 2012).

Although little research has been conducted on the impact of technology on K–12 CLD students, particularly those with HID, teachers need to be cognizant and sensitive to these differences in learning preferences, involve family members when appropriate, and make culturally responsive decisions.

SUMMARY

As technology tools become more readily available and affordable, the possibility of increased communication, independence, and learning of students with HID could increase dramatically. Yet currently many students are never exposed to the tools that could enhance and improve their lives. Fortunately, IDEA requires that all IEP teams consider each individual student's need for assistive technology and that the student's family members are involved in those decisions. Assistive technology must be provided if it is needed for a student to receive a free appropriate public education or to be supported in the least restrictive environment. These federal requirements reflect the notion that the foundations of special education technology have been shaped primarily through legal and policy mandates rather than research-based evidence.

When making AT decisions, IEP teams should consider the student, environment, tasks, and tools (SETT Framework), as well as family and cultural considerations. Not only can AT improve or maintain the functional capacity of a student with a disability, technology in general can enhance knowledge of content through technology integration in the curriculum. The goal for such integration is to link software, media, Internet, and technology tools with specific instructional objectives in ways that facilitate teaching and learning. The process for integration is recursive and includes the steps of selection, acquisition, implementation, and integration.

Parents or family members are critical participants in AT decisions for individual students. Professionals need to consider at least four issues regarding parent involvement: family values, impact of AT on shifting family role, potential for AT abandonment, and family acceptance of AT. Special consideration should be given to CLD families, particularly given that an overriding assumption for AT is that it helps facilitate independence, a value which not all cultures promote. Also, issues related to training and funding options may be particularly important for families from lower socioeconomic backgrounds.

Many technology tools are available to support the cognitive needs of and to provide curricular support for students with HID. In addition, specific technology that has been found to be useful for this population includes video modeling and computer-based instruction. And as online and blended learning continue to gain momentum, more students with disabilities might be served in this way in the future.

REVIEW QUESTIONS

1. Define and provide three examples of assistive technology.

2. Describe the SETT Framework. Identify at least 10 of the questions associated with this Framework.

3. Provide an example of the technology integration process by describing each of the phases and steps involved.

4. Create a related technology goal to this curricular goal: Students will identify the main idea and three to five key details of a text, and explain how the details support the main idea.

5. Describe the importance and legal requirements involving family members with AT selection and implementation.

6. Justify this statement: "The foundations of special education technology have been shaped primarily through legal and policy mandates rather than research-based evidence."

7. Describe video modeling including advantages and disadvantages for students with HID.

8. Define and describe how supported eText and speech-to-text would be helpful for students with HID.

9. Compare and contrast online and blended learning. Include examples.

10. Describe key considerations in involving students and family members in the selection and implementation of technology.

ACTIVITIES

1. Locate websites devoted to assistive educational resources. Rate the usefulness of each site.

2. Create a case study of an IEP team going through the process of selecting AT for a student with HID. Describe what they considered and how they reached their conclusion.

3. Identify, explore, and evaluate supported eText and speech-to-text tools. Write or orally present your recommendations.

4. Investigate the prevalence of online and/or blended learning for students with disabilities through your state, local school district, or neighborhood schools. If possible, interview teachers using online or blended learning. Write a report or present your findings orally.

Council for Exceptional Children (CEC) Standards

The Council for Exceptional Children (CEC) is a premiere national professional organization comprised of special educators, paraeducators, related service personnel, parents, and others interested in individuals with disabilities and/or those with gifts and talents. This organization has generated 10 standards for the preparation of special educators. These standards are listed in each chapter as they relate to the content within the chapter. The standards that apply to Chapter 4 are Standards #3, #5, and #6.

CEC Initial Preparation Standard #3: Curricular Content Knowledge (partial)

3.0 Beginning special education professionals use knowledge of general and specialized curricula to individualize learning for individuals with exceptionalities.

CEC Initial Preparation Standard #5: Instructional Planning and Strategies (partial)

5.1 Beginning special education professionals consider an individual's abilities, interests, learning environments, and cultural and linguistic factors in the selection, development, and adaptation of learning experiences for individuals with exceptionalities.

5.2 Beginning special education professionals use technologies to support instructional assessment, planning, and delivery for individuals with exceptionalities.

5.3 Beginning special education professionals are familiar with augmentative and alternative communication systems and a variety of assistive technologies to support the communication and learning of individuals with exceptionalities.

CEC Initial Preparation Standard #6: Professional Learning and Ethical Practice (partial)

6.3 Beginning special education professionals understand that diversity is a part of families, cultures, and schools, and that complex human issues can interact with the delivery of special education services.

REFERENCES

Allen, K. D., Wallace, D. P., Renes, D., Bowen, S. L., & Burke, R. V. (2010). Use of video modeling to teach vocational skills to adolescents and young adults with autism spectrum disorders. *Education and Treatment of Children, 33*(3), 339–349.

Alliance for Technology Access (2005). Software features. Retrieved from www.ataccess.org

Anderson-Inman, L. (2009). Supported eText: Literacy scaffolding for students with disabilities. *Journal of Special Education Technology, 24*(3), 1–7.

Anderson-Inman, L., & Horney, M. A. (2007). Supported eText: Assistive technology through text transformations. *Reading Research Quarterly, 42*(1), 153–160.

Ashton, T. M., & Hall, K. S. (2000). What to do when technology disrupts your teaching: Suggested Activities and troubleshooting steps for teachers using technology. *Journal of Special Education Technology Practice, 2*(4), 15–20.

Batorowicz, B., Missiuna, C. A., & Pollock, N. A. (2012). Technology supporting written productivity in children with learning disabilities: A critical review. *Canadian Journal of Occupational Therapy, 79*(4), 211–224.

Boisvert, P., & Rao, K. (2015). Video self-modeling for English Language Learners. *TESOL Journal, 6*(1), 36–58.

Bouck, E. C. (2010). Technology and students with disabilities: Does it solve all the problems. In F. E. Obiakor, J. P. Bakken, & A. F. Rotatori (Eds.), *Current issues and trends in special education: Research technology, and teacher preparation* (Vol. 20, pp. 91–104), Bradford, England: Emerald.

Bouck, E. C. (2016). A national snapshot of assistive technology for students with disabilities. *Journal of Special Education Technology, 31*(1), 4–13.

Bouck, E. C., Maeda, Y., & Flanagan, S. (2012). Assistive technology and students with high incidence disabilities: Understanding the relationship through the National

Longitudinal Transition Study-2. *Remedial and Special Education, 33*, 298–308.

Burton, C. E., Anderson, D. H., Prater, M. A., & Dyches, T. T. (2013). Video self-modeling on an iPad to teach functional math skills to adolescents with autism and intellectual disability. *Focus on Autism and Other Developmental Disabilities, 28*(2), 67–77.

Carnahan, C. R., Basham, J. D., Christman, J., & Hollingshead, A. (2012). Overcoming challenges: "Going mobile with your own video models." *TEACHING Exceptional Children, 45*(2), 50–59.

Charlop, M. H., Dennis, B., Carpenter, M. H., & Greenberg, A. L. (2010). Teaching socially expressive behaviors to children with autism through video modeling. *Education and Treatment of Children, 33*(3), 371–393.

Chen, C.-H., (2007). Cultural diversity in instructional design for technology-based education. *British Journal of Educational Technology, 38*(6), 1113–1116.

Creer, T. L., & Miklich, D. R. (1970). The application of a self-modeling procedure to modify inappropriate behavior: A preliminary report. *Behaviour Research and Therapy, 8*, 91–92.

Edyburn, D. L. (1998). A map of the technology integration process. *Closing the Gap, 16*(6), 1, 6, 40.

Edyburn, D. L. (2000). Assistive technology and mild disabilities. *Focus on Exceptional Children, 32*(9), 1–24.

Edyburn, D. L., Higgins, K., & Boone, R. (2005). *Handbook of special education technology research and practice.* Whitefish Bay, WI: Knowledge by Design.

Golden, D. (1999). Assistive technology policy and practice: What is the right thing to do? What is the reasonable thing to do? What is required and must be done? *Journal of Special Education Technology Practice, 1*(1), 12–14.

Greer, D., Rice, M., & Dykman, B. (2014). Reviewing a decade (2004–2014) of published, peer-reviewed research on online learning and students with disabilities.

In R. E. Ferdig & K. Kennedy (Eds.), *Handbook of research on K–12 online and blended learning* (pp. 135–159). Pittsburg, PA: Entertainment Technology Center, Carnegie Mellon University.

Greer, D., Rowland, A. L., & Smith, S. J. (2014). Critical considerations for teaching students with disabilities in online environments. *TEACHING Exceptional Children, 46*(5), 79–91.

Hashey, A. I., & Stahl, S. (2014). Making online learning accessible for students with disabilities. *TEACHING Exceptional Children, 46*(2), 70–78.

Hitchcock, C. H., Prater, M. A., & Dowrick, P. W. (2004). Reading fluency and comprehension: The effects of tutoring and video self-modeling on first grade students with reading difficulties. *Learning Disabilities Quarterly, 27*, 89–103.

Hourcade, J. J., Parette, H. P., & Huer, M. B. (1997). Family and cultural alert: Considerations in assistive technology assessment. *TEACHING Exceptional Children, 30*(1), 40–44.

Israel, M., Marino, M., Delisio, L., & Serianni, B. (2014). *Supporting content learning through technology of K-12 students with disabilities* (Document No. IC-10). Retrieved from http://ceedar.education.ufl.edu/wp-content/uploads/2014/09/IC-10_FINAL_09-10-14.pdf

Jeffs, T., & Morrison, W. F. (2005). Special education technology addressing diversity? A synthesis of the literature. *Journal of Special Education Technology, 20*(4), 19–25.

Kemp, C. E., & Parette, H. P. (2000). Barriers to minority family involvement in assistive technology decision-making processes. *Education and Training in Mental Retardation and Developmental Disabilities, 35*, 384–392.

Kennedy, M. J., & Deshler, D. D. (2010). Literacy instruction, technology, and students with learning disabilities: Research we have, research we need. *Learning Disability Quarterly, 33*, 289–298.

King-Sears, M. E., & Evmenova, A. S. (2007). Premises, principles, and processes for integrating technology into instruction. *TEACHING Exceptional Children, 40*(1), 6–24.

Knight, V., McKissick, B. R., & Saunders, A. (2013). A review of technology-based interventions to teach academic skills to students with autism spectrum disorder. *Journal of Autism and Developmental Disabilities, 43*, 2628–2648.

Knight, V., Wood, C., Spooner, F., Browder, D., & O'Brien, C. (2015). An exploratory study using science etexts with students with autism spectrum disorder. *Research in Autism Spectrum Disorders, 30*(2), 86–99.

Molnar, A. (1997). Computers in education: A brief history. *THE Journal.* Retrieved from http://thejournal.com/Articles/1997/06/01/Computers-in-Education-A-Brief-History.aspx?Page=2

Molnar, A., M., Miron, G., Huerta, L., King Rice, J., Cuban, L., Horvitz, B., . . . Shafer, S. (2013, May). *Virtual schools in the U.S. 2013: Politics, performance, policy, and research evidence.* Boulder, CO: National Education Policy Center. Retrieved from http://nepc.colorado.edu/files/nepc-virtual-2013.pdf

Office of Technology Assessment. (1995). *Teachers and technology: Making the connection.* Washington, DC: U.S. Government Printing Office. Retrieved from http://www.wws.princeton.edu:80/~ota/disk1/1995/9541_n.html

Ortiz, J., Burlingame, C., Onuegbulem, C., Yoshikawa, K., & Rojas, E. D. (2012). The use of video self-modeling with English Language Learners: Implications for success. *Psychology in the Schools, 49*(1), 23–29.

Parette, P. (1999). Transition and assistive technology planning with families across cultures. *Career Development for Exceptional Individuals, 22*, 213–231.

Parette, H. P., Huer, M. B., & Scherer, M. (2004). Effects of acculturation on assistive technology service delivery. *Journal of Special Education Technology, 19*(2), 31–41.

Parette, P., & McMahan, G. A. (2002). What should we expect of assistive technology: Being sensitive to family goals. *TEACHING Exceptional Children, 35*(1), 56–61.

Parette, P., VanBiervliet, A., & Hourcade, J. J. (2000). Family-centered decision making in assistive technology. *Journal of Special Education Technology, 15*(1), 45–55.

Patrick, S., Kennedy, K., & Powell, A. (2013). *Mean what you say: Defining and integrating personalized, blended and competency education.* Vienna, VA: iNACOL.

Pennington, R. C., (2010). Computer-assisted instruction for teaching academic skills to students with autism spectrum disorders: A review of literature. *Focus on Autism and Other Developmental Disabilities, 25*(4), 239–248.

Powell, S. (2014). Choosing iPad apps with a purpose: Aligning skills and standards. *TEACHING Exceptional Children, 47*(1), 20–26.

Prater, M. A., Carter, N., Hitchcock, C. H., Dowrick, P. W. (2011). Video self-modeling to improve academic performance: A literature review. *Psychology in the Schools, 49*(1), 71–81.

Rayner, C., Denholm, C., & Sigafoos, J. (2009). Video-based intervention for individuals with autism: Key questions that remain unanswered. *Research in Autism Spectrum Disorders, 3*, 291–303.

Roblyer, M. D. (2003). *Integrating educational technology into teaching* (3rd ed.). New York, NY: Pearson.

Schwab Learning. (2003). *Assistive technology guide* (3rd ed.). San Mateo, CA: Author.

Seo, Y.-J., Woo, H. (2010). The identification, implementation, and evaluation of critical user interface design features of computer-assisted instruction programs in mathematics for students with learning disabilities. *Computers & Education, 55*, 565–377.

Shadiev, R., Hwang, W.-Y., Chen, N.-S., & Huang, Y.-M. (2014). Review of speech-to-text recognition technology for enhancing learning. *Educational Technology & Society, 17*(4), 65–84.

Smith, S. J., & Basham, J. D. (2014). Designing online learning opportunities for students with disabilities. *TEACHING Exceptional Children, 46*(5), 127–137.

Tonks, D., Weston, S., Wiley, D., & Barbour, M. K. (2013). "Opening" a new kind of high school: The story of the open high school of Utah. *The International Review of Research in Open and Distance Learning, 14*(1), 255–271.

Wang, M. (2007). Designing online courses that effectively engage learners from diverse cultural backgrounds. *British Journal of Educational Technology, 38*(2), 294–311.

Weng, P.-L., Maeda, Y., & Bouck, E. C. (2014). Effectiveness of cognitive skills-based computer-assisted instruction for students with disabilities: A synthesis. *Remedial and Special Education, 35*(3), 167–180.

Weng, P.-L., Savage, M. N., & Bouck, E. C. (2014). iDIY: Video-based instruction using iPads. *TEACHING Exceptional Children, 47*(1), 11–19.

Yell, M. L. (2016). *The law and special education* (4th ed.). Boston, MA: Pearson.

Zabala, J. S. (2005). The SETT Framework: Critical areas to consider when making informed assistive technology decisions. Retrieved from http://www.joyzabala.com

⑤SAGE edge™ • ●

Review ➡ Practice ➡ Improve

Get the tools you need to sharpen your study skills. Access videos, practice quizzes, eFlashcards and more at **edge.sagepub.com/prater.**

©iStockphoto.com/monkeybusinessimages

Assessment for Instruction

Ms. Georgio is preparing a unit on mammals. She knows she needs to create not only the instructional components of her unit, but she needs to decide how she can best assess her students' knowledge about what they learned. She hasn't decided if she should ask students to complete an end-of-the-unit paper-and-pencil test, create a written project, and/or give an oral presentation.

Terrance, a new student transferring in the middle of the year, is assigned to Mr. Jacobowski's third-grade class. Mr. Jacobowski isn't certain where Terrance should be placed in the reading curriculum. He decides to assess his reading ability so that he can be taught at an appropriate instructional level.

Mrs. Horrocks is concerned about Aggie, one of her seventh-grade students. Aggie is not progressing as quickly as other students in her English class. She appears to have some reading and writing problems, although Mrs. Horrocks is not certain what they are. She's considering referring Aggie to be assessed for special education services.

Learning Objectives

- Compare and contrast types of assessment by their function, frequency, formality, and the types of knowledge/skills being assessed.

- Provide an argument for and against the use of standardized tests, including high-stakes accountability assessment. In the argument, provide examples of different types of standardized tests.

- Describe examples in which curriculum-based assessment and behavioral observation assessment would be appropriate. Include all forms of observational recording systems.

- Explain how cultural and/or linguistic diversity can impact the use of assessment and how teachers can work toward reducing or eliminating test bias.

Assessment is a major classroom tool used by teachers every day. Teachers use assessment in the form of tests and other formal and informal formats to make educational decisions such as identifying a student for special education services, placing a student at the appropriate level in the curriculum, or assigning final grades. Teachers of students with high-incidence disabilities (HID) need specialized knowledge and skills in appropriate assessment tools to ensure their students are afforded an appropriate education.

Assessment encompasses the administration of standardized normative and criterion referenced tests, informal inventories, curriculum-based assessment, observations, interviews, and checklists. Authentic assessment generally involves student demonstration of knowledge through performance, products, or exhibits. Examples of authentic assessment include writing samples, scientific experiments, and a speech written and delivered by the student.

Types and Purposes of Assessment

Teachers need a clear understanding of terminology used when discussing assessment. For example, assessment is not testing. Assessment is the process of using any tool or technique to measure student performance and behavior to make educational decisions. **Testing** is the administration of a predetermined set of questions or tasks for which predetermined responses (e.g., correct answers) are sought (Salvia, Ysseldyke, & Bolt, 2013). Tests produce some form of numerical results, such as a score or set of scores. Testing is a subset of assessment. Other types of assessment tools exist, such as observations or interviews. All of these may be referred to as assessment tools.

Assessment may be categorized by four attributes. Assessment tools vary by (1) purpose and how the information will be used (function or reference), (2) how often the assessment occurs (frequency), (3) the formality of the procedures (formality), and (4) the type of knowledge or skill being assessed (knowledge or skill). Each is described in more detail.

Assessment by Function or Reference Point

Teachers use assessment in schools for a variety of purposes. The function of the assessment is usually defined by the purpose for assessing. When teachers assess, they compare one student's performance against (a) another student or group of students, (b) the same student's previous performance, (c) a large domain of knowledge, and/or (d) a specific standard or benchmark.

Another way of conceptualizing the function of assessment is by the reference point. Educators typically refer to tests as being norm-referenced, criterion-referenced, standards-referenced, or domain-referenced. **Norm-referenced assessment** is used to identify an individual's performance relative to a group of individuals. Most of the tests administered to identify eligibility for special education, for example, are norm-referenced. These tests receive this label because they have been designed and standardized based on the performance of a normative group. Norm-referenced tests provide important information, but are limited in guiding the development of an Individualized Education Program (IEP) or instruction. Another limitation is the restrictiveness with which the information can be interpreted. That is, the results reflect an individual's performance only in relationship to the sample of the population used in standardizing the test. If students with disabilities, for example, were not used in the original standardized sample, it would be inappropriate to compare a student with a disability's score with those who do not have disabilities. If Mrs. Horrocks decides to refer Aggie for special education assessment, most of the tests administered will be norm-referenced.

Criterion-referenced assessment or standards-referenced assessment indicates a student's performance relative to a specified criterion level or standard. Scores are reported as whether or not the student met the criterion or standard (e.g., pass or fail) or by the number of correct and incorrect responses. Performance on these tests usually refers directly back to the content being taught. Thus, they are more helpful than norm-referenced tests to classroom teachers designing instruction. With **domain-referenced tests**, representative questions or performances are selected from a larger domain of skills or knowledge. A student's performance on a domain-referenced test is usually reported as a percentage. Assuming the knowledge and skills being assessed are aligned with the curriculum, domain-referenced tests can also be a helpful tool for the teacher. See Table 5.1 for more information about each type of test. These categories are not restrictive to one another. For example, a test can be both norm-referenced and domain-referenced. Most published achievement tests may be characterized as both. Ms. Georgio's assessment given at the end of the unit on mammals will be

TABLE 5.1   Types of Assessment by Function or Reference

Type of Assessment	Purpose	Questions Selected Usually Based on	Scores Usually Reported as	Useful for	Less Useful for	Examples
Norm-Referenced	To indicate an individual's performance relative to a group of individuals	Those which discriminate among individuals (maximizes variability)	An individual's place in the group distribution	Competitive situations Grading on a curve Identifying students who qualify for special education	Instruction	Standardized achievement tests IQ Tests
Criterion- or Standards-Referenced	To indicate an individual's performance relative to a specified criterion level or standard	Curriculum being taught and/or state/district standards	Pass/fail or number correct and incorrect	Determining whether student met a standard Instruction Repeatable	Ranking students Generalization	Teacher made tests State graduation tests
Domain-Referenced	To estimate students' skills or knowledge on all content	Representativeness of the domain of skills or knowledge	Percent of responses correct	Needing to test "everything" Instruction Repeatable Generalization	Specific skill information	End of unit tests

domain-referenced. Mr. Jacobowski's assessment of Terrance's reading level may be characterized as criterion- or standards-based assessment.

Assessment by Frequency

The second attribute of assessment tools is the frequency with which they are administered. Most people think of tests as those administered at the end of instruction. This is called **summative assessment** and these tools demonstrate how much a student has learned. Ms. Georgio's assessment is a good example of summative assessment. In contrast, **formative assessment** is administered frequently and while learning is still occurring. Formative assessment provides teachers with much more information than summative assessment because the former allows teachers to adjust their instruction to assist students in the learning process. Formative assessment will be discussed in more detail later in the chapter. Definitions and examples of summative and formative assessment may be found in Table 5.2.

TABLE 5.2   Assessment Classifications

Assessment Classifications	Definition	Examples of Purposes	Examples
Summative	One-time assessment reflected by the collection of student performance data AFTER instruction has occurred	Determine how well the student learned the content Assign end of term grades	End of the unit test Final exams
Formative	Ongoing frequent assessment reflected by the collection of student performance data WHILE instruction is occurring	Determine whether student is progressing from day to day Determine the effectiveness of the instruction for the individual student	Timed tests on math facts Oral reading passages
Formal	Assessment is formal when tools are used that are standardized. Standardization is based on selection of materials and the administration, scoring, and interpretation of results.	Determine eligibility for special education services Determine specific functioning levels Determine whether student meets state standards for graduation Quantitative observation data required	IQ tests Achievement tests Formal behavior observations Standardized checklists
Informal	Assessment is informal when tools are used that include some, but not all, elements of standardization.	Screening for potential referral for formal assessment Classroom-based decisions	End of the chapter tests Work samples Anecdotal observations
Curriculum-Based	Assessing content directly from the curriculum being taught using materials and procedures used during instruction	Determine whether specific instructional goals have been met Monitor progress through the curriculum	End of chapter test Curriculum-based measurement Portfolio assessment
Behavioral	Direct observation of student behavior	Determine student behavior and interaction patterns	Anecdotal report of 10-minute observation ABC analysis Functional Behavioral Assessment

Assessment by Formality

Educators often differentiate between formal and informal assessment, the third attribute by which assessment tools can be categorized. The formality of assessment, however, may best be conceptualized as a continuum with the degrees of formality based on administration and standardization procedures as well as the purpose for the assessment.

The main factor that differentiates formal from informal assessment is the degree to which the assessment is done in a prescribed and predetermined fashion. **Formal assessment** involves preidentified test items and/or observation procedures and must be administered using standardized procedures. **Informal assessments** do not necessarily involve preidentified items nor use standardized administration or observation procedures. Usually formal assessment requires students to participate in an activity (e.g., taking a pencil/paper achievement test) in which they normally would not participate so that an examiner can observe or score their performance. Conversely, effective teachers embed informal assessment as part of their daily and weekly instructional routine in activities such as verbal reading comprehension questions or daily math assignments.

Special educators engage in both formal and informal assessment. They might use, for example, informal assessment to screen students for potential referral for formal assessment or to make classroom-based decisions, and formal assessments for activities such as determining whether a student is eligible for special education services or meets state standards for graduation. Both formal and informal assessment can be used to compare a student against other students, his previous performance, or a standard.

Another term often used is *standardized testing*. Standardization refers to structuring test materials, administration procedures, scoring methods, and procedures for interpreting results. Standardization makes it possible to give, score, and interpret tests in a controlled manner that minimizes erratic, unpredictable results. This helps to ensure accuracy and consistency in measuring progress, determining levels of performance, and comparing performance to others (Venn, 2014, pp. 57–58).

Formal tests are standardized. Informal tests may include some but not all elements of standardization. Additional detail about formal and informal assessment may be found in Table 5.2.

TEACHER TIP #5.1

DAILY ENTRANCE AND EXIT SLIPS

Students can be informally assessed by asking them to answer specific questions as they enter the classroom and as they leave the classroom. As a preassessment, teachers can get a sense of students' prerequisite knowledge before instruction commences. At the end of class, teachers can use a similar process to gauge what students have learned. Entrance and exit slips don't always need to be written or done individually. Students can work in pairs or small groups and respond in writing, orally, or through demonstration (Joseph et al., 2014).

Assessment by Knowledge and/or Skills Being Assessed

The fourth assessment tool attribute involves the knowledge and/or skills being assessed and includes curriculum-based assessment and behavioral assessment. **Curriculum-based assessment** implies that the student is being assessed on the curriculum being taught in the classroom. Behavioral assessment refers to the direct observation of student behavior. Special educators most frequently engage in these two forms of assessment. Therefore, curriculum-based and behavioral assessment are addressed in more detail later in this chapter. A brief comparison may be found in Table 5.2.

Standardized Tests

Standardized tests have structured materials and systematic procedures for the administration, scoring, and interpretation of results. School employees who administer standardized tests need to be trained in administrative procedures. In most schools, school psychologists or certified school personnel administer individualized standardized tests. Anyone administering standardized tests needs appropriate training to do so.

Many commercially prepared standardized tests are available. First, two major categories of standardized tests are discussed—namely, **intelligence tests** and achievement tests. But before doing so, teachers must understand three basic characteristics related to standardized tests—norms, reliability, and validity.

Standardization Characteristics

Norms

Typically **standardized tests** compare one student's performance against a group of students. In order to make this comparison possible, the test must be taken by a group of students usually called *the norm* or *standardization sample*. How well the individual student's performance can be compared against the group hinges on the characteristics of the norm sample. For example, if intelligence is being measured and the norm group consisted only of students enrolled in a gifted and talented program, an average student may score within the intellectual disabilities range. Norm groups are generally based on the population at large. Proportional representation of the norm sample across the following characteristics is important: gender, age, grade, intelligence, geographic location, and sociocultural considerations (e.g., acculturation of parents, race, and cultural identity) (Salvia et al., 2013). Test developers must also ensure that the normative data provided is consistently updated inasmuch as the population is constantly fluctuating. Normative information should be provided in the test's manual and should be investigated prior to selection of the test.

Reliability

When teachers assess they would like to generalize the results in three ways. They want to assume that the same results would be obtained (a) if the student were given similar but different test questions, (b) if the test were given at a different time (e.g., tomorrow or next week), and (c) if any other qualified examiner administered the test (Salvia et al., 2013). Reliability helps us determine the degree to which these generalizations can be made.

Reliability is defined as the degree of accuracy and consistency of test scores or other assessment measures and is usually reported using a statistic called a reliability coefficient (r) which can vary in value from 0 to 1.00. If $r = 0$, that means there is a total lack of reliability, whereas $r = 1.0$ connotes perfect reliability. In general, reliability coefficients should exceed $r = .90$ in order for the measure to have adequate reliability (Venn, 2014).

Reliability is determined in several ways. When evaluating test–retest reliability the test is administered twice to the same group of individuals and the resulting scores used to calculate a reliability coefficient. Alternate-form reliability is similar except that two forms of the same test are administered to the same group of individuals and a reliability coefficient is computed using the two sets of scores. Split-half reliability involves correlating two halves of the same test. The test is administered only once to the same group. The test items are divided in half and the scores on the halves are compared against one another to estimate reliability (Venn, 2014). Reliability coefficients and the manner in which they were determined should be available in test manuals.

Another form of reliability is interrater or interobserver reliability. This form of reliability is determined when two observers directly listen and/or watch a student and the observers' scores are compared. Some professionals prefer to call this *interrater* or *interobserver agreement* because agreement, rather than reliability, better reflects what is being calculated. The following formula is usually used: Number of agreements/(number of agreements + disagreements) × 100 = percentage of agreement.

Validity

When engaging in assessment, teachers need assurance that they are actually measuring what they think they are measuring. **Validity** is defined as the degree to which the assessment instrument measures what it was designed to measure. Validity is considered the most important technical characteristic of assessment. Assessment instruments can be reliable without being valid, but they cannot be valid without being reliable.

Several forms of validity exist. First, content validity is the degree to which a test covers the domain being assessed. Second, face validity involves whether the measure appears valid on the surface. Third, criterion-referenced validity can be either predictive or concurrent. With predictive validity the question is raised as to how well the test scores predict future behavior. Concurrent validity relates to how well the scores from this test correlate with scores from a valid test in the same content area. A fourth type of validity is construct validity. This refers to how well the instrument assesses the theoretical underpinnings that it was designed to measure (Venn, 2014). As with norms and reliability, validity information should be available in test manuals.

Types of Standardized Tests

Intelligence Tests

The most commonly used intelligence tests used in schools are the *Wechsler Intelligence Scale for Children, 5th Edition* (WISC-V; Wechsler, 2014) and the *Stanford-Binet Intelligence Scale, 5th Edition* (Roid, 2003). Details regarding each may be found in Table 5.3. The *Wechsler Adult Intelligence Scales, 4th Edition* (WAIS-IV) is normed for individuals ages 16+ and is often used in secondary schools (Wechsler, 2008) while the *Batería III Woodcock-Muñoz* (Woodcock, Muñoz-Sandoval, McGrew, & Mather, 2004) is used to assess general intelligence of Spanish-speaking students. Two additional tests are detailed in Table 5.3, the *Test of Nonverbal Intelligence, 4th Edition* (TONI-4; Brown, Shervenou, & Johnsen, 2010) and the *Universal Nonverbal Intelligence Test* (UNIT; Bracken & McCallum, 2015). Both are designed to estimate intelligence using nonverbal measures and are particularly appropriate for students who have difficulty responding verbally or who are negatively impacted by language-loaded tests.

Academic/Achievement Tests

Academic or **achievement tests** measure student performance on knowledge and skills typically taught in school such as reading and mathematics. Schools conduct group administration of academic or achievement tests to all students at least once a year. The use of these tests has increased given the amplified interest and focus on school accountability. Students being identified for or currently receiving special education services are given individually administered tests in the appropriate academic areas. For example, a student referred for written language difficulties may be administered the *Test of Written Language, 4th Edition* (TOWL-4; Hammill & Larsen, 2009) whereas a student receiving special education services for math may be given the *Key-Math 3 Diagnostic*

TABLE 5.3   A Sample of Intelligence Tests

Name	Age Range	Content Covered	Basic Characteristics
Batería III Woodcock-Muñoz (Woodcock, Muñoz-Sandoval, McGrew, & Mather, 2004)	2–90+ years	Fluid reasoning, processing speed, memory, visual-spatial, knowledge, and bilingual	Norm-referenced Administered Spanish language
Stanford-Binet Intelligence Scale, 5th Edition (SB-5; Roid, 2003)	2–85 years	Fluid reasoning, knowledge, quantitative reasoning, visual-spatial processing, and working memory	Norm-referenced Individually administered
Test of Nonverbal Intelligence, 4th Edition (TONI-4; Brown, Shervenou, & Johnsen, 2010)	6–89 years	Abstract reasoning and problem-solving	Norm-referenced Individually administered Language-free test
Universal Nonverbal Intelligence Test, 2nd Edition (UNIT 2; Bracken & McCallum, 2015)	5–21 years	Memory and reasoning subtests	Norm-referenced Individually administered Language-free test
Wechsler Adult Intelligence Scales, 4th Edition (WAIS-IV; Wechsler, 2008)	16–90 years	Verbal comprehension, perceptual reasoning, working memory, and processing speed	Norm-referenced Individually administered
Wechsler Intelligence Scale for Children, 5th Edition (WISC-V; Wechsler, 2014)	6–16 years	Verbal comprehension, visual-spatial processing, working memory, fluid reasoning, and processing speed	Norm-referenced Individually administered

Assessment (Connolly, 2007). Several tests such as the *Comprehensive Inventory of Basic Skills, 2nd Edition* (Brigance, 2010) and the *Woodcock-Johnson IV Tests of Achievement* (Schrank, Mather, & McGrew, 2014) assess a wide range of academic skills. A sample list of academic/achievement tests with additional detail may be found in Table 5.4.

TABLE 5.4   **A Sample of Academic Tests**

Name	Purpose	Grade or Age Levels	Content Covered	Basic Characteristics
Aprenda: La Prueba de Logros en Espanol, Tercera Edicion (2008)	To assess academic skills of Spanish-speaking students	K–12th grade	Reading, math, language, and listening Optional: writing and English	Norm-referenced Individually administered Spanish language
Batería III Woodcock-Muñoz (Woodcock, Muñoz-Sandoval, McGrew, & Mather, 2004)	To assess academic achievement of Spanish-speaking students	K–12th grade	Reading, oral language, math, and written language	Norm-referenced Individually administered Spanish Language
Comprehensive Inventory of Basic Skills, 2nd Edition (Brigance, 2010)	To assess specific academic skills May be used to develop IEPs and monitor student progress.	K–9th grade	Reading, listening, spelling, writing, and math	Curriculum-based Individually administered
Dynamic Indicators of Basic Early Literacy Skills (DIBELS) (Good et al., 2011)	To assess and progress monitor reading skills	K–6th grade	Phonemic awareness, alphabetic principle, accuracy, fluency, reading comprehension, and vocabulary	Curriculum-based Individually administered
Gray Oral Reading Tests, 5th Edition (GORT-5; Wiederhold & Bryant, 2012)	To screen reading proficiency	6–23 years	Oral reading, reading comprehension	Norm-referenced Individually administered
Iowa Tests of Basic Skills (ITBS; Hoover, Dunbar, & Frisbie, 2005)	To screen basic academic skills	K–8th grade	Reading comprehension, word analysis, vocabulary, listening, math, language, social studies, and science	Norm-referenced Group administered

(Continued)

TABLE 5.4   (Continued)

Name	Purpose	Grade or Age Levels	Content Covered	Basic Characteristics
Kaufman Test of Educational Achievement, 3rd Edition (KTEA-3; Kaufman & Kaufman, 2014)	To screen or assess academic achievement	4–25 years	Reading, math, written language, and oral language	Norm-referenced Individually administered
Key-Math 3 Diagnostic Assessment (Connolly, 2007)	To assess mathematics achievement	K–12th grade	Basic math concepts, operations, and applications	Norm-referenced Individually administered
TerraNova SUPERA (2011)	To assess academic skills of Spanish-speaking students	K–12th grade	Reading, language arts, and math	Norm-referenced Group administered Spanish language
Test of Written Language, 4th Edition (TOWL-4; Hammill & Larsen, 2009)	To assess written expression	9–17 years	Spontaneous and contrived written expression	Norm-referenced Individual or group administration
Wechsler Individual Achievement Test, 3rd Edition (WIAT-III; Wechsler, 2009)	To assess achievement for diagnostic academic achievement	4–50 years	Oral language, listening, written expression, reading, and math	Norm-referenced Individually administered
Woodcock-Johnson IV Tests of Achievement (Schrank, Mather, & McGrew, 2014)	To assess academic achievement	2–adults	Oral language, reading, math, spelling, and writing	Norm-referenced Individually administered

Social, Emotional, and Behavioral Assessment

Four types of assessment are typically used to measure social, emotional, and behavioral functioning: behavioral observation, interviewing, situational measures, and rating scales (Venn, 2014). Professionals often use a combination of these techniques. Behavioral observation, often the preferred assessment technique, is discussed in more length later in this chapter. Interviews are used to gain information about the perspectives of those familiar with the student and can fall somewhere across the continuums of structured/unstructured, as well as formal/informal. Interviews usually focus on the student's medical and educational history, academic performance and progress, social-emotional functioning, and community involvement. Situational measures involve peer-acceptance nomination scales and sociometric ranking techniques (e.g., sociograms). Both provide an indication of the student's social status within a specific group (e.g., classroom peers) and capture the attitude of others toward a particular student (Venn, 2014).

TEACHER TIP #5.2

CONDUCTING SOCIOGRAMS

To conduct a sociogram,

- ask students to identify their favorite classmates for work or play situations.

- evaluate the results by counting how often individual students were selected by their peers.

- use this information to strategically pair or group students.

- consider implementing an intervention, such as social skills instruction for students rarely or not selected by their peers.

The fourth type of social and emotional assessment involves rating scales. Behavior rating scales are typically completed by the classroom teacher, parent, and when appropriate, the student. Because the scales rely on the rater's judgment, teachers should not use them solely to make instructional decisions. Behavior rating scales can sometimes be problematic because their norms are based on a limited sample of the population and may present cultural and linguistic biases. For example, when the questions are translated verbally to a non-English speaker, the meanings can change which invalidates the instrument and results. Additionally, two students may respond differently on the same social skills assessment, not necessarily because their skills vary, but because of their social beliefs and values.

Some of the scales have been recently updated and are now available in languages other than English. In addition, some have included diverse populations in updating the norms. Depending upon the stated purpose of the rating scale, they can be used to help (a) identify students having difficulty, (b) identify a student as having a disability, or (c) provide instructional guidance. Examples of Rating Scales are listed in Table 5.5.

Assessment in the Classroom

Much of what has been discussed to this point involves assessment that usually occurs outside of the classroom setting. Most of the remainder of the chapter is devoted to assessments teachers use frequently within the classroom, namely, curriculum-based assessment and behavioral assessment.

Curriculum-Based Assessment

Teachers using curriculum-based assessment (CBA) align their assessment tools to the curriculum or content they are teaching. In CBA, the actual curriculum materials used for instruction are also used for assessment and the direct observation and recording of student performance on a CBA is used to make instructional decisions. CBA can be formal or informal, standards- or domain-referenced, and summative or formative and can take many forms such as authentic or real-life tasks, curriculum-based measurement, educational games, interviews, observations, portfolios, presentations, self-assessment, simulations, student journals, tests, written products, and so forth. Examples of CBA and how each may be characterized may be found in Table 5.6. Curriculum-based measurement and portfolio assessment are examples of CBA that require additional explanation.

TABLE 5.5   Sample of Social and Behavior Rating Scales

Name	Purpose	Content	Respondent(s)	Age Range	Basic Considerations
Achenbach System of Empirically Based Assessment (Achenbach, 2009)	Identify emotional or behavioral problems	Anxiety, depression, somatic complaints, social problems, attention problems, rule-breaking behavior, and aggressive behavior	Parent, teacher, child	$1^1/_2$–90	Translation in 100 languages Multicultural scoring options
Behavior Assessment System for Children, 3rd Edition (BASC-3; Reynolds & Kamphaus, 2015)	Identify emotional, behavioral, social, or adaptive concerns	Externalizing problems, internalizing problems, learning problems, social skills, and adaptability	Parent, teacher, child	2–21	Spanish forms available Web-based or paper administration Screening option available
Behavioral and Emotional Rating Scale, 2nd Edition (BERS-2; Epstein, 2004)	Identify behavioral and emotional strengths and weaknesses	Interpersonal strength, family involvement, intrapersonal strength, school functioning, affective strength, and career strength	Parent, teacher, child	5–18	Separate norms for children diagnosed with emotional or behavioral disorders available
Conners Rating Scale, 3rd Edition (Conners, 2008)	Identify ADHD and other disorders	Inattention, hyperactivity, impulsivity, learning problems, executive functioning, defiance, aggression, and peer relations	Parent, teacher, child	6–18	Score report linked to DSM-5 criteria Web-based or paper administration
Social Responsiveness Scale, 2nd Edition (SRS-2; Constantino & Gruber, 2012)	Identify and evaluate social impairments within the autism spectrum (from nonexistent to severe)	Social cognition, social awareness, social communication, social motivation, restricted interests, and repetitive behavior	Parent, teacher	2.5–18	Multiple forms to monitor symptoms across life span
Social Skills Improvement System Rating Scales (SSIS; Gresham & Elliott, 2008)	Evaluate social skills, problem behaviors, and academic competence	Social skills, problem behaviors, and academic competence	Parent, teacher, child	3–18	Spanish forms available Direct links to interventions

Name	Purpose	Content	Respondent(s)	Age Range	Basic Considerations
Vineland Adaptive Behavior Scales, 2nd Edition (Sparrow, Cicchetti, & Balla, 2005)	Measure adaptive behavior	Communication, daily skills, socialization, motor skills, and maladaptive behavior	Parent, teacher	Birth–90	Spanish forms available

TABLE 5.6 **Examples of Curriculum-Based Assessment**

Curriculum	Examples	Formal	Informal	Standards-Referenced	Domain-Referenced	Formative	Summative
Written Language	Daily formation of letters of the alphabet		X	X		X	
	Daily student journal writing		X	X		X	
	Weekly creative writing passages		X	X		X	
	End of the punctuation unit test		X	X	X		X
	Comprehensive Inventory of Basic Skills (Brigance, 2010)	X		X	X		X
Life Science	Daily matching correct vocabulary terms to definitions		X	X		X	
	Weekly assignments		X	X		X	
	End of the life science textbook chapter test		X		X		X
	State Graduation Test	X		X	X		X

Curriculum-Based Measurement

Ms. Mathys, a third-grade teacher, and Mr. Tumblemann, a special educator, team-teach for a portion of each day. They have arranged to train some fifth-grade students in tutoring and recording reading progress. Once trained, these students come to the third-grade classroom every day for 15 minutes. Each fifth-grade student is assigned two students. The third graders take turns orally reading as the fifth grader prompts and provides corrective feedback. Every Friday, the fifth-grade students collect and chart data on the third graders' reading progress.

Mr. Yeslam observes what is happening in Ms. Mathys's and Mr. Tumblemann's classroom and wants to initiate something similar in his classroom. After receiving training during a professional development conference, he decides to focus on math and implement curriculum-based measurement. After students have demonstrated they can accurately answer math computational problems, Mr. Yeslam wants to build their fluency or the ability to respond automatically. Every day following the math instructional period, the students complete as many problems as they can accurately on an individually prescribed worksheet within 1 minute. They then self-correct, self-record, and self-chart their performance as taught to do so previously by Mr. Yeslam. Mr. Yeslam reviews the charts every day and makes decisions about instruction based on these results.

Curriculum-based measurement (CBM) is a formal type of CBA. Teachers using CBM implement standard procedures including timed tests and charting of student performance. The focus is on fluency or the rate of performance over time. CBM can be distinguished from most forms of classroom assessment by the following factors. First, it is standardized. The behaviors to be measured and the procedures for measuring them are specified. Second, CBM is used over a long period of time with testing procedures and materials remaining constant. And third, each weekly test contains content that reflects performance desired by the end of the year (Fuchs, Fuchs, Hosp, & Hamlett, 2003). For example, Ms. Mathys and Mr. Tumblemann are using CBM to assess reading. They established a long-term goal for each student, that is, performance at a particular grade level. They then identified 30 reading passages of equivalent difficulty at that grade level. Each week the fifth-grade tutors administer one test by asking students to orally read from one passage for 1 minute. The number of words read correctly comprises the score and are graphed against time. Not only can this information provide formative or individual student growth information, but also within a normative framework, student performance at a given point in time can be compared with others to identify risk status (Fuchs et al., 2003).

Curriculum-based measurement scores can be used as a screening tool to identify students who need additional or different forms of instruction. Teachers can also use CBM scores to monitor students' academic progress, as well as to improve their instructional programs. Application of curriculum-based measurement has been researched across grade levels and content areas including reading (e.g., Christ, Silberglitt,

Yeo, & Cormier, 2010), math (e.g., Calhoon & Fuchs, 2003), written language (e.g., Lembke, Deno, & Hall, 2003), social studies (e.g., Beyers, Lembke, & Curs, 2013), and science (e.g., Vannest, Parker, & Dyer, 2011). Literacy and math CBMs have been studied more than other content areas. Literacy CBMs are often technically stronger than math CBMs, and most studies have applied CBMs at the elementary rather than the secondary level (e.g., Foegen, Jiban, & Deno, 2007; Wayman, Wallace, Wiley, Tichá, & Espin, 2007).

Technology Spotlight #5.1

Creating Electronic Quizzes

Creating and using electronic quizzes is an option for assessing classroom performance. The value of an electronic quiz from the teacher's perspective reveals many reasons why teachers should use them on a regular basis. Most quiz authoring tools are simple to use and involve basic skills such as keyboarding, copying and pasting, and saving. Essentially, teachers create a quiz the same way they normally would type a paper-based quiz. The palette of item formats varies by authoring tool, but the common formats include true/false, multiple choice, short answer (one or two words), and matching. After entering each item, the teacher indicates the correct answer. This facilitates electronic feedback and quiz scoring. As a result, the time a teacher spends creating an electronic quiz is amply repaid by eliminating time spent grading student papers.

The value of an electronic quiz can also be considered from the student's perspective. The primary advantage of electronic quizzes for struggling students is that they offer immediate feedback on their performance rather than waiting until the teacher has time to grade a quiz. For students who struggle with the writing aspect of test-taking, electronic quizzes can be more engaging. Finally, e-quizzes help focus student attention on key facts and concepts that a teacher feels they must know. As a result, regular use of electronic quizzes is likely to raise student test scores.

Access issues (i.e., cognition, alternative input, and screen readers) may arise with several common e-quiz tools. As a result, teachers may want to consider specialized software tools that can be used to make accessible quizzes and exams. In particular, these tools are ideal for developing multimedia exams that support struggling students:

- click on a word to hear it,

- click on a prompt to hear and see a definition of a word,

- click on a link to see a picture of the item, and

- click on a link to see a video clip.

One strategy for enhancing performance on tests is to provide students with adequate practice to check their understanding. Recent technology developments in e-quizzes have the potential to impact the technology toolkit of every teacher. To learn more about various e-quiz tools, visit the following sample websites:

ProProfs: www.proprofs.com

QuestionWriter: www.questionwriter.com

Quia: www.quia.com

Portfolio Assessment

Portfolio assessment has received increased attention in recent years. Although different authors define portfolio assessment in a myriad of ways, all have six elements in common. Portfolio assessment

- focuses on valued outcomes.

- requires tasks that are relevant to real life.

- encourages cooperation among students and teacher.

- requires evaluation of student work across multiple dimensions.

- establishes student reflection.

- integrates assessment and instruction. (Venn, 2014)

Spencer Salend (1998) describes six guidelines for using portfolios to assess student performance. These guidelines appear in Table 5.7. Before designing a portfolio assessment, teachers need to know the purpose for creating a portfolio, the most common of which are to (a) display students' best work, (b) show students' growth or progress, or (c) demonstrate the completion of a goal or benchmark. The contents of portfolios are determined by the teacher's purpose.

Teachers and students tend to organize portfolios chronologically by subject areas. A progress portfolio may be organized with work samples within subject areas side by side so viewers can see progress over time. When appropriate, students should have a major role in selecting their work and in preparing the self-reflections that become part of the portfolio (Davies, 2000). Student reflections can be verbal or written, but must be documented as a permanent product. Verbal reflections, then, should be audio recorded, video recorded, and/or dictated. Teachers may need to conference with students individually or in small groups to help them set reasonable goals and select appropriate artifacts for their portfolios (Hedin & Conderman, 2010).

Limited research has been conducted on portfolio assessment with students with disabilities. One study concluded that when self-assessment and self-reflection are taught as part of the portfolio assessment process, students with disabilities increase their internal locus of control or their perception of control over their environment (Ezell & Klein, 2003). Another study found that students with disabilities expressed more ownership, pride, and satisfaction with their portfolio while the teacher reported the students worked harder and actively chose more elements of the assignment (Thompson & Baumgartner, 2008).

Rubrics

Rubrics are typically used to evaluate forms of student work that are difficult to grade. They provide scoring criteria with a rating scale or checklist for evaluating the student product or performance. Rubrics include descriptors that serve as examples which help both the teacher and the student know what elements are being

TABLE 5.7 Guidelines for Using Portfolios to Assess Student Performance

Guidelines	Examples
1. Identify student goals appropriate for portfolio assessment.	• IEP annual goals • General education curriculum benchmarks
2. Determine the type of portfolio to be used.	• Showcase: Represents students' best work • Reflective: Facilitates understanding of various dimensions of student learning • Cumulative: Shows changes in student performance over time • Goal-based: Demonstrates progress or completion of preidentified goals • Process: Represents each element of a process with the last artifact being the final product
3. Establish portfolio organization and format.	• Organized by content areas, chronologically, or both • File folders, three ring binder, videotapes, CD, webpage
4. Select authentic products as artifacts for the portfolio.	• Written language samples • Audio and video recordings • Reports • Artwork • Classroom tests
5. Create a caption statement for each artifact.	• Identify the artifacts by goals, content area, dates, and so forth. • Include student reflection on why they selected the product, what they learned from it, how it differs from other products, and so forth.
6. Periodically review and evaluate the portfolios.	• Students present their portfolios to peers, teachers, parents, and/or other groups. • Formally evaluate the portfolio using rubrics or other tools.

Source: Adapted from S. J. Salend (1998).

used to evaluate the work (Venn, 2014). Rubrics can be either analytical or holistic. Analytical rubrics assess a product or performance by evaluating each essential feature. Holistic rubrics assess using an overall impression of the product or performance (Hall & Salmon, 2003). An example of a rubric used to evaluate written essays appears in Table 5.8.

TABLE 5.8   Example of a Rubric for Written Essays

Conceptual Level	Accuracy and Thoroughness	Writing
4. **Evaluation Level**—The student presents an evaluative judgment of the issue including evidence based on the processes of comparison, discrimination, interpretation, summarization, and conclusion.	4. The discussion is accurate, comprehensive, and thoroughly supported.	4. The essay is clearly organized (e.g., introduction, discussion, and conclusion). No more than 1 grammatical and/or spelling error.
3. **Analysis or Synthesis Level**— The student breaks the concepts into parts and discusses interrelationships then brings the parts together into a different, original, or new whole.	3. The discussion is accurate and most of the important relevant issues are addressed and well supported.	3. The essay is organized with few to no grammatical and/or spelling errors.
2. **Comprehension or Application Level**—The student grasps the meaning of the material and interprets it through paraphrasing and/or providing examples. Also demonstrates the ability to apply rules, methods, and theories in new situations.	2. Most relevant issues are addressed. The information provided is generally accurate and documented.	2. Some organization is evident. Few grammatical and/or spelling errors exist.
1. **Knowledge Level**—The student recalls previously learned knowledge of facts and theories	1. Few relevant issues are addressed. A number of inaccuracies exist. Some documentation is provided.	1. Organization is poor, and multiple grammatical and/or spelling errors exist.
Score:	**Score:**	**Score:**

TEACHER TIP #5.3

DEVELOPING RUBRICS

Use these steps to develop your own rubrics:

- Identify all the essential components of an exemplary response or performance.

- Develop a checklist of those essential components.

- Translate the list into descriptors of the task or project.

- Select the rubric format (e.g., analytic or holistic).

- Describe exemplary to poor levels of responding to the descriptors or components.

- Select the scale (4-point scale is recommended). (Hall & Salmon, 2003)

Although portfolios provide more instructional information than traditional standardized assessment data, the use of portfolios and rubrics are not without problems. The inconsistency and diversity in portfolio responses and artifacts can make them difficult to score (Bures, Barclay, Abrami, & Meyer, 2013). Also, the process of compiling and scoring portfolios is time consuming for students and teachers (Thompson & Baumgartner, 2008). In one study, portfolio reviewers expressed concerns that students may not see personal benefit in the process of creating a portfolio and do not always meaningfully engage in the reflective process (Diller & Phelps, 2008).

Technology Spotlight #5.2

Electronic Portfolios and Rubrics

Portfolios can take many forms, one of which is electronic. Electronic portfolios use digital technology, thereby allowing the student to collect and organize the artifacts in different media types, such as audio, video, graphics, and text. Electronic portfolios are advantageous in that they allow developers and evaluators to use databases or hyperlinks to demonstrate relationships between standards, goals, artifacts, and reflections.

Several tools are available to assist with developing electronic portfolios, including the following:

Online systems allow teachers to keep track of many students' work and have the advantage of creating profiles across student groups (e.g., www.taskstream.com, www.foliotek.com, www.digication.com).

PDF documents are used to store and display documents with or without graphics. These documents are considered "pictures" of pages and are easy to store and share (e.g., Adobe Acrobat).

Web pages may also be posted on the Internet. These pages can support sophisticated media presentations. (e.g., www.wix.com, www.squarespace.com)

Video can be used as either analog (low-cost and linear) or digital (more flexible and interactive) (e.g., Windows Movie Maker, iMovie).

Several Internet sites provide templates for teachers to develop their own rubrics. Here are a few:

- Rubistar: rubistar.4teachers.org
- iRubric: www.rcampus.com/indexrubric.cfm
- Common Core Rubric Creation Tool: www.essaytagger.com/commoncore/step3?rce_ids=400

Developing Formative Curriculum-Based Assessments

The most commonly used assessment tool by special educators is formative curriculum-based assessment. Teachers may apply curriculum-based measurement as discussed earlier, or teachers may develop their own formative CBA tools.

Margaret King-Sears (1994) created a succinct 5-step procedure for developing, implementing, and evaluating formative CBAs. The beginning letters of each step spell the word *APPLY*. Each step is described below.

1. *Analyze the curriculum.*

Regardless of the age or functional level of the students, the first step in developing a CBA is analysis of the curriculum. In this context, curriculum refers to the content being taught. Curriculum for students identified for special education services should be identified primarily through the IEP process. State curriculum guides and standards, as well as the scope and sequence of the content, should also be considered. The curriculum may involve academic, social, behavioral, and/or vocational content.

IEP annual goals and short-term objectives provide a framework for analyzing the curriculum. Teachers should use these goals and objectives to identify a target behavior. This may involve breaking the short-term objective into smaller portions.

A short-term objective for several students in Mrs. Timberlake's class reads as follows: *Given a written math word problem, the student will write the correct answer on 9 out of 10 problems.* Mrs. Timberlake decides that although the outcome of the objective is the correct answer, knowing how students arrived at the answer will assist with instruction. She breaks the objective into these parts: selecting the correct operation, selecting the correct numeric values, and computing the answer correctly.

2. *Prepare items to match curriculum objectives.*

The next step in the process is selecting or creating test items that match the objectives and sequencing them. The sequence may be random, or if the objective deals with completing a task in a specific sequence, then the items may include a checklist of the steps to be followed.

Mrs. Timberlake creates a large pool of math word problems that include varied operations and numeric values so that she can use them with a wide range of student abilities.

3. *Probe frequently.*

The frequency with which formative CBAs are administered may vary, but teachers usually administer CBAs at least weekly and oftentimes they administer them daily. The individual testing periods should be short periods of time. A formative CBA should not take more than 3 minutes for students to complete.

Every Monday, Wednesday, and Friday, Mrs. Timberlake assesses her students' skill on the objective. On these days, students are given eight math word problems at their level of difficulty. They write down the numeric values, operations, and show their computational work within the time period of 2 minutes.

4. *L*ood data using graphs.

Once data are collected, they are recorded on a graph. Then the visual display of their results can be interpreted. Graphing also provides students with motivation and responsibility for improving their own learning, which is discussed in more detail later in the chapter.

> After completing their word problems, students self-correct their answers using correction sheets provided by Mrs. Timberlake. She has taught the students to not only correct their own answers but to record their results on individual graphs, which they do next.

5. *Y*ield to results— revisions and decisions.

Data on student performance are not collected simply as an exercise in collecting data. This information must be analyzed to determine whether the student is progressing. If not, then changes in the instructional program need to occur. Specific decision rules and procedures are described later in the chapter. Based on student performance, the target behavior and/or the assessment tool may need to be revised.

> Mrs. Timberlake taught her students decision-making rules and procedures. If the rules and procedures indicate a change is warranted, they call it to Mrs. Timberlake's attention. Together they discuss whether in fact a change is needed and if so what kind of revision to make.

DIBELS

One curriculum-based assessment that is used prominently in schools and research programs is Dynamic Indicators of Basic Early Literacy Skills (DIBELS). **DIBELS** are a set of procedures and measures for assessing the acquisition of early literacy and math skills from kindergarten through sixth grade. With established benchmarks and cut scores, DIBELS can be administered to all students to identify students at-risk for academic difficulties. Typically, schools administer a DIBELS probe from one to three times a year to all students. In addition, teachers can administer progress-monitoring probes weekly to students receiving reading interventions to assess the effectiveness of the intervention and guide instructional decisions.

Indicadores Dinámicos del Éxito en la Lectura (IDEL) is similar to DIBELS, but based in the Spanish language. The IDEL measures are not a translation of the DIBELS measures, but rather take into account the linguistic structure of the Spanish language. Like DIBELS, the IDEL is a screening tool that includes instructional recommendations and benchmark goals. It provides teachers with information on student skills in the core components of beginning reading.

A growing evidence base exists for DIBELS. For example, predictive validity of DIBELS has been supported with various studies showing significant correlations between oral reading fluency scores in first grade and performance on state tests in third grade (Goffreda & DiPerna, 2010; Johnson, Jenkins, Petscher, & Catts, 2009; Munger & Blachman, 2013). However, a study by Amy Hoffman, Jeanne Jenkins, and S. Kay Dunlap (2009) mirrors a trend in the literature for polarized opinions about the effectiveness and use of DIBELS. Participants responded to a mail-in questionnaire about their perceptions of the advantages and disadvantages of DIBELS. While many respondents indicated that DIBELS is easy to use, identifies at-risk learners, and informs instruction, participants also stated that it took a lot of time to administer and some didn't find the results meaningful. For DIBELS to be effective, teachers need to be well trained not only in how to administer the assessment, but also how to use the data for progress monitoring and adapting instructional materials to meet student needs.

Behavioral Observation Assessment

In addition to curriculum-based assessment, special educators often engage in behavioral assessment in order to develop behavioral intervention plans designed to change student behavior and promote positive student outcomes. A behavioral assessment should include multiple sources of data across varying settings often including, but not limited to, observations of the student, interviews, and behavior rating scales. The first step in behavioral assessment is to identify the behavior that is impeding student performance in the classroom. Problem statements should be concrete, specific, observable, and targeted to one specific behavior (e.g., Jonathan talks out during class without raising his hand). Once the problem has been identified, data are collected to determine baseline levels of behavior as well as to inform intervention plans to target changes in student behavior. Special educators are often included in the behavior assessment process by collecting classroom data.

There are many different data collection methods for monitoring behavior in the classroom. The data collection procedure must be appropriate to the behavior being observed and the type of behavior change desired. Data collection efforts are implemented at the beginning of behavioral assessments and continue through the analysis and intervention processes to determine student progress.

Types of Data

The first step in behavioral assessment is selecting a system of data collection. The data collection procedure must be appropriate to the behavior being observed and the type of behavior change desired. The most common forms of data are frequency, duration, latency, and rate.

Frequency. The **frequency** of a behavior is the number of times the behavior occurred and involves tallying or counting the occurrences of the behavior within an observation period.

- Sharon kicked a classmate four times on Friday.

- Lillian wrote two of her 10 spelling words correctly.

- Juanita blurted out the answer eight times without raising her hand during 10 minutes.

- Zoe greeted a classmate saying, "Hi" three times during the lunch hour.

Not only is the observation period important to note (e.g., 10 minutes, 20 minutes, on Friday), but if the opportunities to engage in the behavior are limited, the number of opportunities should also be noted. For example, knowing Lillian wrote two spelling words correctly is not helpful unless the teacher also knows that she had the opportunity to write 10 words.

Duration. **Duration** is the length of time in which the student engages in the behavior.

- Hawley wrote in his journal for 6 minutes.

- Kamil's tantrum lasted 22 minutes.

- Irene worked with her peer tutor for 15 minutes.

- Ethan played by himself for 31 minutes before interacting with anyone else.

Duration is important when the amount of time a student engages in the behavior is more informative than the number of times the student engaged in the behavior.

Latency. Like duration, latency focuses on length of time. **Latency** refers to the length of time between when instructions or directions are given to perform and the occurrence of the behavior.

- After being provided the directions, Mackenzie took 9 minutes to start her assignment.

- After telling Connor to stop talking, it took him 4 minutes to get back to work.

- Meda was asked to take the class roll to the office and 6 minutes passed before she left the room.

- Thomas was instructed to begin orally reading but didn't start for 45 seconds.

Rate. The **rate** of behavior is the ratio of frequency over time. It is computed by dividing the number of times a behavior occurred by the length of the observation period. Converting frequencies to rate allows teachers to directly compare the frequencies. For example, if Mary read orally a 93-word passage in 3 minutes on Monday and a 68-word passage in 2 minutes on Tuesday, both can be converted to words read per minute (93/3 = 31 words a minute and 68/2 = 34 words a minute).

- Mason wrote 12 addition answers correctly per minute.

- Brandon raised his hand to answer a question 5.2 times per 50-minute class period.

- Carlos got out of his seat 0.3 times per minute.

- Jack worked on the computer 42 minutes per day.

Observational Recording Systems

Observational recording systems are used to record samples of the behavior while it is occurring. The most common observational recording systems include event recording, interval recording, time sampling, duration recording, latency recording, and ABC recording. For examples of observation forms for each see Figure 5.1.

FIGURE 5.1 **Examples of Observational Recording Systems**

Event Recording

Student: _____   Date: _____

Condition: _____

Behavior: _____

Class Period	Observation Period (Beginning and Ending Time)	Observer	Number of Occurrences	Total Number

Comments:

Interval Recording or Time Sampling

Student: _____   Date: _____

Observer: _____   Condition: _____

Behavior: _____

Time Intervals: _____

Date and Time	Intervals															Comments
	1	2	3	4	5	6	7	8	9	10	11	12	13	14	15	

Comments:

Duration Recording

Student: _____   Observer: _____

Behavior: _____

Date	Time Behavior Initiated	Time Behavior Ended	Duration

Comments:

Latency Recording

Student: _____   Observer: _____

Behavior: _____

Date	Time Instruction or Direction Given	Time Behavior Initiated	Latency

Comments:

Event recording. **Event recording** is used to record the frequency or number of times a behavior occurs. This is the most frequently used observational recording procedure and consists of tallying the number of times the behavior is observed within a specified period of time (e.g., 9:00–9:20 a.m. or during school hours). Event recording should be used only if the behaviors being observed are discrete. That means that there is a clear beginning and ending to the behavior so that the observer can discern when one occurrence of the behavior ended and a new one began. Event recording should not be used when the behavior is occurring at very high rates or if the behavior occurs for an extended period of time.

Interval recording. **Interval recording** provides an estimate of the actual frequency of the behavior occurrence. A specific time period is selected between 10 and 60 minutes during which time the behavior will be observed. The observation period selected is divided into equal intervals and should not exceed 30 seconds. Within each interval, the observer records whether the behavior did or did not occur at any time during the interval. Problems with interval recording are that the data provide only an estimate of the frequency. In addition, behaviors that are ongoing, such as putting his or her head on the desk, may occur across more than one interval. An additional problem is that the observer needs to attend fully to watching the student. It is difficult, therefore, to teach or engage in other classroom responsibilities while using an interval recording system. Data are reported in terms of a ratio or percentage of the number of intervals in which the behavior occurred and the total number of intervals.

Time sampling. **Time sampling** is similar to interval recording in that the observer selects an observation period and divides it into equal intervals. However, the intervals are generally larger with time sampling. The observer records whether or not the student engaged in the behavior at the end of the interval. This allows teachers or other observers to engage in other behaviors while observing. It is not uncommon, however, for observers to be distracted and to forget to look at the student at the end of the interval. Audio cues such as electronic timers or prerecorded "beep" tapes can be helpful. As with interval recording, time sampling provides only an estimate. Time sampling is particularly helpful with behaviors that are frequent or of long duration. Data are reported like interval recording procedures, usually as a ratio or percentage of the number of intervals in which the behavior occurred divided by the total number of intervals.

Duration recording. When the length of time the behavior is occurring is the major concern, duration recording may be used. Like event recording, **duration recording** is appropriate for behaviors that have an easily identified beginning and ending. Using a stopwatch is the easiest way to collect duration data. Once the behavior begins, turn on the stopwatch. When the behavior ends, stop the stopwatch. There are two ways to collect duration data. If the behavior occurs regularly, then duration can be collected each time it happens and an average duration time computed. If the concern is how long the student engaged in the behavior on and off in a specified period of time, then the total duration recording method may be used. In this instance, the stopwatch is turned on each time the behavior begins and is turned off each time it ends to represent every occurrence of the behavior within that time limit. A cumulative or total duration time is recorded. Duration is reported in time units and may include seconds, minutes, and/or hours depending on the behavior and the length of the observation period.

Latency recording. **Latency recording** measures how long it takes for a student to initiate a behavior once prompted to do so. The procedures are similar to duration recording. Once the directions or instructions are given, the stopwatch is started. When the student begins initiation of the behavior, the stopwatch is stopped. Latency is usually reported in terms of minutes and/or seconds.

ABC recording. The initialism ABC refers to antecedents, behaviors, and consequences. Antecedent stimuli or events are those that occur prior to the behavioral event. Antecedents may include setting events (e.g., time of day, experiences at home prior to coming to school), the task (i.e., what the student is being asked to do), other persons present (e.g., peers), or instructions given (Kerr & Nelson, 2006). Behavior refers to the student's behavior and the consequences are those events that occur following the occurrence of the behavior (e.g., peers laughed, student threw her book). In conducting an ABC analysis, the observer records anecdotally all of the events that occur within the setting over several observation periods. Formatting the data as shown in Figure 5.2 helps the observer identify patterns among the antecedents, behaviors, and consequences.

FIGURE 5.2   **An Example of an ABC Data Sheet**

Student____*Jay*____ Date____*10/5/16*____ Time ____*10:05–10:20*____

Observer____*Margaret Osborne*____

General Behavior Concerns____*Doesn't follow directions, off-task, out of seat*____

Antecedents	Behavior	Consequences
Teacher tells the class to turn to page 33 in their math books.	Jay plays with a pencil and rubber band.	Teacher repeats directions.
Teacher asks the class "What did I say?"	Jay looks at the teacher.	Teacher takes pencil and rubber band away from Jay.
Teacher tells Jay to turn to page 33.	Jay looks at the teacher.	Teacher turns Jay's book to page 33.
Teacher asks Tammy to find the first story problem and read it out loud.	Jay asks a peer what they are supposed to do.	Teacher tells Jay to be quiet.
Teacher asks Jay to read the next story problem.	Jay asks peer where they are in the book.	Peer points to the problem.
Teacher tells Jay to read the problem.	Jay reads the problem.	Teacher thanks Jay.
Teacher directs students to complete problems 1 to 5 on their own and to raise their hands if they have questions.	Jay looks in his desk.	Teacher closes Jay's desk.
Teacher reminds Jay what he is to do.	Jay starts working on his math problems (3 minutes) then moves over to the window.	Teacher tells Jay to sit down.

Functional Behavioral Assessment

Arguably, the most important step in the behavioral assessment process is answering the question, "Why is the behavior happening?" Information garnered from observations and data collection is used to generate hypotheses about what is maintaining the student's behavior. As discussed in Chapter 3, all behavior takes place in an environmental context and for a specific purpose. **Functional behavioral assessment** is the process of assessing identified problem behavior in the context of environmental variables that occur before, during, and after the target behavior (Kerr & Nelson, 2006). The aim of this process is to identify the **function of student behavior**, or the reason why the student engages in the behavior.

The function of student behavior typically falls into one of four categories: attention, escape, access, and sensory. When attention is the primary function of student behavior, students are reinforced and motivated by social recognition or the attention of parents, teachers, and peers. When escape is the primary function of student behavior, students may do their best to avoid assignments or tasks. Access, or obtaining something desirable such as time or money, may also motivate student behavior. Finally, student behavior may sometimes be explained by unmet sensory needs (e.g., a student scratches his hand on the desk repeatedly because of the textural sensation it provides). Once the primary function of student behavior is identified, interventions may be designed to change and shape student behavior. Often, these behavior plans include a replacement behavior, or a behavior that fulfills the same function as the target behavior in a way that's appropriate for the classroom setting.

IDEA mandates the use of functional behavioral assessments and positive behavior supports and interventions. Research supports its effectiveness for students with high-incidence behavior problems as well as feasibility within schools when school personnel are given expert support (Reid & Nelson, 2002).

Record-Keeping and Decision-Making Procedures

Much attention has been devoted in this chapter to curriculum-based and behavioral assessment. At this point, readers may be asking, "What should teachers do with all of this information?" That is an excellent question and deserves a pointed answer. Teachers should never collect data simply to collect data. They should always use this information to make instructional decisions about whether change is needed. "What kind of changes?" Assuming that the target behavior has been selected appropriately, change would involve modifications to the instruction or behavior program.

Once a CBA has been developed and administered, teachers record the results on a graph similar to that found in Figure 5.3. When collecting academic frequency counts, both corrects and errors should be counted. For example, a student may orally read a passage for 1 minute and the number of words read correctly and the number read incorrectly are recorded. After the student has been assessed three times and the number of corrects and errors are graphed, a learning picture begins to emerge. A variety of learning pictures with suggested instructional modifications is listed in Figure 5.4. These suggestions are based on the assumption that the target behavior and curriculum are at the instructional level and in other ways appropriate for the student.

FIGURE 5.3 Example of a Graph to Record Progress Data

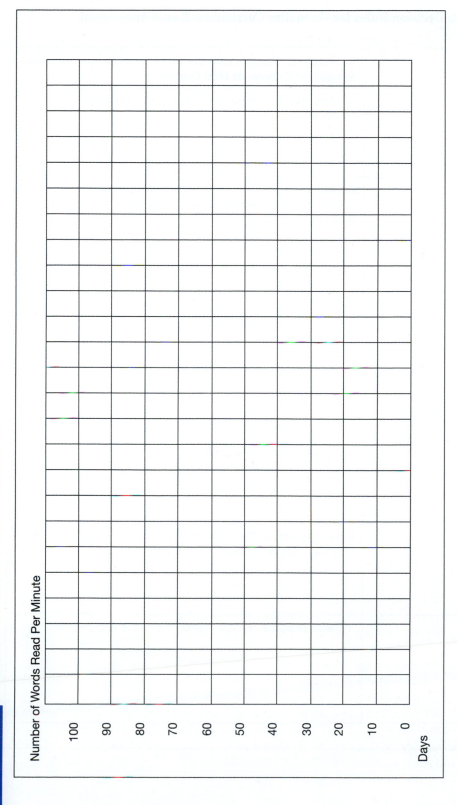

FIGURE 5.4 **Data Decision Rules for Formative Curriculum-Based Assessment**

Pictures	Suggested Change or Modification
	Continue present instruction. Reinforce continued improvement.
	Continue present instruction. Reinforce continued improvement. If errors are a concern, analyze, remediate, and reinforce.
	Continue present program. If necessary, reinforce continued improvement.
	Set daily goals. Increase practice. Reinforce improvement.
	Analyze instructional procedures. Set daily goals. Analyze errors and remediate. Reinforce improvement.
	Increase practice. Set daily goals. Reinforce improvement. If errors are a concern, analyze and remediate.
	Increase practice. Set daily goals. Reinforce improvement.

	Increase practice. Set daily goals. Reinforce improvement. If errors are a concern, analyze and remediate.
	Set daily goals. Reinforce improvement. Increase practice.
	Set daily goals. Reinforce improvement. Increase practice.
	Set daily goals. Reinforce improvement. If errors are a concern, analyze and remediate. Increase practice.
	Set daily goals. Reinforce improvement. If errors are a concern, analyze and remediate. Increase practice.

Key:

——— Number of correct responses

------- Number of incorrect responses (Below the line = 0)

TEACHER TIP #5.4

CREATING DATA-BASED DECISION-MAKING SYSTEMS

Use the following guidelines when creating a data-based decision-making system:

- Use readily available data. Sometimes the data already exist (e.g., weekly spelling tests).

- Design data collection procedures that are easy to use and do not require excessive staff time and resources. One suggested rule of thumb is that data collection should not consume more than 1% of a staff member's time each day.

- Ensure the purpose for data collection relates to ongoing classroom activities.

- Collect data on a small number of behaviors.

High-Stakes Accountability Assessment

As described in Chapter 1, states and districts are required to use large-scale assessments to document the academic achievement of all students for the purpose of accountability. These assessments are used to establish whether students have met district or state standards. In some states, student performance determines if they are advanced to the next grade level or graduate. These assessments have been labeled **high-stakes assessment** because of the serious consequences for students who perform poorly.

IDEA requires that students with disabilities be included in general state and districtwide assessment programs, with accommodations and modifications in administration, if necessary. Under IDEA, students with disabilities must also have access to the general curriculum. The student's IEP team determines the extent to which the general curriculum and assessments of achievement in the general curriculum are appropriate as well as the accommodations and modifications if needed. Appropriate test accommodations and modifications are described in Chapter 7.

In addition to IDEA, the Elementary and Secondary Education Act (ESEA) which most recent revisions were passed in 2015, was relabeled, Every Student Succeeds Act (ESSA). This act requires that states implement a statewide accountability system including test scores of all students in every public school. Students are tested in reading and math in Grades 3 to 8 and once in high school, as well as in science three times between Grades 3 and 12. Test results must be reported by subgroups including economically disadvantaged students, major racial and ethnic groups, students with disabilities, and English learners. One percent of the total student population (estimated to be less than 10% of all students with disabilities) may take alternative assessments based on alternative academic achievement standards. These alternative standards must align with academic content standards, promote access to the general education core, and be designated in the IEP.

Many educators believe the standards and expectations under ESSA are too great to achieve. The legislation has also been criticized for not being flexible enough for students with disabilities. For example, students with disabilities may be forced to take inappropriate tests or schools may become more desirous of excluding students, particularly those with behavior problems (Scheuermann, 2003). Failing a high-stakes test may lead students already vulnerable to having lower self-esteem, increased anxiety, increased likelihood of dropping out of school, and losing educational advancement and career opportunities (Albrecht & Joles, 2003).

Implications for Culturally and/or Linguistically Diverse Students

As discussed in Chapter 1, students from culturally and/or linguistically diverse (CLD) backgrounds are over identified as having disabilities which begins with students from diverse populations being over referred for individual assessment. Once referred, examiners may select inappropriate assessment tools which in turn create inaccurate results and students from diverse backgrounds are falsely identified as having disabilities. Teachers need to understand the potential risk of this cycle. Several safeguards are included in legislation and the courts have provided further interpretation to protect students from discriminatory assessment.

IDEA considers types of discrimination that may occur during assessment activities. First, the law includes safeguards for individual students and guarantees appropriate assessment instruments and techniques are used. The assessment instrument must be validated for the purposes for which they are used. Second, tests and other assessment materials should be administered in the student's native language or other mode of communication. Third, the assessment must be administered by personnel who are trained in accordance with the administration procedures. And fourth, the assessment must be comprehensive and include all areas related to the suspected disability and in specific areas of educational need.

Examiners should avoid using instruments that depend on the specific skills with which the student has difficulty unless the specific purpose of the assessment is to identify and characterize those difficulties. For example, a nonverbal test of intelligence would be more appropriate for a student who has expressive language problems, than the traditional verbally laden intelligence tests. In addition to selecting appropriate assessment instruments, examiners must be careful to avoid bias in administering, scoring, and interpreting test results. Bias during testing can occur in many ways including the examiner being unfamiliar with testing procedures. Also, examiner attitudes can influence expectations for student response. Examiners must communicate directly with students through the student's primary mode of communication. Using interpreters to translate examiner questions and student responses contaminates the standardization administration procedures and influences test result interpretation. Test developers are beginning to provide alternative tests validated in languages other than English.

When developing standardized tests, professionals use a specific population of students who compose the normative group. Examiners need to ensure that the tests used reflect a similar background of students upon whom the test was standardized. Research and court decisions support the fact that many standardized tests include items considered culturally and linguistically biased against students from nonmajority populations. For example, Pacific Islander Americans may be asked to label a picture in which it is snowing. Yet the students have never experienced snow. Conversely, an Alaska Native may be shown a picture of a desert with palm trees and be asked the same thing. These items could be considered biased, particularly if there were no Pacific

Islander or Alaska Native students in the normative group. Fortunately, researchers and publishers are becoming more aware of our increasing diversity and are now (a) including a wider breadth of participants in norming assessment tools, (b) creating norms for specialized groups, and/or (c) creating and norming assessment tools based on languages other than English.

Many other test biases exist. For example, students who come from cultures that emphasize working cooperatively in groups may not be conditioned to do their best when individually assessed; or students may not have been exposed to tests to develop test-taking skills. Including activities in tests such as puzzles and games assumes students have been exposed to these activities and know what they are supposed to do. Gender bias may also exist in tests.

When using rating scales teachers need to recognize that social and behavioral skills cannot be assessed in isolation without considering variables that include the complexities of socialization, such as culture. The social profile of a student can be influenced by the assessment tools selected and the interpretation of test results. Questions or descriptors that are presented through survey or rating scales may be broad and open to interpretation. A parent completing one of these instruments may be interpreting items very differently than a teacher. Teachers need to employ multidimensional assessment and instruction in order to gain a more thorough understanding of students' social strengths and needs.

John Venn (2014) suggests that factors leading to potential bias in testing may be reduced through the use of functional assessment because it involves the direct evaluation of student behavior and performance under existing teaching conditions as well as altering instruction to improve and then monitoring student performance on a continuous basis. "Because functional assessment is direct and continuous, it minimizes bias due to cultural differences" (p. 196).

When administering curriculum-based assessments, teachers can inadvertently build in bias based on cultural or linguistic differences. For example, a teacher may assume an English learner can complete a written test because her oral English is good. Other factors such as cultural norms of helping one another may confuse students who are asked to complete the test on their own. Teachers need to be aware of potential biases in any form of assessment and work toward eliminating them as best they can.

SUMMARY

School professionals use assessment of student performance to make educational decisions every day. Such decisions include identifying a student as having a disability or charting the student's progress throughout the curriculum. Assessment tools can be defined by their function (e.g., norm- vs. criterion-referenced), frequency (e.g., formative vs. summative), formality (e.g., standardized test vs. daily quiz), and the types of knowledge or skills being assessed (e.g., curriculum-based vs. behavioral).

Standardized tests must be administered by trained personnel because the tests must be administered, scored, and interpreted using systematic procedures.

Three basic characteristics of standardized tests include norms (i.e., test has been administered to a norm sample), reliability (i.e., the degree of accuracy and consistency of test scores), and validity (i.e., the test measures what the developers purport it measures). Standardized tests typically compare one student's performance against a group of students. Comparisons are possible because the tests have been normed with strong reliability and validity. Standardized tests are used to identify students as having a disability and to provide an estimate of how an individual or group are achieving in comparison to others. High-stakes accountability assessment use standardized tests.

Teachers who use CBAs align the assessment tool to the actual curriculum being taught in the classroom. Forms of CBAs include curriculum-based measurement which focuses on fluency, portfolio assessments where students create a portfolio of their work which is evaluated using a rubric, and behavioral assessments during which the behavior of a student is observed and recorded. Two commonly used CBAs include DIBELS for academic skills and ABC recording for behavior.

Behavioral assessment is necessary in order to develop behavioral intervention plans designed to change student behavior and promote positive student outcomes. Many different data collection methods are used, including the frequency of the behavior, the duration or how long the behavior lasts, latency or the length of time between when directions are given and the occurrence of the behavior, and rate which is the ratio of frequency over time. Depending upon the type of data collected, different observational recording systems are used including event recording, interval recording, time sampling, duration recording, latency recording, and ABC recording.

Functional behavior assessment is used to ascertain why the behavior is happening. The process involves assessing the problem behavior within the context of environmental variables that occur before, during, and after the behavior. The function of student behavior is usually attention, escape, access, or sensory. Once the primary function of the student behavior is identified, interventions may be designed to change and shape the behavior.

Teachers should never collect data without analyzing it to make instruction decisions. Data are typically recorded on graphs or charts. For example, changes in the frequency of a behavior, such as number of words read correctly in 1 minute can be graphed and the learning patterns that emerge used to make decisions about future instruction or interventions.

States and districts use high-stakes assessment to document the academic achievement of all students for the purpose of accountability. These tests measure whether students have met standards. IDEA and ESSA both require students with disabilities be included in these large-scale assessment efforts.

Students from CLD backgrounds are generally over identified as having disabilities. IDEA has safeguards built in (e.g., assessment should be administered in the student's native language), but over identification continues. Bias can occur as part of the assessment process regardless of the type of assessment being used. Teachers must be aware of potential assessment biases and do their best to eliminate these biases.

REVIEW QUESTIONS

1. Compare and contrast the four functions by which assessment can be categorized. Provide an example for each.

2. Taking into account what IDEA specifies about assessing students with disabilities, what do special educators need to know about standardized tests to ensure compliance with this law?

3. Describe how standardized tests are usually used in schools. Provide at least one example.

4. Present arguments for and against the use of standardized tests, including high-stakes testing, with students with disabilities.

5. Define curriculum-based assessment. Provide an example of how teachers can use CBA to guide instruction.

6. Describe the benefits and challenges of using portfolio assessments in the classroom. How can the challenges be addressed?

7. List the five common behavioral observation systems. Describe educational goals for students with high-incidence disabilities that could be measured using each behavioral observation system.

8. Describe how collecting data on antecedents, behavior, and consequences enable teachers to analyze problem behaviors.

9. Describe the safeguards provided in IDEA to help eliminate assessment bias.

10. Explain how assessment could potentially be biased for students from culturally and linguistically diverse backgrounds beyond the biases safeguarded in IDEA. Describe with examples what teachers can do to help eliminate those biases.

ACTIVITIES

1. Create a graphic organizer that illustrates how assessment information is used to educate students with disabilities. The organizer should include diagnostic assessments as well as ongoing classroom assessments.

2. Suppose you teach mathematics in middle school. Anticipate how you will use assessments to track student performance on an ongoing basis. Write a plan for the types of assessment you will use, describe the assessments including how often you will use them, and how they will fit into your classroom routines.

3. Identify an individual and a behavior you can observe. Ask for permission from the person (or a parent if under 18) to observe, collect data, and analyze the data. Select the proper form based on the type of behavior. Observe the person and record behavior for at least 30 minutes. Submit the data and write-up of your analysis and experience.

4. Interview two special educators who teach in a diverse community. Ask them how standardized and classroom-based assessment practices are influenced by the diversity of students. Write up your interviews.

Council for Exceptional Children (CEC) Standards

The Council for Exceptional Children (CEC) is a premiere national professional organization comprised of special educators, paraeducators, related service personnel, parents, and others interested in individuals with disabilities and/or those with gifts and talents. This organization has generated 10 standards for the preparation of special educators. These standards are listed in each chapter as they relate to the content within the chapter. The standard that applies to Chapter 5 is Standard #4:

CEC Initial Preparation Standard #4: Assessment

Beginning special education professionals use multiple methods of assessment and data sources in making educational decisions.

4.1 Beginning special education professionals select and use technically sound formal and informal assessments that minimize bias.

4.2 Beginning special education professionals use knowledge of measurement principles and practices to interpret assessment results and guide educational decisions for individuals with exceptionalities.

4.3 Beginning special education professionals in collaboration with colleagues and families use multiple types of assessment information in making decisions about individuals with exceptionalities.

4.4 Beginning special education professionals engage individuals with exceptionalities to work toward quality learning and performance and provide feedback to guide them.

REFERENCES

Achenbach, T. M. (2009). *The Achenbach System of Empirically Based Assessment (ASEBA): Development, Findings, Theory, and Applications*. Burlington, VT: University of Vermont Research for Children, Youth and Families.

Albrecht, S. F., & Joles, C. (2003). Accountability and access to opportunity: Mutually exclusive tenets under a high-stakes testing mandate. *Preventing School Failure, 47*, 86–91.

Beyers, S. J., Lembke, E., & Curs, B. R. (2013). Social studies progress monitoring and intervention for middle school students. *Assessment for Effective Intervention 38*(4), 224–235.

Bracken, B. A., & McCallum, R. S. (2015). *Universal Nonverbal Intelligence Test* (2nd ed.). Chicago, IL: Riverside.

Brigance, A. H. (2010). *Brigance Comprehensive Inventory of Basic Skills* (Rev. ed.). North Billerica, MA: Curriculum Associates.

Brown, L., Shervenou, R. J., & Johnsen, S. K. (2010). *Test of Nonverbal Intelligence* (4th ed.). Austin, TX: Pro-Ed.

Bures, E. M., Barclay, A., Abrami, P. C., & Meyer, E. J. (2013). The reality of assessing "authentic" electronic portfolios: Can electronic portfolios serve as a form of standardized assessment to measure literacy and self-regulated learning at the elementary level? *Canadian Journal of Learning and Technology, 39*(4), 1–21.

Calhoon, M. B., & Fuchs, L. S. (2003). The effects of peer-assisted learning strategies and curriculum-based measurement on mathematics performance, *Remedial and Special Education, 24*, 235–245.

Christ, T. J., Silberglitt, B., Yeo, S., & Cormier, D. (2010). Curriculum-based measurement of oral reading (CBM-R): An evaluation of growth rates and seasonal effects among students served in general and special education. *School Psychology Review, 39*, 447–462.

Conners, C. K. (2008). *Conners 3rd Edition Manual*. North Tonawanda, NY: Multi-Health Systems.

Connolly, A. J. (2007). *KeyMath-3 Diagnostic Assessment*. Minneapolis, MN: Pearson.

Constantino, J. N., & Gruber, C. P. (2012). *Social Responsiveness Scale*, second edition (SRS-2). Los Angeles, CA: Western Psychological Services.

Davies, A. (2000). Seeing the results for yourself: A portfolio primer. *Classroom Leadership, 3*(5), 4–5.

Diller, K. R., & Phelps, S. F. (2008). Learning outcomes, portfolios, and rubrics, oh my! Authentic assessment of an information literacy program. *Portal: Libraries and the Academy, 8*, 75–89.

Epstein, M. H. (2004). *Behavioral and Emotional Rating Scale: A strengths-based approach to assessment* (2nd ed.). Austin, TX: PRO-ED.

Ezell, D., & Klein, C. (2003). Impact of portfolio assessment on locus of control of students with and without disabilities. *Education and Training in Developmental Disabilities, 38*, 220–228.

Foegen, A., Jiban, C., & Deno, S. (2007). Progress monitoring measures in mathematics: A review of the literature. *Journal of Special Education, 41*(2), 121–139.

Fuchs, L. S., Fuchs, D., Hosp, M. K., & Hamlett, C. L. (2003). The potential for diagnostic analysis within curriculum-based measurement. *Assessment for Effective Intervention, 28*(3/4), 13–22.

Goffreda, C. T., & DiPerna, J. C. (2010). An empirical review of psychometric evidence for the Dynamic Indicators of Basic Early Literacy Skills. *School Psychology Review, 39*, 463–483.

Good, R. H., III, Kaminski, R. K., Cummings, K., Dufour-Martel, C., Petersen, K., Powell-Smith, K., Stollar, S., & Wallin, J. (2011). *DIBELS Next Assessment Manual.* Eugene, OR: Dynamic Measurement Group.

Gresham, F., & Elliott, S. N. (2008). *Social Skills Improvement System Rating Scales.* Minneapolis, MN: NCS Pearson.

Hall, E. W., & Salmon, S. J. (2003). Chocolate chip cookies and rubrics: Helping students understand rubrics in inclusive settings. *TEACHING Exceptional Children, 35*(4), 8–11.

Hammill, D. D., & Larsen, S. C. (2009). *Test of Written Language–4.* Austin, TX: Pro-Ed.

Hedin, L. R., & Conderman, G. (2010). Teaching students to comprehend informational text through rereading. *Reading Teacher, 63*(7), 556–565.

Hoffman, A. R., Jenkins, J. E., & Dunlap, S. K. (2009). Using DIBELS: A survey of purposes and practices. *Reading Psychology, 30*, 1–16.

Hoover, H. D., Dunbar, S. B., Frisbie, D. A. (2005). *Iowa Tests of Basic Skills.* Itasca, IL: Riverside.

Johnson, E., Jenkins, J., Petscher, Y., & Catts, H. (2009). How can we improve the accuracy of screening instruments? *Learning Disabilities Research & Practice, 24*, 174–185.

Joseph, L. M., Kastein, L. A., Konrad, M., Chan, P. E., Peters, M. T., & Ressa, V. A. (2014). Collecting and documenting evidence: Methods for helping teachers improve instruction and promote academic success. *Intervention in School and Clinic, 50*(2), 86–95.

Kaufman, A. S., & Kaufman, N. L. (2014). *Kaufman Tests of Educational Achievement – Third Edition.* San Antonio, TX: Pearson.

Kerr, M. M., & Nelson, C. M. (2006). *Strategies for addressing behavior problems in the classroom* (5th ed.). Upper Saddle River, NJ: Prentice-Hall.

King-Sears, M. E. (1994). *Curriculum-based assessment in special education.* San Diego, CA: Singular.

Lembke, E., Deno, S. L., & Hall, K. (2003). Identifying an indicator of growth in early writing proficiency for elementary school students. *Assessment for Effective Intervention, 28*(3/4), 23–25.

Munger, K. A., & Blachman, B. A. (2013). Taking a "simple view" of the Dynamic Indicators of Basic Early Literacy Skills as a predictor of multiple measures of third-grade reading comprehension. *Psychology in the Schools, 50*, 722–737.

Reid, R., & Nelson, J. R. (2002). The utility, acceptability, and practicality of functional behavioral assessment students with high-incidence problem behaviors. *Remedial and Special Education, 23*, 15–23.

Reynolds, C. R., & Kamphaus, R. W. (2015). *Behavior and Assessment System for Children* (3rd ed.). Circle Pines, MN: NCS Pearson.

Roid, G. H. (2003). *Stanford-Binet Intelligence Scales* (5th ed.). Itasca, IL: Riverside.

Salend, S. J. (1998). Using portfolios to assess student performance. *TEACHING Exceptional Children, 31*(2), 36–43.

Salvia, J., Ysseldyke, J. E., & Bolt, S. (2013). *Assessment in special and inclusive education* (12th ed.). Stamford, CT: Cengage.

Scheuermann, B. (2003, November). Where's IDEA? *Council for Children with Behavioral Disorders Newsletter, 17*(3), 1–5.

Schrank, F. A., Mather, N., & McGrew, K. S. (2014). *Woodcock-Johnson IV Tests of Achievement.* Rolling Meadows, IL: Riverside.

Sparrow, S. S., Cicchetti, D. V., & Balla, D. A. (2005). *Vineland Adaptive Behavior Scales* (2nd ed.). Circle Pines, MN: American Guidance Service.

Thompson, S. A., & Baumgartner, L. (2008). Exploring portfolios in the elementary classroom with students with disabilities/exceptionalities: Timely or Time-consuming? *Exceptionality Education Canada, 18,* 148–165.

Vannest, K. J., Parker, R. I., & Dyer, N. (2011). Progress monitoring in grade 5 science for low achievers. *Journal of Special Education, 44*(4), 221–233.

Venn, J. J. (2014). *Assessing students with special needs* (5th ed.). Upper Saddle River, NJ: Pearson.

Wayman, M. M., Wallace, T., Wiley, H. I., Tichá, R., & Espin, C. A. (2007). Literature synthesis on curriculum-based measurement in reading. *Journal of Special Education, 41,* 85–120.

Wechsler, D. (2008). *Wechsler Adult Intelligence Scales* (4th ed.). San Antonio, TX: NCS Pearson.

Wechsler, D. (2009). *Wechsler Individual Achievement Test* (3rd ed.). San Antonio, TX: Psychological Corporation.

Wechsler, D. (2014). *Wechsler Intelligence Scale for Children* (5th ed.). San Antonio, TX: NCS Pearson.

Wiederhold, J. L., & Bryant, B. R. (2012). *Oral Reading Tests* (5th ed.). Austin, TX: Pro-Ed.

Woodcock, R. W., Muñoz-Sandoval, A. F., McGrew, K. S., & Mather, N. (2004). *Batería III Woodcock-Muñoz.* Itasca, IL: Riverside.

⑤SAGE edge™ ●

Review ➡ Practice ➡ Improve

Get the tools you need to sharpen your study skills. Access videos, practice quizzes, eFlashcards and more at **edge.sagepub.com/prater.**

©iStockphoto.com/Steve Debenport

Teacher-Directed Instruction

Teachers' teaching styles often vary as greatly as their personalities differ. Some teachers are characterized as flamboyant and exuberant. Others are more reserved. Some teachers use their creative powers in all of their teaching methods. Other teachers are more precise and systematic in the way they approach instruction. Although teacher style may vary based on personality and preference, there are instructional methods that are more effective than others in achieving positive student outcomes. Teacher-directed instruction is one of those.

Teacher-directed instruction includes methodologies in which the teacher is the primary deliverer of instruction, in contrast to student-mediated instruction, in which students take more responsibility for their own learning and the learning of their peers. This chapter focuses on teacher behaviors that lead to higher student achievement, based on the teacher effectiveness literature. Included are direct instruction, lesson planning, and technological tools that support teacher-directed instruction, as well as implications for teaching culturally diverse students. Consider the information presented in this chapter as laying the foundation for teaching students with high-incidence disabilities (HID).

Learning Objectives

- Explain why and provide examples of how teachers can influence student learning by improving allocated and student-engaged learning time.

- Describe the prescribed format teachers should use in lesson presentations. Explain why each element is important and provide examples of objectives, lesson introduction, instruction and modeling, guided practice, independent practice, and closure.

- Discuss the importance of understanding students' culture in context of teacher-directed instruction. Defend whether teacher-directed instruction is culturally responsive.

Teacher Effectiveness Variables

Mr. Ettington is concerned about Josef who comes from a home with one parent and seven other children. Their home is very small and he shares a bedroom with three of his brothers. He comes to school without his homework completed and doesn't appear motivated to do his work even at school. He has made little to no progress in 2 months. Mr. Ettington concludes that Josef isn't doing well in school because of his home environment. After all, his mother works full time to keep the family going. And Josef doesn't get any help at home with his homework.

Student achievement results from the influence and interaction of several factors, including characteristics of the student, the teacher, the school system, and the home. All teachers need to be aware of these factors in their students' lives. Teachers also need to recognize and admit that they are one of these influential factors, and the only factor over which they have direct control. In fact, research indicates that regardless of whether students are rich or poor, male or female, academically gifted or challenged, teachers can make a difference in their academic achievement (Adams & Englemann, 1996).

Although Mr. Ettington cannot change Josef's home life, there are things he can do to improve his school performance. He should reexamine his teaching practices and look for ways to help Josef succeed. Teachers can make a difference in student learning often regardless of the teaching method used or the home or social issues impacting the classroom. For example, research has shown that effective elementary special educators distinguish themselves from less effective ones in the following ways: They conduct activities in the class; they ask questions frequently; they limit independent seatwork (especially silent reading); and they allow time for social interaction with students (Sindelar, Espin, Smith, & Harriman, 1990).

Effective instructional techniques in special education are not very distinct from those that are effective in general education. Instructional principles demonstrated to be effective with students with disabilities are effective whether students are educated in self-contained classrooms, in resource rooms, or in general education classes. On nearly 100 occasions, the author has asked large groups of educators, administrators, and university students to brainstorm a list of characteristics of effective teachers. In every instance, the groups have generated a very long list without my being asked, "What kind of a teacher?" "A teacher of what kind of students?" "What content is the teacher teaching?" or "In what kind of setting is the teacher teaching?" Principles of good teaching apply regardless of the type of students being taught or the setting in which they are being taught (Bost & Riccomini, 2006). Teachers who work with students requiring special education services need, however, to be particularly aware of effective instructional methods in order to be the most effective and efficient teachers possible. Three categories of teacher behaviors that impact student learning are (a) content selected for instruction, (b) amount of time spent in instruction, and (c) amount of active participation by students. Table 6.1 outlines some of the principles of effective instruction.

Content

Mrs. Forum is starting her first year as a special educator. She will be working in a resource room with upper elementary students. Each student has an IEP with reading and math goals. Mrs. Forum has a strong background in science and wants to incorporate some science experiments in the resource rooms to help teach reading and math. She's concerned about whether she can do this since none of the students have science goals on their IEPs.

As discussed in Chapter 1, the majority of states have adopted the Common Core State Standards (CCSS) that define the content to be taught in schools. The CCSS, or other state or district standards, applies to students receiving special education services. Students with disabilities, where possible, should be learning the same content as their typical peers.

Textbooks and other published curricular materials also impact what is taught. Publishers are attending to the CCSS and ensuring that their materials address the standards. Sometimes thick textbooks and massive curricular materials give teachers the impression that they must teach it all. Research indicates, however, that focusing on fewer topics and big ideas results in increased student achievement (McTighe, Seif, & Wiggins, 2004).

In determining instructional content for students with disabilities, special educators need to attend to their locally adopted standards, as well as to the goals prescribed

TABLE 6.1   Principles of Effective Instruction and School Engagement

Principle	Explanation
Active Engagement	Students should be actively engaged in learning tasks that are instructionally appropriate.
Providing the Experience of Success	Students need to experience success early and often.
Content Coverage and Opportunity to Learn	The amount of content covered should be maximized based on student needs.
Grouping for Instruction	Grouping students into smaller groups or providing one-on-one instruction should be determined by lesson objectives and student needs.
Scaffolded Instruction	Teachers should provide a sequenced series of content, materials, tasks, and teacher-supported prompts.
Addressing Forms of Knowledge	All forms of knowledge (e.g., facts, steps to solve problems, when and where to use strategies) should be part of instruction.
Organizing and Activating Knowledge	Connecting and combining prior knowledge to new information increases understanding and application.
Teaching Strategies	Students should be taught "how to learn" as well as "what to learn."
Making Instruction Explicit	Effective teacher-directed instruction includes clearly stating the purpose, providing structured instruction, and presenting content clearly and directly.
Teaching Sameness	Using purposely designed instruction helps students understand patterns and to organize knowledge.

Source: Adapted from L. W. Bost & P. J. Riccomini (2006). Effective instruction. *Remedial and Special Education, 27*(5), pp. 301–311.

on students' Individualized Education Programs (IEPs) (see Chapter 1). IEP goals and state or district standards then should drive the instruction that takes place. Teachers make the ultimate decision about the content taught to their students and often the curricular focus for their students. Special education teachers need to ensure that the content they teach ties directly to the IEP goals, and that these goals are based on their students' needs and the general education curriculum.

The CCSS and other state- or district-adopted standards "specify what students should know and be able to do, but they don't specify how teachers must teach those things" (Barth, 2013, p. 13). The curriculum decisions, or how to teach the content standards, is left to states, districts, school, and teachers to decide.

Mrs. Forum decides that rather than trying to teach the IEP goals using science experiments, she will design a reinforcement system whereby students can participate in the experiments if they achieve prespecified goals in reading and math. She will directly teach reading and math skills and then apply these skills as part of the science experiments at the end of each week.

Time

As a new teacher, Mr. Chapman has been frustrated with the number of interruptions in his classroom. It seems, for example, that he just begins instructing when a note comes from the principal's office or another teacher comes in asking for some assistance. He's not certain what to do about all of these interruptions. Mr. Chapman asks his mentor teacher to observe and collect data on the amount of time Mr. Chapman spends on academic-related tasks in the classroom. He also asks his mentor teacher to provide some suggestions for improving and using his time more directly related to instruction.

Time is a major commodity for schools and teachers. The manner in which teachers organize and utilize time has a direct impact on student learning. School time may be divided into (a) allocated time and (b) engaged learning time.

Allocated Time

Allocated time is defined as the amount of time scheduled for instruction. Research documents that about 50% to 60% of the school day is allocated to academic instruction. The remaining time is consumed by lunch, recesses, announcements, assemblies, housekeeping activities, and so forth. An average school day is about 6 hours; only 3 to 3½ hours a day, then, is allocated to instruction. In one study, special educators were found to spend less than 50% of their school day instructing: 46.0% was spent on instruction, assessment, and discipline; 28.7% on planning, meeting, and paperwork; with the remaining time spent on other school duties or personal time (Vannest, & Hagan-Burke, 2010).

All teachers have generally the same amount of time for instructing students. Yet, as with the content or curriculum covered, teachers vary greatly in their use of time. In one study, the average amount of time allocated to mathematics in general education in second grade varied from 25 to 60 minutes a day. And in fifth grade, reading and reading-related instruction was allocated for 60 to 140 minutes a day (Fisher et al., 2015). If those figures were multiplied by the number of school days in a year, the discrepancies between the teachers would be vast. Great variance also exists among special educators' use of time. In one study, the engaged time in special education classrooms varied from 11 minutes to 3 hours per day (Vaughn, Levy, Coleman, & Bos, 2002).

In a study of second- and fifth-grade general classrooms, researchers discovered that in addition to time allocated to academic instruction, 23% to 24% of the school day is allocated to nonacademic activities such as wait time and transitions; and 17% to 19% of school time is consumed by noninstructional activities (Rosenshine, 2015). In another study, a significant amount of time (17%) in high school was spent waiting for the teacher to start or restart instruction due to housekeeping activities, such as taking attendance or the teacher assisting students individually (Fisher, 2009).

Engaged Learning Time

In a comprehensive review of research that examined variables related to both cognitive and affective school outcomes, Margaret Wang, Geneva Haertel, and Herbert Walberg (1990) concluded that the variables "most important to learning outcomes were those that were directly tied to students' engagement with the material to be learned" (p. 37). This is referred to as **active engagement**. **Engaged learning time** refers to the time during which students are attending to relevant instructional activities with a high rate of success. "Engaged" implies that students are involved actively in an activity or task that (a) relates directly to the material they are learning, (b) is provided at the appropriate level and stage of learning, and (c) can be completed with a high degree of success. Engaged learning time is also sometimes called academic learning time (Fisher et al., 2015). All three criteria must be met to be considered engaged learning time. If students are working on a set of worksheets at their desk as busy work, the students may be considered on task, but they are not actively engaged in learning. If the work, for example, ties directly to a planned review based on maintenance activities and the students are achieving high levels of accuracy and fluency (to be expected with maintenance activities), then they are participating in engaged learning time.

The amount of time students are actively engaged in learning, not just allocated time, is the ultimate goal of all instructional programs. As engaged learning time increases, so does student achievement (Fisher et al., 2015). Some of the instructional techniques described earlier under time-on-task also apply to engaged learning time. If teachers are asking relevant and appropriate-level questions, for example, students will be working on relevant content, working at the appropriate instructional level, and achieving high rates of success. The pacing of instruction and quick transition times contribute to engaged learning. In addition, Robert Marzano (2007) suggests that students need a certain amount of energy level to stay engaged which can be accomplished through physical activity.

Teachers who keep their students actively engaged or participating in their own learning achieve greater class performance than teachers who do not. Teachers can improve the amount of time students spend engaged by improving their (a) teaching behaviors, (b) instructional management, and/or (c) behavior management.

Teaching behaviors. As discussed earlier, what teachers do in the classroom greatly impacts student learning. Teaching behaviors during instruction that make a difference in student achievement include such things as questioning strategies, pacing, and monitoring of student progress.

Questions and responses. Regardless of the content being presented or the type of students being taught, teacher questioning consumes a large portion of group instruction. The way in which teachers ask questions and the type of questions asked are both critical variables that impact student achievement. During group instruction, effective teachers use appropriate questioning techniques. For example, they ask a question, then call on a student to answer (e.g., "What is the capital of Maine?" "David?"), rather than the teacher calling on the student first and then asking the question (e.g., "David, what is the capital of Maine?"). If teachers address questions to a specific student prior to stating the question, other students do not need to pay attention. Effective teachers also avoid using a set order, such as going down a row of desks, for students to read aloud or provide answers. Using such an order gives students time to determine when it will be their turn and to not pay attention until then. For example, a student may notice that she is the fifth student in the row, so she counts to the fifth paragraph (knowing that each student is reading orally one paragraph) and rehearses it until it is her turn.

Also, teachers using effective teaching practices ask students to respond at least sometimes to questions as a group in a choral fashion and other times to answer questions individually. Choral or group responding can be a very effective practice activity when students are in the fluency-building stage of learning. Group responses, however, can get out of control if students do not respond together. The use of verbal signals, such as "What word?" or "Ready, read" or hand signals such as snapping fingers, touching the problem on the board, or clapping hands helps keep group responses together. Choral responding can only be effective with factual information that has only one correct answer and requires a concise response (e.g., one to three words). Also, choral responding may be difficult in large group instruction to ensure full student participation and to identify student errors (Blackwell & McLaughlin, 2005). Choral responding can be helpful when students are at different learning levels because they can learn from one another without being embarrassed for responding incorrectly. In a review of research, choral responding was found to be more effective than individual responding on increasing student time-on-task. These results were particularly true for students with emotional and behavioral disorders, autism, and moderate cognitive disabilities (Haydon, Marsicano, & Scott, 2013).

Response cards are a method of ensuring active student involvement that can also be used to check for student understanding. They can take the form of (a) preprinted materials (e.g., cards with preprinted answers, movable hands on sample analog clock) or (b) write-on materials (chalkboards, dry erase boards, or scrap paper). Response cards are generally easy to prepare and use and they provide students with a large number of opportunities to respond. Response cards, when compared with choral responding or hand-raising, was found in one study to be the most effective responding technique for young children with attention problems (Godfrey, Grisham-Brown, Schuster, & Hemmeter, 2003).

Effective teachers ask more than factual questions. They ask questions that require higher level thinking as well. Reading comprehension questions are often labeled as literal (factual), inferential (interpretative), or evaluative (critical). Effective teachers incorporate all three levels as part of their instruction. Inferential or evaluative questions are often raised as points of discussion. When teachers discuss with students what they have read, inferential and evaluative comprehension increases.

Teachers' presentation style for higher level thinking skills differs from the factual rapid-fire questioning method. If students are engaged in fluency-building activities based on factual information, the latency, or the time between the question being raised and the response of the student is critical. That is, students need to respond quickly in order to demonstrate they know the answer automatically. Some skills should be developed at this level. Higher level thinking skills, however, need think-time. That is, after asking a question, teachers should allow the student some time to think before responding (Freiberg, 2002). Most teachers wait 0.7 to 1.4 seconds for students to respond to a question, when they should wait at least 3 seconds (Marzano, 2007). Students with processing difficulties may require even longer time. Teachers can use a strategy to remind them to provide think-time by saying silently and slowly, "think-time 1-2-3" after asking a question. Research indicates that when teachers allow time for students to formulate their higher level responses, the length of student responses, the number of correct responses, and the quality of student responses improves. In addition, students are more likely

TABLE 6.2   **Words Commonly Associated With Comprehension Levels**

Literal	Inferential	Evaluative
Define	*Compare*	*Appraise*
Identify	*Contrast*	*Argue*
List	*How*	*Assess*
Recite	*Predict*	*Critique*
What	*Relate*	*Decide*
When	*Speculate*	*Defend*
Where	*Support*	*Judge*
Who	*Why*	*Prioritize*

to contribute to another students' response, creating more student–student discussions as opposed to only teacher–student exchanges (Pagliaro, 2011).

When asking questions, other factors are also important. For example, teachers should ensure that the questions asked are clear and succinct and that only one question at a time is asked. Teachers should also distribute their questions so that all students have a chance to participate, including calling on both volunteers and nonvolunteers to answer questions (Pagliaro, 2011).

TEACHER TIP #6.1

ADDITIONAL QUESTIONING TECHNIQUES

Try these additional questioning techniques:

- After placing students in pairs, model the question (e.g., *Ask your partner to list the 4 parts of speech.*), then have them question their partner (McConnell, Ryser, & Higgins, 2000).

- Give one or more tickets to each student. Each time the student answers a question, have them hand you a ticket back. When all their tickets are gone, they cannot respond until everyone's tickets are gone. This will help ensure all students are given an opportunity to

respond and no one monopolizes the discussion (McConnell et al., 2000).

- Use both "thick" and "thin" questions. Thick questions are open-ended big idea questions (e.g., *Why? What if?*). Closed-ended single answers are thin (e.g., *Who?*) (Bintz & Williams, 2005).

- Use questions to solicit students' insights and interpretations. For example, after reading a story ask students to draw a representation of what they learned based on an open-ended question such as, *How did the story make you feel?* (Bintz & Williams, 2005).

Pacing. The teacher's pace is another critical time factor. Individuals who enter the special education profession often have the misconception that special education students need a slower pace of instruction than their typically achieving counterparts. This is not true. Effective teachers, including special educators, maintain a brisk pace through the curriculum, as represented by the amount of content covered in a day, week, month, or year. Teachers who present new information and ask questions at a brisk pace maintain student interest and attention, but do not lose the students by moving too quickly. While moving briskly through the curriculum, effective teachers also maintain high levels of accuracy and fluency (Englert, Tarrant, & Mariage, 1992).

Well-established procedures for daily routine activities, such as handing in assignments and distributing materials, can enhance the pace of a lesson. Instead of the teacher providing directions each time one of these activities takes place, students know what is expected of them. Similarly, transitioning from one part of a lesson (e.g., instruction) to the next (e.g., practice) should be smooth (Marzano, 2007). For example, starting a lesson with the children sitting on the reading rug and then having them move to their tables to practice, then back to the rug for closure requires much unnecessary movement and slows the pace of the lesson.

TEACHER TIP #6.2

SUGGESTIONS FOR IMPROVING TIME-ON-TASK

To improve time-on-task, try the following ideas:

- Veer between quickly paced question-and-answer discussion and quiet time for silent reading or journaling.
- Use unique ways to introduce new content, such as dramatic footage from a video.

- Invite guest speakers to discuss content of interest to students.
- Share your personal stories, passions, vulnerabilities, and love of learning.
- Connect content being learned with students' personal experiences. (Intrator, 2004)

Monitoring student behavior. Another critical element of effective teaching is frequent and active monitoring of student behavior. Teachers monitor student behavior in a variety of ways and on different levels. When it comes to monitoring student behavior, keep in mind that students spend less time actively involved during seat work than when receiving group instruction. Effective teachers are particularly alert to students during seat work. They move around the classroom monitoring work for completeness and accuracy. If the seat work has been assigned at an appropriate level, the help students need should be brief (30 to 40 seconds), and most of the students should not need much assistance.

Monitoring students is also demonstrated through *with-it-ness*—defined as the teacher's awareness of what is going on the classroom, communication of that awareness to the students, and the teacher's attending to two or more events at one time. Eye contact and visual scanning are two strategies that have been found to increase student on-task behavior. Even if eye contact cannot be made at all times, teachers should position themselves and their students so that all students are in the teacher's eyesight at all times.

Instructional management. In addition to teaching behaviors, the second category that affects student on-task behavior is instructional management, or the manner in which teachers design their classroom to enhance the learning process. Several ideas for setting up an effective classroom environment were already addressed in Chapter 3. Instructional management also includes the group structures used in the classroom, such as peer tutoring and cooperative learning groups. Both are discussed at length in Chapter 7 on Student-Mediated Learning.

Elementary-level teachers should set up routines for activities at the beginning of the day such as taking attendance, collecting lunch money, and acknowledging special occasions (such as a student's birthday). Similarly, secondary-level teachers need set routines for taking attendance, dealing with tardy students, and addressing students who missed class the day before. Routines at the end of the day or class period should also be established (e.g., communicating clear expectations for homework, putting materials away, cleaning the room) (Marzano, 2007). Teachers who use effective instructional management also set up routines for students to use if, for example, they are confused about specific seat-work problems, what to do next, or what to do if they complete work early. Students should be taught these routines explicitly. Effective teachers outline the steps and practice them with the students. Teachers may wish to display these steps on a poster and write them on the chalkboard as well.

Effective teachers also set up routines for transitions such as getting materials ready, collecting homework, and preparing to board the bus. A considerable amount of time can be wasted by transition time. In fact, major transitions have been found to constitute about 15% of classroom time in general education (Rosenshine, 2015) and special education (Vaughn et al., 2002) classrooms. Students receiving special education services, in particular, require structure and need to be reinforced for following the routines provided.

Effective teachers also involve students in correcting papers and other housekeeping tasks. Students can, for example, correct their own or another's homework. This can be done with self-correcting materials or keys with the correct responses. Or answers can be corrected orally. Rather than the teacher calling out the answers one student can give the answer, and a second can confirm if the answer is correct. If there is a discrepancy, you can review the item with the class. Other housekeeping jobs can teach responsibility or be used as reinforcers for students' improved behavior. Students often enjoy erasing the chalkboard, delivering messages to the office, or feeding the classroom pet. Teachers can assign these housekeeping needs as jobs or as activities to be earned by students.

Students of effective teachers rarely have to wait for the teacher's help. "Wait time" is a major contributor to the amount of time students spend off task. Teachers should design creative ways for their students to stay on task while waiting for assistance. If appropriate, students can be encouraged to assist one another. A student who needs the teacher or paraeducator's help could place a flag or a card on her desk indicating the need for help. Students should also be encouraged and reinforced for moving on to other seat work, projects, or silent reading, rather than just waiting for help. These instructional management strategies can increase greatly student time-on-task.

Behavior management. Effective teachers are also effective behavior managers. Effective behavior management is a necessary but not a sufficient condition for student learning to occur. That is, effective teacher management sets the stage or provides the opportunity for other variables to influence student achievement.

As discussed in Chapter 3, well-managed classrooms have well-defined rules for appropriate behaviors. The rules are expressed in positive terms and posted in words that the students understand. The rules are explained, discussed, role-played, and the rationale is provided for each rule. In addition, the rules are applied to stop inappropriate behavior promptly. Effective teachers anticipate problem behaviors, communicate their expectations clearly, watch the students closely, intervene promptly and invoke prespecified consequences for behavior. In addition, effective teachers do not attend just to the "rule breaker"; they also attend to the students who are keeping the rules, providing positive attention. More specific information and examples may be found in Chapter 3.

TEACHER TIP #6.3

MANAGING REQUESTS TO LEAVE CLASS

Some students love to leave the classroom and may make excuses to do so. Occasional trips to the restroom or drinking fountain are not disruptive but can become out of hand. At the beginning of each grading period (e.g., 6 weeks), give students two "Get Out of Class Free" cards with their names written in ink (or have them write their own names). Explain that when they need to leave the room they will give you the card, but that since they have only two cards, only two trips per grading period are allowed. In addition, explain that for each card not used, the student can add points to his or her final grade or drop a homework assignment. (McConnell et al., 2000)

In summary, research documents that the amount of time teachers allocate to instruction in a content area is positively associated with the amount of learning in that area. In addition, the more time students spend engaged in learning, the more they will achieve. Teachers can increase student-engaged learning by improving teaching behaviors, instructional management, and behavior management. In these ways, teachers can control much of their students' learning as well as their success rate (Fisher et al., 2015).

Classrooms should be structured so that students are engaged actively in their own learning, whether the specific task is an individual or group undertaking. Organizing students into cooperative learning or pairs for peer tutoring can increase active participation. Self-management strategies, as well, can have powerful effects on students' on-task behavior and academic achievement. With self-management strategies, students are taught ways for monitoring their own behavior and/or academic learning; cooperative learning and peer tutoring are discussed in Chapter 8 and self-management in Chapter 13.

Direct Teaching

Teachers play several roles in the classroom. They may be a classroom manager, facilitator, or instructor, among other roles. As a manager, they arrange the classroom environment and materials to meet their and the students' needs. As facilitators, they help students access information. And as instructors, they directly teach content. This section is devoted to what effective teachers do when they directly teach content. Research has identified the teacher behaviors that lead to effective student learning outcomes in the context of teacher-directed instruction, particularly for the acquisition stage of learning. In fact, direct or explicit instruction has been identified as one of two of the field's most significant advancements for students with HID. "Time and again, studies have shown that while explicit instruction is helpful for typically achieving students, it is essential for students who struggle in learning" (Deshler, 2014, para. 6). A brief description of *Direct Instruction* precedes the discussion on direct teaching principles subtitled *Direct Instruction Lesson Planning.*

Direct Instruction

When individuals use the term **direct instruction,** they may be referring to generic effective teaching principles or *Direct Instruction* principles and commercially produced instructional programs developed by Siegfried Englemann and associates at the University of Oregon (Goeke, 2009). These two interpretations, however, are not mutually exclusive. There are many instructional techniques that overlap (e.g., high rates of responding, brisk pacing, systematic error correction procedures). In order to avoid confusion in this text, *Direct Instruction*, capitalized and italicized, refers to the commercially produced materials, and the lower case designation direct instruction applies to the generic principles.

Direct Instruction encompasses both the delivery of instruction and curriculum design (Tarver, 2000). Although initially designed and evaluated for use with disadvantaged populations, *Direct Instruction* has also been tested and found to be effective with special populations (Adams & Carnine, 2003; Barbash, 2012). The overall goal is to "accelerate learning by maximizing efficiency in the design and delivery of instruction" (Tarver, 2000, p. 201).

> A guiding principle of Direct Instruction is that students can learn what the teacher can teach, and that if students aren't learning, the teacher isn't teaching. In other words, neither race, family background, social class, nor other factors are used to explain low achievement. Either the curriculum is ill-designed (which is unlikely because Direct Instruction curricula are extensively field tested); or the teacher is not following the curriculum exactly (generally because she has not received sufficient prior training or is not receiving timely coaching), or the teacher has not adapted the curriculum (e.g., provided extra practice) based on students' needs revealed by periodic curriculum-based measures ("mastery test"). (Kozioff, LaNunziata, Cowardin & Bessellieu, 2000, p. 59)

Direct Instruction curriculum materials provide explicit step-by-step lesson scripts, error correction procedures, gradual fading from teacher-directed activities to independent work, cumulative reviews, and continuous progress tests to monitor student progress through the curriculum. Concepts are often taught using both positive and negative examples (Tarver, 2000), an important instructional component for conceptual understanding (Prater, 1998). The typical *Direct Instruction* materials contain about 180 lessons for each grade level. A typical lesson can be presented in approximately 45 minutes (Tarver, 2000). Published *Direct Instruction* curricular materials are available in reading (Prekindergarten–adulthood) and math (Prekindergarten–Grade 8) through Science Research Associates (SRA), McGraw Hill Publishing Company.

The *Direct Instruction* approach to teaching has not been without its critics (Adams & Carnine, 2003; Barbash, 2012). The usual criticisms are that *Direct Instruction* stifles students and that the effects dissipate over time. Research has demonstrated, however, that *Direct Instruction* is an effective model of instruction, particularly for students with special needs. For example, *Direct Instruction* was one of nine different instructional approaches implemented in Project Follow Through, an extension of Head Start. Data collected from nearly 100,000 low-income kindergarten through third-grade children showed that the *Direct Instruction* was the only procedure in which these students consistently outperformed their comparison groups (for a discussion of this research see Stein, Kinder, Silbert, & Carnine, 2006).

Other research also supports the effectiveness of *Direct Instruction*. W. A. T. White (1988) conducted an analysis of 25 studies that compared *Direct Instruction* with other instructional procedures using as participants students who receive special education services. Not one of the studies showed results favoring the compared procedures. A review of 34 studies also indicated that *Direct Instruction* showed larger gains than other methods for general and special education studies at both elementary and secondary levels (Adams & Engelmann, 1996). A second review of 17 studies in which students with learning disabilities were taught using *Direct Instruction* received similar results (Adams & Carnine, 2003).

Direct Instruction Lesson Planning

The *Direct Instruction* curriculum materials are based on generic effective teaching principles. The remainder of this chapter is devoted to these teaching principles. The principles are presented within the context of lesson planning. Beginning teachers need a firm foundation in lesson planning. Therefore, a lot of detail in how to write lesson plans and many examples of lesson plans are included throughout the textbook. Once teachers have experienced writing and implementing detailed lesson plans, they will begin to internalize the steps and sequences, requiring them to write less detail in their lesson plans.

A comprehensive overview of the elements of effective teacher-directed lessons may be found in Table 6.3. Based on this list, teachers must include elements such as reviewing, stating the purpose of the lesson, introducing the topic, modeling the expected behavior, providing guided and independent practice, and summarizing, among others.

Table 6.4 provides lesson plan skeletons in two content areas: reading (words with specific syllables) and science (the water cycle). Later, a scripted writing lesson plan (using transition words in writing) provides each step in more detail (see Appendix A).

TABLE 6.3   **Effective Teacher-Directed Lesson Presentation**

Components of Effective Teacher-Directed Lessons

1. Obtains student attention prior to beginning lesson.

2. Provides a review of the previous day's concepts at the beginning of the lesson.

3. Actively assesses students' understanding and retention of previously learned material.

4. Provides a clear overview of the lesson.

5. States or elicits the purpose of the lesson and enlists students' commitments to learn.

6. Familiarizes students with what they will be accountable for knowing and/or doing.

7. Introduces the topic activating prior experiences and knowledge relevant to the information or skills to be learned.

8. Relates lesson topics to existing knowledge.

9. Provides an organizational framework to assist students in organizing the lesson information.

10. Instructs in a clear, concise, and sequential manner.

11. Models the expected behavior of the student as part of instruction.

12. Models self-talk that will help students achieve (e.g., strategies for recall).

13. Provides frequent questions to evaluate student understanding.

14. Requires overt and active participation.

15. Maintains a brisk pace during the lesson.

16. Uses instructional cues and prompts to maintain high accurate responding.

17. Maintains high success rate in teacher-led activities (70% to 90% accuracy).

18. Provides guided practice opportunities only after students demonstrate appropriate levels of understanding.

19. Assists students with guided practice opportunities by monitoring student work, giving feedback, and applying error correction procedures.

20. Provides independent practice opportunities only after students have achieved a high rate of success (90% to 100%) in guided practice.

21. Gives summary of the lesson content and integrates with content of other lessons or experiences.

22. Provides daily, weekly, and monthly reviews.

23. Maintains continuous records and graphs of students' performance and communicates results of evaluation activities to students.

24. Instructs students to generalize and apply knowledge across settings, situations, and conditions.

Source: Adapted from Englert, C. S., (1984). Measuring teacher effectiveness from the teacher's point of view. Focus on Exceptional Children, (12), 17–15.

TABLE 6.4   Sample Teacher-Directed Lesson Plan Skeletons

Objectives	Anticipatory Set/Purpose	Review	Modeling/Guided Practice–Task Analysis Dialogue	Independent Practice	Data Collection
Given 20 two-syllable words with -*tion*, -*ture* and -*ly* suffixes, the students will orally read the words with 90% accuracy.	Hold up a chapter book. Explain that in chapter books there are many two-syllable words. In this lesson, the students will learn skills that will enable them to read two-syllable words.	Flash card review of suffixes (-*tion*, -*ture*, -*ly*, -*ing*, -*ed*, -*ment*) Flash card review of CVC pattern words.	Teacher uses an overhead projector to model and to guide students in using the following process: 1. Underline and read the first syllable. 2. Circle and read the suffix. 3. Touch and read the word.	Students practice reading lists of 10 words to a partner.	Students orally read a list of 20 words to the teacher. Teacher records data.
Given a graphic organizer that depicts the water cycle, students will write the key words that describe the various aspects of the water cycle with 100% accuracy as measured by the teacher's example.	The teacher walks around the class and sprays water in the air. The teacher asks the class if they know how water cycles through the environment. In this lesson, the students will learn how water cycles through the environment and they will learn vocabulary words that describe the water cycle.	Review names for different bodies of water: *lakes*, *oceans*, *rivers*, *streams,* and *ponds.*	Teacher uses an overhead transparency for modeling and guided practice. 1. Water is in lakes, oceans, rivers, streams, and ponds. Water from bodies of water evaporates into the air. (Teacher writes *evaporates* above the picture of the lake and explains the meaning of evaporation). 2. Water in the air condenses to form clouds. (Teacher writes *condenses* next to the picture of the cloud and explains term). 3. Water is released into the air. This is called precipitation. (Teacher writes *precipitation* next to the picture of the rain and explains the terms as meaning rain, sleet, and snow).	Students are given a graphic organizer that depicts the water cycle. Students write the key words that describe the water cycle next to the graphic representation of the word.	Teacher collects the completed organizers and records whether students met the objective.

Special educators design their instruction based on students' needs as described in their Individualized Education Plans (IEPs). The first place to start then is to examine students' goals on their IEPs. Teachers must also take into consideration the general education curriculum and the state or district standards. Based on these pieces of information, instructional units can be planned. From each instructional unit, individual lessons can be created. The focus of the discussion in this chapter is the individual lesson. Unit planning is discussed in Chapter 12.

Behavioral Objectives

Each teacher-directed lesson should include an anticipated student outcome. Outcomes are usually written as behavioral objectives that describe what the student should be able to do following completion of the lesson. In order to determine lesson objectives, the general education curriculum (or the state, district, or core standards) and the student's IEPs goals must be taken in consideration. For example, Steven is a 10th-grade student who is receiving special education services. The general education life skills curriculum includes this goal: *Students will use money to purchase goods.* And one of Steven's annual goals is this: *When given 10 opportunities, Steven will identify coins matching the amount of a purchase price under $1 with 100% accuracy.*

Based on this information, Steven's teacher develops a unit plan on money (see Chapter 12), which she further subdivides into lesson objectives. One of the first skills Steven will need to learn is how to identify the value of each coin. Therefore, one of the lesson objectives is this: *Given four pennies and a numeral under five, Steven will move the correct number of pennies represented by the numeral 5 out of 5 trials.* This objective provides the basis for designing a teacher-directed lesson for Steven acquiring this skill.

Stages of learning. One of the considerations in developing lesson objectives is the students' stage of learning. The first stage of learning is **acquisition**. During this stage, students first learn the knowledge or skill being taught. The goal for acquisition learning is accuracy or frequency of response. Once the skill or knowledge has been acquired, instruction can focus on the second stage of learning, **fluency** or the rate at which the student responds. Fluency is important because some academic and life skills need to be built to the level of automaticity. For example, a fluent reader decodes words without having to stop and sound them out. The last two stages of learning are **maintenance**, the ability to retain the knowledge or skill over time without being retaught, and **generalization** or the ability to apply the knowledge or skill to different conditions, such as materials (e.g., from a worksheet to a textbook), individuals (e.g., different teachers), or settings (e.g., school to home). Table 6.5 lists these stages with the type of instruction and measurement used for each.

After considering the stage of learning, teachers are prepared to write lesson objectives. Lesson objectives must have the following elements: (a) observable and measurable behavior, (b) condition(s) under which the behavior will occur, and (c) criteria for acceptable performance of the behavior. Another consideration for lesson objectives is the students' stage of learning.

Behavior. The lesson objective must describe the behavior to be exhibited by the student, not the teacher, upon completion of the lesson. The student will be observed

TABLE 6.5   Stages of Learning

Stage of Learning	Instruction	Measurement	Example
Acquisition	Explicit instruction with feedback and error correction	• Accuracy • Frequency	• 90% accuracy • 6 times during one hour; 5 out of 5 trials
Fluency	Accurate practice while building rate	• Time with accuracy	• 70 in 1 minute with no more than two errors
Maintenance	Periodic review	• Measured after instruction is completed and time has passed	• Same as above
Generalization	Provide wide range of examples and practice experiences during instruction	• Measured in a different context	• Same as above except new context is added

exhibiting the behavior, and how well the student performed will be measured. Teachers often include activities within a lesson that go beyond or supplement the ultimate objective. These are activities that enhance the lesson; they need not be written as objectives. If the answers to the following questions are no, then the activity should not be listed as a lesson objective:

- Will I as a teacher model the behavior and require that the student practice it?

- Will I as the teacher record (e.g., grade) the student's performance on this objective?

Generally, lessons will contain no more than two objectives. Two objectives may be written in instances where students are working on behavioral-social goals and academic-functional goals simultaneously. Sometimes students who are English learners (ELs) will also need a language goal. Given the difficulty of effectively integrating more than two goals within one lesson, the author recommends that lessons involving EL students integrate behavior-social goals with language goals OR academic-functional goals with language goals.

The behavioral component of the lesson objective must be a verb that is observable. *To know, to understand,* or *to appreciate* are not observable. Teachers often use verbs such as *calculate, read, list,* or *explain.* One cannot visualize, however, what students will be doing when *calculating, reading, listing, or explaining.* Will students be doing the calculations in their heads, or will they be writing the answers on paper? Examples of unobservable, observable but unclear, and observable and clear verbs are listed in Table 6.6.

TABLE 6.6   **Verbs for Behavioral Objectives**

Unobservable	Observable but Unclear	Observable and Clear
to know	to calculate	to write
to learn	to construct	to physically build
to master	to compare	to compare verbally
to appreciate	to list	to list in writing
to understand	to read	to read orally
to realize	to explain	to explain verbally
to like	to classify	to point to
to master	to identify	to circle in writing

Conditions. The conditions under which the student will perform the behavior must also be stated in the objective. Conditions typically include materials, prompts, and instructions. This component of the behavioral objective is often overlooked because the conditions may appear obvious. However, there are special conditions for certain behaviors that must be applied. Suppose the behavior is to write the answers to math problems; some students may require special conditions under which the behavior will be accomplished, perhaps use of compensatory skills such as a number line, times table chart, or calculator. Those items would be written as part of the condition: for example, "Whitney will write the answers to three-digit multiplication problems at 100% accuracy using a calculator."

Criteria. Teachers must also establish the criteria for acceptable performance of the behavior. These are often written in percentages (e.g., 80% or 100% correct). As discussed previously, the criteria should reflect the stage of learning at which the student is expected to perform. If the student is expected to demonstrate only acquisition, then percentages or ratio of items correct (10 out of 10 words) would be appropriate. Sometimes, depending upon the behavior, a percentage or ratio is not appropriate. The student may be expected to demonstrate the behavior a number of times during a specified time period. For example, the objective may be that the student will initiate a conversation four times during the school day. Another approach that is often taken is with the number of trials. The example presented earlier with Steven's objectives includes this type of criterion. He will be asked to move the correct number of pennies represented by the numeral presented five times (five trials) and will be expected to be correct all five times. If the student is demonstrating fluency, time limits and accuracy should be included among the criteria.

Another possibility is the use of specific statements of criteria. This is important, for example, in handwriting skills. It would be impossible to assess *writing her name at 100% accuracy* without knowing what 100% accuracy means. Is the inclusion of every letter the most important criterion? Or does every letter need to be in order? Or is the goal to write the first letter capitalized and remaining letters in lower case? Or is the placement on the paper important, such as having all the letters written on the line? Or is having all letters of proportionate size important? Rather than use an accuracy level, the intended outcomes (e.g., all letters in order and of proportionate size) should be written as the criteria. Examples of objectives using various conditions and criteria for accuracy and for fluency appear in Table 6.7.

> Mr. Young, a new student teacher, has developed a well-designed lesson plan. His cooperating teacher and university supervisor are both observing him today so he is nervous. As he begins his lesson, he forgets to obtain student attention before starting. As he proceeds through the lesson, the students are talking, texting, and otherwise not paying attention to Mr. Young at all.

Attending Cues

Prior to initiating the lesson, teachers must gain student attention through the use of attending cues. Acquiring student attention means that students are not engaged in verbal or motor behavior that may inhibit learning. That is, the students are looking at, listening to, or otherwise focused on the teacher and the lesson content. Teachers can

TABLE 6.7   Examples of Lesson Objectives

Stage of Learning	Sample Objective
Acquisition	*Given teacher recitation*, Brent will **write** 10 spelling words 100% accurately.
	When presented with coins from a purchase, Yvonne will **count the change** and **state verbally** the total amount accurately in 4 out of 5 trials.
	On every written assignment given, Jacob will **write** his name in the upper right-hand corner using a capital *J* and lower case *a, c, o,* and *b*.
	Following completion of a social skills lesson, Nelson will **role-play** accepting negative feedback and score 90% on the observer checklist.
Fluency	*Given a list of survival words*, Winston will **read** them **orally** at a rate of 60 correct with no more than 2 errors in 1 minute.
	When asked, Tommy will **recite verbally** his home address correctly and within 15 seconds.
	Following his tutoring session, Kalei will **write the answers** to mixed facts with 80 digits correct and no more than 2 errors in 1 minute.

Key:

italics = condition

<u>underline</u> = <u>criteria</u>

bold = **behavior**

establish routine signals to cue students to know what the signal implies and behave in the prescribed and pretaught manner (Archer & Hughes, 2011). Teachers who can apply less involved and drastic signals will conserve effort and energy and will maintain greater control of student behavior. One high school special education teacher was observed using a color-coded system. Following the meaning of traffic light colors, when a yellow piece of construction paper was displayed on the front chalkboard, students knew to anticipate the beginning of a lesson. When the teacher changed the yellow paper to a red paper, students had been taught to stop what they were doing immediately and to give attention to the teacher at the front. When a green paper was displayed, students knew they could continue with their small-group and individual work. Other attending cues may be simple verbal statements by the teacher, such as "Get ready," "Look," or "Let's start." Other teachers, particularly with younger children, may teach them a short song or rhyme and when the students hear the teacher start, they join in and know that once it is over, they are to attend to the teacher. Teachers select attending cues based on what is being taught and on the students' age, abilities, experiences, and attending behaviors.

Anticipatory Set

Successful lessons begin with an anticipatory set. **Anticipatory sets** may be viewed as the introduction to the lesson. If designed and implemented well, anticipatory sets take the students' minds off other things and focus their attention on today's lesson. An anticipatory set also can hook into students' past knowledge and trigger a memory or some practice which will facilitate the new lesson (Hunter, 2004). The anticipatory set should be short and consume little of the instructional time. When teaching how and when to dial 911, one teacher set up some scenarios describing "What if?" to motivate the students to learn how to acquire help. Another teacher used similar scenarios with older students to get them motivated to learn to use spell-check on their laptops. A third teacher read a story about a woman who put tomatoes in her fruit salad as an introduction to a lesson about what defines fruits versus vegetables. In a large-group setting, another teacher asked the students, "Imagine seeing a volcano erupt. Write down five things you might see."

When designing anticipatory sets, teachers should ask themselves these questions:

- Is the anticipatory set relevant to the lesson?

- Does it require active participation?

- Does it link past information with new information to be learned?

- Will it motivate students to learn the new material?

Mrs. Osborne is an exceptional special educator. The school district often sends new teachers to observe her. On this particular day, she has three new teachers watching. After observing for about an hour, they meet with Mrs. Osborne for 10 minutes to ask her questions. One of the teachers mentions that she was surprised to see Mrs. Osborne spend so much time talking about the material before even

(Continued)

(Continued)

starting the lesson. She wonders why. Mrs. Osborne explains that what she was doing was making certain the students remembered the previously learned material. She also needs to make certain they have the skills necessary to move to this new material. She also explains how important it is for students to "buy-into" the lesson. In other words, if students don't know why they are learning or should learn this new content, why would they want to learn it? So she spends time asking students how learning this will help them in their lives. If they can't generate ideas, she prompts and gives them ideas.

Review, Prerequisite Checks, and Purpose

Effective teachers review previously learned material, engage in some form of prerequisite check, and state or elicit purposes for learning the current day's content. These three components may fall in differing order and sometimes are similar or overlap. Mrs. Osborne ensures that she includes these elements in each of her lesson presentations.

Reviews are important to tie current information or skills to what has been previously learned. They also provide an opportunity to maintain previously learned information or skills (Goeke, 2009). Reviews are not reteaching or asking students if they remember how to do something. Reviews are intended to ensure that all students recall information or can perform the previously learned task before moving on (Archer & Hughes, 2011). Students' current knowledge needs to be assessed to ensure they are ready to learn the new content. The prerequisite check may be accomplished through the review. In this way, students might be asked a series of questions relating to previously taught information that ties to the current lesson.

Purpose statements are also a critical component of lessons. The purpose of the lesson may be stated by the teacher directly, or it may be elicited from the students. The statement of purpose serves as motivation and may be used to elicit commitment from the students to participate and learn. A teacher who was teaching a learning strategy shared the success of previous students in using this strategy in improving their grades in their general education classes. She then asked the students if they too would like to improve their grades; if so, they were invited to participate in the lesson. The teacher then asked how this learning strategy could be used beyond improving grades in school. The students decided it could be used in specific ways at home or on the job. Thus the teacher elicited responses from the students to identify reasons for acquiring this skill.

Purpose statements can also provide an overview to the lesson which gives students a "mental set" to assist them in anticipating what they will be learning. The purpose statement also provides an organizational framework for students so they are better prepared to integrate, associate, and organize information. Another function of the purpose statement is to inform students what they will be accountable for knowing and/or doing based on this lesson. And possibly the most important reason is to help students connect what they are going to learn to their lives (Hunter, 2004).

One of the other new teachers observing Mrs. Osborne asked why she demonstrates for the students so often. In this lesson she was teaching how to read a graph. Mrs. Osborne presented steps to follow then demonstrated the steps in front of the students using a graph from the computer projector and talking out loud as she completed the steps. The teacher asking the question wondered if this was actually necessary. Mrs. Osborne explained that modeling is a critical element in showing students how to complete the task. Teachers cannot assume that just telling them how to do something is sufficient. Students need to see the actual skill modeled.

Instruction and Modeling

As part of delivering instruction, **modeling** the behavior required in the instructional objective must be included. Modeling may be done by the teacher, a paraeducator, a peer, a parent, a job coach, an employer or anyone who has mastered the skill. Modeling involves *behavioral modeling* and *cognitive modeling*. **Behavioral modeling** includes actual demonstration of the skill. **Cognitive modeling** involves self-talk that assists students in understanding the thought processes of the person modeling (Goeke, 2009). In providing self-talk, teachers state overtly what they are thinking as they are accomplishing the task. This allows the teacher to model not only the task, but the strategies that are used to accomplish the task. For example, a teacher modeling addition with regrouping would self-talk the process of the steps required as she completes the problem. This modeling example is outlined in Table 6.8.

Within teacher-directed lessons, modeling of the skill increases the likelihood of student success. In addition to modeling, teachers should deliver instruction in a manner that is clear, complete, and coherent. They should ask for student responses using prompts and feedback, as needed. Of course, the amount of repetition in instruction will vary and depend on the needs of the individual students and the complexity of the task. In almost all cases, multiple demonstrations are necessary (Archer & Hughes, 2011; Test, Browder, Karvonen, Wood, & Algozzine, 2002).

TEACHER TIP #6.4

REMEMBERING EFFECTIVE INSTRUCTION ELEMENTS

Teachers can use the acronym SCREAM to recall elements of effective delivery of instruction:

S **S**tructure

C **C**larity

R **R**edundancy

E **E**nthusiasm

A **A**ppropriate Rate

M **M**aximum Engagement

Source: Mastropieri & Scruggs, 2002.

TABLE 6.8   **An Example of Modeling Addition With Regrouping With Sample Problem**

$$163$$
$$235$$
$$\underline{+\ 542}$$

Teacher Verbalizes	Teacher Behaves
• "When I'm working an addition problem with regrouping, I first make certain I write my numbers in columns and they are all lined up properly."	• Writes numbers on chalkboard or projector
• "Let me check that the numbers are lined up properly. Yes, they appear to be lined up."	• Scans number columns
• "Now I want to make certain that I draw the addition and equal signs."	• Draws addition and equal signs
• "The next thing I do is add up all the numbers in the ones column. 3 plus 5 equals 8 plus 2 equals 10. Since this number is greater than 9, I need to regroup to the tens column. Therefore, I place the 0, representing zero ones in the ones column and write the 1, representing one ten in the tens column."	• Points to each number while adding; writes 0 under the equal sign in the ones column; writes 1 in the tens column above the other numbers
• "Now I need to add all the numbers in the tens column. 1, which I regrouped, plus 6 equals 7 plus 3 equals 10 plus 4 equals 14. Since this number is greater than 9, I need to regroup to the hundreds column. Therefore, I place the 4, representing four tens in the tens column and write the 1, representing one hundred in the hundreds column."	• Points to each number while adding; writes 4 under the equal sign in the tens column; writes 1 in the hundreds column above the other numbers
• "Next I add all the numbers in the hundreds column. 1, which I regrouped, plus 1 equals 2 plus 2 equals 4 plus 5 equals 9."	• Points to each number while adding; writes 9 under the equal sign in the hundreds column
• "I have now completed my problem."	

Another aspect of Mrs. Osborne's teaching that caught the attention of the new teachers was her use of practice. They asked her to explain why she started helping the students with their assignment and then stopped. Mrs. Osborne explained that after she'd taught and modeled the skill, she worked through three of the problems as a class, asking and answering questions, and making certain every student understood how to do the problems. Once they'd demonstrated they could do it, she allowed them to work the remaining problems alone.

Guided Practice

Once the teacher has modeled the behavior (i.e., the lesson's behavioral objective), the student is given an opportunity to practice the lesson objective under direct supervision. **Guided practice,** therefore, is a strategy where students practice with someone who has mastered the skill (e.g., teacher, paraeducator, peer tutor) readily available to assist them by answering questions, ensuring that errors are not being practiced, correcting errors and re-teaching, if necessary. Mrs. Osborne and the class working together on several problems before asking the students to work independently is a form of guided practice. If guided practice opportunities are provided during group instruction, all students need to be given an opportunity to practice. The major purpose of guided practice is to correct inaccurate responses so that students don't practice errors. A piano teacher once told the author that if a note was misplayed three times, the error was learned. Practice does not make perfect. Only perfect or accurate practice makes perfect. Guided practice involves

- all students practicing alone, but under the intense supervision of someone who has mastered the skill (e.g., teacher, paraeducator, peer tutor).

- students answering in choral responding and individually.

- students practicing in pairs with intense supervision.

Guided practice is not

- only one or two students answering the question or working the problem.

- assignments sent home as homework.

Teachers sometimes do not apply guided practice appropriately. For example, some teachers call on individual students to work math problems or spell a word at the chalkboard. Teachers who apply the principle of guided practice would ask ALL students to work the problem or write the word at their desks and compare their processes and answers with those written by the student on the chalkboard. The teacher would monitor each student's work and provide feedback.

Another excellent strategy for guided practice is to allow students to work in pairs while the teacher monitors each pair. Depending on the characteristics of the students and the skill being developed, students may need to be broken into small groups and assigned a *master* to monitor each group's guided practice. One Head Start teacher, for example, who was teaching the stop/drop/roll procedure for avoiding burns during a fire, divided the class into groups of four and assigned a teacher, the paraeducator, and volunteers to each group. The students practiced stopping/dropping/rolling in their small groups under direct guidance of an adult.

Prompts. **Prompts** are assistance provided to increase the likelihood of the student responding correctly. Prompts should be used only if students have difficulty responding or if the teacher anticipates students will have problems responding correctly. Types of prompts include (a) verbal directions, (b) modeling, (c) physical guidance, and (d) stimulus prompts. Verbal direction prompts may be a sound, a word, or several sentences in length. For example, if a student is reading orally and becomes "stuck," the teacher might assist the student by suggesting he "sound it out" or the teacher might start sounding it out. The teacher might also ask the student "What word do you think it is?"

With modeling prompts, usually the teacher demonstrates the desired behavior so that the student can imitate it. However, modeling prompts are not limited to the teacher or to a human. The model may be presented, for example, through visual illustration, such as a word printed on a card or a drawing of an action to be imitated. Physical guidance prompts involve bodily assistance with an action. A physical education teacher, for example, may guide a student's arm in executing a tennis serve, or a student with fine motor difficulty may require physical guidance in learning to use scissors or write with a pencil. The last type of prompt, stimulus prompts, are used in conjunction with the instructional materials: for example, drawing attention to important points in reading materials by using arrows, bold print, highlighting, color change, and such. Prompts should focus students' attention on the relevant material, not distract from it, and teachers should use the weakest prompt possible that is still effective.

Fading. Prompts are provided when students have difficulty responding correctly. Teachers' use of prompts should be faded until prompts are removed totally. Fading usually involves moving from most to least (e.g., physical guidance to visual prompt to verbal directions) or least to most (verbal prompts to gestures to physical prompts); fading may be in the form of graduated guidance (using physical prompts only when necessary), time delay (delaying the time between presentation of the stimulus and the delivery of the prompt), or fading the stimulus (highlighting or exaggerating a physical aspect of the stimulus, through color, size, and position, and gradually fading that highlighting or exaggeration). Another example of fading is moving from telling the student what to do, to asking the student what she should do, to reminding the student to follow the steps learned (Archer & Hughes, 2011). Teachers should fade prompts as quickly as possible and avoid using unplanned prompts, such as vocal intonation giving away the answer (Alberto & Troutman, 2012). Fading prompts is necessary for students to be prepared for independent practice.

Independent Practice

Independent practice differs from guided practice in that students are expected to perform the task independent of the teacher or with no prompts, and teacher feedback is not provided as quickly as during guided practice. In some respects, independent practice can be equated with "testing" the students' individual performance. Sometimes in traditional instruction, independent practice takes the form of homework. Independent practice should not commence until students have obtained high rates (90% to 100%) of success in guided practice (Englert et al., 1992). This is particularly critical when assigning homework. Teachers who appropriately use homework as independent practice schedule time for guided practice in the classroom. Effective teachers do not assign the homework until students have demonstrated their ability to accomplish the lesson objective at high rates of success. Once students in Mrs. Osborne's class demonstrated they were able to complete the problems accurately with minimal assistance, she allowed them to work the problems independently.

Independent practice does not always take the form of written work. In the previous Head Start example, the teacher "tested" students' recall of the stop/drop/roll procedure the next day by having the students perform it without adult assistance. Those who had difficulty were retaught and given additional opportunities to practice under guidance.

Checking for Understanding

Checking for understanding involves posing questions and checking students' work during group and individual practice. Choral responses and response cards, discussed earlier, are two ways in which teachers can involve all students more actively, as well as checking for all students' understanding of the content simultaneously (Cavanaugh, 1994). Teachers need to determine specific ways in which they will check for understanding and include that information in their lesson plans.

TEACHER TIP #6.5

DOs AND DON'Ts IN CHECKING FOR UNDERSTANDING

When designing and implementing checking for understanding throughout the lesson, remember these tips:

DO

Use group signals (e.g., thumbs up or down).

Use choral responding.

Ask whole group question, then call on a representative sample of students.

Ask students to answer your question in writing. Circulate among students to check answers.

Use electronic devices that allow individual responses but aggregate the results, which can be displayed in front of the classroom through a computer and projector.

Use short quizzes, papers, or performances of the skills.

Use a variety of techniques.

DON'T

Ask, "Does anyone not understand?" or "Everyone understands, right?"

Use the ubiquitous okay? (e.g., "I think we're ready to move on, okay?")

Assume students understand when they don't ask any questions. (Goeke, 2009)

Error Correction

Error correction procedures vary according to the type of practice (guided vs. independent). During guided practice, students require explicit explanation of why their response is incorrect, as well as additional modeling, more examples, and/or reteaching of the skill. In order to be effective, teacher feedback must be as immediate as possible, thus keeping the students from practicing errors.

During independent practice, error correction consists of calling to a student's attention that an error has been made, but additional explanations or reteaching should rarely be necessary since the student has already demonstrated high levels of success during guided practice before moving to the independent practice phase. Teachers need to anticipate the types of errors students will make and build error correction procedures into the lesson planning process.

One of the most important things a teacher can do is provide students with feedback on how well they are doing and how they can improve. Teachers should use corrective feedback by giving students an explanation as to why their response was correct or incorrect. Feedback should be provided in a timely manner with immediate feedback being the most effective. Summative feedback should tell students where they stand in relation to specific skills, not to other students. Teachers can also teach students to effectively monitor their own progress, thus providing some of their own feedback (Marzano, Pickering, & Pollock, 2001).

Closure

Effective teachers provide closure to their lessons by summarizing or reviewing the content and integrating it with previously learned content or experiences. To demonstrate the importance of closure, the author has played a short song on the piano and stopped before the last few bars. Listeners become discontent wanting the song to finish on a dominant chord. Teachers who do not use closure can leave students feeling unsettled similar to the uncompleted song. Teachers also often provide an anticipatory set for the next lesson as part of the closure. For example, students may be told that what they learned today has prepared them for what they will experience the rest of the week. This can be particularly motivating if students are learning small portions of content and need motivation to continue by seeing the ultimate larger outcome. As part of closure, teachers may ask, "What did we learn today?" "Why is this information or skill important, relevant, or helpful?" or "How does what we learned today relate to the larger unit of study?" The latter two questions are particularly important for older students (Goeke, 2009).

Oftentimes, closure doesn't happen because teachers fail to watch the time or misjudge the amount of time needed to complete the lesson. Teachers in secondary classrooms, for example, may be interrupted by the bell ringing while the students are still in guided practice. One teacher used an electronic timer and set it for 45 minutes at the beginning of each class period. When the timer rang, the teacher knew she had 5 minutes to provide lesson closure and to prepare students for transitioning to their next class.

Monitoring Progress

Monitoring student progress is another instructional principle used by effective teachers. Monitoring progress in this context refers to evaluating and recording students' performance on the lesson's behavioral objective. As mentioned previously, one of the criteria for determining whether to include a lesson activity as a behavioral objective is whether the teacher would assess and record student performance. Specific ways of recording student performance were discussed in Chapter 5.

Depending upon the behavioral objective, student performance may be recorded (a) while students are engaged in independent practice, such as the stop/drop/roll example or (b) after the student has submitted a permanent product, such as the worksheet Mrs. Osborne assigned.

In Appendix A, a scripted lesson plan is presented. This lesson plan includes the identified critical elements and a script of what the teacher should say and do, as well as anticipated student responses. A checklist for scripted lesson plans is provided in Table 6.9. This checklist can be used to ensure that all of the critical elements are included. Additional scripted lesson plans are also provided in Chapters 10 through 14.

TABLE 6.9   Scripted Lesson Plan Checklist

Lesson Component	Items to Be Included
Objectives	1. The students' IEP short-term objective from which this lesson was created is included.
	2. No more than two behavioral objectives for this lesson are listed.
	3. Each lesson objective includes an appropriate condition; observable, measurable behavior; and criteria for acceptable behavior.
	4. The criterion makes sense given the behavior and the condition.
	5. Student performance of the lesson objective will be recorded because it is useful information and provides documentation regarding progress toward the IEP objective.
Lesson Introduction	6. The anticipatory set will spark the interest of the student and relates directly to the lesson content.
	7. Review of previously taught information is included.
	8. A prerequisite check has been included to ensure students have the necessary background for this lesson.
	9. The purpose(s) for the lesson are stated by the teacher or elicited from the students.
	10. Expected student performance following completion of this lesson is stated.
Instruction and Modeling	11. The instructions relate directly to the lesson objective.
	12. The instructions are accurate, clear, complete, concise, and sequential.
	13. The teacher (or a "master") models the lesson objective.
	14. Students are asked frequent and appropriate questions to evaluate their understanding.
	15. Anticipated correct and incorrect student responses are included.
	16. Appropriate error correction techniques are included in anticipation of incorrect responses.
Guided Practice	17. All students are provided guided practice opportunities that relate directly to the lesson objective.
	18. Monitoring of student performance is included.

(Continued)

TABLE 6.9   (Continued)

Lesson Component	Items to Be Included
	19. Anticipated correct and incorrect student responses are included.
	20. Appropriate error correction techniques are included in anticipation of incorrect responses.
Independent Practice	21. All students are provided independent-practice opportunities that relate directly to the lesson objective.
Closure	22. A summary and review of the lesson are included.
	23. The content of this lesson is tied to previously learned information.

TEACHER TIP #6.6

SELF-ASSESS YOUR TEACHING

Teachers rarely receive enough ongoing feedback about their teaching to be helpful. One strategy teachers can use is self-assessment. Audio or video record your instruction and then analyze the lesson. One first-year high school teacher did so and set the following goals:

- When asking higher level questions, allow more wait time for student responses.

- Ask a question, wait, and then call on a student.

- Allow students to ask more questions and receive more feedback.

- Narrow the topic.

- Make certain previous concepts are fully reviewed and tied to this new lesson.

- Use more specific praise.

- Quit saying "OK" and "all right."

- Conduct this self-evaluation frequently. (Freiberg, 2002)

Technology Spotlight #6.1

Flipped Classrooms

A recent trend of blending technology with in-person instruction is the use of flipped classrooms. Typically teachers instruct in their classrooms and assign homework for students to practice the skills at home. In a flipped classroom model, the activities are inverted. Students participate in teacher instruction at home, and practice the new skills learned during class time. Teachers convert their instruction to video or audio lessons that can be accessed by students at home. One rule of thumb is to make videos no longer than 60 to 90 seconds per grade level. So a video for seventh grade would be 7 to 9 minutes long (7 x 60 seconds to 7 x 90 seconds) (Bergmann & Sams, 2014). Flipped learning is most effective when teaching knowledge that is procedural (i.e., knowledge about how to do something) (Milman, 2014).

In the context of this chapter, a flipped classroom would consist of the teacher recording the instructional portion of the lesson using all of the effective teaching elements. If guided practice is included on the video, it would consist of the teacher asking the student to complete the tasks along with the teacher. The instructional portion would be recorded and placed on the Internet, CDs, DVDs, or flash drives. Other materials accessed through the Internet (such as science simulations) can be included in the lessons.

Using the elements of effective instruction, students would view the teacher's instruction at home and then complete guided practice opportunities in the classroom. Following the principles of effective instruction, once students have demonstrated high levels of understanding, they can move on to independent practice. Opportunities for higher level application of the skills learned can also occur during class time given the presence of the teacher to facilitate these activities.

Flipped classrooms for students allow them to move at their own pace, have access to instruction all hours of every day, and be better prepared for anticipated 21st century learning.

Also, if multiple teachers make videos addressing the same concepts and students are given access to them, the student can view more than one teacher's instruction to better understand the concepts being taught (Fulton, 2012).

One set of teachers merged flipped learning and mastery learning. Students in their classrooms learned course content through videoed direct instruction and at an individualized pace. When each completed a unit, he or she demonstrated mastery of the learning objective before moving to the next unit. Students with special needs required more time than other students to complete the units. These teachers "front-loaded" the essential concepts and left the "nice to know" lessons to the end of the school year to ensure all students learned what was essential (Bergmann & Sams, 2014).

Advantages of flipped learning for teachers include better understanding of student difficulties, using class time more effectively, and learning from viewing each other's instruction. In addition, family members have access to the instruction (Fulton, 2012). Flipped learning also has disadvantages. For example, teachers need time to create the videos and the quality may not be the best. Students may not have access to the technology necessary to view the lessons at home and may encounter a lot of distractions in that environment. They may also not watch the video or not understand the concept being taught and thus are unprepared for the classroom practice and enrichment (Milman, 2014).

Limited research has been conducted on flipped learning in K–12 schools (Milman, 2014). Some teachers report

(Continued)

(Continued)

that students improve their academic skills (e.g., LaFee, 2013), particularly when compared with a traditional mode of instruction (e.g., Fulton, 2012). Although no research was located in which students receiving special education services were specifically targeted, the advantages of flipped learning (e.g., moving at individual pace, more supervision of practice) indicate there may be promise for this population.

Implications for Culturally and/or Linguistically Diverse Students

Historically, students representing cultural groups outside of the European American middle-class majority have failed to thrive in school. Issues regarding culturally sensitive instruction have arisen as our community and school populations have become less European American, with more emphasis being placed on maintaining cultural identity rather than assimilating diverse individuals into a *melting pot* (Jones, 2004).

As discussed in previous chapters, today's school culture usually reflects European American culture. Thus, schools expect students to be competitive, independent, focused on academics and accomplishments, and future oriented. These values often conflict with those of other cultures, as well as differing abilities of students who represent those cultures. Teachers need to recognize and embrace the cultural and linguistic resources students from culturally and/or linguistically diverse (CLD) backgrounds bring.

Within this section and throughout the book, the characteristics of specific groups are stated as generalizations. These generalizations are provided only to demonstrate the contrast among cultural groups. Teachers must always remember there can be wide variations in characteristics within the same cultural group. No two students or families from the same cultural group will exhibit the same exact beliefs or behaviors. Therefore, teachers need to be careful not to stereotype or make assumptions about students or their families based on cultural group. In order to better understand values and beliefs, teachers need to become acquainted with individual students and their families.

Cultural Differences Impacting Instruction

Cultural backgrounds vary across many dimensions, two of which have particular influence on teacher-directed instruction, namely efficiency and independence. The focus on efficiency is tied directly to cultural perceptions of time. European-based cultures place a great deal of emphasis on using time wisely (e.g., *Time is money*). Other cultures are less time conscience. Teachers should not assume that students who hesitate before answering a question in class do not have the correct answer or are unsure of themselves. Additional think-time, particularly for higher level questions may be needed. For example, Native Americans are taught not only to think before they speak but to be patient and allow others to go first (Nel, 1993). Their culture emphasizes performing correctly. As a result, Native Americans may be reluctant to respond to questions if they feel uncertain about their answer (Morgan, 2010).

Cultural differences impact teachers' perceptions of the students, as well as students' performance in the classroom. Teachers, therefore, need to be aware of potential cultural differences and adjust teaching procedures as appropriate. Teachers who lack sensitivity to cultural values of efficiency may perceive the child as "wasting time." Hispanic students, for example, may focus more on doing a job well than on finishing rapidly so they can move on to the next task (Grossman, 1995). At times, it is appropriate to allow downtime or time off task or to slow down the pace of a lesson to accommodate students' cultural styles.

Although some cultures place less emphasis on time than others, some elements of time may need to be taught and reinforced in schools. In a large-scale survey of Hispanic and non-Hispanic educators examining their beliefs regarding Hispanic students and culture, a very high percentage of these teachers believed that Hispanic students should learn to function in the time frame of the classroom. At the same time, the majority felt that Hispanic students should not be rushed, but that they should also not be allowed as much time as they wanted. Some suggestions for teacher-directed instruction for Hispanic students include the following:

- Require daily assignments while teaching students to plan and organize to complete longer term assignments.

- Adjust pace to allow time to respond and finish, but do not provide all the time they want.

- Provide students with immediate, not delayed, feedback.

- Integrate Hispanic culture and language into the lessons, including Hispanic contributions to society.

- Hold high expectations, especially for students who are academically oriented. (Grossman, 1995)

Some cultures are also more present- than future-oriented. Hispanic, African American, and Pacific Island cultures often value the present more than the future. Students may need daily rather than long-term assignments while teachers assist them in organizing and planning their time to complete long-term assignments.

European Americans value independence and individual autonomy while other cultures rely more on group processes. Students from other cultures, therefore, often benefit from cooperative rather than competitive environments and enjoy learning in groups and from their peers. For example, in Hawaiian and Vietnamese cultures, older siblings often take over the parenting role, making younger children more receptive to an older peer, rather than an adult authority (Cheng, Ima, & Labovitz, 1994). On the other hand, Native American children are considered "autonomous, equal individuals, responsible for their own choices" (Nel, 1993, p. 22). The impact of cultural roles on independence and the issue of competitiveness versus collaboration are discussed in greater detail in Chapter 8.

Direct Teaching Techniques

Even though cultural differences exist which may impact the effectiveness of teacher-directed instruction, most cultural learning styles in some way support the teacher effectiveness principles discussed in this chapter. For example, Asian cultures (e.g., Japanese, Korean, Chinese) value schooling and have high regard for teachers. Students from these cultures are taught to work hard, behave well, obtain good grades, and excel in their schooling (Cheng et al., 1994). In fact, Asian cultures are often similar to European American cultures when it comes to reinforcing high achievement.

Other cultures in their unique ways support the principles of direct instruction. Even though some aspects of African American culture may appear to conflict with the traditional teacher-directed instructional model (Townsend, 2000), these students also come from high-energy and fast-paced home environments with a multitude of simultaneous stimulation and, according to Mary Franklin (1992), find "low-energy, monolithic environments (as seen in many traditional school environments) as less stimulating" (p. 118). Thus, fast-paced instruction supports African American learning style. In addition, many African American students prefer varied instructional presentation formats, particularly techniques that incorporate body movements (Franklin, 1992).

In Hawaiian culture, children are expected to watch and memorize in order to learn how to do something (*By observing, one learns.*) This cultural practice supports the principle of modeling. One teacher learning to adapt to teaching students of Hawaiian and Pacific Island descent stated, "I began to think that anything I could model had a better chance of being learned. So I looked for ways to model more complex and abstract processes . . . . I would think aloud, write aloud, and work aloud" (Tepper, 1992, p. 5). In addition, this teacher learned the importance of repetition and practice for the learner. "Rehearsal became an understood and comfortable mode for all sorts of learning work" (p. 6).

Research supports the effectiveness of teacher-directed instruction with CLD students. For example, in several studies examining the impact of *Direct Instruction* curriculum (i.e., *Reading Mastery* and *Corrective Reading*) as supplemental reading instruction in English, Hispanic students benefitted as much or more than the non-Hispanic students (Gunn, Biglan, Smolkowki, & Ary, 2000; Gunn, Smolkowski, Biglan, Black, & Blair, 2005). Effective teachers apply teacher-directed instruction in the manner described in this chapter. Modest variations may be needed to ensure that students from culturally diverse populations are given opportunities to maximize their potential in a manner to which they are accustomed.

TEACHER TIP #6.7

TEACHING ENGLISH LEARNERS

The number of English learners (ELs) is increasing in both special education and general education. Try these strategies when teaching ELs:

- Allow students who collectively speak a language other than English (e.g.,

Spanish), to use their language among themselves in pairs or cooperative learning groups. Allow students to interpret for one another when necessary and appropriate.

- Incorporate as many visual aids as possible (e.g., pictures, graphs, videos).

- Be aware of students' body language and facial expressions as nonverbal feedback. A questioning look speaks volumes.

- When ELs use English to express their thoughts, assess their understanding, not their language. Do not interrupt them to correct language mistakes. Address common language errors through writing or one-on-one sessions. (Rolon, 2002–2003)

Culturally Responsive Teaching

Culturally responsive teaching refers to methods that support CLD students' cultural and linguistic backgrounds integrated with evidence-based instructional practices (Aceves & Orosco, 2014). The primary goal of culturally responsive teaching and curriculum is to infuse students' prior knowledge and language with learning to build rich cultural and linguistic backgrounds within families and communities (Utley, Obiakor, & Bakken, 2011). **Evidence-based interventions and practices** are instructional practices that have been documented through research to be effective in improving student outcomes. In the context of this chapter, the previously discussed elements of teacher-directed instruction are evidence-based practices. A body of literature is emerging demonstrating the positive impact that culturally responsive teaching coupled with evidence-based practices can have on CLD students.

In a review of literature, Therese Aceves and Michael Orosco (2014) identified relevant themes of culturally responsive teaching to be the following: instructional engagement; culture, language, and racial identity; multicultural awareness; high expectations; critical thinking; and social justice. They also identified emerging evidence-based culturally responsive teaching practices. These practices included modeling, responsive feedback, collaborative teaching, and instructional scaffolding. Then in terms of methods of instruction, teachers who implement culturally responsive teaching engage students in instruction; communicate clear and specific expectations; model skills and strategies; and provide feedback that is supportive, critical, ongoing, and immediate. These elements have been discussed previously in this chapter with the exception of instructional scaffolding.

As with scaffolds used when constructing buildings, instructional scaffolds provide temporary supports while students are learning new content or skills. Teachers who scaffold their instruction break large tasks into smaller tasks and teach to those smaller units providing students with the necessary guided practice providing assistance and praise throughout the process. They may use concrete materials during initial instruction and vary the materials used (Vaughn & Bos, 2012). When teaching CLD students, instructional scaffolding occurs when "teachers control for task difficulty and promote a deeper level of understanding using students' contributions and their cultural and linguistic backgrounds" (Aceves & Orosco, 2014, p. 16). Teachers who scaffold their instruction reference students' culture or primary language while asking different types of questions, providing appropriate wait time, and using supportive instructional materials such as graphic organizers and guided notes. Other recommended culturally responsive strategies include providing visual representations, allowing frequent interactions in pairs, small groups, and whole class, as well as using study guides, taped text and jigsaw reading, concept maps, and other effective teaching strategies (Ford, Stuart, & Vakil, 2014).

Culturally responsive teaching goes beyond using effective teaching practices and ensuring CLD students' culture and language are represented. Culturally responsive teachers "(a) build trust among their students, (b) become culturally literate, (c) use appropriate diagnostic and assessment approaches, (d) use culturally sound questioning techniques, (e) provide effective feedback, (f) analyze content in instructional materials, and (g) establish positive home-school-community relationships." (Utley et al., 2011, p. 9).

SUMMARY

Although student achievement is influenced by many factors, teachers can positively influence student learning, regardless of the characteristics students bring to the classroom. Effective teachers use methods and strategies that research has documented to make a difference. Although effective instructional techniques in special education are not very distinct from those that are effective in general education, teachers who work with students with HID need to be particularly aware of evidence-based practices in order to teach as effectively and efficiently as possible.

Teachers can impact learning in three general ways. First, by selecting appropriate content to be taught. Instructional content should be determined by individual students' IEPs and state or district standards. Second, by maximizing the amount of time spent instructing. Typically, about 50% to 60% of the school day is allocated as instructional time. Teachers can increase this time by decreasing or eliminating noninstructional activities such as transition time and housekeeping efforts. And third, by increasing student engaged learning time. During engaged learning, students are attending to relevant instructional activities with a high rate of success. Teachers influence student engagement through teacher behaviors (e.g., questioning, pacing), instructional management (e.g., establishing routines), and behavior management (e.g., creating class rules). Research shows an association between the amount of time students spend in engaged learning and their academic achievement.

Teacher-directed instruction includes the commercial materials labeled, *Direct Instruction*, which are based on generic effective teaching principles documented through research to be effective. These principles should be used when teachers design their own lesson plans. Basic lesson plan elements include lesson objectives, anticipatory set/purpose statement, review, modeling, instruction, guided practice, independent practice, and closure. When writing lesson objectives, teachers should consider the stage of learning and include an observable behavior, a condition for acceptable performance, and a criterion. Modeling of the desired behavior is a critical element of effective teaching, which is often neglected in the lesson sequence. During modeling, a master of the skill (usually the teacher) demonstrates completion of the task as students observe. Self-talk is used to verbalize thought processes. Students should be provided an opportunity to practice the behavior under guided conditions (guided practice) prior to being required to perform it independently (independent practice). Effective teachers monitor student performance throughout to check for understanding, reteach, and correct errors.

Teachers need to be aware of and sensitive to the cultural backgrounds they bring to the classroom and equally sensitive to the cultures of their students. For example, some differences may be observed regarding the importance of efficiency and independence. Although students from culturally diverse groups often benefit from cooperative, rather than competitive environments, many of these cultures also directly reinforce the teacher effectiveness principles discussed in this chapter. Research has shown, for example, that CLD students benefit from direct instruction to at least the same degree as non-CLD students. Culturally responsive teachers embed their students' cultural and linguistic backgrounds within evidence-based teaching practices. In addition, they build trust among their students and establish positive home-school-community relationships, among other practices.

REVIEW QUESTIONS

1. Why is it important to use both state and district standards and the individual students' IEP goals in determining content to be taught?

2. Explain the difference between allocated and engaged learning time. Why should teachers be concerned about increasing allocated or engaged learning time in the classroom?

3. Provide five examples of how teachers can increase allocated or engaged learning time.

4. What is the overall goal of the *Direct Instruction* model? What assumptions underlie the *Direct Instruction* model?

5. Differentiate between *Direct Instruction* and direct instruction.

6. Why is the stage of learning an important consideration when writing lesson objectives?

7. Rewrite the following to include all elements of a behavior objective: *Angela will read a list of 10 CVC (consonant, vowel, consonant) words correctly.*

8. Outline the major elements of an effective lesson plan. Explain the purpose of each element.

9. What are your attitudes about the use of time and independence? How might your attitudes conflict with the culture of your students? How could these conflicts be managed in the classroom?

10. Define culturally responsive teaching and describe how teacher-directed instruction may be considered culturally responsive.

ACTIVITIES

1. Select five tasks you complete on a daily basis (e.g., brushing teeth, putting on your shoes, making breakfast). Write dialogue for modeling how to complete each task.

2. Locate a lesson plan on the Internet. Evaluate the lesson as compared to the elements of a teacher-directed lesson. What elements are the same, and what elements are different? Redesign the Internet lesson to include all the elements discussed in this chapter.

3. Evaluate a peer's scripted lesson plan. Describe the strengths and weaknesses of the plan. Write at least one suggestion for how the lesson could be improved.

4. Write a scripted lesson plan using all of the necessary elements. In small groups, present the lesson to your peers.

Council for Exceptional Children (CEC) Standards

The Council for Exceptional Children (CEC) is a premiere national professional organization comprised of special educators, paraeducators, relative service personnel, parents, and others interested in individuals with disabilities and/or those with gifts and talents. This organization has generated 10 standards for the preparation of special educators. These standards are listed in each chapter as they relate to the content within the chapter. The standard that applies to Chapter 6 is Standard #5.

**CEC Initial Preparation Standard #5:
Instructional Planning and Strategies (partial)**

Beginning special education professionals select, adapt, and use a repertoire of evidence-based instructional strategies to advance learning of individuals with exceptionalities.

5.1 Beginning special education professionals consider an individual's abilities, interests, learning environments, and cultural and linguistic factors in the selection, development, and adaptation of learning experiences for individuals with exceptionalities.

5.6 Beginning special education professionals teach to mastery and promote generalization of learning.

5.7 Beginning special education professionals teach cross-disciplinary knowledge and skills such as critical thinking and problem solving to individuals with exceptionalities.

REFERENCES

Aceves, T. C., & Orosco, M. J. (2014). *Culturally responsive teaching* (Document No. IC-2). University of Florida, Collaboration for Effective Educator Development, Accountability, and Reform Center. Retrieved from http://ceedar.education.ufl.edu/wp-content/uploads/2014/08/culturally-responsive.pdf

Adams, G. L., & Carnine, D. W. (2003). Direct instruction. In H. L. Swanson, K. R. Harris, & S. Graham (Eds.), *Handbook of learning disabilities* (pp. 403–416). New York, NY: Guilford Press.

Adams, G. L., & Engelmann, S. (1996). *Research on direct instruction: 25 years beyond DISTAR.* Seattle, WA: Educational Achievement Systems.

Alberto, P. A., & Troutman, A. C. (2012). *Applied behavior analysis for teachers* (9th ed.). Boston, MA: Pearson.

Archer, A. L., & Hughes, C. A. (2011). *Explicit instruction: Effective and efficient teaching.* New York, NY: Guilford Press.

Barbash, S. (2012). *Clear teaching.* Arlington, VA: Education Consumers Foundation.

Barth, R. S. (2013). The time is ripe (again). *Educational Leadership, 71*(2), 10–16.

Bergmann, J., & Sams, A. (2014). Flipping for mastery. *Educational Leadership, 71*(4), 24–29.

Bintz, W. P., & Williams, L. (2005). Questioning techniques of fifth and sixth grade reading teachers. *Middle School Journal, 37*(1), 45–52.

Blackwell, A. J., & McLaughlin, T. F. (2005). Using guided notes, choral responding, and response cards to increase student performance. *The International Journal of Special Education, 20*(2), 1–5.

Bost, L. W., & Riccomini, P. J. (2006). Effective instruction: An inconspicuous strategy for dropout prevention. *Remedial and Special Education, 27*(5), 301–311.

Cavanaugh, R. A. (1994). How can I make the shot when I don't get the ball? Improving academic achievement by increasing active student response. *The Forum, 19*(4), 9–11.

Cheng, L. L., Ima, K., Labovitz, G. (1994). Assessment of Asian and Pacific Islander students for gifted programs. In S. B. Garcia (Ed.), *Addressing cultural and linguistic diversity in special education: Issues and trends* (pp. 30–45). Arlington, VA: Council for Exceptional Children.

Deshler, D. D. (2014). Moving in the right direction but at what speed, and how smoothly? *Remedial and Special Education, 36*(2), 72–76. doi: 10.1177/0741932514558093

Englert, C. S., Tarrant, K. L., & Mariage, T. V. (1992). Defining and redefining instructional practice in special education. *Teacher Education and Special Education, 15*, 62–86.

Fisher, C., Berline, D., Filby, N., Marliave, R., Cahen, L., & Dishaw, M. (2015). Teaching behaviors, academic learning time, and student achievement: An overview. *Journal of Classroom Interaction, 50*(1), 6–24.

Fisher, D. (2009). The use of instructional time in the typical high school classroom. *The Educational Forum, 73*, 168–176.

Ford, B. A., Stuart, D. H., & Vakil, S. (2014). Culturally responsive teaching in the 21st century inclusive classroom. *The Journal of the International Association of Special Education, 15*(2), 56–62.

Franklin, M. E. (1992). Culturally sensitive instructional practices for African-American learners with disabilities. *Exceptional Children, 59*, 115–122.

Freiberg, H. J. (2002). Essential skills for new teachers. *Educational Leadership, 59*(6), 56–60.

Fulton, K. P. (2012). 10 reasons to flip. *Phi Delta Kappan, 94*(2), 20–24.

Godfrey, S. A., Grisham-Brown, J., Schuster, J. W., & Hemmeter, M. L. (2003). The effects of three techniques on student participation with preschool children with attending problems. *Education and Treatment of Children, 26*, 255–272.

Goeke, J. L. (2009). *Explicit instruction: A framework for meaningful direct teaching.* Upper Saddle River, NJ: Merrill.

Grossman, H. (1995). *Educating Hispanic students: Implications for instruction, classroom management, counseling, and assessment* (2nd ed.). Springfield, IL: Charles C Thomas.

Gunn, B., Biglan, A., Smolkowski, K., & Ary, D. (2000). The efficacy of supplemental instruction in decoding skills for Hispanic and non-Hispanic students in early elementary school. *The Journal of Special Education, 34*(2), 90–103.

Gunn, B., Smolkowski, K., Biglan, A., Black, C., & Blair, J. (2005). Fostering the development of reading

skill through supplemental instruction: Results for Hispanic and non-Hispanic students. *The Journal of Special Education, 39*(2), 66–85.

Haydon, T., Marsicano, R., & Scott, T. M. (2013). A comparison of choral and individual responding: A review of the literature. *Preventing School Failure, 57*(4), 181–188.

Hunter, M. (2004). *Mastery teaching.* Thousand Oaks, CA: Corwin.

Intrator, S. M. (2004). The engaged classroom. *Educational Leadership, 62*(1), 20–24.

Jones, H. (2004). A research-based approach on teaching to diversity. *Journal of Instructional Psychology, 31*(1), 12–19.

Kozioff, M. A., LaNunziata, L., Cowardin, J., & Bessellieu, F. B. (2000). Direct instruction: Its contribution to high school achievement. *The High School Journal, 84*, 54–71.

LaFee, S. (2013). Flipped learning. *Education Digest, 79*(3), 13–18.

Marzano, R. J. (2007). *The art and science of teaching: A comprehensive framework for effective instruction.* Alexandria, VA: Association for Supervision and Curriculum Development.

Marzano, R. J., Pickering, D. J., & Pollock, J. E. (2001). *Classroom instruction that works: Research-based strategies for increasing student achievement.* Alexandria, VA: Association for Supervision and Curriculum Development.

Mastropieri, M. A., & Scruggs, T. E. (2002). *Effective instruction for special education* (3rd ed.). Boston, MA: Allyn & Bacon.

McConnell, K., Ryser, G., & Higgins, J. (2000). *Practical ideas that really work for students with ADHD.* Austin, TX: PRO-ED.

McTighe, J., Seif, E., & Wiggins, G. (2004). You can teach for meaning. *Educational Leadership, 62*(1), 26–30.

Milman, N. B. (2014). The flipped classroom strategy: What is it and how can it best be used? *Distance Learning, 11*(4), 9–11.

Morgan, H. (2010). Teaching Native American students: What every teacher should know. *Education Digest, 75*(6), 44–47.

Nel, J. (1993). Preventing school failure: The Native American child. *Preventing School Failure, 37*(3), 19–24.

Pagliaro, M. M. (2011). *Exemplary classroom questioning: Practices to promote thinking and learning.* Lanham, MD: Rowman & Littlefield.

Prater, M. A. (1998). Teaching concepts: Procedures for the design and delivery of instruction. In E. L. Meyen, G. A. Vergason, & R. J. Whelan (Eds.), *Educating students with mild disabilities: Strategies and methods* (2nd ed., pp. 417–435). Denver, CO: Love Publishing.

Rolon, C. A. (2002–2003, December /January). Educating Latino students. *Educational Leadership, 60*(4), 40–43.

Rosenshine, B. V. (2015). How time is spent in elementary classrooms. *Journal of Classroom Interaction, 50*(1), 41–53.

Sindelar, P. T., Espin, C. A., Smith, M. A., & Harriman, N. E. (1990). A comparison of more and less effective special education teachers in elementary-level programs. *Teacher Education and Special Education, 13*, 9–16.

Stein, M., Kinder, D., Silbert, J., & Carnine, D. W. (2006). *Designing effective mathematics instruction: A direct instruction approach* (4th ed.). Upper Saddle River, NJ: Merrill Prentice/Hall.

Tarver, S. G. (2000). Direct instruction: Teaching for generalization, application and integration of knowledge. *Learning Disabilities, 10*, 201–207.

Tepper, E. (1992). Culture and a classroom: One teacher's voyage of discovery. *The Kamehameha Journal of Education, 3*(2), 1–21.

Test, D. W., Browder, D. M., Karvonen, M., Wood, W., & Algozzine, B. (2002). Writing lesson plans for promoting self-determination. *TEACHING Exceptional Children, 35*(1), 8–14.

Townsend, B. L. (2000). The disproportionate discipline of African American learners: Reducing school suspensions and expulsions. *Exceptional Children, 66*, 381–391.

Utley, C. A., Obiakor, F. E., & Bakken, J. P. (2011). Culturally responsive practices for culturally and linguistically diverse students with learning disabilities. *Learning Disabilities: A Contemporary Journal, 9*(1), 5–18.

Vannest, K. J., & Hagan-Burke, S. (2010). Teacher time use in special education. *Remedial and Special Education, 31*(2), 126–142.

Vaughn, S., & Bos, C. (2012). *Strategies for teaching students with learning and behavior problems* (8th ed.). Boston, MA: Allyn & Bacon.

Vaughn, S., Levy, S., Coleman, M., & Bos, C. S. (2002). Reading instruction for students with LD and EBD: A synthesis of observation studies. *The Journal of Special Education, 36*(1), 2–13.

Wang, M. C., Haertel, G. D., & Walberg, H. J. (1990). What influences learning? A content analysis of review literature. *Journal of Educational Research, 84*, 30–43.

White, W. A. T. (1988). A meta-analysis of the effects of direct instruction in special education. *Education and Treatment of Children, 11*, 364–374.

$\textcircled{S}$SAGE edge™ ●●

Review ➡ Practice ➡ Improve

Get the tools you need to sharpen your study skills. Access videos, practice quizzes, eFlashcards and more at **edge.sagepub.com/prater.**

Supporting Students in General Education

Importance of General Education Supports

The need for high-quality instruction in the general education classroom has not been stronger than it is today. More students with high-incidence disabilities (HID) are being educated in general classrooms necessitating appropriate supports for their success. Students at risk for and with disabilities are more successful when teachers (a) apply scientifically based instruction in the general classroom, (b) evaluate student progress to determine whether sufficient learning is occurring, and (c) adjust instruction based on individual needs of students. This chapter is focused on instructional strategies used by general education teachers. Special educators play a critical role as they collaborate with general educators to ensure the best education possible for all students, including those with HID.

Within this chapter, four categories of general education support are discussed: (1) multitiered systems of supports (MTSS) (response to intervention and positive behavior instruction and supports), (2) universal design for learning (UDL), (3) differentiated instruction, and (4) adaptations (modifications and accommodations). Typically MTSS is implemented at the school level, while differentiated instruction and adaptations are applied at the classroom level. UDL can be adopted across any level of implementation. The approach for each is different, but the purpose is the same—to help students be successful academically and socially.

Learning Objectives

- Defend the use of the response to intervention framework and describe how it is implemented to support students with academic needs.

- Compare and contrast the following: universal design for learning, differentiated instruction, adaptations, accommodations, and modifications. Provide examples of each.

- Describe considerations teachers should make before providing culturally and/or linguistically diverse students supports in the general education classroom.

Multitiered Systems of Supports (MTSS)

Multitiered systems of supports (MTSS) is an umbrella term that describes an implementation framework for schools to ensure all students are provided high-quality core instruction and the necessary supports when students are not succeeding. Positive behavior interventions and supports (PBIS) and **response to intervention (RTI)** are structures under MTSS. Neither is a curriculum or a single intervention, but frameworks that incorporate **multitiered interventions** and supports. Both focus on preventing student difficulties as well as intervening quickly when problems do occur. PBIS emphasizes social and behavioral supports, while RTI centers on academic supports. Both PBIS and RTI (a) ensure all students receive highly effective core instruction; (b) identify students who are not achieving their potential under those conditions; (c) provide a continuum of services and interventions, including instruction, for those not performing to their ability; and (d) take a team approach (Young, Caldarella, Richardson, & Young, 2012). This overarching model is called multitiered because when designed and implemented properly, multiple levels of instruction and other supports are provided based on individual student needs.

Positive Behavior Interventions and Supports (PBIS)

Typically both PBIS and RTI involve three tiers. Tier 1 is called the universal or primary tier because all students receive Tier 1 instruction and support. For PBIS, this involves schoolwide rules and expectations with positive consequences, proving verbal and written praise as reinforcers, and teaching social skills to all students. Tier 2 interventions are provided to students who need more intensive supports based on performance in Tier 1 or through screening instruments designed to identify targeted students, not for special education services, but for general education intervention. Tier 2 involves individualized and specific behavioral interventions based on an ABC assessment (see Chapter 5). Additional social skills instruction may also be part of Tier 2 interventions. Although specific behaviors are targeted for individual students, interventions are often delivered in small groups. Tier 3 consists of similar interventions to those provided in Tier 2. However, the intensity, dosage, and/or individualization provided may be increased.

Although this chapter focuses on RTI because PBIS was addressed in Chapter 3, strong links have been established between behavioral and academic performance suggesting that behavioral and academic data need to be considered simultaneously (Algozzine, Wang, & Violette, 2011; Benner, Beaudoin, Kinder, & Mooney, 2005). While behavioral and academic supports are often presented separately (as is the case with PBIS and RTI), school teams should always consider the whole child in team meetings and consider both behavioral and academic needs.

Response to Intervention (RTI)

The response to intervention framework has been implemented for two major purposes. First, to help identify students as having a learning disability, and second to provide individualized support to all students in the general education classroom based on their specific needs.

Identifying Learning Disabilities

Like PBIS, RTI provides a structure for ensuring all students receive high-quality core instruction as well as interventions for those not progressing under those conditions. Historically, however, one of the first promotions of RTI occurred with professionals desiring to use an alternative method for identifying students with learning disabilities (LD). When first passed, the Individuals with Disabilities Education Act (IDEA) stated that a wide discrepancy between ability and achievement needed to be demonstrated before a student could be identified as having LD and receive special education services (see Chapter 1). This resulted in having to wait until the student became further and further behind academically in order to qualify for and receive additional support, sometimes referred to as the "wait-to-fail" or discrepancy model.

The reauthorized IDEA now allows states to use an RTI model to identify students with LD. That is, students who receive additional, more intensive, and/or more frequent instruction but do not make adequate progress may qualify as having LD. Some states (e.g., Colorado and Delaware) have made RTI a requirement for identifying LD (Shapiro et al., 2012). Many experts in the field, however, believe that RTI alone should not be used for identifying LD (Hale et al., 2010). Rather, multiple sources of data, including a comprehensive neuropsychological assessment, should be used.

RTI has been characterized as solving many problems associated with the discrepancy model because struggling students can access help more rapidly in the general education classroom, and they can be given additional instruction based on their individual needs. RTI also has the potential of reducing the number of students inappropriately referred to special education and identified as having disabilities (Orosco & Klingner, 2010). However, including RTI as an option for identifying LD does not necessarily mitigate the wait-to-fail problem. Critics of RTI assert that it takes too long for students to receive intensive services and, while educators take a lot of data on student performance, students are not making adequate progress. In response to these criticisms, researchers such as Stephanie Al Otaiba et al. (2014) have looked at implementing intensive interventions sooner based on screening and baseline data. Findings suggest improvements in student academic performance providing some evidence for the need to "fast-track" some students to more intensive interventions.

Implementing RTI for All Students

When designing and implementing RTI, five core components need to be included: (1) multitiered interventions, (2) data-based decision-making, (3) alignment of curriculum and evidence-based intervention, (4) team collaboration, and (5) implementation fidelity. In addition, consideration should be given to whether RTI is being designed for an elementary or secondary school.

Multitiered implementation. RTI is a multitiered system of support typically consisting of three tiers, often depicted visually as a triangle with the majority of students falling in Tier 1 at the base of the triangle and the fewest number of students needing Tier 3 supports at the top of the triangle (Figure 7.1). Varying and increasing levels of supports exist in the three tiers. Tier 1 supports include core instruction and are provided to all students in general and special education. Strategies such as differentiated instruction, which will be discussed in more detail later in the chapter, are a hallmark of Tier 1 instruction. Typically, 80% of students are able to access the general curriculum with only Tier 1 supports. If less than 80% of students achieve grade-level benchmarks or maintain adequate progress, changes should be made to core instruction.

When students continue to struggle (i.e., not meeting benchmarks or falling below 25% of the normative sample on standardized tests), Tier 2 supports may be implemented. These are small-group interventions that typically occur one to two times a week in the content area where the student is struggling. Tier 2 supports do not replace, but supplement Tier 1 instruction. Typically, 10% to 15% of students will need Tier 2 supports.

Building on these supports, Tier 3 interventions are the most intensive and are typically administered in a one-on-one setting four to five times per week. While some researchers conceptualize Tier 3 as special education services, others believe that there should be a fourth tier to capture students identified with disabilities (Averill, Baker, & Rinaldi, 2014; Jenkins, Schiller, Blackorby, Thayer, & Tilly, 2013). Regardless, it is important to note that all students have access to all three tiers of support depending on student need and that a certain amount of flexibility and fluidity is built into tiered supports. For example, students cannot (and should not) be labeled as "Tier 3" or "Tier 2" students. A student may need Tier 3 supports in reading, Tier 2 supports in writing, and Tier 1 supports in math and science. In addition, as the student responds to intervention, supports should be faded from Tier 3 to Tier 2 or from Tier 2 to Tier 1 as the student progresses. Conversely, if the student starts to struggle more academically based on progress monitoring data, more supports may be added.

FIGURE 7.1   **Multitiered Systems of Support Model**

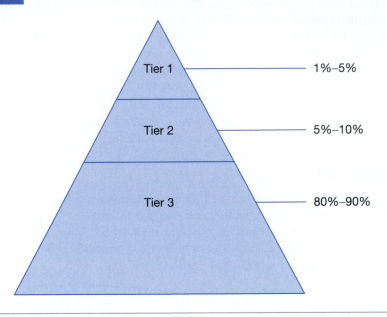

Note: Percentages represent the approximate percentage of students receiving academic (RTI) or behavior/social (PBIS) in each tier.

The support team at Ignacio Elementary have designed a response to intervention program to identify students who are struggling with typical classroom instruction and provide them the support they need to be successful. They design three levels of support as follows. Tier 1 represents evidence-based instructional practices in the general classroom. The teachers undergo professional development to ensure that they have the skills necessary to implement teaching methods and strategies that are known through research to be effective. Students receiving Tier 2 supports are divided into small groups consisting of three to six students meeting two times a week for 30 minutes. In Tier 3, students receive interventions in a one-on-one setting 5 days a week for 50 minutes. Specific interventions vary by content area. One of the evidence-based interventions adopted by the education team is Peer-Assisted Learning Strategies (PALS), a peer tutoring intervention that targets reading and math. This intervention is offered as both a Tier 2 and a Tier 3 intervention depending on the amount of time the student receives the intervention and the setting in which the intervention is received (i.e., small group or one on one).

Data-based decision-making. A core component of RTI is using student performance data to make decisions regarding educational placement, instruction, and interventions. Teams should use multiple sources of data including considerations of teacher judgment when making decisions (Shapiro et al., 2012). Data may include curriculum-based assessments or standardized assessments. As these measures were discussed in depth in Chapter 5, they will only be mentioned here. Educators may also consider conducting "can't do/won't do assessments" to determine if student difficulties are a skill deficit or a problem with motivation (Benner, Kutash, Nelson, & Fisher, 2013).

TEACHER TIP #7.1

CAN'T DO/WON'T DO ASSESSMENT

A simple way to conduct a can't do/won't do assessment is to ask students to complete a short task two times, once with and once without built in motivation. For example, a student may read a 1-minute fluency probe to see how many words correct per minute she can read. Next, she reads the 1-minute fluency probe but this time, she's provided an incentive (e.g., selecting a prize out of a treasure box)

for exceeding her words correct per minute. If the student is able to significantly improve her performance on the task, interventions to target motivation should be considered. If the student is not able to significantly improve her performance on the task, skill-deficit interventions to target reading fluency should be considered.

Universal screening, or collecting data on all students to assess risk status, can help determine which level of tiered supports a student needs in an academic area (Shapiro et al., 2012). Progress monitoring or collecting data throughout the school year, is used to assess student progress. Typically, data are collected for all students three times a year, biweekly for students receiving Tier 2 supports, and weekly for students receiving Tier 3 interventions. When data are collected more frequently, teams can respond efficiently by making necessary adjustments without too much time passing with an intervention that is not working. Responding to these data means making adjustments to instruction or interventions when students are not making adequate progress or continuing with services as designed if students meet goals or demonstrate appropriate progress. Teams may find it helpful to chart or graph student data with goal and trend lines as a means of comparison.

At Ignacio Elementary School, Mrs. Clark's students, JuliAnne, Sebastian, and Asher, receive both Tier 1 (effective instruction) and Tier 2 (PALS peer tutoring) interventions. They are tested twice a month in the materials they are learning. JuliAnne reached the preselected benchmarks so she discontinues participating in peer tutoring. Sebastian is making progress, but has not reached the benchmarks, so he continues in the peer tutoring sessions. Asher also did not reach the benchmarks, but he is not making adequate progress, so he receives additional instruction and support as a Tier 3 intervention (one-on-one instruction and increased peer-tutoring time), while continuing to receive Tier 1 and Tier 2 interventions.

Aligned curriculum and evidence-based interventions. A strong core curriculum and evidence-based interventions are necessary for RTI to be successful. Evidence-based interventions have demonstrated evidence of effectiveness through research and are based on strong theoretical principles. While no intervention is without its faults, choosing an evidence-based intervention means that educators are giving themselves the highest probability for success. In addition, these interventions are often structured or even scripted, helping to save educator time in planning. In addition to being evidence-based, all RTI interventions must (a) have a plan for implementation, (b) include criteria for acceptable performance, and (c) provide means for monitoring progress (Averill et al., 2014).

Technology Spotlight #7.1

Accessing Evidence-Based Interventions Online

A number of online databases exist that include evidence-based interventions for academic and behavioral concerns. These websites often provide background information on the evidence base as well as recommendations for adaptations and progress monitoring.

Best Evidence Encyclopedia: www .bestevidence.org

Florida Center for Reading Research: www.fcrr.org

Intervention Central: www.interven tioncentral.org

National Center on Intensive Intervention: www.intensiveinter vention.org

What Works Clearinghouse: ies.ed .gov/ncee/wwc/

Team collaboration. RTI is a systemic approach to prevention and intervention for student learning and as such, requires a team-based approach to collaboration and decision-making. Schools that implement RTI often have weekly team meetings to discuss individual at-risk students. These team meetings may be referred to as teacher assistance teams, instructional support teams, prereferral intervention teams, problem-solving teams, mainstream assistance teams, or instructional consultation teams (Kovaleski & Black, 2010). Typically involved in these meetings are administrators, intervention specialists, general education teachers, special education teachers, school psychologists, school counselors, and speech language pathologists. Parents may also be included in these meetings. As a team, decisions such as how to modify instruction, when to refer for an evaluation for special education eligibility, and when to increase or fade services are determined. These meetings are most effective when the strengths and weaknesses of the student are considered and the focus of the meeting is on school-based factors that can reasonably be controlled to improve student outcomes. Common pitfalls of these meetings include blaming outside or home factors, complaining about the student, not using data to make decisions, and not selecting evidence-based interventions to help the student (King Thorius, Maxcy, Macey, & Cox, 2014).

In addition to team meetings focused on individual students, schools may also consider having periodic grade-level team meetings to assess the effectiveness of Tier 1 supports (Harlacher, Potter, & Weber, 2015). In these meetings, data are analyzed to see if the core curriculum is appropriate for the majority of students (i.e., 80% of the students reach proficiency). If gaps exist in the majority of students' performance, adjustments to Tier 1 instruction across the grade level are implemented.

TEACHER TIP #7.2

TEAM MEETINGS

Team meetings are most effective and efficient when teachers come prepared with some data already collected on a student. Often schools will have requirements about what is necessary to bring to these meetings; however, if no guidelines are provided, keep in mind that teachers have a lot of data that can be useful in making team decisions and most of it is already being collected as part of the daily school routine.

Information such as attendance, end-of-level test scores, reading benchmarks, in-class work samples, English language proficiency scores, anecdotal behavior logs, on-task/off-task data, and grades can all be helpful in team meetings. Putting together a small folder of student data before the meeting can help streamline the process and provide solid evidence for academic concerns.

When making team decisions, two models have become the most prominent in schools: the problem-solving model and the standard protocol model (Faggella-Luby & Wardwell, 2011; King Thorius et al., 2014; Spear-Swerling & Cheesman, 2011). The problem-solving model is characterized by four steps: (1) problem identification (What is the problem?), (2) problem analysis (Why is the problem happening?), (3) plan identification and implementation (What are we going to do about it?), and (4) plan evaluation (did the solution work?). In this model, interventions are designed on a case-by-case basis and the team collects data to see if the intervention worked. Adjustments are made accordingly and the process is conceptualized as a cycle that educators may go through multiple times. In the standard protocol model, school teams establish standard interventions to be implemented to address a particular need.

Implementation Fidelity

Implementation fidelity (or treatment fidelity) refers to a measure of whether the intervention was delivered as it was designed to be implemented. Interventions are more effective when implemented with fidelity (Nelson, Oliver, Hebert, & Bohaty, 2015), so an element of RTI is ensuring that educators implement interventions with adequate integrity. This means that the intervention is delivered as it was designed to be implemented. Educators may have difficulty assessing fidelity given time constraints and the fact that empirically developed measures to effectively measure implementation integrity continue to be researched and developed (Noltemeyer, Boone, & Sansosti, 2014). Currently, schools most often have educators self-report on a checklist or may occasionally assign outside observers to assess the elements of the intervention (Averill et al., 2014).

Elementary versus secondary schools. RTI implementation can be very different for elementary than for secondary schools. Elementary schools are the most researched setting for RTI because of the impact and focus on early intervention and prevention. In addition, implementation may be easier in elementary given that students are generally assigned to just one classroom. Although the logistics of implementation differ in secondary schools (Vaughn & Fletcher, 2012), research has demonstrated positive effects in secondary settings as well (Faggella-Luby & Wardwell, 2011; Fisher & Frey, 2011). Douglas Fisher and Nancy Frey (2011) describe a case study of RTI implementation in a high school setting. At the participating school, block times were established across the school for interventions to be implemented in various content areas simultaneously. Developing a plan for implementation that works within the school structure is essential for the systemic changes that RTI requires.

TEACHER TIP #7.3

USING AN INTERVENTION BLOCK

Many schools are designating time during the day (e.g., 20 to 30 minutes) in an intervention block where Tier 2 and Tier 3 interventions can be administered to all students needing them. Use the following tips in designing an intervention block.

- Identify assessment and intervention resources available (e.g., curricular materials, professional training of staff).

- Identify areas of student weakness and provide professional development for faculty in those areas (e.g., workshops on reading comprehension or math problem solving strategies).

- Capitalize on personnel resources (i.e., identify which personnel will be involved and determine how to use them to get the most leverage).

- Build time into the schedule for interventions that engage all students and allows for teacher collaboration.

- Maximize the use of space and time (e.g., consider furniture configuration, move teachers instead of students when possible). (Averill et al., 2014)

Models for Supporting Students in General Education

Given the increased number of students with disabilities and those at risk for school failure in the schools today, universal design for learning (UDL) introduced in Chapter 1 can provide the structure teachers need to ensure that all students in their classroom have access to the curriculum. However, no curriculum or materials will ever be totally universally designed. Some adaptations for specific students will always be necessary and thus, teachers will need to know how to best accommodate the needs of their individual students.

Three instructional design and delivery models can be implemented to allow students with HID access to the general curriculum—namely, UDL, differentiated instruction, and adaptations. All three have the same purpose, which is to optimize teaching and learning for all students. All three are also considered Tier 1 interventions in the RTI framework. In addition, all three require preplanning in anticipation of potential problems students may encounter. At the same time, differences among these three models occur at the preplanning stage. Universal design attempts to address all potential difficulties all students will encounter including those with sensory impairments, learning disabilities, multiple disabilities, and so forth. Planning for differentiated instruction considers typical difficulties clusters of students will encounter in their general education classroom. And adaptations are planned at the individual student level, based on the needs of an individual student.

Universal Design for Learning

The concept of UDL began with architecture and engineering. In response to the passage of the Americans with Disabilities Act (ADA) in 1990, public space in the United States began changing. Ramps, elevators, and wider doorways became commonplace. Most buildings needed to be retrofitted which was often expensive and unattractive. Over time, buildings were built with embedded accessibility as part of the plan. Expenses decreased while attractiveness increased. The phrase, *universal design*, was created to represent systems that consider and are designed from the beginning, to be accessible to the broadest range of individuals possible (Pisha & Coyne, 2001).

Universal design for learning is achieved by creating flexible curricular materials and providing built-in alternatives within the instructional design of the materials. Add-on adaptations do not meet the universal design definition. In most cases when teachers have access to universally designed materials, they can use the materials without having to plan adaptations for students with special needs.

Universal design improves systems for both those with and without disabilities. For example, restaurants and department stores that adjust their furniture and racks to permit access to wheelchair users also make accessibility easier for individuals pushing young children in strollers. Cut-down curbs make sidewalks more accessible not only to those in wheelchairs, but to those riding bicycles or skateboards or persons pushing a hand truck. Similarly, universally designed curriculum enhances the compatibility of the materials for learners with diverse needs, including those with and without disabilities. The basic premise is that curricular content should be available in a transformable format or in multiple ways which makes it accessible to all. Universally designed curriculum makes the teacher's job less burdensome by reducing the number of adaptations that need to be made. Outlines principles of UDL with a few examples.

Possible examples of UDL are endless. Below are a few examples from the literature that demonstrate how UDL may be manifested in the classroom. Most of these examples use technology which has enhanced our ability to create universal design for learning.

- Enhanced notebook with text-to-speech features and multimedia opportunities for responses

- Content acquisition podcasts

- Multimedia with narration, video, and animation

- Sets of scaffolded practice problems

- Self-management strategies embedded into the curriculum

- Computer-based read-aloud testing (Kennedy, Thomas, Meyer, Alves, & Lloyd, 2014; King-Sears et al., 2015; Roa, Ok, & Bryant, 2014)

TABLE 7.1   Principles of Universal Design for Learning

Principles	Checkpoints	Examples
Provide options for perception	Offer ways of customizing the information presentation.	Customize with size of text, color used for emphasis, speed of simulations.
	Offer alternatives for auditory information.	Provide visual diagrams, written transcripts, captions for videos.
	Offer alternatives for visual information.	Provide auditory cues; use touch equivalents for key visuals.
Provide options for language, mathematical expressions, and symbols	Clarify vocabulary and symbols.	Preteach vocabulary and symbols; highlight how complex words or equations are composed of simpler ones.
	Clarify syntax and structure.	Provide links between ideas in a concept map; highlight transition words in reading materials.
	Support decoding text, mathematical notions, and symbols.	Allow the use of text-to-speech; provide a list of key terms.
	Promote understanding across languages.	Make all key information in dominant language; embed visuals for vocabulary clarification.
	Illustrate through multiple media.	Present key information in two ways (e.g., text with a video or math equation with animation).
Provide options for comprehension	Activate or supply background knowledge.	Activate prior knowledge with visual imagery, use advanced organizers, and preteach critical concepts through demonstration.
	Highlight patterns, critical features, big ideas, and relationships.	Use outlines, graphic organizers, multiple examples and nonexamples; highlight key elements in text, graphics, diagrams, and formulas.
	Guide information processing, visualization, and manipulation.	Embed strategies for learning within the content; provide scaffolding opportunities.

Source: Adapted from CAST (2011).

Technology Spotlight #7.2

UDL Resources

The best source for technology support of UDL materials is CAST, a nonprofit education, research, and development organization that focuses on expanding learning opportunities for all individuals through UDL. A description of their major projects follows. Although all of these learning tools are free, some of the pages require users to create a free account to access. For more information about CAST, see www.cast.org/about#. VYmwPEa2Ulo.

- **UDL Guidelines**[1] (www.udlcenter .org/): This website discusses the principles of UDL and includes definitions and guidelines, as well as advocacy and research resources. Video clips demonstrating the use of UDL in the classroom are also available.

- **UDL Book Builder**[2] (bookbuilder. cast.org/): Book Builder enables the user to create, share, publish, and read digital books to engage and support diverse learners' needs, interests, and skills.

- **UDL Curriculum Toolkit**[3] (udl-toolkit.cast.org/home): This Web-based platform allows the development and publication of Web-based curricula and other content built using the principles of UDL.

- **UDL Exchange**[4] (udlexchange. cast.org/home): The exchange pages allow educators to create and share instructional resources aligned to the Common Core and based on UDL.

- **UDL iSolveIt**[5] (isolveit.cast .org/home): iSolveIt is a mobile digital learning environment that includes a collection of innovative, researched, tablet-based puzzles that use UDL principles and teach essential math reasoning and problem-solving skills.

- **UDL Studio**[6] (udlstudio.cast.org/): On this site, you can discover projects created by others and work on your own projects. The site also provides tips and resources that include information about text (e.g., free, public domain text sources), audio (e.g., converting audio files to mp3 format), video (e.g., video editing), images (e.g., free online image editors), and animation (e.g., free public domain animations).

---

[1]UDL Guidelines is a registered trademark of the National UDL Center at CAST.

[2]UDL Book Builder is a registered trademark of the National UDL Center at CAST.

[3]UDL Curriculum Toolkit is a registered trademark of the National UDL Center at CAST.

[4]UDL Exchange is a registered trademark of the National UDL Center at CAST.

[5]UDL iSolveIt is a registered trademark of the National UDL Center at CAST.

[6]UDL Studio is a registered trademark of the National UDL Center at CAST.

Differentiating Instruction

Although UDL allows for easier access to the curriculum, not all UDL-based curriculums will meet all students' needs. Additionally, published UDL-based materials are not prominently available necessitating innovative UDL development at the local level. **Differentiated instruction** is more common than UDL for general classrooms. Teachers using differentiated instruction acknowledge and build upon student commonalities and differences by proactively planning and implementing a variety of strategies to match instructional content, process, and product to student differences in readiness, interest, and learning needs (Tomlinson, 2014). Teachers who differentiate their classrooms look for clusters of student needs and adjust instruction accordingly (see Table 7.2). This differs from the concept of individualized instruction where the instructional plan is based on the individual student's needs (Tomlinson & McTighe, 2006). As described by Carol Ann Tomlinson and Jay McTighe, "differentiated classrooms support students who learn in different ways and at different rates and who bring to school different talents and interests. More significantly, such classrooms work better for a wide range of students than do a one-size-fits-all setting" (p. 13).

Mr. Thimm is an exceptional seventh- and eighth-grade math teacher. After Mr. Thimm received a state award for best math teacher of the year, a local newspaper reporter spent a day in his classroom. Below is an excerpt from the reporter's article:

As I walked into the classroom, I thought the principal had given me incorrect directions. This couldn't be Mr. Thimm's classroom. Students were not sitting in desks neatly lined in a row. Instead they were working in small groups. Others were working alone. And two students were seated at a small table being instructed by an adult, who I assumed was the teacher. As I watched, waiting for the teacher to free himself to speak to me, my perspective of what I observed changed. At first I saw disorganization and chaos. Within a few minutes, however, it became clear that each student had an academic task on which he or she was working. Some of the tasks were the same, others were different. Maybe this was Mr. Thimm's classroom after all.

TABLE 7.2   What Differentiated Instruction Is and Is Not

What Differentiated Instruction Is NOT:	What Differentiated Instruction IS:
• The same as individualized instruction	• Proactive
• Chaotic	• More qualitative than quantitative
• Just another way to provide homogeneous grouping	• Rooted in assessment
• A new label for an old process	• Multiple approaches to content, process, and product
	• Student centered
	• A blend of whole-class, group, and individual instruction
	• Dynamic

Source: Tomlinson (2001).

As described throughout this book, student bodies are becoming more and more diverse. Even so, teachers can find commonalities as well as differences in every group of students. Mr. Thimm's classroom looked chaotic. Yet, upon further examination, it wasn't chaotic; rather it was a differentiated classroom with instruction designed to meet the needs of each student in the class.

Mr. Thimm gave the reporter the freedom to speak with the students as he roamed the classroom. The reporter learned that some students were working alone and others by themselves to solve a complex mathematical problem. One student was given a written sheet with prompts about how to solve the problem. He also noted that the complexity of the problem varied across groups and individuals. Some students had the problem printed on green paper, which was different from the problem printed on blue paper. Two students working together told him they were allowed to use manipulatives or calculators and that they will be explaining their solution orally rather than in writing. As he interviewed the teacher, he learned that the two students working with him were being instructed in a simpler mathematical concept than the problem-solving exercise being completed by their classmates.

Differentiated instruction may be conceptualized as adjustments in instruction based on content, process and/or product (Tomlinson, 2014). Mr. Thimm was using all three. He adjusted the content by varying the type and complexity of the mathematical problem. He used process differentiation by providing some students manipulatives, calculators, and written prompts to help them solve the problem, as well as by allowing students to choose to work independently or in groups. Last, he used product differentiation by allowing two students to demonstrate their understanding orally rather than in written work.

Content

Content refers to what students should know, understand, and do as a result of instruction (Tomlinson, 2014). Adapting what is taught may include completely different curriculum (substitute curriculum) or adaptation of the curricular goals (alternate goals). Content changes may also involve the amount or difficulty level of the work to be achieved. One strategy for dealing with content accommodations is to select the core concepts each student must master. From there, teachers can adjust the complexity as needed (Nordlund, 2003).

Teaching the "big ideas" or the major ideas, concepts, or principles rather than detailed information is another example of content adaptation. Not all instructional objectives are equally important to academic development. Focusing on big ideas is essential for students with academic disabilities who have less time left in school to master content than their peers who are not already academically behind. Also, understanding the big ideas help learners connect facts and concepts they have learned (Coyne, Carnine, & Kame'enui, 2011).

Process

Process centers on how the content will be taught and learned. Process accommodations involve how the teacher instructs, how much support is provided to the student, how much time is allotted to instruction, the degree of sophistication of the instruction, and the degree to which the student participates in the task. When modifying instruction, teachers vary activities and strategies needed by individual students. Some students, for example, may require more directed instruction (Nordlund, 2003).

The following are a few examples of process adaptations that could be provided to students with specific learning needs:

- Provide written materials to help focus conceptual understanding and relevant information.

  ○ Guided notes where student fills in the missing words while reading or listening to a presentation
  ○ Graphic organizers that visually display the relationship between concepts being taught
  ○ Study guides with questions student answers
  ○ Written outline of the lesson

- Include visual aids within lessons to emphasize concepts being taught.

- Check for understanding frequently to ensure the student isn't misunderstanding or practicing errors.

- Allow students to use technology, such as recorders or word processors, during instruction.

- Provide short breaks for physical movement so students don't need to attend for long periods of time. (Carter, Prater, & Dyches, 2009)

Product

Product refers to the manner in which the student will be evaluated in terms of depth, amount, or independence of products usually in the form of tests, projects, written work, or oral presentations (Nordlund, 2003). Use of oral or dictated responses is a common product adaptation for students with writing difficulties.

When teachers use large-scale projects as product outcomes, Tomlinson (2001) suggests avoiding the "poster-report-mobile rut of products" (p. 88). Product possibilities are only limited by the teacher's and students' imaginations. Students could, for example, create a series of illustrations, make a video, complete a demonstration, write a song, develop a collection, conduct a debate, create an exhibit, and so forth.

Tomlinson (2001) provides guidelines for projects such as these:

- Ensure the product allows the students to demonstrate what they know, understand, and/or can do.

- Determine expectations for quality in the content (e.g., information), process (e.g., research), and product (e.g., size).

- Consider the students' readiness, interest, and learning profile.

- Use products that help students see the real-world application of knowledge and skills being taught in school.

- Use check-in dates for particularly difficult or lengthy projects.

- Ensure your students have the production skills before assigning the product.

- Use formative and summative peer and self-evaluation based on agreed-upon criteria.

- When possible, arrange for others besides the teacher to view the product.

Adaptations, Modifications, and Accommodations

Differentiated instruction as a label and concept has its roots in general education. General education teachers are taught to apply differentiated instruction to all students in their classroom. Conversely, the concept of adapting curriculum and instruction for students with disabilities stems from the field of special education, and focuses on individualizing instruction to meet the needs of the student with disabilities. Despite these differences, the process and outcome are similar.

While interviewing Mr. Thimm, the reporter became more and more intrigued with the notion of differentiated instruction. He asked questions to better understand and in doing so he learned the following. Mr. Thimm has five students with Individualized Education Programs (IEPs) in his math class: Thelma, Terence, Noah, Keenan, and Walter. Thelma needs visual prompts to help her recall and process information. Otherwise, she can keep up with her classmates. Thelma completes the same homework assignments as the other students except her math textbook and any other individual assignment sheets have handwritten prompts she has been taught to decipher (e.g., arrows indicating which operation to complete first). Terence and Noah have writing difficulties. They understand mathematical concepts, but have difficulty transferring their understanding to paper. Thus, Mr. Thimm allows Terence and Noah to dictate their responses to a peer or to use the classroom computer when appropriate. Keenan and Walter are behind their classmates academically. Mr. Thimm, in consultation with their special educator, implements different curriculum material for them. He relies on classmates, through his peer-tutoring activities, to continue and extend his instruction for Keenan and Walter when needed.

Based on the requirements of IDEA, students with disabilities are to be provided an individualized education, at least to some extent. **Adaptation** is the overarching term that encompasses both modifications and accommodations. **Modifications** refer to changes in the curriculum or standard. Keenan and Walter are receiving modifications because Mr. Thimm is teaching them a different curriculum than their peers. **Accommodations** are adaptations that make the general curriculum and assessment accessible to the student without changing the standard or curriculum. Thelma, Terence, and Noah are receiving accommodations in Mr. Thimm's class because they are working on the same curriculum as their peers, but need some assistance in learning the same content and meeting the same standard.

Selecting Adaptations

Ideally, the differentiated classroom is designed to meet the educational needs of all of the students in the classroom. However, not all teachers design differentiated instruction, and depending upon the subject matter, not all curriculums allow for easy implementation of differentiated instruction. To provide appropriate support for students with disabilities in general education classrooms, IEP teams specify which accommodations and/or modifications a student with disabilities may need. Jeanne Shay Schumm (1999) created eight principles for making adaptations in the general education classroom and organized them using the acronym FLEXIBLE, which stands for Feasible, Lively, Eliminated, Explicit, Intentional, Beneficial, Limelight, and Evaluated. Questions to ask before selecting potential adaptations accompany each principle and sample questions may be found in Table 7.3.

TABLE 7.3   The FLEXIBLE Principle: Questions to Ask Before Selecting Potential Adaptations

Principle	Sample Questions
Feasible	• How feasible are the potential adaptations? • How easily can they be incorporated into the general education classroom?
Lively	• How will the adaptations keep students actively engaged? • Will they help make learning interesting, motivating, and fun?
Eliminated	• How easy will it be to fade the accommodation over time? • Will the student be able to generalize the skill?
Explicit	• What is the purpose of the adaptation and how will I communicate the purpose to the student? • Who else needs to know about the adaptation?
Intentional	• How does this accommodation fit with goals on the student's IEP? • How does this accommodation fit with district or state standards?
Beneficial	• How does this adaptation benefit the targeted student? • Will other students benefit as well?
Limelight	• How can the adaptation be implemented and not place undue attention on the student with the disability?
Evaluated	• How will I evaluate the effectiveness of the adaptation? • How will the evaluation inform changes in the adaptation?

Source: Adapted from Schumm (1999).

TEACHER TIP #7.4

SELF-IDENTIFIED ACCOMMODATIONS

To help students identify which accommodations they prefer, try these two strategies:

- Provide students with a blank sheet of paper with the following written at the top: *What my teacher can do to help me learn.* If necessary, read and explain the sentence to the students. Ask them to draw or write something that shows how you or another teacher can help them learn.

- Create a certificate of accommodations, similar to a contingency contract. Ask the students to write the classroom accommodations they would prefer. Once the accommodations have been finalized, ask the student, parents, and teachers involved to sign the certificate. (Blazer, 1999)

Technology Spotlight #7.3

Accessing Leveled Learning Material on the Internet

Special educators are often challenged to create curriculum accommodations and modifications for students with disabilities. Indeed, this is a challenging task under the best circumstances. However, most special educators have inadequate background in the subject and have too little time to create accessible learning materials.

Recognizing the need to respond to classroom diversity, instructional designers are exploring how technology can personalize the presentation of information and engage readers in learning about a topic. Visit the following websites to obtain a glimpse of the future by exploring how rich instructional content can be presented at tiered levels so that students can decide which level is most appropriate for them.

- Ben's Guide to US Government for Kids (bensguide.gpo.gov/): Ben's Guide provides information about our nation and system of government. You can access information written for kindergarten through 12th-grade students.

- Windows on the Universe (www.windows.ucar.edu/): Available at this site is information on a number of topics including computers, health, and social science. For each topic, information is written at beginner, intermediate, or advanced levels.

Teachers clearly have a responsibility for creating accessible instructional units and lessons. Some resources to explore

(Continued)

(Continued)

to facilitate planning for curriculum accommodations and modifications include the following:

- 4 Teachers (www.4teachers .org/): When you visit this site, click on the equity index and you can access resources and tools

for addressing diversity in your classroom.

- TeAch-nology (www.teach-nology .com/themes): A number of teacher resources are available at this site including lesson plans, organizers, rubrics, and worksheets.

MARCIE model. Another way of conceptualizing adaptations is the use of the MARCIE model, originally the CRIME model (Prater, 2003). The MARCIE model extends adaptations beyond instruction to also examine classroom rules and the environment. The acronym MARCIE stands for

- **M**aterials
- **A**ssessment
- **R**ules
- **C**urriculum
- **I**nstruction
- **E**nvironment

Materials. The first category, materials, encompasses all materials and equipment available to the teacher including classroom supplies, textbooks, supplementary materials, computers, calculators, and so forth. Just as teachers use assessment information to plan instruction, teachers can use assessment information to determine what type of material support students with disabilities may need. If a student's primary disability is reading, then the student may need support that allows the student to access information without having to read grade-level material. Audio-recorded materials, videos, computerized text readers, and simplified versions of the classroom text can address reading problems. Students with information processing problems may need graphic organizers and study guides to enable them to identify important information. Supplemental text materials that define new vocabulary, or outline chapter information can also be helpful. Some students have difficulty completing and turning in assignments. In such cases, self-monitoring checklists and assignment sheets may enhance performance.

Wally has difficulty reading his 11th-grade science, history, and literature textbooks. His special education teacher has acquired copies of the books on CDs. Wally listens to the CDs at home to keep up with the required reading.

Assessment. The second category is assessment. Students with HID may qualify for standardized assessment accommodations. Similarly, they may require accommodations in the classroom assessment processes as well. Assessment in this context refers to the manner in which the student will demonstrate their knowledge and against which the student will be evaluated. Assessment accommodations can vary greatly. The three forms of differentiated instruction include content, process, and product. Assessment adaptations can be represented by any of those forms. For example, the content may be simpler (e.g., easier or fewer spelling words), the process may be adjusted (e.g., allowed to use a number line), or the product may change format (e.g., demonstrate knowledge through tests with short, written answers rather than essays written in full sentences).

> Marilyn's driver education teacher, Mr. Brewster, uses multiple-choice tests to assess basic driving knowledge. He uses assessment sheets where students have to fill in the bubble corresponding to their answer. Marilyn has difficulty tracking and aligning the bubbles to fill in her answers. So, she writes the letter corresponding to her answer on a piece of paper instead of using the bubble sheets.

Rules. All classrooms need rules. Rules that are stated by the teacher and posted in the classroom are explicit rules. As described in Chapter 3, these rules should be observable, measurable, positive, stated in positive terms, and so forth. Consequences for keeping or breaking rules should also be well defined, understood, and delivered consistently.

In addition to explicit rules, implicit rules also exist in classrooms. Implicit rules are those that are unexpressed. For example, a teacher may not have explicit rules about submitting homework assignments or arriving to class on time, yet she may be a very punctual person with the same expectations for her students. She consciously or subconsciously punishes students who are late. Another teacher may be more laid back when it comes to punctuality and willing to allow students more leeway. Students with disabilities are less likely to discern these distinctions between teachers and act accordingly. Therefore, teachers must become conscious of implicit rules operating in their classrooms, particularly the implicit rules that impact students with special needs and make them explicit for students.

Adaptations for rules may involve explicit and/or implicit rules. One good strategy for rule accommodation is the use of contingency contracts (see Chapter 3). A set of rules may apply to all students in the classroom with the exception of the student who has a contingency contract with appropriate adjustments in those rules. These differences in expectation need to be explained to the other students in the classroom.

> Abdul has high-functioning autism and doesn't understand implicit rules. Mrs. Coombs, his special education teacher, has worked with all of his eighth-grade teachers and helped them identify the implicit rules for their classroom and consequences for keeping and breaking the rules. A list of the rules for each teacher is listed in Abdul's notebook. He has learned to refer to the list each time he enters a different teacher's classroom and check off the rules he followed at the end of the class period which the teacher signs. Mrs. Coombs administers the consequences.

Curriculum. Curriculum refers to the content being taught, but may also include state- or districtwide standards students are expected to achieve and goals and objectives identified on student IEPs. Teachers should identify content critical to achieving goals and objectives and eliminate unnecessary content from their curriculum. Once teachers have selected essential content, teachers should select curriculum materials designed to maximize student learning. The overall curriculum design should incorporate effective teaching practices such as assessing student performance, presenting information in a logical and sequential manner, teaching at an instructional level, providing a model, monitoring progress, and incorporating systematic reviews.

In addition, teachers can identify skills necessary for success with a specific subject and include skill instruction in the curriculum. For example, in high school English classes, writing skills are necessary for classroom success. Instruction on how to write a basic paragraph can be included in the curriculum, as well as instruction on how to plan and write literary response papers.

Teachers can also plan to incorporate learning strategies in the year's curriculum. Strategy instruction teaches students how to complete a task, and facilitates learning. In science and social studies classes, students must learn new vocabulary and concepts. Mnemonic strategy instruction teaches students how to remember terms by connecting new information with known information. The benefit of strategy instruction is that students learn new information, and learn how to improve their ability to learn.

Fifth-grader Suri has difficulty understanding all of the concepts from Mr. Wilkinson's science lessons. So Mr. Wilkinson identified in advance the "big ideas" of his lesson that she will be responsible to learn. He provides her a simplified version of the reading materials and makes certain she is involved in all of the small group projects at the level in which she can participate.

Instruction. Instructional needs of students with disabilities vary. Formal and informal assessment information can help teachers determine the best instructional adaptations for their students. Teachers should identify weaknesses that may hinder learning, and adapt instruction accordingly. The possible types of instructional adaptations are unlimited, but include categories such as the manner in which instruction occurs (e.g., cooperative learning groups vs. directed instruction), the modality of instruction (e.g., visual, auditory), and the amount of time or support provided to the student. For example, students with attention deficits focus attention better when instruction is fast paced and interactive, while incorporating visual prompts and varied audiovisual materials in instruction benefits students with auditory processing problems. Students who process information slowly may require more teacher time and attention than other students. After adapting instruction to meet the needs of students with disabilities, the teacher must constantly monitor student progress to verify that the instructional accommodations implemented are appropriate and effective.

Mrs. Haller has three students with HID in her sixth-grade classroom who learn best when they have one-on-one attention and instruction. Rather than singling them out, she decides that for 20 minutes a day, all of the students in her class will engage in either peer tutoring or enrichment activities. Performance on daily quizzes determines who will receive which activity. She ensures that the students with disabilities are given an opportunity to participate in enrichment activities as well.

Environment. The learning environment includes the physical outlay of the classroom, the number and grouping of students, and other physical environmental elements such as temperature, time of day, light, and noise. When examining their classrooms, teachers should consider accessibility to materials, equipment, and other people, as well as reduced distraction areas. Modifications may include seating arrangements, flexible scheduling, and instructional grouping.

Cameron has difficulty staying on task during seatwork. His teacher noticed that he spends a lot of time staring out the window. So she moved him to a desk where he can't see the window and now he is more focused.

Table 7.4 shows the similarities between differentiated instruction and adaptations. Included are the three differentiated classroom categories suggested by Tomlinson (2001), the six categories of the MARCIE model (Prater, 2003), and nine types of accommodation methods recommended by Sandi Cole et al. (2000). *Time* is listed twice because

TABLE 7.4 Differentiated Instruction and Making Adaptations

Differentiated Instruction (Tomlinson, 2014)	MARCIE Model (Prater, 2003)	Accommodations (Cole et al., 2000)	Examples
Content	Curriculum Materials	Size—Amount of content the learner is expected to learn	Reduce the number of vocabulary or spelling words to be learned at one time.
		Difficulty—The difficulty level of a skill or activity	Allow student to use a calculator. Simplifying directions
		Alternate Goals—Adapting the goals or outcome expectations for the student while using the same materials	Adapt the goal of matching states and capitals to recognizing state names.

(Continued)

TABLE 7.4 (Continued)

Differentiated Instruction (Tomlinson, 2014)	MARCIE Model (Prater, 2003)	Accommodations (Cole et al., 2000)	Examples
		Substitute Curriculum—Using different instruction and materials to meet the student's goal	Provide lower vocabulary reading materials.
Process	**Instruction Materials**	**Input**—The manner in which instruction is delivered	Use visual or auditory prompts. Involve student in project. Provide additional structure to the lesson.
		Level of Support—The amount of assistance the student receives	Use personal assistance such as a peer tutor or paraeducator. Provide additional materials such as manipulatives, visual aids, audio-recorded books.
		Time—The amount of time allowed to complete learning	Decrease the pace of instruction.
		Participation—The extent to which the learner is actively involved in the task	Assign different roles in cooperative learning groups.
Product	**Assessment**	**Time**—The amount of time allowed to complete assignments or testing	Increase the amount of time for completing an exam.
		Output—The manner in which the student demonstrates knowledge and skills	Use weekly quizzes instead of end-of-unit exams.
	Rules		Make implicit rules explicit. Use contingency contracts.
	Environment		Provide study carrels. Change time of day instruction is provided.

it fits under both process and product categories. Definitions of the Cole et al. model are provided in the table because they are not described elsewhere in the text.

Mary Anne Prater (2003) provides a framework in which the MARCIE (formally CRIME) model can be used by general and special educators collaborating to meet the needs of students with disabilities in the general classroom. This framework is also an acronym which spells SHE WILL SUCCEED and is presented in Figure 7.2.

FIGURE 7.2   The SHE WILL SUCCEED Process

The SHE WILL SUCCEED Process

Increased number of students with disabilities and those identified as at risk for school failure are being educated in the general education classroom. This necessitates that general and special educators work collaboratively to ensure that the education each student receives is appropriate (see Chapter 2). Below is a 14-step process to assist teachers in making these accommodations to instruction, curriculum, and the learning environment based on individual student's needs.

S **Show concern for the targeted student**. When teachers are genuinely concerned about students and communicate those concerns, students begin to believe in themselves. Show appropriate and genuine concern.

H **Have faith in yourself and your targeted student**. Students who have a history of school failure often expect to fail and become dependent on others to solve their problems. Help the student connect skills and effort to success and failure. Let the student know that you believe she or he can succeed.

E **Examine your classroom**. Using the MARCIE elements discussed in the text, write down statements relating to each category as it relates to your classroom.

MARCIE	My Classroom
Materials	
Assessment	
Rules	
Curriculum	
Instruction	
Environment	

W **Write down the targeted student's strengths and limitations AND**

I **Include skills, learning preferences, and behaviors specific to your classroom.** Identify the student's strengths and limitations in context of your classroom using the three categories of skills, learning preferences, and behaviors.

Categories	Strengths	Limitations
Skills		
Learning Preferences		
Behaviors		

(Continued)

FIGURE 7.2   **(Continued)**

L **Line up student and classroom characteristics as those that facilitate, provide barriers, or are neutral for the individual student's learning success.** Create a matrix using the description of your classroom elements (MARCIE) down the first column and the categories of facilitators, neutral, or barriers to learning across the first row. Fill in the cells with examples of student's strengths and weaknesses where they best fit.

	Facilitators	Neutral	Barriers
Materials			
Assessment			
Rules			
Curriculum			
Instruction			
Environment			

L **List one to three classroom characteristics you could modify and/or skills you could teach.** Once you have identified the student's characteristics as facilitators, barriers, or neutral based on your classroom elements, identify classroom characteristics that you would be willing to modify to accommodate the student.

S **Select and implement adaptation(s) and goal(s).** Once potential adaptations and/or goals have been selected, you are ready to begin implementation.

U **Use effective teaching principles to teach goals.** If you are going to teach a new skill, be certain to use effective teaching principles (see Chapter 6).

C **Collaborate with others as needed.** Seek out others, such as a special education teacher or the student's family members, to assist you with making appropriate accommodations (see Chapter 2).

C **Change adaptations and instruction as necessary AND**

E **Evaluate results**. Teachers don't always "get it right" the first time. Thus, change may be necessary. Continuously evaluate whether the accommodations were successful, and if not, make appropriate adjustments (see Chapter 5).

E **Exit here OR**

D **Do again.** If the accommodations were successful, then more changes may not be necessary. If the student is, however, still struggling, repeat the process focusing on the same barrier for learning or selecting a different barrier, depending on the student's needs.

Source: Prater, M. A. (2003). She will succeed! Strategies for success in inclusive classrooms. *TEACHING Exceptional Children, 35*(5), 58–64.

Lesson Plan Spotlight #7.1

An Example Lesson Plan With Accommodations

Lesson Objective

Following instruction, students will write one paragraph with no convention errors (e.g., spelling, punctuation), describing five possible causes of dinosaur extinction and accurately identify which one has the most scientific support.

Materials

Paragraph graphic organizer for each group, computer, and projector

Anticipatory Set, Review, and Prerequisite Check

Ask who remembers what you've been studying in science and what you've learned thus far. Teach any vocabulary students do not know: *extinction, volcanic eruptions, meteor, supernova, radiation,* and *climate*. Include a brief review of how to write a paragraph using the paragraph graphic organizer.

Purpose

Explain that students will work in their cooperative learning groups to read about the five possible causes of dinosaur extinction. They will then discuss the five possible causes and decide which one has the most scientific support. Students will be individually responsible for writing a paragraph describing these causes. Explain that this information will help prepare them for the field trip to the dinosaur museum next week and that they might even create some additional questions to ask while they're at the museum.

Instruction and Modeling

Model reading one paragraph in the textbook. Ask the following questions and write the answers on the blackboard:

1. "What possible cause for the dinosaur extinction is presented?"

2. "What are some words I would use to describe this possible cause?"

3. "How strong is the scientific support?"

4. "Using the information on the board, what sentence can I write about this possible cause?"

5. "Now that I've written sentences about a possible cause, I will use the paragraph graphic organizer to organize the sentences into a paragraph." (Write the example paragraph on the computer.)

Guided Practice

Remind students to use their assigned roles as they work in their cooperative groups. Ask them to read the next paragraph and answer the same questions you answered. Start with the first question. Prompt them to find the answer. Ask the groups to share their answers. Provide corrective feedback as needed and prompt the groups to continue to respond to the questions and then write their sentence. Monitor the groups and provide corrective feedback as necessary.

(Continued)

(Continued)

Independent Practice

Explain that now they have their individual sentences, they need to write them up as a paragraph. Give each group the paragraph graphic organizer. Students independently write their own paragraphs.

Specific Accommodations

Materials

Provide Harold and Gerry a copy of the vocabulary words with definitions.

Instruction

Assign Judy and Quentin to roles other than reading in their cooperative learning groups.

Assessment

Assign Harold and Gerry to work together in writing their individual paragraphs.

As one writes each sentence, the other provides corrective feedback.

Allow Judy to compose her paragraph on the class computer and use spell-check.

Assign Quentin to draw pictures representing each possible extinction cause and then orally describe his answer.

Resource Information

Five possible causes of dinosaur extinction:

1. Giant meteor hits the earth—has the most scientific support
2. Volcanic eruptions
3. Changes in climate
4. Radiation from a nearby supernova
5. Disease

Other Adaptations

Some teachers rely heavily on students accessing information through textbooks. This is prominent primarily at the secondary school level. Students with HID are often excluded from the general classroom, not because they are unable to understand the concepts, but because they cannot adequately read the textbook and/or the assessment tools aren't designed to adequately measure what they know and can do. Grading is also a particularly difficult issue for teachers working with students with disabilities. A discussion with suggestions related to making textbook, assessment, and grading adaptations follows.

Textbook adoption, instruction, and adaptations. Students vary in their reading ability. As students progress in school, instruction shifts from mastering reading skills to mastering content presented in textbooks (Boyle et al., 2003). When teachers rely heavily on textbook materials, students with poor reading skills have difficulty demonstrating their knowledge of content.

The first strategy to assist students with HID to succeed is to select an appropriate textbook. Sometimes policy requires that teachers use a particular textbook. But if teachers are serving on a selection committee or have individual choice in the matter, care should be taken to ensure the textbook meets appropriate standards and can be adapted for students with disabilities.

Before adopting textbooks, professionals should evaluate them carefully in terms of content, familiarity, interest, and text structures. Readers who have prior knowledge about the content they are reading will comprehend the text better than readers who do not. This familiarity includes both vocabulary and content. How interesting the reader finds the material also impacts comprehension. Specific features such as fast action, concrete details, personal pronouns, analogies, examples, sidebars, and novelty can increase reader's interest levels. This interest, however, must be integral to the text, not an interest-creating feature that is only trivial detail. Text structure also impacts comprehension. The text structure needs to follow a predictable pattern and the structure must be communicated explicitly to the reader. The inclusion of effective strategies within the text structure, such as graphic organizers, also facilitates comprehension. Organizational aids, such as preview statements, outlines, and graphic organizers, aid student learning and are also important considerations in selecting textbooks for diverse learners (Bruhn & Hasselbring, 2013) (see Table 7.5).

Design elements of textbooks can influence students' understanding of content. One study discovered that students with learning disabilities improved their history content acquisition and engagement when using a textbook that used "big ideas" designed primarily around cause/effect, problem-solving, cooperative, and group-success structures. These curricular design principles significantly improved student performance when compared to those using a traditional textbook (Harniss, Caros, & Gersten, 2007).

Given that teachers, particularly in secondary schools, rely heavily on textbooks, they need to know how to use them effectively as well as how to teach students to use them effectively. Teachers often assume students are fluent in using textbooks, but most, even those without disabilities benefit from explicit instruction in this area. Such instruction should first introduce the textbook and then prepare students to read the textbook. Students who use textbooks effectively understand the book's features. Each textbook will vary in what features are included, but standard ones include the table of contents, headings and subheadings, figures and graphs, chapter introductions and summaries, glossary, and index. Other features may include use of color or bold to highlight specific information, sidebar boxes, appendices, learning objectives, review questions, and so forth. After students are initially taught to access the text's features, reviews and reminders need to be provided throughout the year.

Students can be taught to *steal* information from the text by using the THIEVES strategy for previewing texts:

Title

Headings

Introduction

Every

Visuals and Vocabulary

End-of-chapter questions

Summary (Manz, 2002)

Students first examine the Title of a chapter then the Headings. Students then string headings together to create a summary of the chapter prior to reading the chapter.

The next step is to read the Introduction to determine the framework of the chapter. Then they read Every first sentence in important paragraphs. Next, students look for the Visuals and Vocabulary. Translating pictures and illustrations into words and understanding key vocabulary enables students to comprehend the material prior to reading. Finally, they examine the End-of-chapter questions and Summary (Manz, 2002).

TABLE 7.5   Checklist for Textbook Adoption

Content	• Is the content aligned with state/district standards?
	• Is the content accurate and up to date?
	• Does the book include a clear sense of purpose with a scope and sequence of material in a logical fashion?
	• Do the materials focus on the big ideas?
	• Does the content connect to real-life experiences that students can understand and apply?
	• Does the book embed accurate and nonstereotypical multicultural representations (e.g., disability, gender, religion, ethnicity)?
	• Are cultural representations (e.g., disability, ethnicity) accurate and nonstereotypic?
	• Does the content help conceptualization by relating it to the real world?
	• Does the text develop ideas fully so as to promote student understanding?
	• Is the text material written in clear and concise language?
Familiarity	• How familiar are the students with the content already?
	• How much prior knowledge is needed to understand the content?
	• How complex and how many new vocabulary words are included?
Interest	• How engaging is the material?
	• Are concrete and detailed examples provided?
	• How novel is the content?
	• Is the content developmentally appropriate?
Text Structure	• Is the text structure logical and consistent?
	• Is the content previewed and summarized?
	• How many and how effective are the strategies included (e.g., graphic organizers, highlighted information, concept maps, tools for studying)?
	• How conspicuous are the strategies included?
	• Do the materials provide mediated scaffolding?
	• Is judicious review included?
	• Are supplemental materials provided (e.g., assessments, online resources, CDs)?

Source: Adapted from Bruhn & Hasselbring (2013); Carter et al. (2009); Dyck & Pemberton (2002); King-Sears & Duke (2010).

TEACHER TIP #7.5

USING A TEXTBOOK SCAVENGER HUNT

Use a textbook scavenger hunt to teach students how to use their textbook. Create a series of questions about the structure and content of the book. A range of 10 to 20 questions should be asked with at least one question linking the students' personal experience to the textbook content (Conderman & Elf, 2007). Have students complete the hunt either individually or in pairs. The goal of the scavenger hunt is not to see who can complete it first, but for students to complete it accurately (Bruhn & Hasselbring, 2013). A sample of the types of questions follows:

- On what pages do the table of contents, the glossary, and the index start?

When would you choose to use one over another?

- Why are some words bolded in the text? How could this feature help you learn the material?

- How can the headings and subheadings be helpful to you?

- What are the definitions of *zoology*, *radiology*, and *anthropology*? What do these words have in common? Where did you find the definitions?

- Based on the graphic describing the food chain, describe it in your own words.

Norma Dyck and Jane Pemberton (2002) suggested a model for making text adaptations. First, teachers assess whether the student can read and comprehend the selected text. If the student has adequate skills to read and understand the text, adaptations are not necessary. However, if the student will have difficulty learning from the text, the teacher should select another text or provide supports that will enable the student to meet the goals and objectives of the class.

If a student can understand the text when the text is read to him or her, bypass reading is an option (Dyck & Pemberton, 2002). Bypass reading may involve (a) reading the text aloud to the class, (b) allowing a peer to read the text to a student, (c) providing audio versions of the text, or (d) implementing computer text-to-speech technology. Elizabeth Boyle et al. (2003) studied whether secondary students with high-incidence cognitive disabilities improved classroom performance when they listened to audio textbooks. They found that students who used the audio textbooks demonstrated greater improvement in classroom test scores than students who read the textbooks. They concluded that audio textbooks enabled students with mild cognitive disabilities to access high-level content material.

For students who can decode the text, but are not fluent readers, decreasing the amount of material the student is expected to read is an option. A teacher can identify critical portions of the text, and assign the student to read only the selected material. Additionally, the teacher can select an alternative text that covers the same content, but is less demanding for a student with poor reading ability. Textbook publishers often provide parallel textbooks, which may be an appropriate accommodation for some students.

Even with decreased reading demands, some students may fail to comprehend the text. Supported reading, organized reading, and guided reading are options teachers can employ to facilitate comprehension (Dyck & Pemberton, 2002). Sometimes students can read a textbook, but fail to comprehend the material due to the vocabulary demands of the text. Supported reading includes adding definitions of key terms to the margins of a text, and adding cues and questions to help the student focus attention on relevant material. Questions can be written in the margins, or on sticky notes to encourage the student to stop, reflect, and respond to the reading material. These supports placed within the text can increase comprehension.

Another means of improving comprehension is using organized reading supports such as providing graphic organizers of material presented in reading selections or chapters (see Chapter 9) (Dyck & Pemberton, 2002). Visual illustrations can convey essential information in a concise simplified format, which is easier for students with disabilities to process. Hierarchical trees can illustrate main ideas and show how information in the text supports the main idea. Compare and contrast charts can help students perceive similarities and differences between concepts and ideas; and goal maps, which contain information on characters and relationships, can assist students in drawing conclusions and making inferences.

Finally, guided reading supports help students focus on important information in textbooks (Dyck & Pemberton, 2002). Study guides are used to preview material, organize and summarize information, and assist students as they work through the material. Previews are overviews of the reading material, and provide students with a summary of main ideas, key terms, and relevant background knowledge necessary for understanding the selection. Giving a student a blank graphic organizer to complete as he reads can assist the student in organizing the information while reading. Structured

TABLE 7.6   Possible Textbook Adaptations

Student Characteristics	Possible Adaptations
Student cannot read the textbook but can understand the material when read to him or her.	• Teacher reads text to all students. • Peer reads text to student. • Student listens to audio recording of text. • Student listens to computer text-to-speech version.
Student can decode the textbook, but not fluently.	• Decrease the amount of reading expected. • Select an alternative text.
Student can decode, but has difficulty comprehending the material.	• Add definitions of key terms to margins. • Write cues and/or questions in the margins or with sticky notes throughout the text to help student focus on relevant material. • Provide graphic organizers. • Add visual illustrations. • Provide study guides or structured notes.

notes (also discussed in Chapter 9) are used to show the student how to integrate the material from the text with the teacher's lectures.

Alternative texts. In addition to explicitly teaching students the features of their textbook, alternative texts may be considered. Examples of alternative texts include magazines (e.g., Muse Magazine, Weekly Reader News), newspapers, and trade books (e.g., Landmark Books). Alternative texts must be selected carefully ensuring that the content, readability, and interest are appropriate for the student and the curriculum standards. In fact, a team, including the special educator, a content area teacher, and a curriculum or literacy specialist should work together to select, plan, and implement alternate texts. Appropriate reading materials would be selected based on the text connecting to content curriculum. Readability level would also be examined to ensure it matches the students' reading level. When computing readability levels, care must be taken to include text samples throughout the book and to use more than one formula for comparison purposes because results may vary depending on the formula used (King-Sears & Duke, 2010). In addition, teachers should strive to access information about text difficulty levels beyond just readability formulas because readability formula results can vary greatly. For example, in one study researchers found the Dale-Chall formula to be the most reliable one but only for Grades 3–5 (Begeny & Greene, 2014).

Test accommodations. Tests administered to all students for the purpose of determining who graduates, who is promoted to a certain grade, or which school is the strongest in the district are referred to as *high-stakes tests*. In the past, students with disabilities have generally been excluded from participating in state- and districtwide high-stakes tests. That is no longer the case. As discussed in Chapter 1, IDEA mandates that students with disabilities be included in state and districtwide assessment programs. The IEP team has the authority to select individual accommodations needed for students with disabilities to participate in these tests. If the team determines that the student will not participate in a particular assessment or part of an assessment, they must state how the student will be assessed (Lovett & Lewandowski, 2015).

As described in Chapter 5, tests can be standardized or curriculum based. Issues related to making accommodations to standardized tests are complex because any change in procedures can influence the interpretation of test scores. On the other hand, without accommodations, students with disabilities may not demonstrate their full potential. For some individuals with disabilities, test scores underrepresent what they know and can do. The most common types of accommodations for standardized tests are providing extra time, having the test items read aloud, or allowing oral responses.

Grayson, a third grader with high-functioning autism, is required to take the statewide high-stakes exam. Part of his disability is high levels of distraction. The IEP team concluded that he would complete the exam in a separate room and allowed extra time only if he becomes distracted and cannot complete the exam in the same amount of time as his peers. A paraeducator will keep an eye on Grayson and will intervene with routines already established if he becomes distracted and stops attending to the test.

Accommodations for classroom tests should also be determined as part of the IEP process. The goal is the same as with standardized testing, that is, providing accommodations to offset the student's disability. In the classroom, teachers use a variety of tests to assess student learning. The IEP team should determine which accommodation is appropriate based on the subject, the nature of the test, and the skill or knowledge being tested.

Accommodations are not intended to change the nature of the construct being measured; instead, they are meant to lessen the impact of the disability so that the test scores are as accurate as possible (Lai & Berkeley, 2012). Test accommodations refer to changes in the way the test is administered, while test modifications reflect changes in the content of the test (Lovett & Lewandowski, 2015).

Seventh-grader Levi has a learning disability and the IEP team anticipates he will have difficulty reading and writing responses to essay questions on his tests in the general education classes. A reader is assigned to Levi and trained to only read the test, not interact with Levi in other ways. Levi is also allowed to use a speech-to-text function on the computer, rather than handwrite his answers to the essay questions.

Unfortunately, research has demonstrated that accommodation selection is not always based solely on the student's disability, but rather on factors such as the student's comfort level or self-esteem. When IEP teams determine appropriate test accommodations, they must evaluate the student's "inability to access a test because of disability-related functional impairments" (Lovett & Lewandowski, 2015, p. 15). For example, students who have impaired processing speed as diagnosed and demonstrated in classroom work, could be appropriately assigned extra time to complete tests. Extended time is one of the most commonly used test accommodations, but should be used cautiously and only if the student truly needs more time to compensate for his or her disability (Thurlow, Elliott, & Ysseldyke, 2003). Any accommodation should be documented and justified on the IEP and then provided for classroom and high-stakes tests. Table 7.7 lists examples of possible test accommodations.

When selecting test accommodations, IEP teams should follow these guidelines:

- Explicitly identify the knowledge and skills to be measured. Ensure that proposed accommodations do not interfere with the assessment of those skills. For example, if the intent of a writing test is to measure the expression of thought, a scribe would be appropriate. If, however, the intent is to measure handwriting, a scribe would not be appropriate. If the proposed accommodation alters the validity of the test, the adjustment would be a modification, not an accommodation.

- Make certain the accommodation is based on the specific need of the student, not the type of disabling condition or professional judgement alone. Gather data on student performance before making the decision.

- Ensure that the accommodation is necessary and does not provide an advantage to the student over his peers.

TABLE 7.7   Examples of Test Accommodations

Type of Accommodation	Examples
Setting: Change the conditions of the testing situation.	• Small group • Study carrel • Adaptive furniture
Format: Change the format of the test.	• Print size • Braille • Number of items per page
Timing: Change the amount of time or when the test is administered.	• Extended time • Flexible schedule • Frequent breaks
Presentation: Alter how the test is presented.	• Read directions to student. • Provide audio recorded prompts. • Clarify directions.
Response: Adjust how the student responds to the test questions.	• Mark in a book. • Use a scribe. • Use pencil grips.
Scheduling: Schedule the test to accommodate the needs of the student.	• Specific time of day • Across multiple days • Schedule short testing segments.

Sources: Carter et al. (2009); Thurlow et al. (2003).

- Consider whether the student could adapt or be taught skills that would enable him to take the test without accommodations.

- Choose accommodations that are the least intrusive. As an example, if a student cannot write responses, the use of a keyboard and word processor would be less intrusive than a scribe (Bolt & Thurlow, 2004; Lovett, 2010).

In addition to those guidelines, the checklist in Table 7.8 asks important questions to consider when making accommodation decisions.

The following guidelines should be applied by teachers and other school personnel as they prepare for and implement testing accommodations:

- Ensure that the instructional and assessment accommodations align. That is, prior to testing, students should have had opportunities to apply the accommodation during instruction.

- Train those who administer accommodations. Those who act as scribes or readers need prior preparation and instruction, such as making it clear that scribes write down verbatim responses.

- Anticipate and be prepared for challenges associated with accommodations. For example, if tests are reformatted with large print, the tests may cause items to be split across pages.

- Monitor the effects of accommodations on students. In some circumstances, accommodations can be detrimental to the student's performance. (Bolt & Thurlow, 2004)

TABLE 7.8   Checklist for Classroom Test Accommodations Decision-Making

	Questions	Yes	No
Can the student complete the same test . . .	1. At the same level as peers?		
	2. With altered or simpler directions?		
	3. With adapted expectations?		
	4. With a different delivery system?		
	5. With different time constraints?		
	6. With flexible scheduling?		
	7. With additional math learning tools?		
	8. With additional written language learning tools?		
	9. With additional memory tools?		
	10. If the language level is varied?		
Can the student complete objective tests if . . .	11. The multiple-choice items are adapted?		
	12. The matching items are adapted?		
	13. The true/false items are adapted?		
	14. The completion items are adapted?		
Can the student . . .	15. Respond to essay questions if adaptations are made?		
	16. Complete part or specific items of the same exam?		
	17. Respond appropriately with an example provided?		
	18. Be held to the same course content if the type of assessment is varied to suit the individual learner's style?		
Does the student . . .	19. Demonstrate emotional reactions to test taking that need to be considered?		
	20. Need alternative assessment?		

Source: Adapted from Reetz, Ring, & Jacobs (1999).

Grading. Ideally, grades communicate information to students and their parents about a student's achievement, progress in the curriculum, and effort expended on learning (Carter et al., 2009). In practice, however, traditional grading practices may reflect a student's disability more than effort and advancement. Research indicates there are five common problems associated with grading students with disabilities. First, students included in general education classrooms generally receive low or failing grades. Students who constantly receive low grades can be demoralized. This is particularly true of students with disabilities who are included in general education classes and their work is being compared to those of their nondisabled peers. Second, grades serve different purposes for teachers, parents, and students. If effort and individual progress are used to grade students with disabilities this may communicate the wrong message to students and their parents who interpret grades as representations of knowledge and skills attained. Third, teachers feel pressured to give passing grades to students with disabilities because they recognize the work is difficult for students with disabilities. Fourth, the grading system may not be aligned with the adaptations that the student is receiving in the classroom. And fifth, students and parents typically have little to no input into how students will be assigned grades. For students with disabilities, selecting grade adaptations should be done collaboratively with general and special educators, parents, and, if appropriate, the student (Silva, Munk, & Bursuck, 2005).

Grading adaptations can be modifications or accommodations. Modifications are made when the learning objectives on which a student's grade is based are different than the student's peers. If the learning objectives are the same as other classmates, but how the student demonstrates achievement differs, then the grading adaptation is an accommodation.

Grades can be adapted in many ways including the following:

- **Adjust grade weights**. Teachers can adjust the percentage activities or products count toward a final grade. For example, the weight for performance on a written exam could be reduced from 50% to 25%, while individual assignments and projects increased from 50% to 75%.

- **Adapt grades to reflect progress on meeting IEP goals.** When teachers write IEPs, they can specify the curriculum the student will be expected to master, and then include an explanation that the student will be graded on mastery of the curriculum.

- **Modify the syllabi.** With a contract and a modified course syllabi, a student with disabilities can progress through course material at a rate appropriate for the student's skills and abilities.

- **Include improved performance in the grade calculation.** Teachers can track student performance, and award extra points for improvement in academic and self-management behaviors.

- **Add written comments**. To minimize confusion and misperception, teachers can write comments on report cards to clarify their grading criteria.

- **Grade products and performance.** In addition to a letter or number grade representing academic achievement, teachers can give students grades for effort and progress made during a term.

- **Assign pass/fail grades.** Although students with disabilities rated many grade adaptations as unfair, in one survey, low achievers felt a pass/fail grading system was less judgmental than number or letter grades. In order to implement a pass/fail grading system, the teacher would have to determine the criteria for passing the class and communicate the criteria to the student.

- **Use checklists.** Teachers can develop a competency checklist from the student's IEP goals and objectives and attach the checklist to the student's report card. Checklists can allow the student and the parents to see which skills the student mastered during a term: math facts, grammar, addition and subtraction procedures, map work, and so forth.

- **Prioritize content or learning objectives and calculate grade based on those priorities.** Students with disabilities can be evaluated according to the most important content for that student to learn. This may mean the student will not complete full units or not be held accountable for all assignments. (Carter et al., 2009)

TEACHER TIP #7.6

USE PRETESTS

In courses that lend themselves to written exams, instead of administering only posttests, give the same test as a pretest before instruction begins. Then compare student results on the pre- and the posttest to determine whether progress was made. Use this information to help determine grades earned (Gregory & Chapman, 2002).

Implications for Culturally and/or Linguistically Diverse Students

Response to Intervention

One may assume that culturally and/or linguistically diverse (CLD) learners would benefit from RTI as a method for identifying students with learning disabilities, as well as a method for determining interventions for all students. RTI does hold promise for accurately identifying CLD students as having learning disabilities (Haager, 2007). An RTI approach eliminates the need for standardized tests which have traditionally shown bias against this population. Additionally, RTI doesn't require the CLD student to wait to fail before receiving individualized services based on the student's needs. At the same time, RTI is often implemented as a one-size-fits-all approach, which fails to consider the uniqueness of CLD students.

Care must be taken when making any RTI decisions for CLD learners. First, teachers cannot assume that the evidence-based practices selected for Tier 1 intervention have been validated with CLD students. Failure to progress in Tier 1 may be more a reflection of the inappropriate match of the intervention to the student, rather than the CLD student's ability. Second, the experience and knowledge base of the teachers should be considered. In order to provide highly effective instruction, teachers need strong groundings in culturally responsive instruction and second language acquisition. In addition, they must understand the values, beliefs, and practices of CLD students (Orosco & Klingner, 2010).

Socioeconomic status (SES) must also be considered. Students living in poverty may have untreated health problems or move frequently, which impacts their attendance and academic progress (Finch, 2012). In one study of over a million students, students who were receiving free and reduced lunch performed below similarly identified students on all measures of literacy regardless of being an English learner (EL) or having a learning disability (Solari, Petscher, & Folsom, 2014). Although these researchers did not study RTI per se, they documented the significant and critical role SES plays in achievement. School personnel who are aware of these difficulties may need to implement Tier 2 or Tier 3 more quickly with low-SES students than with other students.

Some research has documented that when implemented properly, RTI can be effective for ELs at risk for reading disabilities. Effective interventions have included peer-assisted learning strategies; small-group interventions in Spanish; and explicit, systematic, and intensive interventions in reading (Orosco & Klingner, 2010). Much, however, still needs to be learned about the effectiveness and implications of RTI for CLD students (Haager, 2007).

Supports in General Education

When it comes to providing supports in the general education classroom, students have personal learning preferences. Some students learn best when they are allowed to move around; others prefer to stay in one spot to concentrate. Some students like a "busy" environment, while others find such situations distracting. Some students prefer to learn by reading a passage on their own, while other students learn best when someone reads the passage to them. In addition to personal learning preferences, our cultural background affects how we learn. Culture can influence, for example, whether students

- view time as fixed/rigid or flexible/fluid.

- are more effusive or reserved.

- learn best through a whole-to-part or part-to-whole approach.

- prefer to work in groups or individually.

- value creativity or conformity.

- are more reflective or more impulsive. (Tomlinson, 2001)

Teachers cannot manipulate all personal learning and cultural preferences all of the time. They can, however, recognize that students have different learning approaches and try to incorporate these within the classroom. Effective teachers understand the range of learning and cultural approaches that exist in their classrooms and make the classroom flexible enough to meet these varied approaches to learning (Tomlinson, 2001). For example, they can create a classroom with different "looks" in different corners of the room. One corner may have desks and materials designed for independent work, while another corner has a round table and chairs with group-work materials. When appropriate, students can be given the choice of where they prefer to work.

Teachers in differentiated classrooms have been described as being "more in touch" with their students than other teachers (Tomlinson, 2014). Part of being "in touch" is understanding the cultural and linguistic backgrounds of their students. When determining appropriate accommodations, teachers should consider whether specific accommodations are compatible with a student's cultural heritage and language skills.

For example, the written word is emphasized in Western cultures more than in cultures where oral-language traditions are valued (Chamberlain, 2005). Immigrant children or those who live in poverty may not have had the same exposure to books and other printed materials as their classmates, and therefore have not experienced learning from text materials. English learners (ELs) may have good English-speaking and oral-comprehension skills, but do not read English at the same level. Teachers can promote learning through strategies such as providing supplemental or replacement audiovisual materials, providing materials from which students can access information (e.g., magazines, library books), and teaching students how to preview books and make predictions (Carter et al., 2009).

Students who are not English proficient will need additional supports in aspects of instruction that rely on language (i.e., listening, speaking, reading, and writing). Two general adaptations can be provided. First, ELs benefit from more time spent in oral expression. They may need more opportunities to discuss ideas and explore new concepts than teacher-directed instruction provides. Integrating interactive questions and discussion in small groups or pairs will help build language skills. Second, ELs need to be taught academic language. Academic language differs in structure and vocabulary from everyday spoken language. Academic language is used in formal reading materials like textbooks, as well as on formal tests. Classroom teachers also use academic language orally during instruction. Understanding academic language is critical to success in formal educational settings.

The main barrier to understanding academic language is poor academic vocabulary. Academic vocabulary is both generic and content specific. Many academic words are used across disciplines (e.g., *estimate, evaluate, analyze, summarize*). Other words pertain to specific disciplines (e.g., *angle, ratio, rectangle* for math; *syntax, semantics, expository* for English). Strategies suggested for strengthening academic language include building students' background knowledge; connecting instruction to prior knowledge and real-life experiences; using texts that are engaging, age appropriate, and comprehensible; explicitly teaching about academic language; and providing opportunities to practice academic language through speaking and writing (Fitts & Bowers, 2013).

Virtually all of the differentiated and adapted strategies presented in this chapter apply to CLD students. The keys are to ensure the culture of the student is considered in making those instructional adaptations and that students who are ELs are provided additional language support. Suggested adaptations for ELs are outlined in Table 7.9.

TABLE 7.9   Suggested Adaptations for English Language Learners

Type	Adaptation
Instructional Support	• Provide peer tutoring or tutoring before or after school. • Require less quantity in assignments. • Allow extra time. • Pair with a bilingual student. • Use paraeducators to help one on one, when appropriate. • Avoid calling on student in front of others. • Use technology such as text-to-speech software.
Information Difficulty	• Use visual aids to reinforce concepts being taught. • Label items in the classroom in the student's native language. • Display classroom rules and other important information in multiple languages. • Provide students a vocabulary list of important concepts in the student's native language. • Allow students to draw pictures instead of writing to demonstrate learning. • Allow student to research in the student's native language.
Delivery of Instruction	• Preteach and reteach concepts. • Break complex sentences into shorter, simpler ones. • Avoid using or explain idiomatic expressions (e.g., *as easy as pie, keep an eye on, pop quiz, pulling your leg, make up your mind*). • Pause during instruction to give time to process what was heard. • Use simple, everyday language to explain key words. • Request oral responses rather than written responses. • Provide translated materials. • Include student in presentations to encourage and develop oral language skills. • Encourage reluctant talkers by repeating student's response with *and*. • Focus on content and meaning, not grammar and spelling in written work. • Modify writing assignments.

Source: Adapted from Carter et al. (2009); Solomon, Lalas, and Franklin (2006).

SUMMARY

Students with HID receive instruction in the general classroom to a greater degree than in the past. Multitiered systems of support (MTSS), universal design for learning, differentiated instruction, and adaptations help facilitate student success in the general classroom. MTSS is an umbrella term that describes an implementation framework to ensure all students are provided high-quality instruction and the necessary supports when they are not succeeding. Positive behavior interventions and supports (PBIS) and response to intervention (RTI) are structures under MTSS. PBIS emphasizes social and behavior supports, while RTI centers on academic supports. One of the first promotions of RTI was as an alternative method for identifying students with learning disabilities. In addition, this framework is used to ensure all students receive high-quality instruction and necessary supports to succeed academically.

Universal design for learning provides built-in alternatives within the instructional design of materials to enhance the compatibility of the materials for all learners. The goal is to make the curricular content accessible to literally all students in the classroom. Sometimes, however, that isn't possible and teachers need to provide differentiated instruction. Differentiated instruction occurs when teachers match the student's readiness, interest, and learning needs with the content, process, and product associated with instruction. Typically, general educators are taught to apply differentiated instruction for all students, whereas the concept of adapting curriculum and instruction for students with disabilities stems from the field of special education. These adaptations are determined on an individual basis through the IEP process and include both modifications and accommodations. Modifications refer to changes in the curriculum or standard, whereas accommodations are adaptations that make the general curriculum and assessment accessible to the student without changing the standard or curriculum. Areas of consideration for adaptation include materials, assessment, rules, curriculum, instruction, and environment.

Special consideration should be given to textbook adoption, instruction, and adaptations. For example, the readability and features (e.g., highlighted terms, graphic organizers) of a textbook impact student comprehension of the content. Most students benefit from being explicitly taught the features and how to use the textbook. Teachers should use other textbook supports, such as reading or study guides, when needed to help students focus on important information in the textbook. Alternative texts, if available, can also be considered.

Test accommodations may be needed by some students with HID. The most common types of accommodations for standardized tests are providing extra time, having the test items read aloud, or allowing oral responses. Accommodations for tests should be determined as part of the IEP process and based solely on the student's disability. Adaptations for grading may also need to be made. Grading adaptations may include a modification—changing the learning objectives on which a student's grade is based or an accommodation—the learning objective remains the same but how the student demonstrates achievement changes.

All forms of RTI, UDL, differentiation, and adaptations must consider the wide diversity of culture, language, and experience that students bring to the classroom. An RTI approach to LD identification eliminates the need for standardized tests which have traditionally shown bias against this population. Teachers should consider the cultural practices and language skills of students when applying the principles of these general education supports to ensure compatibility with students' culture and language.

REVIEW QUESTIONS

1. Define, provide examples, and then compare and contrast RTI and PBIS.

2. Describe the components of RTI and why they are critical elements to successful implementation.

3. Define UDL and UDL principles. Provide an example for each. Which principles do you think are most realistic?

4. Define *differentiated instruction* including the three categories for differentiating instruction. Provide examples for each.

5. When would teachers use modifications versus accommodations? Provide examples for each using the MARCIE acronym.

6. Compare and contrast UDL, differentiated instruction, and adaptations. Use examples for each in your response.

7. In what ways could comprehending information in grade-level textbooks be challenging for students with HID? Describe how teachers can help.

8. How can teachers determine which testing accommodations are appropriate and which may invalidate the results of particular tests?

9. Why should teachers consider adapting grading practices for students with disabilities? What adaptations are possible? Which do you believe are the fairest?

10. What factors should teachers consider in using RTI and making adaptations for CLD students?

ACTIVITIES

1. Access the following journal issue: Ludlow, B. L. (Ed.). (2014). Data-based individualization [Special issue]. *Teaching Exceptional Children, 46*(4). Select three articles, read and summarize in writing. Embed information from this chapter throughout the summary.

2. Identify a special educator and a general educator who teach at the same school and educate the same student with a HID. Walk them through the MARCIE model ending with the identification of appropriate accommodations for the student. Write up a summary of your experience.

3. Suppose you are teaching a fourth-grade math class that includes two students with disabilities. These students process information slower than other students and have difficulty understanding directions. Write a paper describing accommodations you can provide that will enable these students to access the math curriculum. Explain your reasons for selecting specific accommodations.

4. Based on this chapter and other reliable sources, generate a list of questions to help teachers select adaptations for students from culturally and/or linguistically diverse backgrounds.

Council for Exceptional Children (CEC) Standards

The Council for Exceptional Children (CEC) is a premiere national professional organization comprised of special educators, paraeducators, relative service personnel, parents, and others interested in individuals with disabilities and/or those with gifts and talents. This organization has generated 10 standards for the preparation of special educators. These standards are listed in each chapter as they relate to the content within the chapter. The standards that apply to Chapter 7 are Standards #2, #3, #4, and #5.

CEC Initial Preparation Standard #2: Learning Environments (partial)

Beginning special education professionals create safe, inclusive, culturally responsive learning environments so that individuals with exceptionalities become active and effective learners and develop emotional well-being, positive social interactions, and self-determination.

2.1 Beginning special education professionals through collaboration with general educators and other colleagues create safe, inclusive, culturally responsive learning environments to engage individuals with exceptionalities in meaningful learning activities and social interactions.

CEC Initial Preparation Standard #3: Curricular Content Knowledge (partial)

Beginning special education professionals use knowledge of general and specialized curricula to individualize learning for individuals with exceptionalities.

3.3 Beginning special education professionals modify general and specialized curricula to make them accessible to individuals with exceptionalities.

CEC Initial Preparation Standard #4: Assessment (partial)

Beginning special education professionals use multiple methods of assessment and data sources in making educational decisions.

4.2 Beginning special education professionals use knowledge of measurement principles and practices to interpret assessment results and guide educational decisions for individuals with exceptionalities.

CEC Initial Preparation Standard #5: Instructional Planning and Strategies (partial)

Beginning special education professionals select, adapt, and use a repertoire of evidence-based instructional strategies to advance learning of individuals with exceptionalities.

5.1 Beginning special education professionals consider an individual's abilities, interests, learning environments, and cultural and linguistic factors in the selection, development, and adaptation of learning experiences for individuals with exceptionalities.

REFERENCES

Algozzine, B., Wang, C., & Violette, A. S. (2011). Reexamining the relationship between academic achievement and social behavior. *Journal of Positive Behavior Interventions, 13*, 3–16.

Al Otaiba, S., Connor, C. M., Folsom, J. S., Wanzek, J. Greulich, L., Schatschneider, C., & Wagner, R. K. (2014). To wait in tier 1 or intervene immediately: A randomized experiment examining first-grade response to intervention in reading. *Exceptional Children, 81*(1), 11–27.

Averill, O. H., Baker, D., & Rinaldi, C. (2014). A blueprint for effectively using RTI intervention block time. *Intervention in School and Clinic, 50*(1), 29–38.

Begeny, J. C., & Greene, D. J. (2014). Can readability formulas be used to successfully gauge difficulty of reading materials? *Psychology in the Schools, 51*(2), 198–215.

Benner, G. J., Beaudoin, K., Kinder, D., & Mooney, P. (2005). The relationship between the beginning reading skills and social adjustment of a general sample of elementary aged children. *Education and Treatment of Children, 28,* 250–264.

Benner, G. J., Kutash, K., Nelson, J. R., & Fisher, M. B. (2013). Closing the achievement gap of youth with emotional and behavioral disorders through multi-tiered systems of support. *Education and Treatment of Children, 36*(3), 15–29.

Blazer, B. (1999). Developing 504 classroom accommodation plans: A collaborative, systematic parent-student-teacher approach. *TEACHING Exceptional Children, 32*(2), 28–33.

Bolt, S. E., & Thurlow, M. L. (2004). Five of the most frequently allowed testing accommodations in state policy. *Remedial and Special Education, 25,* 141–152.

Boyle, E. A., Rosenberg, M. S., Connelly, V. J., Washburn, S. G., Brinckerhoff, L. C., & Banerjee, M. (2003). Effects of audio texts on the acquisition of secondary-level content by students with mild disabilities. *Learning Disability Quarterly, 26,* 203–214.

Bruhn, A. L., & Hasselbring, T. S. (2013). Increasing student access to content area textbooks. *Intervention in School and Clinic, 49*(1), 30–38.

Carter, N., Prater, M. A., & Dyches, T. T. (2009). *Making accommodations and adaptations for students with mild to moderate disabilities.* Upper Saddle River, NJ: Pearson.

CAST. (2011). *Universal design for learning guidelines version 2.0.* Wakefield, MA: Author. Retrieved from http://www.cast.org/our-work/learning-tools.html#.VY8s0Ua2VfY

Chamberlain, S. P. (2005). Recognizing and responding to cultural differences in the education of culturally and linguistically diverse learners. *Intervention in School and Clinic, 40,* 195–211.

Cole, S., Horvath, B., Chapman, C., Deschenes, C., Ebeling, D. G., & Sprague, J. (2000). *Adapting curriculum and instruction in inclusive classrooms: A teacher's desk reference.* Bloomington, IN: The Center for School and Community Integration Institution for the Study of Developmental Disabilities.

Conderman, G., & Elf, N. (2007). What's in this book? Engaging students through a textbook exploration activity. *Reading & Writing Quarterly, 23,* 111–116.

Coyne, M. D., Carnine, D. W., & Kame'enui, E. J. (2011). *Effective teaching strategies that accommodate diverse learners* (4th ed.). Upper Saddle River, NJ: Pearson.

Dyck, N., & Pemberton, J. B. (2002). A model for making decisions about text adaptations. *Intervention in School and Clinic, 38,* 28–35.

Faggella-Luby, M., & Wardwell, M. (2011). RTI in a middle school: Findings and practical implications of a tier 2 reading comprehension study. *Learning Disability Quarterly, 34*(1), 35–49.

Finch, M. E. H. (2012). Special considerations with response to intervention and instruction for students with diverse backgrounds. *Psychology in the Schools, 49*(3), 285–296.

Fisher, D., & Frey, N. (2011). Implementing RTI in a high school: A case study. *Journal of Learning Disabilities, 46,* 99–114.

Fitts, S., & Bowers, E. (2013). Developing academic English with English language learners. In M. B. Arias & C. J. Faltis (Eds.), *Research in second language learning: Academic language in second language learning* (pp. 27–56). Charlotte, NC: Information Age.

Gregory, G. H., & Chapman, C. (2002). *Differentiated instructional strategies: One size doesn't fit all.* Thousand Oaks, CA: Corwin.

Haager, D. (2007). Promises and cautions regarding using response to intervention with English language learners. *Learning Disabilities Quarterly, 30,* 213–218.

Hale, J., Alfonso, V., Berninger, B., Bracken, C., Christo, E., Clark, M., . . . & Yalof, J. (2010). Critical issues in response-to-intervention, comprehensive evaluation, and specific learning disabilities identification and intervention: An expert white paper consensus. *Learning Disability Quarterly, 33,* 223–236.

Harlacher, J. E., Potter, J. B., & Weber, J. M. (2015). A team-based approach to improving core instructional reading practices within response to intervention. *Intervention in School and Clinic, 50,* 210–220.

Harniss, M. K., Caros, J., & Gersten, R. (2007). Impact of the design of U.S. history textbooks on content acquisition and academic engagement of special education students: An experimental investigation. *Journal of Learning Disabilities, 40*(2), 100–110.

Jenkins, J. R., Schiller, E., Blackorby, J., Thayer, S. K., & Tilly, W. D. (2013). Responsiveness to intervention in reading: Architecture and practices. *Learning Disability Quarterly, 36*(1), 36–46.

Kennedy, M. K., Thomas, C. N., Meyer, J. P., Alves, K. A., & Lloyd, J. L. (2014). Using evidence-based multimedia to improve vocabulary performance of adolescents with LD: A UDL approach. *Learning Disability Quarterly, 37,* 71–86.

King-Sears, M. E., & Duke, J. M. (2010). "Bring your textbook!" Using secondary texts to assess reading demands and skills required for students with high-incidence disabilities. *Intervention in School and Clinic, 45*(5), 284–293.

King-Sears, M. E., Johnson, T. M., Berkeley, S., Weiss, M. P., Peters-Burton, E. E., Evmenova, A. S., . . . , & Hursh, J. C. (2015). An exploratory study of universal design for teaching chemistry to students with and without disabilities. *Learning Disability Quarterly, 38*(2), 84–96.

King Thorius, K. A., Maxcy, B. D., Macey, E., & Cox, A. (2014). A critical practice analysis of response to intervention appropriation in an urban school. *Remedial and Special Education, 35,* 287–299.

Kovaleski, J. F., & Black, L. (2010). Multi-tier service delivery. In T. A. Glover & S. Vaughn (Eds.), *The Promise of Response to Intervention* (pp. 23–56). New York, NY: Guilford Press.

Lai, S. A., & Berkeley, S. (2012). High-stakes test accommodations: Research and practice. *Learning Disability Quarterly, 35*(3), 158–169.

Lovett, B. J. (2010). Extended time testing accommodations for students with disabilities: Answers to five fundamental questions. *Review of Educational Research, 80*(4), 611–638.

Lovett, B. J., & Lewandowski, L. J. (2015). *Testing accommodations for students with disabilities.* Washington, DC: American Psychological Association.

Manz, S. L. (2002). A strategy for previewing textbooks: Teaching readers to become THIEVES. *The Reading Teacher, 55,* 434–435.

Nelson, J. R., Oliver, R. M., Hebert, M. A., & Bohaty, J. (2015). Use of self-monitoring to maintain program fidelity of multi-tiered intervention. *Remedial and Special Education, 36*(1), 14–19.

Noltemeyer, A. L., Boone, W. J., & Sansosti, F. J. (2014). Assessing school-level RTI implementation for reading: Development and piloting of the RTIS-R. *Assessment for Effective Intervention, 40*(1), 40–52.

Nordlund, M. (2003). *Differentiated instruction: Meeting the educational needs of all students in your classroom.* Lanham, MD: Rowland & Littlefield.

Orosco, M. J., & Klingner, J. (2010). One school's implementation of RTI with English language learners: "Referring into RTI." *Journal of Learning Disabilities, 43*(3), 269–288.

Pisha, B., & Coyne, P. (2001). Smart from the start: The promise of universal design for learning. *Remedial and Special Education, 22*(4), 197–203.

Prater, M. A. (2003). She will succeed! Strategies for success in inclusive classrooms. *TEACHING Exceptional Children, 35*(5), 58–64.

Reetz, L., Ring, M. M., & Jacobs, G. M. (1999). Examine test modifications. *Intervention in School and Clinic, 35,* 117–118.

Roa, K., Ok, M. W., Bryant, B. R. (2014). A review of research on universal design educational models. *Remedial and Special Education, 35*(3), 153–166.

Schumm, J. S. (1999). *Adapting reading and math materials for the inclusive classroom.* Reston, VA: The Council for Exceptional Children.

Shapiro, E. S., Hilt-Panahon, A., Gischlar, K. L., Semeniak, K., Leichman, E., & Bowles, S. (2012). An analysis of consistency between team decisions and reading assessment data within an RTI model. *Remedial and Special Education, 33,* 335–347.

Silva, M., Munk, D. D., & Bursuck, W. D. (2005). Grading adaptations for students with disabilities. *Intervention in School and Clinic, 41*(2), 87–98.

Solari, E. J., Petscher, Y., & Folsom, J. S. (2014). Differentiating literacy growth of ELL students with LD from other high-risk subgroups and general education peers: Evidence from Grades 3–10. *Journal of Learning Disabilities, 47*(4), 329–348.

Solomon, M., Lalas, J., & Franklin, C. (2006). Making instructional adaptations for English language learners in the mainstream classroom: Is it good enough? *Multicultural Education, 13*(3), 42–45.

Spear-Swerling, L., & Cheesman, E. (2011). Teachers' knowledge base for implementing response-to-intervention models in reading. *Reading and Writing, 25,* 1691–1723.

Thurlow, M. L., Elliott, J. L., & Ysseldyke, J. E. (2003). *Testing students with disabilities: Practical strategies for complying with district and state requirement* (2nd ed.). Thousand Oaks, CA: Corwin.

Tomlinson, C. A. (2001). *How to differentiate instruction in mixed-ability classrooms* (2nd ed.). Alexandria, VA: Association for Supervision and Curriculum Development.

Tomlinson, C. A. (2014). *The differentiated classroom: Responding to the needs of all learners* (2nd ed.). Alexandria, VA: Association for Supervision and Curriculum Development.

Tomlinson, C. A., & McTighe, J. (2006). *Integrating differentiated instruction and understanding by design.* Alexandria, VA: Association for Supervision and Curriculum Development.

Vaughn, S., & Fletcher, J. M. (2012). Response to intervention with secondary school students with reading difficulties. *Journal of Learning Disabilities, 43,* 244–256.

Young, E. L., Caldarella, P., Richardson, M. J., & Young, K. R. (2012). *Positive behavior support in secondary schools.* New York, NY: Guilford Press.

$SAGE edge™ ••

Review ➡ Practice ➡ Improve

Get the tools you need to sharpen your study skills. Access videos, practice quizzes, eFlashcards and more at **edge.sagepub.com/prater.**

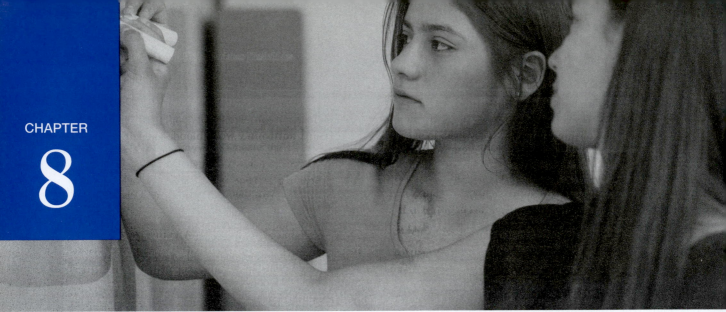

CHAPTER 8

Student-Mediated Instruction

If asked to make an oral presentation in front of classmates, some individuals would prefer to plan and present alone, while others would want to work with at least one other person. Similarly, if given the choice to play a spelling game competing against classmates or as a class team to see how far the class can get without missing a word, some prefer the competition and others prefer working as a whole group.

Teachers can structure their classrooms to emphasize students working competitively against one another on the same goal, cooperatively together in order to achieve a common goal, or individually to accomplish goals unrelated to those of their peers. Although some teachers effectively combine these structures within their classroom, students perceive and teachers practice competitiveness as the predominant force in schools today.

In Chapter 6, effective teaching procedures were discussed from the perspective of large-group, small–group, or one-on-one teacher-directed instruction. This chapter is devoted to grouping students together to promote student-mediated learning. Student-mediated learning implies that students take the primary role in instructing or managing themselves and/or their peers. In teacher-directed instruction, the teacher conveys information and models skills. In student-mediated instruction, the teacher facilitates instructional interactions among students and acts as a resource to students. Two student-mediated processes, cooperative learning and peer tutoring, are used in special education and general education classrooms to facilitate the learning of students including those with high-incidence disabilities (HID).

Learning Objectives

- Define and describe, then compare and contrast cooperative learning and peer tutoring as student-mediated instruction.

- Discuss the benefits and challenges of using student-mediated instruction with students with high-incidence disabilities. Provide examples of how to overcome potential challenges.

- Describe how different cultural values can impact the effectiveness of student-mediated instruction using case study examples.

Cooperative Learning

Mr. Hunt arranges his classroom unlike the other middle school teachers in his school because all of the desks are clustered together. If you were to visit his classroom, you'd see students working together in groups of three to five throughout at least half of each class period. During the rest of the class period, Mr. Hunt is either instructing large or small groups or students are working independently on reading or writing tasks. Mr. Hunt teaches English and in all of his classes he has at least two students who qualify for special education services. He works collaboratively with their special education teacher in making appropriate accommodations for these students. Mr. Hunt is *sold* on using cooperative learning. He has found students remain on task for longer periods of time; and they submit higher quality products. Overall, he feels he can better meet the needs of students with disabilities using cooperative learning.

When teachers use **cooperative learning,** they apply a set of instructional strategies that facilitate student-to-student interactions which result in collective and individual achievement of lesson objectives. Students work in small groups to accomplish shared goals while maintaining individual accountability. "Students perceive that they can reach their learning goals if and only if the other students in the learning group also reach their goals" (Johnson & Johnson, 2005, p. 117). Teachers provide the classroom structure and organization to ensure student success.

Cooperative learning can be applied in any school classroom. Students with HID may experience cooperative learning groups in their general education classroom. Or special educators can create groups in their resource or special education classroom. If structured well, students with HID can benefit from cooperative learning groups by providing them the opportunity to become a contributing member of a group, learn content from peers, and practice collaborative skills learned through teacher instruction.

Elements of Cooperative Learning

Placing students in groups and expecting them to work collaboratively is ineffective. However, when cooperative learning experiences are structured, students are on task at higher rates. They listen and share more ideas and resources than students who are assigned simply to work as a group. Additionally, students in cooperative learning groups have been shown to complete more complex and higher thinking skills when answering specific problem-solving questions (Gillies, 2008).

Cooperative learning applications do not look or sound alike. At the same time, all models of cooperative learning have at least five elements in common. These include (a) a common task or activity suitable for group work, (b) small-group learning, (c) cooperative behavior, (d) positive interdependence, (e) individual accountability and responsibility, and (f) group processing (Davidson, 2002; Gillies, 2014). Each element is described below.

Common Tasks Suitable for Group Work

Cooperative learning is more than putting students together and instructing them to work together or help one another. The group must be working toward a common task (e.g., presentation, written report) or goal (e.g., improving individual members' performance on a test) (Slavin, 2014). All of the cooperative learning models include common tasks accomplished by groups or teams. Sometimes tasks are broken into individual assignments. Using this format, individual students assume specific roles and responsibilities. The students complete their individual work. Then they come together and combine each person's work into one team project. Another format is for individual team members to work collectively to achieve a team goal. For example, each individual in the group may investigate a subtopic. The information acquired by the individuals is shared among group members, and a group report is planned and presented to the whole class. Another application of this element involves members of the groups working together rather than conducting investigations individually. The key element is that in all formats, students are working together toward a common task.

Small-Group Learning

The second element common to all cooperative learning models is the use of small groups to facilitate students' learning. Usually students are assigned to heterogeneous groups of four to six members. The heterogeneous grouping mixes gender, ethnicity, ability, and achievement levels of the students. Later in the chapter, specific ways teachers can group students together will be discussed.

Cooperative Behavior

Successful cooperative learning groups require that students use appropriate cooperative and collaborative skills. Students must know and trust each other, communicate accurately and unambiguously, accept and support one another, and resolve conflicts constructively. Although all cooperative-learning approaches agree on the importance of these behaviors, they differ regarding whether these skills should be taught explicitly. Some advocate direct social-skill instruction. In other approaches, direct teaching of social skills does not occur unless students demonstrate specific needs for social-skill training. Because cooperative behavior is a critical component of successful cooperative learning experiences, additional information regarding what and how to teach these skills is presented later in the chapter.

Interdependence

The fourth element common to all of the cooperative models is interdependence. **Interdependence** is the notion that individuals are linked with each other, and in order for the individual to succeed, the group needs to succeed and vice versa. If interdependence is achieved, students will feel successful only when all members of their group are successful, both individually and collectively as a team. Interdependence may be achieved by setting mutual goals for teams; dividing the labor among group members; dividing and/or sharing materials, information, and/or resources among group members; assigning various roles to students; and providing reinforcement contingent on achieving the goals.

Individual Accountability and Responsibility

The next common element, individual accountability and responsibility, is often left out of cooperative learning which lessens the potential of the experience (Slavin, 2014). Individual accountability and responsibility may take the form of reward or task accountability. **Reward accountability** refers to group members receiving rewards based on a total of individual contributions. For example, the team's score consists of individual team member's scores added together. Each group member's performance is assessed and the results shared with the group attributed to the individual. **Task accountability** refers to each student being accountable to the team for her portion of a team project.

   Individual accountability requires that all students be held responsible for learning the material, as well as for contributing to the group. This avoids the *free ride* effect, where one or more students do the majority of the work and the others get a free ride. Students who free ride may have doubts about their ability or they may be shy or reluctant to be involved. Individual accountability also prevents the *know-it-all* effect where one or two students dominate and tell others the answers.

TEACHER TIP #8.1
DEVELOPING INDIVIDUAL ACCOUNTABILITY

Teachers can ensure individual accountability by implementing one or more of the following:

1. Make certain the group task or goal requires all members to learn and participate.

2. Never select a task or goal that one student could do alone.

3. Frequently remind students that the purpose of cooperative learning is to make certain all students learn, not just get the right answer or finish the task.

4. Discuss with students why individual accountability is fair.

5. Use structures, such as numbered heads together, which reinforce individual accountability.

6. Do not step in too quickly when students struggle. Allow group members to develop interdependence and assist one another. (Slavin, 2014)

Group Processing

Group processing involves the group deconstructing and reflecting on the members' actions that helped or hindered goal attainment and making decisions about what actions to continue or change. Group processing allows members to discuss their progress and maintain healthy working relationships (Gillies, 2014). Some research has shown that when group processing is included in cooperative learning, and the teacher monitors and provides feedback of task progress and group processing, student achievement improves (Bertucci, Johnson, Johnson, & Conte, 2012; Emmer & Gerwels, 2002).

Implementing Cooperative Learning

Creating Groups

Although cooperative-learning approaches vary in the suggested number of group members, four-member teams allow for maximal numbers of interactions within groups. If a large group is not evenly divisible by four and one student remains unassigned, establish one team of five. If two students are left over, create two teams of three, and if three are left over, then build one team of three (Kagan & Kagan, 2009).

Most cooperative-learning approaches advocate the use of heterogeneous grouping within teams. Group assignment can be random or teacher assigned. Random assignment has its advantages in that it is easy and quick, adds variety and stimulation to the class, and avoids resistance because students perceive it as fair. Teachers often use random assignment at the beginning of the year before they know the students well. Random assignment can also be used to create groups temporarily to determine who works well with one another and who should not be placed together. There are also disadvantages to random assignment. Students in a randomly created group could be incompatible in personality or homogeneous in ability. Generally speaking, tasks assigned to randomly-assigned groups should not be graded.

The intent of teacher-assigned groups is to achieve heterogeneity across gender, ethnicity, ability, and achievement (Slavin, 2014). One way of assigning membership in a group is to rank the students according to achievement level, divide the list into fourths, and select one student from each quartile to be a member of a group of four. As group assignments are made, teachers should adjust for gender and ethnicity representation, and avoid placing students together who are either best friends or worst enemies.

In assigning students with disabilities to groups in general education classrooms, also consider the role the students will assume, their potential contribution to the group, and whether they will require assistance from other members of their group. Place no more than one at-risk student in each group.

Most cooperative learning groups remain intact for approximately 6 to 8 weeks. Groups can create a team name, flag, coat of arms, and/or motto to form cohesiveness and express their team personality (Slavin, 2014).

TEACHER TIP #8.2

STUDENTS WITH DISABILITIES IN GENERAL EDUCATION COOPERATIVE LEARNING GROUP

Students with HID may be anxious or fearful about joining a general education cooperative learning group. To help prevent this from happening, try the following:

- Prepare the student by explaining the procedures.
- Make certain the role to be assigned is appropriate for the student.
- Explain the responsibilities of the role carefully.
- Role-play the role the student will be assigned.
- Preteach any social or academic skill important for success in the group. (Mastropieri & Scruggs, 2004)

Teaching Cooperative Behaviors

Cooperative-learning approaches differ on whether cooperative behaviors should or need to be taught directly. Some researchers suggest students be taught skills such as taking turns, sharing materials, helping others, talking politely, checking for understanding and agreement, providing encouragement, listening actively, paraphrasing, managing conflict, providing constructive critiques, accepting individual responsibility, considering others' ideas, and making decisions democratically (Gillies, 2008, 2014; Piercy, Wilton, & Townsend, 2002; Slavin, 2014).

Although teachers should minimally provide participation rules for cooperative learning groups (Kuester & Zentall, 2012), most students with HID need to be explicitly taught the necessary collaborative social skills. The later approach emphasizes social skills as a defining component of a cooperative learning lesson and includes formal social-skill instruction within each lesson. How to teach social skills may be found in Chapter 13.

Assigning Roles

Roles that students assume may be assigned by the teacher or selected by team members. Depending on the composition of the group and the activity, roles may be assigned randomly or deliberately. One random strategy is to ask members of the group to number themselves (e.g., 1 to 4); then randomly assign each number to a role. For example, the student who is number one in each group is the recorder; number two, the reader; number three, the discussion leader; and number four, the materials gatherer. Random role assignment works best when the abilities of individual members of the group are fairly equivalent. Deliberate role assignment is preferred when group membership is more heterogeneous, particularly when students with disabilities are part of the general education cooperative learning group. In the above example, a student with a learning disability who has difficulty reading and writing may function most effectively in the role of a discussion leader or materials gatherer. A wide range of roles may be possible.

Technology Spotlight #8.1

Cooperative Learning and Digital Devices

Many teachers have limited access to digital devices for their students, but often not enough for each student. The limited number of digital devices necessitates a cooperative learning approach. The cooperative learning strategies discussed in this section are relevant for managing the classroom with limited digital devices.

The following are some strategies to keep in mind:

- When groups of students work together at the device, be sure to clarify each person's role (e.g., keyboarder/driver, notetaker, team leader).

- For typical apps and programs, train a group of students to serve as in-class experts to provide technical assistance for any student with a question. This will allow the teacher to work with other students without interruption.

- Search for apps and websites that focus on problems of engaging students in challenging work rather than using products with an individual remedial focus.

- Plan instructional activities that utilize a similar type of productivity tasks (e.g., conduct a Web search, create a poster on the word processor, develop a PowerPoint presentation) to facilitate student skill development over time.

Using Activities, Structures, and Projects

A list of potential activities, structures, and projects for cooperative learning groups would be endless. Those most researched, easiest to implement, and predominantly used include think-pair-share, numbered heads together, and jigsaw.

Think-Pair-Share

In the **Think-Pair-Share** structure, the teacher poses a questions or problem. Each student thinks about the answer for a specified amount of time. Students then form pairs and discuss their answers. The pairs are two members of a team of four. Following the Pair step, teams of four discuss the question or problem. This structure allows for much more student participation. Teams can then share their solutions or answers with the whole class (Kagan & Kagan, 2009).

Numbered Heads Together

Numbered Heads Together may be considered an alternative strategy for teacher questioning. This cooperative learning strategy, which actively engages all of the students in the classroom during teacher-directed instruction, supports informal team coaching for lower achievers to ensure that all group members understand the correct response (Maheady, Michielli-Pendl, Mallette, & Harper, 2002). Numbered Heads Together has been shown to have a positive impact on achievement of students with HID with or without accompanying behavioral incentives (Haydon, Maheady, & Hunter, 2010).

In groups of four, students number themselves one to four. Groups may also be numbered. The teacher poses a question to the entire class. The students in each group put their heads together to determine the group answer. The teacher randomly calls a number from one to four, and then a group number. The student who represents both the group and individual numbers responds for her group. The teacher then asks which of the students who have the same number as the student who just responded agree with the given answer? Those who agree raise their hands. This provides the teacher with a quick check of the responses of the whole class. The teacher may also ask students with the same number as the respondent to expand upon the given answer. The teacher recognizes and reinforces those who provided, agreed with, and expanded upon the correct response (Kagan & Kagan, 2009).

Jigsaw

Jigsaw, a well-known cooperative learning strategy, has many applications. As originally designed, students are assigned to six-member teams with academic material broken into sections. Each team member reads his or her assigned section of the material and then meets with members of different teams who had been assigned the same material. Students then return to their original teams and teach their teammates about their section (Aronson, 2014).

Variations of the original Jigsaw structure can also be used. For example, students can be assigned specific material to read and given *expert sheets* assigning them to a topic on which they are to become the expert. Students with the same topic can meet together to discuss and then return to their classmates to teach them what they have learned. In addition, the Jigsaw structure can be modified, using forms of communication beyond reading to gain information. In one example, a high school teacher used herself as one source of information. She shared information with one member of each of the groups, while others listened to an audio recording or read textual information. Then members from each group rejoined and shared what they learned. Using input other than reading can be critical for students with reading disabilities.

Evaluating students. Cooperative learning outcomes can be evaluated in a variety of ways. In order to promote group cohesiveness, group grades are not uncommon. Group grades are assigned when the group submits one product or performance as a composite of the individual group members' contributions. Each member of the group receives the same grade. Another approach is to evaluate the group based on an average grade. The average grade is computed in terms of individual group members' scores. Averaging grades is most effective with content such as mathematics or spelling for which individual group members may be working at their own appropriate level of difficulty.

Students' reactions to cooperative learning should also be evaluated. Ask students if they would prefer to work individually or cooperatively and what they liked best and least about working cooperatively. Use reflection activities as part of evaluation. Ask students to rate statements such as *My team had clear goals, stayed on task, and made decisions based on views of all* or *My teammates listened well to each other, helped each other, and all participated.* Students can assess themselves and their team members on similar statements. Clarification should be sought when a student's rating differs from the ratings of the other group members. Goals can then be set for increasing that member's contribution to the group.

TEACHER TIP #8.3

TEACH HOW TO GET HELP

Teach students to ask their peers for help during cooperative learning group activities. Specifically teach them the following:

- When to ask for help (e.g., if you don't understand the directions, have completed half of the assignment, or completed the whole assignment)

- How to tell if a peer is available (e.g., sitting next to you, working independently or sitting quietly)

- How to ask for help (e.g., tapping lightly on arm or back, ask if she or he can help you)

- What to say afterward (e.g., thank you for your help) (Wolford, Heward, & Alber, 2001).

Cooperative Learning and Teacher-Directed Instruction

Mr. Hunt, the middle school teacher introduced at the beginning of the chapter, has learned over time how to best integrate cooperative learning throughout his teacher-directed instruction. He has found, for example, that his students learn best when he conducts the instruction and modeling when teaching basic skills. So, although he continues his teacher-directed instruction, he integrates cooperative learning in other parts of the lesson, such as during review, guided practice, and closure. In fact, he almost exclusively uses cooperative learning during guided practice. Students practice within their groups while he monitors closely to ensure they are not practicing errors.

Cooperative learning is not used in isolation from other forms of instruction in the classroom. Neither is teacher-directed instruction. There are many ways in which the two can be combined in effectively teaching students with disabilities. In fact, some research shows that students perform better when teachers have been trained to embed cooperative learning into their lessons (Gillies, 2008). Cooperative learning can be applied very effectively within the structure of a teacher-directed lesson plan. For example, Numbered Heads Together could be used to review previously learned information. As a prerequisite check, groups could use the Think-Pair-Share structure, sharing group answers with the teacher and the whole class. The Jigsaw strategy could be used during instruction. During guided practice, students could practice in pairs or as cooperative groups. Individual performances during independent practice could be used to contribute to group rewards. Cooperative learning strategies can also be used to accomplish closure. Groups could create a visual (e.g., poster) or auditory (e.g., a song) representation of what they have learned. Examples of combining teacher-directed and cooperative-learning approaches are provided in Table 8.1.

TABLE 8.1   Combining Teacher-Directed and Cooperative-Learning Approaches

Instructional Steps	Teacher-Directed Instruction Examples	Cooperative-Learning (CL) Examples
Reviewing	Teacher asks whole group questions about previously discussed material, calling on individual students to respond or using whole-group response techniques.	Numbered Heads Together—Teacher asks question, allows students to discuss answer in CL group. Teacher randomly calls a group number and a person number. The person assigned the called number responds for the group. Teacher asks other students with the same number if they agree or disagree.
Prerequisite Check	Teacher asks whole group questions, calling on individuals or using whole-group response techniques.	In CL group, students create a definition or visual representation of concept to be taught.

(Continued)

TABLE 8.1 **(Continued)**

Instructional Steps	Teacher-Directed Instruction Examples	Cooperative-Learning (CL) Examples
Instruction	Teacher presents new information and monitors student understanding through questioning.	Jigsaw—Students with the same number meet together with the same material. They prepare to take that information back to their CL group to share.
Modeling	Teacher usually models skill, procedure, or behavior.	Peers model skills, procedure, or behavior for those in their CL group.
Guided Practice	Teacher practices with large group and/or individuals work independently with teacher monitoring.	Students practice within CL groups with teacher monitoring.
Independent	Individuals demonstrate skill, procedure, or behavior independently.	Individuals demonstrate skill, procedure, or behavior independently, although individual performance may contribute to group rewards.
Closure	Teacher summarizes.	CL groups create a visual or oral representation of what was learned and present to whole class.

Cooperative Learning With Students With Disabilities

In the move toward full inclusion, educators have advocated the use of cooperative learning groups as a means for educating students with disabilities in general education classrooms (Jenkins & O'Connor, 2003; Murphy, Grey, & Honan, 2005). Yet relatively few studies have examined the effectiveness of cooperative learning for students with disabilities. And the limited number of studies conducted have received mixed results (McMaster & Fuchs, 2002). Some research indicates that students with disabilities demonstrate improved self-esteem and are more socially accepted by their nondisabled peers following heterogeneous cooperative learning group experiences (Jenkins, Antil, Wayne, & Vadasy, 2003).

A few studies have demonstrated increased achievement of students with disabilities participating in cooperative-learning activities. For example, when students participated in the Numbered-Heads-Together questioning approach, they scored higher on daily quizzes when compared with the traditional whole class hand-raising, but equivalently to individual response cards (Maheady et al., 2002). However, Joseph Jenkins and Rollanda O'Connor (2003) conducted a review of studies and concluded that based on research, one cannot gauge the extent to which cooperative learning improves the achievement of students with disabilities.

Although academic gains have yet to be established conclusively, cooperative learning groups seem to provide a structure that may help accommodate inclusion. Providing the structure and involving students with disabilities in that structure, however, is far from adequate in accommodating the needs of the students. Teachers should attend to the specific strengths and needs of students with disabilities, particularly when assigning group membership and role responsibilities to ensure success.

Although not targeted toward students with disabilities, some research has discovered that teachers who implement cooperative learning engage in more mediated-learning interactions with students and make fewer disciplinary remarks. These behaviors may serve as a model for students, given that cooperative-learning group members were found in one study to provide almost twice as many elaborations, short responses, and helping behaviors than students in other small-group work (Gillies, 2006).

One study asked the general educators working with special and remedial education students the benefits of cooperative learning for this population. Results included improved self-esteem, the creation of a safe learning environment, and greater success with classroom tasks and required products (Jenkins et al., 2003). Eighty percent of these teachers ranked cooperative learning as first or second in effectiveness when compared with other instructional approaches. Students for whom cooperative learning was not effective were described as those with behavior and motivational challenges.

Cooperative learning provides opportunities for students to work and interact together in appropriate and productive ways. However, there will always be students who may not work well in these groups. In one study, cooperative learning groups that contained a member at risk for attention-deficit/hyperactivity disorder demonstrated more negative verbalizations (i.e., loud voices, bossiness, and off-task comments), and more off-task motor activity (e.g., running around the room, crawling under the table) than the comparative typical group (Zentall, Kuester, & Craig, 2011). Not all students will willingly participate. There will always be students who may not do the work, are withdrawn, are low achievers, or are disruptive during group processes. Some students may also wish to take control of the group inappropriately. Potential solutions to these problems are listed in Table 8.2.

TABLE 8.2   Challenging Behaviors and Possible Strategies for Cooperative Learning Groups

Challenging Behaviors	Possible Strategies
Lack of Contribution to the Group	• Assign explicit roles and responsibilities to group members. • Ask the group to discuss the problem to ascertain why there is lack of contribution. • Discuss with students not contributing why they are not participating. Problem-solve with them. • Trust the group to resolve the problem without teacher intervention. • Change the way in which group members are evaluated (e.g., base part of the grade on team members' evaluation of each individual's contribution). • Evaluate the quality of the activity students are asked to complete.
Withdrawn Behavior	• Place student with withdrawn behavior in a group with students who are "nurturing and supportive." • Design the activity and materials such that sharing and interaction are required (e.g., provide only one pair of scissors or incorporate Jigsaw structure). • Assign a role or responsibility to the student with withdrawn behavior that is "low risk," but requires participation.

(Continued)

TABLE 8.2   (Continued)

Challenging Behaviors	Possible Strategies
Students With Low Achievement	• Assign "low risk" and appropriate roles and responsibilities. • Coach students in advance to make them experts in a specific area relating to the group assignment. • Ensure that other group members will be helpful and supportive of the student.
Student With Disruptive Behavior	• Avoid assigning other group members who "set the student off" or otherwise contribute to the disruptive behavior. • Preteach other group members strategies for managing the student. • Use the disruptive situation to teach collaborative skills to all students. • Reduce the number of students in the group. Consider using only a partner with students who have disruptive behaviors.
Students Who Dominate the Group	• Assign the student supportive, rather than domineering, roles. • Include the amount and nature of involvement or participation as part of the evaluation criteria (e.g., part of the grade is based on other team members' evaluation regarding equal contribution.)

Source: Adapted from Kelly (2002).

Students with academic or social-skill deficits may detract from group activities in other ways. A student with a disability might provide incorrect information, which is then used by the group. Students with disabilities may require additional help from peers that could detract from the group work being accomplished. Or students may complain about their teammates. Prior to using cooperative-learning groups, the teacher should evaluate whether students need explicit instruction in cooperative-learning behaviors. In one study, students with learning disabilities were shown multiple video clips of appropriate and inappropriate cooperative-learning behaviors which improved their cooperative participation and led to higher level discussion (O'Brien & Wood, 2011). In addition to preparation, when assigning students to groups and roles, the teacher should anticipate any potential problems.

Specific accommodations may be made for students with disabilities who are participating in cooperative-learning groups, particularly if these groups are in an integrated general education classroom. Teachers must determine curricular modifications, such as whether the student will learn the entire general education curriculum, a subset of that curriculum, or different content. Such curricular decisions will impact the cooperative-learning structure. Curriculum modifications can occur in a variety of ways, which include changing response modes, developing functional equivalents, allowing for different completion rates or workloads, or using computer-assisted instruction. The way in which student performance is evaluated should be consistently reviewed and individual and group interactions should be constantly monitored. Students with disabilities may need a personal form of evaluations to compensate for their differences.

Implementation of cooperative learning groups in elementary and secondary classrooms can create an atmosphere of community and connection in which all students feel comfortable and supported. Cooperative learning can also lead to open communication about differences, strengths, and needs. "Cooperative learning can help make diversity a resource rather than a problem" (Slavin, 1995, p. 3). Students learn that everyone has strengths that can be used to help others, as well as that everyone is entitled to assistance and can benefit from help from others. Cooperative-learning structures can contribute to the amount of on-task instructional time in the classroom. In addition, cooperative learning may have particular effects on social acceptance, particularly when compared with competitive and individualized procedures.

Peer Tutoring

Mrs. Sebastian is a veteran teacher who is very organized and who manages her special education classroom very well. Her new student teacher, Mr. Yamaguchi, is amazed at how well activities in the classroom seem to flow, even with students constantly coming and going from the classroom. After spending one day observing, he felt overwhelmed and questioned whether he could match what she is doing when it comes time for him to *solo*. After spending a week in her classroom and discussing her organizational plan, Mr. Yamaguchi begins to understand. In addition to the teacher-directed instruction she provides, Mrs. Sebastian has also set up a peer-tutoring system. Students from other classrooms enter her classroom at varying times during the day and work as tutors for the special needs students. Mrs. Sebastian trained the tutors and organized the schedule to meet the needs of both the tutors and those in her classroom. Initially, it seemed complicated to Mr. Yamaguchi, but now he understands how it works.

Every day students in Ms. Gerhardt's class look forward to reading to each other. Ms. Gerhardt has placed students in pairs and they practice reading to each other for 10 minutes every day. Before starting the program, Ms. Gerhardt taught all of the students the procedures for these 10 minutes. One reads to the other for 3 minutes. The tutor listens carefully reading along and corrects errors if needed. Then they change roles. They were also taught how to keep track of the number of words read and the number of errors. They record this each day in a folder each student individually designed. When asked why they like this activity, they respond because they like to see themselves become better readers and they like working with their friends.

Peer tutoring, another student-mediated teaching strategy, has received wide acceptance in both general and special education. In the context of this chapter, *tutoring* means that a tutor is directly instructing a tutee. *Peer* implies that the students involved are of the same general chronological age and/or grade level. Within the dyad, the role of the tutor and tutee may or may not be reciprocal. Reciprocal tutoring means that the two students involved switch responsibilities. The tutee becomes the tutor and vice versa. Ms. Gerhardt is using reciprocal teaching; Mrs. Sebastian is not.

As with cooperative learning, students with HID may experience peer tutoring in their general education classrooms or special education classrooms. Depending upon the circumstance, they may serve only as the tutor or the tutee or be a member of a reciprocal team. Care should be taken to ensure that students with HID are not always the tutee. Opportunities can and should be created in which they tutor other students (e.g., tutoring younger students or tutoring in an area of strength).

Reciprocal Peer Tutoring

When a pair of students switches roles between being the tutor and the tutee, this is referred to as **reciprocal peer tutoring**. Although teachers can set up a reciprocal peer-tutoring program similar to Ms. Gerhardt, researchers have created and studied three specific reciprocal models including Classwide Peer Tutoring, Peer-Assisted Learning Strategies, and Classwide Student Tutoring Teams. A description of each follows.

Classwide Peer Tutoring (CWPT)

The **Classwide Peer Tutoring (CWPT)** program has four major components: (1) student teams that compete weekly; (2) reciprocal tutoring procedures that are highly structured; (3) daily points, public posting, and reinforcement; and (4) direct practice of instructional content. CWPT was designed as the practice component of instruction; therefore, CWPT focuses on content that has been taught previously through teacher-directed instruction (Maheady & Gard, 2010).

To implement CWPT, students in the class are divided randomly into two teams. Within teams, the teacher assigns dyads who alternate as tutor and tutee. Teachers should match students' ability levels and on how well students work together (Bowman-Perrott, 2009). Students are trained in the procedures for both roles. Teachers organize the content into daily and weekly units in a format conducive for the peer-tutoring sessions. Tutoring sessions typically occur 3 to 5 days a week for 20 to 45 minutes each day (Burks, 2004).

The tutoring dyad typically uses the following procedures. The tutor presents the tutee with the problem (e.g., spelling word, math problem, social studies question). The tutee says and writes the answer. If the answer is correct, the tutor assigns two points. If the answer is incorrect, the tutor follows a structured error correction procedure. The tutor provides the correct response, asks the tutee to write the correct answer three times, and awards the tutee one point if the error is corrected. After a set period of time (5 to 10 minutes), the tutor and tutee change roles. The teacher circulates among the dyads and awards points based on whether the tutor correctly presented material, awarded points, used the error correction procedures, and provided supportive comments and help. Points are awards for the number of items the dyads have completed during the session. After participating in the tutoring session for two to four times a week, the students are individually tested, earning 5 points for each correct answer. All of the cumulative points are added for the two class teams at the end of the week and are recorded and displayed at the front of the classroom (Burks, 2004; Maheady & Gard, 2010).

TABLE 8.3   Benefits of Classwide Peer Tutoring

Benefit Category	Specific Benefits
Instructional Benefits	• One-on-one instruction • Students learn how to teach. • Error correction procedures are provided. • Positive social interactions occur. • Both social and academic goals can be addressed simultaneously.
Benefits for Teachers	• Can reduce teacher work load • Can be implemented with current curriculum • Can be implemented in 30- or 40-minute blocks • Helps with classroom management
Benefits for Students	• Active engagement rates are higher. • Opportunities to respond are frequent. • Student focused • Experience more success • Opportunity to practice important skill of collaboration • Immediate feedback and error correction provided. • Mastery of content increased.

Source: Adapted from Bowman-Perrott (2009).

Peer-Assisted Learning Strategies (PALS)

The **Peer-Assisted Learning Strategies (PALS)** program is an extension of the CWPT, but designed for engaging students in strategic learning activities. It was developed to accommodate diverse learners in general classrooms; be feasible enough to be implemented in general classrooms; and provide students with a set of strategic, challenging, and motivating activities designed to improve academic achievement. Although the PALS strategies vary according to students' grade levels, common features include highly structured activities, high rates of verbal and sometimes written responses between tutor and tutee, and reciprocity of roles (McMaster, Fuchs, & Fuchs, 2002).

The PALS program was originally designed to improve reading skills of students in Grades 2 through 6, but it has been subsequently extended to lower and higher grades and to other academic content. In Grades 2 through 6, a higher and a lower performing student are paired. The teacher uses systematic procedures to train students to use Partner Reading with Retell, Paragraph Shrinking, and Predication Relay.

In Paragraph Reading with Retell, students use teacher-selected literature which they read for 5 minutes each. The stronger reader always goes first to serve as a model. When hearing an error, the tutor says, "Stop you missed that word. Can you figure it out?" If the student cannot in 4 seconds, then the tutor gives the word and asks the tutee, "What word?" Paragraph Shrinking focuses on reading comprehension. While reading orally, each student stops at the end of a paragraph to identify the main idea. In Prediction Relay, the reader makes predictions about what will happen in the next half page to be read, then after reading the tutee confirms or disconfirms the prediction. Specific prompts and error correction procedures are built in to each of these activities (McMaster, Fuchs, & Fuchs, 2006).

Kindergarten and first-grade PAL (K-PAL) reading activities involve phonological awareness, beginning decoding, and word recognition. Pairs of students play games that address rhyming, isolating beginning and ending sounds, blending sounds into words, and segmenting words into sounds. As students progress, sight words and sentences are presented (Fuchs, Fuchs, Al Otaiba et al., 2001).

High school PALS is similar to the PALS for second through sixth grade, differing in only three ways. Students switch partners more frequently, the motivational system is more age appropriate, and students generally read from expository rather than narrative text, which is selected to be more age appropriate (McMaster et al., 2006).

Classwide Student Tutoring Teams (CSTT)

Elements of the Classwide Peer Tutoring (CWPT) program were combined with elements of the Teams-Games-Tournaments cooperative learning strategy to create the Classwide Student Tutoring Teams (CSTT). Students are first placed in heterogeneous cooperative learning groups, in which they remain from 4 to 6 weeks. Each team member receives a study guide consisting of 10 to 30 questions and answers, along with a set of numbered cards. One student draws a card and asks the corresponding study guide question. Each member, except the *tutor*, writes his answer. The tutor checks each answer against the study guide answer sheet, awards 5 points to those who are correct, and provides the correct answer to those who are not correct. Tutees whose responses are incorrect write the answer once or twice; if they do this correctly, they receive 2 points. The tutor's role rotates throughout the group, and the procedure is repeated as each takes a turn. As with CWPT, bonus points and public posting of scores are used. Students are tested individually, and their scores are added to the team's cumulative point total (Maheady, Mallette, & Harper, 2006).

Nonreciprocal Peer Tutoring

Unlike the previously described three models, peer tutoring may be nonreciprocal, with tutors and tutees not exchanging roles. Mrs. Sebastian was using **nonreciprocal peer tutoring** in her classroom. When students are not naturally grouped in classrooms for nonreciprocal peer tutoring, volunteers need to be recruited. Students from older grades can be paired with younger students for a short period of time. As one example, Amy Lingo (2014) demonstrated that high school students with HID could successfully tutor sixth-grade students with HID in oral reading fluency. Adult volunteers can also be used as tutors. Regardless of the age and skill level, tutors need training to ensure that they appropriately provide effective instructional skills, such as direct questioning, checking for understanding, and giving feedback.

Keri Menesses and Frank Gresham (2009) examined the impact of reciprocal and nonreciprocal peer tutoring and discovered that they both produced comparable gains in math facts for both the tutor and the tutee. Also, those engaged in either form of tutoring produced substantially larger academic gains than students engaged in other forms of practice.

A series of steps to be completed when setting up a nonreciprocal peer tutoring program are outlined in Table 8.4. Teachers should initially design and implement a tutoring program using only a few students. Once successful, the program may expand to include more students.

TABLE 8.4 Steps for Implementing Nonreciprocal Peer Tutoring

1. Select participants.

   a. Identify tutees. Consider characteristics such as skill deficits, attentive behaviors, and social-skill needs.

   b. Identify tutors. Consider characteristics such as ability to acquire necessary teaching skills and effective interpersonal skills.

   c. Recruit tutors, by approaching students individually, providing public announcements, or soliciting support from other teachers if necessary.

2. Match tutors and tutees.

   a. Base the match on a differential of about two years in skill area being tutored and on preexisting social relations within the group.

   b. Consider allowing students to express their positive and negative preferences privately or in writing.

   c. Encourage cross-gender and cross-ethnicity pairing.

3. Arrange the environment.

   a. Determine the setting in which the tutoring will occur.

   b. Arrange for adequate personal space.

   c. Consider strategies for reducing noise levels.

   d. Arrange efficient ways of moving students into and out of tutoring sessions.

4. Arrange the tutoring schedule.

   a. Determine the time of day which tutoring will take place.

   b. Identify the duration of tutoring sessions. Sessions generally last from 15 to 30 minutes.

   c. Determine the frequency of sessions. To be effective, they should occur at least three times a week.

   d. Identify how many weeks the tutoring will take place. A minimum of 6 weeks and maximum of 12 weeks is suggested.

(Continued)

TABLE 8.4   (Continued)

5. Select and/or design materials.

    a. Create a script for the tutor to follow including specific error correction procedures.

    b. Consider whether specific reinforcers will be used.

    c. Select procedures for recording performance of skills (e.g., number of words spelled correctly) and/or reinforcers earned.

6. Train the tutors.

    a. Trainers can be teachers, paraeducators, administrators, volunteers, or students who have mastered the tutoring procedures.

    b. Plan a minimum of five 20-minute training sessions.

    c. Use effective instructional techniques to train the tutors (e.g., explain the program objectives, introduce materials, model and practice the procedure).

    d. Provide evaluative feedback to tutors. Implement error correction to eliminate procedural errors.

    e. If necessary, discuss the unique needs of the tutees.

7. Implement.

    a. Supervise the tutoring dyads. Supervision may be conducted by anyone in the school community who is trained to do it.

    b. While monitoring, provide praise and/or other reinforcers to students who are following the tutoring procedures.

8. Evaluate.

    a. Use students' performance on skills being tutored as measures of effectiveness.

    b. Use supervisors' observations as forms of evaluation.

    c. Ask students to provide self-reports of tutoring effectiveness.

TEACHER TIP #8.4

LOCATING VOLUNTEER TUTORS

Sometimes teachers have difficulty locating volunteer tutors for nonreciprocal tutoring. Try accessing tutors through one or more of the following:

- general education classes (ask if their teacher will give them extra credit)

- parents, grandparents, or older siblings
- retired individuals in the community
- after-school clubs
- community organizations
- staff members in the school (e.g., lunch workers, custodian)

Peer Tutoring and Teacher-Directed Instruction

The principles of teacher-directed instruction discussed in Chapter 7 are similar to the procedures suggested for peer tutoring. In some ways, peer tutoring, when used appropriately, can be more effective than teacher-directed instruction because students receive one-on-one instruction and are involved in direct academic materials at the appropriate level of difficulty. Also, the teacher is available to monitor and provide feedback and reinforcement which also increases on-task behavior.

As with cooperative-learning procedures, peer tutoring should be used in conjunction with teacher-directed instruction. For example, the teacher can provide initial instruction which is then practiced through peer tutoring. The CWPT program uses peer tutoring as an opportunity to practice content already directly taught by the teacher (Maheady & Gard, 2010). Peer tutoring can also be used as a review procedure to facilitate maintenance of the skills.

TEACHER TIP #8.5

ERROR CORRECTION PROCEDURES

Accurate error correction procedures can make a big difference in the effectiveness of a tutor. Train tutors to use these procedures. Then monitor to ensure they are implementing them correctly. When an error is made,

- signal (usually nonverbally) the tutee;
- model the correct response;

- lead or prompt the tutee to imitate the correct response;
- ask the tutee to respond independently; and
- at some later point, recheck to make certain the tutee can still respond correctly.

Peer Tutoring and Students With Disabilities

Peer tutoring is documented as an effective peer-mediated strategy for students with HID regardless of the setting (general education or special education classroom) or the content being taught (Okilwa & Shelby, 2010). The Classwide Peer Tutoring model has been studied with a wide range of students, in various settings and with various content areas. For example, CWPT has been shown to improve reading, math, science, social studies, and spelling. It has been effective with elementary, middle, and high school students at risk, students with HID, and students without disabilities (e.g., Bowman-Perrott, 2009; Burks, 2004; Kamps et al., 2008; Menesses & Gresham, 2009; Scruggs, Mastropieri, & Marshak, 2012; Simpkins, Mastropieri, & Scruggs, 2009).

Peer-Assisted Learning Strategies has also been shown to be an effective strategy for students across a wide range of ages and abilities, including students with disabilities, as well as those from culturally diverse and/or poverty backgrounds. For example, PALS has increased reading and prereading skills of students identified with emotional/ behavioral disorders (Falk & Wehby, 2001) and students who are low, average, and high achievers (Fuchs, Fuchs, Yen et al., 2001). Other studies have shown PALS to be effective in math computational skills of students with learning disabilities in Grades 9 through 12 (Calhoon & Fuchs, 2003), social acceptability of students with learning disabilities in general classrooms (Fuchs, Fuchs, Mathes, & Martinez, 2002), and reading performance of English learners with and without learning disabilities in transitional bilingual education classrooms (Saenz, Fuchs, & Fuchs, 2005).

Nonreciprocal peer tutoring has also been demonstrated to be an effective intervention for students with HID. For example, Lingo (2014) studied the impact of high school students tutoring sixth-grade students with HID. Results showed that the tutees improved their oral reading skills and fluency even when the grade-level materials were far above the tutees' instructional reading levels.

In terms of general peer tutoring methods, Vicky Spencer and Giulia Balboni (2003) reviewed 52 peer tutoring studies in which students with intellectual disabilities (ID) were involved. They reported that all studies reported favorable outcomes regardless of whether the student with ID served as a tutor to a peer without disabilities or was involved with reciprocal tutoring. These studies demonstrated that students with ID were successful in tutoring their peers in basic daily living, academic, and self-help skills. In another review, Donald Stenhoff and Benjamin Lignugaris/Kraft (2007) examined the impact of peer tutoring in secondary settings with HID. Generally peer tutoring resulted in improved academic performance. They also discovered that tutors performed better when they were trained on implementation procedures than when no training was offered.

Reviewers of peer tutoring studies agree that these procedures are effective with general education students and with students with disabilities. Both the tutor and the tutee benefit from participation. Tutees gain the benefit of one-on-one individual instruction that promotes improved academic performance and higher levels of engaged learning. Tutors can become more fluent with the skill they are teaching. Tutors can also gain a sense of responsibility for themselves and other students.

A major advantage of peer tutoring is that these procedures empower students with a learning strategy that may be used to approach new learning tasks outside of the original tutoring sessions. In addition, tutors have been shown in some cases to improve their attitudes toward school and toward the content they are teaching (Mastropieri & Scruggs, 2002). More specifically, positive social and emotional benefits are more likely to be obtained when the following conditions are in place: students are selected and trained systematically, the tutoring sessions are designed to be successful for all participants, the participants are appropriately reinforced for good performance, and students' progress is continuously monitored.

Peer tutoring may be used to facilitate effective inclusive classrooms. As discussed previously, merely the existence of any peer-mediated instruction is insufficient in meeting the dynamic and interactive needs of individual students, their peers and teacher. But peer tutoring can provide a starting point for supporting inclusive practices.

Technology Spotlight #8.2

Using Technology Tools With Peer Tutoring

By definition, peer tutoring involves two students, one acting as tutor and the other as tutee. Although peer tutoring is a human-interaction endeavor, technological tools can be helpful in facilitating the tutoring experience. A few examples follow:

- Wireless technology through bug-in-ear (BIE) can deliver immediate feedback to the tutee. With BIE, the tutee wears an earpiece that fits inside the ear and the peer tutor provides feedback while the tutee is engaged in a behavior. For example, in one study, tutors were taught to provide feedback to tutees during their oral presentation. The tutors provided feedback regarding speaking too quickly, rocking behavior, and lack of inflection in their speech. Based on the results, the authors concluded that immediate feedback provided by peer tutors using BIE was more effective than delayed feedback and that the BIE device is an acceptable, unobtrusive means to providing feedback for peers (Scheeler, Macluckie, & Albright, 2010).

- The VoicePod, a portable digital recording and playback system, can be used to facilitate peer tutoring. VoicePod uses multiple, reusable cards that are covered with a clear plastic sleeve where a paper is inserted displaying text. Each card has an identification strip across the bottom that when activated, accesses a recording that is coordinated with a visual prompt on the card. In one study, the VoicePod was used to teach fourth-grade students with learning disabilities vocabulary. For each vocabulary word the following information was recorded: the word, the definition or synonym, a sentence using the word, an identical sentence using the definition or synonym, two sentences containing blanks for one word, and the correct sentence from the previous card. Peer tutors incorporated the VoicePods as part of the tutoring procedures. In comparison with incidental learning, those engaged in peer tutoring with audio prompting made much stronger gains. (Mackiewicz, Wood, Cooke, & Mazzotti, 2011)

Implications for Culturally and/or Linguistically Diverse Students

As discussed in previous chapters, cultural values are the core principles that define desirable behaviors in both individuals and groups of people (Gollnick & Chinn, 2012). A major dimension of cultural variation involves individualism versus collectivism.

Although there may exist great variation within a cultural group, individualism is promoted in most northern and western European and North American cultures, whereas, collectivist values are found in African, American Indian, Asian, Latin American, Middle Eastern, and the Pacific Island cultures (Chan & Chen, 2011; Joe & Malach, 2011; Sharifzadeh, 2011). For example, Latino culture is usually characterized as having a collective orientation that fosters interdependence, cooperation, and group identity with an emphasis on interpersonal relationships (Lynch & Hanson, 2011). As another example, most Middle Eastern cultures identify the collective achievement of family, rather than one's personal achievement, as a source of pride and identity (Sharifzadeh, 2011).

Students' cultural values can greatly impact how they experience school. Students from cultures that encourage collectivism are less motivated by competition and individual achievement, but respond favorably to group participation, such as cooperative learning and peer tutoring. Teachers should not assume, however, that the ethnicity or cultural upbringing of a student determines her ability to apply student-mediated learning strategies. Ethnic groups vary in their approaches to cooperation. In the European and North American culture, each person is generally expected to *carry his or her weight.* In other cultures, group members are expected to make contributions according to ability and need. Students who are being raised in cultures that foster cooperative behaviors may need direction as to when cooperation is appropriate in school. They may, for example, be quick to share their belongings with peers, which could extend to allowing others to copy their school work or answers on examination. Students may view themselves as being helpful or generous, and not interpret the sharing of answers to be inappropriate or problematic (Grossman, 1995).

Research has documented that students from cultures promoting collectivism perform more effectively when engaged in student-mediated instruction. For example, in a review of literature, Debbie Robinson, Janet Schofield, and Katrina Steers-Wentzell (2005) concluded that both peer-tutoring and cross-age tutoring in mathematics had positive academic outcomes for African American and other ethnically diverse students regardless of whether the students were the tutor, the tutee, or both. These authors suggest teachers seriously consider peer tutoring for diverse students because student gains were observed in academic, attitudinal, and socioemotional outcomes.

English learners (ELs) can also benefit from student-mediated instruction. Studies have examined the effectiveness of peer-mediated strategies with English learners with and without disabilities. One study found that Peer-Assisted Learning Strategies improved the reading comprehension of third through sixth-grade Spanish speaking students with and without learning disabilities (Saenz et al., 2005). Another study examined the impact of PALS in first-grade, predominately Hispanic classrooms. Results indicated that those participating in PALS showed statistically significant improvement in literacy skills than those who received traditional instruction. These improvements helped ameliorate the risk status of Hispanic participants (Calhoon, Al Otaiba, Greenberg, King, & Avalos, 2006).

The use of cooperative learning with diverse student populations has also been examined. One study examined the effects of cooperative learning on the Spanish and English reading, writing, and language achievement of ELs. Those participating in the cooperative learning outperformed their comparative group in writing and reading (Calderon, Hertz-Lazarowitz, & Slavin, 1998). Research on the effectiveness of cooperative learning and peer tutoring with CLD students is limited, but these proce-dures seem to hold promise for this population of student.

TEACHER TIP #8.6

COOPERATIVE LEARNING AND ENGLISH LEARNERS

English learners (ELs) can benefit greatly from cooperative learning groups if the teacher structures and monitors the groups properly as follows:

- Structure team-building activities to ensure that ELs have an opportunity to get to know other group members in meaningful ways as well as demonstrate their competence to others.

- Design cooperative-learning activities with tasks that encourage verbal interactions.

- Strategically assign tasks to ELs such as drawing, graphic designer, mime, or translator for other second-language learners in the class.

- When ELs are not participating to the same degree as others, ask a student to tally the number of times that each group member speaks and encourage others to ask the ELs specific questions. (Herrell & Jordan, 2016)

In addition to academic gains, there are additional benefits of using student-mediated strategies for students whose primary language is not English. Language development can be dramatically enhanced by the increased opportunities for individu-alized and personal interaction in pairs or small groups. In particular, cooperative learn-ing and peer tutoring provide multitude opportunities for students to use and practice oral language in natural settings. In classrooms not using group work, ELs may be passive learners not saying much and thus they are not working toward developing their oral language (Fisher, Frey, & Rothenberg, 2011). In addition, working together provides opportunities for ELs to acquaint themselves with others. This can reduce cul-tural and language barriers, and true friendships and positive relationships can develop. As a rule, cooperative learning and peer tutoring are powerful and effective strategies for all students, regardless of disability or cultural background.

SUMMARY

In student-mediated instruction, the teacher facilitates instructional interactions among students. Two forms of student-mediated instruction include cooperative learning and peer tutoring. Cooperative learning typically takes place in small groups of three to five students during which students work together on a common task. For cooperative learning to be effective, students must develop interdependence. In other words, for the individual to succeed, the group needs to succeed and vice versa. Although interdependence is important, so is independence. Students must be held responsible and accountable for their individual learning and contributions. Students, particularly students with HID, need to be explicitly taught collaborative behaviors. Teachers should anticipate potential challenges for students with HID and adjust the cooperative learning experiences as needed.

Peer tutoring is a well-documented, effective peer-mediated strategy for students with HID. In reciprocal models, students switch roles of tutor and tutee in their dyads. In the non-reciprocal model, usually older students serve as the tutors to younger students. Regardless of the model, tutors need to be trained to follow specific procedures while engaged in the tutoring process. Many studies have shown peer tutoring to be an effective instructional strategy for typically developing students and students with disabilities. Both the tutor and the tutee benefit from participation in peer tutoring.

Both cooperative learning and peer tutoring can be implemented effectively within a teacher-directed lesson.

Cooperative learning, for example, could be part of the review, prerequisite check, guided practice, and closure portions of a teacher-directed lesson. Peer tutoring lends itself best to guided practice, although it could also be used as review.

Although limited research has been conducted, the effectiveness of student-mediated strategies for CLD students is emerging. Students from cultures that encourage collectivism are less motivated by competition and individual achievement, but respond favorably to group participation, such as cooperative learning and peer tutoring. English learners (ELs) can benefit from student-mediated instruction given that cooperative learning and peer tutoring provide multitude opportunities for students to use and practice oral language in natural settings. Also, students working together can reduce cultural and language barriers, and true friendships and positive relationships can develop. Both cooperative learning and peer tutoring are effective strategies for all students, including students with HID and those from CLD backgrounds.

REVIEW QUESTIONS

1. What are the six elements common to all cooperative-learning approaches? Why is it important to understand each of these elements prior to organizing cooperative-learning groups?

2. Discuss the advantages and limitations of each of the cooperative structures discussed in the chapter.

3. Compare and contrast teacher-directed instruction with cooperative-learning approaches. Discuss how teacher-directed instruction and cooperative learning can increase engaged learning time.

4. What are the potential benefits and challenges of including students with disabilities in cooperative groups?

5. What strategies can teachers use to address problems associated with including students with disabilities in cooperative-learning groups?

6. Define reciprocal and nonreciprocal peer tutoring. Provide specific examples of when you would use each.

7. Describe how incorporating peer tutoring in a teacher-directed lesson can maximize opportunities for learning.

8. Discuss how students with reading disabilities might benefit from peer tutoring. Which peer tutoring models would be most beneficial for improving reading skills, and why?

9. Why is peer tutoring such an effective strategy for students with HID? Substantiate your answer with a few research findings.

10. Discuss how student-mediated instruction might provide academic support for students from different cultures, as well as EL students.

ACTIVITIES

1. Develop four cooperative-learning activities about providing accommodations for students with disabilities. For each activity, describe the objective of the activity, roles each member of the group will play, and how you will measure the group's performance. Implement in your university classroom.

2. Create a PowerPoint presentation about cooperative learning or peer tutoring. Plan for the presentation to be interactive with the audience participating in at least two activities that you discuss.

3. Locate a teacher implementing cooperative learning or peer tutoring. Observe several sessions. Compare the classroom practices with what you have learned in this chapter. Write up or orally present your report.

4. Evaluate your experience participating in cooperative-learning groups or peer tutoring. Describe how you have benefited and challenges you have encountered as you have worked with other students. As a teacher, how would you address the challenges you have encountered?

Council for Exceptional Children (CEC) Standards

The Council for Exceptional Children (CEC) is a premiere national professional organization comprised of special educators, paraeducators, relative service personnel, parents, and others interested in individuals with disabilities and/or those with gifts and talents. This organization has generated 10 standards for the preparation of special educators. These standards are listed in each chapter as they relate to the content within the chapter. The standard that applies to Chapter 8 is Standard #5.

CEC Initial Preparation Standard 5: Instructional Planning and Strategies

5.1 Beginning special education professionals consider an individual's abilities, interests, learning environments, and cultural and linguistic factors in the selection, development, and adaptation of learning experiences for individuals with exceptionalities.

REFERENCES

Aronson, E. (2014). *The jigsaw classroom*. Retrieved from https://www.jigsaw.org

Bertucci, A., Johnson, D. W., Johnson, R. T., & Conte, S. (2012). Influence of group processing on achievement and perceptions of social and academic support in elementary inexperienced cooperative learning groups. *The Journal of Educational Research, 105,* 329–335.

Bowman-Perrott, L. (2009). Classwide peer tutoring: An effective strategy for students with emotional and behavioral disorders. *Intervention in School and Clinic, 44*(5), 259–267.

Burks, M. (2004). Effects of classwide peer tutoring on the number of words spelled correctly by students with LD. *Intervention in School and Clinic, 39*, 301–304.

Calderon, M., Hertz-Lazarowitz, R., & Slavin, R. (1998). Effects of bilingual cooperative integrated reading and composition on students making the transition from Spanish to English reading. *Elementary School Journal, 99*, 153–165.

Calhoon, M. B., Al Otaiba, S., Greenberg, D., King, A., & Avolos, A. (2006). Improving reading skills in predominately Hispanic Title I first-grade classrooms: The promise of peer-assisted learning strategies. *Learning Disabilities Research and Practice, 21*(4), 261–272.

Calhoon, M. B., & Fuchs, L. S. (2003). The effects of peer-assisted learning strategies and curriculum-based measurement on the mathematics performance of secondary students with disabilities. *Remedial and Special Education, 24*, 235–245.

Chan, S., & Chen, D. (2011). Families with Asian roots. In E. M. Lynch & M. J. Hanson (Eds.), *Developing cross-cultural competence: A guide for working with children and their families* (4th ed., pp. 234–318). Baltimore, MD: Paul H. Brookes.

Davidson, N. (2002). Cooperative and collaborative learning: An integrative perspective, In J. S. Thousand, R. A. Villa, & A. I. Nevin (Eds.), *Creativity and collaborative learning: The practical guide to empowering student, teachers, and families* (2nd ed., pp. 181–195). Baltimore, MD: Paul H. Brookes.

Emmer, E. T., & Gerwels, M. C. (2002). Cooperative learning in elementary classrooms: Teaching practices and lesson characteristics. *The Elementary School Journal, 103*(1), 75–91.

Falk, K. B., & Wehby, J. H. (2001). The effects of peer-assisted learning strategies on the beginning reading skills of your children with emotional or behavioral disorders. *Behavioral Disorders, 26*, 344–359.

Fisher, D., Frey, N., & Rothenberg, C. (2011). *Implementing RTI with English learners.* Bloomington, IN: Solution Tree.

Fuchs, D., Fuchs, L. S., Al Otaiba, S. A., Thompson, A., Yen, L., & McMaster, K. L. (2001). K-PALS: Helping kindergarteners with reading readiness: Teachers and researchers in partnerships. *TEACHING Exceptional Children, 33*(4), 76–80.

Fuchs, D., Fuchs, L. S., Mathes, P. G., & Martinez, E. A. (2002). Preliminary evidence on the social standing of students with learning disabilities in PALS and No-PALS classroom. *Learning Disabilities Research, 17*, 205–215.

Fuchs, D., Fuchs, L. S., Yen, L., McMaster, K. L., Swenson, E., & Yang, N. (2001). Developing first-grade reading fluency through peer mediation. *TEACHING Exceptional Children, 34*(2), 90–93.

Gillies, R. M. (2006). Teachers' and students' verbal behaviours during cooperative and small-group learning. *British Journal of Educational Psychology, 76*, 271–287.

Gillies, R. M. (2008). The effects of cooperative learning on junior high school students' behaviours, discourse and learning during a science-based learning activity. *School Psychology International, 29*(3), 328–347.

Gillies, R. M. (2014). Cooperative learning: Developments in research. *International Journal of Educational Psychology, 3*(2), 125–140.

Gollnick, D. M., & Chinn, P. C. (2012). *Multicultural education in a pluralistic society* (9th ed.). Boston, MA: Pearson.

Grossman, H. (1995). *Educating Hispanic students* (2nd ed.). Springfield, IL: Charles C Thomas.

Haydon, T., Maheady, L., Hunter, W. (2010). Effects of numbered heads together on the daily quiz scores and on-task behavior of students with disabilities. *Journal of Behavioral Education, 19*, 222–238.

Herrell, A. L., & Jordan, M. (2016). *50 strategies for teaching English language learners.* Boston, MA: Pearson.

Jenkins, J. R., Antil, L. R., Wayne, S. K., & Vadasy, P. F. (2003). How cooperative learning works for special education and remedial students. *Exceptional Children, 69*, 279–292.

Jenkins, J. R., & O'Connor, R. E. (2003). Cooperative learning for students with learning disabilities: Evidence

from experiments, observations, and interviews. In
H. L. Swanson, K. R. Harris, & S. Graham (Eds.),
Handbook of learning disabilities (pp. 417–430),
New York, NY: Guilford Press.

Joe, J. R., & Malach, R. S. (2011). Families with American
Indian roots. Families with Asian roots. In E. M. Lynch
& M. J. Hanson (Eds.), *Developing cross-cultural
competence: A guide for working with children and
their families* (4th ed., pp. 110–139). Baltimore,
MD: Paul H. Brookes.

Johnson, D. W., & Johnson, R. T. (2005). Cooperative
learning. In S. W. Lee (Ed.), *Encyclopedia of school
psychology* (pp. 117–120), Thousand Oaks, CA: Sage.

Kagan, S., & Kagan, M. (2009). *Kagan cooperative
learning.* San Clemente, CA: Kagan.

Kamps, D. M., Greenwood, C., Arreaga-Mayer, C.,
Veerkamp, M. B., Utley, C., Tapia, Y., . . . & Bannister, H.
(2008). The efficacy of classwide peer tutoring in middle
schools. *Education and Treatment of Children, 31*(2),
119–152.

Kelly, B. (2002). Student disruptions in the cooperative
classroom. In J. S. Thousand, R. A. Villa, & A. I. Nevin
(Eds.), *Creativity and collaborative learning: The
practical guide to empowering students, teachers, and
families* (2nd ed., pp. 223–233). Baltimore, MD:
Paul H. Brookes.

Kuester, D. A., & Zentall, S. S. (2012). Social interaction
rules in cooperative learning groups for students at risk
for ADHD. *The Journal of Experimental Education,
80*(1), 69–95.

Lingo, A. S. (2014). Tutoring middle school students
with disabilities by high school students: Effects on
oral reading fluency. *Education and Treatment of
Children, 37*, 53–75.

Lynch, E. W., & Hanson, M. J. (2011). *Developing cross-
cultural competence: A guide for working with children
and their families* (4th ed.). Baltimore, MD:
Paul H. Brookes.

Mackiewicz, S. M., Wood, C. L., Cooke, N. L., & Mazzotti,
V. L. (2011). Effects of peer tutoring with audio prompting
on vocabulary acquisition for struggling readers.
Remedial and Special Education, 32(4), 343–354.

Maheady, L., & Gard, J. (2010). Classwide peer tutoring:
Practice, theory, research, and personal narrative.
Intervention in School and Clinic, 46(2), 71–78.

Maheady, L., Mallette, B., & Harper, G. F. (2006). Four
classwide peer tutoring models: Similarities, differences,
and implications for research and practice. *Reading &
Writing Quarterly, 22*, 65–89.

Maheady, L., Michielli-Pendl, J., Mallette, B., & Harper, G. F.
(2002). A collaborative research project to improve the
academic performance of a diverse sixth grade science
class. *Teacher Education and Special Education,
25*, 55–70.

Mastropieri, M. A., & Scruggs, T. E. (2002). *Effective
instruction for special education* (3rd ed.). Boston,
MA: Allyn & Bacon.

Mastropieri, M. A., & Scruggs, T. E. (2004). *The inclusive
classroom: Strategies for effective instruction* (2nd ed.).
Upper Saddle River, NJ: Pearson.

McMaster, K. L., & Fuchs, D. (2002). Effects of
cooperative learning on the academic achievement
of students with learning disabilities: An update of
Tateyama-Sniezek's review. *Learning Disabilities
Research and Practice, 17*, 107–117.

McMaster, K. L., Fuchs, D., & Fuchs, L. S. (2002). Using
peer tutoring to prevent early reading failure. In
J. S. Thousand, R. A. Villa, & A. I. Nevin, (Eds.),
*Creativity and collaborative learning: The practical
guide to empowering students, teachers, and families*
(2nd ed., pp. 235–246). Baltimore, MD: Paul H. Brookes.

McMaster, K. L., Fuchs, D., & Fuchs, L. S. (2006).
Research on peer-assisted learning strategies: The
promise and limitations of peer-mediated instruction.
Reading & Writing Quarterly, 22, 5–25.

Menesses, K. F., & Gresham, F. M. (2009). Relative
efficacy of reciprocal and nonreciprocal peer tutoring for
students at-risk for academic failure. *School Psychology
Quarterly, 24*(4), 266–275.

Murphy, E., Grey, I. M., & Honan, R. (2005). Co-operative
learning for students with difficulties in learning: A
description of models and guidelines for implementation.
British Journal of Special Education, 32, 157–164.

O'Brien, C., & Wood, C. L. (2011). Video modeling of cooperative discussion group behaviors with students with learning disabilities in a secondary content-area classroom. *Journal of Special Education Technology, 26*(4), 25–40.

Okilwa, N. S. A., & Shelby, L. (2010). The effects of peer tutoring on academic performance of students with disabilities in grades 6 through 12: A synthesis of the literature. *Remedial and Special Education, 31*(6), 450–463.

Piercy, M., Wilton, K., & Townsend, M. (2002). Promoting the social acceptance of young children with moderate-severe intellectual disabilities using cooperative-learning techniques. *American Journal of Mental Retardation, 107*, 352–360.

Robinson, D. R., Schofield, J. W., & Steers-Wentzell, K. L. (2005). Peer and cross-age tutoring in math: Outcomes and their design implications. *Educational Psychology Review, 17*(4), 327–362.

Saenz, L. M., Fuchs, L. S., & Fuchs, D. (2005). Peer-assisted learning strategies for English language learners with learning disabilities. *Exceptional Children, 71*, 231–247.

Scheeler, M. C., Macluckie, M., & Albright, K. (2010). Effects of immediate feedback delivered by peer tutors on the oral presentation skills of adolescents with learning disabilities. *Remedial and Special Education, 31*(2), 77–86.

Scruggs, T. E., Mastropieri, M. A., & Marshak, L. (2012). Peer-mediated instruction in inclusive secondary social studies learning: Direct and indirect learning effects. *Learning Disabilities Research & Practice, 27*(1), 12–20.

Sharifzadeh, V. S. (2011). Families with Middle Eastern roots. In E. M. Lynch & M. J. Hanson (Eds.), *Developing cross-cultural competence: A guide for working with children and their families* (4th ed., pp. 392–436). Baltimore, MD: Paul H. Brookes.

Simpkins, P. M., Mastropieri, M. A., & Scruggs, T. E. (2009). Differentiated curriculum enhancements in inclusive fifth-grade science classes. *Remedial and Special Education, 30*(5), 300–308.

Slavin, R. E. (1995). *Cooperative learning: Theory, research, and practice* (2nd ed.). Boston, MA: Allyn & Bacon.

Slavin, R. E. (2014). Making cooperative learning powerful. *Educational Leadership, 72*(2), 22–28.

Spencer, V. G., & Balboni, G. (2003). Can students with mental retardation teach their peers? *Education and Training in Developmental Disabilities, 38*, 32–61.

Stenhoff, D. M., & Lignugaris/Kraft, B. (2007). A review of the effects of peer tutoring on students with mild disabilities in secondary settings. *Exceptional Children, 74*(1), 8–30.

Wolford, P. L., Heward, W. L., & Alber, S. R. (2001). Teaching middle school students with learning disabilities to recruit peer assistance during cooperative learning group activities. *Learning Disabilities Research and Practice, 16*, 161–173.

Zentall, S. S., Kuester, D. A., & Craig, B. A. (2011). Social behavior in cooperative groups: Students at risk for ADHD and their peers. *The Journal of Educational Research, 104*, 28–41.

$SAGE edge™ •••●

Review ➡ Practice ➡ Improve

Get the tools you need to sharpen your study skills. Access videos, practice quizzes, eFlashcards and more at **edge.sagepub.com/prater.**

9

Strategies for Learning

Strategies for Learning

The overall purpose of education is to prepare students to reach their potential for learning both during and after formal schooling. In the previous two chapters, teacher-directed and student-mediated instruction were discussed. Both instructional approaches are essential for students to reach their potential for learning. The development of strategic learning processes, the topic discussed in this chapter, is also necessary for successful learning.

> Madison, a seventh-grade student with learning disabilities attends the general education content courses and receives support from a special educator. Madison is required to take all the standardized tests with her nondisabled peers, but she's frightened that she will do poorly. Her parents and teachers assure her that she knows the content, but that doesn't seem to help Madison feel prepared for these tests.

Learning Objectives

- Defend why students with high-incidence disabilities need strategy instruction based on the notion of strategic learner.

- Define attention and mnemonic strategies and describe how to teach them. Provide examples for on-task attention, selective attention, acronyms, acrostics, rhymes, keywords, and pegwords.

- Compare and contrast organizing strategies, study strategies, test-taking strategies and notetaking strategies. Provide multiple examples of each and describe when and how they should be taught.

- Describe why learning strategies may be particularly helpful to English learners.

Strategies refer to how students think and act when planning, executing, and evaluating their performance while completing an academic task or solving a problem (Hughes, 2011). Strategies usually consist of a series of steps to complete a task or solve a problem. They involve both cognition and behavior and may be thought of as how one approaches the task rather than the actual skill or knowledge used to accomplish the task. Madison knows the content on which she will be tested. What she lacks are the test-taking strategies she needs to demonstrate her knowledge on the test.

To be academically successful, students need content, strategic, and metacognitive knowledge. **Metacognition** refers to our broad general awareness and knowledge of cognition (i.e., what we know) and cognitive processes (i.e., how we know). Metacognitive skills help students to select, monitor, and implement strategies.

> Strategic learners (a) know what strategies are within their repertoire, (b) hypothesize which strategy is appropriate given the task at hand, (c) remember the sequence of steps to follow and how to apply them, (d) have an outcome goal in mind, (e) evaluate whether the strategy is effective in meeting the goal and make needed adjustments if they are not meeting it, and (f) decide when the outcome goal has been reached. (Hughes, 2011, pp. 1–2)

Strategies are not instructionally significant until they are associated with a specific problem or task. Task-specific strategies are used in conjunction with cognitive strategies and may be designed to accomplish specific tasks such as skill development in reading or mathematics. Specific task strategies, for example, may include various word-attack skills applicable to teaching reading. Additional discussion regarding the development and use of task strategies in teaching academic, social, and life skills may be found in Chapters 10 through 14.

Strategic learners, in general, possess and implement a large repertoire and variety of strategies. Many learners are capable of creating or finding strategies on their own, often inducing optimal strategies through trial and error. That is, students without learning difficulties often create or look for strategies on their own. For example, a student may find a rhyme to remember information better (e.g., *Columbus sailed the ocean blue in fourteen hundred and ninety-two.*). If the rhyme helps, he will continue to use rhymes with new information. If the rhyme doesn't help, he won't use it again.

Generally speaking, students with high-incidence disabilities (HID) do not create or look for strategies to help them learn (Hughes, 2011). Therefore, strategy instruction for students with disabilities is particularly needful and is most efficient when made explicit to the learner. Although students need explicit strategy instruction, the ultimate goal in teaching strategies is to help students to become more responsible for their learning and to learn *how-to-learn*.

The teaching of strategies may be categorized as direct or indirect. Direct teaching involves teacher selection of an efficient and effective strategy for accomplishing a task and teaching the student to apply that strategy. Indirect teaching involves prompting and guiding students in their strategy use. Students with HID are less likely than their typical peers to be efficient and effective strategy users, yet the ultimate goal of strategy instruction is to develop lifelong, self-sustaining learners. Strategy instruction with this population, therefore, needs to incorporate a combination of both direct and indirect approaches.

In this chapter, strategies for learning are presented: strategies for attention, remembering (mnemonic), organizing, test-taking, and notetaking. In addition, how students can be taught to self-manage their own behavior and learning is discussed. As in previous chapters, implications for culturally and/or linguistically diverse learners as they relate to strategies for learning are also presented.

Attention Strategies

Ten-year-old Brayden struggles in school. He was diagnosed as having attention–deficit/hyperactivity disorder at age 8 and started taking medication at that time. His behavior improved, but he still has difficulty paying attention for the length of time his peers can attend. Once he is distracted by something like a person entering the classroom or the teacher's phone ringing, he doesn't get back on task. It's becoming more problematic because he's beginning to distract other students and getting them off task.

Many students with HID have difficulty attending to tasks. In order to perform successfully, student attention must be gained, maintained, and refocused. Jon Saphier, Mary Ann Haley-Speca, and Robert Gower (2008) define five categories of teacher behaviors related to gaining, maintaining, and refocusing student attention—namely, desisting, alerting, enlisting, acknowledging, and winning. These behaviors may be conceptualized moving along a continuum from authoritative (desistive) to attraction (winning). Teachers should be familiar with each behavior and select them when needed.

Desistive teacher behaviors are corrective and direct. They inform students that they are engaged in inappropriate behavior and specify the appropriate behavior (e.g., *Joe either give me your toy or put it away and finish your assignment.*). Alerting behaviors are usually targeted toward groups of students and focus on keeping the group alert and in anticipation (e.g., eye-to-eye contact, looking at one student while talking to another student). There are no direct messages given. The third category, enlisting, involves attempts at soliciting the voluntary involvement of an individual or a group to participate in the activity (e.g., varying voice to add interest, using physical objects as part of a lesson). Acknowledging requires sensitivity on the teacher's part to be familiar with events outside the current activity that may affect the students' inattentive behavior and to acknowledge those events (e.g., *I know you are excited about the game after school, but right now you need to help your partner.*). The last category, winning, is similar to enlisting except that the teacher behavior forces student attention on the teacher rather than the activity (e.g., teacher demonstrates encouragement, enthusiasm, or praise). Given that students have different needs and respond differently, skillful teachers select their interventions based on the individual student and circumstances.

Brayden's teacher, Mr. Gordon, knows Brayden needs to be refocused several times a day. Mr. Gordon may stand close to him or call on him to answer a question with advance notice (*"Brayden, not this question but the next one will be for you."*). In addition, when needed, Mr. Gordon reminds all students what they are supposed to be doing and praises those who are on task. Brayden usually responds to these strategies. When he does not, Mr. Gordon provides correction and direction (*"Brayden, you need to stop looking out the window and watch me."*). Mr. Gordon has also placed tape on the floor in a square around Brayden's desk and chair. Brayden knows that he's allowed to stand, kneel or sit but that he must stay within the square. Mr. Gordon has set up a behavior management system to reinforce Brayden for doing so.

The types of attention students are required to perform in school may be divided into at least two categories, on-task attention and selective attention.

On-Task Attention

Students are considered *on-task* when they are engaged in relevant school-related tasks. As described in Chapter 3, teachers can increase the amount of time students spend on task by improving their teaching behaviors, instructional management, and/or behavior management. For example, teachers can increase time on task by reducing transition time, giving short periods of time-off-task, prompting students throughout the lesson, and randomly calling on students to answer questions, among many other behaviors.

All of the above examples, including those provided by Saphier et al. (2008), are teacher-directed. They require that the teacher initiate the behavior to ensure that student attention is gained, maintained, and refocused. It is preferable, when possible, to teach students to gain, maintain, and refocus their own attention. Students can be taught, for example, to self-monitor their on-task behavior (See Chapter 13).

Selective Attention

Selective attention refers to the ability to select the appropriate stimuli, focus on those stimuli, and ignore all other irrelevant stimuli. The relevant and irrelevant stimuli in this sense may be environmental and/or academic. Typical environmental stimuli in classrooms may be categorized as visual, auditory, or both. If the teacher is giving oral directions and other people are talking, the student needs to select the teacher's voice, focus on what the teacher is saying, and ignore everyone else's voice. Or, if a student is reading a poem she wrote while the lawn mower outside the classroom can be heard, the other students need to select the student's voice, focus on her voice, and ignore the sound of the lawn mower. Both of these examples involve auditory stimuli. Environmental stimuli may also be visual. Suppose that the classroom is soundproof and it isn't the lawn mower noise distracting students but the movement of the lawn mower across the lawn. In this example, the visual movement of the lawn mower is the irrelevant stimulus. Students should ignore the movement while focusing on the appropriate stimulus (e.g., book being read, movie being shown, teacher talking).

Irrelevant stimuli may also be academic. For example, *distracters* are often included in mathematical story or word problems. Unnecessary information is provided to determine if the student is *paying attention* or focusing on what is necessary and relevant. An example of a word problem follows. *Larry had 3 cats, 2 birds, 4 toy trucks, and 1 dog. How many pets did he have altogether?* Students who do not attend to the relevant stimuli include the 4 toy trucks in their equation and respond that Larry had 10 pets, rather than the correct answer of 6 pets.

Fluent readers who are reading for comprehension often underline or highlight material in the text. Underlining and highlighting are selective-attention strategies. The reader identifies the most important information (selecting the appropriate stimuli), highlights or underlines it (focuses on those stimuli), and upon rereading or studying for an exam, reads only the highlighted or underlined portions while ignoring the rest of the text (ignoring other irrelevant stimuli). Highlighters can also be used to mark relevant information in advance. For example, prior to completing a math worksheet with mixed operations, students can be taught to highlight each of the operation signs, even using different colors if needed for different signs (Stormont, 2008). This helps focus the students' attention on the relevant operation sign. Sticky notes can also be used to support and improve selective attention. For example, such a note can mark where the student stopped within an assignment before taking a break (Stormont, 2008). They can also be used to cover answers or irrelevant information or distracting elements of a book. Creative teachers can find many uses of typical classroom materials to help students in improving their attention.

There are several strategies that teachers can employ with students with HID who have selective attention difficulty. Most strategies involve (a) telling the student what is relevant, (b) using focusing strategies to emphasize the relevant information, and/or (c) teaching students how to identify the relevant stimuli. A list of examples under these three categories appears in Table 9.1.

TABLE 9.1   **Examples of Strategies for Improving Selective Attention Difficulties**

Category	Specific Strategy
Teacher Identifies Relevant Stimuli	• Tell students what information is important for them to recall or remember. • Emphasize relevant information through vocal intonation and/or volume. • Provide students with both an oral and written summary of relevant information (i.e., provide lecture notes, write important information on the chalkboard). • Identify relevant information (e.g., highlight with a marker, underline, color code, draw arrows).
Focusing Strategies	• Eliminate extraneous distracting environmental stimuli (e.g., use study carrels). • Eliminate distracting academic information (e.g., use window boxes over worksheets or other written material). • Periodically ask students about that to which they should be attending. • Keep students engaged actively through meaningful content and briskly paced presentations.
Teach Students to Identify Relevant Stimuli	• Teach students to use strategies provided within textbooks (e.g., bolding, italics). • Teach students to identify cues to verbally presented materials (e.g., lists, seriation). • Teach students to identify distracters in academic material.

TEACHER TIP #9.1

ALLOWING MOVEMENT WITHOUT DISTRACTION

Many students have difficulty sitting still. To reduce distraction in the classroom, try these tips:

• Some students like to tap their fingers or pencils on their desk. Give them a mouse pad or a piece of shelf paper to place on their desk against which to tap. This will reduce the noise level.

• Provide students soft squeeze balls to keep their hands busy.

• For students who like to stand by their desk and move around, use brightly colored tape to create a boundary around their desks. Allow enough room to get up and move a little, but not enough space to bother other students.

• Provide a certain number of free-movement passes for students to use when they need to move around the classroom. Use visual cues (pictures or words) to describe the specific behaviors the passes can be used for (e.g., getting a drink). (McConnell, Ryser, & Higgins, 2000; Stormont, 2008).

Mnemonic Strategies

Twelve-year-old Makayla has an intellectual disability. She is behind her nondisabled peers in academic skills, and she has limited reading and writing skills. Makayla is currently enrolled in a middle school history class. Her teacher makes adjustments in Makayla's assignments so they are more on her level. The biggest difficulty she has in this class is recalling specific historical information.

Many tasks in school require that students recall information. Yet, one of the characteristics of students with HID is difficulty in recalling important information. Strategies that help students remember information are called mnemonic strategies. A **mnemonic** is a technique or device for improving or strengthening memory. Commonly used mnemonic strategies include acronyms, acrostics, rhymes, keywords, and pegwords.

Acronyms and Acrostics

Acronyms and acrostics can be used to recall lists or sets of information. **Acronyms** are created by taking the first letter of each piece of information to create another word or words. An acronym used to recall the five great lakes, for example, is HOMES (Huron, Ontario, Michigan, Erie, and Superior). **Acrostics** are similar to acronyms except that the first letters of words in the list are used to create new words to represent a phrase or sentence. For example, to recall the planets of our solar system, students may learn: **M**y **V**ery **E**ager **M**other **J**ust **S**erved **U**s **N**oodles (**M**ercury, **V**enus, **E**arth, **M**ars, **J**upiter, **S**aturn, **U**ranus, and **N**eptune).

Sometimes it is important for students to recall a list of items in a specific order. Other times the order is not relevant. For example, if one needs to remember the five Great Lakes in no particular order, the acronym HOMES is convenient because it spells a word. On the other hand, the previously stated acrostic for recalling the planet names lists them in their order from the sun. Keeping the words in this sequence assists recall of both the planet name and their order from the sun. Acronym strategies may also facilitate recall of order. The name **ROY G. BIV** (**R**ed, **O**range, **Y**ellow, **G**reen, **B**lue, **I**ndigo, **V**iolet) represents the spectrum of the colors of the rainbow. Another acrostic example in which order is important are the names of the notes on the lines of the treble clef represented by the sentence **E**very **G**ood **B**oy **D**oes **F**ine.

Acronyms and acrostics are helpful only if the learner is able to recall the word that the letter represents. In other words, the *H* in HOMES can assist the learner to recall Huron, only if the student has previously associated the *H* with Huron. Accompanying acronyms and acrostics with visual pictures (e.g., a picture of homes on the great lakes) may be more successful than teaching the acronyms alone. Depending upon the needs of students, teachers may give students specific acronym and acrostic strategies or they may teach students to create their own strategies.

Acronyms, or in this context, first letter mnemonics are also used to teach and recall a series of steps for students to complete. These steps are usually embedded in academic content. For example, the first letter mnemonic, POW, was developed for a student with autism to help him plan and organize the writing process. **P** stood for **P**ick my ideas, **O** for **O**rganize my notes, and **W** for **W**rite and say more (Asaro & Saddler, 2009). In another example, Laura Buchan, Trisha Fish and Mary Anne Prater (1997) created a strategy for elementary-age students with HID to help them with creative writing assignments. The strategy was **N**inja **T**urtles **C**ounting **P**izza **T**oppings. The first letter of each word represented an aspect of their writing for them to check prior to submitting them: **N**ame, **T**itle, **C**apitalization, **P**unctuation, **T**ransition words. More examples of acronyms and acrostics appear throughout this and future chapters.

Rhymes

Rhymes can also be used to facilitate recall. Commonly learned rhymes such as *Thirty days hath September, April, June, and November* and *I before E except after C* continue to be used by adults although learned in their childhood. Related to rhyming is the use of rhythm or music. *The Alphabet Song*, for example, is taught to young children to facilitate recall of the letters of the alphabet. The use of rap has also been used to facilitate recall of information. Ideas that teachers have found helpful can be located through quick searches on the Internet.

Keywords

The **keyword** strategy facilitates the associative recall of at least two pieces of seemingly unrelated information. Examples include state names and capitals, English and Spanish words, composer and composition title, among others. A long line of research conducted with students with disabilities indicates that the keyword method is a powerful tool for facilitating recall (Scruggs & Mastropieri, 2000).

The keyword procedure requires three steps: (1) recoding, (2) relating, and (3) retrieving. Recoding involves associating an unfamiliar word into an acoustically similar and familiar word. For example, the keyword for Pennsylvania could be *pen*; and the keyword for Pennsylvania's capital, Harrisburg, *hairy*. The second step, relating, involves associating the keywords in an interactive, memorable visual image, for example, a hairy pen. Retrieving, the last step, involves recalling the capital's name when given the state's name or vice versa.

Even more complex content information can be recalled using the keyword method. *Oxalis* is the scientific name that refers to the genus of clover-like plants. Students would first need to understand ox and clover-like plant. They would be taught the keyword for oxalis (ox) and shown a visual image of the ox eating a clover-like plant (Scruggs, Mastropieri, Berkeley, & Marshak, 2010). After teachers introduce how keywords work, why they should use them, and the content that will help students remember (e.g., understanding the scientific name for plants), teachers would implement a teaching sequence similar to this: "Remember that plants have scientific names.

The keyword for oxalis is *ox*. When I say oxalis, remember the picture of the ox (for oxalis) eating the clover-like plant. What is the scientific name for clover-like plants?" Teachers may need to prompt some students through these steps. For example, if they don't answer correctly, ask, "What was the keyword for oxalis?" "That's right, it was ox." "What do you remember about the picture with the ox?" "Yes, the ox was eating the clover-like plant." "What did the ox stand for?" "Oxalis is correct." "So what does oxalis mean?"

Pegwords

The **pegword** method is similar to the keyword method, but includes numbers as part of the factual information being taught. Examples include, the 10 reasons dinosaurs became extinct in order of probability, presidents of the United States and their presidency number, or the periodic table of the elements. The numbers 1 through 10 are recoded to well-known and acoustically similar words:

one = bun or sun	six = sticks
two = shoe	seven = heaven
three = tree	eight = gate
four = door or floor	nine = vine or line
five = hive	ten = hen

The procedure for teaching pegwords is similar to that used in the keyword method. The student is taught the *rhyming* pegwords. The unfamiliar information is then associated with the number through the pegword.

A form of the pegword method may also be used to facilitate recall of information that goes beyond number 10. Presidents of the United States, for example, may be taught following the pegword method above, but adding a season in which the interaction is occurring. The first decade of Presidents would be placed in a spring garden, the second decade on a beach (representing summer), the third at a Thanksgiving Dinner (fall), and the fourth decade would include a snowman (winter). For example, the sixteenth president of the United States was Abraham Lincoln. The keyword for Lincoln could be links. The keyword for six is sticks. Since Lincoln served in the second decade of Presidents, the easily visualized interaction may be toasting sausage links (for Lincoln) on sticks (representing six) on a beach (summer or second decade) (See Figure 9.1.) In addition, pegwords can be combined with keywords. For example, to help students recall that Monroe was the fifth president, they can be shown a picture of *money*, the keyword for Monroe, being carried by bees to a *hive* (pegword for five) (Scruggs & Mastropieri, 2000). Another example would be carbon (keyword car) being associated with six (pegword sticks) because carbon is atomic number 6 on the periodic table. So a visual representation could be a car made out of sticks (Reid, Lienemann, & Hagaman, 2013).

FIGURE 9.1   **An Example of a Pegword Mnemonic Strategy**

Source: Illustration created by Dena Plant, 2005.

Other pegwords that have been used with numbers beyond 10 include the following:

Number Pegword Visual Representation

   twelve elf (elf)

   sixteen mixing (mixing spoon)

   eighteen baiting (fishing reel)

   twenty twin-T (twins)

   thirty dirty (dust)

   forty warty (warts)

   fifty gifty (bow)

   sixty witchy (witch) (Wood & Frank, 2000)

Makayla is learning about the founding fathers in her history class. She's having difficulty remembering major contributions of each (e.g., George Washington—general in the Revolutionary War; Thomas Jefferson—wrote the Declaration of Independence). Using keywords, Makayla's teacher and her paraeducator create keywords for the names and contributions (e.g., washing machine—jeans, tom cat—declare) and mnemonic pictures where the two keywords are interacting (e.g., jeans being placed in the washing machine, a tom cat declaring independence). Makayla is then taught what the keywords stand for and to remember the interaction between them in the pictures. Although it takes some time for Makayla to learn these associations, she appears delighted when she recalls the correct information after being quizzed.

A substantial amount of research has demonstrated the effectiveness of mnemonic strategies for students with disabilities. In fact, mnemonic instruction has been found to be one of the most effective methods reported in the special education literature (Forness, 2001). In an analysis of studies implemented in secondary content areas (e.g., science, social studies), mnemonic strategies was the strongest instructional technique only exceeded by explicit teacher-directed instruction (Scruggs, Mastropieri, Berkeley & Graetz, 2010). Extensive research has demonstrated the effectiveness of the keyword method, in particular, in facilitating recall of factual information in the academic content areas such as vocabulary development (e.g., Uberti, Scruggs, & Mastropieri, 2003), science (e.g., Therrien, Taylor, Hosp, Kaldenberg, & Gorsh, 2011), and social studies (e.g., Mastropieri, Sweda, & Scruggs, 2000). Keyword strategy training has been successfully used with students when applied in both special education self-contained classrooms (Terrill, Scruggs, & Mastropieri, 2004) or general education classrooms (e.g., Fontana, Scruggs, & Mastropieri, 2007).

Organizing Strategies

In addition to applying appropriate remembering or mnemonic strategies, effective teachers and learners use strategies for organizing content information, in particular, three strategies for organizing information, namely—graphic organizers, advance organizers, and study guides.

Graphic Organizers

Graphic organizers visually represent knowledge by arranging facts and concepts in an associative organization. Using graphic organizers can reduce the cognitive demand on students by providing them a visual display of the most significant information (Singleton & Filce, 2015). They are appropriate for upper elementary through high school.

Graphic organizers help students (a) focus on relevant information while ignoring isolated details, (b) integrate prior knowledge with new knowledge, (c) highlight key concepts, and (d) understand relationships between concepts from teacher presentations and text materials (Dexter, Park, & Hughes, 2011). In addition, graphic organizers can help teachers plan for instruction and they can serve as an assessment tool.

Graphic organizers must be consistent, coherent, and creative. Students with HID benefit from consistent routines and structure. Therefore, teachers should establish a routine for using graphic organizers and create a standard and consistent set of graphic organizers to use in the classroom. To be coherent, graphic organizers must (a) clearly label the relationships between concepts, (b) limit the number of ideas covered, and (c) avoid unnecessary distractions. Teachers can find creative ways to implement graphic organizers, such as during cooperative-learning groups or as part of homework (Baxendell, 2003).

There are at least six types of graphic organizers:

1. hierarchical, sometimes called top-down, in which the information is arranged by major and minor categories similar to an outline;

2. conceptual maps where a central idea or category is tied together with details or subcategories;

3. sequential diagrams, which represent the chronological order or a sequence of events;

4. cyclical organizers, used to represent a continuous sequence of events with no beginning or ending;

5. Venn diagrams, which depict different and similar attributes or characteristics of a concept; and

6. matrices, appropriate for classifying categories of information across topics.

An example of each appears in Figure 9.2. Also, different types of information warrant different types of graphic organizers. For examples, see Table 9.2.

FIGURE 9.2   Examples of Graphic Organizers

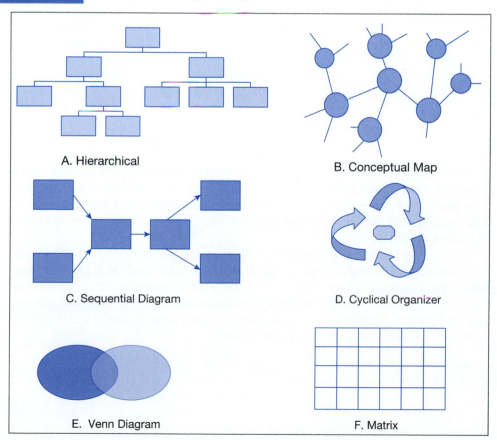

A. Hierarchical

B. Conceptual Map

C. Sequential Diagram

D. Cyclical Organizer

E. Venn Diagram

F. Matrix

TABLE 9.2	Examples of Graphic Organizer Use

Types of Organizer	Examples
Hierarchical	• Classifying plants or animals • Associating types of instruments in an orchestra • Classifying government agencies
Conceptual Maps	• Describing associations between characters in a story • Describing key concepts in a science textbook chapter • Describing different math formulas that represent the same numeral
Sequential Diagrams	• Explaining issues leading to an event in history • Describing a problem-solving process • Describing the evolution of air transportation
Cyclical Organizers	• Describing the rain cycle • Describing the food chain • Describing the life cycle of an animal
Venn Diagrams	• Comparing and contrasting two stories in literature • Comparing similarities and differences between a book and the movie • Examining similarities and differences between two individuals' points of view
Matrices	• Describing the impact of several historical events on different countries • Documenting the results of a scientific experiment • Describing the changes over time across various environmental situations

When using graphic organizers, teachers need to explicitly teach the use of the organizer. That is, just providing the visual display is not sufficient. Students need to be taught how concepts are related, how to recognize main ideas from subordinate ideas, and how to put all the pieces together into the global concept being taught (Dexter et al., 2011).

Graphic organizers can be developed by the students, the teacher, or both. Students, for example, can be asked to create a graphic organizer individually or in groups to represent their conceptual understanding of a topic prior to instruction. This can serve as a pretest of prerequisite and/or lesson content knowledge. Students could also develop their own graphic organizer while reading a text chapter or at the end of a unit to document their understanding of the concepts learned.

TEACHER TIP #9.2

CREATING AFFINITY DIAGRAMS WITH STUDENTS

Teach students to use affinity diagrams to organize large amounts of information using these steps:

- Students brainstorm individually or in groups on a specific topic (e.g., animals).

- For each idea, students write one to three words on a note card.

- All notes are placed on a desk or wall where they may be viewed.

- Students arrange ideas into columns by groups that reflect similarities.

- Students discuss why these ideas are similar and create a label for the column. (Haselden, 2003)

Advance Organizers

Before teaching a lesson on natural disasters, Mr. Sato shared an experience he'd had while living in Hawai'i. An earthquake had occurred in the Pacific Ocean and a tsunami alert was sounded in the morning throughout the islands. The tsunami was expected later that afternoon. All schools and most businesses closed. Signs were posted across all affected beaches warning people to stay away until a certain time period had passed. Mr. Sato shared that although tsunamis can be very dangerous and that alerts should be taken very seriously, this was one time when the tsunami never came. He was not, however, unhappy because he got out of a day of school! Before moving forward with his lesson, Mr. Sato quickly surveyed the students to see how many of them had personally experienced a tsunami, earthquake, tornado, or hurricane. He told them that they would have the opportunity later in the lesson to share their experiences.

Prior to attending a field trip, Mr. Ruddy reviewed a previous lesson on pioneers who settled the western United States. He then asked students to review a map of the pioneer village they would visit. He asked the students to become familiar with the route they would walk and the buildings they would visit. Mr. Ruddy also showed pictures of pioneers working in the fields, the homes, and the various shops in the village. They discussed briefly what each person was doing and why.

Advance organizers are verbal or written techniques used to activate prior knowledge about a topic and provide a general description of the entire lesson. They prepare students for future learning. Advance organizers are not intended to be summaries or overviews, but to bridge the gap between what students already know and what is to be learned or experienced. They help students develop a mental framework for organizing and connecting new knowledge with prior knowledge (Swanson & Hoskyn, 2001).

Educators and researchers often use the term, *advance organizers*, to mean the introduction of the lesson designed to gain students' attention, state the instructional objective, review information, and activate prior knowledge (e.g., Bryant, Smith, & Bryant, 2008). Some professionals also equate advance organizers with anticipatory sets, the latter of which was discussed in Chapter 6. Advance organizers may be simple or complex in format depending upon the amount of content and difficulty of the material to be learned (Berg & Wehby, 2013). They help prepare students to be better consumers of the new information and later recall that information. They can engage students by motivating them to learn more about the topic (Dell'Olio & Donk, 2007). Advance organizers are developed and implemented by the teacher and should be kept to a minimum amount of time, particularly when designed for a one-day lesson.

Mr. Sato has just begun his advance organizer. After gaining students' attention through a personal story related to the topic being studied, he moves to the other portions of the lesson's introduction as described in Chapter 6. Similarly, Mr. Ruddy's advance organizer provides students a framework about what they will be experiencing on their field trip. He also tells the students what he expects them to learn from this trip and how they will demonstrate what they learned.

TEACHER TIP #9.3

PLANNING ADVANCE ORGANIZERS

When planning advance organizers, keep the following in mind:

- Focus the advance organizer on what is important, not what is unusual.

- "Higher level" advance organizers may be more effective than "lower level" ones.

- Advance organizers are most helpful with information that is not well organized.

- Different kinds of advance organizers produce different results. (Marzano, Pickering & Pollock, 2001)

Study Strategies

As students progress throughout their schooling, the expectation of independent learning increases. This can be particularly evident as students move from elementary to secondary schools. Often students, with and without disabilities, are unprepared for these increased demands. One of the difficulties students with HID demonstrate is the inability to study independently. Their lack of organization also inhibits their ability to demonstrate all they know and can do.

Effective study skills are particularly important for adolescent learners. Students with HID need explicit instruction in study skills (Paulsen & Sayeski, 2013). In particular, they need to learn how to develop effective study habits and routines as well as how to use study guides.

Study Habits and Routines

Students can be taught study habits and routines that will help them become more efficient and effective in completing homework and studying for tests. Study skills are particularly important for secondary-age students but can begin to be introduced in the upper elementary grades. Teachers should teach and encourage the following study habits as part of their instruction:

- Encourage students to establish routines, such as a specific time of the day or evening to complete their homework and study for tests.

- Help students select a place at home to study that is not distracting. Solicit parent support as well.

- Provide a means (e.g., a checklist) to ensure the students take all of the necessary materials home and have these materials accessible before studying begins.

- Teach students to begin a long-term project as soon as it is assigned.

- Instruct students how to break a long-term project into smaller units that can be accomplished in a day or two.

- Teach students to study for a specified time (e.g., 50 minutes) and take a 5 to 10 minute break and to return to studying after the break.

- Instruct students to use positive self-talk while they are studying (e.g., "I'm doing a great job." "I'm making great progress on this assignment and will get it turned in on time."). (Lambert & Nowacek, 2006)

Students can also be given tools to help them organize and structure their study habits. For example, a sample homework study sheet can be found in Figure 9.3. The sheet outlines the assignments and tests for each week. Students would insert the due dates for each class, as well as what homework they will complete each day to ensure they are prepared. Note that a specific time is also listed for each day of homework. Teachers can create study sheets to meet the needs of the students. For example, some students may need daily sheets, while others need a weekly, monthly, or semester planner.

First-letter mnemonic strategies can help students remember to complete forms or assignment sheets. Here are two examples.

TRICK BAG: Take out your assignment sheet, **R**ecord the assignment in the right place, **I**nsert important details (e.g., book, worksheet), **C**ircle the materials needed, **K**eep materials in your folder, **B**e certain you can read what you wrote, **A**sk a partner to read it as a check, and **G**o put it in your backpack. (Scott & Compton, 2007)

PROJECT (BEST): **P**repare your forms, **R**ecord and ask questions if needed, **O**rganize (**B**reak the assignment into parts, **E**stimate the number of study sessions, **S**chedule the sessions, **T**ake your materials home), **J**ump to it, **E**ngage in the work, **C**heck your work, and **T**urn in your work. (Hughes, Ruhl, Schmaker, & Deshler, 2002)

FIGURE 9.3 **Sample Completed Homework Study Sheet**

Week: January 10-17					
Days	**Monday**	**Tuesday**	**Wednesday**	**Thursday**	**Weekend**
Study Times	6–8 pm	3–5 pm	6–8 pm	3–5 pm	Sat. 9–11 am
Assignments & Tests Due					
	Monday	**Tuesday**	**Wednesday**	**Thursday**	**Friday**
English		Chapter 3			Reaction paper
Math			Page 58		Quiz
Science					(poster due next Monday)
History					WWII paper
Other					
Homework					
	Monday	**Tuesday**	**Wednesday**	**Thursday**	**Weekend**
English	Read Chapter 3		Write reaction paper		
Math		Page 58		Review for quiz	
Science			Design poster	Add content to poster	Finish poster
History	Work on WW II paper	Finish draft of WW II paper	Edit WW II paper	Complete WW II paper	
Materials Needed					
	Monday	**Tuesday**	**Wednesday**	**Thursday**	**Weekend**
	English book History book Computer	Math book History book Paper & pencil	English book Science book Computer Printer	Math book History book Computer Printer	Computer

TEACHER TIP #9.4

ORGANIZING SCHOOL MATERIALS

Students with HID often need assistance organizing their school materials. Here are some organizational ideas:

- Tell students to organize their subjects by color. For example, if English is yellow, then the notebook, highlighter, and folder for English class are all yellow.

- Teach students to use post-it flags in each subject color. When homework is assigned, students can flag the page in their book by the colored flag. This will help students remember they have homework which they can locate easily.

- Teach students to use a calendar, planner, or some other organizer. Help them learn to use the same system in all classes.

- Identify one folder as the "take home folder." (McConnell et al., 2000)

Study Guides

Study guides enhance instruction by leading students through academic information using questions or activities. They are usually used to help students learn and retain information from textbooks by providing an organized framework of the content. Study guides can be effective at varying points in a lesson. For example, they can be used to introduce new vocabulary, review newly introduced concepts, integrate previous information with new content, guide content-specific reading, help students discriminate between relevant and less relevant information, and organize information for studying purposes (Conderman & Bresnahan, 2010).

Study guides vary in format depending upon the purpose of the guide and the sophistication of the learner. They usually contain a series of questions students answer based on the material read. Study guides can also be designed to help guide students through textual information providing clues as to where to find the information (e.g., "Look at the bolded words."). Sometimes study guides include a summary or an outline of the material, definitions of vocabulary words, or activities for students to complete (Conderman & Bresnahan, 2010). The steps for creating a study guide may be found in Table 9.3.

Examples of study guides may be found in Figures 9.4 and 9.5. Figure 9.4 is a study guide for this chapter on learning strategies, while Figure 9.5 is a science study guide. The steps needed to complete the science study guide are listed in Figure 9.6 in the form of self-talk. Using the teacher-directed instruction model (see Chapter 6), the instructor would model the steps by talking aloud while completing an example projected on the board. Then students would practice using the strategy with guidance from the teacher, followed by independent practice of the strategy.

TABLE 9.3   Creating a Study Guide

Step 1	Identify the main or big ideas of the content being studied.
Step 2	Match the content standards to the big ideas to refine content to be included.
Step 3	Create an outline and select an organizer that best fits the structure of the information.
Step 4	Identify important vocabulary, concepts, and details under the main ideas.
Step 5	Develop short answer and/or fill-in-the-blank questions. If appropriate, include graphic organizers on which students write answers (e.g., compare/contrast table, Venn diagram).
Step 6	If needed, include clues to help students locate the information.
Step 7	Write a key to the study guide with correct answers. This may be used for correction by the teacher or peer or for self-correction by the student.

FIGURE 9.4   A Sample Study Guide for This Chapter

Study Guide – Learning Strategies

PURPOSE: *This chapter introduces strategies for learning. Students with disabilities often fail to independently develop effective learning strategies. Teachers of students with high-incidence disabilities can incorporate strategy instruction into most any lesson.*

Key Topics

Attention Strategies
Mnemonic Strategies
Organizing Strategies
Study Strategies
Test-Taking Strategies
Notetaking
Creating Learning Strategies
Implications for CLD Students

New Vocabulary

Strategy—

Metacognition—

Mnemonic—

Attention Strategies

On Task—	
Selective—	

Mnemonic Strategies

Type of Mnemonic	Definition	Example
Acronym		
Acrostic		
Rhymes		
Pegword		
Keyword		

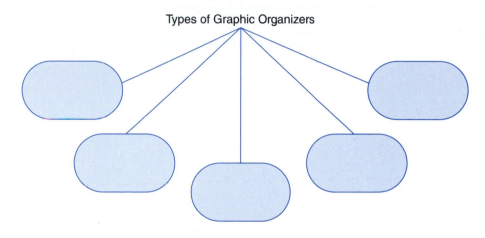

Types of Graphic Organizers

Advance Organizer

Major Points:

-
-
-
-
-
-
-
-

Study Guides

Major Points:

-
-
-
-
-
-

(Continued)

FIGURE 9.4   (Continued)

Test-Taking	Notetaking
FORCE	CALL-UP
PIRATES	"A" NOTES
ANSWER	SAND
	CUES

Implications for CLD Students

FIGURE 9.5   An Example of a Study Guide

Study Guide: The Chemistry of Life

Section 2.1 The Nature of Matter

Name _____   Date_____

Vocabulary – Write the definition of each word.

nucleus –

electron –

isotope –

compound –

ionic bond –

covalent bond –

molecule –

Questions – Write your answer in complete sentences.

Describe the structure of the atom. _____
_____
_____

What is a covalent bond? An ionic bond? _____
_____
_____

How are compounds related to molecules?

_____
_____

FIGURE 9.6 **Self-Talk Students Can Be Taught for Using the Study Guide in Figure 9.5**

Using the Study Guide

- When I receive my study guide I put my name on the paper.
- Then, I complete each section of the study guide. Completing each section of the study guide will help me identify material that I need to know for the section test.
- For section 1 of the study guide, I write the definition of the terms listed. To do this, I
  - look for the **bolded** word in the subsections of this chapter section.
  - read the definition that surrounds the word and then I write it on my paper.
- For section 2, I write answers to the questions. To do this, I
  - read the question or statement and identify a key word that the question is about.
  - find the key word in the text.
  - reread the question or statement.
  - read the section with the key word to find the answer.
  - write the answer.

Organizational strategies have been documented to be effective for students with disabilities. Most of the research has been conducted with students with learning disabilities in secondary schools, although some research has also documented effectiveness with students with autism (e.g., Zakas, Browder, Ahlgrim-Delzell, & Heafner, 2013). Research has documented that graphic organizers can improve the performance of students in science (e.g., Dexter et al., 2011), mathematics (e.g., Ives, 2007), social studies (e.g., Swanson, Hairrell, Kent, Ciullo, Wanzek, & Vaughn, 2014), and English/reading (e.g., Dexter & Hughes, 2011). In addition, there exists some evidence that advance organizers play a meaningful role in promoting student learning (Preiss & Gayle, 2006); and that teaching study habits and using study guides improve homework production and quality (e.g., Hughes et al., 2002).

TEACHER TIP #9.5

USING REMINDER NOTES

Provide students reminder notes several days before tests and projects are due. Print them on bright paper so they are not lost. Include the due date and the material the test will cover or the type of project. If helpful, ask parents to sign the note and assign students bonus points for returning the note signed (McConnell et al., 2000).

Test-Taking Strategies

Students with HID need effective test-taking strategies particularly to facilitate success in general education classrooms. Madison, the seventh-grade student introduced at the beginning of the chapter is experiencing some test anxiety. Being afraid of taking tests, she could benefit from learning test-taking strategies which are important in order for students to perform to the best of their ability on standardized schoolwide tests, as well as on curriculum-based tests.

Students who demonstrate effective test-taking strategies are considered *testwise*. Testwise students exhibit behaviors such as wise use of time, elimination of obviously incorrect choices on multiple choice tests, and marking uncertain answers to review before submitting the test. The testwise student will perform better than another student who is not testwise, but who has equal knowledge of the content.

Teachers can help students become more testwise by teaching strategies to reduce text anxiety, making instruction and assessment explicit, providing appropriate testing accommodations, and teaching test-taking strategies. A discussion of three of these four follows. (Testing accommodations was presented in Chapter 7.)

Test-Anxiety Reduction

Research documents that between 10% to 33% of all school students experience some form of text anxiety; and students with disabilities demonstrate test anxiety at higher rates than those without disabilities (Datta, 2014; Whitaker Sena, Lowe, & Lee, 2007). Test-anxious students commonly experience lower standardized achievement test scores, poor motivation, negative self-evaluation, difficulty learning new material, and trouble concentrating (Woods, Parkinson, & Lewis, 2010).

Most people feel some stress when faced with preparing for or taking a test. A little anxiety can motivate students to work hard and try their best. At the same time, too much anxiety inhibits the student's ability to use cognitive processes necessary for good test performance. Students who have had a history of poor test performance usually develop unpleasant feelings about testing which results in nervousness and dread when faced with taking a test (Banks & Eaton, 2014).

Signs of text anxiety can be categorized as physical, behavioral, and affective symptoms. Elementary students are more likely to show physical signs, while secondary students show behavioral and affective symptoms (Whitaker et al., 2007). Physical symptoms include changes in the physical body (e.g., increased heartbeat, muscle tension, flushed skin color, sweaty palms). Behaviorally, test anxiety is manifested in cognitive difficulties (e.g., retrieving information, organizing answers), off-task behaviors (e.g., making inappropriate comments, tapping fingers or a pencil), and feigning illness or being absent on the day of the test. Affective symptoms relate to student attitudes and motivation (e.g., making excuses for poor performance, being apathetic, making negative self-statements) (Salend, 2011). Test anxiety can be reduced by teaching anxiety-reduction strategies, providing accommodations if appropriate, and teaching test-taking strategies.

Students can be taught to initiate anxiety-reduction strategies to apply before and during the testing situation. For example, often talking to other students about the test can increase anxiety. Students can be taught to arrive just in time to take the test and to avoid false rumors about the test. They can also learn to engage in positive self-talk, focus on past successes, and take deep breaths in order to relax. During the test, they can learn to sit in nondistracting areas of the room; roll their shoulders, neck, and head; or tense and relax their muscles (Salend, 2011).

Teachers can increase testwiseness by being explicit about what content will be on the test. That is, if students know what they will be accountable for knowing, they can focus their studying on those elements. Teachers can also share the type of test questions that will be used (i.e., essay, true/false, matching, or multiple choice) and the directions for answering the questions. Providing experience with test formats and the directions in advance will help lessen anxiety and provide more time for students to actually answer the questions.

Specific Test-Taking Strategies

Another means for improving test performance is teaching students test-taking strategies. To perform well on a test, students must have knowledge of the content and knowledge of how to take the test. Study habits, routines, and guides as discussed previously can help facilitate students' preparation for learning the content to be tested. Here are some examples of general test-taking strategies that students can be taught:

- Review the test to get a sense of the length, sections, and type of questions being asked.

- Read the comprehension questions prior to reading the passage.

- Answer the easier questions first. Some tests get more difficult as the exam progresses. Other tests intersperse easy questions.

- Anticipate the answer and then look for that answer in the choices provided.

- Consider all options in the choices provided.

- Recognize that choices using absolute words like *always, every,* and *never* are usually false, while other words such as *generally, usually,* and *sometimes* are often included in the correct answer. (Conderman & Pedersen, 2010)

Different test formats require different strategies. For example, selecting the right answer in a multiple choice or true/false question differs significantly from knowing how to write the response to an essay question. Table 9.4 delineates some test-taking strategies by the type of questions on a test.

First letter mnemonics have also been created to help students develop stronger test-taking skills. For example, FORCE was designed to help students prepare for test-taking. PIRATES was designed for implementation while taking a test. And, ANSWER was developed specifically for essay tests. These three first-letter mnemonics and the steps they represent are listed in Table 9.5. Appendix B provides a sample lesson plan for teaching a test-taking strategy. When students with HID are instructed early (e.g., late elementary or middle school) in test-taking strategies, the more likely they will become testwise and be able to apply these strategies with both standardized and classroom-based tests (Carter et al., 2005).

Most research has examined the effectiveness of test-taking strategies with students who have learning disabilities (e.g., Therrien, Hughes, Kapelski, & Mokhtari, 2009).

| TABLE 9.4 | Examples of Test-Taking Strategies Categorized by Type of Test Question |

Test Item Types	Test-Taking Strategies
Multiple Choice	• Before reading the choices, try to answer the question. • Consider all choices carefully. • Eliminate choices. • Look for clue words (statements like *always* or *rarely*). • Compare the choices with each other and the relationship to the stem statements.
Sentence Completion	• If unsure of the answer, guess. • Fill in at least partial information. • Make the sentence consistent and logical.
Essay	• Answer every item. • Use your time wisely. • If writing your answers, use your best penmanship.

| TABLE 9.5 | Examples of Test-Taking Strategies |

Test Preparation	**FORCE** (Wehrung-Schaffner & Sapona, 1990)
	Find out (what the test will cover and what types of questions will be asked)
	Organize (by collecting all the necessary materials to study)
	Review the material
	Concentrate and make a cue sheet
	Early exam (Practice by drilling or having a partner ask you questions)
During the Test	**PIRATES** (Hughes et al., 1993)
	Prepare to succeed
	Inspect the instructions
	Read, remember, reduce
	Answer or abandon
	Turn back
	Estimate
	Survey
	ANSWER (Hughes, Schumaker, & Deshler, 2005)
	Analyze the action words in the question
	Notice the requirements of the question
	Set up an outline
	Work in detail
	Engineer your answer
	Review your answer

However, a few studies have shown that test-taking strategy instruction is effective with other high-incidence disabilities, including students with autism (e.g., Songlee, Miller, Tincani, Sileo, & Perkins, 2008) and students with emotional/behavioral disorders (e.g., Hughes, Schumaker, Deshler, & Mercer, 1993).

Notetaking Strategies

Ms. Ho begins her class each day reviewing what she has already taught her students about how to take notes. The class generated a list of steps they need to follow to effectively take notes from the material she presents in class. They then created a first letter mnemonic to remember the steps. Each day the students write the mnemonic on their paper as a prompt to remember what to do. Ms. Ho has observed a noticeable increase in the students' performance since teaching this notetaking strategy.

Students with HID have difficulty taking notes regardless of whether they are listening to instruction (e.g., teacher lecture, video presentation) or reading material (e.g., textbook). The quality of notetaking is influenced by both the notetaker's background knowledge of the subject as well as the skills for taking notes. Effective notetakers identify and distinguish between main ideas and details, paraphrase by condensing information and putting it in their own words, avoid random or verbatim notes, integrate new information with old information, identify various words or graphic structures (e.g., headings, bolded or italicized words), and organize notes by placing information in appropriate groups or patterns. They also record important vocabulary, recognize teacher cues regarding important information, and review the notes after the lecture (Boyle, 2011).

Improved notetaking can occur by teaching notetaking skills, modifying instruction to facilitate notetaking, and using guided notes. All three are discussed below.

Notetaking Skills

General education content teachers continue to use whole-class, teacher-led lecture predominantly in their classrooms (Scruggs, Mastropieri, & McDuffie, 2007). One researcher, for example, discovered that 79% of high school science teachers reported to lecture either regularly or mostly (Vogler, 2006). Students can be taught specific steps to take notes successfully. For example, two notetaking first-letter mnemonics, CALL UP and "A" NOTES were developed by Elaine Czarnecki, Delores Rosko, and Elaine Fine (1998) (See Table 9.6). The CALL UP strategy teaches students to listen for cue words and copy main ideas that the teacher has written from the board or on a projected image. Then students listen and look for details which they add to their notes. Each time a question is asked by the teacher or student, students write it down marking it with a *Q*. They then look for the answer, write it down, and mark it with an *A*. Students use their textbooks for review. They write text information in their own words within their notes. A brief lesson plan for teaching this strategy may be found in the Lesson Plan Spotlight 9.1.

The second strategy, "A" NOTES, was designed for reviewing notes after class presentations (see Table 9.6). In the first step, students ask themselves if they have a date and topic. Then the main ideas and details are "named" and highlighted. The third step involves reviewing the notes again comparing them with the textbook. The STAR substrategy is then used. Students star important information, connect them with arrows, and number the major ideas in order. The last STAR step involves noting an abbreviation (e.g., *def.* for *definition*) next to the information. Students then review their notes to fix unclear or missing information and summarize the overall idea in a sentence or two at the bottom of the notes (Czarnecki, Rosko, & Fine, 1998).

As another example, Joseph Boyle (2011) taught middle school students with and without learning disabilities the CUES first-letter mnemonic. The *C* prompted students to record lecture ideas into clusters of three to six related topics. The *U* reminded them that teachers use lecture cues (e.g., "first", "second"), and the *E* to enter their vocabulary words in the appropriate area of the notetaking paper provided. The *S* represented the summarize step during which students wrote a summary word or phrase to represent the clustered ideas.

TABLE 9.6   **Notetaking Strategies**

Mnemonic	Steps
CALL UP (Czarnecki et al., 1998)	**C**opy from board or projection. **A**dd details. **L**isten and write the question. **L**isten and write the answer. **U**tilize the text. **P**ut it in your own words.

"A" NOTES and **SAND**
(Czarnecki et al., 1998)
	Ask yourself if you have a date and a topic.
	Name the main ideas and details.
	Observe ideas also in text.
	Try margin noting and use **SAND** strategy:
	  • **S**tar important ideas.
	  • **A**rrange arrows to connect ideas.
	  • **N**umber key points in order.
	  • **D**evise abbreviations and write them next to the item.
	Examine for omissions or unclear ideas.
	Summarize key points.

CUES (Boyle, 2011)	**C**luster three to six main ideas. **T**eachers **U**se lecture cues. **E**nter vocabulary words on your sheet. **S**ummarize clustered main ideas.

Lesson Plan Spotlight #9.1

Notetaking Skills

Lesson Objective

When given a worksheet with the acronym CALL UP listed, students will follow the steps with 100% accuracy including copying information written on the board, writing a sentence that adds details, writing the lecture question and answer, reading a paragraph from their text, and writing a short summary in their own words.

Materials

CALL UP Strategy Prompt Sheet—The prompt lists the steps of the CALL UP strategy and provides blank lines for

(Continued)

(Continued)

practicing the skill described for each step. An independent practice sheet with the letters of the strategy printed next to blank lines.

Anticipatory Set, Review, and Prerequisite Check

"When you are studying for a test and you want to remember something we've discussed in class, will you be able to call me up and ask me questions on the phone? Probably not. I don't think I'll be available after school hours. Instead, you'll want to read your class notes, and CALL UP information from your notes. If you take good notes, there will be no reason to call me.

"Yesterday, we practiced copying information quickly and accurately. I've written three topics on the board (reptiles, birds, and mammals). Take out your notebooks and pencils and copy the information as quickly as you can. We also practiced writing phrases that summarized information. I will tell you two sentences and I want you to write a brief summary of my sentences (Mammals are animals that give birth to live animals. When reptiles reproduce, they lay eggs)."

Purpose

"Today you will learn the CALL UP strategy for taking notes. Why is learning to take notes important?"

Instruction and Modeling

"I will use the CALL UP strategy to help me take notes in class. First, I will explain the steps of the strategy."

1. "First, I **C**—Copy important information from the board. Teachers usually write important information on the board. For example, I have a definition of amphibians written on the board. To take good notes, I would copy this definition into my notes." (Demonstrate.)

2. "Next, I **A**—Add details. During a lecture, a teacher will tell more information about the topic. To add details, write summary statements of the information the teacher provides. If the teacher says, 'When amphibians are young, they live in the water,' the summary statement I would write would be, 'Young amphibians live in water.'" (Demonstrate.)

3. "Then, I **L**—Listen and write the question. Sometimes, when teachers present information, they ask questions. If a teacher asks a question during a lecture, it's probably an important question, so you'll want to write the question. If the teacher asks, 'How are amphibians able to be both land and water animals?' when I use this strategy, I would write that question in my notes." (Demonstrate.)

4. "The next step is **L**—Listen and write the answer. When a teacher poses a question during a lecture, the teacher will most likely answer the question. When the teacher gives the answer, write the answer in your notes. If the teacher says, 'When amphibians are young, they live in the water like fish. But, as they grow older they lose their fishlike characteristics and change to become land animals,' I would write that information in my notes." (Demonstrate.)

5. "The last steps of the strategy are to **U**—Utilize your text, and **P**—Put it in your own words. After the teacher finishes the lecture, he

or she will probably assign you a section to read in your textbook. When you read the text selection, add information from the text to your notes by putting the information in your own words. We've practiced this before so you know how to do this. Let me demonstrate." (Demonstrate.)

Guided Practice

"Now, we'll practice using this strategy together. Here's your copy of the steps of the strategy. Before we practice using the strategy, let's read the steps together a few times." (The teacher and class read the steps 3-4 times. The teacher can require the student to repeat the steps from memory.)

"Now that we know these steps, let's practice using this strategy. In this section of the chalkboard, I have some new information about amphibians written. We'll use this information to practice the strategy."

1. "First, let's **C**—Copy. Please read this information and then copy it on your strategy sheet." (Teacher and class read and copy.)

2. "Now, we **A**—Add details. I will tell you two sentences about amphibians. We will write these details in our strategy sheet." (Say, "Amphibians have smooth skin instead of fur, scales, or feathers. They breathe with gills, lungs, and skin"). "Let's write these details on our sheet."

3. "Next, **L**—Listen and write the question. The question is 'When do amphibians develop these characteristics?' We write this question on our sheet."

4. "The next **L** is listen and write the answer. The answer is 'When amphibians are young, they live in the water and have gills and tails. When they grow older, they lose their tails and gills and grow limbs.' Let's write this answer on our sheet."

5. "The final steps are to **U**—Utilize the text, and **P**—Put it in your words. On the board is a short section of the text (Amphibian larvae move like fish—they wiggle their bodies and flatten their tails to move. Adult amphibians use their front and back legs to move). Let's read this together and then we'll write a summary in our own words." (Teacher and class read the section and then they write summary statement on the prompt sheet.)

Have three or four more guided practice examples ready. Practice the strategy with the class until the class can independently follow the steps of the strategy and fill in the prompt sheets. Fade prompts as the students complete the steps of the strategy.

Independent Practice

Have a final example ready. Present the information, and have the students write the notes using a blank CALL UP sheet.

Reproduction facts for independent practice:

Females lay eggs in water. Females can release as many as 200 eggs. After females release eggs, males fertilize them. Frog eggs are sticky and attach to underwater plants. The sticky substance makes it difficult for predators to grasp the eggs. Most amphibians abandon their eggs after they lay them.

Technology Spotlight #9.1

Inspiration

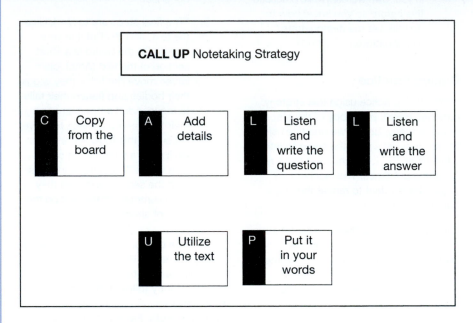

Creating great looking graphic organizers, visual prompts, and mnemonic devices does not have to be a difficult task. The above example was created using the computer program Inspiration®. Inspiration® is a program designed for helping students and teachers create graphic organizers, outlines, and visual representations of concepts and content information. The program is easy to use and is a great resource for implementing the concepts discussed in this chapter. In fact, Inspiration®[1] is so easy to use that students in Grades 6–12 can quickly learn program features and create their own visual learning supports. For younger children (Grades K–5), Kidspiration®[2] provides an easy way to apply the proven principles of visual learning. With Kidspiration®, students build graphic organizers by combining pictures, text, and spoken words to represent thoughts and information (Inspiration Software, 2016).

1 Inspiration is a registered trademark of Inspiration Software, Inc.

2 Kidspiration is a registered trademark of Inspiration Software, Inc.

Teacher Instruction to Facilitate Notetaking

The structure and delivery of teacher lectures and presentations impact student notetaking. The tighter, clearer, and more explicit the presentation, the easier it is to take notes. For example, teachers who talk in circles without defining vocabulary or the main ideas are hard to follow, particularly for students with HID. If students can't follow the flow of the lecture, then they won't understand the concepts being taught, and thus be unable to take notes. On the other hand, teachers who use a concise and direct outline to structure their presentation are much easier to understand, follow, and take notes from. Thus, some responsibility rests on teachers to make their instruction explicit and clear enough from which to take notes. Teachers also have responsibility to clarify the content on which students will be held accountable. That is, sometimes discussion occurs in the classroom for enrichment and creative thinking to occur, yet students will not be tested on this exchange of ideas. Clarifying this for students helps them focus on what to take notes on and what content to study. Table 9.7 lists additional ideas for structuring lectures to facilitate notetaking.

Guided Notes

Guided notes are another tool to help students take notes. Guided notes generally consist of outlines and/or graphic organizers with blank spaces in which students can write main ideas, vocabulary, concepts, and/or relationships. Guided notes represent the overall content and structure of the content being learned. The study guide that appears in Figure 9.3 could also be used as guided notes.

TABLE 9.7   **Structuring Lectures to Facilitate Notetaking**

Ideas for Structuring Lectures
• Distinguish between times when students should and should not take notes. Tell students the difference. When not taking notes, students can just listen for understanding and ask questions. Then provide them ample time to copy notes from the chalkboard or generate their own outlines.
• Provide students audio cues during lecturing, such as "This is important." "You should write this down." "These are the five reasons and you need to know this for the test."
• Provide students visual cues, such as writing key vocabulary words on the board or projecting key ideas at the front of the classroom.
• For selected students, provide them a copy of the lecture outline or slides.
• Allow time for students to go over their notes immediately following instruction to ensure they understand. Then answer any questions they may ask.
• Set up the lectures to make them *student friendly* and easy for taking notes. This promotes students' strategy use and also requires that teachers become aware of how they have organized and presented the content.

Tips for developing and using guided notes are outlined in Table 9.8. Figure 9.7 provides the self-talk students can be taught to use with guided notes.

TABLE 9.8   Developing Guided Notes

Developing and Using Guided Notes

- Use existing lecture notes including main ideas, key terms and phrases, and definitions.

- Use a consistent format including columnar format (comparative information) and skeletal format (outline) that parallels the sequence of the lecture.

- Project completed guided notes at the front of the classroom. Reveal each section only as it is being discussed.

- Provide visual cues, such as individual blanks for each word to be filled in or a list of numbers under a heading, on the students' copies to convey the amount and type of information used.

- Distribute the blank spaces throughout the notes to encourage active engagement.

- Give students the guided notes for a whole unit or chapter before discussing.

- Randomly select students' guided notes at the beginning of class. Review the content and clarify misunderstandings.

- Model how to fill out the guided notes by using a short (3 to 5 minute) prerecorded lecture with the guided notes projected at the front of the classroom.

- For students with writing difficulties, consider modifying the guided notes by having them write fewer words, giving them choices to circle, or allowing them to use assistive technology (e.g., word processing).

Source: Adapted from Konrad, Joseph, & Itoi (2011); Lazarus (1996).

FIGURE 9.7   Self-Talk for Using Guided Notes

Using Guided Notes

- When I take guided notes, I clear my desk and have only my notes and a pencil on my desk.

- I listen to the teacher and watch what he or she does.

- When the teacher writes, I write what he or she writes.

- After I've written what the teacher writes, I check my notes for accuracy and completeness.

- If I have any questions about my notes, I ask them.

Research supports the effectiveness of notetaking and notetaking strategies. Notetaking not only provides a permanent product from which students can study, research shows that those who take notes increase their attention; active engagement; ability to paraphrase, elaborate and seek clarification; comprehension; later recall of information; and performance on tests (Boyle, 2010). Generally speaking, teachers should not hand out complete notes as a replacement for students taking notes. Studies show that listening and then being given the notes is not as effective as taking notes (Porte, 2001).

Studies have examined the effectiveness of notetaking instruction on students with learning disabilities (e.g., Boyle, 2011), emotional/behavioral disorders (e.g., Patterson, 2005), and attention-deficit/hyperactivity disorder (e.g., Evans, Pelham, & Grudberg, 1995). Results indicate that students with HID can be taught to use notetaking strategies which in turn lead to better academic performance on tests. Research also documents that guided notes can facilitate increased learning (e.g., Lazarus, 1996).

Technology Spotlight #9.2

Tools for Learning Strategies

An increasing number of technological supports for the classroom can be used to create and use learning strategies to aid student achievement. Below are examples of these technological tools.

Graphic Organizers (Ciullo & Reutebuch, 2013)

Research has documented that computer-based graphic organizers (e.g., Inspiration®) can support student learning, particularly to enhance explicit instruction, to expand concepts from readings, or as a study guide. For an example, see Technology Spotlight #9.1.

Notetaking (Boyle, Forchelli & Cariss, 2015)

- **Digital pens** or **smartpens** can be used to upload notes as digital images and pictures or audio record a lecture in synch with the written notes.
- **Handheld tablets** (e.g., iPads) can help students organize and store information in one place. Some transfer handwriting to type-font and allow synching written notes with audio recording.
- **Apps** are readily available to help facilitate notetaking (e.g., AudioNote, Notability, Notes Plus, Penultimate). They vary in capability and should be selected based on the needs of the student.

Teaching Strategies (Lancaster, Schumaker, Lancaster, & Deshler, 2009)

Learning strategies instruction (i.e., test-taking strategy) has been shown to be effective when delivered through computer-based instruction. When converted to this format, teacher instructional time can be reduced from 3 hours to 1½ hours. This format could provide more individualized instruction but it does not relieve the teacher from instructional activities such as monitoring students.

Creating Learning Strategies

Numerous learning strategies have been created by researchers and teachers. Yet, only a few examples are provided within the context of this chapter. Teachers can create their own strategies and, if appropriate, teach students to create them as well. Strategies that are specific to the needs of the setting, content, and learner can be powerful tools in increasing learning capabilities. Features of an effective learning strategy include the following. First, they form a first-letter mnemonic strategy that is easy to remember. All of the steps in the strategy need to be in the students' repertoire, so if they are unable to complete an individual step, it needs to be taught. Second, each step should be short with only the essential words. Third, each step should begin with a verb or a keyword related to the cognitive or behavioral task. Fourth, no more than seven steps should be included. Fifth, the first-letter mnemonic should relate to the overall strategy. And sixth, familiar and simple vocabulary words should be used (Hughes, 2011; Lenz, Ellis, & Scanlon, 1996).

The STRATEGY first-letter mnemonic was designed to teach students to create their own learning strategies. These steps can also be helpful to teachers as they create strategies for their students:

- **S**tart by choosing a learning or behavior outcome.

- **T**ask analyze it.

- **R**earrange the wording of the steps.

- **A**sk if you can make a word from the first letters.

- **T**ry to find a word that relates to the task.

- **E**xamine possible synonyms to get the first letter.

- **G**et creative.

- **Y**es, you can make your own strategies. (Heaton & O'Shea, 1995, p. 34)

TEACHER TIP #9.6

SIM (STRATEGIC INSTRUCTION MODEL)

The University of Kansas Center for Research on Learning has developed the Strategic Instruction Model (SIM) which includes learning strategies curriculum.

Teachers can learn specific instructional strategies by enrolling in courses at the institute. Strategies in their curriculum include the following:

Strategies for Reading

- Inference Strategy
- Paraphrasing Strategy
- Self-Questioning Strategy
- Visual Imagery Strategy
- Word Identification Strategy
- Word Mapping Strategy

Strategies for Studying

- FIRST-Letter Mnemonic Strategy
- LINCS Vocabulary Strategy
- Listening and Notetaking
- Paired Associate Strategy

Strategies for Writing

- EDIT Strategy
- InSPECT Strategy
- Paragraph-Writing Strategy
- Sentence-Writing Strategy (Fundamentals)
- Sentence-Writing Strategy (Proficiency)
- Theme Writing (Fundamentals)

Strategies for Improving Performance

- Assignment-Completion Strategy

- Essay Test-Taking Strategy
- Strategic Tutoring
- Test-Taking Strategy

Strategies for Effectively Interacting with Others

- BUILD Strategy
- Focusing Together
- Following Instructions Together
- LEARN Strategy
- Organizing Together
- SCORE Skills
- SLANT: A Starter Strategy for Class Participation
- Taking Notes Together
- Talking Together
- Teamwork Strategy
- THINK Strategy

Strategies for Motivation

- Possible Selves: Nurturing Motivation
- Self-Advocacy Strategy

Strategies for Math

- Strategic Math Series

Source: Strategic Instruction Model (2016); (sim.kucrl.org/products).

Implications for Culturally and/or Linguistically Diverse Students

Although research examining the effectiveness of learning strategies for culturally and/or linguistically diverse (CLD) students is limited, educators advocate the use of these strategies given the structure and support they provide. In particular, organizing, notetaking, and mnemonic strategies may be helpful.

Graphic organizers, such as concept maps, can capitalize on CLD students' cultural experiences. They may be particularly helpful for students who are English learners (ELs) because they provide a visual representation connecting ideas with limited use of language and they can be created in English, the students' primary language, or both. Teachers can use graphic organizers in cooperative learning groups with each group creating their graphic organizers representing the relationships between the concepts learned. Discussing the topics with their peers helps them expand their speaking and listening skills (Hart, 2009).

Graphic organizers can also be used to assess EL students' knowledge. For example, in one study, elementary EL students created concept maps before and after a 4-week science unit on plants. They were given three general concept words, asked to add four words that represent important changes that plants go through and, based on these seven concepts, draw a concept map using connecting words (e.g., verbs and prepositions). Results showed increases in students' scientifically accurate concepts and scientific vocabulary (Stoddart, 2006).

Guided notes can be extremely helpful to EL students given that attending to both the language and the content simultaneously during teacher presentations can be very difficult. With guided notes, the structure of the lesson is provided and they need to only write a few words or phrases, making the notetaking experience easier to accomplish (Konrad et al., 2011).

Mnemonic strategies can facilitate recall of information for EL students. One study examined the impact of mnemonic strategies on EL students' recall of social studies content. When the secondary-age students were taught mnemonic strategies, they performed significantly higher on curriculum-based assessment, were on task to a greater degree, and reported more strategy use as compared to receiving teacher-directed instruction. Also, both the teachers and their students reported they learned more and preferred mnemonic strategies over explicit instruction (Fontana et al., 2007).

Although limited research has been conducted with CLD students, and particularly CLD students with HID, it seems reasonable that they would benefit from learning-strategies instruction given that they provide the structure and guidance often needed by this population. Clearly additional research is needed to substantiate the power of learning strategies on CLD students with and without disabilities.

SUMMARY

Strategies are plans, actions, steps, and processes that allow students to accomplish a learning or problem-solving task. Effective strategies encompass both cognitive and behavioral elements. Students with HID need to be taught strategies explicitly, as well as prompted and guided in using strategies for learning. Major categories for strategies include attention, mnemonic, organizing, study, test-taking, and notetaking strategies.

Students with HID often need assistance with maintaining on-task attention and selective attention. On-task attention may be maintained through teacher-directed prompts or taught through self-monitoring, while teacher-directed strategies for improving selective attention include helping students focus, identifying the relevant stimuli for students, and teaching students to identify the relevant stimuli themselves.

Mnemonic strategies that assist with recall include acronyms, acrostics, rhymes, keywords, and pegwords. These strategies help students retrieve factual information commonly taught in content-focused classrooms. Teachers can create mnemonic strategies or students may be instructed in generating their own strategies. A substantial amount of research supports the effectiveness of mnemonic strategies for students with HID.

Organizing strategies include graphic and advance organizers. Graphic organizers visually represent knowledge by arranging information in an associative organization. They may be developed by the students, the teachers, or both; and they may be used effectively before, during, or after instruction. Advance organizers are delivered at the beginning of instruction and are similar to anticipatory sets.

Effective study habits and routines are critical for student success. Study guides can also help students with HID learn new vocabulary, guide reading, review newly introduced concepts, integrate previous information with new content, practice specific skills, and/or review for a test. In order to be successful in general education classrooms, students with HID also need effective test-taking and notetaking strategies. Test-taking strategies include reducing test anxiety, as well as using specific test-taking strategies (e.g., PIRATES). Students can also be taught explicit notetaking strategies (e.g., CUES), or provided guided notes. In addition, teachers can modify their teaching style to better accommodate notetaking.

Although limited research has examined the effectiveness of learning strategies for CLD students, some evidence has demonstrated that organizing and mnemonic strategies can have a positive impact. Given the structure and guidance learning strategies provide, professionals believe they can be helpful, particularly for EL students.

REVIEW QUESTIONS

1. Define *strategies* and *strategic learner*. Explain why students with HID need instruction in the use of strategies.

2. Explain the five categories of teacher behaviors related to gaining, maintaining, and refocusing student attention. Give an example of each teacher behavior, and discuss skills teachers would need to manage student attention while instructing.

3. Explain teachers' options for addressing students' selective attention difficulties.

4. Develop an outline for teaching a mnemonic strategy. Create visual representations if needed.

5. Describe strategies you use to remember information. How are your strategies similar to or different from the memory strategies discussed in this chapter?

6. What should be considered when using a graphic organizer in the classroom?

7. Compare and contrast advance organizers, graphic organizers, and study guides. Provide examples of each.

8. Explain why students with disabilities need to learn strategies for taking notes and tests and how you would teach them.

9. How can teachers structure instruction to facilitate notetaking?

10. What can teachers do to make learning strategies particularly helpful for students who are English learners?

ACTIVITIES

1. Create a graphic organizer representing the content of this chapter.

2. Work with a classmate to create mnemonic keywords and/or pegwords to facilitate recall of information in this book. Use them to help recall information. Share your results.

3. Create a chart and then track your study habits. After 3 days, implement a strategy to improve your habits. Continue to track your progress for at least 2 weeks. Report the results.

4. Access a secondary school textbook. Analyze the book for ways in which strategies are embedded, prompted, and/or encouraged in the book. Generate at least five examples of how learning strategies would help students learn the content.

5. Interview at least three adolescent students about the learning strategies they use to attend, remember, organize, study, take tests, and take notes. Ask them how teachers can help them with these strategies. Present the results.

Council for Exceptional Children (CEC) Standards

The Council for Exceptional Children (CEC) is a premiere national professional organization comprised of special educators, paraeducators, relative service personnel, parents, and others interested in individuals with disabilities and/or those with gifts and talents. This organization has generated 10 standards for the preparation of special educators. These standards are listed in each chapter as they relate to the content within the chapter. The standard that applies to Chapter 9 is Standard #5.

CEC Initial Preparation Standard #5:
Instructional Planning and Strategies (partial)

Beginning special education professionals select, adapt, and use a repertoire of evidence-based instructional strategies to advance learning of individuals with exceptionalities.

5.1 Beginning special education professionals consider an individual's abilities, interests, learning environments, and cultural and linguistic factors in the selection, development, and adaptation of learning experiences for individuals with exceptionalities.

5.4 Beginning special education professionals use strategies to enhance language development and communication skills of individuals with exceptionalities.

5.6 Beginning special education professionals teach to mastery and promote generalization of learning.

5.7 Beginning special education professionals teach cross-disciplinary knowledge and skills such as critical thinking and problem solving to individuals with exceptionalities.

REFERENCES

Asaro, K., & Saddler, B. (2009). Effects of planning instruction on a young writer with Asperger Syndrome. *Intervention in School and Clinic, 44*(5), 268–275.

Banks, T., & Eaton, I. (2014). Improving test-taking performance of secondary at-risk youth and students with disabilities. *Preventing School Failure, 58*(4), 207–213.

Baxendell, B. W. (2003). Consistent, coherent, creative: The 3 c's of graphic organizers. *TEACHING Exceptional Children, 35*(3), 46–53.

Berg, J. L., & Wehby, J. (2013). Preteaching strategies to improve student learning in content area classes. *Intervention in School and Clinic, 49*(1), 14–20.

Boyle, J. R. (2010). Note-taking skills of middle school students with and without learning disabilities. *Journal of Learning Disabilities, 43*(6), 530–540.

Boyle, J. R. (2011). Strategic note-taking for inclusive middle school science classrooms. *Remedial and Special Education, 34*(2), 78–90.

Boyle, J. R., Forchelli, G. A., & Cariss, K. (2015). Note-taking interventions to assist students with disabilities in content area classes. *Preventing School Failure, 59*(3), 186–195.

Bryant, D. P., Smith, D. D., & Bryant, B. R. (2008). *Teaching students with special needs in inclusive classrooms.* Upper Saddle River, NJ: Pearson.

Buchan, L., Fish, T., & Prater, M. A. (1997). Ninja Turtles counting pizza toppings: A creative writing learning strategy. *Teaching Exceptional Children, 28*(2), 40–43.

Carter, E. W., Wehby, J., Hughes, C., Johnson, S. M., Plank, D. R., Barton-Arwood, S. M., & Lunsford, L. B. (2005). Preparing adolescents with high-incidence disabilities for high-stakes testing with strategy instruction. *Preventing School Failure, 49*(2), 55–62.

Ciullo, S. P., & Reutebuch, C. (2013). Computer-based graphic organizers for students with LD: A systematic review of literature. *Learning Disabilities Research & Practice, 28*(4), 196–210.

Conderman, G., & Bresnahan, V. (2010). Study guides to the rescue. *Intervention in School and Clinic, 45*(3), 169–176.

Conderman, G., & Pedersen, T. (2010). Preparing students with mild disabilities for taking state and district tests. *Intervention in School and Clinic, 45*(4), 232–241.

Czarnecki, E., Rosko, D., & Fine, E. (1998). How to CALL UP note taking skills. *TEACHING Exceptional Children, 30*(6), 14–19.

Datta, P. (2014). Test anxiety research: Students with vision impairments and students with mild intellectual disabilities. *International Journal of Special Education, 29*(2), 68–74.

Dell'Olio, J. M., & Donk, T. (2007). *Models of teaching: Connecting student learning with standards.* Thousand Oaks, CA: Sage.

Dexter, D. D., & Hughes, C. A. (2011). Graphic organizers and students with learning disabilities: A meta-analysis. *Learning Disabilities Quarterly, 34*(1), 51–72.

Dexter, D. D., Park, Y. J., & Hughes, C. A. (2011). A meta-analytic review of graphic organizers and science instruction for adolescents with learning disabilities: Implications for the intermediate and secondary science classroom. *Learning Disabilities Research & Practice, 26*(4), 204–213.

Evans, S. W., Pelham, W. E., & Grudberg, M. V. (1995). The efficacy of notetaking to improve behavior and comprehension of adolescents with attention deficit hyperactivity disorder. *Exceptionality, 5*(1), 1–17.

Fontana, J. L., Scruggs, T. E., & Mastropieri, M. A. (2007). Mnemonic strategy instruction in inclusive secondary social studies classes. *Remedial and Special Education, 28*(6), 345–355.

Forness, S. R. (2001). Special education and related services: What have we learned from meta-analysis? *Exceptionality, 9,* 185–197.

Hart, J. E. (2009). Strategies for culturally and linguistically diverse students with special needs. *Preventing School Failure, 53*(3), 197–206.

Haselden, P. (2003). Use of affinity diagrams as instructional tools in inclusive classrooms. *Preventing School Failure, 47*(4), 187–189.

Heaton, S., & O'Shea, D. J. (1995). Using mnemonics to make mnemonics. *TEACHING Exceptional Children, 28*(1), 34–36.

Hughes, C. A. (2011). Effective instructional design and delivery for teaching task-specific learning strategies to students with learning disabilities. *Focus on Exceptional Children, 44*(2), 1–16.

Hughes, C. A., Ruhl, K. L., Schumaker, J. B., & Deshler, D. D. (2002). Effects of instruction in an assignment completion strategy on the homework performance of students with learning disabilities in general education classes. *Learning Disabilities Research & Practice, 17*(1), 1–18.

Hughes, C. A., Schumaker, J. B., Deshler, D. D., & Mercer, C. D. (1993). *The test-taking strategy.* Lawrence, KS: Edge Enterprises.

Hughes, C. A., Schumaker, J. B., & Deshler, D. D. (2005). *The essay test-taking strategy.* Lawrence, KS: Edge Enterprises.

Inspiration Software. (2016). Retrieved from http://www.inspiration.com/

Ives, B. (2007). Graphic organizers applied to secondary algebra instruction for students with learning disabilities. *Learning Disabilities Research & Practice, 22*(2), 110–118.

Konrad, M., Joseph, L. M., & Itoi, M. (2011). Using guided notes to enhance instruction for all students. *Intervention in School and Clinic, 46*(3), 131–140.

Lambert, M. A., & Nowacek, J. (2006). Help high school students improve their study skills. *Intervention in School and Clinic, 41*(4), 241–243.

Lancaster, P. E., Schumaker, J. B., Lancaster, S. J. C., & Deshler, D. D. (2009). Effects of a computerized program on use of the test-taking strategy by secondary students with disabilities. *Learning Disability Quarterly, 32,* 165–179.

Lazarus, B. D. (1996). Flexible skeletons: Guided notes for adolescents with mild disabilities. *Teaching Exceptional Children, 28*(3), 36–40.

Lenz, B. K., Ellis, E. S., & Scanlon, D. (1996). *Teaching learning strategies to adolescents and adults with learning disabilities.* Austin, TX: PRO-ED.

Marzano, R. J., Pickering, D. J., & Pollock, J. E. (2001). *Classroom instruction that works: Research-based strategies for increasing student achievement.* Alexandria, VA: Association for Supervision and Curriculum Development.

Mastropieri, M. A., Sweda, J., & Scruggs, T. E. (2000). Teacher use of mnemonic strategy instruction. *Learning Disabilities Research and Practice, 15,* 69–74.

McConnell, K., Ryser, G., & Higgins, J. (2000). *Practical ideas that really work for students with ADHD.* Austin, TX: PRO-ED.

Patterson, K. B. (2005). Increasing positive outcomes for African American males in special education with the use of guided notes. *Journal of Negro Education, 74*(4), 311–320.

Paulsen, K., & Sayeski, K. L. (2013). Using study skills to become independent learners in secondary content classes. *Intervention in School and Clinic, 49*(1), 39–45.

Porte, L. K. (2001). Cut and Paste 101: New strategies for notetaking and review. *TEACHING Exceptional Children, 34*(2), 14–20.

Preiss, R. W., & Gayle, B. M. (2006). A meta-analysis of the educational benefits of employing advanced organizers. In B. M. Gayle, R. W. Preiss, N. Burrell, & M. Allen (Eds.), *Classroom communication and instructional processes: Advances through meta-analysis* (pp. 329–340). Mahwah, NJ: Erlbaum.

Reid, R., Lienemann, T. O., & Hagaman, J. L. (2013). *Strategy instruction for students with learning disabilities* (2nd ed.). New York, NY: Guilford Press.

Salend, S. J. (2011). Addressing test anxiety. *TEACHING Exceptional Children, 44*(2), 58–68.

Saphier, J., Haley-Speca, M. A., & Gower, R. (2008). *The skillful teacher: Building your teaching skills* (6th ed.). Acton, MA: Research for Better Teaching.

Scott, V. G., & Compton, L. (2007). A new TRICK for the trade: A strategy for keeping an agenda book for secondary students. *Intervention in School and Clinic, 43*(5), 280–284.

Scruggs, T. E., & Mastropieri, M. A. (2000). The effectiveness of mnemonic instruction for students with learning and behavior problems: An update and research synthesis. *Journal of Behavioral Education, 10*, 163–173.

Scruggs, T. E., Mastropieri, M. A., Berkeley, S. L., & Graetz, J. E. (2010). Do special education interventions improve learning of secondary content? A meta-analysis. *Remedial and Special Education, 31*(6), 437–449.

Scruggs, T. E., Mastropieri, M. A., Berkeley, S. L., & Marshak, L. (2010). Mnemonic strategies: Evidence-based practice and practice-based evidence. *Intervention in School and Clinic, 46*(2), 79–86.

Scruggs, T. E., Mastropieri, M. A., & McDuffie, K. A. (2007). Co-teaching in inclusive classrooms: A metasynthesis of qualitative research. *Exceptional Children, 73*(4), 392–416.

Singleton, S. M., & Filce, H. G. (2015). Graphic organizers for secondary students with learning disabilities. *TEACHING Exceptional Children, 48*(2), 110–117.

Songlee, D., Miller, S. P., Tincani, M., Sileo, N. M., & Perkins, P. G. (2008). Effects of test-taking strategy instruction on high-functioning adolescents with autism spectrum disorders. *Focus on Autism and Other Developmental Disabilities, 23*(4), 217–228.

Stoddart, T. (2006). *Using concept maps to assess the science understanding and language production of English language learners*. Proceedings of the Second International Conference on Concept Mapping, San José, Costa Rica. Retrieved from http://cmc.ihmc.us/cmc2006Papers/cmc2006-p103.pdf

Stormont, M. A. (2008). Increase academic success for children with ADHD using sticky notes and highlighters. *Intervention in School and Clinic, 43*(5), 305–308.

Strategic Instruction Model. (2016). Retrieved from http://sim.kucrl.org/products

Swanson, E., Hairrell, A., Kent, S., Ciullo, S., Wanzek, J. A., & Vaughn, S. (2014). A synthesis and meta-analysis of reading interventions using social studies content for students with learning disabilities. *Journal of Learning Disabilities, 47*(2), 178–195.

Swanson, H. L., & Hoskyn, M. (2001). Instructing adolescents with learning disabilities: A component and composite analysis. *Learning Disabilities: Research & Practice, 16*(2), 109–119.

Terrill, M. C., Scruggs, T. E., & Mastropieri, M. A. (2004). SAT vocabulary instruction for high school students with learning disabilities. *Intervention in School and Clinic, 39*(5), 288–294.

Therrien, W. J., Hughes, C., Kapelski, C., & Mokhtari, K. (2009). Effectiveness of a test-taking strategy on achievement in essay tests for students with learning disabilities. *Journal of Learning Disabilities, 42*(1), 14–23.

Therrien, W. J., Taylor, J. C., Hosp, J. L., Kaldenberg, E. R., & Gorsh, J. (2011). Science instruction for students with learning disabilities: A meta-analysis. *Learning Disabilities: Research and Practice, 26*(4), 188–203.

Uberti, H. Z., Scruggs, T. E., & Mastropieri, M. A. (2003). Keywords make the difference: Mnemonic instruction in inclusive classrooms. *TEACHING Exceptional Children, 35*(3), 56–61.

Vogler, K. E. (2006). High school graduate examination on Tennessee science teachers' instructional practices. *American Secondary Education, 35*(1), 33–57.

Wehrung-Schaffner, L., & Sapona, R. H. (1990). May the FORCE be with you: A test preparation strategy for learning disabled adolescents. *Academic Therapy, 25,* 291–300.

Whitaker Sena, J. D., Lowe, P. A., & Lee, S. W. (2007). Significant predictors of test anxiety among students with and without learning disabilities. *Journal of Learning Disabilities, 40*(4), 360–376.

Wood, D. K., & Frank, A. R. (2000). Using memory-enhancing strategies to learn multiplication facts. *TEACHING Exceptional Children, 32*(5), 78–82.

Woods, K., Parkinson, G., & Lewis, S. (2010). Investigating access to educational assessment for students with disabilities. *School Psychology International, 31*(1), 21–41.

Zakas, T. L., Browder, D. M., Ahlgrim-Delzell, & Heafner, T. (2013). Teaching social studies content to students with autism using a graphic organizer intervention. *Research in Autism Spectrum Disorders, 7,* 1075–1086.

$SAGE edge™ • ●

Review ➜ Practice ➜ Improve

Get the tools you need to sharpen your study skills. Access videos, practice quizzes, eFlashcards and more at **edge.sagepub.com/prater.**

©iStockphoto.com/Solovyova

Strategies for Reading and Writing Instruction

Reading and Writing Disabilities

Opal is just entering kindergarten. She is the oldest of three children in her home. Opal has been slow to develop spoken language but can now converse sufficiently with others. She has not been exposed to books or reading in the home. Her kindergarten teacher is concerned that Opal appears unaware of the connection between written and spoken language, but she is hopeful that Opal will grasp these concepts quickly to catch up with her peers.

Ellis, a sixth grader identified as having an intellectual disability, has learned enough phonic skills to decode words on his reading level (e.g., *ball, rush, feet*). But he struggles with words that cannot be "sounded out" (e.g., *was, one, eye*); and as he is reading a passage he often stumbles on words and needs to stop to sound them out which interferes with his ability to read the passage fluently. When asked comprehension questions, he gets about 50% of the answers correctly. His teacher attributes his comprehension difficulties to both his lack of fluency and having a limited vocabulary.

C. J. is an eleventh grader with autism. He likes to orally share factual information about his favorite topics, but writing them down is difficult. In particular, he has limitations with handwriting and spelling. His special education teacher, Mr. Warburton, first transcribed C. J.'s thoughts through a keyboard. But now he is teaching C. J. to use speech-to-text software to convert his oral thoughts to written language.

Learning Objectives

- Describe the types of difficulties students with high-incidence disabilities may encounter in learning to read and write and accompanying strategies to facilitate student learning.

- Define and describe the importance of mastering skills in phonemic awareness, phonics, fluency, vocabulary development, text comprehension, handwriting, spelling, grammar, and text structure and composition. Provide examples of how to teach each.

- Create scripted lesson plans to teach reading and writing concepts following the steps described for teacher-directed instruction.

- Explain the role of culture and language in reading and writing and the implications culturally and/or linguistically for diverse students. Discuss how to teach reading and writing to students from diverse backgrounds.

Prevalence

Reading disabilities are one of the most commonly identified disabilities in schools. For example, reading disabilities appear in about 80% of all students identified with learning disabilities (LD) (Eden & Vaidya, 2008), between 25% and 40% of students with attention-deficit/hyperactivity disorder (ADHD) (Samuelsson, Lundberg, & Herkner, 2004), and approximately one third of the students identified with emotional/behavioral disorder (EBD) (Mattison, 2008). Also, students with intellectual disabilities and many students with autism perform below their peers in reading (Fautsch-Patridge, McMaster, & Hupp, 2011; Spector & Cavanaugh, 2015).

Similarly, students with high-incidence disabilities (HID) often have difficulties learning to write. However, the prevalence of writing disabilities has not been studied to the degree it has been for reading disabilities. Some recent research documents that the prevalence of writing disabilities rivals, and may exceed, the prevalence of reading disabilities (Costa, Edwards, & Hooper, 2016). Students with writing disabilities generally have difficulty transferring what they can communicate through speech to writing. In addition to handwriting challenges, students may struggle with organizing thoughts and using syntax structure and grammar while writing. Although handwriting problems are only one facet of written expression disabilities, studies have documented that handwriting problems among school-age students varies between 5% and 33% (Overvelde & Hulstijn, 2011).

Contributing Factors

Although each student is unique, students who struggle to learn to read generally experience difficulty related to word recognition, fluency, and/or comprehension. Underlying cognitive abilities impacting reading include attention regulation, language, and memory. Students with writing disabilities have difficulties with planning, translating, and revising written text. Contributing factors include fine-motor skills, attention regulation, language abilities, visual-spatial abilities, and memory (Costa et al., 2016). Table 10.1 describes specific problems students with reading disabilities exhibit as they engage in reading tasks. Many of these difficulties carry over into written expression disabilities. A brief discussion of the impact of memory, attention, auditory processing, visual processing, and language on reading and written expression disabilities follows.

Memory

Reading and writing proficiency relies on strong memory skills. Beginners must memorize letters and sounds, remember how to decode or recognize combinations of letters and sounds in words, and continue to add new words to their long-term memory. As discussed in Chapter 1, a common concern for students with HID is their poor memory skills. For these students, the most troublesome bottleneck in learning to read is the lack of proficient word identification. Students with memory deficits need many more repetitions as normally achieving students (Mercer & Pullen, 2008). Hence, students with disabilities need explicit, intensive and supportive instruction, including practice and application opportunities of sufficient frequency and duration.

Attention

Students with HID often have difficulty sustaining attention to academic tasks such as reading and writing. Yet maintaining attention during the instructional sequence is critical for students to benefit from such instruction. Research has shown that when students demonstrate both reading and attention problems, reading interventions are less effective (Cho et al., 2015). In addition to sustained attention, selective attention skills contribute to reading and writing performance. Selective attention requires students to disregard irrelevant and distracting factors (both internally and externally) in order to focus their attention on what is relevant. Auditory and visual processing skills (described below) are impacted by the quality of a student's selective attention (Erbay, 2013).

TABLE 10.1   Common Difficulties That Affect Reading Performance of Students With Reading Disabilities

Learning Difficulty	Skills
Processing Speed	• Rapid Naming—Is slow naming letters, sounds, numbers and is also slow in identifying familiar pictures • Word Recognition—Does not quickly and accurately recognize words • Fluency—Overall fluency rate is slower than peers
Visual Discrimination/ Memory	• Visual Discrimination—Difficulty distinguishing the difference between similar letters such as *b* and *d* • Visual Memory—Problems remembering how to form letters and words and remembering how words are configured
Memory	• Short Term Memory Deficits—Difficulty retaining meaning long enough to comprehend a passage • Long Term—Struggles with learning and retrieving letter and sound information
Phonological Processing	• Phonological Memory—Impaired ability to remember sounds and sounds within words, such as individual sounds in words or syllables in multisyllable words • Phonological Retrieval—Difficulty retrieving words, may substitute words such as *knife* for *fork*, or may overuse nonspecific words like *thing* or *stuff* • Segmenting—Problems perceiving sounds within words and breaking words into syllables • Blending—Difficulty blending sounds together to form words • Rhyming—Difficulty producing rhymes for words • Sound splitting—Inability to drop sounds in words (e.g., saying *hat* without the *h* sound) • Oddity—Difficulty identifying different sounds such as recognizing *bat* as being different from *big*, *pig*, and *fig*
Phonics and Spelling	• Letter/Sound correspondence—Does not learn the letter representations for various sounds • Decoding—Problems decoding new or unfamiliar words • Spelling—Does not reflect phonics knowledge, inability to accurately sequence the sounds of words, writing has many spelling errors
Language Comprehension	• Vocabulary—Poorly developed vocabulary creates decoding and comprehension problems • Grammar/Syntax—In speaking or writing, the construction of sentences is not complex, and the same sentence construction is used to express thoughts (e.g., *I saw a dog. I saw a tree. I saw a cat.*) • Text-level processing—Deficits in grammar/syntax and vocabulary contribute to difficulty constructing meaning from printed material or comprehending what is read

Sources: Bell, S. M., McCallum, S., & Cox, E. A. (2003); Catts, H. W., & Hogan, T. P. (2003); Joshi, R. M. (2003).

Auditory Processing

Many students with HID, particularly those with LD and ADHD, demonstrate a weakness in their ability to understand and use auditory information. Auditory processing skills are vital for reading, and deficits in this area may be manifested in the following ways: (a) inability to recognize, compare, and distinguish separate sounds in words (auditory discrimination); (b) difficulty identifying important sounds from a noisy background (auditory figure-ground discrimination); (c) poor short-term and long-term auditory memory; and (d) difficulty understanding and recalling the order of sounds and words (auditory sequencing) (Cortiella & Horowitz, 2014).

Visual Processing

As with auditory processing deficits, students with HID often exhibit difficulty understanding and using visual information. These difficulties may include (a) inability to recognize, compare, and distinguish visual symbols (visual discrimination); (b) difficulty identifying a shape or symbol from its background (visual figure-ground discrimination); (c) poor short-term and long-term visual memory; (d) difficulty seeing and distinguishing the order of symbols or words (visual sequencing); (e) inability to recognize an object when only parts of it are visible (visual closure); and (f) difficulty understanding how objects are positioned in space (spatial relationships) (Cortiella & Horowitz, 2014). In addition, difficulties with visual-motor integration or the coordination and assimilation of visual perception and fine motor movement can contribute to handwriting problems, which interfere with students' ability to compose on paper (Dunn & Finley, 2010).

Language

Language exists in both oral and written forms and across receptive and expressive formats. Receptive language is used to receive and understand communication from another source, while expressive language communicates thoughts or ideas to others. By the time most students start school, they have acquired sufficient oral skills to converse in their native language. That is, they can carry on a conversation by speaking (expressive) and listening (receptive). Although oral skills continue to improve as students develop, academic instruction typically focuses on written forms of communication, namely reading and writing.

Oral language skills are a critical precursor to the development of reading and writing. Students who struggle with verbal vocabulary and listening comprehension often develop poor reading and written expression skills. The breadth of a student's vocabulary is particularly important for reading comprehension (Cho et al., 2015).

Reading and Writing Foundations

Reading and writing are complex cognitive behaviors that require recognizing and making sense of the written symbols that represent speech. Writing is the process of using these symbols to make a tangible record of thoughts. Reading is essentially the reverse; that is, reading requires students to decipher the symbols to bring the written word back into speech form, either orally or silently. All modern languages have written symbol systems, though they vary greatly in form. Alphabetic languages like English or Russian use a few symbols and combinations of symbols to represent the sounds of speech. Logographic languages like Chinese or Japanese use a combination of characters or drawings to variously represent ideas, objects, or sounds. The common feature in all written language is the use of symbols to represent the spoken word.

Reading involves not only correctly decoding written symbols, it also involves extracting meaning while decoding. Breakdowns in decoding the symbol system and in deriving the intended meaning are the two general causes of reading problems. Both have been studied extensively, and the accumulated results of these studies provide a great deal of insight into what is required to learn to read and read well. The most influential analysis of these studies resulted in a report by the National Reading Panel ([NRP], 2000). The NRP study analyzed over 100,000 studies. The results of this comprehensive research review indicate that students must master skills in five areas to become good readers:

1. **Phonemic awareness**—recognition that spoken language can be broken into smaller units, such as discrete sounds

2. **Phonics**—the ability to match sounds to letters in order to read and write

3. **Fluency**—the skill of reading accurately, at an appropriate rate, and with expression

4. **Vocabulary development**—the knowledge and use of words that make up a language

5. **Text comprehension**—the ability to understand and use information that is read

Reading requires effective learning and integration of these five skills. How to instruct in each of these five areas is discussed in the next section.

Much less attention has been devoted to writing disabilities; the field knows less about skills that contribute to beginning writing than to beginning reading. Research does support, however, that the cognitive processes of written expression involve two subcomponents: text generation and transcription (i.e., handwriting and spelling). When students lack the transcription skills, they devote their attention to spelling and forming letters which takes their attention and cognitive efforts away from composing text. Spelling and handwriting, therefore, play a crucial role in developing written expression (Puranik & Al Otaiba, 2012).

Writing is a complex activity that requires the use of many cognitive abilities in order to think, organize, and record one's thoughts (Carretti, Motta, & Re, 2016). In fact, writing may be one of the most complex human activities. Although written language is essential to the way we learn, interact, and progress in educated societies, the ability to write well does not develop naturally and must be taught. In order for students to learn to write effectively, they need to understand, learn, and master five skills: handwriting, spelling, grammar, text structure, and composition. Each skill is discussed later in the chapter.

Reading Instruction

Historically, fourth grade has been viewed as a critical point in reading development. After third grade, the emphasis on reading instruction begins to fade in the general education classroom with the focus shifting from learning to read to reading to learn. Reading materials become more complex and the use of textbooks increases. Remediating reading difficulties after third grade becomes particularly challenging necessitating the importance of quality reading instruction in the early grades (Wanzek et al., 2013). At the same time, 5% to 10% of students acquire reading problems for the first time after third grade (Etmanskie, Partanen, & Siegel, 2016).

Students at risk or struggling with learning to read need explicit or teacher-directed instruction as described in Chapter 6. During modeling, teachers demonstrate the skill or strategy and include think-alouds where the teacher verbalizes thought processes or the steps of a strategy. Teachers guide students as they practice these skills and strategies and once high levels of success are achieved, students demonstrate them on their own. Research has documented the effectiveness of explicit instruction on teaching young children (e.g., Kamps et al., 2008) as well as adolescents (e.g., Shippen, Houchins, Steventon, & Sartor, 2005) to read. Research also demonstrates that explicit instruction is effective with students identified as having learning disabilities (e.g., Seifert & Espin, 2012), emotional/behavioral disorders (e.g., McDaniel, Houchins, & Terry, 2011), intellectual disabilities (e.g., Allor, Mathes, Roberts, Cheatham, & Al Otaiba, 2014), and autism (e.g., Roux, Dion, Barrette, Dupéré, & Fuchs, 2015).

At-risk readers need to learn explicit and systematic strategies necessary for decoding words. The most phonemically explicit interventions produced the strongest growth in word reading ability in at-risk students. They also need more intensive instruction including increased teaching/learning opportunities. Learning opportunities increase when teachers devote more time to reading instruction, promote students in small instructional groups, and incorporate peer-tutoring and peer-assisted learning strategies in instructional routines (see Chapter 8). At-risk readers need more supportive instruction with ample positive reinforcement and increased teacher guidance. Instruction for at-risk students should have two types of support or scaffolding: carefully sequenced instruction designed to build skills gradually, and teacher–student interactions that support the student in processing and thinking through tasks (Torgesen, 2002). A list of commercially available curricular materials supported through research appears in Table 10.2.

Phonemic Awareness

Students with phonological awareness recognize that spoken language can be broken into units ranging from entire words to syllables to smaller **phonemes** or discrete sounds. The deepest level of phonological awareness is ***phonemic awareness***, defined as the ability to hear, recognize, and manipulate the single distinctive sounds of language (Armbruster, Lehr, & Osborn, 2001). Phonemic awareness is the most crucial to reading and spelling success. For example, a student must be able to isolate the phoneme /p/ in the words *pat, pin,* and *pot* in order to fully understand that the letter *p* represents the /p/ sound and use this information when attempting to decode a word such as *put.* Although phonological awareness takes several years to mature, most children begin

TABLE 10.2	Research Validated Reading Programs Designed to Remediate Reading and Spelling Disabilities

Program Name	Target Group/ Program Type	Description
Corrective Reading (www.mheducation.com/preK-12)	Designed for students with the following reading difficulties: misidentified words, confusion of similar words, word omissions or insertions, lack of attention to punctuation, and poor comprehension; appropriate for students enrolled in Grades 4 and above	Teaches decoding and comprehension, which may be taught separately or together.
Lindamood-Bell Phoneme Sequencing Program (lindamoodbell.com)	Phonemic Sequencing; best used with younger students	Teaches oral motor awareness as an aid to processing phonological information during reading and writing activities.
Reading Mastery Programs (www.mheonline.com) (www.nifdi.org/programs/reading/reading-mastery)	Designed for K–5; appropriate as a core program or for at-risk students	Teaches phonemic awareness, letter–sound correspondence, sounding out words, word recognition, vocabulary, oral reading fluency, and comprehension. Program aligns 95% with the Common Core State Standards in English Language Arts.
Reading Wonders (www.mhreadingwonders.com)	Designed for K–6 for all students in a general classroom	Teaches foundational skills, close reading, writing, and fluency, among other skills, through highly scaffolded and scripted instruction. Provides supports for English learners. Built on the Common Core State Standards in English language arts.
Spelling Mastery (www.mheducation.com/preK-12)	Designed for K–6 for all students in a general classroom, but may be delivered to individuals as well as small groups	Teaches spelling skills by blending the phonemic, morphemic, and whole-word approaches. Provides scripted lessons in scaffolded steps to help students finish each concept before a new one is presented.
Wilson Reading Systems (www.wilsonlanguage.com)	Three programs Fundations—K–3 for prevention and intervention Just Words—Grades 4–12 for students with word-level deficits Reading System—Grade 2–adult for those not making progress or needing more intensive instruction	Focuses on phonemic awareness skills, decoding, spelling, and comprehension.

to develop an awareness of the phonemes in spoken language between ages 2 and 4, which prepares them to learn to read with the alphabetic system (Troia, 2004). Students with poor phonemic awareness are at great disadvantage and are at serious risk for reading and spelling difficulties (Compton, 2002). Opal, the kindergarten student in the case study presented earlier, will need to develop phonemic awareness before she can successfully learn to read.

Initial sound fluency and phoneme segmentation fluency can be used to assess phonemic awareness. Assessment of initial sound fluency is useful for preschool and kindergarten children who have not yet learned to read and can be measured by having students identify the beginning sound in words that are cued by looking at pictures. Phoneme segmentation fluency can be assessed with any age of reader and requires students to hear a word and then say the individual sounds, such as hearing *sat* and saying /s/ /a/ /t/. Other phonemic awareness tasks include recognizing the same sound in different words (e.g., *pet, pan, pill*), choosing a dissimilar sounding word from a group (e.g., *dog, did, ran*), blending sounds to say a word (/k/ /i/ /k/ = *kick*), adding a sound to a word to make a new word (/f/ + /lag/ = *flag*), and substituting one sound for another to make a new word (e.g., *tub, tug*).

Mrs. Ortega understands how important phonemic awareness skills are for reading. When she designed her kindergarten program, she planned to explicitly teach phonemic awareness and basic phonics. In addition to formal instruction, Mrs. Ortega incorporates phonemic awareness activities in general classroom routines. For example, each morning during circle time, she selects a student's name and says the name to the class but leaves off the first sound (e.g., Elissa for Melissa). Or she adds a sound to a student's name (e.g., Bian for Ian). The students in her class enjoy guessing the name and providing the missing or added sound.

Phonemic awareness can be taught by having students identify, categorize, blend, segment, delete, add, or substitute phonemes as they learn to recognize and manipulate sounds of English language. For the time-limited teacher, however, concentrating efforts on phoneme segmentation and phoneme blending may be most beneficial (Armbruster et al., 2001). Teachers should introduce and teach segmentation by modeling a word and its separate sounds several times, then saying it with the students, and then prompting students to do it themselves. Choral responding works well for this type of exercise since there is only one right answer and hearing other students repeat the task corrects and reinforces each student's responses. The same can be done for blending exercises, when the teacher says several sounds and then blends them to form a word, followed by students replicating the task. An example may be found in Table 10.3.

When students are learning handwriting in kindergarten or first grade they should be taught to write each sound or word after segmenting or blending it orally. This introduces the phonic principle as students learn to hear, say, read, and write sounds represented by letters.

TABLE 10.3   **An Example of Teaching Segmentation and Blending**

Segmentation

Teacher: The word is *bat.* Say *bat.*

Students: *Bat.*

Teacher: Listen as I say the sounds in *bat*—/b/ /a/ /t/. (repeat several times)

Teacher: Let's all say the sounds in *bat.*

Teacher and students: /b/ /a/ /t/

Teacher: Now you say the sounds in *bat.*

Students: /b/ /a/ /t/. (repeat several times, teacher reinforces correct responses)

Teacher: (Repeat several times with a variety of words to provide ample practice.)

Blending

Teacher: Listen as I say some sounds: /l/ /e/ /t/.

Teacher: These sounds said together make the word *let.* (repeat several times)

Teacher: Now let's all say the sounds together.

Teacher and students: *let.*

Teacher: Listen to these sounds: /d/ /i/ /g/. Say the word.

Students: *dig.*

Teacher: (Repeat with a variety of words; reinforce correct responses.)

TEACHER TIP #10.1

A PHONEMIC AWARENESS STRATEGY

Teach the STOP strategy which builds phonological awareness by incorporating both segmenting and blending skills. The strategy involves the following steps:

S—**S**tare at the unknown word.

T—**T**ell yourself each letter sound.

O—**O**pen your mouth and say each letter.

P—**P**ut the letters together to say the word. (Boyle, 2008)

Phonics

Phonics differs from phonemic awareness. Instruction in phonemic awareness focuses on helping students master the sounds in the language. Once letters are added to the instruction, it becomes phonics (Pullen & Lloyd, 2007). **Phonics** refers to the ability to match phonemes (sounds) with graphemes (spellings) to read or write. Students must have skills in phoneme segmenting, or breaking words and sounds into phonemes, as well as blending, reassembling the sounds back together to make words. These skills, however, are insufficient. Students must also be able to connect sounds with printed letters and words. Phonemic awareness and phonics have a reciprocal relationship in that phonemic awareness promotes phonics knowledge while phonics knowledge improves phonemic awareness (Pullen & Lloyd, 2007). Students who have not yet mastered phonics or letter–sound correspondence have great difficulty learning to read (Torgesen, Rashotte, & Alexander, 2001).

Phonics skill assessment consists of students pointing to and reading letter names as well as reading nonsense words. Nonsense words consist of phonetically regular vowel–consonant and consonant–vowel–consonant pseudowords like *ut* and *min*. Research has documented a strong relationship between the ability to read pseudowords and the ability to read real words (Good, Baker, & Peyton, 2009).

The purpose of phonics instruction is to help students learn and use sound–spelling relationships for fluent reading. Reading and writing require students to master the systematic associations and sequences that make written language understandable. Given the variety of possible spellings for some phonemes, English may seem unsystematic, and critics downplay the usefulness of phonics instruction for this reason. However, predictable structures underlie English orthography as they do in other languages. As students learn and remember word spellings, they can read and spell those words accurately, and they add to their knowledge as they learn more sophisticated words and spellings (Armbruster et al., 2001).

Systematic phonics teaching means that teachers use explicit sequential instruction to model and teach sound–spelling relationships, and then carefully monitor associated student application to reading and writing. This approach consistently produces better decoding and word identification skills for poor readers than less explicit methods. In the English language, there exist at least 40 phonemes represented by 26 letters. Some letters are used rarely and some spoken sounds are represented by the same letters (e.g., In the word, *cease*, the letter *c* represents the /s/ sound, whereas in *cat*, the letter c represents the /k/ sound). Given the complexity of the English language, phonics instruction needs to be explicit, systematic, and scaffolded in order for the alphabetic principle to be transparent (Pullen & Lloyd, 2007).

Paige Pullen and J. W. Lloyd (2007) recommend the following guidelines for teaching phonics systematically:

- Teach the most common sound for a new letter beginning with letters and sounds that are used most frequently. Separate the introduction of letters and sounds that are auditorily or visually similar.

- Provide practice of reading text using words that contain sounds students have learned.

- Teach two-letter and consonant–vowel–consonant words that are easiest to decode. Continuous sounds (e.g., /m/, /a/ /n/) are easier to blend than stop sounds (e.g., /b/, /d/, /k/).

- Extend phonics instruction to letter combinations (e.g., *oo, ai, ar*), more complex patterns (e.g., vowel–consonant–"silent" e), and multiple syllable words.

- Extend instruction to more complex structures such as suffixes, prefixes, and so forth.

New letters should be introduced at a rate that facilitates mastery before new ones are taught, which might consist of one new letter every second or third day. The teacher should not introduce new letters until students can reliably produce the sounds of the letters already taught. When students make errors, correction procedures should include modeling the correct sound and prompting student responses until the sound is correct. The teacher then assesses student learning by prompting with the target letter followed by alternately prompting with other letters until students can accurately sound each letter each time it is presented (Carnine, Silbert, Kame'enui, & Tarver, 2010).

TEACHER TIP #10.2

BLENDING WHEELS

A blending wheel can be created to help students practice blending sounds to make words. The wheel consists of three concentric circles held together with a brass fastener. Letters are written around each circle such that when lined up horizontally they spell a word, some of which may be pseudowords. The circles are moved into various positions to create these words (e.g., *hat* can transform to *mat, sat, rat, hit, hip, hid,* and so forth). For beginning readers, use consonant–vowel–consonant combinations. As readers advance, consonant clusters (e.g., *br, spl, th*) can be used for the beginning and end of the words with vowel diagraphs (e.g., *ar, ou, ea*) in the middle. Even more advanced blending wheels can be used to create multisyllabic nonsense words (e.g., *pre+tash+er*). Both sides of the wheel can be used. After teaching students how to correctly manipulate the wheels to make words, students can engage in paired or individual practice activities as well as working in small groups. Multiple copies of the same wheel work best when used in groups. (Lane & Pullen, 2015)

Fluency

Fluency, an automatic processing skill, is the ability to read accurately, at an appropriate rate, and with expression (Kubina & Hughes, 2007). Fluent reading results from effortless recognition of familiar words coupled with proficient use of phonics to decode unfamiliar words. In addition to reading words quickly and accurately, fluent readers also understand and use expression to understand and enjoy what they read (NRP, 2000).

Ellis, the sixth-grade student introduced at the beginning of the chapter, stumbles on his words and stops to sound them out. He is not yet a fluent reader.

Reading fluency is highly associated with reading comprehension because fluent readers are able to place cognitive effort on the content rather than the decoding of the written word. Accuracy is essential for fluency, but rate is relative, depending on the type of text and the purpose for reading (Armbruster et al., 2001). Speed for recreational reading may be quite different than speed for studying text books or instructional manuals where vocabulary and information are comparatively new or complex. In the previous case study, Ellis is struggling with reading fluency because he stops to sound out too many words. This in turn impacts his reading comprehension.

Fluency is best measured by counting the number of words read correctly within a specified amount of time (e.g., 1 minute). A common method involves the test administrator directing the student to read orally while the tester marks errors on a second copy as the student reads. After 1 minute, the tester stops the student, marks the last word read, counts the number of words read correctly and incorrectly, and computes the number of words read correctly per minute for that reading level (Good, Kaminski, & Dill, 2002). This procedure can be used as often as teachers wish to measure and report student progress.

A teacher who implements effective fluency instruction does the following:

- **Provides models of fluent reading.** Students need to hear accurate, expressive, appropriately paced reading. Teachers who read aloud to their students can model fluent reading as well as build students' vocabulary.

- **Engages students in repeated readings.** Rereading to improve fluency requires that students have accurately read the passage at least once. If the readings are at the right level, students should be able to build their fluency with about four repeated readings.

- **Provides assisted reading.** Assisted reading can take the form of choral reading (i.e., groups or pairs reading orally together) or a form of reading buddies in which support and feedback are provided to one another.

- **Incorporates phrase-cued reading.** Students can be instructed to draw a slash mark at the end of each phrase and practice reading the text using these phrases.

- **Uses text at the appropriate level.** Students should be able to read with 90% to 95% accuracy and answer at least 75% of the comprehension questions accurately. Also, the length of the text should be short and should be of interest to the student.

- **Provides ongoing fluency lessons and practice.** Just like any other important skills, learning to read fluently requires plenty of opportunities to practice. (Lee & Yoon, 2015; Wilson, 2012)

After students have mastered enough phonics to read simple sentences combined into paragraphs, Mr. Dubinsky models oral reading fluently in small groups. This is followed by students orally reading the passage as a group along with Mr. Dubinsky multiple times. Then the students join into pairs and practice reading the same passage together. Mr. Dubinsky monitors the pairs and makes corrections as needed. Lastly, Mr. Dubinsky listens to each student read it independently and tracks how the number of words read correctly and incorrectly in 1 minute. Error correction or reteaching occurs if needed.

A common useful approach to improving reading fluency involves timed rereading. To implement this process, teachers must select a passage that (a) students have read at least once, so they are familiar with the words; and (b) is longer than they can read in 1 minute. Students are assigned to orally read the passage until the teacher stops them at the end of 1 minute and makes a mark after the last word read. This is repeated two more times with the same passage, marking the ending word each time. Students then count and record the number of words for each reading on a chart of vertical columns corresponding to the number of words read. This procedure provides both reading practice and an incentive for speed while giving students and teachers a visual running account of progress.

Researchers have determined grade level fluency indicators to use as guidelines. Work by Roland Good and Ruth Kaminski (2002) on Dynamic Indicators of Basic Early Literacy Skills (DIBELS) produced benchmark fluency levels for narrative text in first through third grades. End-of-year rates have been identified as 40 or more words per minute in first grade, 90 or more in second grade, and 110 or more in third grade. The DIBELS materials are an excellent resource. For further information about DIBELS, see Technology Spotlight #10.1 in this chapter.

Vocabulary Development

Vocabulary is defined as the words that make up a language. Understanding and being able to use vocabulary words both orally and in text is critical to students' academic success. Although most students learn the meaning of words indirectly, through everyday experiences with language, students with HID need vocabulary-rich environments, as well as a strong vocabulary-development program, particularly in the elementary grades (Carnine et al., 2010). Most beginning readers have a much larger speaking vocabulary than reading vocabulary (Armbruster et al., 2001), and early reading is enhanced when students recognize and read printed words that are conversationally familiar. Vocabulary is important to both fluency and comprehension. As students readily recognize more words, fluency increases; as understanding of word meaning grows, comprehension improves.

Vocabulary recognition can be measured by having students read from graded lists to see how many words they recognize. Word lists are available in a variety of commercially published reading inventories, such as *Classroom Reading Inventory* (Wheelock & Campbell, 2011) and *Analytical Reading Inventory* (Woods & Moe, 2015). Vocabulary comprehension can be reliably measured by using the maze method, wherein a reading passage has occasional words left out and students select from three choices to supply the correct missing word (Shin, Deno, & Espin, 2000).

Students learn vocabulary through incidental word learning and purposeful instruction. Incidental word learning occurs when students are exposed to words during independent reading, oral discussions, and books read aloud (Vadasy & Nelson, 2012). Students who struggle to read independently should particularly be given opportunities to hear advanced vocabulary through discussions and books read aloud. To constantly develop students' vocabulary, books they listen to read should be written on a vocabulary level two grades ahead of the students' listening comprehension (Layne, 2015). For example, if a fourth-grade student with HID reads on a second-grade level but has the listening comprehension of a typical fourth grader, the reading level of read-aloud books should be at the sixth grade assuming the content is appropriate for fourth graders.

Purposeful instruction to teach vocabulary involves teacher-directed instruction, mnemonic devices, and graphic depictions. Students with HID should be given multiple exposures to words in various contexts to promote deeper understanding (Bryant, Goodwin, Bryant, & Higgins, 2003). Explicit instruction helps build vocabulary in two important ways. First, students master the reading and spelling of a continually growing vocabulary, and second, they learn to use word structure strategies to become proficient decoders.

The more words students can instantly recognize, the more fluent will be their reading. Likewise, the more words students understand, the stronger their reading comprehension. **General vocabulary** includes commonly used words for everyday speaking, reading, and writing. **Content-specific vocabulary** refers to words for discussing, reading, or writing specific expository information. The purpose of vocabulary instruction is to help students learn new general and content-specific vocabulary, and to understand what the words mean and how they are used. Continuous vocabulary enrichment is essential for building reading capacity in the elementary years.

Teachers who strengthen their students' vocabulary engage in the following:

- **Provide vocabulary-rich classrooms** by using slightly higher vocabulary (and providing synonyms or definitions) in naturally occurring conversations, reading aloud to the students, visually displaying vocabulary words, and so forth.

- **Teach vocabulary through explicit instruction.** Students who do not read well or often, or who have difficulty with new learning, benefit greatly from direct instruction for new vocabulary. Such instruction is effective when teachers carefully model word meaning and usage and provide students with multiple exposures to new words over time.

- **Use synonyms and definitions** to teach and clarify the meaning of words student encounter. Provide definitions when appropriate.

- **Teach the identification and use of morphological patterns** (e.g., base words, suffixes, prefixes) to help determine meaning.

- **Teach strategies for acquiring new vocabulary** such as semantic mapping and keyword mnemonics (see Chapter 9).

- **Teach students to infer the meaning** of an unknown word from the surrounding language (e.g., In the sentence, "A deadly *plague* caused thousands of people to sicken and die," the reader can use the context clues *thousands*, *sicken*, and *die* to connote that a plague is a deadly contagious illness that affects many people.). (Bryant et al., 2003; Carnine et al., 2010; Troia, 2014)

TEACHER TIP #10.3

WORD OF THE DAY STRATEGY

The following strategy can be used after explicitly teaching a set of vocabulary words and their definitions:

- Select one of the vocabulary words to be word of the day.

- Instruct students to listen for the word of the day to be spoken and to tally a mark each time the word is heard next to the word which they will write on their paper.

- Have students write the word and a box around the word representing the word's configuration or shape.

- Begin using the word, preferably 15 to 20 times.

- Teach students to prompt usage of the word (e.g., by framing questions requiring the word to be spoken).

- Ask students to add their tallies at the end of the day.

- If students are slower at recognizing that the word has just been spoken, do not penalize them for marking tallies just because they see other students doing so. (Vesely & Gryder, 2009)

Text Comprehension

All of the reading skills discussed so far contribute to the purpose of reading, which is to understand and use the information read. Yet phonological awareness, reading fluency, and scope of vocabulary are not sufficient to produce comprehension. Text comprehension involves the integration of decoding, vocabulary knowledge, prior knowledge, and strategies to understand the text (Brigham, Berkeley, Simpkins, & Brigham, 2007). Maintaining interest and motivation also play a role in comprehension. The National Reading Panel (2000) report emphasizes *text* comprehension to differentiate between it and other means of deriving meaning, such as illustrations, pictures, and diagrams. Although visual text enhancements certainly add interest and understanding to reading, they can also confound assessment of whether or not students actually comprehend the written word. Materials used for reading assessment and instruction must be designed to ensure students can gain information only through reading.

Reading comprehension tasks vary according to the type of text and the purpose for reading. The purpose of narrative text is to tell a story, whether real or imaginary, with characters, a plot, and setting. Narrative text has traditionally been considered easier to comprehend because most students enjoy stories and can readily follow sequential events. Expository text conveys information in forms other than narrative.

Textbooks are the most common form of expository text in schools, although students also obtain information from encyclopedias, almanacs, news sources, and topical nonfiction books on a wide range of subjects.

Narrative text comprehension can be reliably measured by having students read passages orally or silently and then answer a variety of comprehension questions. There are four basic types of passage comprehension. **Literal comprehension** means understanding what the author said. **Inferential comprehension** means inferring what the author meant, but did not directly state. **Critical comprehension** means critiquing the author's writing to determine if it is fact or opinion, fiction or nonfiction, possible or not possible. **Creative comprehension** means creatively extending the author's message, either by putting oneself in the story or by predicting what might happen beyond the story's conclusion. An example of reading comprehension questions is provided in Table 10.4.

Expository text differs from narrative text in that it is designed to educate readers with factual information. Expository text is considered more difficult for students to read for several reasons: (a) the material is typically not as sequential or predictable as narrative, (b) the text structures can be complicated and unfamiliar, (c) the purpose is to locate and synthesize information to understand the topic or to answer questions, and (d) readers are expected to read to learn rather than read for enjoyment (Bakken & Whedon, 2002). Assessment for expository comprehension usually involves recalling or summarizing information (literal comprehension) and using information to make predictions or solve problems (inferential comprehension). Expository text can be complex because it usually contains new vocabulary, new declarative information, and new concepts that affect comprehension. Elementary school reading tends to involve more narrative than expository text until students reach middle and high school, when reading from expository textbooks becomes more frequent.

Students may comprehend one type of text and not another. Students who do well with narrative texts may have difficulty locating information in textbooks or synthesizing facts from several sources to write about something like the life cycle of a butterfly or the events leading up to the fall of the Alamo. Teachers need to be cognizant of the different type of comprehension demands on understanding narrative and expository texts. Designing and administering tasks for students to perform using each type of text can provide teachers with information on the students' strengths and needs from which instruction can be designed and implemented.

TABLE 10.4 **Examples of Types of Comprehension Questions**

Reading Comprehension Questions for *The Scarlet Letter* by Nathanial Hawthorne

- Literal: "What letter was Hester required to display on her gowns?"
- Inferential: "What was the townspeople's attitude toward adultery?"
- Critical: "Would people actually put someone in jail for having a child out of wedlock?" "Why or why not?"
- Creative: (Self) "What would you have done if Hester was your best friend?"
- Creative: (Prediction) "What do you think Hester would tell her daughter about this incident when Pearl becomes a teenager?"

Mr. Bradford had several students with HID in his 11th-grade American history class. A number of students in his class struggled to understand the textbook. Mr. Bradford created guided notes to help all students in his class identify important information in each chapter. Whenever possible, he also included graphic organizers in the guided notes packets. Mr. Bradford provided explicit, but brief instruction on how to use these tools. A few of his students still didn't grasp how to use the tools, so he paired them with students who did understand and they worked through the guided notes together until all students understood and could use them independently.

Good readers know the purpose for their reading and they actively process what they read (NRP, 2000). Active mental processing is best facilitated by strategies or conscious plans that readers use to make sense of the material (Armbruster et al., 2001). Research studies have documented that reading fluency and vocabulary training contribute to comprehension, yet they are not sufficient to adequately develop comprehension skills. Comprehension can improve if educators teach effective strategies, carefully design instruction, provide guidance and feedback, and monitor student progress.

Comprehension instruction can take several forms including a (a) fundamental reading skills approach, (b) text enhancements approach, and (c) self-questioning approach (Berkeley, Scruggs, & Mastropieri, 2010). Explicit or teacher-directed instruction may be used to teach all forms. For example, teachers can present new vocabulary words with meanings as a fundamental reading skill through explicit instruction. Similarly, students can be taught to use or create text enhancement techniques such as bolding, highlighting, mnemonic techniques, study guides, concept maps, and so forth through teacher-directed instruction. These text enhancements help students separate the essential from the nonessential in text, as well as guide them to locate, analyze, and synthesize information relevant to the reading purpose. However, students with HID are unlikely to transfer the use of text enhancement devices to other settings or purposes unless they are specifically taught to do so and receive sufficient practice opportunities to internalize the procedures. More information on these techniques may be found in Chapter 9.

Teachers can also use explicit instruction to teach self-questioning strategies. As discussed in Chapter 1, most students with HID have difficulty creating or applying effective cognitive strategies to help facilitate their learning. The absence of strategy use leads to poor reading comprehension for many students.

Researchers who have analyzed studies for the last few decades have reached conclusions about best approaches to reading comprehension instruction for students with learning disabilities, in particular. For example, Margo Mastropieri and Thomas Scruggs (1997) discovered that the strongest outcomes occurred with teacher-led questioning and self-questioning, followed by text enhancement, and basic skills instruction. Sheri Berkeley, Scruggs, and Mastropieri (2010) replicated the previous review with research published since the previous review and concluded that teaching any or all three techniques can result in improved student reading comprehension. The common attribute across the studies they examined were that the instruction taught students to improve their attention and to think more carefully and systematically about the text they were reading. Another set of researchers analyzed studies examining the impact of reading comprehension instruction on middle school students with learning disabilities. They concluded that all three approaches were also helpful, particularly the use of summarization or main idea strategy instruction, mnemonics, mapping, and questioning, as well as explicit instruction (Solis et al., 2012).

In order for text comprehension instruction to be successful, students must have the necessary reading prerequisite skills. Based on research, teachers who implement the following help students improve their reading comprehension:

- **Teach strategies using explicit and systematic instruction** with adequate modeling, guided and independent practice, and feedback (see Chapter 6). Provide explanations of the purpose of the strategy and how students can attribute success or failure to use of the strategy.

- **Teach summarization and main idea strategies** for both expository and narrative readings. Strategies for expository readings (e.g., textbooks) should be embedded within the content being read (see Chapter 12).

- **Use appropriate teacher-led comprehension strategies** by asking students varying types of questions both before and after reading. Asking questions before they read helps guide their attention to the content they are reading.

- **Teach self-questioning strategies,** with **self-monitoring** where appropriate. For example, teach acronyms that represent steps students need to independently undertake to ask themselves questions about what they have read.

- **Use materials that include enhancements** to facilitate reading recall (e.g., highlighting, bolding). (Berkeley et al., 2010; Solis et al., 2012)

Teachers who use these guidelines can locate or develop strategies to help their struggling readers. An example of a teacher-directed comprehension lesson is provided in Appendix C. Improved reading comprehension will help students have greater access to the general curriculum and prepare them for successful independent lives.

TEACHER TIP #10.4

THE MAIN IDEA STRATEGY

The main idea strategy was developed to help students identify inferential main ideas (in contrast to literal main ideas). Steps to teach this strategy include (a) pretest and gain students, commitment to learn the strategy, (b) introduce prerequisite knowledge and the skills, (c) teach the strategy by modeling the steps and verbally practicing the steps of the strategy, (d) teach paraphrasing in the same way, (e) provide guided practice opportunities using reading passages at students' readability level, (f) provide independent practice opportunities using students' grade-level texts, and (g) posttest and facilitate generalization to other readings and settings. The steps of the strategy are the following:

- **M**ake the topic known—Identify a word or short phrase that represents the topic.

- **A**ccent at least two essential details—These are details that relate directly to the topic.

- **I**nk out the nonessential clarifying details—Draw a line through details that are helpful but not essential.

- **N**otice how the essential details are related—Identify how the sentences go together and what the author is saying "between the lines."

- **I**nfer the main idea—Put the main idea in your own words. (Boudah, 2013)

Technology Spotlight #10.1

Tools for Teaching and Assessing Reading

Many students with HID experience considerable difficulty learning to read and write. As a result, a wide variety of assistive technology interventions have been developed to support instruction and facilitate performance. In this spotlight, several common assistive technology tools for reading are highlighted.

A student's oral reading fluency has been found to be a reliable predictor of reading achievement. An innovative tool for collecting, analyzing, and monitoring students' oral reading fluency is known as the Reading Assistant (readingassistant.com). Students start by previewing and reading a passage silently and answering guided questions. Then the Assistant reads the passage while the student follows along. The student then orally reads the passage with the Reading Assistant intervening when the student struggles with a word. The Assistant reads the correct word; the student rereads that word and continues.

At the end, a quiz is administered and Reading Assistant creates a report for the student's teacher.

A number of products are useful instructional interventions. Start to Finish Books (donjohnston.com) are leveled reading books that come in print, audio, and computer based in order to provide students with supports for their reading. Simon Sounds It Out (donjohnston. com) is an engaging reading instruction program that features branching and data collection. This program focuses on reading and spelling phonetically and matching words to pictures for comprehension. Comprehensive products like Kurzweil 3000-firefly (www.kurzweiledu.com), WYNN and PAL (Promoting Academic Learner) (www.freedomscientific.com) allow a printed text to be read to the student and supply additional tools to facilitate comprehension (e.g., highlighting, talking dictionary, note cards). Many apps have been developed for developing

(Continued)

(Continued)

reading skills, particularly phonemic awareness and phonics. Tips for selecting apps may be found in Chapter 4.

Regardless of the type of instructional intervention used, procedures should be in place for monitoring reading progress. One research-based tool that has been developed for this purpose is known as The Dynamic Indicators of Basic Early Literacy Skills (DIBELS) (dibels.uoregon. edu). DIBELS are short (1 minute) fluency measures for regularly monitoring of prereading and early reading (K–3) reading skill development (available free by downloading).

Writing Instruction

Lifelong success in formal education and most careers in educated societies relies on written expression skills. Students use writing to demonstrate, support, and deepen their content knowledge. Strong writing skills aid students' performance on high-stakes tests in writing and other domains. Writing also acts as a gateway for employment and as a means to communicate socially. Despite the importance of writing for lifelong success, approximately 75% of all students are judged to be below grade-level expectations in written expression (Troia, 2014).

Based on a review of 20 research syntheses on writing instruction, the following elements were identified as essential components of effective writing instruction:

- Writing must be an essential part of school curriculum. In addition, providing supportive environments for writing is critical to student success (e.g., use of personally relevant and authentic writing tasks, providing successful writing experiences).

- Students need to be explicitly taught writing skills. They should be given ample opportunities to practice writing across the curriculum which can enhance their content knowledge (e.g., history, science). Writing instruction should also promote independent and reflective writings.

- Writing instruction should focus on the (a) process of writing (e.g., planning, drafting, revising), (b) text or product (e.g., considering audience, using creativity), and (c) elements of writing (e.g., handwriting, typing, grammar).

- Writing instruction should take advantage of technology as tools to remove barriers as well as to facilitate the writing process.

- Writing assessment should use explicit criteria (e.g., rubrics) and provide quality feedback (Troia, 2014).

Five skills necessary for successful written expression include handwriting, spelling, grammar, text structure, and composition and are discussed below.

Handwriting

Mrs. Bracken uses teacher-directed instruction to teach her students beginning handwriting skills. Prior to teaching letter formation, she taught her students to draw straight, diagonal, and curved lines. When she started teaching letters, she taught one letter at a time. She started with the letter *a,* and then taught *c, d, g, q, s* because the starting point for each of these letters is the same. Mrs. Bracken was careful to provide accurate models for her students. After she modeled the new letter, Mrs. Bracken provided guidance and feedback as her students learned to write the new letter. When her students demonstrated that they could accurately form the new letter, she allowed her students to independently practice.

Handwriting, or penmanship, is the basic tool skill people use to record their thoughts on paper. School work requires much handwriting; and even in this age of rapidly advancing computer and text messaging technology, many facets of adult life necessitate writing. Handwriting may constrain the development of beginning writers in several ways. First, poor legibility limits accessibility of the students' thoughts to others. Second, illegibility can influence the evaluation of content. Third, when concentrating on formation of letters, thoughts are focused on the handwriting, not the content of the composition. And fourth, difficulty with handwriting minimizes the use of effective writing processes, such as revising (Graham et al., 2008). Students who master handwriting have distinct advantages over those who struggle because they can focus on composition rather than letter formation; and they are more likely to successfully copy information and take notes (Mercer & Pullen, 2008). For most students, handwriting skills improve until about sixth grade. But some students have great difficulties learning to write at all (Berninger, Abbott, Abbott, Graham, & Richards, 2002).

The goals of handwriting instruction are simply legibility and fluency. Students need to learn to write so others can read what they've written, and they need to write as smoothly and accurately as possible. But instruction for handwriting is not simple. Good handwriting requires correct paper placement on the writing surface, appropriate pencil grip, and adept eye–hand coordination. In addition, the writer must remember not only the shape and formation of the letters, but also the motor movements that produce them. Learning this rather complicated task requires patient, explicit instruction in letter and word formation, with much guided and independent practice.

Manuscript and cursive letters are comprised of various combinations of vertical, horizontal, slanted, and curved lines in combination with loops, dots, arcs, and circles. Teachers are responsible for helping students learn the correct formation of letter parts as prescribed by the manuscript or cursive style used in the particular school or district. Letter formation should be taught one letter at a time so that students can master formation, size, alignment, spacing, slant, and rate of production. Student progress with each of these elements can be assessed by obtaining frequent student writing samples and comparing them to the models in the particular writing style method book used for instruction.

Handwriting instruction lends itself well to explicit, sequential instruction. Steve Graham, Karen Harris and Barbara Fink (2000) found that of nine instructional variables considered as possible predictors of handwriting success, the following were the most powerful predictors of success: teacher modeling, high rates of student responding, and a variety of practice activities. These elements align directly with the teacher-directed instruction format addressed in Chapter 6.

The most common methods for teaching letter formations is the Zaner-Bloser approach (www.zaner-bloser.com/zaner-bloser-handwriting) and the D'Nealian handwriting program (dnealian.com) (Graham et al., 2008). With Zaner-Bloser, students are taught a manuscript alphabet that approximates fonts most widely used in printed text which helps promote literacy development. The program also includes instruction for cursive writing. An e-Toolkit lesson builder is available that can be used to integrate handwriting into content-area lessons. These tools can be used for short, custom handwriting skill-development and include resources such as animated letter models and games. The D'Nealian handwriting program uses manuscript letters that prepare students for transitioning to cursive writing. In fact, 87% of D'Nealian lower case letters are the same as their cursive version.

Even though many more students have access to computers than even a few years ago, handwriting continues to be an important part of the elementary curriculum, and should be taught to mastery. Whatever method is used to teach handwriting, consistent teacher modeling followed by many opportunities for student practice with feedback is essential. Correct practice helps students learn letter formations and gain fluency in the motor movements required for fluent and legible handwriting. Given the availability and use of word processing as a means for written expression, in addition to handwriting, students need to learn keyboarding skills. Computer keyboarding skills can be taught to very young children, although it is recommended that keyboarding instruction begin in third or fourth grade (Donne, 2012).

Research documents that the following instructional strategies help students learn handwriting skills:

- **Introduce letters in a logical order**, not in order of the alphabet. Introduce confusable letters (e.g., *b* and *d*) and sounds (e.g., sound /a/ as in *mat* and sound /e/ as in *bed*) separately.

- **Teach the mechanics** of proper grip, posture, and paper position.

- In guided practice, have students **trace and copy letters**. Also **use numbered arrows** to guide the order and direction for letter formation.

- Once students can form letters, **build fluency through speed drills**.

- **Monitor students** while writing to **provide corrections** about letter formation, spacing, slant, alignment, and line quality.

- Teach students to **self-identify their best handwriting**. Require that they **set goals** for improving specific aspects of their handwriting.

- **Instruct handwriting separately as well as integrated** with other content (e.g., writing a science or social studies report).

- **Provide different types of paper and writing tools** to increase generalizability.

- **Begin handwriting instruction early** (i.e., kindergarten) before bad habits develop. (Hart, Fitzpatrick, & Cortesa, 2010)

Spelling

Written language includes accepted orthographic, or spelling, conventions that must be mastered for students to become successful writers. While students with disabilities may spend cognitive effort on how to spell (Puranik & Al Otaiba, 2012), skilled writers rarely think about spelling (Graham & Harris, 2016). Thus, spelling doesn't detract from skilled writers' cognitive effort that could be used for composition. As with reading instruction, spelling instruction begins with phonemic awareness. In addition, students need to know the names of the letters and to recognize that the letters have direct associations to sounds (i.e., the alphabetic principle). This knowledge leads to phonological awareness and recognition that phonemes can be related to graphemes (i.e., letters and letter combinations that represent a phoneme) (Williams, Walker, Vaughn, & Wanzek, 2016).

In English, there exist hundreds of ways to write about 43 different sounds (e.g., the variation in spellings for the sound /f/ in the words *for, taffy, phantom,* and *rough*). English spelling is not always phonetically predictable (e.g., phonetically the word *was* should be written *wuz;* the word *of* should be written *uv,* and the word *thorough* presents several sound-spelling problems). The great disparity between the number of phonemes, or sounds, in the English language and the number of graphemes, or letter combinations used to represent those sounds, can make spelling a difficult task.

A teacher-guided spelling lesson should include the essential elements of explicit instruction, especially for students who have difficulty mastering the words. These elements include careful and explicit oral and visual teacher modeling, prompting for oral student responses followed by written responses, proofing with a written model for accuracy, and then oral and written rehearsal until mastery is attained. Teaching letter sound writing and oral word segmentation, as well as implementing the commercial materials, Spelling Mastery (see Table 10.2), have been documented as effective interventions for students with disabilities (Williams et al., 2016).

The cover, copy, and compare (CCC) strategy and the model, cover, copy, and compare (MCCC) strategy have also been shown to effectively teach students with HID to spell. The CCC and MCCC strategies use the principles of self-management (see Chapter 13). Using the second strategy, students (a) view and copy the word, (b) view and study the correct spelling of a word, (c) cover the word and write it from memory, and (d) check to see if the word was written correctly. The CCC strategy simply eliminates the first step, copying the word from a model. Research has shown these strategies to be effective for students with and without disabilities not only for spelling, but for other academic content such as math facts (Joseph et al., 2012).

The following instructional elements and approaches yield the greatest improvements in spelling for students with disabilities:

- **Select spelling words based on student's instructional level,** which for students with HID is often lower than their current enrolled grade level. Providing words too difficult can lead to frustration and words too easy will not challenge the student.

- **Teach using explicit spelling instruction** (see Chapter 6). Relegating spelling instruction to homework or independent work is insufficient.

- **Include rule- and morpheme-based instruction.** Morphemes are the smallest units of speech that have meaning (e.g., *re* means again, *s* means more than one, *ed* means past tense). Teachers should systematically teach only a few rules at a time.

- **Teach learning strategies** to help students practice, such as the copy-cover-compare procedure.

- **Schedule ample practice opportunities that are distributed.** Students will more likely recall and retain information when sufficient practice opportunities are provided; and distributed practice is more effective than massed or one-time practice.

- **Teach students to identify and correct their errors** in spelling using strategies, spelling checkers, and other means. Give hints on how to spell a word instead of spelling it for students.

- **Provide immediate feedback** on spelling accuracy. In particular, use error correction procedures, including practicing the words correctly, when words are misspelled. Using peer tutors allows students more opportunities to practice and to receive immediate feedback (see Chapter 8). (Graham & Harris, 2016; Sayeski, 2011; Troia, 2014; Wanzek et al., 2006)

TEACHER TIP #10.5

SPELLER STRATEGY

In inclusive classrooms, teachers can use peer tutoring (see Chapter 8) and the SPELLER strategy to help students with HID improve spelling skills. The steps of SPELLER include the following:

- **S**pot the word and say it.
- **P**icture the word with eyes open.
- **E**yes closed, visualize the word.
- Open eyes and **L**ook to see if right.
- **L**ook away and write the word on the SPELLER sheet.

- **E**xamine it and check against the flash card.
- **R**epeat or Reward.

After teaching the SPELLER strategy, assign and train students to work in pairs where one student is the tutor and the other is the tutee for 10 minutes. Then students switch roles for another 10 minutes. Each dyad is given SPELLER practice sheets, a SPELLER cue card, colored pencils, flash cards with the spelling words, and a timer. The tutor shows the tutee the first spelling word and prompts the tutee to complete each step of the SPELLER strategy for the word. When complete, the tutor checks the tutee's work for accuracy. Students work on words for 10 minutes and then switch roles. Be certain to monitor the students as they work. (Keller, 2002)

Grammar and Text Structure

Grammar instruction helps students learn the proper use of word order (**syntax**) and vocabulary (**semantics**) to create understandable sentences. Accomplishing this link between structure and meaning has moved the field of writing instruction away from the decontextualized memorization of grammar rules and parts of speech toward emphasis on the function of grammar for composition (Sams, 2003). Researchers have discovered that isolated memorization of grammar rules does not positively impact composition skills (Gregg & Hafer, 2001; Weaver, McNally, & Moerman, 2001). Inasmuch as the basic unit of written language is the sentence, sentence and paragraph writing are now the structures through which grammar is taught and learned. Educators should teach grammar as a part of learning to express oneself in writing which is an authentic approach teachers advocate today (Troia, 2014).

Prose writing begins by creating meaningful sentences to express ideas (Sams, 2003). Writing instruction commences with sentence construction and sentence writing can be task analyzed and taught just like any other academic skill. Through explicit teacher modeling, prompting, and practice with feedback, students can be taught to first recognize and then write basic statement, question, exclamation, and command/request sentences. First-word capitalization and end punctuation should be taught as part of sentence structure instruction. After students have learned to recognize and write basic sentences proficiently, teachers can model how to combine two sentences into a complex sentence followed by students practicing this skill. Writing instruction must be accompanied by immediate authentic writing practice so students are not struggling to grasp grammar concepts or sentence structure in isolation (Graham & Harris, 2016). Several research-based strategies for writing instruction are detailed in the literature today. For example, the PLEASE mnemonic acronym strategy can be helpful to students as they learn to compose paragraphs (Welch & Jensen, 1991) (see Table 10.5).

Skilled writers also understand and apply strategies for different types of text they write (Graham & Harris, 2016). As introduced earlier in the chapter, the two general classifications of text commonly used for English are narration and exposition. Narrative writing is (a) story telling through prose or poetry; (b) usually fictional; and (c) organized around a story sequence with a recognizable beginning, middle, and end (Bakken & Whedon, 2002). Narrative text is familiar to young students because most elementary basal readers and children's literature books are in story or poetry format. Expository text conveys factual information. The most common exposition assignments in school today are essays and research papers (Gersten & Baker, 2001).

Learning to write narrative and expository text requires students to understand the various text structures for different genre. Text structure refers to formats that are used to accomplish specific purposes. Narrative text includes structures like character description, setting, plot, events, feelings, and conclusion. Expository text structures include main idea (focus on a single topic), list (succession of descriptors about a topic), sequence (steps or events in order), comparison (describing similarities and differences),

TABLE 10.5   Mnemonic Acronym Strategies for Writing

Type of Writing	Acronym	Strategy
Planning Writing (Troia & Graham, 2002)	**STOP & LIST**	**S**top **T**hink **O**f **P**urpose **L**ist **I**deas **S**equence **T**hem
Writing Process (Englert, Raphael, Anderson, Anthony, & Stevens, 1991)	**POWER**	**P**lan **O**rganize **W**rite **E**dit **R**ewrite/**R**evise
Paragraph Writing (Welch & Jensen, 1991)	**PLEASE**	**P**ick a topic **L**ist ideas **E**valuate ideas **A**ctivate ideas **S**upply supporting ideas **E**nd with closing sentence/**E**valuate
Persuasive Writing (Mason, Kubina, Valasa, & Cramer, 2010)	**TREE**	**T**opic sentence **R**easons—three or more **E**xplanations to support reasons **E**nding/Summary
Opinion Essay Writing (De La Paz & Graham, 1997)	**DARE**	**D**evelop position statement **A**dd supporting arguments **R**eport and refute counter arguments **E**nd with strong conclusion
Narrative Writing (Troia & Graham, 2002)	**SPACE**	**S**etting **P**roblems **A**ction **C**onsequences **E**motions
Revising Writing (Sherman & De La Paz, 2015)	**FIX**	**F**ocus on essay elements **I**dentify problems e**X**ecute changes

contrast (describing differences), and classification (arranging into categories) (Bakken & Whedon, 2002). These structures can be used to inform, persuade, or express opinions in single or multiple paragraph compositions.

Students need to learn to recognize and write both narrative and expository compositions. Inasmuch as early reading and writing have traditionally been narrative, researchers and practitioners recommend moving young students to a more balanced curriculum of narrative and expository text for both reading and writing. The concern is that exclusively reading and writing fiction fails to prepare students for the more sophisticated tasks of expository writing. Essays, in particular, require students to analyze information, synthesize their thoughts, and then compose statements about social and political issues of the past and present (Gersten & Baker, 2001). Such complex thinking and writing requires careful instruction and practice to learn and develop.

The following elements are important components for effectively teaching grammar and text structure:

- **Provide authentic opportunities for students to learn to use grammar knowledge**. That is, teach grammar in the context of actual writing, rather than memorizing grammar rules.

- **Teach sentence and paragraph construction** that are grammatically correct and convey intended meaning.

- **Start writing instruction with simple sentences**, then move to more complex sentences followed by multiple sentences to create paragraphs.

- **Teach students to identify and correct their grammar errors** using strategies, grammar checkers, and other means.

- **Teach mnemonic acronym strategies** for writing paragraphs (e.g., PLEASE) and different types of text structures (e.g., TREE, DARE, SPACE) (see Table 10.5). (Graham & Harris, 2016; Welch & Jensen, 1991)

Composition

Composition requires authors to synthesize the elements of writing. Of the elements described earlier, handwriting (or keyboarding) and spelling are typically called *transcription* skills, meaning the tool skills used to transcribe, or put words on paper in accurate and readable ways (Maki, Vauras, & Vainio, 2002). Sentence grammar and text structure are *frameworks* for composition that guide purposeful expression. Using knowledgeable transcription within an appropriate compositional framework makes good writing possible. In other words, skillful use of processes results in a desired product. This *process–product* conceptualization of writing is characterized by sequential steps or stages that lead authors to accomplish their writing goals. These stages of writing can be generally labeled *prewriting*, or the planning stage; *writing*, or the composition stage; and *postwriting*, or the feedback and editing stage. The stages do not represent a linear model so much as a recursive one, in which the stages are revisited as needed to refine the work (Wong, 2000). A description of each stage follows.

Prewriting

The prewriting stage includes the preparatory activities that effective writers go through before they begin composition. The most important author behaviors at this stage are setting the writing goal or purpose, generating ideas, and organizing ideas for the intended audience and type of writing (Troia & Graham, 2002). Goal-setting seems to be important both for understanding the purpose of the writing and for motivation. Setting the purpose not only guides the process, but also serves as a checkpoint for students and teachers as they evaluate the accomplishment of the task. Anytime a teacher can help students see that they did what they set out to do, effort and sense of self-efficacy is reinforced (Gersten & Baker, 2001).

When the purpose is understood, authors must then generate ideas about the topic. Teachers can guide this process first by modeling their thoughts out loud and then through thought-provoking question and answer or through brainstorming, during which ideas are listed by individual students or by a group of students for everyone to see (Troia & Graham, 2002; Wong, 2000). Idea generation should be accompanied by discussion so students can clarify their thoughts through listening to the ideas of the teacher and other students. Gary Troia and Steve Graham reported that teacher feedback on the appropriateness of ideas for the writing task led to better student work than open brainstorming with no feedback.

The final phase of prewriting is to organize ideas to accomplish the purpose of the composition. This requires that students are familiar with the genre and have learned the salient characteristics of a finished piece so their planning matches the writing purpose. Mnemonic acronym strategies have been documented as useful tools to help students with the writing process. A sample of these strategies found in the research literature may be found in Table 10.5.

Writing

Composition is the process of putting thoughts into sentences and paragraphs to accomplish an expressive purpose. Writing is a complicated cognitive process that requires deciding what to say and how to say it, as well as fluent motor and text production skills, (i.e., handwriting or keyboarding, spelling, grammar, capitalization, and punctuation). Simultaneous use of composition and transcription skills is the hallmark of effective writers. Writing problems, like reading problems, emerge early in a student's career and usually continue through the school years. Fortunately, ample research evidence indicates that good instruction and carefully monitored practice can build and sustain writing capacity in students both with and without disabilities (Graham & Harris, 2016; Matsumura, Patthey-Chavez, Valdés, & Garnier, 2002).

Student writers typically launch into composition without forethought or planning. They use a random think and write process wherein one thought leads more or less to another, usually ending in unsatisfactory results (Graham, Harris, & Larsen, 2001). Learning to plan and then to use frameworks for composition are necessary to overcome this tendency. Students must also learn that writing is a process, not an event, and that all authors revisit drafting and revising as often as necessary to achieve the desired result. All of this is best accomplished by using a curriculum of explicit instruction in skills and processes balanced with opportunities for student choice and free thought in expression (Strickland et al., 2001).

Explicit composition instruction should begin with teacher modeling, including *thinking aloud* to make inaudible thinking processes audible, and using charts or diagrams to make invisible thinking visible. Generally, the teacher should first model alone, and then model while prompting for student responses to make certain they can follow the process. Repetition at this and other stages is essential, especially for students with learning difficulties who often need many more trials to achieve mastery than normally achieving students. The teacher should also prompt students to write independently while carefully monitoring for confusion, guiding where necessary, and reinforcing student success.

Postwriting

During postwriting, teachers or other authors provide feedback to guide student revision of drafts. Students learn much when they receive teacher feedback and use it to revise the content or structure of their work (Matsumura et al., 2002). Feedback may also be provided by peers who are trained in this skill. Postwriting activities teach students that any writing is a work in progress, and that improvement is gained through input from knowledgeable others. Interestingly, elementary teachers tend to provide feedback regarding the mechanical or stylistic aspects of student writing, such as spelling, punctuation, or grammar, almost to the exclusion of feedback regarding content, the flow of ideas, or the logical progression of the work, although the latter are more meaningful to excellent writing (Matsumura et al., 2002). Whether feedback is provided by the teacher, by peers, or both, students must learn to use the information to improve their work.

The following instructional elements and approaches should be included when teaching students the writing process:

- **Teach students that writing is a process** by explicitly instructing them to plan, draft, revise, edit, and share their work through the prewriting, writing, and postwriting stages.

- **Use mnemonics structures** to help students complete the writing process (e.g., STOP & LIST, POWER, FIX) (see Table 10.5).

- **Structure instruction so that students can receive feedback** from both the teacher and peers (as appropriate).

- **Provide dedicated and sufficient time to writing** and writing instruction including embedding writing across the curriculum.

- **Encourage students to be self-regulatory**, doing as much writing as they can on their own.

- **Provide a positive writing environment** that is supportive, motivating, encouraging to students. (Graham, Harris & Chambers, 2015; Sherman & De La Paz, 2015)

TEACHER TIP #10.6

SELF-REGULATED STRATEGY DEVELOPMENT (SRSD)

The Self-Regulated Strategy Development (SRSD) model provides a framework for teachers to explicitly teach planning, drafting, and revising strategies. The model also focuses on building students' attributions for effort. The SRSD instructional stages include the following:

Stage 1—Develop background information. Teachers need to ensure students have the prerequisite knowledge and skills and to teach them if they don't.

Stage 2—Discuss it. During this stage, teachers discuss students' current writing performance and understanding of the writing process. This information provides a foundation for discussing the purpose and potential benefits of learning the strategy.

Stage 3—Model it. Teachers model how to use the strategy using the think-aloud process.

Stage 4—Memorize it. Students need to know the steps to use them automatically, so they memorize them. Prompts can be provided for students who have difficulty memorizing the steps.

Stage 5—Support it. During this stage, students practice the strategy with scaffolded support from the instructor. The practice may occur in pairs or small groups.

Stage 6—Independent performance. The ultimate goal is for students to be proficient in the use of the strategy over time, in multiple settings, and with a variety of tasks and content. (Santangelo, Harris, & Graham, 2008)

Reading/Writing Language Arts Standards

The most universally adopted set of language arts standards are the Common Core State Standards which include foundational skills for reading, literature reading, informational text reading, writing, speaking, listening, language, and literacy in history/social studies, science, and technical subjects. The development of these standards was led by the U.S. governors and education commissioners through the National Governors Association (NGA) Center for Best Practices and the Council of Chief State School Officers (CCSSO). Educators and parents from across the country also provided input into the development of the standards. Implementation of the standards (e.g., how the standards are taught, curriculum and materials used) is determined entirely at the state and local levels (NGA & CCSSO, 2010). A small sample of these standards for both reading and writing are listed in Table 10.6.

Given that students with disabilities need access to the general curriculum, knowledge of general education standards has become important for special educators to understand and apply in their teaching. When developing Individualized Education Plans (IEPs), teachers need to consider standards, whether they be the Common Core or other state- or district-adopted standards, as the IEP team develops goals and the

TABLE 10.6   Sample Common Core Standards for Reading and Writing

Foundational Reading Standards	Reading Literature Standards	Writing Standards
Kindergarten	**Grade 3**	**Grade 8**
Print Concepts	**Key Ideas and Details**	**Text Types and Purposes**
• Demonstrate understanding of the organization and basic features of print.	• Ask and answer questions to demonstrate understanding of a text, referring explicitly to the text as the basis for the answers.	• Write arguments to support claims with clear reasons and relevant evidence.
• Follow words from left to right, top to bottom, and page by page.	• Recount stories, including fables, folktales, and myths from diverse cultures; determine the central message, lesson, or moral and explain how it is conveyed through key details in the text.	• Write informative/explanatory texts to examine a topic and convey ideas, concepts, and information through the selection, organization, and analysis of relevant content.
• Recognize that spoken words are represented in written language by specific sequences of letters.		
• Understand that words are separated by spaces in print.	• Describe characters in a story (e.g., their traits, motivations, or feelings) and explain how their actions contribute to the sequence of events.	• Write narratives to develop real or imagined experiences or events using effective technique, relevant descriptive details, and well-structured event sequences.
• Recognize and name all upper- and lowercase letters of the alphabet.	**Craft and Structure**	**Production and Distribution of Writing**
Phonological Awareness	• Determine the meaning of words and phrases as they are used in a text, distinguishing literal from nonliteral language.	• Produce clear and coherent writing in which the development, organization, and style are appropriate to task, purpose, and audience.
• Demonstrate understanding of spoken words, syllables, and sounds (phonemes).	• Refer to parts of stories, dramas, and poems when writing or speaking about a text, using terms such as *chapter*, *scene*, and *stanza*; describe how each successive part builds on earlier sections.	
• Recognize and produce rhyming words.		• With some guidance and support from peers and adults, develop and strengthen writing as needed by planning, revising, editing, rewriting, or trying a new approach, focusing on how well purpose and audience have been addressed.
• Count, pronounce, blend, and segment syllables in spoken words.		
• Blend and segment onsets and rimes of single-syllable spoken words.	• Distinguish their own point of view from that of the narrator or those of the characters.	
• Isolate and pronounce the initial, medial vowel, and final sounds in three-phoneme (consonant–vowel–consonant) words.	**Integration of Knowledge and Ideas**	• Use technology, including the Internet, to produce and publish writing and present the relationships between information and ideas efficiently as well as to interact and collaborate with others.
Phonics and Word Recognition	• Explain how specific aspects of a text's illustrations contribute to what is conveyed by the words in a story.	
• Know and apply grade-level phonics and word-analysis skills in decoding words.		

(Continued)

TABLE 10.6   **(Continued)**

Foundational Reading Standards	Reading Literature Standards	Writing Standards
• Demonstrate basic knowledge of one-to-one letter–sound correspondences by producing the primary sound or many of the most frequent sounds for each consonant. • Associate the long and short sounds with the common spellings (graphemes) for the five major vowels. • Read common high-frequency words by sight (e.g., *the, of, to, you, she, my, is, are, do, does*) • Distinguish between similarly spelled words by identifying the sounds of the letters that differ. **Fluency** • Read emergent-reader texts with purpose and understanding.	• Compare and contrast the themes, settings, and plots of stories written by the same author about the same or similar characters. **Range of Reading and Level of Text Complexity** • Read and comprehend literature, including stories, dramas, and poetry, at the high end of the Grades 2–3 text complexity band independently and proficiently.	**Research to Build and Present Knowledge** • Conduct short research projects to answer a question drawing on several sources and generating additional related, focused questions that allow for multiple avenues of exploration. • Gather relevant information from multiple print and digital sources, using search terms effectively; assess the credibility and accuracy of each source; and quote or paraphrase the data and conclusions of others while avoiding plagiarism and following a standard format for citation. • Draw evidence from literary or informational texts to support analysis, reflection, and research. **Range of Writing** • Write routinely over extended time frames and shorter time frames for a range of discipline-specific tasks, purposes, and audiences.

Source: Common Core State Standards for Language Arts (www.corestandards.org/ELA-Literacy/).

teachers develop lesson plans. One way to define access to the general curriculum is to ensure students have meaningful opportunities to achieve the same standards, the Common Core or other standards, as those without disabilities. Standards offer a foundation for developing the understanding and skills students need to be college- and career-ready. Yet, standards do not teach, nor do they direct teachers how to teach. Standards simply state what students should be taught to know and do. For a complete list of the Common Core State Standards for Language Arts, see www.corestandards .org/ELA-Literacy/.

Technology Spotlight #10.2

Tools for Writing Instruction

Although developing legible handwriting remains an important instructional outcome, keyboarding skills have become more and more a necessity in today's world. Both commercial and free keyboarding instructional tools are available (Donne, 2012). Below is a list of a few free online resources:

- Byte Back: byteback.org/typing/ (18 text-based lessons with extra practice sessions available)

- Dance Mat Typing: www.kidztype. com (three activities for four stages using cartoon format)

- Learn2Type for Kids: learn2type. com (14 text-based lessons, requires login)

- Sense-Lang.org: sense-lang.org (15 lessons, teacher can enter specific text for practice exercises)

One of the first obstacles to writing is deciding what one wants to write about and how to organize the ideas. Valuable tools for prewriting are software products Kidspiration and Inspiration (www.inspiration.com) which allow users to randomly place ideas on the screen and then organize them. This task is often modeled with the whole class as students learn how to engage in the process of brainstorming and planning. Upon completion, the software provides an outline based on the ideas generated and organized. This visual process provides a powerful alternative to traditional outlining.

After students have developed their ideas, the process of getting their ideas on paper, often presents another series of obstacles for reluctant writers. Some students might benefit from a predictive word processor such as Co:Writer (donjohnston.com) which tries to predict each word being typed (e.g., type *T* and a list of t words will appear such as *the*) and can be selected and inserted from a list. Predictive word processors appear especially valuable for students who are poor or slow typists or have difficulty with spelling. Special designed word processors like WYNN (www.freedomscientific.com/LSG/index. asp) offer text-to-speech so writers can listen to what they have written, talking dictionary and thesaurus, as well as study aids (e.g., highlighting, bookmarking, notes).

Implications for Culturally and/or Linguistically Diverse Students

As discussed throughout this book, the United States is experiencing increasing numbers of students from diverse backgrounds, including those for whom English is not their first language. Thus, our nation's schools and teachers are educating more and more students who are learning the English language. Approximately 100 languages other than English are spoken in these students' homes, with about three fourths of them speaking Spanish (Klingner & Soltero-Gonzalez, 2009).

Each English learner (EL) is unique in first language, level of English language proficiency, ethnic background, socioeconomic status, and quality and quantity of previous schooling. Given these unique characteristics, ELs need to be evaluated individually and provided the most appropriate instruction that matches their needs. Second language acquisition is a very complex process influenced by many factors (e.g., cultural values, first language proficiency) which may lead to misidentification of high-incidence disabilities (Baca, Fletcher, & Hoover, 2016). At the same time, it isn't necessary to wait for ELs to develop their English language skills before ruling out language as a cause for their difficulties. If a student has a true disability, then it should manifest itself in all the student's languages (Hamayan, Marler, Sánchez-López, & Damico, 2013).

Educators know much about reading and writing instruction for monolingual students due to extensive studies conducted with this population. Less is known about similar instruction for ELs, although the amount of research is increasing quickly. For example, researchers have studied whether ELs should (a) learn to read in their native language first, then learn English; (b) learn to read in their native language simultaneous to learning English; or (c) be instructed in English only. Some research indicates ELs benefit more from bilingual instruction than instruction in English only (Slavin & Cheung, 2004). However, Alan Cheung and Robert Slavin (2012) analyzed studies examining effective reading programs for Spanish-dominant ELs and reported that the quality of instruction was more important than the language of instruction.

Researchers are beginning to document that instruction recommended for monolingual students with reading disabilities is appropriate for at-risk ELs. Current knowledge leads professionals to believe that reading interventions recommended for monolingual students with reading disabilities (e.g., intense small-group explicit instruction in phonemic awareness, phonics, and other reading skills) may also be appropriate for ELs (Cheung & Slavin, 2012; Richards-Tutor, Baker, Gersten, Baker, & Smith, 2016; Slavin & Cheung, 2004).

Special educators may teach students with a HID who are also ELs. Specialists who have training in understanding the instructional needs of ELs should also be instructing and supporting the ELs with disabilities; and special educators and other specialists should be working collaboratively to ensure the highest quality instruction possible for ELs with HIDs.

English learners are not the only group of diverse students who need special attention related to literacy instruction. Students from low-income families often experience difficulties in both oral language/vocabulary and printed/phonological knowledge, which can be related to insufficient experience with the printed word (Vernon-Feagans et al., 2010). Students who come from homes where books are integrated into family activities (e.g., parents reading to children, families visiting libraries) are better prepared to learn reading and writing skills.

The following strategies have been found to be helpful in improving the reading and writing skills of students from culturally and/or linguistically diverse backgrounds:

- **Choose printed materials (e.g., books, quotes, stories, poems) that relate to students' lives**. Teachers have many choices in selecting reading materials and should select books that connect with the lives of their students. For example, one study found that the reading rates of African American second graders were greater when they read culturally responsive reading passages versus nonculturally responsive passages (Cartledge, Bennett, Gallant, Ramnath, & Keesey, 2015).

- **Use teacher-directed, systematic, small-group instruction**. Explicitly teaching skills has been found to benefit all students, including English learners. Small-group instruction provides extended opportunities for students to use English and interact with the teacher (Richards-Tutor et al., 2016).

- **Focus instruction on the five skills identified by the National Reading Panel (2000).** Although these skills are important for reading instruction of ELs, they may not respond similarly as students whose first language is English. For example, ELs may not be accustomed to hearing or distinguishing English sounds or recognizing English orthographies. They may read more slowly and be confused by common words, such as those with multiple meanings. In addition, their prior experience or cultural differences can impact their reading comprehension abilities (Klingner & Geisler, 2016).

- **Teach reading behaviors explicitly.** Not all students come from backgrounds that prepare them to participate in traditional reading programs. For example, students from other countries may not be accustomed to the adult–student question and answer interactions common in American classrooms. Teachers should explicitly teach reading behaviors required for school success. When teachers directly explain behavioral expectations, students in multicultural classrooms can better understand (a) why a teacher requires particular behaviors and responses, and (b) that literacy expectations at school may differ from language experiences in the home and community (Meier, 2003).

- **Take advantage of students' interest and ability with social literacy to build their academic literacy**. Social literacy (e.g., text or e-mail messages, comic books, personal journals) is easier to learn than academic literacy because it deals with more concrete ideas, has referents easily accessible to the learner, and is used often. Academic language, on the other hand, is more abstract, complex, and cognitively demanding. Academic language is used in textbooks, literature, instructions, encyclopedia entries and so forth (Hamayan et al., 2013).

- **Teach vocabulary before starting the lesson and provide repeated exposures to new vocabulary**. Students need five to 20 repetitions to fully understand new words. Frequent exposure should occur soon after new words are introduced. Over time, the exposure can be less frequent but should occur periodically (Vadasy & Nelson, 2012).

- **Use repeated reading** where students hear the passage read, then read the passage to a partner three to five times. New vocabulary should be taught before the readings begin. Repeated readings increase reading rate and accuracy and can help develop greater comprehension (Herrera, Perez, & Escamilla, 2015).

- **Incorporate visual materials** to support reading comprehension. For example, graphic organizers can help students conceptualize how the concepts being discussed connect and illustrations can assist students to develop conceptual and vocabulary understanding. Fade the applications of visual materials, particularly illustrations, so students need to rely on the text alone (McCollin & O'Shea, 2005).

- **Include language objectives as part of lesson plans.** Lesson plans can include both content objectives (e.g., "Students will classify the changes that matter undergoes when given a description of the shape and volume.") and language objectives related to the content (e.g., "Students will define *matter, states of matter, solid, liquid,* and *gas.*"). Lesson plans can also include objectives related to the use of language (e.g., "Students will verbally describe the change of state of water using subject/verb agreements accurately.") (Echevarria, Frey, & Fisher, 2015).

- **Make books come alive.** Students can form powerful attachments to books when teachers provide opportunities for students to experience and connect with literature. Students form attachments to books when they relate to the characters, are allowed to either read or hear a story numerous times, and when they engage in meaningful discussions about stories and books (Meier, 2003).

- **Expose students to a broad range of fiction and nonfiction.** Successful literacy programs expose students to a broad range of material. Teachers should provide time for students to read and listen to a variety of books so that students build listening and reading vocabularies, improve their information base, and have opportunities to enjoy reading (Hoover & Fabian, 2000; Layne, 2015).

SUMMARY

Reading and writing disabilities are commonly identified disabilities in school, particularly for students with HID. This is not surprising given that reading and writing are complex cognitive behaviors that require recognizing and making sense of the written symbols that represent speech. Underlying cognitive processes that impact students' abilities with the written word include attention regulation, language, memory, fine-motor skills, language abilities, and visual-spatial abilities.

Based on a thorough analysis of over 100,000 research studies conducted in reading instruction, the National Reading Panel (NRP, 2000) concluded that students must master skills in five areas to become good readers. They include phonemic awareness, phonics, fluency, vocabulary development, and text comprehension. Students with phonemic awareness recognize that spoken language can be broken into smaller units, such as discrete sounds. Phonics is the ability to match sounds to letters in order to read and write, while fluency is the skill of reading accurately, at an appropriate rate and with expression. Students' vocabulary or knowledge and use of words and their text comprehension, the ability to understand and use information that is read, are also critical elements of being a proficient reader. Students struggling with learning to read need to acquire these elements through explicit or teacher-directed instruction. Such instruction should also be scaffolded by carefully sequencing instruction to build skills gradually and supporting the student through thinking through tasks.

Five skills necessary for successful written expression include handwriting, spelling, grammar, text structure, and composition. Handwriting and spelling continue to be basic tool skills even in the times of rapidly advancing computer and text messaging technology. Grammar and text structure instruction helps students learn the proper use of word order and vocabulary to create understandable written communication. Students also need to be taught that writing is a process in planning, drafting, revising, editing, and sharing their work through the prewriting, writing, and postwriting stages. As with reading instruction, students with HID need explicit or teacher-directed instruction when learning to write. Additionally, mnemonic acronyms have been shown to help students recall elements of the writing process.

General education standards are important for special educators to understand and apply in their teaching, particularly because students with HID need access to the general curriculum. The most universally adopted set of language arts standards are the Common Core State Standards which include foundational skills for reading, literature reading, informational text reading, writing, speaking, listening, language, and literacy in history/social studies, science, and technical subjects.

Given the increased number of English learners in the schools, researchers are focusing on studying the best instructional strategies for teaching ELs reading and writing in English. Currently, professionals believe that reading interventions recommended for monolingual students with reading disabilities (e.g., explicit instruction, small groups, phonics, and other reading skills) may also be appropriate for ELs.

REVIEW QUESTIONS

1. Explain why and how characteristics of students with HID (e.g., memory, attention difficulties) impact learning to read and write.

2. What are the five elements of reading identified by the NRP as critical? Define and provide examples of each.

3. Describe one strategy each for teaching phonemic awareness, phonics, fluency, and vocabulary.

4. Compare and contrast the differences between narrative and expository text. Provide examples of appropriate comprehension questions for each.

5. Create an outline for teaching one aspect of reading using the teacher-directed model of instruction.

6. What are the five skills necessary for successful written expression? Define and provide examples of each.

7. Defend teaching handwriting, spelling, and grammar in today's advancing technological tools for communicating.

8. Create an outline for teaching a mnemonic acronym for writing using the teacher-directed model of instruction.

9. Describe the three stages of composition with examples of instructional strategies for each stage.

10. Based on current knowledge, how should ELs be evaluated and taught reading and writing skills?

ACTIVITIES

1. Three times a week for 2 weeks, visit an elementary school classroom and volunteer to read with a student who is struggling with reading. Keep a log of your experience.

2. Analyze the reading comprehension strategies you use when you read new material at different difficulty levels. Write down your thought processes.

3. Visit a community literacy center. Identify what reading program they implement and which elements of effective reading instruction are included in their program. Present your experience and analysis orally in writing.

4. Interview a teacher who teaches English literacy skills to students whose first language is not English. Identify the strategies the teacher finds most helpful for this population. Orally present the findings.

Council for Exceptional Children (CEC) Standards

The Council for Exceptional Children (CEC) is a premiere national professional organization comprised of special educators, paraeducators, relative service personnel, parents, and others interested in individuals with disabilities and/or those with gifts and talents. This organization has generated 10 standards for the preparation of special educators. These standards are listed in each chapter as they relate to the content within the chapter. The standards that apply to Chapter 10 are Standards #1, #3, #5, and #6.

CEC Initial Preparation Standard 1: Learner Development and Individual Learning Differences

Beginning special education professionals understand how exceptionalities may interact with development and learning and use this knowledge to provide meaningful and challenging learning experiences for individuals with exceptionalities.

1.1 Beginning special education professionals understand how language, culture, and family background influence the learning of individuals with exceptionalities.

1.2 Beginning special education professionals use understanding of development and individual differences to respond to the needs of individuals with exceptionalities.

CEC Initial Preparation Standard #3: Curricular Content Knowledge (partial)

Beginning special education professionals use knowledge of general and specialized curricula to individualize learning for individuals with exceptionalities.

3.1 Beginning special education professionals understand the central concepts, structures of the discipline, and tools of inquiry of the content areas they teach, and can organize this knowledge, integrate cross-disciplinary skills, and develop meaningful learning progressions for individuals with exceptionalities.

3.2   Beginning special education professionals understand and use general and specialized content knowledge of teaching across curricular content areas to individualize learning for individuals with exceptionalities.

CEC Initial Preparation Standard #5: Instructional Planning and Strategies (partial)

Beginning special education professionals select, adapt, and use a repertoire of evidence-based instructional strategies to advance learning of individuals with exceptionalities.

5.1   Beginning special education professionals consider an individual's abilities, interests, learning environments, and cultural and linguistic factors in the selection, development, and adaptation of learning experiences for individuals with exceptionalities.

5.4   Beginning special education professionals use strategies to enhance language development and communication skills of individuals with exceptionalities.

5.7   Beginning special education professionals teach cross-disciplinary knowledge and skills such as critical thinking and problem-solving to individuals with exceptionalities.

CEC Initial Preparation Standard #6: Professional Learning and Ethnical Practice (partial)

Beginning special education professionals use foundational knowledge of the field and their professional Ethical Principles and Practice Standards to inform special education practice, to engage in lifelong learning, and to advance the profession.

6.3. Beginning special education professionals understand that diversity is a part of families, cultures, and schools, and that complex human issues can interact with the delivery of special education services.

REFERENCES

Allor, J. H., Mathes, P. G., Roberts, J. K., Cheatham, J. P., Al Otaiba, S. (2014). Is scientifically based reading instruction effective for students with below-average IQs? *Exceptional Children, 80*(3), 287–306.

Armbruster, B. B., Lehr, F., & Osborn, J. (2001). *Put reading first: The research building blocks for teaching children to read, kindergarten through grade 3*. Jessup, MD: National Institute for Literacy.

Baca, L. M., Fletcher, T., & Hoover, J. J. (2016). Conclusion: Putting the pieces together. In J. J. Hoover, L. M. Baca, & J. K. Klingner (Eds.), *Why do English learners struggle with reading?* (2nd ed., pp. 163–172), Thousand Oaks, CA: Corwin.

Bakken, J. P., & Whedon, C. K. (2002). Teaching text structure to improve reading comprehension. *Intervention in School and Clinic, 37*, 229–233.

Berkeley, S., Scruggs, T. E., & Mastropieri, M. A. (2010). Reading comprehension instruction for students with learning disabilities, 1956–2006: A meta-analysis. *Remedial and Special Education, 31*(6), 423–436.

Berninger, V. W., Abbott, R. D., Abbott, S. P., Graham, S., & Richards, T. (2002). Writing and reading: Connections between language by hand and language by eye. *Journal of Learning Disabilities, 35*, 39–56.

Boudah, D. J. (2013). The main idea strategy: A strategy to improve reading comprehension through inferential thinking. *Intervention in School and Clinic, 49*(3), 148–155.

Boyle, J. R. (2008). Reading strategies for students with mild disabilities. *Intervention in School and Clinic, 44*(1), 3–9.

Brigham, R., Berkeley, S., Simpkins, P., & Brigham, M. (2007). Reading comprehension strategy instruction. *Current Practice Alerts #12*. Division for Learning Disabilities and Division for Research of the Council for Exceptional Children. Retrieved from http://teachingld.org

Bryant, D. P., Goodwin, M., Bryant, B. R., & Higgins, K. (2003). Vocabulary instruction for students with learning disabilities: A review of the research. *Learning Disability Quarterly, 26*, 117–128.

Carnine, D. W., Silbert, J., Kame'enui, E. J., & Tarver, S. (2010). *Direct instruction reading* (5th ed.). Boston, MA: Merrill/Pearson.

Carretti, B., Motta, E., & Re, A. M. (2016). Oral and written expression in children with reading comprehension difficulties. *Journal of Learning Disabilities, 49*(1), 65–76.

Cartledge, G., Bennett, J. G., Gallant, D. J., Ramnath, R., & Keesey, S. (2015). Effects of culturally relevant materials on the reading performance of second-grade African Americans with reading/special education risks. *Multiple Voices for Ethnically Diverse Exceptional Learners, 15*(1), 22–43.

Cheung, A. C. K., & Slavin, R. E. (2012). Effective reading programs for Spanish-dominant English language learners (ELLs) in the elementary grades: A synthesis of research. *Review of Educational Research, 82*(4), 351–395.

Cho, E., Roberts, G. J., Capin, P., Roberts, G., Miciak, J., & Vaughn, S. (2015). Cognitive abilities, attention, and self-efficacy of adequate and inadequate responders in a fourth grade reading intervention. *Learning Disabilities Research and Practice, 30*(4), 159–170.

Compton, D. L. (2002). The relationships among phonological processing, orthographic processing, and lexical development in children with reading disabilities. *The Journal of Special Education, 35*, 201–210.

Cortiella, C., & Horowitz, S. H. (2014). *The state of learning disabilities: Facts, trends and emerging issues* (3rd ed.). New York, NY: National Center for Learning Disabilities.

Costa, L. C., Edwards, C. N., & Hooper, S. R. (2016). Writing disabilities and reading disabilities in elementary school students: Rates of co-occurrence and cognitive barriers. *Learning Disability Quarterly, 39*(1), 17–30.

De La Paz, S., & Graham, S. (1997). Effects of dictation and advanced planning instruction on the composing of students with writing and learning problems. *Journal of Educational Psychology, 89*, 203–222.

Donne, V. (2012). Keyboarding instruction for students with a disability. *The Clearing House, 85*, 201–206.

Dunn, M. W., & Finley, S. (2010). Children's struggles with the writing process: Exploring storytelling, visual arts, and keyboarding to promote narrative story writing. *Multicultural Education, 18*(1), 33–42.

Echevarria, J., Frey, N., & Fisher, D. (2015). What it takes for English learners to succeed. *Educational Leadership, 72*(6), 22–26.

Eden, G. F., & Vaidya, C. J. (2008). ADHD and developmental dyslexia: Two pathways leading to impaired learning. *Annals of the New York Academy of Sciences, 1145*, 316–327.

Englert, C. S., Raphael, T. E., Anderson, L. M., Anthony, H. M., & Stevens, D. D. (1991). Making writing strategies visible: Cognitive strategy instruction in regular and special education classrooms. *American Educational Research Journal, 28*, 337–372.

Erbay, F. (2013). Predictive power of attention and reading readiness variables on auditory reasoning and processing skills of six-year-old children. *Educational Sciences: Theory and Practice, 13*(1), 422–429.

Etmanskie, J. M., Partanen, M., & Siegel, L. S. (2016). A longitudinal examination of the persistence of late emerging reading disabilities. *Journal of Learning Disabilities, 49*(1), 21–35.

Fautsch-Patridge, T., McMaster, K. L., & Hupp, S. C. (2011). Are current reading research findings applicable to students with intellectual disabilities? In S. J. Samuels & A. E. Farstrup (Eds.), *What research has to say about reading instruction* (4th ed., pp. 215–235). Newark, DE: International Research Association.

Gersten, R. & Baker, S. (2001). Teaching expressive writing to students with learning disabilities: A meta-analysis. *The Elementary School Journal, 101*, 251–272.

Good, R. H., Baker, S. K., & Peyton, J. A. (2009). Making sense of nonsense word fluency: Determining adequate progress in early first-grade reading. *Reading & Writing Quarterly, 25*, 33–56.

Good, R. H., & Kaminski, R. A. (2002). Nonsense Word Fluency. In R. H. Good & R. A. Kaminski (Eds.), *Dynamic Indicators of Basic Early Literacy Skills* (6th ed.). Eugene, OR: Institute for the Development of Educational Achievement. Retrieved from https://dibels .uoregon.edu/

Good, R. H., Kaminski, R. A., & Dill, S. (2002). DIBELS oral reading fluency. In R. H. Good & R. A. Kaminski (Eds.), *Dynamic indicators of basic early literacy skills* (6th ed.). Eugene, OR: Institute for the Development of Educational Achievement. Retrieved from https://dibels .uoregon.edu/

Graham, S., & Harris, K. R. (2016). A path to better writing: Evidence-based practices in the classroom. *The Reading Teacher, 69*(4), 359–365.

Graham, S., Harris, K. R., & Chambers, A. B. (2015). Evidence-based practice and writing instruction. In C. A. MacArthur, S. Graham, & J. Fitzgerald (Eds.), *Handbook of writing research* (2nd ed., pp. 211–226), New York, NY: Guilford Press.

Graham, S., Harris, K. R., & Fink, B. (2000). Is handwriting causally related to learning to write? Treatment of handwriting problems in beginning writers. *Journal of Educational Psychology, 92*, 620–633.

Graham, S., Harris, K. R., & Larsen, L. (2001). Prevention and intervention of writing difficulties for students with learning disabilities. *Learning Disabilities Research & Practice, 16*, 74–84.

Graham, S., Harris, K. R., Mason, L., Fink-Chorzempa, B., Moran, S., & Saddler, B. (2008). How do primary grade teachers teach handwriting? A national survey. *Reading & Writing, 21*, 49–69.

Gregg, N., & Hafer, T. (2001). Disorders of written expression. In A. M. Bain, L. L. Bailet, & L. C. Moats (Eds.), *Written language disorders. Theory into practice* (2nd ed., pp. 103–136). San Antonio, TX: Pro-ed.

Hamayan, E., Marler, B., Sánchez-López, C., & Damico, J. (2013). *Special education considerations for English language learners* (2nd ed.). Philadelphia, PA: Caslon.

Hart, N. V., Fitzpatrick, P., & Cortesa, C. (2010). In-depth analysis of handwriting curriculum and instruction in four kindergarten classrooms. *Reading & Writing, 12*, 673–699.

Herrera, S. G., Perez, D. R., & Escamilla, K. (2015). *Teaching reading to English language learners: Differentiated literacies* (2nd ed.). Boston, MA: Pearson.

Hoover, M. R., & Fabian, E. M. (2000). Problem-solving—struggling readers: A successful program for struggling readers. *Reading Teacher, 53*, 474–476.

Joseph, L. M., Konrad, M., Cates, G., Vajcner, T., Eveleigh, E., & Fishley, K. M. (2012). A meta-analytic review of the cover-copy-compare and variations of this self-management procedure. *Psychology in the Schools, 49*(2), 122–136.

Kamps, D., Abbott, M., Greenwood, C., Wills, H., Veerkamp, M., & Kaufman, J. (2008). Effects of small-group reading instruction and curriculum differences for students most at risk in kindergarten. *Journal of Learning Disabilities, 41*(2), 101–114.

Keller, C. L. (2002). A new twist on spelling instruction for elementary school teachers. *Intervention in School and Clinic, 38*, 3–7.

Klingner, J. K., & Geisler, D. (2016). Helping classroom reading teachers distinguish between language acquisition and learning disabilities. In J. J. Hoover, L. M. Baca, & J. K. Klingner (Eds.), *Why do English learners struggle with reading?* (2nd ed., pp. 83–100), Thousand Oaks, CA: Corwin.

Klingner, J., & Soltero-Gonzalez, L. (2009). Culturally and linguistically responsive literacy instruction for English language learners with learning disabilities. *Multiple*

Voices for Ethnically Diverse Exceptional Learners, 12(1), 4–20.

Kubina, R. M., & Hughes, C. A. (2007). Fluency instruction. *Current Practice Alerts #15.* Division for Learning Disabilities and Division for Research of the Council for Exceptional Children. Retrieved from http://teachingld.

Lane, H., & Pullen, P. C. (2015). Blending wheels: Tools for decoding practice. *TEACHING Exceptional Children, 48*(2), 86–92.

Layne, S. L. (2015). *In defense of read-aloud.* Portland, ME: Stenhouse.

Lee, J., & Yoon, S. Y. (2015, September 25). The effects of repeated reading on reading fluency for students with reading disabilities: A meta-analysis. *Journal of Learning Disabilities.* doi: 10.1177/0022219 415605194

Maki, H. S., Vauras, M. M. S., & Vainio, S. (2002). Reflective spelling strategies for elementary school students with severe writing difficulties: A case study. *Learning Disability Quarterly, 25,* 189–207.

Mason, L. H., Kubina, R. M., Valasa, L. L., & Cramer, A. M. (2010). Evaluating effective writing instruction for adolescent students in an emotional and behavior support setting. *Behavioral Disorders, 35(2),* 140–156.

Mastropieri, M. A., & Scruggs, T. E. (1997). Best practices in promoting reading comprehension in students with learning disabilities 1976–1996. *Remedial and Special Education, 18,* 197–213.

Matsumura, L. C., Patthey-Chavez, G. G., Valdés, R., & Garnier, H. (2002). Teacher feedback, writing assignment quality, and third-grade students' revision in lower- and higher-achieving urban schools. *The Elementary School Journal, 103*(1), 3–25.

Mattison, R. E. (2008). Characteristics of research disability types in middle school students classified ED. *Behavioral Disorders, 34*(1), 27–41.

McCollin, M., & O'Shea, D. (2005). Increasing reading achievement of students from culturally and linguistically diverse backgrounds. *Preventing School Failure, 50*(1), 41–44.

McDaniel, S. C., Houchins, D. E., & Terry, N. P. (2011). Corrective reading as a supplementary curriculum for students with emotional and behavioral disorders. *Journal of Emotional and Behavioral Disorders, 21*(4), 240–249.

Meier, T. (2003). "Why can't she remember that?" The importance of storybook reading in multilingual, multicultural classrooms. *The Reading Teacher, 57,* 242–252.

Mercer, C. D., & Pullen, P. C. (2008). *Students with learning disabilities* (7th ed.). Upper Saddle River, NJ: Pearson.

National Reading Panel. (2000). *Report on research-based approaches to reading instruction.* Bethesda, MD: Author.

Overvelde, A., & Hulstijn, W. (2011). Handwriting development in grade 2 and grade 3 primary school children with normal, at risk, or dysgraphic characteristics. *Research in Developmental Disabilities, 32,* 540–548.

Pullen, P. C., & Lloyd, J. W. (2007). Phonics instruction. *Current Practice Alerts #14.* Division for Learning Disabilities and Division for Research of the Council for Exceptional Children. Retrieved from http://teachingld.org

Puranik, C. S., & Al Otaiba, S. (2012). Examining the contribution of handwriting and spelling to written expression in kindergarten children. *Reading and Writing, 25,* 1523–1546.

Richards-Tutor, C., Baker, D. L., Gersten, R., Baker, S. K., & Smith, J. M. (2016). The effectiveness of reading interventions for English learners: A research synthesis. *Exceptional Children, 82*(2), 144–169.

Roux, C., Dion, E., Barrette, A., Dupéré, V., & Fuchs, D. (2015). Efficacy of an intervention to enhance reading comprehension of students with high-functioning autism spectrum disorder. *Remedial and Special Education, 36*(3), 131–142.

Sams, L. (2003). How to teach grammar, analytical thinking, and writing: A method that works. *English Journal, 92*(3), 57–65.

Samuelsson, S., Lundberg, I., & Herkner, B. (2004). ADHD and reading disability in male adults: Is there a connection? *Journal of Learning Disabilities, 37*(2), 155–168.

Santangelo, T., Harris, K. R., & Graham, S. (2008). Using self-regulated strategy development to support students who have "trubol giting thangs into werds." *Remedial and Special Education, 29*(2), 78–89.

Sayeski, K. L. (2011). Effective spelling instruction for students with learning disabilities. *Intervention in School and Clinic, 47*(2), 75–81.

Seifert, K., & Espin, C. (2012). Improving reading of science text for secondary students with learning disabilities: Effects of text reading, vocabulary learning, and combined approaches to instruction. *Learning Disability Quarterly, 35*(4), 236–247.

Sherman, C. K., & De La Paz, S. (2015). FIX: A strategic approach to writing and revision for students with learning disabilities. *TEACHING Exceptional Children, 48*(2), 93–101.

Shin, J., Deno, S. L., & Espin, C. (2000). Technical adequacy of the maze task for curriculum-based measurement of reading growth. *Journal of Special Education, 34*, 164–172.

Shippen, M. E., Houchins, D. E., Steventon, C., & Sartor, D. (2005). A comparison of two direct instruction reading programs for urban middle school students. *Remedial and Special Education, 26*(3), 175–182.

Slavin, R. E., & Cheung, A. (2004). How do English language learners learn to read? *Educational Leadership, 61*(6), 52–57.

Solis, M., Ciullo, S., Vaughn, S., Pyle, N., Hassaram, B., & Leroux, A. (2012). Reading comprehension interventions for middle school students with learning disabilities: A synthesis of 30 years of research. *Journal of Learning Disabilities, 45*(4), 327–340.

Spector, J. E., & Cavanaugh, B. J. (2015). The conditions of beginning reading instruction for students with autism spectrum disorder. *Remedial and Special Education, 36*(6), 337–346.

Strickland, D. S., Bodin, A., Buchan, K., Jones, K. M., Nelson, A., & Rosen, M. (2001). Teaching writing in a time of reform. *Elementary School Journal, 101*, 385–397.

Torgesen, J. K. (2002). The prevention of reading difficulties. *Journal of School Psychology, 40*(1), 7–26.

Torgesen, J. K., Rashotte, C. A., & Alexander, A. (2001). Principles of fluency instruction in reading: Relationships with established empirical outcomes. In M. Wolf (Ed.), *Dyslexia, fluency, and the brain* (pp. 333–355). Parkton, MD: York Press.

Troia, G. A. (2004). Phonological awareness acquisition and intervention. *Current Practice Alerts #9*. Division for Learning Disabilities and Division for Research of the Council for Exceptional Children. Retrieved from http://teachingld.org/

Troia, G. A. (2014). *Evidence-based practices for writing instruction* (Document No. IC-5). University of Florida, Collaboration for Effective Educator, Development, Accountability, and Reform Center. Retrieved from http://ceedar.education.ufl.edu/tools/innovation-configuration/

Troia, G. A., & Graham, S. (2002). The effectiveness of a highly explicit, teacher-directed strategy instruction routine: Changing the writing performance of students with learning disabilities. *Journal of Learning Disabilities, 35*, 290–305.

Vadasy, P. F., & Nelson, J. R. (2012). *Vocabulary instruction for struggling students.* New York, NY: Guilford Press.

Vernon-Feagans, L., Gallagher, K., Ginsberg, M. C., Amendum, S., Kainz, K., Rose, J., & Burchinal, M. (2010). A diagnostic teaching intervention for classroom teachers: Helping struggling readers in early elementary school. *Learning Disabilities Research & Practice, 25*(4), 183–193.

Vesely, P. J., & Gryder, N. L. (2009). Word of the day improves and redirects student attention while supporting vocabulary development. *Intervention in School and Clinic, 44*(5), 282–287.

Wanzek, J., Vaughn, S., Scammacca, N. K., Metz, K., Murray, C. S., Roberts, G., & Danielson, L. (2013). Extensive reading interventions for students with reading difficulties after grade 3. *Review of Educational Research, 83*(2), 163–195.

Wanzek, J., Vaughn, S., Wexler, J., Swanson, E. A., Edmonds, M., & Kim, A. (2006). A synthesis of spelling and reading interventions and their effects on the spelling outcomes of students with LD. *Journal of Learning Disabilities, 39*(6), 528–543.

Weaver, C., McNally, C., & Moerman, S. (2001). To grammar or not to grammar: That is not the question! *Voices from the Middle, 8*(3), 17–33.

Welch, M., & Jensen, J. B. (1991). Write P.L.E.A.S.E: A video-assisted strategic intervention to improve written expression of inefficient learners. *Remedial and Special Education, 12,* 37–47.

Wheelock, W. H., & Campbell, C. J. (2011). *Classroom reading inventory* (12th ed.). New York, NY: McGraw-Hill.

Williams, K. J., Walker, M. A., Vaughn, S., & Wanzek, J. (2016). A synthesis of reading and spelling interventions and their effects on spelling outcomes for students with learning disabilities. *Journal of Learning Disabilities.* doi: 10.1177/0022219415619753

Wilson, J. K. (2012). Brisk and effective fluency instruction for small groups. *Intervention in School and Clinic, 47*(3), 152–157.

Wong, B. Y. L. (2000). Writing strategies instruction for expository essays for adolescents with and without learning disabilities. *Topics in Language Disorders, 20*(4), 29–44.

Woods, M. L., & Moe, A. J. (2015). *Analytical reading inventory* (10th ed.). Upper Saddle River, NJ: Prentice Hall.

$SAGE edge™ ••

Review ➡ Practice ➡ Improve

Get the tools you need to sharpen your study skills. Access videos, practice quizzes, eFlashcards and more at **edge.sagepub.com/prater.**

Strategies for Mathematics Instruction

Individuals succeeding in the world today, regardless of their specific circumstances, apply mathematics daily. Reading the clock, measuring ingredients for a recipe, or estimating how long it will take to get ready and travel to a specific destination all involve math skills. Similarly, knowing whether you have enough cash in your wallet or money deposited in your debit account to make specific purchases is a survival skill in today's world. Yet not all students learn these skills easily.

Mathematics Disabilities

LaVonda was diagnosed with intellectual disabilities when she entered kindergarten. She is now an eighth grader. In middle school, she has been educated about three quarters of the day in the general education classrooms. She also attends a special education class and receives some small-group and one-on-one support throughout the day. LaVonda attends a general education math class and also receives additional math instruction and support from her special education teacher. Her teachers have noticed that poor working memory is hampering her ability to recall facts and procedures when needed to solve mathematical computations or word problems.

Sheldon is a fourth-grade student who has been identified as having a learning disability. He has specific difficulties with visual-spatial organization. Although he seems to understand grade-level math concepts, he continues to reverse both letters and numbers when reading and writing and he has problems recognizing right from left and top from bottom. His spatial difficulties hamper his math performance in areas such as number alignment and regrouping numbers while completing computations. Sheldon performs poorly on written math assignments and tests.

Learning Objectives

- Describe the types of difficulties students with high-incidence disabilities may encounter in learning mathematics and accompanying strategies to facilitate student learning.

- Create scripted lesson plans to teach math concepts following the steps described for teacher-directed instruction.

- Define, provide examples of, and describe how the following strategies can be applied to mathematics instruction: self-regulation, mnemonic strategies, and graphic representations.

- Explain the role of culture and language in mathematics and the implications for teaching culturally and/or linguistically diverse students.

Prevalence

Studies have documented that approximately 5% to 10% of the school-age population demonstrate mathematical disabilities, which are manifested in difficulties with number sense, mathematical computation, and/or mathematical problem solving (Dennis, Sorells, & Falcomata, 2016; Shin & Bryant, 2015; Swanson & Jerman, 2006). Even though students receiving special education services may not have been diagnosed with math disabilities, a large portion of students with high-incidence disabilities (HID) will demonstrate difficulty with mathematics. Even so, until most recently, research on mathematics disabilities fell behind research examining reading disabilities. A decade ago, critical gaps existed in our knowledge of math disabilities (Mazzocco & Meyers, 2003); the ratio of reading disabilities to mathematics disabilities being studied was

5 to 1 from 1996 to 2006 and 16 to 1 in the prior decade (Jayanthi, Gersten, & Baker, 2008). Although many researchers are now studying mathematics disabilities, there still exists far less information on mathematics than reading disabilities and instruction (Watson & Gable, 2012).

Contributing Factors

Mathematics is a complex subject and in order for students to succeed, they need efficient cognitive functions as well as specific skills. Some of the current research has demonstrated that mathematic disabilities are not heterogeneous. That is, students demonstrate difficulty in a myriad of areas. As an example, one study discovered six different subtypes of mathematical learning difficulties (Bartelet, Ansari, Vaessen, & Blomert, 2014). However, in general most educators and researchers agree that students with math disabilities experience difficulties in the following areas: computational skills, conceptual understanding, strategy selection for problem-solving, and self-monitoring/self-regulation of thinking while problem-solving (Wei, Lenz, & Blackorby, 2012). The lack of mathematical skill development could be influenced by cognitive-learning characteristics often observed in students with HID (see Chapter 1). For example, mathematic difficulties may be attributed to challenges with memory, attention, visual perception, language, and behavioral and emotional issues.

Memory

Educators and researchers agree that many different cognitive processes are involved in the acquisition of mathematical concepts and procedural skills. Many have hypothesized that different processes hamper students' mathematical understanding and skill development. Most experts, however, believe memory difficulties are a primary factor (Watson & Gable, 2012). LaVonda's memory skills seem to be hampering her abilities to maintain facts and procedures needed to move forward in the math curriculum.

As discussed in Chapter 1, working memory is a limited capacity system that allows temporary storage and manipulation of information for complex cognitive tasks (e.g., comprehension, reasoning). Weaknesses in working memory have been documented for students with math disabilities (Martin et al., 2012). The ability to remember and retrieve information related to numbers, and numeric operations is essential for math success. Efficient memory is needed to master basic facts, to recall steps and sequences of math procedures, and to retrieve numeric information needed to solve problems (Geary, 2004). For example, the process of copying numbers from the board or from a textbook may be extremely difficult for some students who are unable to retain visual images long enough to write them on paper. Even if given problems on a worksheet, some students are still unable to retain enough information to perform the computations accurately and quickly (Bley & Thornton, 2001). Teachers can help by making the learning meaningful to the student, using graphic organizers, using multiple representations to teach a concept, and teaching specific mnemonic strategies (Riccomini, Smith, Hughes, & Fries, 2015; Silva, 2004).

Students with HID may experience difficulties in the following areas due to memory challenges:

- Retaining math facts or algorithm steps

- Recalling the meaning of mathematical vocabulary or symbols

- Completing multistep word problems or computational problems

- Telling time (Mercer & Pullen, 2009)

Attention

As with any academic task, students must stay on task long enough to complete their work. Students who are easily distracted, particularly if they are unmotivated to remain on task can easily drift their attention elsewhere. This is true for any academic work. Attention difficulties, however, may have a direct bearing on math disabilities. For example, some research has shown that students experiencing math difficulties tend to exhibit higher levels of attention problems (Raghubar et al., 2009; Wu, Willcutt, Escovar, & Menon, 2014). This research, however, shows only an association between math challenges and attention and neither can be inferred to cause the other without additional research.

Inadequate selective attention can impact performance in mathematics. Selective attention is the ability to filter out irrelevant information and process relevant information with which students with disabilities often have difficulty (see Chapter 1). Math operations require significant selective attention in basic counting procedures and simple operations such as whether to add or subtract, as well as in complex operations where attention must be focused to track and complete sequences of steps (Geary, 2004).

Selective attention skills are also necessary for solving word problems. Word problems frequently include relevant and irrelevant information in the presentation of the problems. Attention skills are needed to filter out irrelevant information and attend only to that information needed to solve the problem. Suppose students were given this word problem: *Harriet went to the store. She bought 2 apples, 5 bananas, 1 candy bar, and 3 oranges. How many pieces of fruit did she buy?* Students with poor selective attention skills will most likely answer 11. A common error is to add all the numbers without attending to and selecting only the relevant information based on the specific question. This word problem is also a good example of the role language not specific to math vocabulary plays in word problems. If students don't understand the concept *fruit*, they won't be able to decipher that the only pieces of fruit in the word problem are apples, bananas, and oranges.

Student with HID may demonstrate these kinds of difficulties related to attention challenges:

- Using algorithm steps

- Completing multistep computational or word problems

- Identifying the proper operation (e.g., add vs. subtract)

- Identifying and using only relevant information in word problems (Geary, 2004)

Visual Perception

Visual perception, or the ability to perceive and understand accurately what one sees, is necessary for success in all academic areas. Visual perception encompasses the ability to discriminate between different visual stimuli, as well as spatial orientation. Sheldon's general visual-spatial orientation difficulties inhibit his performance in all academic areas of reading, writing, and mathematics. Visual-spatial skills are needed to perform math operations, form concepts such as numeric magnitude, and to represent and manipulate information in spatial form such as in a mental number line. Reading graphs, aligning numbers in place value columns, interpreting and understanding diagrams and geometric pictures all require visual-spatial skills (Geary, 2004).

Students with visual perception difficulties may experience these types of challenges:

- Differentiating between numbers (e.g., 6 vs. 9; or 17 vs. 71), coins, the operations symbols, clock hands

- Using directional aspects of math, such as up/down (e.g., addition), left/right (e.g., regrouping; positive/negative numbers on number line), aligning numbers (e.g., place value)

- Copying problems or shapes, or losing place on worksheet (Mercer & Pullen, 2009)

> Sheldon's teacher found that providing him a template with a box cutout to place over individual math problems in his textbook and graph paper on which columns are color coded (e.g., hundreds—blue, tens—yellow, ones—red) helped him transfer number problems to line up properly.

Language

Language skills are an integral factor in math achievement. Language symbolically represents mathematical information and math symbols represent numeric language concepts. Language skills are needed to complete math calculations, solve word problems, and engage in higher mathematical thinking. In computing, language is used to recall and use math rules, steps, and facts. Word problems cannot be solved without language skills as words must be processed and converted to math symbols and operations. Understanding the vocabulary involved in understanding higher mathematical thinking is also critical. A sample list of vocabulary words for Grades 1–3 and 6–8 in Table 11.1 demonstrates the role language skills play in understanding mathematical concepts.

Students with HID may have difficulty with mathematical vocabulary in the following ways:

- Understanding mathematical terms (e.g., *minus, place value, regroup*)

- Understanding words with multiple meanings (e.g., *times, product*), homonyms (e.g., *pi* vs. *pie*), or concepts expressed in more than one way (e.g., 15 minutes after the hour vs. quarter past)

- Difficulty expressing mathematical concepts or verbalizing steps in solving mathematical problems (Riccomini et al., 2015)

TABLE 11.1   Sample of Mathematical Vocabulary for Grades 1–3 and 6–8

Grades 1–3

Number and Number Sense	Measurement	Geometry	Probability and Statistics	Patterns, Functions, and Algebra
place value	penny	circle	picture graph	pattern
estimate	nickel	square	table	equality/inequality
fraction	dime	triangle	tally marks	number line
less than	quarter	rectangle	pictograph	calculator
greater than	dollar	right angle	line plot	dot cubes
equal to	ruler	side/vertex	certain	equal sign
ordinal numbers	kilogram/grams	symmetry	likely/unlikely	identity property
round	pound/ounces	sphere	impossible	commutative
Computation and Estimation	cup/pint/quart	cube		property
addition	gallon/liter	plane figure		
subtraction	foot/inches	solid figure		
multiply	clock/minute/hour	cylinder		
divide	balance scale	congruent		
number sentence	volume	noncongruent		
regroup/rename	calendar	line segment		
mixed number	thermometer	point		
		ray		

Grades 6–8

Number and Number Sense	Computation and Estimation	Geometry	Probability and Statistics	Patterns, Functions, and Algebra
ratio	proportion	congruent figures	probability	equation
absolute value	scale factor	quadrilaterals	tree diagram	expression
percent	unit rate	parallelogram	mean	variable
equivalent relationships	square root	rhombus	median	coefficient
exponential form	Measurement	trapezoid	mode	term
perfect squares	perimeter	right triangle	range	constant
powers of ten	area	Pythagorean Theorem	bar graph	inequality
scientific notation	pi	coordinate plane	line graph	like terms
natural numbers	circumference	rotation	stem-and-leaf plot	relations
integers	vertex	reflection	circle graph	functions
rational numbers	pyramid	translation	histogram	domain range
irrational numbers	prism	dilation	scatterplot	dependent variable
real numbers	cone			independent variable
	cylinder			

Source: Virginia Department of Education, doe.virginia.gov/instruction/mathematics/resources/vocab_cards/. All rights reserved. Used with permission.

TEACHER TIP #11.1
TEACHING MATHEMATICAL VOCABULARY

Language skill deficits can hamper learning important mathematical vocabulary. The following methods can be used to teach students essential math vocabulary:

- Teach vocabulary explicitly through teacher-directed instruction. Follow the steps described later in this chapter.

- Implement mnemonic strategies, particularly the keyword strategy (see Chapter 9).

- Incorporate frequent but brief (5–10 minutes) opportunities to practice math vocabulary. This will help students build their fluency and maintain their understanding.

- Use game-like educational activities (e.g., Jeopardy).

- Apply technology (e.g., apps, computer simulations) to reinforce math vocabulary (Riccomini et al., 2015)

Behavioral and Emotional Issues

Many students with HID have developed learned helplessness toward mathematics (Mercer & Pullen, 2009). Students with **learned helplessness** believe they cannot learn. Given their history of failure with mathematics, they begin to think there is no relationship between the effort they put into something and the grades they receive. Teachers can help students make the connections between their effort and task success or failure by linking outcomes to effort and application of skills and strategies (Prater, 2003).

One study discovered that students, even as young as second and third grade, who had difficulty with math also demonstrated significant math-specific anxiety. In addition, low math achievement was significantly associated with negative externalizing behaviors such as inattention, rule-breaking, and aggression (Wu et al., 2014). Demonstrating relationships among math anxiety, externalizing behaviors, and low math performance, however, do not imply one causes the others.

Teachers may observe students with math disabilities experiencing the following:

- Learned helplessness (e.g., not trying)

- Math anxiety (e.g., avoiding math, physical symptoms)

Mathematics Content

All students need to develop **number sense**, which refers to an ability to understand numbers, numerical relationships, and how to use information about numbers to perform math operations (Robinson, Menchetti, & Torgesen, 2002). For example, students need to be able to estimate quantity, compare numbers, perceive numeric patterns, and have a sense of the magnitude of various numbers. Number sense begins developing during preschool years as children informally interact with parents and siblings. By age 5, children demonstrate the use of counting skills, use strategies to compute, and understand that words symbolically represent numbers (Geary, 2004). Number sense leads to automatic use of math information and is a key ingredient in solving basic arithmetic computations. Beyond developing number sense, the purpose of effective math instruction is to enable students to acquire sufficient mathematic skills to function in society.

Number Sense and Numerical Power

Several years ago, the National Council of Supervisors of Mathematics generated a monograph describing specific ways in which mathematics curriculum and instruction should shift toward *numerical power* (Charles & Lobato, 1998). Given that emerging evidence indicates that students with math disabilities often have difficulty with number sense (Dennis et al., 2016), special educators can benefit from understanding the characteristics of numerically powerful students and what strategies they can deliver to help students develop stronger number sense. In general, **numerically powerful students** use procedural strategies accurately and know how to make sense of numerical and quantitative situations (see Table 11.2).

Students with HID can be explicitly taught the concepts of numbers and operations they will need for solving both basic and complex math computations (Dennis et al., 2016). In addition, teachers who promote numerical power in their instruction implement the following:

- Provide sufficient opportunities to develop meaning for numbers and operations before teaching computational algorithms or basic facts.
- Provide frequent opportunities to estimate and use mental math strategies.
- Encourage multiple solution approaches.
- Encourage students to communicate their reasoning.
- Solicit and address students' ideas.
- Create an atmosphere of sense-making.
- Develop concepts and skills through problem-solving.
- Provide opportunities to demonstrate numerical reasoning during instruction and practice.
- Assist students in connecting numbers to the quantities that the numbers are used to measure.
- Encourage students to develop logic and reasoning as verification. (Charles & Lobato, 1998)

The characteristics of a numerically powerful student provide a backdrop to the mathematical skills all students need to develop. As described in Chapter 1, given recent legislation emphasizing standards-based education, special educators need to identify means for meeting both standards and individualization in the education of students with HID.

TABLE 11.2   What It Means to Be Numerically Powerful

A Numerically Powerful Student:	
Develops meaning for numbers and operations.	Meaningfully connects numerals with situations from life experiences
	Knows that numbers have multiple interpretations
	Understands that number size is relative
	Connects addition, subtraction, multiplication, and division with actions arising in real-world situations
	Understands the effects of operation on numbers
	Can create appropriate representations for numbers
	Can create appropriate representations for operations
Looks for relationships among numbers and operations.	Can decompose or break apart numbers in different ways
	Knows how numbers are related to other numbers
	Understands how the operations are connected to each other
Understands computational strategies and uses them appropriately and efficiently.	Can perform the steps in an algorithm correctly and can discuss the underlying ideas and important relationships used
	Makes a conscious effort to complete calculations using prior knowledge and simpler calculations
	Uses a variety of calculation strategies, even when computing calculations involving the same operation
	Chooses appropriate calculation techniques to obtain exact answers and to estimate
	Calculates with accuracy
	Calculates with relative efficiency
Makes sense of numerical and quantitative situations.	Expects numerical calculations to make sense
	Connects numbers to the quantities that the numbers are used to measure
	Relates the operations of addition, subtraction, multiplication, and division to a range of quantitative situations
	Seeks to understand relationships among quantities in real-world situations
	Relates computations to quantities in real-world situations
	Assesses whether the result of a calculation makes sense in the context of the numbers and real-world quantities involved

Source: Charles, R., & Lobato, J. (1998). *Future basics: Developing numerical power.* Golden, CO: National Council of Supervisors of Mathematics.

TEACHER TIP #11.2

TEACHING NUMBER SENSE

Below are some suggested activities to help teach students number sense:

- Daily review numbers 11 to 19 because they don't follow the same pattern as the numbers 20 and above. (e.g., We don't say "ten one" for 11 like we say "twenty one" for 21).

- Use a number list or line with corresponding chips to teach counting, one-on-one correspondence and **cardinality**.

- Use a cardinality chart to illustrate that the number with the most squares is the bigger of two numbers.

- 1 2 3 . . . 10

- Illustrate with a number line and chips that the next number in the count sequence is always one more than the previous number and the number before is always one less. Use this process to teach concepts of more, less after, before, which leads to addition and subtraction. (Dyson, Jordan, & Glutting, 2011)

Mathematics Standards

The National Council for Teachers of Mathematics (NCTM) created standards for the study of mathematics in 1989. Since then, standards have received widespread adoption across many disciplines. As discussed in previous chapters, the most shared set of K–12 academic standards in the United States is the Common Core State Standards. Mathematical standards have been identified for kindergarten through eighth grade, as well as for high school. A sample of these standards for Grades 3 and 8 are listed in Table 11.3.

Given that students with disabilities need access to the general curriculum, knowledge of general education standards has become important for special educators to understand and apply in their teaching. When developing Individualized Education Programs (IEPs), teachers need to consider standards, whether they be the Common Core or other state- or district-adopted standards, as the IEP team develops goals and the teachers develop lesson plans. One way to define access to the general curriculum is to ensure students with disabilities have meaningful opportunities to achieve the same standards, the Common Core or other standards, as those without disabilities. Standards offer a foundation for developing the understanding and skills students need to be college- and career-ready. Yet, standards do not teach, nor do they direct teachers how to teach. Standards simply state what students should be taught to know and do. For a complete list of the Common Core State Standards for Mathematics, see http://www.corestandards.org/Math/.

TABLE 11.3	Sample of the Common Core State Standards for Mathematics: Grades 3 and 8

Grade 3	Grade 8
Operations and Algebraic Thinking • Represent and solve problems involving multiplication and division. • Understand properties of multiplication and the relationship between multiplication and division. • Multiply and divide within 100. • Solve problems involving the four operations, and identify and explain patterns in arithmetic. **Number and Operations in Base Ten** • Use place value understanding and properties of operation to perform multi-digit arithmetic. **Number and Operations—Fractions** • Develop understanding of fractions as numbers. **Measurement and Data** • Solve problems involving measurement and estimation of intervals of time, liquid volumes, and masses of objects. • Represent and interpret data. • Geometric measurement: understand concepts of area and relate area to multiplication and to addition. • Geometric measurement: recognize perimeter as an attribute of plane figures and distinguish between linear and area measures. **Geometry** • Reason with shapes and their attributes.	**The Number System** • Know that there are numbers that are not rational, and approximate them by rational numbers. **Expressions and Equations** • Work with radicals and integer exponents. • Understand the connections between proportional relationships, lines, and linear equations. • Analyze and solve linear equations and pairs of simultaneous linear equations. **Functions** • Define, evaluate, and compare functions. • Use functions to model relationships between quantities. **Geometry** • Understand congruence and similarity using physical models, transparencies, or geometry software. • Understand and apply the Pythagorean Theorem. • Solve real-world and mathematical problems involving volume of cylinders, cones, and spheres. **Statistics and Probability** • Investigate patterns of association in bivariate data.

Source: Common Core State Standards for Mathematics, http://www.corestandards.org/Math/.

Effective Instruction for Students With Math Disabilities

Teaching Mathematical Concepts

Mathematical concepts are abstract. This textbook's author experienced a mathematics professor making this point on the first day of a college class. He wrote the numeral *2* on the chalkboard and asked the class what it was. All of the students responded, "The number 2." He informed the students they were incorrect and stated that what he wrote on the chalkboard was the numeral *2*, only a symbol for the concept *2*. He then asked,

"What exactly is 2?" After additional prodding and questioning, class members began to understand that the *2* he wrote on the board is only a numeral representing the abstract concept *2*. This professor deliberately stretched the idea of math abstraction to make an impression on his students.

Since students with HID often exhibit difficulty with abstract concepts, an effective approach in helping them learn math concepts is to use the concrete, representational, abstract (CRA) teaching sequence. That is, students often need concrete manipulatives to help them grasp new mathematical concepts. Manipulatives are then replaced by representations (e.g., pictures) and then followed with abstract replacements (e.g., numerals) (Mercer & Pullen, 2009). Research shows that this sequence has been effective in improving basic math skills of students experiencing math difficulties (Flores, 2010), even secondary-age students with HID (Strickland & Maccini, 2013)

Concrete Instruction

In mathematics, **concrete instruction** involves manipulating objects to represent numerals and operations. For example, if teaching the concept 3, the student may be given 3 blocks or 3 toy cars to count. If teaching the concept of addition, the student may be given 2 pencils, asked how many there are, then given 1 more pencil and asked how many there are now.

Concrete instruction does not only occur in the primary grades. For example, secondary-age students may be given models of geometric shapes and figures like parallelograms or trapezoids to help them solve geometry problems. Pattern blocks, algebra tiles, fraction strips, and geoboards are also examples of manipulatives helpful for teaching mathematical concepts. Research has shown that students who use concrete materials develop stronger cognitive representations and deeper understanding of math concepts, better apply math concepts to real-life situations, and demonstrate stronger motivation and on-task behaviors (Dobbins, Gagnon, & Ulrich, 2014).

Although teaching mathematical concepts by first giving students manipulatives or concrete objects is considered a fundamental instructional math procedure, manipulatives are not often used in classrooms. When asked, teachers report not using manipulatives for several reasons including lack of materials or administrative support or being overwhelmed with other responsibilities. Manipulatives are, however, an important element of learning mathematical concepts, particularly for students with HID. In fact, the amount of time wasted on reteaching concepts outweighs the amount of time needed to teach with manipulations because the latter helps students learn the concepts more effectively in the first place (Moch, 2001). Even though using manipulatives is an effective practice for teaching both computation and word problems, teachers need to be cautious in overusing them. Once students have grasped the concepts through manipulatives, they need to move to representational instruction and eventually to abstract instruction.

Representational Instruction

Rather than the actual blocks, toy cars, or pencils, during **representational instruction,** the student may be given visual representations, whether tally marks, dots, or pictures of blocks or cars. If using dots and students were adding 3 + 2, they would be instructed to draw three dot marks next to the 3, two dots marks next to the 2, and then count the total number of dots to solve the problem. The same can be done with higher math skills.

For example, the models of parallelograms and trapezoids can be followed with drawings of the shape. The emphasis here is to associate the visual models with symbolic processes. Many students with HID need to practice at the representational level to master a concept or fact (Mercer & Pullen, 2009).

The use of virtual manipulatives falls within the category of representational instruction. Virtual manipulatives may be accessed through the Internet (See Technology Spotlight #11.1). Limited research indicates the use of virtual manipulatives holds promise for teaching students with HID (e.g., Satsangi & Bouck, 2015).

Mrs. Dunkel learned about the CRA process in her teacher preparation program but hasn't used it for years. As her students are struggling this year with place values, she knows she needs better concrete and representational ways of teaching the concept. She knows there are a lot of commercial materials she could buy, but she has exhausted her school supply money for the year. So, she gets online and finds an idea of writing numerals on the rim of plastic cups which she makes. Each student receives 3 cups with the numerals 0-9 written sideways and spaced evenly around the rim. One cup also has one 0 and the plus sign written to the right of each numeral and one cup has two 0's and a plus sign to the right of the numerals. The cups can then can be stacked and laid on their side to represent the numbers being taught. For example, for the number 62, the cup with one zero is placed inside the cup with no zeros. Students rotate the cups until they make the equation 60 + 2. After teaching that the 6 represents 6 tens, the two cups can be stacked closer together to make the number 62. Mrs. Dunkel implements this strategy with her students and to her delight, the students begin to understand and appear excited to learn about place value.

Abstract Instruction

Once students understand the concrete and representations of the mathematical concepts, they are ready to move to the **abstract instruction**, or the use of symbols. When students move to the last level, the abstract level, they no longer rely on visual representations to solve problems. Only symbols are used, including numeric (e.g., 2, 5, 7), algebraic (e.g., $=$, $\sim$, $<$), statistical (e.g., $\sum$, μ, σ), and geometric (e.g., π, $\parallel$, $\perp$) symbols.

TEACHER TIP #11.3

TOUCHMATH

TouchMath (Innovative Learning Concepts) is a commercially available curriculum designed to teach students the four basic operations. TouchMath is considered a dot-notation method where dots are associated with each numeral 1 to 9. Students learn the positions of the dots on each numeral. Then when teaching addition, students are taught to select the highest number (e.g., 4), say the number, and then continue counting the dots on the second number (e.g., 3) to achieve the answer (e.g., 7). Once students are proficient using these steps, the dots are removed and the students continue counting the positions of the removed dots. Research conducted with students with intellectual disabilities and learning disabilities has found TouchMath to be an effective instructional strategy for teaching basic operations (Simon & Hanrahan, 2004).

Teacher-Directed Instruction

Teachers generally use either the constructivist or the explicit approach to mathematics instruction. When using a constructivist approach, students construct their own meaning and students' new learning is dependent upon their existing understandings. Social interactions and authentic learning tasks become critical to the instruction. Some refer to the constructivist approach as an inquiry- or discovery-oriented approach (Przychodzin, Marchand-Martella, Martella, & Azim, 2004). In contrast, explicit instruction requires the teacher to plan and direct the instructional sequence using elements such as clear objectives, modeling, guided practice, independent practice, and progress monitoring. (See Chapter 6 for a thorough discussion of these elements.)

In numerous reviews of literature, researchers have documented that explicit or teacher-directed instruction is an effective way to teach students with HID basic facts and procedures, concepts, and problem-solving (Gersten et al., 2009; Jones, Wilson, & Bhojwani, 1997; Kroesbergen & van Luit, 2003; Maccini & Hughes, 1997). For example, Russell Gersten and his colleagues (2009) studied the impact of instructional methods from 42 studies on the mathematical proficiency of students with learning disabilities. They discovered that explicit instruction on direct mathematical skills resulted in significant increased student learning regardless of whether other instructional components were included. General math strategy instruction, students' verbalization of their math reasoning (i.e., self-talk), and the use of visual representations, particularly when used in combination with other instructional components, were also very effective.

Based on research on math instruction, Nancy Stein, Diane Kinder, Jerry Silbert, and Douglas Carnine (2006) created nine steps necessary to designing effective mathematics instructions. The steps are listed in Table 11.4.

Short-Term and Lesson Objectives (Step 1)

All students with disabilities must have IEPs with goals and short-term objectives or benchmarks specific to the student's individual needs and these objectives must take into consideration the general education curriculum. The first of nine steps necessary to designing effective math instruction involves specifying objectives relative to the math content to be learned (see Chapter 6).

Procedural Strategies, Prerequisites, and Skills (Steps 2–4)

A major characteristic of students with HID is their inability to spontaneously generate and apply strategies to facilitate their own learning. Thus, students need to be given procedural strategies or routines to apply. Computational routines can be fairly straightforward and simple to devise and follow. Application strategies, on the other hand can be very difficult (Stein et al., 2006).

TABLE 11.4   Nine Steps to Designing Effective Mathematics Instruction

Step	Brief Description
1. Write short-term and lesson objectives.	Write the short-term objective and lesson objectives that lead to accomplishment of the IEP goals.
2. Design procedure strategies.	Decide what skills need to be taught and in what order.
3. Determine prerequisites.	Plan to teach/check prerequisite skills.
4. Sequence the skills.	Write the steps for completing the new skill.
5. Select a teaching procedure.	Select a teaching procedure: motor, label, strategy.
6. Write a scripted lesson plan.	Use concise, consistent language throughout the lesson plan.
7. Select examples.	Plan all instructional examples to include in the lesson plan.
8. Plan for practice and review.	Prepare practice problems and include review problems for subsequent lessons.
9. Design procedures for monitoring progress.	Create a data collection system that allows you to monitor the students' progress.

Sources: Stein, Kinder, Silbert, & Carnine (2006).

Students with disabilities benefit from step-by-step instruction that teaches both computational routines and application strategies. Teachers can task-analyze to develop lessons that include step-by-step instruction. **Task analysis** refers to breaking a task into smaller manageable parts or steps, teaching steps as separate objectives, and then combining all steps to complete the entire task (Alberto & Troutman, 2012). The first step of task analysis is to determine what skills or concepts the learner must possess to learn the new task. For example, if the objective is for students to learn to add two-digit by two-digit numbers with regrouping, students must understand place value before they can add the columns and regroup. The second step involves considering whether any materials are needed to perform the task. If the task is counting with manipulatives, then manipulatives would be required to perform the task. Third, each step of the task is listed in the order it is to be performed. Finally, which steps will be taught together as a daily objective is determined. Once all steps of the process have been learned, the students complete the entire task (Alberto & Troutman, 2012). A sample task analysis appears in Table 11.5.

TABLE 11.5 Sample Task Analysis

Task Analysis: Two-Digit by Two-Digit, With Regrouping the Tens Place			
Step 1: Prerequisite skills	Step 2: Materials	Step 3: Sequence of steps to complete the skills	Step 4: Decide which steps to teach as a daily objectives
Number recognition Addition skills Place value Writing numbers Write numbers in columns Recognize addition sign	Pencil Paper Manipulatives (if needed)	1. Touch the ones column. 2. Read the numbers in the ones column and read the operation (4 plus 3). 3. Add the numbers (equals 7). 4. If the number is less than 10, write the number under the ones column (write 7). 5. If the number is greater than 10, regroup. 6. Write + (and then the amount regrouped) above the tens column. 7. Read all the numbers in the tens column and state the operation; include the regrouped number. 8. Add the numbers. 9. Write the answer below the tens column.	1. Day 1—Teach steps 1–4. 2. Day 2— Review steps 1–4. Add steps 5–9 to the process. 3. Day 3— Review entire process.

Sequencing skills involves determining the optimum order for introducing new skills and strategies. Stein et al. (2006) suggest three sequencing guidelines to include (a) prerequisite skills of a strategy should be taught before the strategy, (b) easier skills should be taught before harder ones, and (c) skills and strategies that may be confused should not be introduced consecutively. The third guideline is particularly important and often ignored by teachers. Any mathematical concept being taught that is similar to another mathematical concept should not be presented consecutively. A good example of the last guideline is the confusion students often make between the numerals 6 and 9. Given their physical similarity, the introduction of the numerals 6 and 9 should be separated over time.

As Ms. Jiménez worked with her class, she observed that several students made errors computing simple addition facts. She decided to task-analyze addition and teach a simple task analysis to reduce computation errors. Ms. Jiménez's task analysis was	1. Circle the smallest number. 2. Write tallies above the number to represent the number. 3. Touch and say the largest number. 4. Touch each tally and count out loud. 5. Write and say the answer.

Teaching Procedure (Step 5)

There exist three types of tasks in mathematics instruction: motor tasks, labeling tasks, and strategy tasks (Stein et al., 2006). With motor tasks, students memorize and state procedural rules, as well as write numerals. Labeling tasks involves stating words that correctly label an object (e.g., saying, "five" when shown the numeral 5). Strategy tasks require integrating a series of steps to create a generalizable strategy. The instructional sequence for each varies slightly and these steps are outlined in Table 11.6.

TABLE 11.6   Direct Instruction Sequence to Use

Type of Mathematical Task	Instructional Sequence	Example
Motor Tasks	**Model:** Teacher demonstrates the task.	"My turn to count by 2s: 2, 4, 6, 8, 10."
	Lead: Teacher helps students make the desired response.	"Now, let's do it together: 2, 4, 6, 8, 10." Teacher continues until students can do it alone.
	Test: Teacher asks students to make response without help.	"Now it's your turn to do it by yourself."
	Delayed Test: Students complete the task several minutes later after an "interference" task.	After working on some addition problems, the teacher returns to asking students to count by 2s independently.
Labeling Tasks	**Model:** Teacher points to the symbol, tells the student the label, asks student to repeat.	"This is a triangle. What is it?"
	Alternating Test: Teacher alternates pointing between this symbol and symbols previously taught.	"Remember these shapes we already practiced? What is this? (square) What is this? (circle) What is this? (triangle)."
	Delayed Test: Teacher asks student to identify the new symbol later in the lesson.	After working on a new task, the teacher returns to asking students to identify the triangle.

Type of Mathematical Task	Instructional Sequence	Example
Strategy Tasks	**Model:** Teacher demonstrates how to work the problem, asking questions to prompt each step.	"This is how you find the common denominator. First, look at the two denominators. Are they the same or different? If they are the same, you don't need to find a common denominator. If they are different, will the smaller denominator divide evenly into the larger denominator? . . ."
	Guided Practice: The teacher prompts the students less while continuing to ask strategy-based questions as they complete the problems.	"Now you that you have watched me complete these problems, let's do several together. What is the first step? . . ."
	Test: Students complete their work independently, but supervised by the teacher.	"Great! You can do most of these without any help at all. Now it's your turn to do it without my helping you. I am going to watch to make certain you are following all of the steps you learned."

Source: Stein et al., 2006

Scripted Lesson Plan (Step 6)

A scripted lesson plan provides the specifics of what a teacher will say and do and some anticipated student responses. Correction procedures for errors and examples to be presented to the students are particularly important components of mathematics scripted lesson plans. Preparing the lesson in this format in advance allows the teacher to focus full attention on the students during instruction rather than trying to think of additional examples or the next steps. (For more detailed information on writing scripted lesson plans, see Chapter 6.) A scripted lesson plan demonstrating teaching fractions using teacher-directed instruction may be found in Appendix D.

Examples (Step 7)

Step 7 refers to selecting problems to be used for instructional purposes. Based on their review of literature, Gersten et al. (2009) stated that the sequence of examples appears to be the most important during early acquisition of new math skills, whereas the range of examples taught is most critical to support transfer of newly acquired information.

Stein et al. (2006) suggest two guidelines for selecting examples. First, include only problems that students can solve using strategies they already know. Second, include not only problems of the type being currently taught, but previously learned problems that are similar. The second step helps students learn to discriminate between problem types. The importance of mixing problem types cannot be overemphasized.

Practice and Review (Step 8)

Enough opportunities for practice and review must be provided to ensure retention of skills over time. In determining the necessary amount of practice and review, use the following guidelines:

1. Provide enough practice until mastery is reached. Mastery is attained when the student is able to work problems accurately and fluently. Fluency is particularly important for basic math facts.

2. Provide systematic review. Once mastery is achieved, gradually decrease the number of problems of that type, but don't eliminate them altogether. Reintroduce problem types previously learned. Sometimes this requires deliberate planning. Other times it is more natural because the previously learned problem type is a prerequisite for a more advanced problem type (Stein et al., 2006).

Scaffolding can be an effective technique during practice to help support student learning. Four types of scaffolding for mathematics include the following:

- Conceptual scaffolds assist students in focusing on critical content. (e.g., prompts through think-alouds).

- Metacognitive scaffolds help students self-regulate the learning process (e.g., evaluating the task).

- Procedural scaffolds support the student when engaged in a complex task (e.g., multistep word problems) by showing them how to use tools (e.g., graph, diagram, checklist).

- Strategic scaffolds alert students to different methods for solving problems. (Jitendra, 2013)

Continuous Monitoring (Step 9)

Select problems for assessment that are similar to those used during instruction. Implement curriculum-based measurement to evaluate student progress over time. (For more information on continuous progress monitoring see Chapter 5.)

In addition to designing one's own lessons, commercially prepared curricula are available that use an explicit or teacher-directed approach to teaching mathematics. The curricula listed in Table 11.7 are teacher directed and are appropriate for students with math disabilities and those who are at risk for math difficulties.

Specific Mathematics Strategies

Many students with HID have difficulty organizing and remembering organizational frameworks. In addition, they do not spontaneously generate strategies to facilitate their own learning. Thus, strategy instruction is extremely important for this population.

TABLE 11.7 **Commercially Available Math Curriculum Using Teacher-Directed Instruction**

Program Name	Target Group	Description
Connecting Math Concepts www.mheonline.com	Designed for K–5 Appropriate as a core program or for at-risk students	Combines facts, procedures, conceptual understanding, applications, and problem-solving skills based on the Common Core State Standards in mathematics.
DISTAR Arithmetic www.mheonline.com	Designed for K–2 Designed for low-performing students but could be used with all students	Lessons are designed around major skill tracks and delivered in small groups. Covers basic addition, subtraction, multiplication, and fractions, as well as ordinal counting, algebra operations, concepts of more and less, and simple picture and story problems.
Corrective Mathematics www.mheonline.com	Designed for Grade 3–adult Appropriate for remedial or developmental work	Lessons develop the skills, strategies, automaticity, accuracy, and recall of facts that are key to understanding what the operations mean. Also addresses strategies for solving word problems and how to work with fractions. Materials serve as a foundation for future work with complex algebraic expressions.

Technology Spotlight #11.1

Tools for Mathematics Instruction

Many students with disabilities struggle in mathematics. As a result, the field has devoted considerable attention to harnessing the potential of technology for facilitating mathematics instruction. One of the most common tools available for teachers and students involves the use of a spreadsheet. Teaching students how to use a spreadsheet to create formulas to solve specific types of math problems can be a valuable lifelong tool.

The following list summarizes a variety of strategies and technology tools that hold promise for helping students with disabilities improve their math skills:

When students need visuals to make math concepts concrete—

Scholastic Keys: http://www.scholastic.com/administrator/funding/fundingconnection/pdf/KeysProductOverview.pdf

National Library of Virtual Manipulatives: nlvm.usu.edu/en/nav/vlibrary.html

When students need to practice math facts to build fluency—

Funbrain: www.funbrain.com

AplusMath Flashcards: aplusmath.com/Flashcards/index.html

Fastt Math: http://www.hmhco.com/products/fastt-math/

When students have difficulty learning to make change—

Money Instructor, Counting and Making Change Worksheets, Lesson Plans, Lessons:

moneyinstructor.com/change.asp

Enchanted Learning, US Coins: enchantedlearning.com/math/money/coins/

When students have difficulty learning to tell time—

Teaching Time: teachingtime.co.uk/

Time for Time: time-for-time.com/interactive.htm

When students need tools to compensate for calculation and formula application difficulties—

WebMATH: webmath.com

Math.com, Online Calculators: math.com/students/calculators/calculators.html

(See Table 4.5 for additional math tools)

Studies have documented, for example, that teaching students with learning disabilities general mathematical strategies effectively improves their math performance (Gersten et al., 2009). Students can learn basic math facts, as well as problem-solving, through the use of strategies. Instructional strategies discussed in previous chapters, such as peer tutoring, cooperative learning, and learning strategies apply to mathematics. The focus within this chapter is to delineate a few examples specific to teaching and learning mathematics.

Self-Regulation

Self-regulation in this context refers to students' ability to guide their own learning. Self-regulation strategies are needed for students to be effective mathematical problem-solvers and encompass self-instruction, self-questioning, and self-monitoring. These strategies help students gain access to strategic knowledge, as well as guide their application and regulate their use of strategies and their overall performance as they solve problems (Montague, Warger, & Morgan, 2000).

Self-management, for example, has been found to be helpful for students with HID. Students can be taught to record and evaluate their math performance. Recording their scores on a tablet allows the results to be sent to a database accessible to the teacher's computer and graphed for display (or the graphs can be hand drawn) (Mulcahy, Krezmien, & Maccini, 2014). Recording, displaying, and analyzing math performance data can help students learn the mathematical principles and operations involved.

The typical approach to solving mathematical word problems (e.g., read the problem, decide what to do, solve it, and check your answer) is insufficient for students with learning difficulties. They need additional self-regulation strategies. The SOLVE IT! program was designed to provide the extra instructional assistance students with HID need. In this program, students are taught how to "read the problem for understanding, paraphrase by putting the problem into their own words, visualize the problem by drawing a picture or making a mental image, set up a plan for solving the problem, estimate the answer, and compute and verify the solution" (Montague et al., 2000, p. 111). In addition, students are taught self-regulation strategies (i.e., self-instruction, self-questioning, and self-monitoring) needed for effective problem-solving. SOLVE IT! has been documented to be effective for students with HID, including those with learning disabilities (Krawec, Huang, Montague, Kressler, & de Alba, 2012), intellectual disabilities (Chung & Tam, 2005), and autism (Whitby, 2012). Table 11.8 outlines procedures for using self-regulation strategies for mathematical problem-solving from the SOLVE IT! program.

TABLE 11.8   **Cognitive Processes and Self-Regulation Strategies for Mathematical Problem-Solving Instruction**

Read (for understanding).

Say: "Read the problem. If I don't understand, read it again."

Ask: "Have I read and understood the problem?"

Check: For understanding as I solve the problem.

Paraphrase (your own words).

Say: "Underline the important information. Put the problem in my own words."

Ask: "Have I underlined the important information? What is the question? What am I looking for?"

Check: That the information goes with the question.

Visualize (a picture of a diagram).

Say: "Make a drawing or diagram."

Ask: "Does the picture fit the problem?"

Check: The picture against the problem information.

Hypothesize (a plan to solve the problem).

Say: "Decide how many steps and operations are needed. Write the operation symbols (+, -, x, ÷)."

Ask: "If I do ____, what will I get? If I do ____, then what do I need to do next? How many steps are needed?"

Check: That the plan makes sense.

Estimate (predict the answer).

Say: "Round the numbers, do the problem in my head, and write the estimate."

Ask: "Did I round up and down? Did I write the estimate?"

Check: That I used the important information.

Compute (do the arithmetic).

Say: "Do the operations in the right order."

(Continued)

TABLE 11.8	(Continued)

Ask:	"How does my answer compare with my estimate? Does my answer make sense? Are the decimals or money signs in the right places?"
Check:	That all the operations were done in the right order.
Check (make sure everything is right).	
Say:	"Check the computation."
Ask:	"Have I checked every step? Have I checked the computation? Is my answer right?"
Check:	That everything is right. If not, go back. Then ask for help if I need it.

Source: Montague, M., Warger, C., & Morgan, T. H. (2000). Solve It! Strategy instruction to improve mathematical problem solving. *Learning Disabilities Research and Practice, 15*, 110–116.

Mnemonic Strategies

Mathematical vocabulary can be taught using mnemonic keywords. As discussed in Chapter 9, the keyword procedure requires three steps: (a) recoding, (b) relating, and (c) retrieving. Recoding involves associating an unfamiliar word into an acoustically similar and familiar word. For example, the keyword for multiplier could be *pliers*; and the keyword for multiplicand could be *hand*. The second step, relating, involves associating the keywords in an interactive, memorable visual image. In these examples,

> pictures could then be constructed of *pliers* forming the multiplication sign, next to the multi<u>plier</u>, and the multiplicand written on (or by) a *hand*. Likewise, for a division problem, the di<u>visor</u> could be wearing a *visor*, the divi<u>den</u>d could be *in* the *den* (i.e., inside the division lines), and the *quotient* could be written in *quotation* marks. (Mastropieri & Scruggs, 1991, p. 86)

Retrieving, the last step, involves recalling the vocabulary word with its meaning or vice versa.

Pegwords can also be used to teach mathematics, such as the multiplication tables. As discussed in Chapter 9, pegwords are matched numbers with similar sounding words that can be easily visualized. (Sample pegwords were presented in Chapter 9.) Once students learn these pegword associations, then pictures representing the multiplication fact can be presented. For example, to teach 8 x 4 = 32, a gate (eight) leading to a door (four) could be visualized next to a dirty (thirty) shoe (two).

Rhymes and acronyms can be used to teach mathematical procedures. The phrase, *My Dear Aunt Sally*, can help students remember the sequence of operations (multiply and divide, add and subtract) (Mastropieri & Scruggs, 1991). Or the following sentence can help students recall the progression of the metric system: King Henry died Monday drinking chocolate milk (kilometer, hectometer, decameter, meter, decimeter, centimeter, millimeter) (Silva, 2004). Because there are two words that start with the same letter (died = decameter, drinking = decimeter, and meter = Monday, milk = millimeter) students may need additional strategies to identify which word is linked to which word. For example, in the alphabet the *a* (in decameter) comes before the *i* (decimeter).

Two acronym strategies that have been demonstrated to be effective in teaching math are the LAP and SOLVE strategies. LAP is designed to teach students how to add and subtract fractions with and without common denominators (Test & Ellis, 2005); and SOLVE helps students problem-solve (Freeman-Green, O'Brien, Wood, & Hitt, 2015). The steps for each acronym follow:

LAP (add and subtract fractions)

Look at the sign.

Ask yourself, "Are the denominators the same?"

Pick the process for the fraction type.

SOLVE (problem-solving)

Study the problem,

Organize the facts,

Line up a plan,

Verify your plan with action, and

Evaluate your answer.

FIGURE 11.1 **Adding and Subtracting Fractions With LAP**

STEP 1 – L – look at the sign. Is it a plus or minus?

STEP 2 – A – ask yourself. **A.** Are the denominators the SAME? **B.** Are they DIFFERENT and the smaller denominator <u>CAN</u> be divided into the larger denominator? **C.** Are they DIFFERENT and the smaller denominator <u>CANNOT</u> be divided into the larger denominator?

STEP 3 – P – pick the process for the fraction type.

(Continued)

FIGURE 11.1 (Continued)

A. The DENOMINATORS are the SAME	B. The denominators are DIFFERENT and the SMALLER denominator <u>CAN</u> be divided evenly into the LARGER denominator	C. The denominators are DIFFERENT and the smallest denominator <u>CANNOT</u> be divided evenly into the larger denominator.
1. After the equal sign, write a fraction line and write the denominator (it stays the same). 2. If the sign is plus, add the numerators and write the answer above the denominator. 3. If the sign is minus, subtract the smaller numerator from the larger numerator and write the answer above the denominator.	1. Draw a box around the smallest denominator. 2. Ask how many times the smaller denominator can be divided into the larger denominator. 3. Write the answer next to the boxed number, AND next to the numerator on top of the boxed number. 4. Multiply the numerator times the number you wrote. Write the answer next to this fraction. Draw a fraction line under the answer. Multiply the boxed number times the number you wrote, and write it under the new numerator. 5. CROSS OUT THE FRACTION THAT HAS THE BOXED NUMBER. 6. Add or subtract the numerators and write your answer. The denominator stays the same.	1. Draw a fraction line under each original fraction. Multiply the denominators and write the answer under the fraction lines. 2. Look at the first original fraction. Draw a box around the denominator. Ask how many times this denominator goes into the new denominator number. Write the answer next to the numerator. Multiply the numbers and write the answer on top of the new denominator. 3. Look at the second original fraction. Draw a box around the denominator. Ask how many times this denominator goes into your new denominator number. Write the answer next to the numerator. Multiply the numbers and write the answer on top of the new denominator. 4. CROSS OUT THE ORIGINAL FRACTIONS. 5. Add or subtract the numerators of the new fractions and write your answer. The denominator stays the same.

Source: Test, D. W., & Ellis, M. F. (2005). The effects of LAP fractions on addition and subtraction of fractions with students with mild disabilities. *Education and Treatment of Children, 28*, 11–14.

Graphic Representations

Graphic representations can help students' ability to understand and solve word problems. In using this strategy, students are taught how to identify the problem schemata, draw a representation, and then solve the problem (Jitendra, 2002). There are at least three classifications of schemata: change, group, and compare. Examples of these three may be found in Figure 11.2.

TEACHER TIP #11.4

MAGICAL 9'S RULE

Did you know there is a "magical" 9's rule of multiplication? The sum of the digits adds up to 9—for example, 9 x 2 = 18. 1 + 8 = 9. Students can be taught this rule to check their answers. In addition, students can use their prior knowledge of all one digit numbers that add to 9 (i.e., 1 + 8, 2 + 7, 3 + 6, 4 + 5) and count backward to find the first answer. So, if the problem were 9 x 8, the student would count backward from 8 and obtain 7. The second digit would be what needs to be added to 7 to make 9 (answer: 2 or 72). This second application may be more difficult for some students than just learning the fact that 8 x 9 = 72 (Meltzer et al., 1996).

FIGURE 11.2 **Examples of Graphic Representations for Teaching Word Problems**

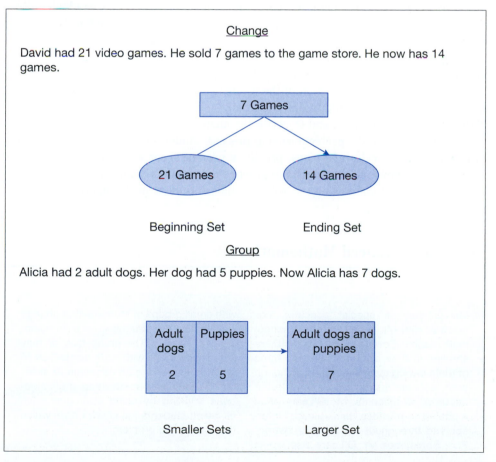

Change

David had 21 video games. He sold 7 games to the game store. He now has 14 games.

7 Games

21 Games   14 Games

Beginning Set   Ending Set

Group

Alicia had 2 adult dogs. Her dog had 5 puppies. Now Alicia has 7 dogs.

Adult dogs	Puppies	Adult dogs and puppies
2	5	7

Smaller Sets   Larger Set

(Continued)

FIGURE 11.2 (Continued)

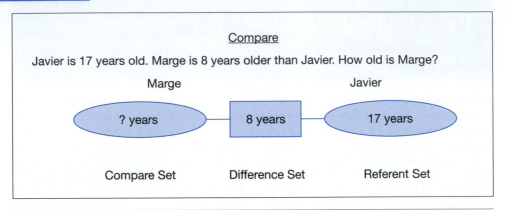

Source: Marshall, S. P. *Schemas in Problem Solving.* Copyright © 1995 Cambridge University Press. Reprinted with the permission of Cambridge University Press. (p. 135).

Using teacher-directed methods, students are taught to identify each of these schematic designs. Teachers should first teach one problem type and then gradually introduce the others until the students can accurately discern each problem type. Once students can identify the type of problem, teach them how to draw a diagram to visually represent information in the word problem and then follow the steps for solving the problem. These steps include (a) find the object that represents the whole, (b) select an arithmetic operation (if the whole is unknown, subtract to find the parts; if the whole is unknown, add to find the total), (c) solve the problem, (d) check to see if the answer makes sense, and (e) write the answer. Use direct-instruction methods to teach the steps of the problem-solving process. Model the process, guide students in memorizing the rules and steps, provide a prompt sheet with the rules and steps listed, fade prompts, allow students to practice independently, and check for mastery. As students apply the strategy to solve problems student performance needs to be constantly monitored.

Teaching Advanced Mathematics

Mr. O'Leary, a special educator, co-teaches with Mr. Fahmi, the high school math teacher. Seven students with HID are enrolled in their algebra class with three of them having math disabilities. Although both teachers instruct and attend to the needs of all students, Mr. O'Leary often models and provides "think-alouds" interspersed throughout Mr. Fahmi's instruction. Sometimes Mr. O'Leary also works with small groups of students that change weekly who are struggling on a particular concept or skill. The group may or may not include those with math disabilities. In addition to working on concepts or skills, Mr. O'Leary tries to develop their algebraic thinking by using strategies such as giving students the answer from which they create the problem.

The Common Core State Standards (CCSS) include a set of standards for high school students which includes algebra, geometry, statistics, and probability, among other content. Although little research has been conducted on teaching students with HID these higher level math skills, teaching algebraic concepts has received some recent attention, perhaps because algebra is considered a gateway to advanced mathematical understanding (Impecoven-Lind & Foegen, 2010). Research has documented that generally speaking students perform poorly in algebra because they (a) lack understanding that a variable (e.g., an x used as a placeholder for an unknown number) represents a value or a relationship between variables; (b) attempt to use informal, intuitive means to answer the problem rather than formal methods necessary in algebra; and (c) lack understanding of notation and conventions used in algebra (e.g., coefficients, negative numbers) (Impecoven-Lind & Foegen, 2010). All of these areas are prerequisite knowledge for algebra. Additional prerequisites have been identified as fluency in computation, strong understanding of rational numbers (including fractions, decimals, and percentages) and integers, and knowledge of measurement (Dougherty, Bryant, Bryant, Darrough, & Pfannenstiel, 2015).

Based on limited research with students with HID, researchers have found the following to be effective in increasing their algebra proficiency: classwide peer tutoring (CWPT), learning strategies, and content enhancement routines (CERs) (Impecoven-Lind & Foegen, 2010). These strategies are addressed fully in in Chapters 8 and 9.

Another approach to algebraic instruction is using explicit questioning to deepen student understanding. Reversibility, flexibility, and generalization are the three types of questions used to help students focus on critical aspects of problems and make connections across them (see Table 11.9). Given that this instructional approach will be different for most students, Barbara Dougherty, Diane Bryant, Brian Bryant, Rebecca Darrough, and Kathleen Pfannenstiel (2015) recommend teachers use this approach but within the framework of teacher directed instruction and student-mediated strategies:

- Use explicit instruction to teach students how to respond to these questions using modeling and "thinking aloud."

- Use think-pair-share or other small group or pairs to formulate answers.

- Use the type of questions provided in Table 11.9.

- Give students prompts when they get stuck ("What kind of model can you use to answer this question?").

Math Response to Intervention

As discussed in Chapter 7, response to intervention (RTI) is a multitiered system of support typically consisting of three tiers. Tier 1 supports are delivered to all students and include math core instruction with differentiated instruction when needed. Students who are unable to make adequate gains in math are provided additional intervention or Tier 2 supports. Tier 2 math interventions typically consist of additional math instruction using teacher-directed instruction, drill and practice with cumulative review, additional reinforcement for motivational support, peer-mediated instruction,

TABLE 11.9   Types of Questions for Developing Algebraic Thinking

Type of Question	Advantages	Examples	Instructional Sequence
Reversibility Students are given the answer and they create the problem.	• Challenges students' perceptions that math is a series of linear, sequential steps. • There are an infinite number of solutions. • Having to create the problem generates deeper thinking.	• What are two integers whose sum is –2? • What are two fractions whose product is 3/8?	• Provide the answer to the type of problems being taught. • Ask to create the problem to get to the answer. • Ask to model or show how to solve the problem (e.g., manipulatives, number line). • Ask if it would help to make a table, draw a picture, etc.
Flexibility Students identify how problems are different and alike. Students are asked to solve a problem multiple ways.	• Helps students look for similar problems before attempting to solve the current problem. • Helps students recognize there are ways other than computation for solving problems.	• If I know 5 + (–12) is –7, then how do I know 5 + (–10) is –5 without using computation? • Solve this problem in multiple ways: –5 + (–12) =	• Ask how a similar problem has been solved before. • Ask how they can use what they know about this problem to solve another one. • Ask if the student can solve the problem in a different way with a model. • Have students share how they arrived at the same answer but in different ways.
Generalization Students create statements about patterns which can be used to predict answers or check responses or create a specific problem from a generalization.	• Promotes generalization of knowledge to future problems. • Helps students who repeat computational errors to review the reasonableness of their answer.	• If I were to add 2/3 and 3/5, would my answer be greater or less than 1? How do I know?	• Ask students to identify patterns. • Ask students to identify representations that have been used to solve the problem (e.g., pictures, diagrams, timelines). • Ask what strategies could be used to solve the problem.

Source: Adapted from: Dougherty, B., Bryant, D. P., Bryant, B. R., Darrough, R. L., & Pfannenstiel, K. H. (2015). Developing concepts and generalizations to build algebraic thinking: The reversibility, flexibility, and generalization approach. *Intervention in School and Clinic, 50*(5), 273–281.

and/or concrete-representational-abstract instruction (Dobbins et al., 2014; Pool, Carter, Johnson, & Carter, 2012). One study discovered that when groups of three to six students received 30 additional minutes of math intervention 3 to 5 days a week, significant gains in student math performance were achieved (Fuchs, Fuchs, & Hollenbeck, 2007). Tier 3 interventions are the most intensive and are typically administered in a one-on-one or dyad setting four to five times per week. Similar interventions to those applied in Tier 2 are implemented; the frequency and intensity, however, are increased.

As data are collected on student performance, students may move in and out of various tiers; and students not succeeding in Tier 3 are typically referred for special education services. As students move into higher tiers, they continue to receive the previous tier(s) interventions. Thus, a student receiving Tier 3 supports also receives supports from Tiers 2 and 1.

TEACHER TIP #11.5
SPECIFIC MATH STRATEGIES

General techniques for teaching mathematics to students with disabilities include the following:

- Use manipulatives and visuals.
- Use boxed templates to isolate problems on a page.
- Assign fewer math problems.
- Minimize or eliminate copying problems from the textbook or board.
- Use colors to code different steps (e.g., underline the directions in green to remind students to read them first).

- Allow students to finger-trace.
- Capitalize on patterns and other associations.
- Use motivating games to reinforce learning of small steps.
- Provide samples for those who need them such as a number line, flip charts with sample problem completed, sample problem completed at the top of a worksheet, and/or a list of procedural steps. (Bley & Thornton, 2001)

Implications for Culturally and/or Linguistically Diverse Students

Without much thought, it may seem as though mathematics deals with quantities and is therefore devoid of cultural influences. However, mathematics is truly an extension of culture. Mathematical concepts have been created to meet the needs of a particular culture. For example, the Gregorian calendar used today was designed to plan and coordinate Christian-based religious celebrations. Other calendars (e.g., Chinese, Jewish, Muslim) have been created throughout the ages for other purposes.

Historically all traditional short-distance measurement systems were based on the human body. For example, the *inch* originally represented the width of a thumb and the *foot* was the length of a human foot. Although the English Customary System of Measurement has standardized these lengths, other cultures continue to use measurement systems based on the human body. For example, the Yup'ik Eskimo people of southwest Alaska base short distances on the following:

- *Yaqneq*—distance from fingertip to fingertip of opposite hands while arms are stretched outward.

- *Taluyaneq*—distance from the middle of the chest to the fingertip of an outstretched arm.

- *Tallinin*—distance from the armpit to the end of a clenched fist of an outstretched arm.

These distances are particularly important for activities such as traveling, hunting, and fishing. The Yup'ik developed other measurement systems connected to their needs. A *fish rack full of drying salmon* and *scoop of berries*, for example, are units of measure in their culture (Lipka, Shockey, & Adams, 2003). These examples are provided to illustrate how mathematics has evolved out of the customs, traditions, and needs of a particular culture. In fact, mathematics may be considered a byproduct of culture.

Other aspects of culture, such as language, can influence the learning of mathematics. For example, the superiority of Asian students in mathematical performance has received much attention. Many have suggested reasons for their success including the structure of Japanese, Korean, and Chinese languages (Jao, 2012). These Asian students who learn mathematics in their native language have one advantage over those learning mathematics using the English language. The organization of the numeral names is congruent with the base-10 system. For example, in Japanese the number labels correspond with their numeric values. A sample of number names follows:

1   ichi

2   ni

3   san

10   juu

11   juu-ichi

20   ni-juu

21   ni-juu-ichi

30   san-juu

Japanese students learn more easily that $10 + 1 = 11$, because the word representing 11 is exactly that—10 (juu) and 1 (ichi) or juu-ichi (11).

Language impacts mathematical performance of culturally and/or linguistically diverse (CLD) students in other ways. As addressed previously in this chapter, language skills are an integral factor in math achievement in that vocabulary comprehension is needed to complete math calculations, solve word problems, and engage in higher mathematical thinking. As compared with native English-speaking students, the number of studies examining best math instructional practices for CLD students is limited. One instructional sequence that was designed to help English learners solve word programs has been researched and shows promise in this area (Orosco, Swanson, O'Connor, & Lussier, 2011). The steps follow:

- Preteach math concepts by introducing key concepts and terminology that the student does not understand. Provide the definitions and place the words in context of the word problem.

- Model the completion of the problem by reading it aloud and solving the problem on the board. Ask students to repeat this process.

- Teach the following problem-solving strategies:

  ○ Know—Ask "What do I already know about the problem?"
  ○ Find—Locate the important vocabulary and numbers in the word problem.
  ○ Set up—After reading each sentence, determine if the information is relevant to solving the problems.
  ○ Solve—Solve the word problem.
  ○ Check for understanding—Student asks and answers questions about what they read, as well as summarizes key ideas in solving the problems and checks if solved correctly.

- Once students can use these strategies, place them in dyads or small groups to practice the steps. (Orosco, 2014)

TEACHER TIP #11.6

LANGUAGE AND MATH INTEGRATION

Integrate another language into the math curriculum. For example, students can learn to count from 0 to 10 in Spanish: *cero, uno, dos, tres, cuatro, cinco, seis, siete, ocho, nueve, diez.* Then teach them the Spanish words for plus (*mas*), minus (*menos*), and are (*son*). Orally state a problem for students to solve in Spanish (e.g., *siete mas dos*). Ask students to repeat the answer in Spanish (e.g., *seite mas dos son nueve*). Have students take turns creating the number problems for a partner. (Benning, Bonenberger, Hickey, & Steward, 2000)

Culture impacts mathematical learning in other ways. As discussed in previous chapters, many ethnically diverse students respond best to holistic, multisensory, group experiences based on real-life experiences. Yet, it has been suggested that problems in mathematics textbooks are more relevant to the authors of the textbooks than to many students, particularly for poor students living in urban settings (Ensign, 2003). Given that textbook mathematical problems may be irrelevant for many students, teachers can use different strategies to identify culturally relevant mathematical problems, such as having students supply their own personal examples or examining the literature and current events of the communities in which the students reside for real-life experiences.

Mr. Weston's math students are a mix of African American, Asian American, and White. He tries to make his instruction culturally responsive, including using group experiences and authentic problems. One event that students from his area understand and have experienced is Hurricane Katrina. Mr. Weston sets up cooperative-learning groups who work on mathematical problem solving exercises involving real-life experience. An example follows: *When Katrina was first declared a hurricane, it had sustained winds of 40 miles per hour. The winds increased to 175 mph and then when it hit landfall along the Louisiana-Mississippi border, the winds slowed to 120 mph. What percentage change occurred in the winds between each of these measurements?*

In addition to making mathematical problems culturally relevant, teachers can select culturally oriented learning activities to be studied along with mathematics topics. For example, the geometric patterns of Northern Plains Native American star quilts can be studied along with the history and customs of those who created them. Students can create designs using the patterns adopted by this group while researching historical background, investigating the tools used to cut the pieces and sew the quilt at the turn of the century (Neumann, 2003). Or the bead patterns used by some Native American tribes to decorate clothing, containers, bags, and other items can be studied as an art, math, and cultural lesson (Arnason, McDonald, Maeers, & Weston, 2001).

TEACHER TIP #11.7

USING CULTURAL ART FORMS

Some Islamic sects forbade the depiction of humans or animals in art form. Artists, therefore, made geometric figures and floral designs coupled with Arabic calligraphy of writing selections from the Qur'an (Koran) to adorn the walls of mosques and palaces. The geometric patterns constructed with a compass and straight-edge are called *tessellations*. Students can study, emulate, or create their own tessellation patterns (Zaslavsky, 2002).

Mathematics is an outgrowth of culture. Culture has influenced the evolution of mathematical concepts we know today and it will continue to impact the field of mathematics. Teachers must recognize the role culture plays in mathematical concepts and ensure that their methods of teaching and the curriculum they use are congruent with the culture of the students they are teaching.

SUMMARY

Approximately 5% to 10% of the school-age population demonstrate mathematical disabilities, which includes many students with HID. The learning characteristics of students with HID contribute to the challenges they may experience with mathematics. Some of these characteristics include difficulties with memory, attention, visual perception, and language. Language skills are needed, for example, to complete math calculations, solve word problems, and engage in higher mathematical thinking. Students with HID may also have behavioral and emotional issues that impact math, such as learned helplessness or math anxiety.

Number sense, or the ability to understand numbers, numeric relationships, and how to use numeric information to solve mathematical problems, is essential for learning math. Emerging evidence indicates that students with math disabilities have difficulty with number sense. Teachers should use teaching strategies that help promote numerical power. Numerically powerful students use procedural strategies accurately and know how to make sense of numerical and quantitative situations.

The CCSS are the most shared set of K–12 academic standards for mathematics. Given that students with HID must have access to general education curriculum, special educators need to be knowledgeable about the CCSS or their local state- or district-adopted standards.

Research has documented that teacher-directed instruction is the most effective way of teaching mathematics to students with HID. Teachers should ensure that all of the elements of effective teaching (e.g., modeling, guided practice, independent practice) are part of mathematical instruction. In addition, students with HID benefit from being taught math concepts using the concrete-representational-abstract sequence. Specific strategies also facilitate learning in mathematics. Self-regulation (e.g., SOLVE IT! program), mnemonic strategies (e.g., pegwords and acronyms), and graphic representations (e.g., graphic organizers representing word problems) have been found to help students learn mathematical facts and procedures.

Students with HID may advance to higher level mathematics. One area that has received recent attention is algebra. To successfully learn algebra, students need prerequisite knowledge such as computational skills and understanding of rational numbers and integers. Several instructional methods, such as peer tutoring and learning strategies have been shown to help students with HID learn algebra. Another approach is to use questioning procedures designed to deepen students' understanding, including reversibility, flexibility, and generalization types of questions.

Given that mathematical concepts were created to meet the needs of a particular culture, mathematics may be considered a by-product of culture. When selecting curriculum materials and designing instruction, teachers are encouraged to use instructional styles compatible with diverse cultures, couple mathematics lessons with culturally oriented learning activities, and consider the appropriateness of textbook mathematical problems. English learners need particular attention given that math is laden with both everyday and content-based vocabulary.

REVIEW QUESTIONS

1. Discuss learning characteristics of students with HID that impact math achievement and address instructional strategies that can be implemented to overcome these learning difficulties.

2. Justify why number sense is important for learning and understanding math.

3. How can teachers help students acquire number sense, or become numerically powerful?

4. Why do students with disabilities benefit from instruction that begins at a concrete level and then moves to an abstract level? Provide a teaching example of moving from the concrete level to an abstract level.

5. Describe the process you would use to task analyze a math operation.

6. Which elements of effective math lessons are most critical and why?

7. Describe the steps suggested by Stein et al. (2006) for designing effective mathematics instructions. Create one example using these steps.

8. Describe how you could incorporate student-mediated instruction, graphic organizers, mnemonics, and self-instruction strategies into teacher-directed math lessons. Provide examples.

9. Explain how teachers can design math instruction to address the needs of students from diverse cultures.

10. Describe the role of language in mathematics and address how you would teach math to students who are English learners.

ACTIVITIES

1. Select five math skills. Task analyze each of the five skills.

2. From the list of standards for third-grade math, select five math skills to teach. Form a group with your peers and discuss how you would teach each skill. Identify which strategies and teaching methods you'll use. Justify why you selected specific strategies and methods.

3. Teach a direct-instruction math lesson to other students in your class. Have the students evaluate your lesson. Write a summary of your experience and their comments.

4. Write a one-page summary of the main concepts of this chapter. Address the following: (a) what you learned about math instruction, (b) effective methods for teaching math to students with disabilities, and (c) which strategies you would use in your classroom, and why.

Council for Exceptional Children (CEC) Standards

The Council for Exceptional Children (CEC) is a premiere national professional organization comprised of special educators, paraeducators, relative service personnel, parents, and others interested in individuals with disabilities and/or those with gifts and talents. This organization has generated 10 standards for the preparation of special educators. These standards are listed in each chapter as they relate to the content within the chapter. The standards that apply to Chapter 11 are Standards #1, #3, #5, and #6.

CEC Initial Preparation Standard #1: Learner Development and Individual Learning Differences

Beginning special education professionals understand how exceptionalities may interact with development and learning and use this knowledge to provide meaningful and challenging learning experiences for individuals with exceptionalities.

1.1. Beginning special education professionals understand how language, culture, and family background influence the learning of individuals with exceptionalities.

1.2. Beginning special education professionals use understanding of development and individual differences to respond to the needs of individuals with exceptionalities.

CEC Initial Preparation Standard #3: Curricular Content Knowledge (partial)

Beginning special education professionals use knowledge of general and specialized curricula to individualize learning for individuals with exceptionalities.

3.1. Beginning special education professionals understand the central concepts, structures of the discipline, and tools of inquiry of the content areas they teach and can organize this knowledge, integrate cross-disciplinary skills, and develop meaningful learning progressions for individuals with exceptionalities.

3.2. Beginning special education professionals understand and use general and specialized content knowledge of teaching across curricular content areas to individualize learning for individuals with exceptionalities.

CEC Initial Preparation Standard #5: Instructional Planning and Strategies (partial)

Beginning special education professionals select, adapt, and use a repertoire of evidence-based instructional strategies to advance learning of individuals with exceptionalities.

5.1. Beginning special education professionals consider an individual's abilities, interests, learning environments, and cultural and linguistic factors in the selection, development, and adaptation of learning experiences for individuals with exceptionalities.

5.7. Beginning special education professionals teach cross-disciplinary knowledge and skills such as critical thinking and problem solving to individuals with exceptionalities.

CEC Initial Preparation Standard #6: Professional Learning and Ethical Practice (partial)

Beginning special education professionals use foundational knowledge of the field and their professional Ethnical Principles and Practice Standards to inform special education practice, to engage in lifelong learning, and to advance the profession.

6.3 Beginning special education professionals understand that diversity is a part of families, cultures, and schools, and that complex human issues can interact with the delivery of special education services.

REFERENCES

Alberto, P. A., & Troutman, A. C. (2012). *Applied behavior analysis for teachers* (9th ed.). Upper Saddle River, NJ: Pearson.

Arnason, K., McDonald, J. J., Maeers, M., & Weston, J. H. (2001). *Interweaving mathematics and indigenous cultures.* Paper presented at the International Conference on New Ideas in Mathematics Education, Queensland, Australia. (ERIC Document Reproduction Service No. ED 472097)

Bartelet, D., Ansari, D., Vaessen, A., & Blomert, L. (2014). Cognitive subtypes of mathematics learning difficulties in primary education. *Research in Developmental Disabilities, 35,* 657–670.

Benning, J. D., Bonenberger, L., Hickey, K. A., & Steward, C. (2000). Ole for math. *Teaching Children Mathematics, 6,* 560–561.

Bley, N. S., & Thornton, C. A. (2001). *Teaching mathematics to students with learning disabilities* (4th ed.). Austin, TX: Pro-Ed.

Charles, R. I., & Lobato, J. (1998). *Future basics: Developing numerical power.* Golden, CO: National Council of Supervisors of Mathematics.

Chung, K. K. H., & Tam, Y. H. (2005). Effects of cognitive-based instruction on mathematical problem solving by learners with mild intellectual disabilities, *Journal of Intellectual & Developmental Disability. 30*(4), 207–216.

Dennis, M. S., Sorrells, A. M., & Falcomata, T. S. (2016). Effects of two interventions on solving basic fact problems by second graders with mathematics learning disabilities. *Learning Disability Quarterly, 39*(2), 95–112.

Dobbins, A., Gagnon, J. C., & Ulrich, T. (2014). Teaching geometry to students with math difficulties using graduated and peer-mediated instruction in a response-to-intervention model. *Preventing School Failure, 58*(1), 17–25.

Dougherty, B., Bryant, D. P., Bryant, B. R., Darrough, R. L., & Pfannenstiel, K. H. (2015). Developing concepts and generalizations to build algebraic thinking: The reversibility, flexibility, and generalization approach. *Intervention in School and Clinic, 50*(5), 273–281.

Dyson, N. L., Jordan, N. C., & Glutting, J. (2011). A number sense intervention for low-income kindergartners at risk for mathematics difficulties. *Journal of Learning Disabilities, 46*(2), 166–181.

Ensign, J. (2003). Including culturally relevant math in an urban school. *Educational Studies, 34*, 414–423.

Flores, M. M. (2010). Using the concrete-representational-abstract sequence to teach subtraction with regrouping to students at risk for failure. *Remedial and Special Education, 31*(3), 195–207.

Freeman-Green, S. M., O'Brien, C., Wood, C. L., & Hitt, S. B. (2015). Effects of the SOLVE strategy on the mathematical problem solving skills of secondary students with learning disabilities. *Learning Disabilities Research and Practice, 30*(2), 76–90.

Fuchs, L. S., Fuchs, D., & Hollenbeck, K. N. (2007). Extending responsiveness to intervention to mathematics at first and third grades. *Learning Disabilities Research and Practice, 22*(1), 13–24.

Geary, D. C. (2004). Mathematics and learning disabilities. *Journal of Learning Disabilities, 37*, 4–15.

Gersten, R., Chard, D. J., Jayanthi, M., Baker, S. K., Morphy, P., & Flojo, J. (2009). Mathematics instruction for students with learning disabilities: A meta-analysis of instructional components. *Review of Educational Research, 76*(3), 1202–1242.

Impecoven-Lind, L. S., & Foegen, A. (2010). Teaching algebra to students with learning disabilities. *Intervention in School and Clinic, 46*(1), 31–37.

Jao, L. (2012). The multicultural mathematics classroom. *Multicultural Education, 19*(3), 2–10.

Jayanthi, M., Gersten, R., & Baker, S. (2008). *Mathematics instruction for students with learning disabilities or difficulty learning mathematics: A guide for teachers.* Portsmouth, NH: RMC Research Corporation, Center on Instruction.

Jitendra, A. K. (2002). Teaching students math problem-solving through graphic representations. *TEACHING Exceptional Children, 34*(4), 34–38.

Jitendra, A. K. (2013). Understanding and accessing standards-based mathematics for students with

mathematics difficulties. *Learning Disability Quarterly, 36*(1), 4–8.

Jones, E. D., Wilson, R., & Bhojwani, S. (1997). Mathematics instruction for secondary students with learning disabilities. *Journal of Learning Disabilities, 30*, 151–163.

Krawec, J., Huang, J., Montague, M., Kressler, B., & de Alba, A. M. (2012). The effects of cognitive strategy instruction on knowledge of math problem-solving processes of middle school students with learning disabilities. *Learning Disability Quarterly, 36*(2), 80–92.

Kroesbergen, E. H., & van Luit, J. E. (2003). Mathematics interventions for children with special educational needs: A meta-analysis. *Remedial and Special Education, 24*, 97–114.

Lipka, J., Shockey, T., & Adams, B. (2003). Bridging Yup'ik ways of measuring to western mathematics. *Yearbook (National Council of Teachers of Mathematics), 64*, 180–192.

Maccini, P., & Hughes, C. A. (1997). Mathematics interventions for adolescents with learning disabilities. *Learning Disabilities Research and Practice, 12*, 168–176.

Martin, R. B., Cirino, P. T., Barnes, M. A., Ewing-Cobbs, L., Fuchs, L. S., Stuebing, K. K., & Fletcher, J. M. (2012). Prediction and stability of mathematics skill and difficulty. *Journal of Learning Disabilities, 46*(5), 428–443.

Mastropieri, M. A., & Scruggs, T. E. (1991). *Teaching students ways to remember: Strategies for learning mnemonically.* Cambridge, MA: Brookline.

Mazzocco, M. M., & Meyers, G. F. (2003). Complexities in identifying and defining mathematics learning disability in the primary school-age years. *Annals of Dyslexia, 53*, 218–253.

Meltzer, L. J., Roditi, B. N., Haynes, D. P., Biddle, K. R., Paster, M., Taber, S. E., & Ciccarelli, A. J. (1996). *Strategies for success: Classroom teaching techniques for students with learning problems.* Austin, TX: Pro-ED.

Mercer, C. D., & Pullen, P. C. (2009). *Students with learning disabilities* (7th ed.). Upper Saddle River, NJ: Pearson.

Moch, P. L. (2001). Manipulatives work! *The Educational Forum, 66,* 81–87.

Montague, M., Warger, C., & Morgan, T. H. (2000). Solve it! Strategy instruction to improve mathematical problem solving. *Learning Disabilities Research & Practice, 15,* 110–116.

Mulcahy, C. A., Krezmien, M., & Maccini, P. (2014). Teaching mathematics to secondary students with emotional and behavioral disorders: Challenges and practical suggestions for teachers. *Preventing School Failure, 58*(2), 69–79.

National Governors Association Center for Best Practices, Council of Chief State School Officers. (2010). *Common Core State Standards for Mathematics.* Washington, DC: Author.

Neumann, M. D. (2003). The mathematics of Native American star quilts. *Mathematics Teaching in the Middle School, 9,* 230–236.

Orosco, M. J. (2014). Word problem strategy for Latino English language learners at risk for math disabilities. *Learning Disability Quarterly, 37*(1), 45–53.

Orosco, M. J., Swanson, H. L., O'Connor, R., & Lussier, C. (2011). The effects of dynamic strategic math on English language learners word problem solving. *The Journal of Special Education, 47*(2), 96–107.

Pool, J. L., Carter, G. M., Johnson, E. S., & Carter, D. R. (2012). The use and effectiveness of a targeted math intervention for third graders. *Intervention in School and Clinic, 48*(4), 210–217.

Prater, M. A. (2003). She will succeed! Strategies for success in inclusive classrooms. *TEACHING Exceptional Children, 35*(5), 58–64.

Przychodzin, A. M., Marchand-Martella, N. E., Martella, R. C., & Azim, D. (2004). Direct instruction mathematics programs: An overview and research summary. *Journal of Direct Instruction, 4*(1), 53–84.

Raghubar, K., Cirino, P., Barnes, M., Ewing-Cobbs, L., Fletcher, J., & Fuchs, L. (2009). Errors in multi-digit arithmetic and behavioral inattention in children with math difficulties. *Journal of Learning Disabilities, 42*(4), 356–371.

Riccomini, P. J., Smith, G. W., Hughes, E. M., & Fries, K. M. (2015). The language of mathematics: The importance of teaching and learning mathematical vocabulary. *Reading & Writing Quarterly, 31,* 235–252.

Robinson, C. S., Menchetti, B. M., & Torgesen, J. K. (2002). Toward a two-factor theory of one type of mathematics disabilities. *Learning Disabilities Research and Practice, 17,* 81–89.

Satsangi, R., & Bouck, E. C. (2015). Using virtual manipulative instruction to teach the concepts of area and perimeter to secondary students with learning disabilities. *Learning Disability Quarterly, 38*(3), 174–186.

Shin, M., & Bryant, D. P. (2015). A synthesis of mathematical and cognitive performances of students with mathematical learning disabilities. *Journal of Learning Disabilities, 48*(1), 96–112.

Silva, J. A. (2004). *Teaching inclusive mathematics to special learners, K–6.* Thousand Oaks, CA: Corwin.

Simon, R., & Hanrahan, J. (2004). An evaluation of the TouchMath method for teaching addition to students with learning disabilities in mathematics. *European Journal of Special Needs Education, 19,* 191–209.

Stein, M., Kinder, D., Silbert, J., & Carnine, D. W. (2006). *Designing effective mathematics instruction: A direct instruction approach* (4th ed.). Upper Saddle River, NJ: Pearson.

Strickland, T. K., & Maccini, P. (2013). The effects of the concrete-representational-abstract integration strategy on the ability of students with learning disabilities to multiply linear expressions within area problems. *Remedial and Special Education 34*(3), 142–153.

Swanson, H. L., & Jerman, O. (2006). Math disabilities: A selective meta-analysis of the literature. *Review of Educational Research, 76*(2), 249–274.

Test, D. W., & Ellis, M. F. (2005). The effects of LAP fractions on addition and subtraction of fractions with students with mild disabilities. *Education and Treatment of Children, 28*, 11–24.

Watson, S. M. R., & Gable, R. A. (2012). Unraveling the complex nature of mathematics learning disability: Implications for research and practice. *Learning Disability Quarterly, 36*, 178–187.

Wei, X., Lenz, K. B., & Blackorby, J. (2012). Math growth trajectories of students with disabilities: Disability category, gender, racial, and socioeconomic status differences from ages 7 to 17. *Remedial and Special Education, 34*(3), 154–165.

Whitby, P. J. S. (2012). The effects of Solve It! on the mathematical word problem solving ability of adolescents with autism spectrum disorders. *Focus on Autism and Other Developmental Disabilities, 28*(2), 78–88.

Wu, S. S., Willcutt, E. G., Escovar, E., & Menon, V. (2014). Mathematics achievement and anxiety and their relation to internalizing and externalizing behaviors. *Journal of Learning Disabilities, 47*, 503–514.

Zaslavsky, C. (2002). Exploring world cultures in math class. *Educational Leadership, 60*(2), 66–69.

$SAGE edge™ •••

Review → Practice → Improve

Get the tools you need to sharpen your study skills. Access videos, practice quizzes, eFlashcards and more at **edge.sagepub.com/prater.**

CHAPTER 12

Strategy Application in Other Content Areas

Key Topics

Mr. Worthington, a middle school special educator, is preparing for a new teaching assignment. He will be team teaching mathematics and science with general educators who have students with disabilities included in their classrooms. He will also teach one functional math class for students who don't have the prerequisite skills to be included in the general education classes. Mr. Worthington has been asked to represent special educators on a districtwide textbook and materials adoption committee. He is excited about the opportunity to help other teachers view commercially prepared educational materials from the perspective of the special educator and the students they teach.

Learning Objectives

- Describe the process and elements of curriculum design in order to meet the learning needs of students with high-incidence disabilities (HID).

- Explain why students with HID need text-based support and provide examples of specific vocabulary development and reading comprehension strategies that teachers can use.

- Compare and contrast the textbook-based and activities-based approach to instruction providing examples of strategies in each for science and social studies.

- Explain how teachers can make homework a vital component of an individual student's learning.

- Describe the importance of integrative curriculum, as well as the importance of embedding cultural diversity contributions, issues, and perspectives across the curriculum.

Curriculum Design and Unit Development

As discussed in Chapter 1, curriculum is defined and used in many ways. Within the context of this book curriculum is defined as an interrelated set of instructional plans and activities based on specified content that when implemented lead to student learning outcomes. The design and evaluation of curriculum constitutes a large subset of the field of education in general. Curriculum design is presented in this chapter within the context of providing students with high-incidence disabilities (HID) access to general education curriculum, which is required by the Individuals with Disabilities Education Act (IDEA). Access involves more than having the curriculum available to students. Access means providing students an opportunity to interact with the curriculum in meaningful ways in order to learn, which may require additional student support.

Curricular materials that meet six principles of effective curriculum design support alternative access (Kame'enui & Simmons, 1999). These principles may also be used to adapt instruction and materials. The six principles include big ideas, conspicuous strategies, mediated scaffolding, strategic instruction, judicious review, and primed background knowledge.

- **Big ideas** are the major ideas, concepts, or principles that serve as anchors for additional or more information. Not all objectives and instructional activities are equally important. Focusing on big ideas is essential for students with academic disabilities who have less time left in school to master content than their peers who are not already academically behind.

- **Conspicuous strategies** or useful steps for accomplishing a goal or task should be provided to students. In the absence of conspicuous strategies, many students may develop their own. As discussed in

Chapter 1, however, students with disabilities do not create strategies spontaneously. Expecting them to do so can waste a considerable amount of time and be frustrating to both teacher and student. Learning is most efficient when teachers make strategies explicit (see Chapter 9).

- **Mediated scaffolding** refers to instructional guidance given to students as they acquire new information. This guidance may be provided by teachers, peers, materials, or tasks. For example, a mathematics textbook that provides more examples of completed problems is providing more scaffolding. The degree of scaffolding changes as the needs of the student, goals of instruction, and complexities of the task change and should be considered temporary. The ultimate goal is to remove scaffolding so the learner can become independent and self-regulatory.

- **Strategic instruction** is the carefully controlled combination of what students already know with what they need to learn so that the relationship between these two elements is clear and the instruction results in knowledge. Strategic instruction increases the likelihood of comprehension and generalization of higher level skills.

- **Judicious review** consists of structured opportunities for the students to recall or apply previously taught information. During such review, students should be able to perform the task without hesitation. Judicious review should be distributed over time, cumulative, and varied.

- **Primed background knowledge** means the curriculum takes advantage of students' previous knowledge. Preexisting knowledge affects new learning. The curriculum should be aligned with learner knowledge and expertise, consider necessary preskills, and prepare the learner for successful performance.

Curricular materials that are universally designed are planned from the beginning to be accessible to the broadest range of individuals possible. Such materials are flexible and include built-in alternatives in the materials. Add-on adaptations do not meet the universal design definition. When teachers have access to universally designed curricular materials, they can use them without having to plan to adapt the materials for students with special needs. Although the concept of universal design provides a framework for curriculum developers to strive toward, the field is far from achieving that goal in curricular materials currently available. Thus, teachers must critically evaluate instructional materials before purchasing or adopting them. (Additional information on universal design for learning [UDL] may be found in Chapters 1 and 7.) A major consideration for curriculum adoption is adaptability for students with disabilities.

Content teachers typically use textbooks not only as curricular materials, but to guide their instruction (Bruhn & Hasselbring, 2013). Students read information in their textbooks, answer end-of-the-chapter questions, complete worksheets, and take tests. Although teachers often rely heavily on textbooks, textbooks can create significant obstacles for students with HID, particularly those who struggle with reading (Mastropieri, Scruggs, & Graetz, 2003). This is not surprising given that textbooks are generally not well designed or written for students with varying levels of reading ability (King-Sears & Duke, 2010).

The curriculum, as an interrelated set of instructional plans and activities, usually represents a large amount of content, such as the social studies or science curriculum for a particular grade level. This curriculum is divided into smaller parts, each referred to as a *unit*. **Unit**s are learning experiences that take place over several days or weeks. They are broader in scope than daily lessons and incorporate multiple learning objectives (Lenz & Deshler, 2004). Meeting multiple objectives requires careful planning. An effective tool for planning units is a Unit Organizer (Boudah, Lenz, Bulgren, Schumaker, & Deshler, 2000; Lenz & Deshler, 2004).

Before teachers plan instructional units, they should answer these three questions:

1. **What should students know or understand at the conclusion of the unit?** By asking and answering this question, teachers can focus on key concepts and foundational understanding rather than specific activities or information.

2. **How will students demonstrate understanding and knowledge?** There exist many options for assessing students, which can range from informal quizzes and questions to formal tests and curriculum-based projects.

3. **What skills or enabling knowledge are necessary to achieve the unit objectives?** For example, without adequate reading skills, students frequently experience difficulty meeting the demands of curricular materials.

The second step in planning a content unit is using the information from the previous questions to complete a **Unit Organizer**. A sample Unit Organizer may be found in Figure 12.1. The Unit Organizer is divided into seven categories, each of which is described below (Lenz & Deshler, 2004).

- **Making Connections**—The first element of the Unit Organizer is making connections. The key concept of the new unit is listed and how the new concept relates to the *Big Picture*, previous units, and subsequent units is identified. By connecting the current focus with previous knowledge and the bigger picture, students' prior knowledge is activated, which promotes comprehension and understanding.

- **Unit Map**—The main part of the Unit Organizer is the Unit Map which consists of two parts: a unit paraphrase, and a graphic organizer. The unit paraphrase statement summarizes the central point or meaning of the unit and the graphic organizer illustrates the main parts of the unit that support the main idea.

- **Unit Relationships**—The purpose of the Unit Relationships section is to identify relationships and to promote higher order thinking. After analyzing unit concepts, the best strategy for promoting higher order thinking and examining relationships is determined. Educators can teach concepts by examining cause and effect, categorizing information, comparing and contrasting, presenting pros and cons, ranking concepts by relative importance, and examining sequences or processes.

- **Unit Questions**—Questions the students should be able to answer at the conclusion of the unit are listed in the Unit Questions section. The purpose of writing unit questions is to focus the student's attention on central themes and concepts.

- **Unit Schedule**—The Unit Schedule includes a list of tasks, assignments, and activities the students must complete during the course of the unit.

FIGURE 12.1 **Unit Organizer**

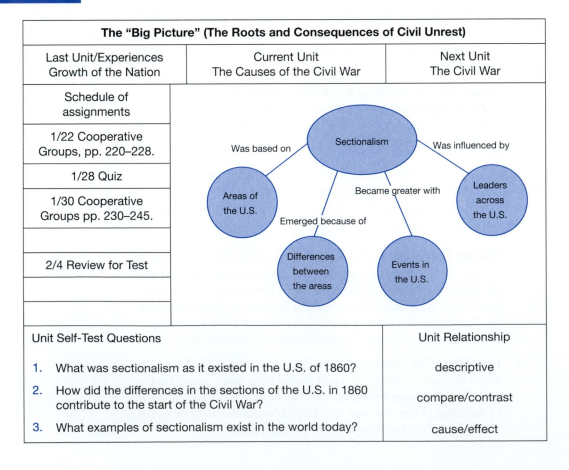

The "Big Picture" (The Roots and Consequences of Civil Unrest)		
Last Unit/Experiences Growth of the Nation	Current Unit The Causes of the Civil War	Next Unit The Civil War

Schedule of assignments

1/22 Cooperative Groups, pp. 220–228.

1/28 Quiz

1/30 Cooperative Groups pp. 230–245.

2/4 Review for Test

Was based on — Sectionalism — Was influenced by

Became greater with

Areas of the U.S.

Leaders across the U.S.

Emerged because of

Differences between the areas

Events in the U.S.

Unit Self-Test Questions	Unit Relationship
1. What was sectionalism as it existed in the U.S. of 1860?	descriptive
2. How did the differences in the sections of the U.S. in 1860 contribute to the start of the Civil War?	compare/contrast
3. What examples of sectionalism exist in the world today?	cause/effect

Expanded Unit Map

The Causes of the Civil War

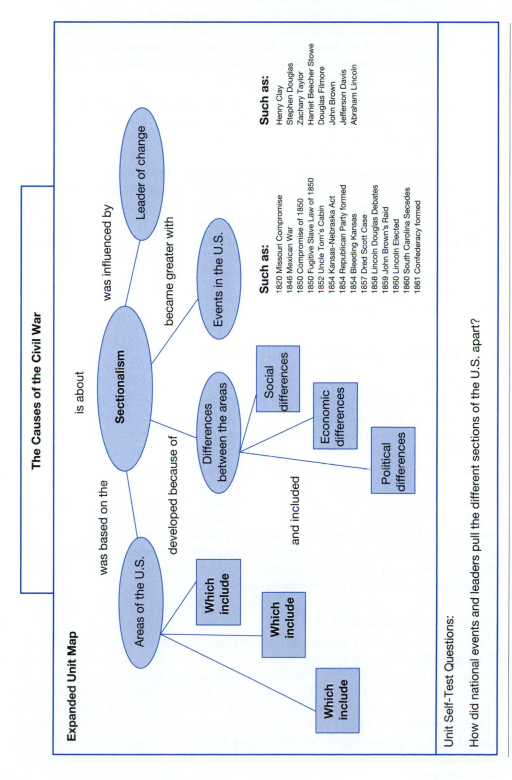

Sectionalism
- is about
- was influenced by → Leader of change
- became greater with → Events in the U.S.
- was based on the → Areas of the U.S.
- developed because of → Differences between the areas
- and included

Areas of the U.S.
- Which include
- Which include
- Which include

Differences between the areas
- Social differences
- Economic differences
- Political differences

Events in the U.S.

Such as:
1820 Missouri Compromise
1846 Mexican War
1850 Compromise of 1850
1850 Fugitive Slave Law of 1850
1852 Uncle Tom's Cabin
1854 Kansas-Nebraska Act
1854 Republican Party formed
1854 Bleeding Kansas
1857 Dred Scott Case
1858 Lincoln Douglas Debates
1859 John Brown's Raid
1860 Lincoln Elected
1860 South Carolina Secedes
1861 Confederacy formed

Leader of change

Such as:
Henry Clay
Stephen Douglas
Zachary Taylor
Harriet Beecher Stowe
Douglas Filmore
John Brown
Jefferson Davis
Abraham Lincoln

Unit Self-Test Questions:

How did national events and leaders pull the different sections of the U.S. apart?

Source: Boudah et al (2000), p. 52.

- **Expanded Unit Map**—The second page of the Unit Organizer is to be used while teaching the unit. The purpose of the Expanded Unit Map is to add information not included in the overview Unit Map. The Expanded Unit Map can facilitate notetaking during class discussions and activities as students add details, subtopics, and vocabulary to the original Unit Map.

- **Unit Self-Test Questions**—Any questions that arise as the students study the unit are included in the Unit Self-Test Questions section.

Once the Unit Organizer has been completed, classroom routines for using it must be established (Lenz & Deshler, 2004). To do so, teachers can present a blank Unit Organizer to the students and discuss how using the Unit Organizer will impact learning. Once students are familiar with the elements of the Unit Organizer, the Unit Organizer is introduced at the beginning of each new unit. Instruction time is then devoted to discussing each section of the organizer as the unit content is previewed. A completed Unit Organizer or a partially completed organizer that the students fill in can be used for previewing the unit. As students progress through unit material, the organizer helps them take notes and review the content because succinct concepts and relationships are represented.

General Strategies Across Content Areas

Many of the strategies discussed throughout previous chapters of this book can be applied to teaching science, social studies and other subject matter. Research has found, for example, that the following are effective in teaching students with HID content materials: explicit teacher-directed instruction, learning strategies, graphic organizers, study aids, mnemonic strategies, hands-on activities, peer mediation, and computer-assisted instruction (Scruggs, Mastropieri, Berkeley, & Graetz, 2010). Information about each may be found in Chapters 4 through 9.

Most students with HID have difficulty reading content textbooks necessitating teaching content-specific vocabulary and specific reading comprehension strategies, as well as using **Content Enhancement Routines (CERs)**. CERs are routines that combine effective teaching practices, reading comprehension strategies, and visual learning strategies. A brief discussion of vocabulary development, specific reading comprehension strategies, CERs, and homework strategies follows.

Vocabulary Development

Vocabulary development within the academic language of a discipline is essential. Students with HID require purposeful instruction to learn vocabulary. Generally, this is done through explicit teacher-directed instruction, mnemonic strategies, and visual and graphic depictions. The more words students can instantly recognize, the more fluent will be their reading. Students must be able to understand and use content-specific vocabulary in order to read, discuss, and write content-related information. The purpose of vocabulary instruction is to help students learn new general and content-specific vocabulary and to understand what the words mean and how they are used.

An instructional strategy helpful to developing content-related vocabulary is to pre-teach them. This is done by strategically selecting words that are central to the lesson, barriers for comprehending the main idea, or potentially problematic for those who lack background knowledge. Somewhere between five and 10 vocabulary words or phrases should be selected. The number will depend upon the sophistication of the learners and the lesson objectives. These words or phrases are then taught through explicit teacher-directed instruction (Berg & Wehby, 2013).

The acronym strategy, CLUE, was developed to help students use the context while reading material to ascertain the meaning of words they do not know. CLUE stands for **C**heck for words that are highlighted or bolded, **L**ook for clues in the sentences around the word by reading them, **U**se the word in a sentence to test whether you understand the meaning, and **E**xpand your resources such as a glossary or asking a friend, if needed (Hairrell et al., 2011).

TEACHER TIP #12.1

USING A RELATIONSHIP CHART FOR VOCABULARY DEVELOPMENT

One way to preview key vocabulary and main ideas of a lesson is to use a relationship chart following these procedures:

- Teacher creates a chart with important vocabulary down the first column and words representing important lesson concepts across the top of the chart.

- If students know the definition for any of the words, they are asked to provide it. Otherwise the teacher provides the definition.

- Students are then asked to provide examples of the important concepts based on their experiences.

- Then students predict the relationships between the lesson concepts and vocabulary as positive, negative, no relationship, or unsure. Symbols can be written in the intersecting cells (+, −, 0, ?).

- After instruction the students review their chart and revise the relationships as needed either individually or as a group. (Berg & Wehby, 2013)

Also important is the students' ability to identify and use common terms and abbreviations (e.g., ref—reference, w/o—without, i.e.—that is, e.g.—for example), as well as symbols (e.g., @—at/per, #—pound or number, &—and, %—percent). Teachers must explicitly teach students these terms, abbreviations, and symbols, help them recognize them in their textbooks, and use them during instruction (Paulsen & Sayeski, 2013). More about vocabulary development may be found in Chapter 10.

Reading Comprehension Strategies

Many content disciplines center on **text-based instruction**, or instruction that is based on students reading a textbook independently to gain information. This approach presents problems for students who struggle with reading comprehension. Fortunately, research shows that explicit instruction in comprehension strategies produces significant gains for students with HID. Margo Mastropieri, Thomas Scruggs, and Janet Graetz (2003) identified the most effective comprehension strategies as the following:

- **Text Structure Strategies**—Teacher-directed instruction in text structure strategies significantly improves students' abilities to comprehend text. Text strategies include (a) finding the main idea plus supporting details, (b) identifying the general topic and listing characteristics of the topic, (c) examining relationships between two or more things, and (d) classifying information into categories (Bakken & Whedon, 2002).

- **Summarizing and Self-Questioning Strategies**—Summarizing and self-questioning strategies promote engaged interaction with text material. For example, students can be taught to identify the main ideas of paragraphs and then to self-check their work against the textbook headings. One strategy for summarizing is to teach students to ask what each paragraph is about, what happens, and then state or write a one-sentence summary of the paragraph. Another strategy is to use the acronym, QRAC, which stands for **Q**uestion (turn the headings into questions), **R**ead the section and stop, **A**nswer your question, and **C**heck to be sure your answer was correct. Researchers have demonstrated this strategy to be effective in facilitating reading comprehension of content-based textbooks (Berkeley & Riccomini, 2011).

- **Activating Prior Knowledge**—Activating prior knowledge involves making students cognizant of what they already know about a subject that will help them connect new knowledge. Activities to activate prior knowledge must be purposeful and direct for students with HID. They may include brainstorming, asking questions, and holding discussions. Teachers should identify key prerequisite facts students need and focus the discussion accordingly. Broad questions ("What is a tropical climate like?") are less effective than specific questions ("What words describe a tropical climate?"). One method for activating prior knowledge is to use an anticipation guide, a set of teacher-generated questions used as a pre- and postassessment (Berg & Wehby, 2013).

- **Main Idea and Self-Monitoring**—Students can be taught a main idea strategy that also includes self-monitoring procedures. This involves teaching them how to generate main idea statements and how to select main ideas when given multiple choices. As students read passages, they mark a cue card to show they (a) read the passage, (b) used prompts provided to recall strategy steps, (c) applied the strategy to construct or identify the main idea, and (d) selected or wrote the main idea. Asha Jitendra, Mary Kay Hoppes, and Yan Ping Xin (2000) found that students using this strategy not only outperformed other students, they also maintained their skills six weeks after instruction.

Students need explicit instruction in the features of their textbooks as well as how to read expository text. A thorough discussion of textbook adoption, instruction, and adaptations appears in Chapter 7; and a discussion of expository text instruction may be found in Chapter 10.

Content Enhancement Routines

Content Enhancement Routines (CERs) combine effective teaching practices, reading comprehension strategies and visual learning strategies. CERs are instructional routines designed to support student comprehension of content by linking effective instruction with a visual device or organizer (e.g., graphic organizers, mnemonic devices, advanced organizers) (Aceves & Fritschmann, 2016). CERs help educators (a) teach academically diverse groups of students while meeting group and individual needs, (b) engage students actively in their learning, and (c) maintain the integrity of the content material (Bulgren, Deshler, & Lenz, 2007). Various routines have been developed and collectively are referred to as CERs, including Concept Anchoring Routine (Bulgren, Deshler, Schumaker, & Lenz, 2000), Concept Comparison Routine (Bulgren, Lenz, Shumaker, Deshler, & Marquis, 2002), and Question Exploration Routine (Bulgren, Marquis, Deshler, Lenz, & Shumaker, 2013), among others. As an example, the Question Exploration Routine was developed to support comprehension, analyze sources, summarize, determine cause and effect, and explain understandings. A graphic organizer template is developed on which these questions are raised:

- What is the critical question?

- What are the key terms and explanations?

- What are the supporting questions and answers?

- What is the main idea answer?

- How can we use the main idea?

- Is there an overall idea? Is there a real-world use? (Bulgren, Graner, & Deshler, 2013)

Research has documented CERs to enhance elementary and secondary students' content knowledge in inclusive settings and in multiple content areas including history (Bulgren et al., 2007), science (Bulgren et al., 2000), and language arts (Bulgren, Marquis et al., 2013).

TEACHER TIP #12.2

THINKING SKILL STRATEGY

The learning strategy acronym, PROVE, can be used to help students with HID learn new information and critical thinking skills. This strategy is well suited for any content-area class that requires integrating knowledge such as English, science, social studies, and vocational education and involves the following steps:

Present knowledge.

Reveal information that supports the knowledge.

Offer evidence.

Verify the evidence.

Express the verified knowledge.

(Continued)

(Continued)

The first step of this strategy is to write a complete sentence that **P**resents knowledge to be proved. The sentence should include what the student knows or believes about a concept, event or person. For example, *Thomas Jefferson was an effective president* is a statement that introduces the subject and presents information that can be defended or verified. The next step is to **R**eveal information that supports the knowledge and provides the rationale of why the student believes what has been expressed (e.g., *Jefferson purchased Louisiana*.). After the student writes a rationale statement, he or she offers evidence that supports the rationale. The evidence should demonstrate how the knowledge presented is correct by directly supporting the rationale (e.g., *This purchase allowed for access to the Port of New Orleans, free navigation on the Mississippi River and opened up western expansion*.). As with all proofs, the evidence presented must be **V**erified. In this strategy, the student verifies evidence either with an example, or by citing class notes or a book. The final step of the strategy is to **E**xpress the verified knowledge in a summary statement (e.g., *Thomas Jefferson was an effective president because he made the Louisiana Purchase which allowed access to the Port of New Orleans and free navigation on the Mississippi River, as well as leading to western expansion of the United States*.). (Scanlon, 2002)

Homework Strategies

Homework can be a hot topic. Some professionals and parents advocate strongly for its use and others argue against it for various reasons including questioning its relevance and overburdening of students during noninstructional time. Others attack homework as contributing to a competitive U.S. culture that places work above and to the detriment of building personal and familial relationships (Marzano & Pickering, 2007). Another argument against homework is that it can marginalize students who come from economically disadvantaged homes (Carr, 2013). Regardless of one's opinion, research has shown a positive relationship between the amount of homework students complete and their academic achievement (Cooper, Robinson, & Patall, 2006). Homework can be an effective instructional tool when it aligns with the academic needs of the student and is assigned in moderation. One rule of thumb is to assign homework that should take minutes to complete that ranges between 5 and 10 times the student's grade (e.g., fifth grade = (5), $5 \times 5 = 25$ and $5 \times 10 = 50$, therefore, homework assigned for fifth graders should take 25–50 minutes to complete). The focus, however, should be on the amount of homework the student completes, not just how much time is spent (Marzano & Pickering, 2007).

If used properly homework helps students complete unfinished schoolwork and practice skills learned in the classroom. In addition, homework acts as a communication tool between the school and home. Yet getting students to complete and return homework can be an unpleasant task for students, parents, and teachers. Students with HID have particular difficulty completing and returning homework for reasons such as not viewing homework as important, forgetting to take their homework home, or lack of motivation to start or finish their homework.

A variety of strategies to improve homework completion and submission have been advocated and a few have been studied. One major strategy is improved communication among teachers, parents, and students. All three parties share responsibility for effective communication between the home and school. They must communicate clearly and effectively with one another about homework policies, expectations, student performance, difficulties, and concerns. Teachers should allow some time in class to work on homework assignments to ensure that the students have solidified their understanding.

Otherwise they may be lost or practicing errors at home. Homework responsibilities and strategies for teachers, parents, and students follow:

Teacher and School Responsibilities

- Ensure the homework is relevant to the student's IEP and to the state or district curriculum standards.

- Before assigning homework, make certain the student has already demonstrated the ability to do the work independently. Do not expect the parents to have the curricular knowledge and skills to help.

- If the student requires an accommodation (e.g., using a computer) for the type of work being assigned, ensure the student has access to the accommodation at home.

- Explicitly explain homework expectations to both students and their parents at the beginning and throughout the school year.

- Create a homework communication process, such as assignment notebooks, between the school, the parent, and the student.

- Communicate with other teachers to avoid overloading students with homework.

- Be sensitive to stressors placed on families besides homework completion. Do not assign homework to students whose family situations interfere with their ability to complete the work at home.

- Don't assume families have access to materials and supplies, such as magazines and colored markers, to complete homework assignments.

Special Educator Responsibilities

- Assist general education teachers in modifying homework for students with HID based on the individual student's learning needs.

- Help monitor homework completion and accuracy at school.

- Assist students with their homework when appropriate, either individually or in small groups.

Home and Family Responsibilities

- Monitor student's homework completion by prompting the student to start and stay on task, helping problem-solve basic skills (e.g., reading directions), and praising student for staying on task and task completion.

- Communicate with teachers on a regular basis including attending conferences and completing any homework forms requested.

- Establish and follow through with consequences when students do not complete homework assignments.

Student Responsibilities

- Take primary responsibility of completing and submitting homework assignments when due.

- Ask for assistance at school if the directions or content of the homework is unclear.

- Follow through with communication between home and school. For example, deliver written notes responsibly.

- Maintain assignment notebooks taking it between home and school daily.

Teacher Strategies for Improving Homework Completion

- Vary the amount and type of homework assigned.

- Only assign homework that students have a reasonable probability of completing independently.

- Assign homework in smaller units.

- Write assignments on the board for students to copy.

- Remind students of homework assignments.

- Create highly motivating homework assignments related to real-life experiences.

- Provide prompt feedback on homework assignments.

- Promote a positive attitude about homework in your classroom.

- Include homework completion and submission as part of your classroom management plan.

- Consider using contingency contracts for students with particular difficulties completing and returning homework.

- Use peer-mediated strategies such as peer checking and cooperative homework groups.

- Establish and follow homework routines for assigning, collecting, grading, and returning homework assignments.

- Teach study and organizational strategies such as goal setting, time management, using assignment sheets, selecting an environment conducive for studying at home, seeking for clarification, and using available and appropriate resources. (Hampshire, Butera, & Hourcade, 2014; Jayanthi, Bursuck, Epstein, & Polloway, 1997; Salend & Gajria, 1995; Steele, 2008)

Science

Gabriel is 12 years old, in sixth grade, and will enter the intermediate school next year. He was diagnosed with high functioning autism as a preschooler. He has been fully integrated in his elementary class. Currently, the special educator co-teaches with his sixth-grade teacher part of the day. The team from the elementary and intermediate schools meet together to create Gabriel's IEP for the school. His parents are particularly concerned about him having different classes and teachers throughout the day.

Most students with HID receive special education services for reading and/or mathematics instruction, but not for content areas such as science and social studies. Traditionally, less attention has been given in the special education literature to content-area learning (Mastropieri et al., 2009). Recently educators have been increasingly interested in how to best provide instruction in science and social studies to students with HID particularly given the need to provide access for all students to the general education curriculum.

Science Knowledge, Skills, and Standards

State Departments of Education are responsible for identifying core curriculum standards to be used in the state. However, a set of Common Core State Standards (CCSS) have been developed for English language arts/literacy and mathematics and have been adopted by the majority of states (see Chapter 1). The English language arts/literacy standards include literacy standards for only Grades 6 through 12 in science and technical skills. A sample of the CCSS literacy standards in science and technical skills for Grades 9 and 10 follow.

- Analyze the structure of the relationships among concepts in a text, including relationships among key terms (e.g., *force, friction, reaction force, energy*).

- Follow precisely a complex multistep procedure when carrying out experiments, taking measurements, or performing technical tasks, attending to special cases or exceptions defined in the text.

- Assess the extent to which the reasoning and evidence in a text support the author's claim or a recommendation for solving a scientific or technical problem.

The New Generation of Science Standards are the science standards that apply to all students (New Generation of Science Standards [NGSS] Lead States, 2013). These standards were designed to make science education resemble the manner in which scientists think and work in the disciplines of physical science, life science, earth and space science, and engineering design. Each standard includes the following three dimensions:

- Scientific and engineering principles—scientific and engineering methods (e.g., planning and implementing investigations, analyzing data, reaching conclusions based on the data)

- Crosscutting concepts—broad themes that are relevant across science content areas (e.g., patterns, cause and effect, structure and function, stability and change)

- Disciplinary core ideas—core content under the four disciplinary areas (Scruggs, Brigham, & Mastropieri, 2013)

Samples of the NGSS across elementary, middle school, and high school for each of the four disciplines may be found in Table 12.1.

TABLE 12.1   A Sample of the National Science Education Content Standards

Content Standard (Sub Standard)	Students in 3rd grade who demonstrate understanding can:	Students in middle school who demonstrate understanding can:	Students in high school who demonstrate understanding can:
Physical Science (Motion and Stability: Forces and Interaction)	• Plan and conduct an investigation to provide evidence of the effects of balanced and unbalanced forces on the motion of an object. • Make observations and/or measurements of an object's motion to provide evidence that a pattern can be used to predict future motion.	• Apply Newton's Third Law to design a solution to a problem involving the motion of two colliding objects. • Plan an investigation to provide evidence that the change in an object's motion depends on the sum of the forces on the object and the mass of the object.	• Analyze data to support the claim that Newton's second law of motion describes the mathematical relationship among the net force on a macroscopic object, its mass, and its acceleration. • Use mathematical representations to support the claim that the total momentum of a system of objects is conserved when there is no net force on the system.
Life Science (Ecosystems: Interactions, Energy, and Dynamics)	• Construct an argument that some animals form groups that help members survive.	• Analyze and interpret data to provide evidence for the effects of resource availability on organisms and populations of organisms in an ecosystem. • Construct an explanation that predicts patterns of interactions among organisms across multiple ecosystems.	• Use mathematical and/or computational representations to support explanations of factors that affect carrying capacity of ecosystems at different scales. • Construct and revise an explanation based on evidence for the cycling of matter and flow of energy in aerobic and anaerobic conditions.
Earth and Space Science (Earth's Systems)	• Represent data in tables and graphical displays to describe typical weather conditions expected during a particular season.	• Develop a model to describe the cycling of Earth's materials and the flow of energy that drives this process.	• Develop a model based on evidence of Earth's interior to describe the cycling of matter by thermal convection.

Content Standard (Sub Standard)	Students in 3rd grade who demonstrate understanding can:	Students in middle school who demonstrate understanding can:	Students in high school who demonstrate understanding can:
	• Obtain and combine information to describe climates in different regions of the world.	• Analyze and interpret data on the distribution of fossils and rocks, continental shapes, and seafloor structures to provide evidence of the past plate motions.	• Develop a quantitative model to describe the cycling of carbon among the hydrosphere, atmosphere, geosphere, and biosphere.
Engineering Design	• Define a simple design problem reflecting a need or a want that includes specified criteria for success and constraints on materials, time, or cost. • Generate and compare multiple possible solutions to a problem based on how well each is likely to meet the criteria and constraints of the problem.	• Evaluate competing design solutions using a systematic process to determine how well they meet the criteria and constraints of the problem. • Develop a model to generate data for iterative testing and modification of a proposed object, tool, or process such that an optimal design can be achieved.	• Analyze a major global challenge to specify qualitative and quantitative criteria and constraints for solutions that account for societal needs and wants. • Design a solution to a complex real-world problem by breaking it down into smaller, more manageable problems that can be solved through engineering.

Source: Next Generation Science Standards (NGSS) (2013). ngss.nsta.org/AccessStandardsByTopic.aspx.

Science Instruction

In Gabriel's IEP meeting, his parents learn from his future science teacher, Mr. Shupe, that he teaches using both a textbook and hands-on instruction. The team decides that Gabriel's decoding and comprehension level will allow him to read and understand most of the text, but that he will need more hands-on instruction to fully develop abstract concepts addressed. After hearing about Gabriel's learning needs, Mr. Shupe agrees to create some hands-on activities that in some cases all students will experience and in other cases they will be tailored specifically for Gabriel. Mr. Shupe also commits to providing Gabriel a peer buddy to work with. In fact, he likes the idea so well he's going to incorporate more structured peer learning for all students in his class. Gabriel's future special education teacher, Mr. Arnold, will work closely with Mr. Shupe to adapt materials and instruction as needed.

Science can be a difficult subject for many students particularly given the vast number of science vocabulary terms and facts that students need to learn. In addition teachers often expect students to acquire this information through reading the textbook. As addressed earlier, heavy reliance on textbooks clearly disadvantages most students with HID. Many of them lack the literacy skills to learn effectively from science textbooks (Cawley & Parmar, 2001). Hands-on or activities-based instruction is often advocated for students with disabilities and fortunately many teachers approach science instruction in this way. Activities-based instruction relies on fieldwork, laboratory work, or simply manipulation of physical materials (e.g., plants, rocks), rather than textbooks (Scruggs, Mastropieri & Okolo, 2008).

Textbook-Based Instruction

Science textbooks may be the most challenging of all school disciplines. For example, research has documented that when compared with other content-area textbooks, science textbooks contain more complex expository text structures, are more conceptually dense, and include higher concentrations of novel and technical vocabulary. They also require rich background knowledge of science concepts (Mason & Hedin, 2011). All of these areas can make access and comprehension difficult for students with HID.

When compared with literacy and numeracy instruction, relatively little research has been conducted examining effective elements of science instruction for students with HID and most of it has been conducted with students with learning disabilities (LD). In a review of studies examining science instruction, researchers have discovered that teaching students the meaning of textbook vocabulary words had the greatest impact on comprehension, and that effective vocabulary instruction focused on semantic mapping, explicit instruction, or mnemonic strategies (Kaldenberg, Watt, & Therrien, 2015). Other researchers have documented that establishing prior knowledge, enhancing the text, and promoting strategy use can help students with LD learn from science texts (Mason & Hedin, 2011). These strategies include embedding graphic representations and spatial organizers and inserting mnemonic illustrations in science textbooks (Brigham, Scruggs, & Mastropieri, 2011).

The term ***textbook enhancements*** refers to teacher practices that help the organization of content information to facilitate students' comprehending and recalling information from the textbook. These may include concept maps, compare/contrast activities, visualization, mnemonic strategies, science-based posters, and so forth. Research has shown the effectiveness of science textbook enhancements to include instructing how to use text illustrations, creating representational illustrations, and applying mnemonic strategies (Mason & Hedin, 2011).

Mnemonic strategies. Mnemonic strategies such as acronyms, keywords, and pegwords are effective in helping students learn and recall science content (see Chapter 9). In particular, mnemonic strategies are powerful in facilitating recall of verbally based science instruction (Scruggs et al., 2008). For example, studies have demonstrated the efficacy with recall of science vocabulary, mineral hardness levels, and dinosaur names and facts (Wolgemuth, Cobb, & Alwell, 2008). The robustness of mnemonic strategies has been documented across educational settings, student ages, and types of disability.

Research also supports that mnemonic strategies are effective when incorporated into activities-based science instruction and teacher application of mnemonic instruction (Scruggs et al., 2008; Wolgemuth et al., 2008).

TEACHER TIP #12.3

USING KEYWORD AND PEGWORD MNEMONICS

When using keyword and pegword mnemonic strategies keep in mind the following:

- Implementing mnemonics as part of instruction is easy. Developing materials takes time and effort.

- Not all mnemonics are easy to create. For example, creating mnemonics with multiple correct answers can be challenging.

- Modeling for students the use of mnemonics is a critical instructional step.

- Students generally enjoy mnemonics, particularly using them with peer tutoring.

- Mnemonics are effective for all kinds of students including English learners.

- Mnemonics are especially effective for students with HID. (Scruggs, Mastropieri, Berkeley, & Marshak, 2010)

Graphic organizers. Research documents that graphic organizers and semantic maps are effective for initial acquisition and retention of science content. More intensive organizers help students in immediate factual recall, whereas simpler organizers can be used for review and help students recall what has been learned. Examples of science graphic organizers include a cyclical graph (e.g., the water cycle), linear graphs (e.g., the layers of the earth), and Venn diagram (e.g., compare and contrast an animal species), among many others (see Chapter 9).

Students must be taught explicitly how to use organizers. In particular, they need to be taught the differences between main and subordinate ideas and how to put all of the information together into the big idea. This instruction is best done using the teacher-directed instruction model (see Chapter 6) (Dexter, Park, & Hughes, 2011).

Activities-Based Instruction

A textbook approach differs from **activities-based instruction** in which students work with objects and apparatus in science activities. Text-based instruction usually requires students to read independently, learn an enormous number of difficult vocabulary words and factual information, and understand concepts through abstract presentations. Activity-based instruction, on the other hand, teaches students science concepts through concrete, hands-on experiences. Typically students will need to read directions, carry out the activities in a systematic manner, record and analyze data, stay on task, and use materials appropriately, all of which can be challenging for students with HID (Brigham et al., 2011). Activities-based instruction has been documented to be effective, particularly for students with learning disabilities (Therrien, Taylor, Hosp, Kaldenberg, & Gorsh, 2011) and emotional/behavioral disorders (Therrien, Taylor, Watt, & Kaldenberg, 2014), as long as there exists enough structure to ensure student engagement.

Activities-based instruction is also sometimes referred to as inquiry-based instruction. However, inquiry-based instruction can range from open discovery learning with no teacher direction or feedback to structured or guided inquiry learning that provides teacher structure and direction, specific feedback, and uses effective teaching principles (Watt, Therrien, Kaldenberg, & Taylor, 2013). In this book, the term *activities-based instruction* will be used in lieu of structured inquiry-based instruction. For activities-based science instruction to be effective, students with HID need the teacher to focus on the big ideas rather than on extraneous facts, provide formative feedback, allow for various forms of demonstrating understanding, and provide additional support to keep students engaged (Therrien et al., 2011).

Although creating big ideas can take time and effort, if done properly, a teacher can narrow a large number of lesson objectives (e.g., 60) into two to four big ideas for the school year. For students with HID, big ideas can build connections for both science instruction and life skills, as well as provide adaptations for students who need them. For example, if teaching the big idea of "living things need water," one student could grow plants and gain an importance of watering them, while another could study how hydration is important for athletes (Watt et al., 2013).

Peer tutoring. Several research studies have documented that classwide peer tutoring that uses materials designed to meet the learning needs of individual students can be very effective in teaching science content to students with HID, particularly in inclusive classrooms (Scruggs et al., 2008). For example, one study examined the effectiveness of classwide peer tutoring with hands-on activities against teacher-directed instruction. Students in the first group outperformed students in the second group on both unit posttests and end-of-year high-stakes tests (Mastropieri et al., 2006). Several other studies have been conducted in which students with HID were taught with activities-based materials solely or in combination or comparison with text-based instruction. Students learned more when taught with activities-based materials. Students also report overwhelmingly that they enjoy activities-based more than text-based instruction; but teachers report that activities-based instruction required considerably more preparation time (Mastropieri, Scruggs, & Magnusen, 1999).

Laboratory and field experiences. Whether teachers use a text-based or an activities-based approach, science instruction usually involves some form of laboratory and field experiences. Special consideration for students with HID must be taken in these environments. Some suggestions from the National Science Teacher Association appear in Table 12.2.

TABLE 12.2	**Sample Guidelines for Teaching Science to Students with HID from the National Science Teachers Association.**

Setting	Sample Guidelines to Consider
Laboratory	• Clearly label equipment, tools, and materials. Color code them to make them easier to recognize. • Introduce the lab equipment individually prior to the class activity. • Provide structured and simplified activity instructions. • Provide cue cards listing the steps to apply. • When dealing with abstract concepts, provide visuals such as charts and graphs. • In paired situations, monitor students carefully to ensure both are contributing equally. • If a student must be denied access to the equipment or the learning task is too difficult, provide an alternative that leads to the same learning objective.
Field Experiences	• Discuss with the student any needs, problems, or alternatives he or she might need in the field environment. • Arouse students' interest in the activity through simulations. • Be clear and direct in explaining expectations of appropriate behavior in advance of these experiences. Use role play. • Allow students to use devices to gather field notes. • Use a peer-buddy system. • Gradually increase the student's participation, particularly if the student is confused or fearful. • Positively reinforce student's appropriate participation and contribution.

Source: http://www.nsta.org/disabilities/intellectual.aspx.

TEACHER TIP #12.4

EFFECTIVE INCLUSIVE SCIENCE INSTRUCTION USING DIS$_2$ECT

Students with HID often receive their science instruction in the general education classroom with a science educator and a special educator co-teaching. The following steps lead to effective instruction for all students in the science classroom:

Design instruction—

Identify learners.

Identify curriculum priorities.

Design assessment framework.

(Continued)

(Continued)

Create learning activities.

Individualization—Keep in mind the learning characteristics of individual students.

Scaffolding & **S**trategies—Build in bridges to help students move from current to higher levels of understanding (e.g., alternative texts, text organizers, semantic maps, mnemonics).

Experiential Learning—Include opportunities to explore and experiment under controlled conditions, particularly before formal instruction begins.

Cooperative Learning—Develop pairs or groups in which students work together.

Teamwork—Co-teachers need to work collaboratively as a team. (Spaulding & Flannagan, 2012)

STEM Instruction

During the last 20 years, there has been a strong push toward preparing students in STEM content (science, technology, engineering, and mathematics). This emphasis has been at least partially based on recent declines or otherwise lack of growth in student STEM performance in this country. Typically, students with HID have underperformed in STEM coursework because of both student characteristics and instructional practices. STEM education should not be considered isolated and decontextualized facts within these four disciplines, but rather an approach to learning that emphasizes student-centered, collaborative learning. Students with HID typically receive STEM instruction in the general education classroom so the role of the special educator will vary. The special educator may co-teach STEM content with a content teacher, provide small-group or individualized explicit instruction, or be responsible for supplemental activities that promote content understanding (Israel, Maynard, & Williamson, 2013).

Instead of STEM, some professionals promote STEAM by adding an A for the arts (e.g., visual arts, music, dance) believing that technical skills and creativity are both important. Traditional STEM fields focus on convergent skills, whereas the arts focus on divergent skills and both are necessary. In fact, the push for STEAM from the technical fields comes from the lack of graduates' creativity, innovation, and curiosity, all of which can be fostered through the arts (Land, 2013).

Technology Spotlight #12.1

Resources for Science and Social Studies

Many technology-based resources exist that teachers can use to supplement their science and social studies instruction.

Simulations (Israel et al., 2013; Wright-Maley, 2015)

Simulations provide students the opportunity to experience and interact with concepts virtually.

They can be particularly helpful to students with HID because they allow abstract concepts to be visualized. Simulations represent real-life processes, events, or phenomena that actively engage the students and provide an opportunity to teach something specific and meaningful.

Annenberg Learner (arts, foreign language, math, science, and social studies): http://learner.org

Gizmos (science and math): www .explorelearning.com/

Know-It-All (science and career development): www.knowitall.org/

PhET (science and math): phet. colorado.edu/

Text-Based Material (Ciullo, 2015):

Alternative source material other than the textbook can be accessed. Sometimes these other source materials are written at lower reading levels.

Go Social Studies Go! (social studies): www.gosocialstudiesgo.com/

Kids Discover (science and social studies): www.kidsdiscover.com

Read Works (arts, culture, science, social studies): www.readworks.org/

Video Games (Marino, Becht, Vasquez, Gallup, Basham, & Gallegos, 2014)

Students are generally highly motivated to participate in video games. If structured properly, games can help students learn complex and interrelated concepts. Teachers should design instruction such that the game is integrated into the curriculum, not just as reinforcement. Lesson implementation should follow the steps of teacher-directed instruction including the teacher modeling game play with self-talk for problem-solving and reflection. Game play time should be limited to no more than 20 minutes.

Dan-Ball (Earth, space, biology, chemistry, physics): dan-ball.jp/en/

The Incredible Machine (physics): www.freegameempire.com/games/ The-Incredible-Machine

Wolf Quest (life science): www .wolfquest.org/

Virtual Field Trips (Zanetis, 2010)

Virtual field trips can be provided over the Internet and/or video conferencing equipment. Examples may include touring a historic site or museum, viewing live demonstrations of science experiments, attending cultural festivals, and so forth. They can be delivered either asynchronously or synchronously. A sample of a few virtual field trips follows.

Arctic Adventure: www.polarhusky. com/

Colonial Williamsburg: www.history .org/history/teaching/eft/index.cfm

Smithsonian Natural History Museum: www.naturalhistory.si.edu/VT3/

Web-Based Videos

Videos can be used effectively if they are selected and used carefully. Videos should come from a reliable source and previewed to ensure the content aligns with the curriculum. Short videos (3–5 minutes) can be used to introduce a lesson or topic. Lengthier videos should be broken into segments (6–10 minutes) and shown as the content aligns with the content being taught.

American Ride (American history): www.byutv.org/

Annenberg Learner (arts, foreign language, math, science, and social studies): www.learner.org

BrainPop (science, social studies, English, math, arts and music, health, engineering and technology): www .brainpop.com

History Channel "Classroom" (social studies): www.history.com/ shows/classroom

Smithsonian Museum (science, social studies, culture): www .smithsonianchannel.com/videos

How Things Work (science): www .howthingswork.com

Social Studies

Social Studies Knowledge, Skills, and Standards

The primary purpose for social studies is to promote "civic competence—the knowledge, intellectual processes, and democratic dispositions required of students to be active and engaged participants in public life" (National Council for the Social Studies, 2010, p. 3). Social studies involves the integration of several fields including anthropology, archaeology, economics, geography, history, law, philosophy, political science, psychology, religion, and sociology.

As stated earlier, State Departments of Education are responsible for identifying core curriculum standards for their state; and states look to professional organizations, such as the National Council for the Social Sciences for appropriate standards in their specific discipline. This organization has developed the National Curriculum Standards for Social Studies (NCSSS) across ten themes:

- Culture

- Time, continuity, and change

- People, places, and environments

- Individual development and identity

- Individuals, groups, and institutions

- Power, authority, and governance

- Production, distribution, and consumption

- Science, technology, and society

- Global connections

- Civic ideals and practices

A sample of the NCSSS for the culture theme is listed in Table 12.3.

In addition to the national standards for social studies, the literacy standard of the Common Core State Standards includes history and social studies literacy standards for only Grades 6 through 12. This implies that secondary social studies teachers must imbed content reading and teach literacy practices to facilitate student use and understanding of social studies texts (Swanson & Wanzek, 2013). Below is a sample of the CCSS literacy standards in history and social studies for middle school:

- Determine the central ideas or information of a primary or secondary source; provide an accurate summary of the source distinct from prior knowledge or opinions.

- Identify aspects of a text that reveal an author's point of view or purpose (e.g., loaded language, inclusion or avoidance of particular facts).

- Distinguish among fact, opinion, and reasoned judgment in a text.

TABLE 12.3 **A Sample of Social Skills Content Standards: Culture**

Early Grades	Middle Grades	High School Level
Knowledge – Learners will understand:		
• "Culture" refers to the behaviors, beliefs, values, traditions, institutions, and ways of living together of a group of people. • How peoples from different cultures develop different values and ways of interpreting experience. • (4 more)	• That culture may change in response to changing needs, concerns, social, political, and geographic conditions. • That language, behaviors, and beliefs of different cultures can both contribute to and pose barriers to cross-cultural understanding. • (6 more)	• That culture as an integrated whole that explains the functions and interactions of language, literature, the arts, traditions, beliefs, values, and behavior patterns. • How people from different cultures develop diverse cultural perspectives and frames of reference. • (7 more)
Process – Learners will be able to:		
• Explore and describe similarities and differences in the ways various cultural groups meet similar needs and concerns. • Describe the value of both cultural unity and diversity within and across groups. • (3 more)	• Evaluate how data and experiences may be interpreted differently by people from diverse cultural perspectives and frames of reference. • Explain how patterns of behavior reflect cultural values and beliefs. • (5 more)	• Compare and analyze behaviors for preserving and transmitting culture even while adapting to environmental or social change. • Analyze historic and current issues to determine the role that culture has played. • (7 more)
Products – Learners demonstrate understanding by:		
• Interviewing and reporting on observations, and developing a description of a sub-culture to which they belong or have access (e.g., friends, school, or neighborhood). • Role-playing ways in which cultural differences between two or more groups can cause conflict, or can contribute to solving problems. • (2 more)	• Selecting a social group and investigating the commonly held beliefs, values, behaviors, and traditions that characterize the culture of the group; hypothesizing about how those elements of culture contribute or fail to contribute to meeting the needs of the members of that group; and preparing an oral presentation to present findings. • (2 more)	• Researching and presenting a position paper on a current or past problem or issue through an analysis of the cultural patterns of the groups involved and the ways in which these contribute or present obstacles to finding solutions. • Presenting a media documentary about the cultural contributions of a local, regional, national, or international cultural group. • (2 more)

(Continued)

TABLE 12.3	(Continued)

Student PEP Strategy Prompt Sheet		
STEP #1 – Identify whether the paragraph is about a person, place, or event.		
STEP #2 – Answer the questions for the category.		
Person (man or woman)	Event (something happened)	Place (location)
• What s/he did.	• What happened.	• Where it took place
• Why s/he did it.	• Why it happened.	• What it is like.
• When and where it was done.	• When and where it happened.	• Why it is special.
• Important words.	• Who the players were.	• Important words.
• Something to connect to what you already know.	• Important words.	• Something to connect to what you already know.
	• Something to connect to what you already know.	

Sources: National Council for the Social Studies, (2010); Katims, D. S. & Harmon, J. M. (2000). Strategic instruction in middle school social studies: Enhancing academic and literacy outcomes for at-risk students. *Intervention in School and Clinic, 35(5),* 280–289.

As one state's example of social studies standards, Utah has defined the social studies fifth-grade course as follows:

> Students will enlarge the study of history, government, economics, and geography as they study the United States. There is neither an intention nor a possibility of successful "coverage" of all of United States history and geography or all of the social, economic, and political movements that have helped create the story of America. Rather, students should "discover" and "uncover" this story, with attention to the overarching concepts of global interconnectedness, the processes of continuity and change over time, the rights and responsibilities we all share, and the systems of power, authority, and governance we create. Primary source documents and literature that recounts the stories of exemplary character and life skills will help students understand their own place in the continuing saga of America. (Utah State Office of Education, 2010)

The State of Utah provides five standards with several objectives under each. One example follows:

- Standard IV: Students will understand that the 19th century was a time of incredible change for the United States, including geographic expansion, constitutional crisis, and economic growth.

  ○ Objective 1: Investigate the significant events during America's expansion and the roles people played.

- Objective 2: Assess the geographic, cultural, political, and economic divisions between regions that contributed to the Civil War.
- Objective 3: Evaluate the course of events of the Civil War and its impact both immediate and long-term.
- Objective 4: Understand the impact of major economic forces at work in the post-Civil War.

Each of these objectives can become instructional units.

Social Studies Instruction

Students with HID experience difficulty accessing social studies content for a number of reasons. First, social studies instruction is not unlike science in that text-based instruction is typically used (Spencer, Scruggs, & Mastropieri, 2003), although some teachers are relying more on original or source documents (e.g., The Declaration of Independence, Federalist Papers, The Constitution). Secondary social studies textbooks generally cover too much content sacrificing breadth for depth, assume students have a significant amount of background knowledge, misalign illustrations and pictures with the text, and are written at reading levels beyond the ability of many students with disabilities (De La Paz & MacArthur, 2003). Source or original documents can be even more difficult for students with HID to read and access information than a textbook. Second, teachers frequently present information in lecture format and many students with disabilities lack skills to obtain information from lectures. Third, social studies curriculum often requires higher order reasoning and writing skills such as comparing and contrasting information, supporting arguments, and critically evaluating information, skills that are often difficult for students with disabilities. Finally, students with disabilities experience difficulty synthesizing information from multiple sources and then generalizing concepts to a broader context (De La Paz & MacArthur, 2003).

Social studies instruction may be viewed at four different levels: factual learning, conceptual learning, procedural learning, and investigative learning. Factual knowledge is knowing key people, events and dates, as well as specialized vocabulary. Conceptual knowledge involves an understanding of key elements of social studies concepts, such as democracy, migration, and free speech. Procedural knowledge is knowing how to perform a task. In social studies, procedural knowledge may involve knowing how to estimate the population of a state or locate a city on a map. The last level, investigative knowledge, involves activities such as research investigations or explorations that solidify the other three levels through application in real-life situations (Scruggs et al., 2008).

Social studies instruction should focus on helping students with disabilities access content and develop skills necessary for critically evaluating information. Many research studies have focused on teaching general literacy skills and learning strategies in the context of social studies instruction. Learning strategies that teach students to understand text, organize lecture information, improve notetaking skills, and recall information are all effective instructional practices for improving social studies performance for students with disabilities (De La Paz & MacArthur, 2003).

Textbook-Based Instruction

Although textbooks are only one way to acquire social studies content, they remain the primary source for instruction in social studies classes (Berkeley, King-Sears,

Hott, & Bradley-Black, 2014). Yet, the quality of social studies textbooks vary widely on factors such as readability, structure and organization, and breadth versus depth of information covered (Scruggs et al., 2008). Reading comprehension strategies for expository text discussed earlier in this chapter and in Chapter 10 can facilitate learning in social studies.

Learning strategies such as graphic organizers and mnemonics can help all students, but particularly those with HID, learn and apply social studies content. In particular, mnemonic strategies facilitate the acquisition and recall of answers to who, what, where, and when social studies questions; graphic organizers help students answer why and how questions (Hall, Kent, McCulley, Davis, & Wanzek, 2013).

Mnemonic strategies. Although social studies involves more than factual information, sometimes extracting facts and information from textbooks is a critical skill in social studies disciplines. Various mnemonic strategies can be helpful in teaching students how to locate and recall information from social studies textbooks. In particular, acronyms, keywords, and pegwords can be beneficial.

> Mr. Forester was a new special education teacher assigned to co-teach a U.S. history class. As Mr. Forester collaborated with Ms. Weingarten, his co-teacher, to design curriculum that would serve the needs of students with and without disabilities in the class, Mr. Forester suggested that unit organizers would be beneficial for all students in the class. His co-teacher agreed, and both worked to create unit organizers for each instructional unit. As they analyzed the text and developed unit organizers, both Mr. Forester and his co-teacher realized that students with disabilities might have difficulty identifying key information from the textbook. They decided they would teach all students in their class the PEP Talk strategy (Katims & Harmon, 2000).

The PEP Talk strategy was designed to teach students to locate facts from social studies textbooks (Katims & Harmon, 2000). *PEP* is an acronym for Person Event Place. To implement PEP, students are taught to decide whether they will be reading about a person, event, or place before reading a new section of the text. Once they decide the category, they focus on questions related to the topic (See Figure 12.2). Once they become familiar with the strategy, students can work collaboratively to construct graphic organizers that represent information from text passages. David Katims and Janis Harmon found the PEP strategy to be an effective intervention for helping at-risk and special education students in general education classes.

Keyword and pegword mnemonic strategies can also help. For example, in one study peg- and keyword mnemonic strategies combined with computer-assisted instruction enabled students with learning and cognitive disabilities to learn basic math facts (Irish, 2002). In another study, students with and without disabilities in an elementary inclusive classroom effectively learned information about the exploration and settlement of the New World using mnemonic strategies (Mastropieri, Sweda, & Scruggs, 2000). In this study, teachers did indicate, however, that students with HID needed more direction and explicit instruction in order to use the mnemonic strategies effectively.

The PEP Talk Strategy

Think **PEP**. Ask questions. Look for answers. Keep notes.

Person (man or woman) Read and find:

   What s/he did

   Why s/he did it

   When and where it was done

   Important words

   Something to connect to what you already know

Event (something happened) Read and find:

   What happened

   Why it happened

   When and where it happened

   Who the players were

   Important words

   Something to connect to what you already know

Place (location) Read and find:

   Where it took place

   What it is like

   Why it is special

   Important words

   Something to connect to what you already know

Source: Adapted from Katims & Harmon, 2000.

Graphic organizers. Graphic organizers are particularly useful for social studies instruction given they can help students comprehend important concepts, as well as consider multiple perspectives associated with learning citizenship, government, economics, geography, and history (Gallavan & Kottler, 2007). Concept maps are graphic organizers that show the relationships between main idea and details or between concepts and subordinate concepts. For example, in social studies, a concept map may include a main idea (e.g., the U.S. Revolutionary War), with subtopics of people (e.g., George Washington) and events (e.g., the shot heard round the world). Each of those subtopics could then become the concept and additional detail added.

   Teachers or students can create graphic organizers and use them throughout the instructional process as a means for pre- or postassessing student knowledge. They can also be used in conjunction with a textbook as a tool for taking notes or during brainstorming group discussions. Graphic organizers can be used in many other ways such as to help students predict outcomes, share ideas, and recall information. In social studies, graphic organizers are commonly used to help students learn to

- compare and contrast concepts (e.g., values and beliefs of different cultural groups),

- link cause and effect of events (e.g., the impact of dropping the atomic bomb on today's U.S. foreign policy), and

- sequence events (e.g., timeline of the events that led to U.S. Civil Rights legislation). (Hall et al., 2013)

When using graphic organizers as a tool for taking notes from the textbook, teachers should do the following:

1. Select a graphic organizer that matches the structure of the chapter.

2. Explain to students how the graphic organizer can help them comprehend the readings.

3. Instruct students in how to enter information onto the graphic organizer. Use explicit instruction including modeling and guided practice.

4. Allow students to complete the graphic organizer on their own or in pairs.

5. Ask students to explain the relationships represented in the organizer. (Hall et al., 2013).

TEACHER TIP #12.5

PREVIEWING HISTORY TEXTBOOKS

Textbook previews can help students establish a relationship with a textbook. Use the following to guide students during their preview:

- Based on the title, what do you think the author will emphasize? How far back in history will it go?

- What are the credentials of the author?

- How is the book organized? Is it chronological or theme based?

- What chapter or unit sounds the most interesting?

- What chapter or unit do you know the most about?

- Flip through the book and find an amazing fact. (Myers & Savage, 2005)

Activities-Based Instruction

In addition to teaching U.S. history using the textbook, Mr. Forester and Ms. Weingarten know students will benefit greatly from peer tutoring. As they design their units, they embed the use of peer tutoring as a means for students to acquire and practice both factual and conceptual knowledge. During some of the sessions students will be given the opportunity to explore assigned simulations or video games that directly align with the content being taught. Mr. Forester and Ms. Weingarten also include on-site and virtual field trips throughout the year.

Although students with HID may struggle with literal comprehension, they may struggle even more understanding multiple perspectives and divergent points of view about social studies issues. In fact, "perhaps more than other school subjects, social studies requires students to contemplate abstract concepts and principles that include economic systems, government, culture, civic roles and responsibilities, geography, and change and continuity, to name a few" (Scruggs et al., 2008, p. 10). Most students have limited experience to build knowledge of social studies' basic principles. Adding experiences such as real-life or virtual field trips, videos, guest speakers, and so forth to supplement the textbook can be of great benefit to many students including those with HID.

As discussed previously, activities-based learning is a framework for learning in which students engage in learning activities, explore concepts or information, and then explain, apply, and evaluate new knowledge (Dalton, Morocco, Tivnan, & Mead, 1997). These learning activities can be effective in not just science, but social studies classes as well. For example, Ralph Ferretti, Charles MacArthur and Cynthia Okolo (2001) reported students with disabilities improved their ability to learn about historical periods by completing activities-based units. Students were first given background information and introduced to broad concepts relating to a historical period. Next, students worked in collaborative groups and studied primary and secondary sources to find information about a specified topic. Then, multimedia was used to present background information about the historical period and to provide students with a source of information for their inquiries. As students acquired information, teachers provided learning supports by teaching students evaluative strategies such as compare/contrast. Finally, students discussed their findings with peers and with the teacher.

Peer tutoring. Peer tutoring has been shown to be an effective student-mediated instructional method in social studies classrooms whether teachers use it for text-based or activities-based learning. For example, Margo Mastropieri, Thomas Scruggs, Vicky Spencer, and Judith Fontana (2003) compared whether peer tutoring or teacher-guided notes was more effective for helping students with learning disabilities learn world history. Tutors were taught general rules and procedures for responding to oral reading errors, for using a summarization strategy, completing self-monitoring checklists and review sheets, and for implementing point sheets. Students who participated in peer-tutoring conditions outperformed students who participated in teacher-guided note sessions on content-area tests. Not only were the academic results impressive, the students reported they enjoyed the peer-tutoring sessions. In a similar study, students in inclusive U.S. history secondary classes participated in classwide peer tutoring with specialized materials (including self-recording materials). Both students with and without disabilities outperformed students who did not participate and student feedback was consistently positive (Scruggs, Mastropieri, & Marshak, 2012). In general, research has demonstrated that peer tutoring is an effective intervention for enhancing academic success of secondary-age students with learning problems in different subject areas, including social studies (Anderson, Yilmaz, & Washburn-Moses, 2004).

Field trips. School-sponsored field trips are learning experiences aligned with the curriculum that are conducted outside of the school. Although field trips can connect to any part of the school curriculum, they often align with the arts, science, or social studies. Quality field trips are real experiences rather than contrived ones. They are not pure entertainment or meaningless sightseeing tours. Field trips should provide learning experiences where students can create new ideas, think logically and critically, and deepen their understanding of the curriculum being studied. They should not be used as reinforcement. They should be offered to all students, particularly those who need the experience. For students with disabilities, field trips can provide them the opportunity for concrete, hands-on experiences. In fact, field trips can motivate reluctant students who may have difficulty with text-based materials to return to those materials more motivated to learn (Merritt, 2015).

Typically field trips consist of walking tours, travel trips, virtual field trips, and museums. Planning is a critical part of conducting field trips and the impact on students with disabilities should be part of that planning. For example, off-campus sites need to be accessible to those with mobility issues, and some students may need more direct assistance to ensure they benefit from the experience. Also, parents of students with disabilities may have questions about the field trip for their child that need to be answered.

Integrative Curriculum

Another process that may benefit students with disabilities is the use of integrating instruction across the curriculum. Many models for curriculum integration have been created (Drake & Burns, 2004), but no one clear formula for creating curriculum integration exists. Nonetheless, **curriculum integration** means moving instruction away from teaching isolated content toward combining objectives, activities, and outcomes across disciplines often to provide more real-life experiences for students. Curriculum integration can involve assimilation of academic skills with occupational skills, social skills, the arts, or other academic skills. For example, in terms of social skills and academic instruction integration, conflict resolution and violence prevention can be assimilated within any curriculum where conflicts are found, such as literature, history, social studies, government, civics, economics, and so forth (Stevahn, 2004). Educators also advocate integrating the arts within other curriculum. One teacher combined a science lesson about pictographs and petroglyphs with the visual arts, by first teaching the academic content and then teaching students to create their own symbols in clay which were painted and fired in the kiln (Mason & Steedly, 2006). As a third example of curriculum integration, the inclusion of literacy standards for science and technical skills, as well as for history and social studies within the Common Core State Standards reflects the importance of both literacy and the integration across academic fields of study.

Integration of skills may be conceptualized and planned using a matrix. List one set of knowledge and skills (e.g., academic skills) across the top row and another set down the first column (e.g., specific life skills). Then objectives, activities, and/or outcomes can be created in the cells intersecting the two curricular areas. Table 12.4, provides an example of how a life-skill standard and four academic discipline standards can be integrated. The life-skill standard is independent living with the subskill being participation in a simulated car purchase. Activities and outcomes related to both the life and academic standards appear in individual cells. Teachers engaging students in these activities and outcomes will be demonstrating that students can accomplish both types of skills through one objective, activity, or outcome.

TABLE 12.4   A Sample of Life Skills Integrated Across the Curriculum

Overall Standard: Students will examine the essential components of independent living.

Subset Skill: Students will participate in a simulated car purchase.

Life Skills Based on Standard	Language Arts	Mathematics	Science and Health
Identify advantages and disadvantages of owning a car.	Write a paper comparing the advantages and disadvantages of owning three different car models.[1]	Compare a high-deductible versus a low-deductible automobile insurance policy using reasonable chances of having a minor or a major accident.[4]	
Use reference materials to judge the performance of a car.	Read Consumer's Report. Identify their criteria. Create a list of guidelines.[2]		Use reference manuals or information systems to find car's specifications.[6]
Debate whether it is better to purchase a used car or a new car.		Compute the costs of a used vs. new car initially and over time.[5]	
Select a car to purchase.	Compare cars in Consumer's Report. Read the newspaper to locate ads. Defend personal decision in a verbal presentation.[3]		Evaluate the car's quality based on safety features.[7]

Sources: Common Core State Standards (CCSC) <corestandards.org> and the Utah State Office of Education Core Curriculum (USOECC) <uen.org/core>

[1]<u>Writing</u>: Write narratives to develop real or imagined experiences or events using effective technique, well-chosen details, and well-structured event sequences. (CCSS.ELA-Literacy.W.9-10.3)

[2]<u>Writing</u>: Conduct short as well as more sustained research projects to answer a question (including a self-generated question) or solve a problem; narrow or broaden the inquiry when appropriate; synthesize multiple sources on the subject, demonstrating understanding of the subject under investigation. (CCSS.ELA-Literacy.W.9-10.7)

[3]<u>Speaking:</u> Present information, findings, and supporting evidence clearly, concisely, and logically such that listeners can follow the line of reasoning and the organization, development, substance, and style are appropriate to purpose, audience, and task.. (CCSS.ELA-Literacy.SL.9-10.4)

[4]<u>Mathematics</u>: Evaluate and compare strategies on the basis of expected values. (CCSS.Math.Content.HSS.MD.B.5.b)

[5]<u>Mathematics</u>: Analyze decisions and strategies using probability concepts. (CCSS.Math.Content.HSS.MD.B.7)

[6]<u>Technical Education</u>: Use reference manuals or information systems to find service procedures and specifications. (USOECC Introduction to Automotive, Standard 2, Objective 4)

[7]<u>Health</u>: Students will demonstrate the ability to apply prevention and intervention knowledge, skills, and processes to promote safety in the home, school, and community. (USOECC Health Education, Standard 4)

[8]<u>Social Studies</u>: Identify and examine persisting issues involving the rights, roles, and status of the individual in relation to society.

Implications for Culturally and/or Linguistically Diverse Students

Students from culturally diverse backgrounds are often unaware of the role of their culture and individuals in the specific disciplines being taught in our schools today. This may lead to a lack of identity for students who are, for example, ethnically or religiously diverse. Teachers need to include people and contributions from diverse cultures in the curriculum. Exposing and teaching students about diverse people and their contributions can strengthen the curriculum in at least four ways. First, students who come from similar backgrounds will have access to role models in an otherwise Eurocentric curriculum. Second, the curriculum can become more relevant to diverse students. For example, writings from African or Asian authors may bridge the world of literature with students' lives. Understanding the work of scientists outside of the traditional American and European backgrounds can help students from these diverse backgrounds develop pride in their culture and at the same time broaden the perspective of all students. A sample of individuals who have made major contributions in the arts, government, and science is listed in Table 12.5.

Students learning about their own and other cultures is a common standard of social studies curriculum. Learning about different cultures should include activities from a

TABLE 12.5   **A Sample of Noted Individuals From Ethnically Diverse Backgrounds**

Curricular Area	Names	Ethnicity Background
Art and Architecture	Jose Aruego	Filipino American
	Judy Baca	Mexican American
	J. Max Bond, Jr.	African American
	Jean-Michel Basquiat	Haitian/Puerto Rican American
	Maya Lin	Chinese American
	Norma Merrick Sklarek	African American
	Minoru Yamasaki	Japanese American
Government	Ben Nighthorse Campbell	Cheyenne – Native American
	Daniel Inouye	Japanese American
	Thurgood Marshall	African American
	Carole Moseley-Braun	African American
	Barack Obama	African American
	Colin Powell	African American
	Dalip Singh Saund	Indian Asian American
	Donna Shalala	Arab American
	Nydia M. Velázquez	Puerto Rican American

Curricular Area	Names	Ethnicity Background
Literature	Julia Alvarez	Dominican American
	Sandra Cisneros	Mexican American
	Charles A. Eastmond (Ohiyesa)	Sioux—Native American
	Le Ly Hayslip	Vietnamese American
	Zora Neale Hurston	African American
	N. Scott Momaday	Kiowa—Native American
	Toni Morrison	African American
	Bharati Mukherjee	Indian Asian American
	Michael Ondaatje	Sri Lankan American
	Amy Tan	Chinese American
	August Wilson	African American
Music	Louis Armstrong	African American
	Ray Charles	African American
	Sammy Davis, Jr.	African American/Puerto Rican American
	Gloria Estefan	Cuban American
	Scott Joplin	African American
	Tania Leon	Cuban American
	Jennifer Lopez	Puerto Rican American
	Yo-Yo Ma	Chinese American
	Zubin Mehta	Indian Asian American
Science	Luis Alvarez	Spanish American
	George Washington Carver	African American
	Elias Corey	Lebanese American
	Charles Drew	African American
	Mario J. Molina	Mexican American
	Ellison Onizuka	Japanese American
	Norbert Rillieux	African American
	Samuel C. C. Ting	Chinese American
	Eugene Huu-Chau Trinh	Vietnamese American
	Ahmed H. Zewail	Egyptian American

worldwide perspective and include contributions of diverse populations to the evolution of our current society. Curriculum used in U.S. schools, even in social studies, has not always included such contributions. For example, even the concept of settling "the West" was a Eurocentric idea. For those coming from Asia, they were headed to settle, not the West, but the East (Banks, 2007).

Not only is learning about culture important in social studies, cultural diversity issues and perspectives should be embedded across the curriculum. Making connections between science and the cultural backgrounds of students can be accomplished by using activities and materials that

- examine different cultural origins of science,

- discuss scientific practices and solutions used in various parts of the world,

- include the achievements of scientists from culturally and linguistically diverse backgrounds, and

- incorporate a variety of culturally diverse practical applications. (Salend, 1998)

The rewriting of curriculum standards in recent years has been done with a broader perspective than in the past. More attention has been placed on the needs of all students, including those with disabilities and culturally and/or linguistically diverse (CLD) students. The New Generation Science Standards (NGSS), for example, offers a vision of science learning for all students, particularly those groups that have traditionally been underrepresented. And in order to meet that vision, teachers will need to know and implement effective instructional strategies for all students regardless of ability, cultural, linguistic, and socioeconomic backgrounds (NGSS Lead States, 2013).

SUMMARY

As mandated by IDEA, students with HID must have access to the general education curriculum and this curriculum usually represents a large of amount of content, such as the science or social studies curriculum for a particular grade level. A year-long curriculum is divided into smaller units, and units are distributed into daily lesson plans. Curriculum planning incorporates effective teaching principles in planning instructional units and the curriculum for the entire school year.

Most content teachers use textbooks not only as curricular materials but to guide their instruction. Yet, the extensive use of textbooks creates barriers to students with HID. Most have difficulty reading content textbooks necessitating using content-specific vocabulary

development strategies, specific reading comprehension strategies, and Content Enhancement Routines.

Although some argue against the use of homework, research documents a positive relationship between the amount of homework students complete and their academic achievement. Homework can be an effective instructional tool when it aligns with the academic needs of the student and is assigned in moderation. The teacher, student, and parents need to work collaboratively to make homework an effective instructional tool.

State Departments of Education are responsible for identifying core curriculum standards to be used in the state. The New Generation of Science Standards and the National Curriculum Standards for Social Studies were created by professional organizations and provide guidance to states in the development of their standards.

Most students with HID receive special education services for reading and/or mathematics instruction, but not for content areas such as science and social studies. Science can be a difficult subject for many students particularly given the vast number of science vocabulary terms and facts, as well as the predominant reliance on textbooks. Teachers also rely on the use of textbooks in social studies; yet, texts generally cover too much information, assume students have the necessary background knowledge, and are written at reading levels beyond the ability of most students with HID.

Teachers may use a textbook-based approach and/or an activities-based approach to instruction. If textbooks are used, teachers should implement textbook enhancements by explicitly teaching content-based learning strategies, such as mnemonic strategies and graphic organizers. Activities-based instruction relies less on textual materials and focuses on engaging in hands-on learning experiences. This may include working with materials and objects or engaging in laboratory work or field trips. Peer tutoring can also be an effective instructional strategy whether students are engaged in textbook-based or activities-based approaches.

Rather than relying on teaching isolated content, integrating content across the curriculum can be helpful to students with HID. Curriculum integration can involve assimilation of academic skills with occupational skills, social skills, the arts, or other academic skills.

Curriculum should include people from diversity and the contributions they made to specific disciplines. Doing so will make the curriculum more relevant to diverse students and help validate their cultural background. Also, discussing these culturally diverse contributions exposes and can broaden the perspective of all students. Students learning about their own and other cultures is a common expectation of social studies curriculum, but cultural diversity issues and perspectives should be embedded across all disciplines of the curriculum.

REVIEW QUESTIONS

1. Describe the six principles of effective curriculum design and the unit organizer elements. Why are these principles and elements important for instructing students with HID?

2. Create an example of using a vocabulary development strategy and an effective comprehension strategy in science or social studies.

3. Describe Content Enhancement Routines.

4. What can teachers do to ensure homework benefits the individual student?

5. Explain who is responsible for content-specific standards and sources used to develop these standards.

6. Define textbook-based and activities-based approaches to instruction. What are advantages and disadvantages of each for students with HID?

7. Compare and contrast the textbook-based and activities-based approaches to instruction providing examples of strategies in each for science and social studies.

8. Describe how integrative curriculum can be helpful to both teachers and students. What do you think teachers should consider when using this approach with students with HID?

9. Defend the embedding of cultural diversity contributions, issues, and perspectives across the curriculum.

10. Describe how teachers can ensure that their students' cultures are represented in the classroom and the curriculum.

ACTIVITIES

1. Create a unit organizer for a unit on the solar system using an elementary- or secondary-level science textbook.

2. Identify one grade-level group of social studies standards from your state's standards. Select at least three standards. Create one activity to teach each of the three standards. Provide an outline of a lesson plan to demonstrate how the activities would be used as part of instruction.

3. Create two graphic organizers—one that illustrates a science concept and another cause and effect in a social studies area.

4. Identify at least 10 resources available on the Internet for virtual field trips in science or math. Create a spreadsheet describing and evaluating these sites. Include categories such as sponsor, URL, cost or free, grade level, content covered, potential challenges for students with HID, and so forth.

5. Using the format of Table 12.4 and state standards, create a table demonstrating how science and literacy can be taught in an integrative fashion.

Council for Exceptional Children (CEC) Standards

The Council for Exceptional Children (CEC) is a premiere national professional organization comprised of special educators, paraeducators, relative service personnel, parents, and others interested in individuals with disabilities and/or those with gifts and talents. This organization has generated 10 standards for the preparation of special educators. These standards are listed in each chapter as they relate to the content within the chapter. The standards that apply to Chapter 12 are Standards #3 and #5.

CEC Initial Preparation Standard 3: Curricular Content Knowledge

Beginning special education professionals use knowledge of general and specialized curricula to individualize learning for individuals with exceptionalities.

3.1 Beginning special education professionals understand the central concepts, structures of the discipline, and tools of inquiry of the content areas they teach, and can organize this knowledge, integrate cross-disciplinary skills, and develop meaningful learning progressions for individuals with exceptionalities.

3.2 Beginning special education professionals understand and use general and specialized content knowledge for teaching across curricular content areas to individualize learning for individuals with exceptionalities.

3.3 Beginning special education professionals modify general and specialized curricula to make them accessible to individuals with exceptionalities.

CEC Initial Preparation Standard 5: Instructional Planning and Strategies (partial)

Beginning special education professionals select, adapt, and use a repertoire of evidence-based instructional strategies to advance learning of individuals with exceptionalities.

5.1 Beginning special education professionals consider an individual's abilities, interests, learning environments, and cultural and linguistic factors in the selection, development, and adaptation of learning experiences for individuals with exceptionalities.

5.4 Beginning special education professionals use strategies to enhance language development and communication skills of individuals with exceptionalities.

5.6 Beginning special education professionals teach to mastery and promote generalization of learning.

5.7 Beginning special education professionals teach cross-disciplinary knowledge and skills such as critical thinking and problem solving to individuals with exceptionalities.

REFERENCES

Aceves, T. C., & Fritschmann, N. S. (2016). Content enhancement routines. Current Practice Alerts: Issue 24. Division for Learning Disabilities (DLD) and Division for Research (DR) of the Council for Exceptional Children. Retrieved from s3.amazonaws.com/cmi-teaching-ld/alerts/33/uploaded_files/original_DLD_Alert24_go_rev.pdf?1455827583

Anderson, S., Yilmaz, O., & Washburn-Moses, L. (2004). Middle and high school students with learning disabilities: Practical academic interventions for general education teachers—A review of the literature. *American Secondary Education, 32*(2), 19–38.

Bakken, J. P., & Whedon, J. P. (2002). Teaching text structure to improve reading comprehension. *Intervention in School and Clinic, 37*, 229–233.

Banks, J. A. (2007). *Educating citizens in a multicultural society*. New York, NY: Teachers College.

Berg, J. L., & Wehby, J. (2013). Preteaching strategies to improve student learning in content area classes. *Intervention in School and Clinic, 49*(1), 14–20.

Berkeley, S., King-Sears, M. E., Hott, B. L., & Bradley-Black, K. (2014). Are history textbooks more "considerate" after 20 years? *The Journal of Special Education, 47*(4), 217–230.

Berkeley, S., & Riccomini, P. J. (2011). QRAC-the-Code: A comprehension monitoring strategy for middle school social studies textbooks. *Journal of Learning Disabilities, 46*(2), 154–165.

Boudah, D. J., Lenz, B. K., Bulgren, J. A., Schumaker, J. B., & Deshler, D. D. (2000). Don't water down! Enhance content through the unit organizer routing. *TEACHING Exceptional Children, 32*, 48–56.

Brigham, F. J., Scruggs, T. E., & Mastropieri, M. A. (2011). Science education and students with learning disabilities. *Learning Disabilities Research & Practice*, *26*(4), 223–232.

Bruhn, A. L., & Hasselbring, T. S. (2013). Increasing student access to content area textbooks. *Intervention in School and Clinic*, *49*(1), 30–38.

Bulgren, J. A., Deshler, D. D., & Lenz, B. K. (2007). Engaging adolescents with LD in higher order thinking about history concepts using integrated content enhancement routines. *Journal of Learning Disabilities*, *40*, 121–133.

Bulgren, J. A., Deshler, D. D., Schumaker, J. B., & Lenz, B. K. (2000). The use and effectiveness of analogical instruction in diverse secondary content classrooms. *Journal of Educational Psychology*, *92*(3), 426–441.

Bulgren, J. A., Graner, P. S., & Deshler, D. D. (2013). Literacy challenges and opportunities for students with learning disabilities in social studies and history. *Learning Disabilities Research & Practice*, *28*(1), 17–27.

Bulgren, J. A., Lenz, B. K., Schumaker, J. B., Deshler, D. D., & Marquis, J. G. (2002). The use and effectiveness of a comparison routine in diverse secondary content classrooms. *Journal of Education Psychology*, *94*(2), 356–371.

Bulgren, J. A., Marquis, J. G., Deshler, D. D., Lenz, B. K., & Schumaker, J. B. (2013). The use and effectiveness of a question exploration routine in secondary-level English language arts classrooms. *Learning Disabilities Research & Practice*, *28*(4), 156–169.

Carr, N. S. (2013). Increasing the effectiveness of homework for all learners in the inclusive classroom. *School Community Journal*, *23*(1), 169–182.

Cawley, J. F., & Parmar, R. S. (2001). Literacy proficiency and science for students with learning disabilities. *Reading & Writing Quarterly*, *17*, 105–125.

Ciullo, S. (2015). Improving access to elementary school social studies instruction: Strategies to support students with learning disabilities. *TEACHING Exceptional Children*, *48*(2), 102–109.

Cooper, H., Robinson, J. C., & Patall, E. A. (2006). Does homework improve academic achievement? A synthesis of research, 1987–2003. *Review of Educational Research*, *76*(1), 1–62.

Dalton, B., Morocco, C. C., Tivnan, T., & Mead, P. L. M. (1997). Supported inquiry science: Teaching for conceptual change in urban and suburban science classrooms. *Journal of Learning Disabilities*, *30*, 670–684.

De La Paz, S., & MacArthur, C. (2003). Knowing the how and why of history: Expectations for secondary students with and without learning disabilities. *Learning Disability Quarterly*, *26*, 142–154.

Dexter, D. D., Park, Y. J., & Hughes, C. A. (2011). A meta-analysis review of graphic organizers and science instruction for adolescents with learning disabilities: Implications for the intermediate and secondary science classroom. *Learning Disabilities Research & Practice*, *26*(4), 204–213.

Drake, S. M., & Burns, R. C. (2004). *Meeting standards through curriculum development*. Alexandria, VA: Association for Supervision and Curriculum Development.

Ferretti, R., MacArthur, C. D., & Okolo, C. M. (2001). Teaching for historical understanding in inclusive classrooms. *Learning Disability Quarterly*, *24*, 59–71.

Gallavan, N. P., & Kottler, E. (2007). Eight types of graphic organizers for empowering social studies students and teachers. *The Social Studies*, *98*(3), 117–123.

Hairrell, A., Simmons, D., Swanson, E., Edmonds, M., Vaughn, S., & Rupley, W. H. (2011). Translating vocabulary research to social studies instruction: Before, during, and after text-reading strategies. *Intervention in School and Clinic*, *46*(4), 204–210.

Hall, C., Kent, S. C., McCulley, L., Davis, A., & Wanzek, J. (2013). A new look at mnemonics and graphic organizers in the secondary social studies classroom. *TEACHING Exceptional Children*, *46*(1), 47–55.

Hampshire, P. K., Butera, G. D., & Hourcade, J. J. (2014). Homework plus: A tool for promoting independence. *TEACHING Exceptional Children*, *46*(6), 158–168.

Irish, C. (2002). Using peg- and keyword mnemonics and computer-assisted instruction to enhance basic multiplication performance in elementary students with learning and cognitive disabilities. *Journal of Special Education Technology, 17*(4), 29–40.

Israel, M., Maynard, K., & Williamson, P. (2013). Promoting literacy-embedded, authentic STEM instruction for students with disabilities and other struggling learners. *TEACHING Exceptional Children, 45*(4), 18–25.

Jayanthi, M., Bursuck, W., Epstein, M. H., & Polloway, E. A. (1997). Strategies for successful homework. *TEACHING Exceptional Children, 30*(1), 4–7.

Jitendra, A., Hoppes, M. K., & Xin, Y. P. (2000). Enhancing main idea comprehension for students with learning problems: The role of a summarization strategy and self-monitoring instruction. *Journal of Special Education, 34*, 127–139.

Kaldenberg, E. R., Watt, S. J., & Therrien, W. J. (2015). Reading instruction in science for students with learning disabilities: A meta-analysis. *Learning Disability Quarterly, 38*(3), 160–173.

Kame'enui, E. J., & Simmons, D. (1999). *Toward successful inclusion of students with disabilities: The architecture of instruction.* Arlington, VA: The Council for Exceptional Children.

Katims, D. S., & Harmon, J. M. (2000). Strategic instruction in middle school social studies: Enhancing academic and literacy outcomes for at-risk students. *Intervention in School and Clinic, 35*, 280–289.

King-Sears, M. E., & Duke, J. M. (2010). "Bring your textbook!" Using secondary texts to assess reading demands and skills required for students with high-incidence disabilities. *Intervention in School and Clinic, 45*(5), 284–293.

Land, M. H. (2013). Full STEAM ahead: The benefits of integrating the arts into STEM. *Procedia Computer Science, 20*, 547–552.

Lenz, B. K., & Deshler, D. D. (2004). *Teaching content to all: Evidence-based inclusive practices in middle and secondary schools.* Upper Saddle River, NJ: Pearson.

Marino, M. T., Becht, K. M., Vasquez, E., Gallup, J. L., Basham, J. D., & Gallegos, B. (2014). Enhancing secondary science content accessibility with video games. *TEACHING Exceptional Children, 47*(1), 27–34.

Marzano, R. J., & Pickering, D. J. (2007). The case for and against homework. *Educational Leadership, 64*(6), 74–79.

Mason, L. H., & Hedin, L. R. (2011). Reading science text: Challenges for students with learning disabilities and considerations for teachers. *Learning Disabilities Research & Practice, 26*(4), 214–222.

Mason, C. Y., & Steedly, K. S. (2006). Lessons and rubrics for arts integration. *TEACHING Exceptional Children Plus, 3*(1), Article 1.

Mastropieri, M. A., Berkeley, S., McDuffie, K. A., Graff, H., Marshak, L., Conners, N., . . . Cuenca-Sanchez, Y. (2009). What is published in the field of special education? An analysis of 11 prominent journals. *Exceptional Children, 76*(1), 95–109.

Mastropieri, M. A., Scruggs, T. E., & Graetz, J. E. (2003). Reading comprehension instruction for secondary students: Challenges for struggling students and teachers. *Learning Disability Quarterly, 26*, 103–116.

Mastropieri, M. A., Scruggs, T. E., & Magnusen, M. (1999). Activities-oriented science instruction for students with disabilities. *Learning Disability Quarterly, 22*, 240–249.

Mastropieri, M. A., Scruggs, T. E., Norland, J. J., Berkeley, S., McDuffie, K., Tornquist, E. H., & Connors, N. (2006). Differentiated curriculum enhancement in inclusive middle school science: Effects on classroom and high-stakes tests. *Journal of Special Education, 40*(3), 130–137.

Mastropieri, M. A., Scruggs, T. E., Spencer, V., & Fontana, J. (2003). Promoting success in high school world history: Peer tutoring versus guided notes. *Learning Disabilities Research & Practice, 18*, 52–56.

Mastropieri, M. A., Sweda, J., & Scruggs, T. E. (2000). Putting mnemonic strategies to work in an inclusive classroom. *Learning Disabilities Research & Practice, 15*, 69–74.

Merritt, R. D. (2015). Field trips. Research Starters: Education (Online Edition). Ipswich, MA: Salem.

Myers, M. P., & Savage, T. (2005). Enhancing student comprehension of social studies materials. *The Social Studies*, *96*, 18–24.

National Council for the Social Studies (2010). *National curriculum standards for social studies: A framework for teaching, learning, and assessment*. Silver Spring, MD: Author.

New Generation of Science Standards Lead States (2013). *Next generation science standards: For states, by states*. Washington, DC: The National Academies Press.

Paulsen, K., & Sayeski, K. L. (2013). Using study skills to become independent learners in secondary content classes. *Intervention in School and Clinic*, *49*(1), 39–45.

Salend, S. J. (1998). Using an activities-based approach to teach science to students with disabilities. *Intervention in School and Clinic*, *34*(2), 67–72, 78.

Salend, S. J., & Gajria, M. (1995). Increasing the homework completion rates of students with mild disabilities. *Remedial and Special Education*, *16*, 271–278.

Scanlon, D. (2002). PROVE-ing what you know: Using a learning strategy in an inclusive class. *TEACHING Exceptional Children*, *34*(4), 48–54.

Scruggs, T. E., Brigham, F. J., & Mastropieri, M. A. (2013). Common core science standards: Implications for students with learning disabilities. *Learning Disabilities Research & Practice*, *28*(1), 49–57.

Scruggs, T. E., Mastropieri, M. A., Berkeley, S., & Graetz, J. E. (2010). Do special education interventions improve learning of secondary content? A meta-analysis. *Remedial and Special Education*, *31*(6), 437–449.

Scruggs, T. E., Mastropieri, M. A., Berkeley, S., & Marshak, L. (2010). Mnemonic strategies: Evidence-based practice and practice-based evidence. *Intervention in School and Clinic*, *46*(2), 79–86.

Scruggs, T. E., Mastropieri, M. A., & Marshak, L. (2012). Peer-mediated instruction in inclusive secondary social studies learning: Direct and indirect learning effects. *Learning Disabilities Research & Practice*, *27*(1), 12–20.

Scruggs, T. E., Mastropieri, M. A., & Okolo, C. M. (2008). Science and social studies for students with disabilities. *Focus on Exceptional Children*, *41*(2), 1–24.

Spaulding, L. S., & Flannagan, J. S. (2012). DISSECT: A framework for effective inclusive science instruction. *TEACHING Exceptional Children*, *44*(6), 6–14.

Spencer, V. G., Scruggs, T. E., & Mastropieri, M. A. (2003). Content area learning in middle school social studies classrooms and students with emotional or behavioral disorders: A comparison of strategies. *Behavioral Disorders*, *28*, 77–93.

Steele, M. M. (2008). Helping students with learning disabilities succeed. *The Science Teacher*, *75*(3), 38–42.

Stevahn, L. (2004). Integrating conflict resolution training into the curriculum. *Theory into Practice*, *43*, 50–58.

Swanson, E., & Wanzek, J. (2013). Applying research in reading comprehension to social studies instruction for middle and high school students. *Intervention in School and Clinic*, *49*(3), 142–147.

Therrien, W. J., Taylor, J. C., Hosp, J. L., Kaldenberg, E. R., & Gorsh, J. (2011). Science instruction for students with learning disabilities: A meta-analysis. *Learning Disabilities Research & Practice*, *26*(4), 188–203.

Therrien, W. J., Taylor, J. C., Watt, S., & Kaldenberg, E. R. (2014). Science instruction for students with emotional and behavioral disorders. *Remedial and Special Education*, *35*(1), 15–27.

Utah State Office of Education. (2010). Core Standards for Social Studies. Retrieved from schools.utah.gov/CURR/socialstudies/Core/Grades36.aspx

Watt, S. J., Therrien, W. J., Kaldenberg, E., & Taylor, J. C. (2013). Promoting inclusive practices in inquiry-based science classrooms. *TEACHING Exceptional Children*, *45*(5), 40–48.

Wolgemuth, J. R., Cobb, R. B., & Alwell, M. (2008). The effects of mnemonic interventions on academic outcomes for youth with disabilities: A systematic review. *Learning Disabilities Research & Practice*, *23*(1), 1–10.

Wright-Maley, C. (2015). What every social skills teacher should know about simulations. *Canadian Social Studies*, *48*(1), 8–23.

Zanetis, J. (2010). The beginner's guide to interactive virtual field trips. *Learning & Leading with Technology*, *37*(6), 20–23.

⑤SAGE edge™ ....●

Review ➜ Practice ➜ Improve

Get the tools you need to sharpen your study skills. Access videos, practice quizzes, eFlashcards and more at **edge.sagepub.com/prater.**

©iStockphoto.com/Highwaystarz-Photography

CHAPTER 13

Social and Emotional Learning

Mary Anne Prater and Ellie Young

Key Topics

Importance of Social and Emotional Learning (SEL)
  Definition
  Prevalence
  Externalizing and Internalizing Concerns
  Social and Emotional Competence and
    Academic Learning
Promoting Prevention and Early Intervention
  Multitiered Systems of Support for SEL
  Creating Emotionally Healthy Classrooms

Identifying Students With Social and
  Emotional Concerns
    Screening
    Individual Assessments
Teaching Social and Emotional
  Competence
Emotional Regulation
Social Skills
Self-Management
Implications for Culturally and/or Linguistically
  Diverse Students

Importance of Social and Emotional Learning (SEL)

Rivera, a seventh-grade student who transferred to her new school in the middle of the year, was identified in elementary school as having a learning disability. Although her difficulties with reading are well documented, four of her six teachers are concerned that she is often withdrawn and isolated in class. She won't ask questions when she doesn't understand the lesson. When she is assigned to work with a lab partner, she doesn't contribute and prefers to let her partner run the experiment. Mr. Howard, her science teacher, doesn't quite know what to do to help her. He's tried offering encouragement, praising her efforts, and anticipating her questions, but it doesn't seem to make much of a difference. Mr. Howard doesn't know what to do next; after all, he's the science teacher, not the school psychologist.

Learning Objectives

- Describe the importance of social and emotional learning (SEL) in school settings including the connections between SEL and academic outcomes.

- Justify the need for prevention and early intervention strategies for students with social, emotional, and behavioral challenges in school settings; and compare and contrast when and how professionals (a) screen and (b) individually assess students for these challenges.

- Describe how and under what circumstances professionals would teach emotional regulation, social skills, and self-management. Provide examples of each.

- Delineate implications of SEL assessment and instruction for culturally and/or linguistically diverse students.

When discussing the social-emotional needs of students, educators often raise many questions about the value of and place for teaching skills that contribute to emotional well-being. They may ask questions such as "Is it the schools' responsibility to teach students social and emotional strategies and skills?" "Aren't the problems a result of poor parenting or issues at home, so shouldn't the parents be responsible for fixing these problems?" "And if it is the school's responsibility, how do teachers balance the time needed to teach academic content with developing self-esteem and relationship skills?" "Since most teachers haven't received training in teaching social skills or similar topics, where can they find lessons and evidence-based curricular materials?" "How do they measure social and emotional learning outcomes?" Clearly, addressing social, emotional, and behavioral issues in schools is complex.

As has been addressed in previous chapters, mastering academic content such as literacy and numeracy is highly valued, the focus of many assessments, the way most teachers are evaluated, and the explicit purpose of schooling. Given the strong emphasis on academic outcomes, educators may believe they have little, if any time, to address social-emotional learning in their classrooms. Most teachers may have had little coursework or professional development about how to teach social skills, emotional regulation, or similar topics (Reinke, Stormant, Herman, Puri, & Goel, 2011).

Common core standards, benchmarks, state testing, and federal legislation clearly define what students should be learning in school in the areas of language arts, science, social studies, and math. In contrast, the social, emotional, and behavioral standards of learning are rarely found in state standards for K–12 settings (Dusenbury et al., 2015). When compared to academic content, curricular materials and clear guidelines for teaching and evaluating for SEL are limited. This paucity of standards, materials, and guidelines does not, however, negate the importance of SEL for all students.

This chapter focuses on why all students need instruction that improves social, emotional, and behavioral well-being, including those with high-incidence disabilities (HID). Social and emotional learning is first defined followed by an overview of the research that supports strong connections between social-emotional competence and academic outcomes. The chapter concludes with ideas about how teachers can create emotionally healthy classrooms and explicitly teach effective coping and social skills.

Definition

Social and emotional learning (SEL) is defined as the way individuals manage emotions and appropriately identify and respond to the feelings of others. Setting and achieving goals, creating and maintaining healthy relationships, and making conscientious decisions are also included in many SEL definitions. Maurice Elias (1997) wrote that

> social and emotional competence is the ability to understand, manage, and express the social and emotional aspects of one's life in ways that enable the successful management of life tasks such as learning, forming relationships, solving everyday problems, and adapting to the complex demands of growth and development. (p. 2)

Social-emotional learning curriculum and interventions include social skills instruction. Social skills are the personal skills individuals need for successful social interactions and relationships, such as knowing how to make friends, negotiate, or give feedback. SEL instruction also includes character education, violence or bullying prevention, mental health promotion, and/or positive behavioral interventions and supports (Collaborative for Academic, Social, and Emotional Learning [CASEL], 2015; Merrell & Gueldner, 2010). Developing positive peer interactions, friendships, and relationships with teachers, parents, and other authority figures also are integrated into SEL instruction. Being aware of one's emotions, displaying empathy, and identifying feelings in self and others are included in the intrapersonal or emotional part of SEL. Social-emotional instruction includes efforts to (a) promote resiliency, (b) teach specific skills to improve coping strategies, (c) support students who are responding to difficult life challenges (e.g., parental divorce, traumatic events), (d) develop healthy self-esteem, and (e) address character education.

Prevalence

As discussed in Chapter 1, students with emotional/behavioral disabilities (EBD) represent about 0.5% of the total school population (United States Department of Education [USDOE], 2014). Prevalence rates, however, are estimated to be much higher. For example, some researchers and government agencies report that 10% to 20% of all school-age students exhibit emotional distress or impairment (Hanchan & Allen, 2013) and would qualify for a mental health diagnosis (e.g., generalized anxiety disorder, major depressive disorder). If these students are not being identified as having EBD and receiving special education services, then most of the students who need SEL instruction and support are within the general education population. In fact, in each classroom of about 25 students, approximately five students probably have notable mental health needs. School systems cannot hire enough additional support personnel to meet the needs of these students, so implementing prevention and intervention strategies in each classroom is one aspect of addressing these concerns and helping all students achieve positive educational outcomes (Doll, Zucher, & Brehm, 2004).

Externalizing and Internalizing Concerns

Jude, a seventh-grade student, has been receiving special education services since fourth grade. Since then, he has improved his focusing and academic skills. However, his teachers are concerned that his aggressive behaviors are escalating. He has been called into the principal's office twice in 4 months for fighting with classmates and he is often argumentative with his teachers.

For students who have social, emotional, or behavioral concerns, their behaviors tend to be either externalizing or internalizing problems; and some students demonstrate both types. **Externalizing behaviors** are observable and include aggressive, noncompliant, argumentative, hyperactive, impulsive, and disruptive behaviors. A student with externalizing concerns may have difficulty making and keeping friends because they struggle to understand the perspective of others; they may often get in fights and disagree with authority figures and peers. They may become angry easily and believe that adults are singling them out for punishment. When faced with their inappropriate behavior, they may deny that they have done anything wrong. Many choose fighting (either physical or verbal) as their preferred way of solving problems. They commonly lack insight about their behavior and may struggle to identify positive alternative behaviors. And even if they can identify alternate behaviors, their impulsive nature may make it difficult for them to consider consequences of decisions before making a choice. The rate at which students demonstrate externalizing behaviors can vary from occasionally to many times a day. And appropriate interventions can range from individual counseling to schoolwide social skill instruction (Nigg & Barkley, 2014). Jude's argumentative and fighting behaviors are externalizing behaviors.

Internalizing behaviors may be difficult for teachers to recognize because of their covert, inwardly redirected nature. Students with internalizing behaviors may not get teachers' attention because their behaviors are usually not disruptive or hurtful to others. Observable behaviors of students with internalizing concerns include acting fearful or sad, not participating in activities, not communicating or interacting with other students and teachers, exhibiting low activity levels, or not attempting to do unfamiliar or difficult work (Walker, Severson, & Feil, 2014). Students with internalizing concerns may be afraid of making mistakes so they procrastinate starting their work. They may avoid asking questions because they do not want to look stupid to peers or teachers. A few students may feel so insecure about their skills that they are easily overwhelmed and cannot decide when or how to start a project. Some students may express unrealistic fears such as being fearful of a tornado when tornados rarely happen in that area of the country. Other students may not know how to join in games and struggle to make friends. As with students with externalizing concerns, internalizing behaviors occur along a continuum, and the interventions can vary, for example, from individual counseling to teachers prompting them to use effective coping strategies. Rivera, the student introduced at the beginning of the chapter is exhibiting internalizing behaviors.

Social and Emotional Competence and Academic Learning

In addition to difficulties with interpersonal relationships, students with emotional and behavioral problems also demonstrate difficulties with academic achievement in all content areas (Nelson, Benner, Lane, & Smith, 2004; Reid, Gonzalez, Nordness, Trout, & Epstein, 2004). Teachers often view students with academic problems as also having behavior problems (Algozzine, Wang, & Violette, 2011). Students with behavior problems miss academic instruction time because of their inappropriate behavior, possibly putting them even further behind their peers. Also, teachers are often stressed due to the demands of dealing with students who are noncompliant, display extreme emotions, have frequent intense conflicts, and so forth (Jones, Bouffard, & Weissbourd, 2013).

A strong research base clearly establishes that SEL contributes to improved school attitudes, school behavior, and school performance. A compelling meta-analysis by Joseph Durlak, Roger Weissberg, Allison Dymnicki, Rebecca Taylor, and Kriston Schellinger (2011) included over 270,000 students who participated in 213 universally delivered programs; the authors reported that K–12 students significantly improved emotional and social skills, behavior, attitudes, and academic achievement. In fact, students' achievement had an 11-point percentile gain when they were involved in SEL programs. Attitude toward self and others and positive social behaviors improved while emotional distress and conduct problems decreased. In another study, teacher-assessed social skills in third-grade students were found to be better predictors of academic achievement in eighth grade than third-grade achievement test scores (Caprara, Barbaranelli, Pastorelli, Bandura, & Zimbardo, 2000). Another study showed first-grade students who were involved in a teacher-led intervention to increase positive, socially acceptable behaviors had significantly lower rates of suicidal thoughts throughout their childhood, adolescence, and young adulthood (Wilcox et al., 2008).

Promoting Prevention and Early Intervention

Multitiered Systems of Support for SEL

Improving the social and emotional skills and knowledge of students can be accomplished by promoting prevention and early intervention. As discussed in Chapter 7, multitiered systems of supports (MTSS) provide a framework for schools to ensure all students receive high-quality core instruction and the necessary supports when they are not succeeding. To help ensure success of social and emotional instruction, it should be delivered under the MTSS umbrella.

All students will benefit from learning effective coping, social, and self-management skills and strategies. Some students may need intensive individual instruction. Just as every classroom has a continuum of excellent to struggling readers, each classroom also has a continuum of happy, engaged students to students who are struggling to manage aggressive impulses. This continuum of needs requires that a continuum of services be available.

Similar to teaching academic content, providing a universal level of SEL instruction for all students throughout the school year is considered a Tier 1 strategy. Teachers may teach social skills such as how to make friends, join in, or follow directions; school psychologists may teach the whole class what worrying is and how to effectively deal with worrying; or school social workers may teach how to have a healthy self-concept. Even though teachers may not have extensive backgrounds in teaching social skills, or coping strategies for worry, or in calming aggressive, upset students, teachers can learn ways to incorporate SEL into their classroom routines so that all students have foundational knowledge. SEL instruction can be embedded into the general curriculum. For example, a high school health teacher could connect lessons on staying physically healthy to lessons on staying socially and emotionally healthy. Later in the chapter, specific SEL curricular materials are introduced. Any of these materials could be used universally for all students in a classroom.

Another example of a Tier 1 intervention to build SEL is the use of **bibliotherapy**. Using carefully selected stories, characters can introduce and model appropriate strategies to help facilitate changes in students' thoughts, feelings, and behaviors (Heath, Dyches, & Prater, 2013). Depending upon the students' age and reading ability, the book may be read independently or read aloud as a group. Students would engage in activities related to the reading. For example, during reading, students could keep a journal about how they think a character feels and how the students themselves would feel and what they would do in that situation. Postreading activities could involve creating a collage of pictures and words describing how the character felt or selecting a portion of the story to rewrite resulting in a different ending. Within these activities, the appropriateness of emotions, social interactions, and behaviors, as well as consequences based on those elements can be discussed (Prater, Johnstun, Dyches, & Johnstun, 2006). The instructional model, Book in a Bag, is similar to bibliotherapy. This model allows teachers to integrate literacy, social studies, and social skills instruction through a piece of literature (Marchant & Womack, 2010). Limited research shows that using stories and books as bibliotherapy can help improve students' emotional and behavioral problems, such as aggression (Shechtman, 2006), bullying (Teglasi, Rahill, & Rothman, 2007), and depression (Stice, Rohde, Seeley, & Gau, 2008).

Tier 1 interventions also include providing explicit social skill instruction and ensuring emotionally healthy classrooms. First, social and emotional skills and knowledge can be taught and learned through direct instruction with opportunities for practice with helpful feedback similar to teaching academic content. If fact, teachers report that teaching a social-emotional curriculum helps them understand the social and emotional components of learning which increases their understanding of the students and of how to better facilitate behavior change and provide support to students (Hallam, 2009). Having an explicit curriculum with lessons and activities places SEL in the same category as reading, writing, arithmetic, and essentially all academic subjects (Merrell & Gueldner, 2010). Specific curriculum will be discussed later in the chapter, as will the second element of Tier 1 interventions and support, creating emotionally healthy classrooms.

Mr. Armstrong, a tenth-grade physical education and health teacher in a rural high school, understands that the health curriculum mandated by the state requires him to address emotional health as well as physical health. Mr. Armstrong uses

(Continued)

(Continued)

the *Strong Teens* curriculum (Merrell, Carrizales, Feuerborn, Gueldner, & Tran, 2007) to teach students about understanding their emotions and the emotions of others, dealing with anger, letting go of stress, resolving conflict, and setting goals. All students in the school are required to pass health, so this is a Tier 1 strategy. When all teachers and administrators know the strategies Mr. Armstrong teaches, they can prompt students to use the strategies in specific situations rather than just know the strategies to pass the health class. For example, if Mrs. Manewitz, the assistant principal, is working with Esera who just got sent to the office because he punched another student in his chemistry class, Mrs. Manewitz can ask Esera to remember and use the strategies for dealing with anger and problem-solving.

Tier 2 interventions focus on supporting small groups of students; the intervention centers on explicit instruction on deficit skills or to address a specific concern such as dealing with parents' divorce. Tier 2 interventions usually last a short time, about 6 to 8 weeks depending on the students' needs. Approximately 15% of students typically need Tier 2 services. School-based mental health professionals such as school counselors, psychologists, and social workers usually lead these interventions. Even when the small groups are led by school-based mental health professionals, collaboration with teachers helps ensure that the learning transfers from the small-group experience to the classroom and beyond.

Students with significant needs receive Tier 3 interventions, which include interventions and supports similar to Tier 2, but they are usually delivered individually. About 5% of students may need Tier 3 interventions. Some, but not all, of these students most likely receive special education services. Usually a team that includes parents, administrators, classroom teachers, school-based mental health professionals, and the student collaborate to identify the specific problem, implement, and then evaluate interventions that target very specific behaviors and interventions.

Supporting students with significant social, emotional, and behavioral concerns can be challenging, especially if teachers believe they need to address the problems all by themselves. Most schools have access to specialists that can provide ongoing encouragement and expertise when needed. School psychologists, counselors, and social workers have training in understanding the needs of high-risk students and can help teachers find resources needed to address the needs of students who have concerning behaviors.

TEACHER TIP #13.1

GETTING HELP FROM OTHER PROFESSIONALS

When working with students who have social, emotional, or behavioral challenges, teachers can get help from other professionals in the following ways:

- Most schools have Teacher Assistance Teams (TAT) where a variety of school-based professionals (e.g., special education teacher, school psychologist, or counselor, instructional coaches, and administrators) provide intervention ideas, strategies for collecting data to help make decisions, and provide ongoing support.

- Feedback from classroom observations completed by colleagues or specialists can provide insights about what is working so teachers can do more of what's working. Classroom observations can also help teachers identify small changes that may have a big impact.

- When working in a rural area, the state department of education usually has specialists available to provide consultation and help teachers identify resources to meet the needs of the student.

- When preparing to collaborate, teachers should come with specific questions and data. For example, rather than describing a student as aggressive and difficult to get along with, define the behaviors and collect data on those behaviors (e.g., Rex has been in trouble with the playground supervisor for 3 out of the last 5 days because he hits peers when they won't let him play kickball.)

Creating Emotionally Healthy Classrooms

All students can be supported through the creation and maintenance of warm, caring classrooms and through a school culture that teaches healthy emotional strategies. Teaching these skills is similar to providing the polio vaccine to inoculate students when stressors occur. Classrooms that promote emotional well-being have the following two characteristics:

1. **Clearly written behavioral expectations with consistent reinforcement for appropriate behavior and explicit consequences for inappropriate behavior.**

Classroom rules that communicate clear expectations for positive behaviors generate a sense of safety and clarity for students. When students know what behaviors are needed in the classroom, they may have less anxiety because they understand behavioral boundaries. Effective rules help students learn to show respect for others, demonstrate ways to work together to achieve goals, and value learning, which are characteristics of productive citizens in any community.

As described in Chapter 3, a maximum number of five rules should be developed at the beginning of the school year with assistance of the students, if appropriate. The behaviors in the rules should be observable, measurable, and positive; and they should be posted in the classroom. The consequences for keeping or breaking rules should be well defined and understood by each student; and teachers must deliver consequences consistently for keeping or breaking the rules. In teaching the rules, teachers should demonstrate examples and nonexamples of the rules. In addition, rules should be reviewed and if necessary revised throughout the school year.

When students are struggling to follow the classroom rules, teachers should consider what environmental factors may be influencing the student's behavior. For example, the teacher should consider where the student sits, how the student is being reinforced for misbehavior, or whether the student is embarrassed to ask for help. For additional information on classroom rules see Chapter 3.

2. **Teachers focus on building positive, warm relationships with all students.**

Learning happens in the context of relationships and the teacher–student relationship should be the core of developing social-emotional competency for all students (Shriver & Buffett, 2015). Teachers who communicate that they value their students and that all students can learn will find that students will work diligently to improve and work on difficult tasks (Doll, Zucker, & Brehm, 2004). Caring teachers talk with students, listen to their viewpoints and perspectives, help them with tasks, and communicate a sense of fairness and warmth. Teachers know about the student's lives, provide encouragement, and communicate empathy. For example, if a student shares that she is angry about the way a peer has treated her, a teacher might say, "Being angry is understandable when someone says something that is not kind. Let's talk about what you can do next."

A warm teacher–student relationship creates a sense of safety and security for students so that they can explore the learning environment and engage in learning activities, especially those activities that are challenging and feel risky for students. When students believe that their teacher is a predictable, warm, fair, considerate person, they are more likely to engage positively in the classroom and show that they are motivated to learn. This warm relationship communicates to students that they are capable of improving, fixing mistakes, and contributing positively to the community. Because students with social-emotional-behavioral challenges frequently struggle to build relationships, focusing on ways to build warmth, understanding, and encouragement with the teacher–student relationship is vital (Roorda, Koomen, Spilt, & Oort, 2011).

Identifying Students With Social and Emotional Concerns

Screening

When schools are implementing a multitiered system of support, they need procedures to identify students who are at risk for developing social-emotional or behavioral concerns. **Screening** is a systematic way of gathering teacher perceptions about students' concerning behaviors. Screening results help teachers and others know which students need Tier 2 or Tier 3 services. Screening results can also help them evaluate schoolwide intervention strategies (Young, Caldarella, Richardson, & Young, 2011). If screening data show that 40% of students have significant risk factors and need Tier 2 or 3 interventions, then the school team could assume that Tier 1 strategies are ineffective and more work needs to be done to enrich the schoolwide prevention and early intervention instruction. Designing Tier 2 and 3 interventions that would involve 40% of the school population is unrealistic.

Schoolwide screening helps teams understand specifically what interventions are needed. For example, if the screening measure shows that a good number of students are struggling with being worried, then the team may want to develop ways to teach all students ways of dealing with anxiety. Or if the screening results show that many students are exhibiting aggressive behaviors, the universal strategies could include teaching ways

TABLE 13.1   Examples of Screening Instruments

Title, (Author, Year)	Description	Grade Level and Types of Behavior	Comments
Student Risk Screening Scale—Internalizing Externalizing (SRSS-IE) (Drummond, 1994; Lane et al., 2011)	Teachers rate students on seven externalizing and five internalizing behaviors using a 4-point Likert-type scale. Strong validity for K–5; validity for 6–12 currently under review	K–12 Externalizing and internalizing behaviors	Teachers can complete the scale on a classroom of students in about 15 minutes.
Systematic Screening for Behavior Disorders, Second Edition (SSBD) (Walker et al., 2014)	Teachers nominate and then rank students with concerning behaviors. Highly ranked students may be considered for additional teacher ratings.	PreK–9 Externalizing and internalizing behaviors	Teachers can complete this screening online. Considered the gold standard of screening measures.
Social Skills Improvement System: Performance Screening Guide (Elliott & Gresham,, 2008)	Teachers report information about students' social skills as they relate to school success.	Pre-K–12 Pro-social behaviors Motivation to learn Reading and math skills	Intended to be used with the social skills interventions designed by the same authors.

to recognize anger, implement strategies for calming themselves, and then problem-solve (Lane, Menzies, Oakes, & Kalberg, 2012).

Screening is different than diagnosis. The purpose of screening is to cast a wide net and identify students who have some or many risk factors for developing social, emotional, or behavioral disorders. Interventions are then implemented so that the risk factors do not develop into full-blown disorders. Screening does not identify students as having a specific disorder or prescribe individualized interventions. Students are screened in groups, while diagnostic assessment occurs individually. The ultimate purpose of screening is to make instructional decisions for students identified as at risk (Young et al., 2011).

Screening procedures should be universal, comprehensive, repeated and continuous, technically adequate, and pragmatic (Glover & Albers, 2007). A description of each follows:

- **Universal**. Schoolwide screening should consider the needs of all students, and both internalizing and externalizing behaviors should be included.

- **Comprehensive**. Screening measures are available for depression, suicide, substance abuse, bullying, and so forth. Rather than screening separately for a disorder (unless there is a specific reason to do so), school teams should select a screening instrument that focuses on general levels of risk.

- **Repeated and Continuous**. Screening should occur throughout the school year. On a traditional school schedule, screenings should be completed in October, January, and April. Because students' needs change throughout the school year and some interventions are short term, repeated screening helps to ensure students' needs are identified and they have access to interventions.

- **Technically Adequate.** The norms should be up to date and represent the characteristic of the school. The instrument should have adequately reliable scores and evidence of validity for the purpose it is being used (see Chapter 5).

- **Pragmatic.** Screening instrument should be administered quickly, as well as easy to score, summarize, and interpret. Teams may be unlikely to screen if the process is unwieldy.

Individual Assessments

When data show that a student's needs have not been effectively addressed through tiered interventions, the team may consider if an individual assessment is needed. Such assessment can determine if the student qualifies as having EBD and what individualized interventions and accommodations are needed in both the general and special education classrooms (see Chapter 1).

Typically, school psychologists or other mental health professionals in the schools take the lead in completing evaluations for students suspected of having EBD. They document the student's difficulty with interpersonal relationships, inappropriate behaviors, moods of unhappiness/depression, or fearfulness. Academic and cognitive or IQ testing may also be completed during the evaluation, if these are specific areas of concern. Teachers contribute to the evaluation process by sharing information about the student's strengths, social relationships, classroom behaviors, and interventions used, and data from the intervention outcomes. Several structured classroom observations are needed, and these observations should be at different times of the school day and in different settings in the school. Data from observations are most helpful if the observations occur at times when the student usually is successful and at times when they may display difficult behaviors. Teachers may be asked to help document the student's academic skills and classroom achievement by summarizing current grades, previous testing results, or other information about the student's academic proficiency.

Both parents/guardians and teachers usually complete behavior rating scales that provide information about both general and specific areas of concerns. The school psychologist may interview teachers, parents, and the student to help the team understand (a) interventions that worked in the past; (b) the student's educational and developmental history, strengths, and weaknesses; and (c) specific concerns of the adults. The interview with the student helps the team understand the student's school experience. For example, some students may feel that they have few, if any, friends, that their teacher does not like them, or that they are experiencing bullying. Given this information, the team may then focus on developing interventions that contribute to helping the student develop positive relationships through social skill instruction and practice.

Interventions often include behavior management strategies that target teaching appropriate behaviors (e.g., using words to solve problems rather than physical aggression) and then reinforcing students when they use the appropriate behaviors. Other interventions may focus on teaching social skills or emotional regulation based on the student's specific needs. School-based mental health professionals may teach these skills in small groups and work with teachers and others to be sure that the student is prompted to use the skill in other settings. Students greatly benefit when teachers collaborate to design and implement the interventions.

Teaching Social and Emotional Competence

Helping students develop social and emotional competence may be viewed as something students learn at home and is primarily the responsibility of parents. School personnel may assume that the students have positive models in their homes and that from these models students learn appropriate behaviors. Often neither assumption is true. A few students seem to gain emotional competency with little effort and support, and at the other end of the continuum, some students consistently struggle to demonstrate these skills despite the best efforts of caregivers and teachers. Even students who generally display healthy social and emotional competence have times when they have difficulty regulating their emotions, using appropriate social skills, and practicing self-management.

Given that all students will need support to increase their social and emotional competence, the most efficient and effective means to achieve positive SEL outcomes is through teacher-directed instruction. Effective social and emotional instruction has several components that contribute to positive outcomes. First, the lessons focus on teaching behaviors rather than characteristics. Some curricula emphasize the importance of constructs such as honesty, respect, kindness, or fairness. Just discussing these constructs does not teach students how to show honest, respectful, kind, or fair behavior. Students will demonstrate respectful behavior when they learn and practice explicit examples of showing respect. Successful lessons have specific examples (e.g., listening when adults are talking, taking turns with peers) and nonexamples (e.g., interrupting others when they are talking, pushing others away to be first in line) of how to show respect (Knoff, 2003).

Second, the teacher instructs using the teacher-directed instruction framework. For example, teachers identify lesson objectives, model the behaviors, and provide guided and independent practice through role-playing. Practicing skills in several different settings (e.g., lunch room, hallways, and the classroom) is especially important to ensure that the skills are transferred to each setting where the skill is needed. Other important components of teacher-directed instruction include correcting errors and providing feedback.

Third, the skills and strategies are taught as part of a comprehensive and developmentally appropriate curriculum across the school, if possible, so that it creates a common language with consistent expectations for all students, teachers, administrators, and other school adults. Having a common language is a way of creating consistent expectations and ways to teach and reinforce those expectations across the school. For example, all students learn that showing respect for others means being quiet and attentive while the teacher is talking, when the lunchroom workers are giving directions, or during the schoolwide assembly. All students learn the same skills at approximately the same time so that expectations are consistent across grade levels. Furthermore, the lessons and activities build upon previously taught concepts so that a comprehensive and integrated curriculum is used rather than teaching one lesson about honesty and another about emotional regulation without any follow up or connection among the lessons that are taught (Hess, Short, & Hazel, 2012).

Anyone would have difficulty delineating all of the social and emotional competencies one would need to succeed in life, including career- and college-readiness skills. Compared to academic content, limited standards and curricular materials exist for SEL which adds to the challenge of knowing which specific skills to teach. General and special educators should collaborate with the school mental health professionals to select the social and emotional skills students need. Examples of important social and emotional competencies are embedded in the following discussion under the categories of emotional regulation, social skills, and self-management.

TEACHER TIP #13.2

SOCIAL SKILLS IDENTIFIED BY TEACHERS

Sometimes it is difficult to determine which social skills are the most important to teach. Although the following skills have been identified by teachers as necessary to succeed in school, these skills are not unlike those needed to do well in other settings, such as at home, on the job, or participating in the community:

- Self-control
- Cooperation

- Following directions
- Attending to teacher instruction
- Controlling your temper when having a conflict with a peer
- Controlling conflicts with adults
- Responding appropriately to physical aggression from peers (Lane, Pierson, & Givner, 2003)

Emotional Regulation

Emotional regulation involves being able to identify and label emotional states and then decide if and how to act on the emotions. Students who can share when they are sad or angry and then intentionally make choices about what to do with that emotion are students who are demonstrating emotional regulation skills. These skills also help students know how to move from feeling overwhelmingly sad with crying to still feeling sad, but able to contain their emotions and continue with their school work. Emotional regulation is focused on modulating the expression of emotions. Students who have healthy emotional regulation skills recognize that emotions vary in intensity and that situations influence how emotions are expressed and managed (Eisenberg, Hofer, Sulik, & Spinrad, 2013).

Leading researchers have identified the integral components of emotional regulation to include self-awareness, self-management, social awareness, relationship skills, and responsible decision-making. Each of these competencies contributes to social/emotional learning (Weissberg, Durlak, Domitrovich, & Gullotta, 2015). Helping students master these skills requires focusing on each component and then explicitly teaching how the skills are connected and integrated by taking them apart and then practicing connecting the parts.

Emotional regulation can be managed through internal processes (e.g., awareness of being angry, awareness of tightness in our shoulders that probably indicates feelings of stress) or through environmental controls (e.g., being asked to leave the room when explosive behaviors are shown, or choosing to leave a stressful situation to calm down). When students are explosive and need to be removed from classrooms, adults are attempting to externally manage the emotions of the student. As caregivers, teachers strive to help students develop adaptive and healthy internal or self-regulation of emotions (Zeman, Cassano, Perry-Parrish, & Stegall, 2006).

Some students may over- or underregulate their emotions. Students with tendencies to overregulate their emotions may not show emotions; they may feel stressed and overwhelmed but want to appear strong and in control. On the other hand, students who demonstrate explosive and aggressive behaviors demonstrate underregulated emotions (Zeman et al, 2006). One of the first steps in teaching emotional regulation skill includes helping students understand that having emotions is part of being human, that some emotions are comfortable, and others are uncomfortable. Learning the ways to recognize, label, and talk about feelings can help adults and students productively discuss, understand, and accept each other's emotions, which is a foundational piece of healthy relationships (Merrell, Carrizales et al., 2007). When students are overwhelmed with feelings that they find difficult to regulate, they may appear unmotivated. When emotions are intense, the ability to think and problem-solve are quite difficult, if not impossible, until students use strategies to calm themselves.

Numerous programs are available to teach emotional regulation, and typically these skills are embedded in broader curricula. Two examples are listed in Table 13.2 and include MindUP (MindUP, 2011) and *Strong Kids* (Merrell, Carrizales et al., 2007). Both are designed primarily for classroom teachers but may be implemented by mental health professionals as part of Tier 2 or 3 interventions. (See Table 13.3 for an abbreviated lesson plan on teaching the emotional regulation strategy of calming yourself.) School psychologists, counselors, and social workers are familiar with curricula and strategies that teach emotional regulation. These professionals can work with classroom teachers to find lessons that meet the specific needs of their students and are usually available to teach or co-teach the lessons. No matter what lessons are chosen and taught, finding ways to practice the skills over time and in various settings is vital to having students actually use and master the skills.

A research base is growing which provides evidence of the effectiveness of social/emotional curricula, especially when some of the lessons address emotional regulation. For example, in one study students at risk for emotional concerns decreased their internalizing behaviors based on teacher ratings when the *Strong Kids* (Merrell, Carrizales et al., 2007) lessons were delivered to all students in an elementary school (Kramer, Caldarella, Young, & Warren, 2014). In a similar study, second-grade students had fewer teacher-reported internalizing problems when they participated in the *Strong Start* (Merrell, Parisi, & Whitcomb, 2007) curriculum (Caldarella, Christensen, Kramer, &

Kronmiller, 2009). Preliminary and promising research also shows that mindfulness helps youth learn emotional regulation skills (Flook et al., 2010; Huppert & Johnson; 2010). While these studies show solid evidence that students will likely improve when direct instruction about emotional regulation occurs, there have been limited large-scale research studies using randomized control design; this lack of rigorous research about specific strategies and programs is typical of a good number of social/emotional learning programs.

TABLE 13.2 A Sample of Evidence-Based Commercially Available Curriculum to Teach Emotional Regulation and Social Skills

Title (Authors, Year) Publisher	Grade Level	Description	Sample of Behaviors and Skill Taught
MindUp (MindUp, 2011) Scholastic	PreK–8	• Three sets of materials based on grade level (PreK–2, 3–5, 6–8) • 15 comprehensive lessons • Scaffolds core academic programs, delivering a set of social, emotional, and self-regulatory strategies and skills • Available in both hard copy and e-book form	Improve focus, concentration, and academic performance Reduce stress and anxiety Handle peer-to-peer conflicts Manage emotions and reactions Develop greater empathy toward others Choose optimism
Skillstreaming (McGinnis, 2011) Research Press	PreK–12	• Three sets of materials based on grade level (early childhood, elementary, adolescent) • Appendixes provide all forms needed, plus leader and observer checklists	Classroom survival Friendship-making Dealing with feelings Alternatives to aggression Dealing with stress
Social Skills in Pictures, Stories and Songs (Serna, Nielsen, & Forness, 2007) Research Press	PreK–2	• Uses stories, mnemonics, coloring books, songs, role-playing, and visual aids • Built around four original stories and songs, featuring animal characters	Following directions Sharing Managing your behavior Problem-solving
Strong Kids (Merrell, Carrizales et al., 2007) Paul H. Brookes	PreK–12	• Five books for various grade levels: • Strong Start—PreK, K–2 • Strong Kids—3–5, 6–8 • Strong Teens—9–12 • CD-ROM with all handouts, worksheets, and assignments as reproducible PDF documents	Understanding your and others' feelings Dealing with anger Clear thinking Power of positive thinking Solving people problems Letting go of stress Setting goals and staying active

TABLE 13.3   An Example of an Emotional Regulation Lesson

Lesson on Calming Yourself

Objective 1: Students will (a) identify 2 times when they have felt an uncomfortable emotion and 2 times when they have felt a comfortable emotion, (b) identify the intensity of each emotion on a scale of 1 to 5 (intense emotions = 5 and low intensity emotions = 1), and (c) identify the behaviors associated with all 4 experiences.

Objective 2: Students will identify ways that they can calm themselves and develop plans for using those strategies.

Anticipatory Set: Introduce the topic using examples with which students can relate. For example, state, "Last night the girls' basketball team won the state championship. What emotions do you think the players were feeling? And the boys' basketball team lost the semifinal game. What emotions do you believe those players were feeling?"

Review: Remind students about the previous lesson that discussed that having feelings is part of the human condition. We all have feelings, which is healthy. We can make healthy or unhealthy decisions about what to do with our feelings.

Purpose Statement: Tell students they will learn how to identify comfortable and uncomfortable emotions, and when emotions are intense and uncomfortable they will learn ways to calm themselves.

Objective 1

Modeling/Instruction: Share a recent time when you had an (a) emotional reaction to an experience, (b) if it was an uncomfortable or comfortable feeling, and (c) the intensity of the feeling. For example, "Someone took my assigned parking spot just as I turned into the parking lot this morning. I was already running late for school. I groaned out loud and gently hit the steering wheel of my car. I was upset because now I was probably going to be late for class. I identified this frustration as an *uncomfortable feeling* and using an intensity scale where 5 is extremely intense and 1 is slightly intense, I would label it about a 4. The intensity was probably a 4 because I groaned loudly and lightly hit the steering wheel with my hand. If I had just shrugged my shoulders and thought, 'It's not a big deal. That person probably needs a close parking spot right now. I'm sure I'll find another spot soon.' I would have identified that the intensity was low, probably a 1, on the feelings scale."

Then share an example of a positive experience and the intensity of that experience based on observable behaviors.

Using a sample of examples across a range of intensity of emotion, discuss as a group whether those feelings are comfortable or uncomfortable and where they probably fit on the feelings scale and why. Create a poster as a group delineating behaviors that might be associated with each rating.

Guided Practice. Provide additional examples for students, in pairs ask them to identify recent feelings as comfortable/uncomfortable and rate them on the feelings scale. Monitor students' answers. Praise them for accurate identification of emotions.

Independent Practice. Ask students to identify 2 uncomfortable feelings and 2 comfortable feelings they have experienced and how they would rate them on the intensity scale. Provide feedback and reteach if necessary.

Objective 2

Modeling/Instruction: Remind the students how you responded to the two examples provided earlier. For example, "I realized I was frustrated and upset. But I did not want to start my day with negative feelings so I started breathing deeply to calm myself. I told myself that I really had plenty of time to find a different parking space." Emphasize the behaviors taken (took deep breaths) and the considerations of how the situation could end positively (I have time). Explain that you could have chosen unhealthy behaviors (e.g., scolding the teacher who parked there, leaving a negative note on the windshield, slashing the tires), but that you didn't because none of those would have solved the problem and would not have calmed you down.

Share other self-calming strategies that can be used at school (e.g., deep breathing, asking to take a break, asking to talk to an adult that can help). Also discuss calming strategies for home (e.g., physical exercise, talking to friends, stretching, taking a shower).

(Continued)

TABLE 13.3   **(Continued)**

Guided Practice: Ask each pair to generate a list of healthy calming strategies for both school and home. Write them on a poster to display in the classroom.

Independent Practice: With their partners, ask students to identify 2 healthy ways they will use to calm themselves at school and 2 healthy ways they will use to calm themselves at home.

Source: Based on a lesson from Merrell et al., 2007 Merrell, K. W., Carrizales, D., Feuerborn, L., Gueldern, B. A., & Tran, O. L., (2007). *Strong kids: Grades 3-5.* Baltimore, MD: Brookes.

TEACHER TIP #13.3

ANGER MANAGEMENT OR PROBLEM-SOLVING

For students who need help with anger management or problem-solving, the following first-letter mnemonic strategies can be taught using the teacher-directed instruction format:

CALM—Anger Management

Can you identify if you're starting to get angry?

Are there some techniques you can use to calm yourself down?

Look at these techniques, choose the best one, and try it.

Monitor yourself. Is it working? If not, try it again.

ICAN—Problem-Solving

Identify the problem.

Can you identify some solutions?

Analyze the solutions.

Now, pick one and try it. If it doesn't work, try it again. (Williams & Reisberg, 2003)

Social Skills

Social skills involve the personal skills needed for successful social interactions and relationships (e.g., beginning a conversation, negotiating, and coping with being left out). In order to teach social skills, each individual skill is task analyzed, or broken into steps that students are taught to master. Students memorize and practice each step, then put them back together (Cumming, 2010). In school, strong social skills help students achieve academically, while students' problem behaviors lower levels of academic achievement (Gresham, 2015). Traditionally, most social skills instruction has been reserved for small group or individual instruction. Such instruction has been delivered as Tier 2 or Tier 3 interventions (Gresham, 2015), although it could also be delivered to all students in a classroom or schoolwide as a Tier 1 or universal intervention (Simonsen et al., 2012).

As mentioned previously, the most efficient and effective means for teaching social skills is through explicit teacher-directed instruction. Teachers can create their own lesson plans using the format discussed in Chapter 7. (For an example of a scripted lesson plan to teach the social skill of how to make a request, see Appendix F.) Or teachers can rely on available commercial materials. For example, the *Skillstreaming*

(McGinnis, 2011) curriculum uses a teacher-directed approach to teaching skills such as friendship-making, alternatives to aggression, and dealing with stress. Another commercially available curriculum designed for young students is *Social Skills in Pictures, Stories and Songs* (Serna et al, 2007). This curriculum uses a multimedia approach to teach skills such as following directions and problem-solving. More detail about these commercially available social skills curriculum may be found in Table 13.2. The list provided in Table 13.2 is not exhaustive. When finding other curricular materials, teachers are urged to ensure they are evidence-based, that the materials have been tested in schools and found to be effective for the same population of students as those being taught in the teacher's classroom or school.

Students can be taught social skills separately or imbedded as part of academic content. This is best done by creating one lesson objective for the academic content and one for a social skill. For example, when teaching students to edit one another's papers, students can learn the editing process as well as how to give positive and negative feedback. A social studies lesson that involves students working in collaborative groups on a project could have an objective about forms of government and an objective focused on compromise or negotiation. An example of a brief lesson plan demonstrating instruction in science inquiry with a social skills component may be found in Table 13.4.

TABLE 13.4 **An Example of an Academic Lesson With a Social Skill Component**

Science Inquiry Lesson with Social Skills Component

Objective 1: When asked to work with a partner to determine the pH of 10 substances, each person in the partnership will alternate taking turns until each person has determined and written the pH for 5 of the substances.

Objective 2: Given 10 substances and 5 pieces of pH paper, students will place a drop of each substance on the pH paper and will write the pH level for each substance with 100% accuracy as measured against the teacher's answer key for the substances.

Anticipatory set: Hold up a glass of orange juice and ask the class to guess if the orange juice is a base or an acid.

Review: Show the pH scale. Have the students write which numbers indicate a substance is an acid, and which numbers indicate a substance is a base.

Purpose statement: In this lesson, you will learn how to measure the pH of various substances. As part of completing this assignment, you will also learn how to take turns.

Objective 1

Modeling/Instruction for social skill:

"For this activity, you will work with a partner. Before we begin the activity, you will learn to take turns. Alisha, would you come up and be my partner as I demonstrate how to take turns and how to complete this science lab?

1. To take turns, you have to first decide who's going first. In your partnership, one of you will ask the other if they'd like to go first. I will ask Alisha if she'd like to go first. 'Alisha, would you like to go first?'

2. Alisha said yes. She'd like to go first. So, I let Alisha take her turn, and I wait and watch. If Alisha would have said that she didn't want to go first, then I would have taken my turn and she would have waited.

3. After the first person finishes taking his/her turn, we switch and the other person gets to take a turn. Since Alisha went first, it's my turn now. I take my turn putting the paper towels on the lab table and Alisha watches and waits."

(Continued)

TABLE 13.4   (Continued)

Guided practice:

"Get with your assigned partner. Now we'll practice this social skill as we put the paper towels out for our experiment.

1. First, decide who goes first. (Prompt the students to ask their partner who'd like to go first).
2. Next, the person who wants to go first takes his/her turn, and the other person watches and waits.
3. Now, we switch and the person who didn't take a turn gets a turn."

Continue to practice this social skill as he/she prompts the class to put out more materials for the experiment.

Independent practice will occur as the partners continue to take turns but without prompting from the teacher.

Objective 2

"Now you'll practice the skill of taking turns as you learn the procedures for the lab. Before we practice taking turns, I'll model the procedures."

Modeling/Instruction for science lab:

While saying the following demonstrate each step:

1. "First, I set out the pH papers on top of the paper towels.
2. Second, I will measure the first substance on my list. I put the substance in front of me and I use the medicine dropper to get some of the substance out of the bottle. I put the dropper in the bottle of the substance and I squeeze the top of the dropper to extract some of the substance.
3. Then, I hold the dropper over the first piece of pH paper and squeeze the dropper to drop some of the substance on the paper.
4. Next, I watch the paper and see if it turns color. The color the paper turns will tell me the pH number. When the paper has turned a color, I put the paper next to the wide-range pH scale and line it up with where it matches color on the scale. Where it matches tells me the pH for the substance.
5. Once I have found where it matches. I look at the number on the scale and write the number."

Demonstrate with 3 more substances.

Guided Practice:

Give the students a list of substances to measure. Throughout this section complete the steps along with the student and provide prompts as needed.

"Before we start measuring, you have to practice the taking-turns social skill. With your partner, decide who will go first. Once you've decided who will go first, that person will practice these procedures and the other person will watch and wait.

1. For the people who are going first, first, we set out the pH papers on top of the paper towels.
2. Second, we will measure the first substance on our list. We put the substance in front of us, and then we use the medicine droppers to get some of the substance.
3. Then, we hold the dropper over the first piece of pH paper and squeeze the dropper to drop some of the substance on the paper.
4. Next, we watch the paper and see if it turns color. When our papers have finished turning color we put the paper next to the wide-range pH scale and line it up with where the colors match.

5. Once we have found where it matches, we look at the number on the scale and write the number.

6. Now it's your partner's turn."

Repeat the process with the partners. Repeat the process 2 more times to give each student a chance to practice the procedure.

Independent Practice:

Give the students the list of 10 items and instruct them to follow the procedures they've practiced for taking turns and for determining the pH for the substances. Instruct them that each person in the partnership will determine the pH for 5 of the items on the list.

Many, if not most, students could benefit from social skills instruction. Effectiveness of the two examples of published curricular materials, *Skillstreaming* (McGinnis, 2011) and *Social Skills in Pictures, Stories, and Songs* have been documented with at-risk students (Serna et al., 2007). Additional studies support the success of social skills instruction with students with HID. For example, such instruction has been demonstrated to improve the social skills of students with EBD (e.g., Cook et al., 2008), and students with autism (e.g., Lopata, Thomeer, Volker, & Nida, 2006; White, Koenig, & Scahill, 2010). However, only emerging evidence exists with modest improvements in social behavior based on social skills instruction. As with studies on emotional regulation, more studies are needed to solidify the evidence of social skill instruction effectiveness.

TEACHER TIP # 13.4

EXPERIENTIAL ADVENTURE ACTIVITIES

Try implementing adventure activities, a social problem-solving approach for teaching students social skills using problem-solving and trust-building activities.

1. Select activities that promote student cooperation (not competition), are fun, and require few props. (For example, Add on Tag is played just like the traditional tag game where one person who is "it" tags another person; but in this version, the person tagged must hold the hand of the person who tagged him and the two try to tag a third person who also must join the two by holding hands. This continues until all players are holding hands.)

2. Introduce the activity and explain the rules:

    i   Work as a team.

    ii Keep each other safe (emotionally and physically).

    iii Give and accept appropriate feedback.

    iv Avoid putting anyone, including yourself, down.

    v   If something bothers you, get over it quickly.

3. Implement the activity.

4. Debrief by asking students to rate the activity and evaluate their performance in keeping the rules. Lead them toward specific issues important to improving their social skills. Ask them what they learned. (Forgan & Jones, 2002)

Self-Management

Richelle has autism and attends general education classes in her high school with special education support. Her English and math teachers have been concerned about her lack of focus and failure to turn in her weekly assignments. Mr. Haskins, her special education teacher, participated in a district-sponsored workshop and learned about self-monitoring, a method of teaching students to monitor their own behavior. The presenter indicated that this method, if taught and implemented properly, can drastically change students' on-task behavior and improve their academic skills. After hearing about Richelle's difficulties in her general education classes, Mr. Haskins is excited to try this technique.

Self-management is an umbrella term that encompasses many procedures in which students manage their own behavior and learning. Traditional behavior management programs (e.g., token economies, contingency contracts) require external behavior control because the teacher monitors the student's behavior and grants the tokens and the reinforcers (see Chapter 3). Self-management training moves students away from external teacher control and toward self-regulation by requiring that students participate actively and take responsibility for their own behavior and learning. Self-management teaches students to be more independent and self-directed. Self-monitoring is the most prominently used and studied self-management strategy.

Self-monitoring procedures involve the application of two other self-management strategies: self-assessment and self-recording. When self-assessing, the student judges whether a behavior occurred. For example, if students are self-assessing their academic or vocational work, they ask themselves predetermined question such as, *Did I finish my homework?* Or *Did I finish wiping my tables?* They may also ask themselves questions related to their work behavior such as *Was I on task?* Or *Did I complete my homework?*

The second component of self-monitoring, self-recording, involves recording the occurrence or nonoccurrence of the behavior. Generally, a self-monitoring sheet is used on which students record their answers. Students can be instructed to make their own sheets. Several samples of self-monitoring charts appear in Figure 13.1.

Prompts are an important feature in self-management procedures. For monitoring on-task behaviors, for example, students are commonly presented with an auditory prompt spaced at random intervals. Students listen and when they hear the prompt, ask themselves, *Was I on task?* and then record their response. Individual students using this procedure can use earphones with a handheld device in order to not disturb other students. Commercial tools are also available that prompt students. For example, the MotivAider is a simple electronic device that can be programmed to vibrate on a fixed or variable schedule at different duration and intensity levels (habitchange.com). Visual prompts may also be most helpful. The self-monitoring sheet may act as a visual prompt. Some students may need additional visual prompts, such as a poster displayed on the classroom wall.

Fading of the prompts is a necessary component of self-management training. The ultimate goal is to internalize the behavior. Consequently, the prompts (e.g., the audio tones) should be faded systematically by reducing the frequency of and eventually eliminating the audio prompts.

FIGURE 13.1   **Samples of Self-Monitoring Charts**

A.M. Self-Monitoring Sheet

Name: _____   Date: _____

Subjects: Reading, Math, Writing, Spelling

Subjects and Assignments	Behavior Check
Reading ☐ Read selection ☐ Answered comprehension questions ☐ Completed one timed reading and recorded time	**Target behavior** ☐ Stayed in seat ☐ Raised hand for assistance
Writing ☐ Wrote 3 paragraphs in response journal ☐ Completed writing skills worksheet ☐ Completed writing challenge assignment	**Target behavior** ☐ Stayed in seat ☐ Raised hand for assistance
Math ☐ Completed a math facts timing ☐ Completed all independent practice problems	**Target behavior** ☐ Stayed in seat ☐ Raised hand for assistance
Spelling ☐ Wrote spelling words 3 times each ☐ Wrote each spelling word in a sentence	**Target behavior** ☐ Stayed in seat ☐ Raised hand for assistance

Homework Completion – MATH

Name: _____   Week of: _____

Day of the Week	Assignment	Turned In	Score
Monday	pp. 110–112 #3–45 (even)	☐	
Tuesday	pp. 115–117 #1–25 (all)	☐	
Wednesday	pp. 121–122 #3–6 & 10–25 (all)	☐	
Thursday	pp. 125–126 #1–30 (odd)	☐	
Friday	pp. 130–131 Chapter Test – (all)	☐	

Total Turned in _____   Average Score _____

Comments:

(Continued)

FIGURE 13.1   **(Continued)**

Behavior Monitoring Chart

Name: _____ Date: _____ Time Period: From_____ to _____

Target Behavior: On Task

On task is:

- Eyes on teacher or on work,
- Sitting in chair,
- Using correct materials,
- Working silently

On task is NOT: Talking with neighbors, leaving your seat, not working

Directions:

1.   Each time the tape beeps, mark whether you are on task.
2.   If you are on task put an X in the box.
3.   If you are not on task, put a 0 in the box.

TOTAL Xs _____   TOTAL 0s _____

TABLE 13.5   **Types of Self-Management Strategies**

Types	Definition	Examples
Self-monitoring	Students self-assess whether they are engaged in a specific behavior. They then record their answer.	Harold uses an audio beep to prompt him to self-assess his behavior, which he then records.
Self-assessment	Students ask themselves questions about their behavior or performance.	When Patrick hears the beep, he asks himself if he was on task.
Self-recording	Students record their behavior or performance.	Gerrilynn records her daily math assignment scores on a self-monitoring sheet.
Self-graphing or charting	Students record their behavior or performance on a graph to show progress.	After self-recording her score, Evie draws a dot representing her score on the graph.
Self-reinforcement	Students identify and then administer reinforcers after achieving a goal.	Every day Quentin completes his homework, he lets himself watch 30 minutes of television.

Students need specific instruction and training in self-monitoring procedures. The instructional procedures are listed in Table 13.6.

TABLE 13.6   **Steps for Implementing Self-Monitoring of On-Task Behavior**

Implementing Self-Monitoring of On-Task Behavior
1. Identify student(s), setting, and behaviors.
2. Determine procedures to collect data on student performance.
3. Collect, compute, and graph baseline data.
4. Gather and/or create needed materials.
5. Teach students to self-monitor.
a. Explain the purpose and enlist commitment from each student.
b. Define behaviors (e.g., on task, off task, completion of homework).
c. Model examples and nonexamples of the behaviors through role-playing.
d. Have students demonstrate examples and nonexamples of the behaviors.
e. Teach students the following sequence they should follow (e.g., hear the tone, ask yourself, *Am I on task?*, then record).
f. Demonstrate using the materials (e.g., audio recording, self-monitoring sheets).
6. Initiate the self-monitoring program.
7. Continue to collect data on student performance.
8. Fade prompts.
a. Reduce the number of prompts (e.g., increase the time between audio prompts).
b. Eventually eliminate the prompts.
c. Have students self-record when they think about it.
d. Eventually eliminate the self-recording.
9. Continue to collect data on student performance. If student performance decreases to an unacceptable level, repeat the process.

Mr. Haskins taught Richelle to self-monitor her on-task behavior using a MotivAider. When she feels the device vibrate, she asks herself if she's on task. Then she self-records her answer on the self-monitoring sheet. Mr. Haskins has also begun a self-monitoring of homework completion procedure. He designed a monitoring sheet with the steps Richelle needs to complete and submit her homework (e.g., Make certain I understand the assignment; Ask questions if needed; Put my book and assignment in my backpack; Take my backpack home; Complete the assignment; Put it in my backpack; Take my backpack to school; Return the assignment to the teacher). As she completes each step, she checks it off the sheet. Mr. Haskins works with the English and math teachers to collect data on Richelle's on-task and assignment completion behavior before and during the self-monitoring intervention. This helps them know whether the self-monitoring is making a difference.

Studies have found self-management training to be effective across a wide range of student characteristics and behaviors. For example, studies have shown self-management training to be effective for students with attention-deficit/hyperactivity disorders (e.g., Barry & Messer, 2003), behavioral disorders (e.g., Cancio, West, & Young, 2004), learning disabilities (e.g., Shimabukuro, Prater, Jenkins, & Edelen-Smith, 1999), intellectual disabilities (e.g., Wadsworth, Hansen, & Willis, 2015), and autism (e.g., Lee, Simpson, & Shogren, 2007). These procedures have also been demonstrated across a wide range of ages, from elementary students (e.g., McDougall & Brady, 1998) to those in high school (e.g., Clemons, Mason, Garrison-Kane, & Wills, 2016). In addition, self-management training has been used with a variety of behaviors including increasing compliance (Wadsworth et al., 2015), time-on-task (e.g., Clemons et al., 2016), academic productivity (e.g., Trevino-Maack, Kamps, & Wills, 2015), and academic achievement (Shimabukuro et al., 1999).

TEACHER TIP #13.5

"I WILL" CARD STRATEGY

The "I Will" card strategy can be used to prompt students to use appropriate behavior rather than relying on others to prompt or direct them. The following steps are used to implement this strategy:

- Identify a target social skill and situation (e.g., ignore and walk away rather than fight or argue).

- Identify what the student would need to say to himself or herself regarding each targeted behavior identified.

- Write script cards for each behavior. Include the situation and "I will" statements (e.g., When someone bothers me, I will . . . not say anything, look away, walk away).

- Teach the student to read the cards and use them when appropriate.

- Review the cards with the student each day. Ask when the cards were used and if not, why not. Ask when the student will use the card next time.

- Provide appropriate feedback including instruction on how and when to use the cards next time as well as praise for using the cards when needed. (Boutot, 2009)

Technology Spotlight #13.1

Using Technology With Social Emotional Learning

Social Skills

Social skills instruction requires modeling and role-playing specific interaction skills. Technology can play a role. For example, teachers can create short video clips

(30–60 seconds) of students modeling the skills being taught using models of the same age and ethnicities as the students learning the skills. For example, in one study researchers created videos of students in a neighboring school role-playing the skills being taught. The video accompanied an adapted *Skillstreaming* social skills curriculum (McGinnis, 2011) focusing on starting and continuing a conversation and joining in an activity. Participants included Latino fourth- and fifth-grade students whose primary language was Spanish. Results demonstrated that participants increased the number of interactions they had with non-Latino students on the playground. The authors attributed the inclusion of the videos as at least partially contributing to the students' success (Lo, Correa, & Anderson, 2015).

In addition to teachers creating videos, they can go a step further in involving students in the video production. In doing so, students can learn technology skills and social skills at the same time. First, students would be placed in small groups and each assigned a specific role (e.g., director, camera operator, scribe). They would write and enact role-plays based on the social skill being learned. At the end of the week, students would screen their movies for other class members. One study found that using these procedures, middle school students with EBD increased their motivation and improved their social skills (Cumming et al., 2008).

Self-Monitoring

When engaged in self-monitoring, technological tools are almost always used. Audio prompts for students may involve a kitchen timer set to ding at a certain interval, a prerecorded sound on a hand held device, or a commercial tool that vibrates (e.g., MotivAider). Given the widespread availability of cell phones and tablets (e.g., iPads), students are beginning to use these as they self-record and self-chart their own behavior. Mobile devices are particularly useful for prompting students given their acceptability and portability. Care must be taken to ensure, however, that school policy allows for the use of the devices, particularly cell phones, for this purpose and that the device is only used for the intended purpose.

Typically when self-monitoring, students hear an audio cue which prompts them to self-record on a paper form. Now technology can be used to not only provide the prompts but to self-record the behavior. CellF-Monitoring is a clever play-on-words idea to describe the use of cell phones for both prompting the student to self-assess and to self-record. Teachers can set up automated text messages through social media programs as prompts (e.g., "Are you on task?") to be sent to the student at certain intervals. The cell phone is set on vibrate to alert the student. The student then responds to the text message with a yes or no. The teacher can review the data on the cell phone or the message log on the social media website (Bedesem & Dieker, 2014).

Implications for Culturally and/or Linguistically Diverse Students

Emotional well-being and social-emotional learning, just like any kind of learning happens within a cultural context. As has been discussed in previous chapters, culture is much more than race or ethnicity. Culture is like a lens that provides information about how individuals see and interact within their environment. Cultural influences can play a role in how teachers view students' behavior. For example, in some cultures eye contact may be avoided as a sign of respect while in other cultures lack of eye contact may be interpreted as a sign of disinterest. Teachers' cultural backgrounds influence how they view the behaviors of students, which necessitates exploration of their cultural biases and the cultural influences of student's behavior.

Cultural differences can impact both SEL assessment and SEL instruction. A good amount of subjectivity exists in rating student behavior which can lead to subtle and nuanced biases. Professionals need to be particularly careful when all members of the team represent the same cultural background which is different than the students being rated. Teachers are urged to collaborate with professionals or paraeducators who represent the same cultural background as the student to reduce bias when both assessing and designing instruction for CLD students. Also, when using standardized assessment, the normative group should have included cultural groups similar to the students' cultural group (see Chapter 5).

Extensive documentation exists about cultural issues regarding office discipline referrals, suspensions, and behaviorally based referrals to special education. For example, African American elementary students are twice as likely to be referred to the office as White students, and in middle school, African American students are almost four times as likely to be referred to the office. Similarly, African Americans and Latinos are more likely to experience out-of-school suspension and expulsion for the same behaviors demonstrated by their White peers (Skiba et al., 2011). This and other research heightens our awareness of how ethnicity, as one aspect of culture, may contribute to the way some students experience school.

For over 40 years, a major controversy has centered on the disproportionate representation of students of color in special education. Cultural differences (e.g., values, beliefs, attitudes) among students, families, and teachers impact teacher expectations and deficit thinking which can lead to over referrals which then leads to overrepresentation (Ford, 2012). For example, African American students are identified with EBD and intellectual disabilities in higher proportions than other ethnic groups (U.S. Department of Education, 2014). In addition, African Americans are overrepresented in restrictive special education settings (e.g., self-contained or unit classrooms) and underrepresented in less restrictive settings (e.g., general education classrooms) (Skiba, Poloni-Staudinger, Gallini, Simmons, & Feggins-Azziz, 2006).

Understanding the complexities of culturally different students helps teachers and other personnel provide needed support. For example, in one study, some Hispanic students who were identified as at risk were also targets of aggressive behaviors from peers. They may have been called racially derogatory names outside of teachers' awareness or had inflammatory notes left in their locker. If the Hispanic students responded similarly, they believed they were more likely than the White students to be sent to the office and punished (Balagna, Young, & Smith, 2013). Understanding the perspective of the student and considering a multiplicity of reasons for the behaviors of students that could be related to culture are vital to providing culturally competent services.

When engaged in SEL, teachers also need to deliver culturally responsive instruction. Five important features of culturally responsive social skills instruction include (1) ensuring the skills being taught are important to the students, (2) using culturally relevant materials, (3) providing culturally competent peer models, (4) integrating students' personal experiences, and (5) providing authentic opportunities to apply the skills being taught (Robinson-Ervin, Cartledge, & Keyes, 2011). (For additional information on culturally responsive teaching, see Chapter 6.)

SUMMARY

Social and emotional learning (SEL) is defined as the way individuals manage, interpret, and respond to their own and others' feelings. Although students with social, emotional, and behavioral concerns may be identified as EBD, many other students are not and could benefit from instruction in these areas. In fact, 10% to 20% of all school-age students exhibit emotional distress or impairment. Students may exhibit externalizing (e.g., fighting, verbal taunts) or internalizing (e.g., withdrawal, acting sad) behaviors or both. Internalizing behaviors are more difficult to identify because these students turn inward with their concerns, worries, and problems. Social and emotional competence impacts relationships, self-esteem, and academic performance. That is, students who are socially competent have better school attitudes, behavior, and performance.

A key element of SEL is promoting prevention and early intervention under the MTSS framework. Similar to teaching academic content, all students receive Tier 1, a universal level of instruction. Those who need additional support may receive more intensive instruction or Tier 2, which usually means more time on the skills with a small group of students with similar needs. Students with significant needs may need individual counseling or Tier 3 intervention. School mental health workers, such as school psychologists, generally provide Tier 2 and 3 interventions. Part of promoting prevention is creating and maintaining emotionally healthy classrooms where teachers have clear behavioral expectations and deliver reinforcing or punishing consequences. Teachers in supportive classrooms also have positive, warm relationships with all students.

Identifying students with social and emotional concerns occurs at two levels: screening and individual evaluation. All students are screened to identify at-risk students who could particularly benefit from intervention. Screening procedures should be universal, comprehensive, repeated and continuous, technically adequate, and pragmatic. Students are individually evaluated when their needs have not been addressed through tiered interventions. Such assessment can determine if the student qualifies as having EBD and thus receives special education services.

All students need support to improve their social and emotional competence. The most efficient and effective means to achieve positive outcomes is through teacher-directed instruction. Students may be taught how to regulate their emotions and/or specific social skills. Published curriculum is available for both or teachers can create their own lessons using the teacher-directed instruction format. These skills can also be integrated into the academic curriculum so that students are learning both simultaneously.

Students with HID also benefit from self-management instruction in which students learn to manage their own behavior and learning. Self-monitoring is a commonly used strategy where students are taught to self-assess whether they are engaged in a specific behavior and then self-record their answer. Students can be taught self-management strategies through teacher-directed instruction.

Emotional well-being and SEL must be considered within a cultural context. Culture influences how teachers view student behavior. Diverse students have more office discipline referrals, suspensions, and behaviorally based referrals to special education which may be due to the mismatch between teachers' cultural perspectives and that of the students. Teachers need to ensure that their SEL instruction includes culturally appropriate models, examples, materials, and opportunities to practice.

REVIEW QUESTIONS

1. What is SEL and why is it important for all students to have SEL competencies?

2. Compare and contrast externalizing and internalizing behaviors. Provide multiple examples of each.

3. In what ways is SEL connected to academic outcomes?

4. Describe MTSS with examples for each tier. Justify why MTSS is an important framework to use for SEL.

5. Compare and contrast SEL screening and individual assessment. Include the purposes, types of instruments, and how the results can be used.

6. Delineate the three important components of effective social and emotional instruction that contribute to positive outcomes.

7. Define *emotional regulation* and *social skills*, provide multiple examples and nonexamples, and describe how one would teach emotional regulation and social skills.

8. Describe how teachers can teach social-emotional skills simultaneously with academic content. Provide examples.

9. Generate an example of when a student should be taught a self-monitoring procedure. Outline the lesson plan.

10. Describe the role of culture in the identification and instruction of students with emotional and social problems.

ACTIVITIES

1. Question 50 adults asking them to list their top 10 emotional regulation and social skills that they believe contribute to lifetime success. Based on the result, select the top three you would teach to students. Write a paper summarizing the results and justifying your selection.

2. Search on the Internet for emotional regulation curriculum and social skills curriculum not mentioned in this chapter. Then search for empirical evidence validating the effectiveness of the curriculum. Make an oral report of your findings.

3. Identify a behavior you wish to change. Create a self-management strategy for yourself. Implement the strategy and report on the results.

4. In a school that educates a high percentage of culturally diverse students, observe a teacher or school mental health specialist teach a social emotional lesson. Interview the teacher or specialist about the curriculum and skills selected and whether the diversity of the students influenced their selection. Write up your experience.

Council for Exceptional Children (CEC) Standards

The Council for Exceptional Children (CEC) is a premiere national professional organization comprised of special educators, paraeducators, relative service personnel, parents, and others interested in individuals with disabilities and/or those with gifts and talents. This organization has generated 10 standards for the preparation of special educators. These standards are listed in each chapter as they relate to the content within the chapter. The standard that applies to Chapter 13 is Standard #5.

CEC Initial Preparation Standard #5: Instructional Planning and Strategies (partial)

Beginning special education professionals select, adapt, and use a repertoire of evidence-based instructional strategies to advance learning of individuals with exceptionalities.

5.1   Beginning special education professionals consider an individual's abilities, interests, learning environments, and cultural and linguistic factors in the selection, development, and adaptation of learning experiences for individuals with exceptionalities.

5.4   Beginning special education professionals use strategies to enhance language development and communication skills of individuals with exceptionalities.

5.6   Beginning special education professionals teach to mastery and promote generalization of learning.

5.7   Beginning special education professionals teach cross-disciplinary knowledge and skills such as critical thinking and problem solving to individuals with exceptionalities.

REFERENCES

Algozzine, B., Wang, C., & Violette, A. S. (2011). Reexamining the relationship between academic achievement and social behavior. *Journal of Positive Behavior Interventions, 13*(1), 3–16.

Balagna, R. M., Young, E. L., & Smith, T. B. (2013). School experiences of early adolescent Latinos/as at risk for emotional and behavioral disorders. *School Psychology Quarterly, 28*(2), 101–121.

Barry, L. M., & Messer, J. J. (2003). A practical application of self-management for students diagnosed with attention-deficit/hyperactivity disorder. *Journal of Emotional and Behavioral Disorders, 12*, 9–22.

Bedesem, P. L., & Dieker, L. A. (2014). Self-monitoring with a twist: Using cell phones to cell-monitor on-task behavior. *Journal of Positive Behavior Interventions, 16*(4), 246–254.

Boutot, E. M. (2009). Using "I will" cards and social coaches to improve social behaviors of students with Asperger syndrome. *Intervention in School and Clinic, 44*(5), 276–281.

Caldarella, P., Christensen, L., Kramer, T. J., & Kronmiller, K. (2009). Promoting social and emotional learning in second grade students: A study of the strong Start curriculum. *Early Childhood Education Journal, 37*(1), 51–56.

Cancio, E. J., West, R. P., & Young, K. R. (2004). Improving mathematics homework completion and accuracy of students with EBD through self-management and parent participation. *Journal of Emotional and Behavioral Disorders, 12*, 9–22.

Caprara, G. V., Barbaranelli, C., Pastorelli, C., Bandura, A., & Zimbardo, P. G. (2000). Prosocial foundations of children's academic achievement. *Psychological Science, 11*(4), 302–306.

Clemons, L. L., Mason B. A., Garrison-Kane, L., & Wills, H. P. (2016). Self-monitoring for high school students with disabilities: A cross-categorical investigation of I-Connect. *Journal of Positive Behavior Interventions, 18*(3), *145–155.* doi: 10.1177/1098300715596134

Collaborative for Academic, Social, and Emotional Learning. (2015). *What is social and emotional learning?* Retrieved from http://www.casel.org/social-and-emotional-learning/

Cook, C. R., Gresham, F. M., Kern, L., Barreras, R. B., Thornton, S., & Crews, S. D. (2008). Social skills training for secondary students with emotional and/or behavioral disorders. *Journal of Emotional and Behavioral Disorders, 16*(3), 131–144.

Cumming, T. M. (2010). Using technology to create motivating social skills lessons. *Intervention in School and Clinic, 45*(4), 242–250.

Cumming, T. M., Higgins, K., Pierce, T., Miller, S., Tandy, R., & Boone, R. (2008). Social skills instruction for adolescents with emotional disabilities: A technology-based intervention. *Journal of Special Education Technology, 23*(1), 19–33.

Doll, B., Zucker, S., & Brehm, K. (2004). *Resilient classroom: Creating healthy environments for learning.* New York, NY: Guilford Press.

Drummond, T. (1994). *The Student Risk Screening Scale (SRSS).* Grants Pass, OR: Josephine County Mental Health Program.

Durlak, J. A., Weissberg, R. P., Dymnicki, A. B., Taylor, R. D., & Schellinger, K. B. (2011). The impact of enhancing students' social and emotional learning: A meta-analysis of school-based universal interventions. *Child Development, 82*, 405–432.

Dusenbury, L. A., Newman, J. Z., Weissberg, R. P., Goren, P., Domitrovich, C. E., & Mart, A. K. (2015). The case for preschool through high school state learning standards for SEL. In J. A. Durlak, C. E. Domitrovich, R. P. Weissberg, & T. P. Gullotta (Eds.), *Handbook of social and emotional learning: Research and practice* (pp. 532–548). New York, NY: Guilford Press.

Eisenberg, N., Hofer, C., Sulik, M. J., & Spinrad, T. L. (2013). Self-regulation, effortful control, and their socioemotional correlates. In J. J. Gross (Ed.), *Handbook of emotion regulation* (2nd ed.; pp. 157–218). New York, NY: Guilford Press.

Elias, M. J. (Ed.). (1997). *Promoting social and emotional learning: Guidelines for educators.* Alexandria, VA: Association for Supervision and Curriculum Development.

Elliott, S. N., & Gresham, F. (2008). *Social Skills Improvement System (SSIS) Performance Screening Guide,* Upper Saddle River, NJ: Pearson.

Flook, L., Smalley, S. L., Kitil, M. J., Galla, B. M., Kaiser-Greenland, S., Locke, J., . . . Kasari, C. (2010). Effects of mindful awareness practices on executive functions in elementary school children. *Journal of Applied School Psychology, 26*(1), 70–95.

Ford, D. Y. (2012). Culturally different students in special education: Looking backward to move forward. *Exceptional Children, 79*(4), 391–405.

Forgan, J. W., & Jones, C. D. (2002). How experiential adventure activities can improve students' social skills. *TEACHING Exceptional Children, 34*(3), 52–58.

Glover, T. A., & Albers, C. A. (2007). Considerations for evaluating universal screening assessments. *Journal of School Psychology, 45*(2), 117–145.

Gresham, F. (2015). Evidence-based social skills interventions for students at risk for EBD. *Remedial and Special Education, 36*(2), 100–104.

Hallam, S. (2009). An evaluation of the Social and Emotional Aspects of Learning (SEAL) programme: Promoting positive behaviour, effective learning and well-being in primary school children. *Oxford Review of Education, 35*(3), 313–330.

Hanchan, T. A., & Allen, R. A. (2013). Identifying students with emotional disturbance: School psychologists' practices and perceptions. *Psychology in the Schools, 50*(2), 193–208.

Heath, M. A., Dyches, T. T., & Prater, M. A. (2013). *Classroom bullying prevention, preK–4th grade: Children's books, lesson plans, and activities.* Santa Barbara, CA: Linworth.

Hess, R. S., Short, R. J., Hazel, C. E. (2012). *Comprehensive children's mental health services in schools and communities.* New York, NY: Routledge.

Huppert, F. A., & Johnson, D. M. (2010). A controlled trial of mindfulness training in schools: The importance of practice for an impact on well-being. *The Journal of Positive Psychology, 5*(4), 264–274.

Jones, S. M., Bouffard, S. M., & Weissbourd, R. (2013). Educators' social and emotional skills vital to learning. *Phi Delta Kappan, 94*(8), 62–65.

Knoff, H. M.. (2003). Character education vs. social skills training: Comparing constructs vs. behavior. *Communiqué, 32*(3), 32.

Kramer, T. J., Caldarella, P., Young, K. R., & Warren, S. (2014). Implementing *Strong Kids* school-wide to reduce internalizing behaviors and increase prosocial behaviors, *Education and Treatment of Children, 37*(4), 659–680.

Lane, K. L., Menzies, H. M., Oakes, W. P., & Kalberg, J. R. (2012). *Systematic screenings of behavior to support instruction: From preschool to high school.* New York, NY: Guilford Press.

Lane, K. L., Oakes, W. P., Ennis, R. P., Cox, M. L., Schatschneider, C., & Lambert, W. (2011). Additional evidence for the reliability and validity of the student risk screening scale at the high school level: A replication and extension. *Journal of Emotional and Behavioral Disorders, 21*(2), 97–115.

Lane, K. L., Pierson, M. R., & Givner, C. C. (2003). Teacher expectations of student behavior: Which skills do elementary and secondary teachers deem necessary for success in the classroom? *Education and Treatment of Children, 36*, 413–430.

Lee, S.-H., Simpson, R. L., & Shogren, K. A. (2007). Effects and implications of self-management for students with autism: A meta-analysis. *Focus on Autism and Other Developmental Disabilities, 22*, 2–13.

Lo, Y., Correa, V. I., & Anderson, A. L. (2015). Culturally responsive social skill instruction for Latino male students. *Journal of Positive Behavior Interventions, 17*(1), 15–27.

Lopata, C., Thomeer, M. L., Volker, M. A., & Nida, R. E. (2006). Effectiveness of a cognitive-behavioral treatment on the social behaviors of children with Asperger disorder. *Focus on Autism and Other Developmental Disabilities, 21*(4), 237–244.

Marchant, M., & Womack, S. (2010). Book in a bag: Blending social skills and academics. *TEACHING Exceptional Children, 42*(2), 6–12.

McDougall, D., & Brady, M. (1998). Initiating and fading self-management interventions to increase math fluency in regular education classes. *Exceptional Children, 64*, 151–166.

McGinnis, E. (2011). *Skillstreaming* (3rd ed.). Champaign, IL: Research Press.

Merrell, K. W., Carrizales, D., Feuerborn, L., Gueldner, B. A., & Tran, O. L. (2007). *Strong kids: Grades 3–5.* Baltimore, MD: Paul H. Brookes.

Merrell, K. W., & Gueldner, B. A. (2010). *Social and emotional learning in the classroom: Promoting mental health and academic success.* New York, NY: Guilford Press.

Merrell, K. W., Parisi, D. M., & Whitcomb, S. A. (2007). *Strong Start* grades K–2: A social and emotional learning curriculum. Baltimore, MD: Paul H. Brookes.

MindUP. (2011). New York, NY: Scholastic.

Nelson, J. R., Benner, G. J., Lane, K. L., & Smith, B. (2004). Academic achievement of k-12 students with emotional and behavioral disorders. *Exceptional Children, 71*, 59–73.

Nigg, J. T., & Barkley, R. A. (2014). Attention-deficit/hyperactivity disorder. In E. J. Marsh & R. A. Barkley (Eds.), *Child Psychopathology* (3rd ed., pp. 75–144). New York, NY: Guilford Press.

Prater, M. A., Johnstun, M. L., Dyches, T. T., & Johnstun, M. R. (2006). Using children's books as bibliotherapy for at-risk students: A guide for teachers. *Preventing School Failure, 50*(4), 5–13.

Reid, R., Gonzalez, J. E., Nordness, P. D., Trout, A., & Epstein, M. H. (2004). A meta-analysis of the academic status of students with emotional/behavioral disturbance. *Journal of Special Education, 38*, 130–143.

Reinke, W. M., Stormont, M., Herman, K. C., Puri, R., & Goel, N. (2011). Supporting children's mental health in schools: Teacher perceptions of needs, roles, and barriers. *School Psychology Quarterly, 26*(1), 1–13.

Robinson-Ervin, P., Cartledge, G., & Keyes, S. (2011). Culturally responsive social skills instruction for adolescent black males. *Multicultural Learning and Teaching, 6*(1), Article 7. doi: 10.2202/2161–2412.1075

Roorda, D. L., Koomen, H. M., Spilt, J. L., & Oort, F. J. (2011). The influence of affective teacher-student relationships on students' school engagement and achievement: A meta-analytic approach. *Review of Educational Research, 81*(4), 493–529.

Serna, L. A., Nielsen, M. E., & Forness, S. R. (2007). *Social skills in pictures, stories, and songs.* Champaign, IL: Research Press.

Shechtman, Z. (2006). The contribution of bibliotherapy to the counseling of aggressive boys. *Psychotherapy Research, 16*(5), 631–636.

Shimabukuro, S. M., Prater, M. A., Jenkins, A., & Edelen-Smith, P. (1999). The effects of self-monitoring of academic performance on students with learning disabilities and ADD/ADHD. *Education and Treatment of Children, 22*, 397–414.

Shriver, T. P., & Buffett, J. (2015). The uncommon core. In J. A. Durlak, C. E. Domitrovich, R. P. Weissberg, & T. P. Gullotta (Eds.), *The handbook of social and emotional learning* (pp. xv-xvi). New York, NY: Guilford Press.

Simonsen, B., Myers, D., Everett, S., Sugai, G., Spencer, R., & LaBreck, C. (2012). Explicitly teaching social skills schoolwide: Using a matrix to guide instruction. *Intervention in School and Clinic, 47*(5), 259–266.

Skiba, R. J., Horner, R. H., Chung, C.-G., Rausch, M. K., May, S. L., & Tobin, T. (2011). Race is not neutral: A national investigation of African American and Latino disproportionality in school discipline. *School Psychology Review, 40*(1), 85–107.

Skiba, R. J., Poloni-Staudinger, L., Gallini, S., Simmons, A. B., & Feggins-Azziz, R. (2006). Disparate access: The disproportionality of African American students with disabilities across educational environments. *Exceptional Children, 72*(4), 411–424.

Stice, E., Rohde, P., Seeley, J. R., & Gau, J. M. (2008). Brief cognitive-behavioral depression prevention program for high-risk adolescents outperforms two alternative interventions: A randomized efficacy trial. *Journal of Consulting Clinical Psychology, 76*(4), 595–606.

Teglasi, H., Rahill, S., & Rothman, L. (2007). A story-guided peer group intervention for reducing bullying and victimization in schools. In J. E. Zins, M. J. Elias, & C. A. Maher (Eds.), *Bullying, victimization, and peer harassment: A handbook of prevention and intervention* (pp. 219–237). New York, NY: Haworth.

Trevino-Maack, S. I., Kamps, D., & Wills, H. P. (2015). A group contingency plus self-management intervention targeting at-risk secondary students' class-work and active engagement. *Remedial and Special Educator, 36*(6), 347–360.

United States Department of Education. (2014). *Thirty-sixth annual report to Congress on the implementation of the Individuals with Disabilities Act.* Washington, DC: Author. Retrieved from http://www2.ed.gov/about/reports/annual/osep/2014/parts-b-c/36th-idea-arc.pdf

Wadsworth, J. P., Hansen, B. D., & Wills, S. B. (2015). Increasing compliance in students with intellectual disabilities using functional behavioral assessment and self-monitoring. *Remedial and Special Education, 36*(4), 195–207.

Walker, H., Severson, H. H., & Feil, E. G. (2014). *Systematic screening for behavior disorders (SSBD) technical manual: Universal screening for preK–9* (2nd ed.). Eugene, OR: Pacific Northwest.

Weissberg, R. P., Durlak, J. A., Domitrovich, C. E., & Gullotta, T. P. (2015). Social and emotional learning: Past, present, and future. In J. A. Durlak, C. E. Domitrovich, R. P. Weissberg, & T. P. Gullotta (Eds.), *The handbook of social and emotional learning* (pp. 3–19). New York, NY: Guilford Press.

White, S. W., Koenig, K., & Scahill, L. (2010). Group social skills instruction for adolescents with high-functioning autism spectrum disorders. *Focus on Autism and Other Developmental Disabilities, 25*(4), 209–219.

Wilcox, H. C., Kellam, S. G., Brown, C. H., Poduska, J., Ialongo, N. S., Wang, W., & Anthony, J. C. (2008). The impact of two universal randomized first- and second-grade classroom interventions on young adult suicide ideation and attempt. *Drug and Alcohol Dependence, 95,* S60–S73.

Williams, G. J., & Reisberg, L. (2003). Successful inclusion: Teaching social skills through curriculum integration. *Intervention in School and Clinic, 38,* 205–210.

Young, E. L., Caldarella, P., Richardson, M. L., & Young, K. R. (2011). *Positive behavior support in secondary schools: A practical guide.* New York, NY: Guilford Press.

Zeman, J., Cassano, M., Perry-Parrish, C., & Stegall, S. (2006). Emotion regulation in children and adolescents. *Journal of Developmental and Behavioral Pediatrics, 27*(2), 155–168.

$SAGE edge™

Review → Practice → Improve

Get the tools you need to sharpen your study skills. Access videos, practice quizzes, eFlashcards and more at **edge.sagepub.com/prater.**

©iStockphoto.com/Steve Debenport

CHAPTER 14

Life Skills and Transition

Transition Services

Julia is a 17-year-old student who has an emotional/behavioral disorder (EBD). She is interested in the health occupations and has focused her vocational education classes in this area. Mr. Donaldson is the transition coordinator and has the responsibility of coordinating field experiences to accompany the life career and life skills curricula for approximately 25 students with Individualized Education Programs (IEPs). Julia is one of those students. Last year, during Julia's sophomore year, she participated in six job-shadowing experiences. She was paired with an employee at each site for one week. The work sites included two different hospital units, a nursing home, a doctor's office, a diagnostic imaging lab, and an immunization clinic. She is now in her junior year and has participated in four paid internships (job sampling) for 2 months each. Of all the jobs she has observed and tried, she likes the lab the best. Therefore, with the help of Mr. Donaldson, her senior year will include investigating the program requirement for Diagnostic Medical Imaging Programs at several technical colleges in their state. She will also participate in a full-year youth apprenticeship with a local firm. While Julia gains practical work experience and takes the courses and tests necessary for college entry, Mr. Donaldson will contact the Disability Services Departments at each of the colleges to ensure that Julia has the support she needs upon entry into postsecondary education.

Learning Objectives

- Describe the purpose of transition planning for students with high-incidence disabilities (HID) and the requirements under IDEA.

- Explain the roles and importance of learning, working, living, and playing in the transition process; and demonstrate how examples of each of these areas can be explicitly taught and integrated into other classroom instruction.

- Describe the importance of student and other stakeholders' involvement in the transition IEP process and how person-centered planning can enhance the process.

- Explain why sensitivity to family cultural differences may impact the IEP transition process to a larger degree than pretransition IEP experiences. Create examples of how family desires of a student's future may differ from the European-American perspective.

One of the primary reasons students attend public school is to prepare them for adult roles and responsibilities. Students with disabilities have been guaranteed support through the Individuals with Disabilities Education Improvement Act (IDEA) to help them make the transition from secondary schooling to adulthood. And although improved services have led to improved outcomes, vast improvements are still needed.

- In 2010, 21% of working-age individuals with disabilities were employed either full-time or part-time, as compared with 59% of those without disabilities. This represents a 38% difference between the two populations. In 1998, the difference was 50% (National Organization on Disability, 2010).

- The proportion of students with disabilities dropping out of school has improved, but is still at alarmingly high rates. For example, in the 2003–2004 school year, 52% of students with emotional behavioral disorders (EBDs) dropped out as compared with 35% ten years later. Dropout rates for students with learning disabilities (LD), intellectual disabilities (ID), and autism have also decreased from 52% to 29%, 29% to 18%, and 13% to 7% respectively in that same time period (U.S. Department of Education, 2015).

- Approximately 45% of individuals without disabilities are enrolled in postsecondary education as compared with 28% of those with disabilities for ages 18–25 (Smith, Grigal, & Sulewski, 2012).

- The median annual earnings for people with a disability was $20,855 in 2015, compared with $30,928 for those without a disability (U.S. Census Bureau, 2015).

- Over 45% of individuals with disabilities are living in poverty compared with 17% of people with no disability (Brault, 2012).

- About 20% of adults (ages 18 and older) without disabilities live with family members (e.g., parent, sibling) as compared with 44% of adults with developmental disabilities, 62% of adults with cognitive disabilities, and 73% of adults with developmental and cognitive disabilities (Larson, Lakin, Anderson, & Kwak, 2001).

IDEA and Transition

Interest in the transition process from secondary school to successful adult life for students with disabilities has resonated throughout special education policy for more than 30 years (Riesen, Morgan, Schultz, & Kupferman, 2014). Studies documenting the activities and lifestyles of former special education students led to the federal government mandating transition services for every student receiving special education services through the Individuals with Disabilities Education Improvement Act (IDEA).

Under IDEA, **transition services** is defined as a coordinated set of activities for a child with a disability that

- is designed from and within a results-oriented (formerly outcome-focused) process, that is focused on improving the academic and functional achievement of the child with a disability to facilitate movement from school to postschool activities, including postsecondary education; vocational education; integrated employment (including supported employment); continuing and adult education; adult services; independent living or community participation; and

- is based on the individual child's needs, taking into account the child's strengths, preferences, and interests.

Beginning not later than the first IEP to be in effect when the child turns 16, or younger if determined appropriate by the IEP team, and updated annually, thereafter, the IEP must include the following:

- Appropriate measurable postsecondary goals based upon age-appropriate transition assessment related to training, education, employment, and independent living, where appropriate;

- Specific transition services needed to assist the child in reaching those goals, including courses of study; and

- Beginning not later than one year before the child reaches the age of majority under state law, a statement that the child has been informed of his/her rights relative to transition service access and delivery, if any, and that will transfer to the child upon reaching the age of majority.

In addition the child's transition IEP must consider the global academic, developmental, and functional needs of the child and include the following:

- A statement of measurable annual goals that will support the child's involvement and participation in the general education curriculum;

- A description of how the child's progress toward meeting those annual goals will be measured; and

- A description of when periodic reports of progress the child is making toward meeting the annual reports, or other periodic reports, concurrent with the issuance of report cards. (U.S. Department of Education, 2006)

When students graduate or "age out" of special education, IDEA requires that the school provide a Summary of Performance (SOP) that includes recommendations for helping the student meet postsecondary goals. The SOP must be completed during the student's final year and should be completed as part of the transition IEP process with the student actively participating, if appropriate. It must include a summary of academic achievement and functional performance and recommendations for assisting the student in meeting his or her postsecondary goals. IDEA does not provide substantive details, so there exists substantial variation in how states and districts operationalize the SOP (Shaw, Dukes, & Madaus, 2012).

TEACHER TIP #14.1

DEVELOPING AND IMPLEMENTING THE SUMMARY OF PERFORMANCE (SOP)

Best practices are beginning to be advocated for the SOP, particularly given the vagueness of IDEA. Consider the following:

- Use the IEP team to develop the SOP as part of the transition components. Ensure appropriate stakeholders are a part of the team.

- If appropriate, have the student lead the SOP discussion while also providing meaningful input.

- Develop the SOP early, rather than using it as a culminating event in the student's transitioning.

- Provide a checklist or other record of transition assessment data.

- Include the following elements:

    Background information on the student

    Student's postsecondary goals

    Summary of academic and functional performance

    Recommendations (e.g., accommodations, adaptive devices)

    Student input (Shaw et al., 2012)

Section 504 and ADA

While students with high-incidence disabilities (HID) are receiving special education services in elementary and secondary schools, they are protected under the mandates of IDEA. Once they move to postsecondary environments, they are protected under **Section 504 of the Rehabilitation Act** of 1973 and the **Americans with Disabilities Act (ADA)** of 1990.

Section 504 of the Rehabilitation Act banned all federally funded programs from discriminating against persons with disabilities.

> No otherwise qualified person with a disability in the United States . . . shall, solely on the basis of disability, be denied access to, or the benefits of, or be subjected to discrimination under any program or activity provided by an institution receiving federal financial assistance or under any program or activity conducted by any Executive Agency or by the U.S. Postal Service. (29 U.S.C. Section 794)

Section 504 also extended the concept of rehabilitation beyond just employment to all domains of living in a community (Flexer, Baer, Luft, & Simmons, 2013).

The purpose of the ADA was to provide "a clear and comprehensive national mandate for the elimination of discrimination" and "clear, strong, consistent, enforceable standards addressing discrimination" (42 U.S.C. Section 12101). This Act extends protection by prohibiting discrimination and ensuring equal opportunity for persons with disabilities in employment, state and local government services, public accommodations, commercial facilities, transportation, and telecommunications (Morgan & Riesen, 2016).

The definitions of disability under Section 504 and ADA are broader than those under IDEA and require the individual to provide documentation of the existence of a disability. Individuals with a disability cannot assume that the diagnosis provided through IDEA and the schools is recent enough or aligns with the definitions used for Section 504 or ADA (Shaw et al., 2012).

Evidence-Based Transition Practices

A variety of transition services and supports could be made available to students. For example, students could be taught vocational, self-determination, travel, and/or independent living skills. They could participate in work study or career awareness programs. In addition, they could be prepared for college with academic study and self-advocacy skills. Any form of education or training that occurs after students graduate or age-out of public schools is considered **postsecondary education**. Knowing which services and supports are most powerful in improving students' postschooling outcomes would help IEP teams know which services and supports to select. David Test, Catherine Fowler, and colleagues (2009) reviewed high-quality research and identified 32 evidence-based practices that improve postschool performance. However, only 2 of the 32, teaching life skills and teaching purchasing skills, had a strong level of evidence. Twenty-eight practices had moderate evidence and two were identified as having potential (see Table 14.1). Additional high-quality research is needed to expand our knowledge base in evidence-based transition interventions.

| TABLE 14.1 | **Transition Practices With Strong, Moderate, and Potential Levels of Evidence** |

Strong Evidence-Based Practices	Moderate Evidence-Based Practices	Potential Evidence-Based Practices
Student-Focused Planning		
Teaching life skills Teaching purchasing skills	Involving students in IEP meetings Self-advocacy strategies Self-directed IEP	
Student Development		
	Teaching the following: Banking skills Completing a job application Cooking skills Employment skills using community-based instruction Food preparation skills Functional math skills Functional reading skills Grocery shopping skills Home maintenance skills Leisure skills Life skills using community-based instruction Life skills using computer-assisted instruction Life skills using self-management Job-specific employment skills Purchasing using the "one more than" strategy Restaurant purchasing skills Safety skills Self-advocacy skills Self-determination skills Self-management for employment skills Social skills	Teaching job-related social communication skills
Program Structures		
	Provide community-based instruction Structure program to extend services beyond secondary school	Implement *Check & Connect* program

Test, Valerie Mazzotti et al. (2009) also identified in-school predictors of postschool outcomes for students with disabilities in the areas of education, employment, and independent living. Stated another way, students who experienced certain interventions improved certain postschool outcomes, although it remains unclear whether the improved outcome was caused by the intervention. Of the 16 predictors, 11 significantly correlated with postsecondary education, 5 with independent living, and 16 with employment (see Table 14.2). Four predictors improved outcomes in all three areas—namely, inclusion in general education, paid employment/work experience, parent expectations, and student support.

TABLE 14.2   Evidence-Based Predictors of Post-School Successes Based on Correlational Research

Predictors/Outcomes	Education	Employment	Independent Living
Career Awareness	X	X	
Community Experiences		X	
Exit Exam Requirements/High School Diploma Status		X	
Goal-Setting	X	X	
Inclusion in General Education	X	X	X
Interagency Collaboration	X	X	
Occupational Courses	X	X	
Paid Employment/Work Experience	X	X	X
Parent Expectations	X	X	X
Parental Involvement		X	
Program of Study		X	
Self-Advocacy/Self-Determination	X	X	
Self-Care/Independent Living	X	X	X
Social Skills	X	X	
Student Support	X	X	X
Transition Program	X	X	
Travel Skills		X	
Vocational Education	X	X	
Work Study		X	
Youth Autonomy/Decision-Making	X	X	

Note: Correlational research means there is an association, but causation cannot be inferred. Empty boxes means no correlational research was located.

Source: Test, Fowler, & Kohler (2013)

TEACHER TIP #14.2
PREPARING FOR TRANSITION IEP MEETINGS

When preparing for the student's first transition plan, consider holding a 60- to 90-minute meeting prior to the formal IEP meeting. In this initial meeting, the student would use multimedia to make a 20- to 30-minute presentation in his or her voice using an outline such as the following:

- introducing self and family
- journaling a typical day
- sharing joys and sorrows
- celebrating accomplishments

- visualizing my future
- setting my goals
- expressing appreciation
- committing to growth and change

Invite about seven to nine individuals to attend including professionals, family members, and significant others selected by the student. After the student presents, allow time for round-robin participant affirmation, as well as questions, discussion, and suggestions. (Skouge, Kelly, Roberts, Leake, & Stodden, 2007)

Learn, Work, Live, and Play

The remainder of this chapter is organized to provide a straightforward view of transition and transition services from a person-centered quality of life, results-oriented perspective—a perspective that can best be identified by comprehensively examining the needs, preferences, and goals that enable and support a student with disabilities to live a productive, independent adult life to the maximum extent possible. The chapter is structured around four global themes—*Learn*, *Work*, *Live*, and *Play*—each of which are beneficial to transition planning and implementation for students with disabilities.

The first theme, *Learn*, considers IDEA's emphasis on access and progress in general education curricula and learning elements that support access to and full participation in postsecondary education. The second theme, *Work*, focuses on employment skills and services necessary to ensure access to and full participation in vocational education, service learning, and community work experience. The third theme, *Live*, considers interdependent living objectives and interpersonal relationships; and the fourth theme, *Play*, takes into account the opportunities to participate in age-appropriate recreational and leisure activities as part of a self-satisfying normalized lifestyle.

Learn

Jeremy, a high school student identified with attention-deficit/hyperactivity disorder (ADHD) and learning disabilities (LD), attended a resource classroom one period each day. His teacher, Mr. Takahashi, taught him and five other students study skills and learning strategies. Mr. Takahashi worked closely with several general education teachers to ensure that Jeremy and the other students had access to the general education curriculum and that accommodations were made where necessary. During his senior year, Jeremy was given testing accommodations and passed his state's mandatory high school exit exam. His goal was to enroll in the state university near his home. Because he had followed an academic track during high school, vocational education was not part of his studies. He was focusing on academic classes that would prepare him for the liberal education core courses at the university level. Jeremy anticipated that he may need some help at the university level. He wanted to make certain there was someone available to modify the college curriculum if necessary, like Mr. Takahashi had done during high school. He also knew that unlike his high school experience, he would not have a care coordinator in college. Therefore, Mr. Takahashi contacted the Office of Student Affairs and made an appointment for Jeremy to meet the university's Disability Services Coordinator before he exited high school. This coordinator helped Jeremy complete the proper forms which qualified him for accommodations such as extended time on tests, a tutor, advanced registration, and audio textbooks. Jeremy was well prepared for entering the university setting.

Transitional services include preparation for postsecondary education, which most broadly described includes any program whose emphasis is further education or institution-based vocational and technical training and includes two- and four-year colleges and universities, private vocational schools, apprenticeship programs, and trade or adult education programs (Sitlington, Neubert, & Clark, 2010). Completion of postsecondary training or education enhances job prospects; provides social opportunities; postpones adult obligations such as marriage, financial independence, and employment; and leads to higher income and better quality of life (Webster & Queen, 2008). When preparing students for postsecondary education, IEP teams need to consider how transition and academic standards can be taught simultaneously, as well as specific preparation for postsecondary studies including eliminating barriers and teaching specific information and skills, among other preparation.

Transition and Academic Standards

Recent educational reform and legislation have focused on college and career readiness for all students, including students with disabilities. While achieving academic standards remains critical for students with HID, other transition skills must also be taught (e.g., daily living, employment, and self-determination skills). In some cases, an emphasis on the academic standards has eliminated other transition skill development due to lack of time to teach both. However, research has shown that students can learn both academic and secondary transition skills simultaneously (Bartholomew, Papay, McConnell, & Cease-Cook, 2015).

For example, in one study, middle school students with HID were taught self-advocacy and writing skills at the same time (Cuenca-Carlino & Mustian, 2013). As part of the self-advocacy instruction, they learned the acrostic, "Don't Go Sneaking Past Any Mad Elephants" which stood for the seven self-determined behaviors: Decision making, Goal setting, Self-awareness, Problem-solving, Self-Advocacy, Self-Monitoring, and Self-Efficacy. They were then taught how they could advocate for themselves using persuasive writing, a common core writing standard (e.g., Write arguments to support claims with clear reasons and relevant evidence.). This was followed with instruction on persuasive writing using the POW+TREE strategy: **P**ick my idea, **O**rganize my notes, **W**rite and say more, **T**opic sentence, **R**easons, **E**xplanations, **E**nding (see Chapter 10 on strategies for writing). Results demonstrated significant improvement in the students' essays. Student interviews documented that they made the connection between self-advocating and persuasive writing.

Where possible, teachers are urged to find ways in which students' transition needs and academic standards can both be met. Doing so can be difficult, but not impossible. Table 14.3 presents examples of how transition objectives can simultaneously meet common core standards.

Postsecondary Schooling

Special education services and supports are mandated by IDEA until the student completes high school, or reaches the age of 21. Students with disabilities and their parents are often unaware that IDEA does not require similar supports and services in postsecondary settings. Transition services and supports become much more unpredictable and nonuniform once the student moves out of the public school system. In addition to a loss of the protective public school environment, college-bound students with disabilities are

TABLE 14.3	Examples of Integrating Transition Objectives Within Common Core Standards

Content	Common Core Standard	Transition Objective
English Language Arts	**Text Types and Purposes** 9-10.1: Write arguments to support claims in an analysis of substantive topics or texts, using valid reasoning and relevant and sufficient evidence.	Compare and contrast two types of health insurance identifying the advantages and disadvantages of each. Choose the best package and create an advertisement that summarizes the plan.
	Research to Build and Present Knowledge 9-10.7: Conduct short as well as more sustained research projects to answer a question or solve a problem. (partial)	Research possible independent residences by answering given questions. Select one possible location to move.
Math	**Ratio and Proportional Relationships** 6.RP.A: Understand ratio concepts and use ratio reasoning to solve problems.	Calculate cost differences based on unit prices when purchasing for 2, 4, 10, or 100 people at a grocery store.
	Linear, Quadratic, and Exponential Models HSF-LE.A: Construct and compare linear, quadratic, and exponential models and solve problems.	Given a room and feature dimensions (e.g., windows and doors) and the cost of paint per square foot, compute the cost of painting the room. Write an estimate quote for completing the painting job.

Sources: National Technical Assistance Center on Transition (NTACT); Transition Objectives and Common Core English Language Arts: transitionta.org/sites/default/files/Transition_Skills_and_CCSS_in_ELA_2013.pdf; Transition Objectives and Common Core Mathematics: http://transitionta.org/sites/default/files/Transition_Skills_and_CCSS_in_Mathematics_2013_online.pdf

likely to encounter many of the same transitional problems as their nondisabled peers. For example, academic competition increases while the ratio of teachers to students decreases. Students are expected to be much more self-directed and responsible for their learning. Table 14.4 outlines some of the major differences in assistance provided in secondary versus postsecondary schools.

Preparing students for postsecondary schooling. Secondary special educators should implement instructional programs that have a direct effect on the real tasks that students will be facing as postsecondary education students. To help students with disabilities successfully transition to postsecondary education, secondary special educators and other transition stakeholders need to teach students with disabilities the following:

- **Understanding their disabilities**. Postsecondary institutions are only required to provide reasonable accommodations and supports to students with self-disclosed, documented disabilities. Federal law offers no guidelines, however, on what documentation provides evidence of disability. Nor does the law indicate what academic accommodations might be needed by postsecondary students. Students must initiate specific requests for disability support services in postsecondary education. To do so, they need to be able to explain their disability, how it impacts their learning, and what accommodations and supports work for them. They also need to know their legal rights and know how to be courageous, assertive, and communicative and how to advocate for themselves.

TABLE 14.4   Overview of Differences in Assistance Across Secondary School and Postsecondary School

	Secondary School	Postsecondary School
Legal	Assistance mandated by the Individuals with Disabilities Education Act and due process requirements	Assistance directed by Section 504 of the Rehabilitation Act and the Americans with Disabilities Act
Identifying Disabilities	Schools are obligated to identify students with disabilities and provide appropriate services.	Postsecondary schools are not obligated to identify students with disabilities; students are not obligated to disclose their disability unless requesting services.
Services Directed By	Individualized Education Programs (IEP) led by the school personnel usually with limited student involvement	Students must self-advocate for services.
Amount and Quality of Services	Special education and supplemental transitional services to provide "benefit" and "success"	"Reasonable" accommodations to assist "equal access" as defined by the ADA and Section 504
Success	Success generally measured in terms of educational benefit (externally managed)	Success measured in terms of postschool competence and long-term goals (internally managed)

- **Taking responsibility for their successes and failures.** Postsecondary education differs greatly from K–12 schooling in that all students must take primary responsibility for their education. They need to be proactive in seeking out information and supports. It is also their responsibility to ensure implementation and the ongoing evaluation of the quality of the supports. Federal disability laws guarantee students equal opportunity to participate, but the student must take responsibility for the success or failure of that opportunity. Special educators can help prepare students by teaching self-management skills and increasing their personal responsibilities.

- **Learning appropriate preparatory skills.** As students transition to postsecondary education, their academic success will rely highly on their ability to apply effective study, time management, and technology skills. Special educators can prepare students by explicitly teaching these skills throughout the curriculum. Students need to begin to be held responsible for implementing study and time-management skills long before completing high school. Emphasizing the importance of basic skills, such as reading and writing, can also prepare students for postsecondary education. Students should begin using computers and other electronic devices as soon as possible to increase their familiarity and comfort levels (Connor, 2012; Duncan & Ali, 2011b; Lehmann, Davies, & Laurin, 2000).

Other supports that can be helpful to students with disabilities to prepare them for postsecondary education include the following:

- **Exposing students to the college campus and success stories in advance.** Take a field trip to show students the campus including where they would live, study, and eat. Arrange for a meeting with the disabilities support staff to become acquainted and to learn about services available firsthand. Also, arrange for currently enrolled students with disabilities to share their stories of struggles and successes. Literature, media, and guest speakers can also be used in the classroom to provide a view of college life of others with disabilities.

- **If appropriate, enrolling students early.** Some postsecondary institutions allow students to register for courses while still in high school. Another option is enrolling during the summer after having completed high school as a way to transition into the new environment including living in dorms, eating in dining halls, and locating classrooms across multiple buildings (Connor, 2012; Duncan & Ali, 2011b).

Postsecondary accommodations and supports. Although legally all postsecondary education institutions must provide access and reasonable accommodations to students with disabilities, the quantity and quality of those educational supports and accommodations varies within and across postsecondary settings. Some institutions are more *student friendly* than others. The student support services provided may fall across a continuum of lightly to highly structured programs. Lightly structured supports may include accommodations such as extended time and altered methods of evaluation, whereas, highly structured services may include opportunities for students with disabilities to design learning plans and courses of study specific to their learning styles and adult outcome needs.

In terms of accommodations and modifications, institutions are not required to make an academic adjustment that alters or waives essential academic requirements. They also do not need to make changes that would fundamentally change the nature of a service, program, or activity or cause undue financial or administrative burden on the institution. Once the student self-identifies as having a disability and provides the required written documentation to substantiate the disability, the student should meet with an advisor or counselor trained to assist students with disabilities to determine appropriate services, including accommodations. Once the aids and services have been identified, institutions may not require the student with disabilities to pay part or all of the costs, although reimbursement from an outside third party may be applied. If the accommodations and services are not working, it is the student's responsibility to notify the institution as soon as possible so that adjustments can be made (Duncan & Ali, 2011a).

The appropriate academic accommodation or adjustment should be made based on the student's disability and needs. Appropriate adjustments include "arranging for priority registration; reducing a course load; substituting one course for another; providing notetakers, recording devices, sign language interpreters, extended time for testing . . . equipping school computers with screen-reading, voice recognition, or other adaptive software or hardware." The postsecondary school does not have to provide "personal attendants, individually prescribed devices, readers for personal use or study, or other devices or services of a personal nature, such as tutoring and typing" (Duncan & Ali, 2011a, n.p.).

In one study, students with disabilities enrolled in postsecondary education rated their satisfaction with the accommodations that were provided. The top five included assistive reading technology, testing with accommodations, text conversion services, reader/writer/interpreter, and assistive listening technology. The accommodations receiving the lowest satisfaction scores were academic advisement and counseling, assignment extensions/modifications, recorded lectures, academic accommodation planning, tutorial support/one-one-one assistance, and classroom accommodations. The researchers concluded that the accommodations receiving lower scores was not delivered by the disabilities service personnel, but required a third-party involvement (e.g., the instructor) (Reinschmiedt, Buono, Sprong, Upton, & Dallas, 2013).

The first time students use a specific accommodation or support should not occur at the postsecondary environment. That is, students should be given an opportunity to learn and apply the types of accommodations that will be provided postsecondary (Connor, 2012). In fact, some students may need explicit instruction on how to implement an accommodation which should be learned while enrolled in K–12.

Eliminating barriers to postsecondary education. Although IDEA requires postsecondary educational goals be created and transition supports provided, many students with HID, particularly those with intellectual disabilities (ID), have not held hopes of postsecondary schooling. Traditionally, two categories of barriers have inhibited access. First, personal barriers such as lack of self-advocacy skills, socialization skills, and coping-with-stress strategies have interfered. Most of these barriers can be reduced or eliminated through careful and explicit instruction during students' K–12 schooling.

The second type of barrier, systematic barriers, can be challenging to overcome. Such barriers may include lack of university-based supports, limited funding for nontraditional participation (e.g., part-time, auditing, continuing education), and federal funding limits (VanBergeijk & Cavanagh, 2012). These barriers were somewhat overcome, particularly for students with ID, with the passage of the Higher Education Opportunities Act (HEOA) in 2008. The Act allows students with ID to apply for federal support (e.g., Pell Grants) even though they may not meet typical eligibility criteria (e.g., high school diploma) (Lee, 2009). However, to be eligible for these funds, the student must be attending an approved Comprehensive Transition Program (CTP) (Boyle, 2012). Although currently over 220 postsecondary programs that support students with disabilities are listed on the ThinkCollege.net website, to date, less than 20 have been approved as CTPs.

Although students with ID may not graduate from a college or university program, there are many ways they can be enriched by enrolling. Generally speaking, their goals are the same as their peers. They want to be independent, have friends, go to class and social events, and get a job. A postsecondary campus is an ideal place to prepare and experience some of these goals. In fact, some research documents positive job and increased life satisfaction of students with ID enrolled in postsecondary education (Kleinert, Jones, Sheppard-Jones, Harp, & Harrison, 2012).

Enrolling students with ID and other disabilities on the postsecondary education campus also benefits the university or college. Their presence broadens the student body's diversity and provides a richer environment and schooling experience for all students (Kleinert et al., 2012).

TEACHER TIP #14.3

PREPARING STUDENTS FOR POSTSECONDARY EDUCATION

Teachers can help students prepare for their future by helping reduce barriers to enrolling in postsecondary education by engaging in the following types of activities in the classroom:

- Role-play ways of communicating to college faculty and disability services staff precise descriptions concerning the nature of their disability and the nature and purpose of the adaptations (accommodations and/or modifications) they will be requesting.

- Inform students about the disability documentation requirements of local postsecondary institutions before their senior year in high school.

- Provide students with information concerning the three most common types of accommodations likely to be provided within and across postsecondary educational settings. Practice implementing these accommodations.

(Continued)

(Continued)

- Provide students with opportunities to develop self-determination skills related to assumption of personal responsibility for goals, accomplishments, and setbacks, including personal elements of assertiveness, self-advocacy, career choices, and life pursuits.

- Discuss the connection of postsecondary education to jobs/careers and independent living.

Work

John is an 18-year-old with intellectual disabilities (ID) who also has some health concerns. His family has been exploring the kinds of jobs that would be well suited to John's interests and abilities. He gets very nervous around new people, so working with the general public may not be a good match for John. He also has a strong need for consistency in his world. With the help of a Small Business Administration counselor, John's mother established a candle business. John helps manufacture the candles by pouring the wax into molds. John is gainfully employed and is a productive citizen.

Much of adult life is spent in work or work-related activities. In addition to promoting financial well-being, employment provides increased opportunity to interact with others, improved self-esteem and self-worth, increased independence and self-determination, and enhanced opportunities to connect with and contribute to the community (Lee & Carter, 2012). The act of working generates the respect of others and may be a source of pride, satisfaction, and personal fulfillment, making it important for *all* persons. For persons with disabilities, working can enhance quality of life by influencing the perceptions of others. Thus, by demonstrating that they are productive and integral parts of society, individuals with disabilities *increase* the likelihood of acceptance by those without disabilities, and these experiences may also help *decrease* the stigma associated with having a disability. For young adults with HID, then, obtaining and maintaining competitive employment is a worthy societal goal. Yet, the greatest school-to-work barrier has been identified as students' lack of employment skills such as work completion, task accuracy, punctuality, self-regulation, and social skills necessitating greater attention to developing these skills while in school (Riesen et al., 2014).

Continuum of Employment Options

Employment options may be conceptualized as lying along a continuum from most to least integrated within the community. Individuals with HID should be placed in the most integrated setting possible. The options can be grouped into the following categories: sheltered, supported, subsidized, transitional, competitive, and self-employment. A description of each follows.

Sheltered employment is the least integrated type of employment and is considered the least desirable placement option for students with disabilities. This category of employment usually entails working in a segregated center like a sheltered workshop or adult day program. Employees receive subminimum wage, and have little, if any, contact with coworkers without disabilities (Flexer et al., 2013). The major disadvantages of sheltered employment include segregation from persons without disabilities, excessive dependence on workshop personnel, little relevancy to preparing for today's labor force, and lack of mobility from the workshop situation to more integrated employment.

Supported employment lies between competitive employment and sheltered employment programs on the placement continuum. This option provides training of employees at the job site by professional staff where individuals receive the necessary services and assistance to learn specific job skills and develop interpersonal skills as well as other job-related skills. Supported employment has three essential elements: wages are paid (although sometimes it is less than minimum wage), work is performed in an integrated setting, and ongoing support services including a job coach or employment specialist are provided (Flexer et al., 2013). At first, a job coach or employment specialist provides continuous one-to-one assistance. The coach/specialist may work with only one person at a work site or may direct a supported work crew or group. Whether one or several employees receive on-site assistance, the principle of supporting workers with disabilities in community employment is the same. As time passes and the employee gradually learns the job, the coach fades from the work site and the employee increasingly begins to work independently. Supervision is gradually turned over to coworkers and supervisors of the company. After a substantial period of time, the coach/specialist provides only follow-up and support services through occasional visits or phone calls. Supported employment is a viable option for individuals with disabilities who may have difficulty with unsupervised competitive employment and need ongoing support.

On the job placement continuum, **competitive employment** offers the highest degree of integration and independence and has many advantages over sheltered or supported employment. Competitive employment involves placement in community-integrated settings where the employee receives at least minimum wage, interacts with coworkers without disabilities, produces valued goods or services, and has opportunities for increased earnings and responsibilities. This employment option is the most preferred outcome for young adults with HID because it establishes the economic and personal foundation necessary for an integrated, independent life. It provides an opportunity to enjoy and engage in work that fulfills individual and societal needs. Competitive employment is an achievable goal for most individuals with HID (Flexer et al., 2013).

Other employment models have been used such as subsidized and supported self-employment. **Subsidized employment** is similar to competitive employment and may be seen as a short-term alternative. It involves providing subsidies to the employer during an initial adjustment or probationary period for the employee with a documented disability. These subsidies provide opportunities for employees who may know the job skills, but are unable to complete these tasks at the required rate of production. **Supported self-employment** is a form of competitive employment where the student (often with help of family members or adult-service agencies) creates their own small business. This form of employment is gaining popularity among individuals with disabilities and their families (Flexer et al., 2013).

Individuals with disabilities have been found to be self-employed in professions such as selling arts and ceramics, landscaping, home maintenance and repair, and motivational speaking. Not unlike self-employed individuals without disabilities, individuals with disabilities indicate the primary advantage to **entrepreneurship** includes a sense of independence derived from owning your own business and the primary disadvantage is fluctuating income. Materials and information for creating an entrepreneurship can be obtained through federal and state Small Business Administration (SBA) offices. In the case presented earlier, John's mother established a small candle making business for John with a loan from the SBA. Before contacting the SBA, students should have an idea of the type of business or product they wish to market. They offer orientation sessions as well as on-line material regarding various loans and considerations to make prior to starting a business (see www.sba.gov/starting-business/how-start-business/business-types/people-disabilities).

Instructional Content and Strategies

Teachers should not wait for students to reach the age of transition planning before teaching them about work. In fact, work concepts can be easily integrated into classroom instruction at the elementary, middle, and secondary levels. For example, teachers at the elementary level can provide exposure to different types of occupations. Parents and community members may talk to students about different career areas so that students are exposed to a wide variety of potential vocations. Field trips may also be arranged so students can compare different occupations. Students may become involved in community service activities (e.g., clean-up projects, visiting nursing homes) or may sample different types of jobs around the school like helping to clean blackboards, watering plants, taking messages in the office, reshelving books, emptying trash, or helping the grounds crew (Wehman, 2001). Within the classroom, teachers can introduce concepts such as money, responsibility, dependability, and the importance of work. Teachers may also set up different *work* stations within the classroom where students have specific responsibilities.

At the middle school level, communication should continue with parents and community members while more emphasis is placed on developing general work habits such as appropriate work appearance, appropriate response to criticism, getting along with others, teamwork skills, time management, and on-task behavior at work stations. At the middle school level students should develop a repertoire of general employability skills and work attitudes so that secondary teachers may concentrate on more specific vocational skills and competencies. Students may have increasing responsibilities at the school library, office, lunch room, and school fundraising events (e.g., plays, concerts, bake sales), and community service-learning projects. Students can become more active in school events and at the same time learn valuable work skills through activities such as taking tickets at games and dances, selling refreshments at school functions, delivering audiovisual equipment, and stocking supplies at the school store (Wehman, 2001).

Enrollment and success in vocational education has been identified as an important component for high school students and their transition to competitive employment. If the student desires to enter the workforce directly upon exiting high school, specific vocational training and work experience must be provided. In the early high school years, practical work experience may take the form of job shadowing where the student follows an employee to see the daily work tasks of various occupations.

Job sampling may also be undertaken where the student actually works at several jobs (each for a short period of time) to get firsthand experience with the types of tasks employees in that occupation perform on a daily basis. Job sampling assessments can reveal a great deal about students' likes and dislikes in terms of future work. These assessments may also reveal how well students perform in *different* work situations, and provide information about work habits, stamina, and social skills. Students then have the opportunity to acquire hands-on exposure to job requirements before actually entering the market. The job sampling stage is a great opportunity to also assess the student's job-seeking skills (i.e., application and interview skills) and job keeping skills (e.g., punctuality and response to supervision). Instruction should focus on the areas in which students need to improve. For example, use peer tutoring to improve the students' abilities to interview for employment (Bobroff & Sax, 2010). As the student approaches graduation practical work experience should take the form of one specific job so the student may build a work history.

Service Learning

Service learning can also be used to promote job-related skills. **Service learning** is an instructional strategy that integrates meaningful community service with instruction and reflection. The goals of service learning are to enrich the learning experience, teach civic responsibility, and provide community service (Dymond, Chun, Kim & Renzaglia, 2013). Service-learning activities can be integrated with transition goals and used as a way to expose students to future employment or build their job skills through authentic, real-life experiences. Service learning can also be used as a means for teaching responsibility and helping students become more integrated into the community.

Students with HID can be involved in service-learning activities in a variety of ways. They can be encouraged to volunteer and given assignment credit. Or these activities can be required as they align with the students' IEP goals (Cease-Cook, Fowler, & Test, 2015). In a survey of coordinators of inclusive high school service-learning programs, they indicated the following elements were the most important: (a) expect students to participate, (b) place students with disabilities in situations where they will be successful, (c) offer a variety of activities, (d) give students choices, (e) allow student ownership of the project, and (f) allow students to have an active role in decision making (Dymond et al., 2013).

In addition to exposure to and experience with work skills, students need to develop strong work habits and appropriate interaction skills in order have successful employment. For example, research documents that poor work habits, social skills, and difficulty generalizing skills from the classroom to the workplace often inhibit individuals' ability to acquire and maintain employment, not the lack of work skills (Nochajski & Schweitzer, 2014). For example, employers of youth tend to emphasize strong social and interpersonal skills in their search for employees. The social-related challenges of students with autism and other related HID, make employment prospects particularly difficult (Lee & Carter, 2012). Thus, teaching responsibility, self-determination, persistence, and appropriate social behaviors should be embedded in transition services.

| TABLE 14.5 | Examples of Infusing Transition Into the Classroom |

Topic	Instruction and Support
Self-Determination	
Grades and Grading	Explicitly teach how grades are determined and the importance of grades. Explain how grades are connected to learning and schooling.
Level of Effort	Teach the connection between effort and outcome. Have students self-evaluate their level of effort.
Level of Support	Identify tasks the teacher does for the student. With student involvement, plan to teach independence of the task or provide an accommodation.
Choice-Making	Provide opportunities for students to make choices. Guide them on making appropriate choices. If needed, provide explicit instruction on how to weigh pros and cons and make the best choice.
Problem-Solving	Explicitly teach the problem-solving process of recognizing a problem exists, identifying potential solutions, evaluating these solutions, selecting a solution, implementing the solution, and evaluating the impact of the solution.
Career Development	
Career Day	Involve students to the degree possible in sponsoring a career day. Students can research possible careers across various industries and those in their communities. Invite representatives to attend and engage students in activities related to their field.
Career Interviews	Students generate a list of questions about various careers in advance. Representatives of various industries are then interviewed and asked these questions.
Live and Virtual Field Trips	Provide opportunities to visit in person or through technology, various job sites. Prepare students in advance to what they might experience and then afterward, to reflect orally or in writing what they did experience.
Individual Technology Use	Support and enhance student use of technology in career exploration.
Work Readiness	Ensure that the following skills are taught as part of the curriculum: written, oral and nonverbal communication, cooperation, collaboration, accepting responsibility, taking initiative, being prompt, completing tasks on time, and making decisions.
Cooperative Learning	Engage students in cooperative learning in which they are each assigned a responsibility to complete for their group. Reinforce their taking responsibility.
Journals	Require students to keep a journal in which they reflect on their current and long-term interests.
Classroom Responsibilities	Assign students classroom responsibilities such as taking attendance, passing out materials, being line leader, cleaning up, and so forth. Define these roles and rotate them throughout the classroom to ensure all are given an opportunity. Discuss the importance of taking responsibility to help yourself and the group.

Source: Adapted from Papay, Unger, Williams-Diehm, & Mitchell (2015); Thomas & Dykes, (2011).

TEACHER TIP #14.4

SELECTING, APPLYING, AND INTERVIEWING FOR JOBS

Teachers can use current job openings to teach the process of applying for employment.

1. Teach students how to locate job openings through the Department of Work Force Services, local newspapers, or other easily accessible websites.

2. Teach students how to match their job interests and skills with the job announcements.

3. Using a mock application, have students apply for one or more jobs.

4. Use role-playing to practice applying for the job(s).

Technology Spotlight #14.1

Using Technology to Prepare for Transition

The everyday use of technology can help students with HID prepare for postsecondary outcomes. Devices used by the populace at large can be particularly helpful to students with HID. For example, GPS (global positioning system) can help direct users to their destination and apps can allow users to create shopping lists, prompt them when it's time for their appointment, or record the number of steps they've taken. Additional technology applications for transition of students with HID follow:

Assistive Technology

Transition IEP teams must consider assistive technology devices when planning for special education services. Also to be considered is the transfer of these devices from the school setting to the postsecondary setting. Teams should ask question such as

- Will the device follow the student out of secondary education?

- What options are available for funding new or replacement devices?

- Who are the key support personnel in postsecondary settings?

- How will assistive technology be maintained? (Asselin, 2014)

Digital Portfolios

One strategy suggested for teaching and promoting self-advocacy is the use of student-generated digital portfolios. Using portfolios in general requires students to decide on the purpose and intended audience, then collecting, selecting, and organizing artifacts documenting their work (e.g.,

(Continued)

(Continued)

assignment and writing samples; student explanations about preferences, needs, and learning styles; photos or videos of completed projects; transition plans). Digital portfolios are more compact, provide flexible storage and portability, and demonstrate students' technology skills. They can be Web-based, although portfolios stored on CDs, DVDs, or USB flash drives are more secure and simpler to create. Digital portfolios can be shared during IEP meetings and, based on feedback from team members, revisions can be made. Minimally the portfolio should be updated at least once each school year (Black, 2010).

Digital Simulations

Digital simulations provide experiences with real-world tasks and situations. The use of simulations can meet both technology and transition goals of students and can be easier to implement than community-based instruction. They provide self-pacing, repetitively consistent practice with variable conditions, and immediate feedback. Research has documented success with selecting jobs and social training, as well as shopping and self-help skills. Digital simulations are available in the form of software simulations or online simulations. For example, the MECA (Microcomputer Evaluation of Careers and Academics) Work Samples are hands-on simulations of actual workplace activities. They allow the user to be exposed to many different potential career areas (www.conovercompany .com/education/meca/) (Zionch, 2011).

Instructional Games

Instructional games can provide students a fun way in which they are exposed to postsecondary options. For example, several online programs offer games for students to develop their work skills as well as to explore career options. Examples include the following:

- Virginia Career VIEW (Vital Information for Education and Work), offers teaching and learning activities related to career development for K–8: vacareerview.org/k5/

- Office of Citizen Services and Innovative Technologies, U.S. General Services Administration, contains a list of careers with videos and interactive games designed for students K–8: kids.usa.gov

Live

Talmadge is preparing to leave his family home as he transitions from high school to dormitory life at the local community college. He was diagnosed with emotional/behavioral disorders (EBD) when he was 10 and although he was also identified as gifted, he has difficulties self-regulating his emotions which sometimes interferes with his academic performance. In preparation for living away from home, he needs to build his social and emotional skills for interacting with his peers, particularly future roommates. So, his transition IEP goals include items such as learning how to generate and self-monitor implementation of a plan for shared responsibilities with others, how to give and receive feedback appropriately to peers, and so forth.

Transition in the context of this chapter refers to change in status from being a student to emerging toward adult life, which includes postsecondary education and employment as well as maintaining a residence, becoming involved in the community, and experiencing positive personal and social relationships. Within this section, residential environments and social/interpersonal and social/intrapersonal relationships are addressed.

Continuum of Residential Environments

Living arrangements for all individuals in communities vary. The same is true for individuals with disabilities. Some live alone with or without support. Some live in group homes or supervised apartments. Some live with family members. **Independent living** is usually defined as living with minimal reliance on others in making decisions and performing everyday activities. Reliance on others is considered minimal because no one lives in a vacuum. All individuals depend on others for various aspects of living such as tax preparation, medical and health care, household maintenance, and so forth, or **interdependent living**. In other words, everyone lives interdependently rather than independently. Individuals with disabilities are no different. As with the continuum of employment options presented earlier, residential living options also fall along a continuum from most restrictive or least integrated to least restrictive or most integrated.

In **group homes** several individuals with disabilities live together in a residential home with at least one trained caregiver who is available 24 hours a day. Group homes are the most restrictive and typically serve people with more significant disabilities. The amount of choice, freedom, and independence varies from home to home depending on the focus population. Activities are typically structured for the residents who must go along with the group. Parents and concerned others have been comfortable allowing these individuals to live away from home in group homes because they offer direct supervision and a safe environment. However, with current movements toward self-determination and empowerment of individuals with disabilities, less restrictive residential options are gaining popularity. Among these more integrated residential options are supervised apartments, living support, and independent living with no outside support.

Supervised apartments offer more freedom and choices than group homes. Support staff is available close by but are only present in the resident's home a few hours a day for support and training in daily living skills such as housekeeping and cooking, and for interpersonal and recreational skills training. Residents typically live in a separate apartment with a roommate, as opposed to the group-home model where all residents share common areas such as dining and leisure areas.

Living support is an even less restrictive option with the support worker visiting *as needed*. This is an appropriate and attractive option for individuals with disabilities and waiting lists may be several years. Therefore, arrangements should be made well in advance before the student leaves secondary school. In living support programs, periodic visits are made by an adult services worker (the frequency of the visits depends on the amount of support needed) to help the resident with tasks such as shopping, paying bills, making appointments, or other areas in which the resident may need assistance. The adult services worker does not live with the resident, which offers a much greater degree of independence. This model provides a truly integrated residential situation, where the individual is living in the community independently with a safety net. Living support is very appealing for individuals with disabilities who desire independence, but may need assistance with tasks such as dealing with utility companies, balancing a bank account, comparative shopping, completing insurance and tax forms, parenting skills, and so forth.

Independent living is the goal for most young adults. The difference between supported and independent living is that there are no social service agencies associated with independent living. Just like young adults without disabilities, the resident must rely on family or friends for assistance. While independent living is a goal for young adults with disabilities, they, like their counterparts without disabilities, may run into barriers. Barriers to achieving fully independent living are related primarily to financial and practical concerns. Financial concerns may include the high cost of rent compared to relatively low wages, and the high costs of utilities, home furnishings, food, and other necessities. Independent living includes living alone or with a spouse, significant other, or roommate(s) (Sitlington et al., 2010). Choosing the right residential option is important, so there are many things that should be discussed when considering a home for a person with disabilities. The following should be considered when helping students with disabilities and their families make independent living choices:

- Independent living skills—level of self-care, cooking, and home maintenance skills

- Transportation—access to public transportation or obtaining a driver's license and automobile

- Personal and behavioral supports—availability of mental health and behavioral self-control assistance

- Financial supports—availability of low-cost housing and supplemental income if wages are low

- Community/natural supports—friends, coworkers, and neighbors who can provide assistance

- Recreational and social needs—integration in community activities and organizations

- Health and safety concerns—adequate medical care and knowledge of community risk factors

In addition, the following considerations should be discussed when designing individualized housing supports:

- providing support to people in their own apartments

- matching individuals with disabilities to roommates without disabilities or with families who may be compensated for providing assistance

- providing in-home supports for those individuals who choose to stay in their family home

- helping people with disabilities to become homeowners

Students with disabilities need specific skills to succeed in independent living. These skills include the following:

- personal and financial management (e.g., budgeting, online banking),

- housing and household maintenance (e.g., basic housekeeping and repair skills),

- health maintenance (e.g., grooming, hygiene, nutrition, exercise),

- sexuality and family living (e.g., birth control, parenting skills),

- interpersonal social skills (e.g., sharing space and responsibilities with roommates), and

- leisure and recreation skills (e.g., joining a local sports or hobby club).

In addition, community-access skills such as obtaining a driver's license or learning how to read the bus schedule should be taught before students exit school. Teachers can use independent living skills as a guiding theme across content areas to make the curricula more relevant, thus increasing students' interest in learning. Interpersonal social skills may also be infused within content areas by reinforcing concepts such as honesty, cooperation, respect, friendliness, and kindness (Sitlington et al., 2010).

The most effective way to teach students skills necessary for independent living is through teacher-directed instruction. A sample scripted lesson plan for teaching how to compute a tip may be found in Appendix G.

Social and Interpersonal Networks

The establishment of social and interpersonal networks remains a critical transition goal. The presence or absence of a network of friends will often have a profound influence on a person's sense of well-being. Individuals with disabilities need to have access to the same experiences and environments as their peers without disabilities so that they can select their own friends and acquaintances. Dimensions of human relationships include daily communication, self-esteem, family support, emotional maturity, friendship, and intimate relationships.

Strong interpersonal relationship skills affect every area of life. Individuals with HID may need social skills training to facilitate the development of meaningful interpersonal relationships. A thorough presentation of social and emotional learning is addressed in Chapter 13. Therefore, social skill instruction is only briefly discussed in this chapter.

Adolescents with HID are highly concerned about peer acceptance, making and keeping friends, and developing intimate relationships (Sitlington et al., 2010). Using peer-initiated interventions for youth with disabilities is a promising approach. Peer-initiated interventions may involve, for example, socially competent peers making specific social initiations to youth with disabilities to engage them in extended, positive social interactions and provide a context for the acquisition of basic social skills. Oftentimes, high-prestige peers are effective in increasing the target student's popularity and social integration within the school. Creating a receptive environment, particularly through integrated settings, promotes interactions with socially responsive peers and promotes generalization to other settings such as the community and workplace. While it is recommended that peer initiated intervention strategies should be used in elementary and middle schools, older students may also need this initial assistance to benefit from opportunities to develop friendships in naturally occurring settings such as the workplace.

The quality of intimate relationships formed with others can influence self-worth and self-esteem (Shany, Wiener, & Assido, 2012). Therefore, another aspect of transition preparation is sexuality education. Teachers need to help students be aware of clothing, actions, and how to express sexuality appropriately. Sexuality education may be included in lessons about healthy lifestyles and interpersonal relationships. All students, with and without disabilities, need to learn about personal responsibility and preventing vulnerability to victimization within the sexual sphere. Teachable moments as well as planned lessons can focus on this important area of adult life.

With the transition from school to adult life, society expects young adults to follow existing social rules in an independent and mature manner. Teachers can help in this process by teaching students appropriate social skills and providing experiences for social participation with peers in school and in the workplace (e.g., coworkers). Teachers should also help students

- understand and practice social reciprocity (e.g., the give-and-take involved in maintaining friendships);

- increase their perspective-taking ability;

- learn to express their sexuality in socially appropriate and safe ways; and

- learn skills for decision-making, conflict resolution, and anger management.

Learners must be taught basic social skills (polite interactions, appropriate greetings, personal space, eye contact), as well as subtle social responses (how to wait for an appropriate time to enter a group who is already engaged in a conversation/activity, and how to modify behavior based on situational cues). Teachers and other service providers must assist youth with disabilities in developing skills that will enable them to communicate and interact appropriately within community contexts and social/recreational activities. See Chapter 13 for more information on social and emotional learning.

Play: Recreation and Leisure

Gabriella is fourteen years old and has been diagnosed with high-functioning autism. Just this past year, she has begun to become fascinated with the game of golf. She watches it on television and once her father took her to a local tournament. Her strong interest in the game was discussed during her most recent IEP meeting and the team decided that they would teach her about golf, including golf etiquette, how to swing a club, putting, teeing off, and the rules of the game. Other skills such as transportation to golf courses, paying fees, renting clubs, and selecting and wearing appropriate clothing will also be integrated into her instruction.

Everyone likes to have fun. Persons with disabilities are no different; they should be included in their communities socially as well as physically. They should not be excluded from any educational or extracurricular program or activity, or any specific course of study. All people, with or without disabilities, have the right to participate fully in community activities and programs.

Although IDEA identifies recreation as one of the related services for students with disabilities, recreation and leisure are often overlooked (Sitlington et al., 2010). Most organizations that work with individuals with disabilities, including schools, focus on specific areas of concern such as education, employment, communication, counseling, and medical care. How a person spends his or her free time is not often a priority. However, recreation is big part of living a full and participatory life.

Everyone can benefit from participation in recreation and leisure. Such participation helps us intellectually, socially, emotionally, and physically. Recreation and leisure activities promote health, growth, development, and independence through self-rewarding recreational and leisure pursuits. Schools should teach students specific skills needed to participate in recreational activities. But instruction should not stop there. Teachers can promote positive attitudes toward leisure, provide information about recreation opportunities, and develop attitudes and skills that facilitate independent, satisfying leisure experiences. Government, private-for-profit, and private nonprofit organizations provide a variety of social, recreational, and leisure activities for people with and without disabilities. However, it is important to recognize the element of choice. Oftentimes individuals with disabilities participate in enforced leisure where the group is taken on bowling or swimming excursions or are scheduled to participate in arts and crafts during a set period of time. True leisure is not imposed upon anyone. Youth with disabilities should start identifying hobbies and interests they want to pursue outside of school.

One study focused on adolescents with autism found that 35% of the students performed volunteer work, 31% took lessons or classes outside of school, 27% were involved in a religious youth group, 16% participated on a sports team, and 9% were involved with a performing group (Shattuck, Orsmond, Wagner, & Cooper, 2011). Although these percentages are low when compared with peers without disabilities, they demonstrate that students can and should be involved in recreational and leisure activities. Becoming involved in these outside activities before leaving secondary schools can help prepare students for their future lives.

Including recreation and leisure goals into a transition IEP can facilitate participation in activities in integrated settings with nondisabled peers, development of self-determination, enhancement of self-concept and social skills, and opportunities to apply skills learned in school in the community.

Involving Stakeholders

To provide successful transition services to students with disabilities, coordination is required with all stakeholders. Composition of all IEP teams include members such as the special education teacher, family members, and if appropriate, the student, among others (see Chapter 1). Other team members may represent future postsecondary education institutions, employment, or residential units. For example, if a student is transitioning to college and plans to move into the dorms, a counselor from the college who advises and supports students with disabilities and the college's residence advisor may attend the IEP meeting. Future or current job representatives may include job coaches or employers. Vocational rehabilitation agency representatives may also be involved. Maintaining a multidisciplinary transition IEP team is critical and membership should be based on the individual student's needs and interests. For example, the school's guidance counselor who advises all students on college admissions could be invited to attend the meeting of those students interested in postsecondary education (Trainor, 2005).

In one study, students with disabilities reported that their families were more influential than their teacher in their selected postsecondary outcomes (Trainor, 2005). These results substantiate the importance of involving family members in the transition process. At the same time, family members may not have the background knowledge or experience to help the student make informed decisions. School personnel need to help educate family members on the implications of enrolling in specific programs, such as early release for work experience and exit test exemption (Trainor, 2005).

Effective collaboration requires appropriate interactive communication skills, knowledge and application of problem-solving processes, as well conflict resolution skills. All of these collaboration principles addressed in Chapter 2 apply to working with stakeholders in transition planning and implementation.

TEACHER TIP #14.5
INVOLVING FAMILY MEMBERS AND STUDENTS

Family members and students themselves are critical stakeholders in transition planning. Implement these tips to ensure their involvement in the process:

- When possible, prepare students to lead at least the transition portion of the IEP meeting. In advance, share with them the results of transition assessments and discuss their likes, dislikes, and interests.

- Invite students with disabilities currently enrolled in college to speak to the students and their family members about their advice and first-hand experiences at college.

- Inform family members about transition plans far in advance of the student's 16th birthday. Keep abreast of issues such as the cost of tuition for postsecondary schooling and requirements for school and work.

- Hold a futures night for students and family members during which information is presented about transition related issues. Invite service providers to make short presentations or serve on a panel. (Kellems & Morningstar, 2010)

Student Involvement

Student involvement as discussed in this section refers to the student's active participation in choice-making as IEP transition goals and services are being decided. As addressed in Chapter 1, students beginning not later than 16 years must be invited to attend their IEP meetings. Many students with HID need explicit instruction in how to participate actively in their transition meetings (see Chapter 1). The discussions and decisions that occur in the meetings must reflect student interests and preferences. In addition, students' postsecondary aspirations should provide direction to the plan of study and needed transition services. Unfortunately, many IEP teams fail to invite students and when students do participate, they are not prepared to self-advocate or to make significant contributions to their IEPs (Martin, Marshall, & Sale, 2004).

Students with HID are capable of and have the right to express personal preferences and to choose a variety of life activities including their place of residence and work. Yet, some students often depend on others to decide their career, residential situation, recreation and leisure activities, and even their friends. Along these same lines, job placement personnel often determine where the person should work based on availability of service programs rather than by the individual's choice or preference. In designing and implementing transition programs, it is of utmost importance that service providers, parents, teachers, and advocates provide opportunities for youth with disabilities to express choices and make decisions that affect outcomes in their lives. Part of this programming, then, should be informing individuals with disabilities about their adult options, allowing them to make independent decisions and to speak for themselves, and providing opportunities where they can express personal preferences and practice self-direction. Students should also be encouraged to invite members of their home communities to their transition IEP meetings (Trainor, 2005).

In addition to learning to self-advocate and participate in the meeting, students with HID need explicit instruction in self-determination and communication skills in order to participate fully in their current and future lives. Self-determined individuals act as casual agents in their lives to make things happen through the choices and decisions they make. Teachers can focus on the following components of self-determined behavior to assist students in the transition to adult living:

- choice-making skills and decision-making skills,

- problem-solving skills,

- goal-setting and attainment skills,

- self-management skills (e.g., self-evaluation, self-instruction),

- independence, risk-taking, and safety skills,

- self-advocacy and leadership skills,

- internal locus of control,

- positive attributions of efficacy and outcome expectancy, and

- self-awareness and self-knowledge. (Wehmeyer & Shogren, 2013)

TEACHER TIP #14.6

STUDENT STRATEGIES FOR IEP INVOLVEMENT

Teach students the following mnemonic strategies to apply prior to and during their IEP meeting:

I PLAN (Hammer, 2004):

Inventory your strengths, areas to improve or learn, goals, and choices for learning or accommodations

(Continued)

(Continued)

Provide your inventory information	**H**ave a pleasant tone of voice
Listen and respond	**A**ctivate your thinking (tell yourself to pay attention, participate, and compare ideas)
Ask questions	
Name your goals	**R**elax (don't look uptight; tell yourself to stay calm)
SHARE (Hammer, 2004)	
Sit up straight	**E**ngage in eye communication

Person-Centered Planning

Before high school graduation, Alicia had received special education services because of her learning disability. Except for language arts, she attended all general education classrooms. Alicia participated in person-centered planning during her IEP transition planning meetings. She attended the meetings and acted as a full participant sharing data, answering questions, expressing her opinion, and contributing ideas. When the transition planning began at age 16, she came prepared with answers to questions about her postsecondary aspirations and where she saw herself in 5 to 10 years after graduating. She indicated a desire to be an elementary school teacher. Her parents agreed that this would be a terrific career for their daughter. Alicia's teachers shared their data on Alicia's skills and suggested what the school could offer to better prepare her for postsecondary education to become a licensed elementary teacher. In addition to academic goals, they decided to work on Alicia's self-advocacy skills and test-taking skills so she could pass the qualifying exam. At the last IEP meeting before graduation, a disability counselor from the postsecondary institution Alicia will attend participated via videoconferencing.

During person-centered planning, the student and others familiar with the student (e.g., family members, friends, peers, teachers) share information to help create a future vision for the student (Wells & Sheehey, 2012). Student, parent, and teacher interviews are essential to person-centered planning. Students are asked about interests and leisure-time activities, the types of work they do at home, and any part-time or summer jobs they have held. During the student interview, knowledge about their aspirations for careers can be tapped. Parent interviews are important to understand aspirations for their child's future employment and schooling. Parents can also provide a wealth of information about their child's strengths and weaknesses in community settings. Teachers who have worked with the student can provide a great deal of information about (a) the individual's cognitive and affective skills, (b) his or her work-related behaviors such as attention and task completion, (c) how the student likes to approach and complete tasks, and (d) the best methods of instruction for that student. Employers may also be interviewed to determine the quantity and quality of work expected, and the social skills necessary for effective job performance.

Typically, questions such as the following are asked as part of the person-centered planning process: Who is the student? What are the student's strengths, greatest challenges, and needs? What are the student's and our dreams for the student? What are our and the student's biggest fears? Students should be asked about interests and leisure-time activities, the types of work they do at home, and any part-time or summer jobs they have held. Through creating a personal history, knowledge about students' and parents' aspirations for future employment and schooling can be tapped. The kind of social or personal life the student wants should not be ignored. Professionals too often focus on employment and residential settings in post-high school planning. Social aspects should be brought into this vision of the future. Figure 14.1 presents a sample of the results of a person-centered planning process.

FIGURE 14.1   **Person-Centered Planning**

Person-Centered Planning

Who is Kaleo?

Kaleo is the middle child in his family. He has an older sister who lives away from home while she is attending college. He has a younger brother who is in eighth grade.

Kaleo is a sophomore in an inclusive high school who loves to play computer games at home. He likes to go camping, fishing, and hiking whenever he can. He also likes riding his skateboard around the neighborhood.

Kaleo gets uncomfortable around large groups of people, but feels good when he's around just a few close friends and/or family.

Kaleo has a very supportive family.

What are Kaleo's dreams?

To have a close circle of supportive friends

To live as independently as possible, to get married, and have a family of his own

To have a meaningful career

To regularly enjoy recreation and leisure activities of his choosing

What are our nightmares?

For Kaleo to be taken advantage of by other people due to his caring and trusting nature

For Kaleo to work and live in segregated environments away from people without disabilities

What are Kaleo's strengths, gifts, and abilities?

His memory and retention of facts

Expressing himself, when allowed time to do it

His skills on the computer

His love of nature, animals, and genuine caring for people

(Continued)

FIGURE 14.1   (Continued)

What are Kaleo's greatest challenges?

Getting around independently in the community

Gainful employment and a career

Being able to calm himself when he gets stressed

What supports are needed for Kaleo?

Travel training

Empowerment and/or self-determination curriculum

Computer literate teacher or peer

Calculator, writing software to strengthen writing skills

Source: Adapted from Wehman (2001). Based on a lesson from Merrell et al., 2007 Merrell, K. W., Carrizales, D., Feuerborn, L., Gueldern, B. A., & Tran, O. L., (2007). *Strong kids: Grades 3-5.* Baltimore, MD: Brookes.

Several person-centered planning methods have been developed including Making Actions Plans (MAPS) (O'Brien, Pearpoint, & Kahn, 2015). MAPS is a comprehensive planning process that was designed initially for students with severe disabilities. But it has since been demonstrated to be relevant and effective with students of various disabilities including those with HID (Wells & Sheehey, 2012). In addition to the student, family members, and teachers, MAPS includes peers in the process. A facilitator convenes a meeting where these individuals discuss questions about the student's future. Questions specific to transition planning may include the following:

- Where will the student live and work at age 21?

- What community activities will the student engage in?

- What leisure activities will the student enjoy?

- How will the student get around the community?

- Who will the student's friends be?

- What might a typical day look like? (Wells & Sheehey, 2012)

The answers to these questions are used as a basis for developing transition plans.

Implications for Culturally and/or Linguistically Diverse Students and Families

Transition to adult life can be difficult for all students with HID, but particularly for those with diverse backgrounds. Research indicates that when compared to Whites with disabilities, youth with disabilities who are African American or Hispanic have significantly lower percentages of employment and postsecondary education (Newman,

Wagner, Cameto, & Knokey, 2009). Also, the postsecondary employment for students who are English learners (EL) with disabilities has been found to be significantly lower than other students with disabilities (Trainor, Murray, & Kim, 2016). Other research has documented that postsecondary transition planning experiences for culturally and/or linguistically diverse (CLD) students differ from their White counterparts (Trainor, 2002), necessitating the need to instruct students in the social context of the cultural identity and disability (Banks, 2014). Given the increasing numbers of students from culturally and/or linguistically diverse (CLD) populations in the schools, special educators are likely to teach high numbers of students from diverse populations, which requires that they be prepared in culturally responsive transition planning and implementation.

Gary Greene (2011) identified the following transition knowledge and skills that all personnel involved with transition of CLD students should demonstrate:

- family values, beliefs, and practices

- family integration and acculturation status

- family attitudes and beliefs about disabilities

- family interpersonal communication style

- promoting active involvement of CLD family members in the student's education

- family understanding of legal aspects of transition

Culture is not just race or ethnicity. Culture also includes language, religion, patterns of social and interpersonal relationships, and family expectations that have a great influence on an individual's interests, abilities, and aptitudes, as well as preferences in residential environment, community integration, and occupational choice. Therefore, culture plays a very large role in the kinds of transition activities that will best match a student's personal and family values. In particular, culture influences two key areas of transition: (a) family/student involvement in the transition planning process, and (b) occupational choice and interdependent living.

Family/Student Involvement in the Transition Planning Process

The families in which all students live are cultural groups that have values, beliefs, and experiences of their own. These commonalities are shaped by family priorities and perspectives. Among other factors, having an individual with a disability as part of the family group can greatly impact the family's priorities and perspectives. Experiencing the emotional climate of discrimination or poverty, and other culturally related experiences, also influences family priorities and perspectives. Given each family's uniqueness related to culture, the most influential factors in making the transition planning process culturally relevant are involving both students and family members in the process.

IDEA's mandate for transition planning promotes a European American perspective of actively preparing for the future. In fact, transition planning is based on independence, achievement, time consciousness, and an assertive style of verbal and nonverbal behavior. Yet, as discussed in Chapter 2, cultural groups vary across at least four dimensions: efficiency, independence, equity, and communication styles. All of these dimensions can impact transition planning and implementation. Given the potential mismatch between the values embedded in transition planning and implementation, special educators need to be particularly sensitive to differences among their students' family cultures.

Research shows that challenges experienced by CLD families can create barriers to their involvement in transition planning. Some of these barriers include (a) limited understanding about legal requirements for transition, (b) lack of understanding and respecting the family's culture, (c) lack of acknowledging the family's hopes and dreams for the student's future, (c) language or immigration issues, (e) cultural and racial stereotypes and biases, and (f) differences in cultural perceptions and expectations impacting views of transition for the student, among others (Greene, 2011).

Given that parents and other family members of their students need to understand transition plans and services in order to fully participate, school personnel should consider providing training for families in a less formal setting than the school (e.g., their home, a public auditorium). Family preparation should center on (a) parents' rights and responsibilities in transition planning and implementation, (b) understanding all aspects of special education and related laws, (c) the importance of support groups or mentors for students and their families, and (d) the use and role of bilingual and bicultural interpreters who should be requested if needed throughout the transition planning process (Greene, 2011).

Postsecondary Education, Occupational Choice, and Independent/Interdependent Living

Biases of school personnel can greatly impact the future lives of their students. For example, some research indicates that CLD students with disabilities, particularly African American and Hispanic students, are being steered by school personnel away from college preparation tracks and enrolled in vocational education although the students expressed desire to attend college (Trainor, 2005; Pellegrino, Sermons, & Shaver, 2011). Additionally, many postsecondary African American students with disabilities have been found to not seek evaluation to document disabilities, disclose their disability, or seek accommodations because of faculty members' attitudes toward race and disability (Banks, 2014; Durodoye, Combes, & Bryant, 2004; Pellegrino et al., 2011).

Most career development theories view a person's occupational choice as a highly individual-centered activity, based on individual preferences, an opportunity for self-expression, and even as a part of personal identity. These career development theories, however, are based on European American culture. As has been discussed throughout this book, many students come from cultures that promote interdependence over individualism, cooperation over competition, and present verses future concepts of time, among other differences. Some young people may be more concerned with the social environment and prefer activities and occupations that allow for more personal relationships and working cooperatively with others. They may not succeed well in work settings involving competition, individual task completion, and rigid time deadlines.

Many cultures believe that the family should take care of their own. Their willingness to accept assistance from outside agencies, especially independent living agencies, may even be viewed as evading family responsibilities. A family's view of disability may also make them unwilling to accept help from disability services agencies. Taking care of a family member with a disability may be seen as a family matter, where help from outside agencies is an intrusion.

In some cultures, individuals with disabilities are not expected to work or to live independently. They are expected to assume certain roles within the family that are seen as equally valued. Male and female role expectations as well as expectations in the areas of responsibilities to the family and the group may also prohibit independent living. Teachers must be sensitive to these values and not impose personal values by making plans for individuals to work or live independently without first consulting the family and eliciting their views. At the same time, teachers can help individuals and their family members prioritize transition-related preferences, strengths, and needs with their own cultural values (Trainor et al., 2016).

TABLE 14.6   Cultural Considerations When Planning Transition

Cultural Considerations When Planning Transition for CLD Students	
Independence and Cooperation	What are the family's norms for independence?
	Does the student's family and culture value cooperation rather than competition?
Views on Family and Disability	What constitutes a family based on their culture (e.g., extended family included)?
	What child-rearing practices does the family use (e.g., authoritarian or children make decisions for themselves)?
	How might their views of family and child-rearing practices impact the transition process?
	How does the family view disabilities and how might these views impact transition planning?
Family Work Expectations	What work related goals are held by the family for the student?
	Is the student expected to work in a family business or traditional family occupation?
	Does the family have certain expectations as to what occupations are and are not appropriate for the student?
Occupations	Has the student been exposed to a wide variety of careers, or has most of their observational learning about jobs consisted of family jobs that are all in the same occupational cluster?
	What jobs are valued and not valued?
	Would some jobs be seen as shameful to the family?
Communication	What language is spoken at home and what is the literacy level of family members?
	What communication style does the family promote?
	Does the student prefer to remain relatively quiet and speak only when spoken to?
Educational Aspirations	Does the family have certain expectations about the type of postsecondary education appropriate for the student?
	Does the family want the student to attend a certain kind of school after high school (e.g., university or technical school)?
	Can the student's family financially afford a 4-year college education?
	Considering the career goals of the student and family, would a community college or technical school provide a more appropriate education at less expense to the family?

(Continued)

TABLE 14.6   (Continued)

Cultural Considerations When Planning Transition for CLD Students	
Residence	What are the residential patterns in the family (e.g., extended families live together, 18-year-olds move out before married)?
	What residential goals does the family hold for the student?
	If the student selects a job not available in the local community, does the family view moving away as acceptable?
Environmental conditions and events, past learning experiences, how the student approaches tasks, and preferred learning style are also important in determining a person–occupation match.	

Educators and transition personnel need to be competent in culturally responsive communication and collaborative processes. Culturally responsive communication can facilitate the transition process by team members (a) providing the necessary training for their participation, (b) becoming familiar with the family's cultural background and beliefs about transition to adult life, (c) listening to family members and respecting their perspectives, and (d) supporting the family's hopes and dreams for the student's future even if they differ from other team members' ideas (Greene, 2011; Greene, 2014).

SUMMARY

IDEA mandates that all students receiving special education services must have transition goals and services included in their IEP by age 16. Transition services focus on improving the student's academic and functional achievement to facilitate movement from school to postschool activities. These services may include teaching skills such as career awareness, life skills, self-advocacy, goal-setting, and social skills, as well as collaborating with agencies and/or postsecondary education personnel for current or future services. As with all IEPs, schools should seek the involvement of students and their family members in the development and implementation of transition plans.

While students with disabilities are receiving special education services in K–12 schools, they are protected under the mandates of IDEA. Once they move to postsecondary settings, they are protected under Section 504 and ADA. At that time, the responsibility is placed on the individual to provide documentation of

the disability and to self-advocate for accommodations and services.

When designing transition services and goals, IEP teams should consider these four aspects of the student's life: learning, working, living, and playing. Some students will enroll in postsecondary education, whether it be vocational training or college. Care must be taken to ensure postsecondary education matches the interest, abilities, and preferences of the student. Teachers can help students prepare for postsecondary schooling by helping them understand their disability and take responsibility for their successes and outcomes, among other things. Systemic barriers for students with HID attending college can be challenging to overcome. The HEO Act passed in 2008 provides support to students identified as ID to attend a college or university program.

Employment or the working aspect of life plays a critical role in adult living, and there are several employment options available for individuals with HID that span a continuum from least integrated (sheltered employment) to most integrated (competitive employment). Teachers can prepare students in elementary, middle, and high schools for employment by incorporating work concepts into classroom instruction. Service learning can also provide an opportunity to promote job-related skills as well as providing service to the community.

Transition planning is incomplete without attending to where the student will live. Living arrangements also fall across a continuum from least integrated (group homes) to most integrated (independent living) settings. Other community access skills such as transportation should be taught before students exit schools. The establishment of social and interpersonal networks remains critical to transitioning to adult life. Students with HID may need social skills training and peer-initiated interventions to help them integrate into the community.

Although recreation (playing) is identified in IDEA as one of the related services, IEP teams often overlook it. Recreation is a big part of living a full and participatory life. Schools should teach specific skills needed to participate in recreational activities, as well as promote attitudes and skills that facilitate independent, satisfying leisure experiences that are based on the student's choices.

Students with HID are capable of and have the right to express personal preferences and to choose a variety of life activities including their future schooling, work, place of residence, and recreational activities. All stakeholders must be involved in the transition IEP process, including students and their family members. Using person-centered planning can help the student and others familiar with the student share information to help create a future vision for the student. Visions for the future are greatly influenced by cultural values, beliefs, and practices. Thus, involvement of CLD students and families and sensitivity to their vision are particularly critical to transition planning and implementation.

REVIEW QUESTIONS

1. Define *transition* as stated in the Individuals with Disabilities Education Act (IDEA). Include when a student with a disability must have a transition plan and what it must contain.

2. What laws impact adults with disabilities? How do they compare with IDEA?

3. Provide an example of a common core standard and transition objective and describe how both outcomes can be met simultaneously.

4. What are some of the barriers to postsecondary education for students with HID? How can

secondary teachers prepare them to overcome these barriers? Provide at least three examples.

5. Describe the continuum of employment and residential options from most to least restrictive.

6. Provide examples of how teachers can prepare students for postsecondary employment in elementary, middle, and high schools.

7. What is the importance of student and other stakeholders' involvement in the transition process? How can person-centered planning enhance the process?

8. How could teachers involve students in their IEP meeting? In what ways would they need to be prepared for that involvement?

9. Describe why it is particularly important for culturally and/or linguistically diverse families

to become involved in their student's transition planning.

10. Provide examples of how culturally and/or linguistically diverse family desires of a student's future may differ from the European American perspective.

ACTIVITIES

1. Contact a high school transition specialist or special educator. Obtain information on the transition services the specialist or teacher can provide for students with HID. Write a report.

2. Through a high school transition specialist or special educator, identify a mentor or supervisor for job placement programs. Interview the individual. Identify how the employer provides job training for students with disabilities. Orally present your results.

3. Find a website for your state office of rehabilitation services. Write a summary report of information

the site provides about services for persons with disabilities.

4. Investigate options for assisted living in your state. List information that describes options for persons with disabilities.

5. Interview parents of a young adult with disabilities. Ask what types of transition services were provided to support their child and the parents' level of satisfaction with those services. Identify services that were helpful and those that could be improved. Report your results.

Council for Exceptional Children (CEC) Standards

The Council for Exceptional Children (CEC) is a premiere national professional organization comprised of special educators, paraeducators, relative service personnel, parents, and others interested in individuals with disabilities and/or those with gifts and talents. This organization has generated 10 standards for the preparation of special educators. These standards are listed in each chapter as they relate to the content within the chapter. The standards that apply to Chapter 14 are Standards #1, #2, #3, #5, and #6.

CEC Initial Preparation Standard 1: Learner Development and Individual Learning Differences

Beginning special education professionals understand how exceptionalities may interact with development and

learning and use this knowledge to provide meaningful and challenging learning experiences for individuals with exceptionalities.

1.1. Beginning special education professionals understand how language, culture, and family background influence the learning of individuals with exceptionalities.

1.2. Beginning special education professionals use understanding of development and individual differences to respond to the needs of individuals with exceptionalities.

CEC Initial Preparation Standard #2: Learning Environments (partial)

Beginning special education professionals create safe, inclusive, culturally responsive learning environments so that individuals with exceptionalities become active and effective learners and develop emotional well-being, positive social interactions, and self-determination.

2.1. Beginning special education professionals through collaboration with general educators and other colleagues create safe, inclusive, culturally responsive learning environments to engage individuals with exceptionalities in meaningful learning activities and social interactions.

2.2. Beginning special education professionals use motivational and instructional interventions to teach individuals with exceptionalities how to adapt to different environments.

CEC Initial Preparation Standard #3: Curricular Content Knowledge (partial)

Beginning special education professionals use knowledge of general and specialized curricula to individualize learning for individuals with exceptionalities.

3.1. Beginning special education professionals understand the central concepts, structures of the discipline, and tools of inquiry of the content areas they teach and can organize this knowledge, integrate cross-disciplinary skills, and develop meaningful learning progressions for individuals with exceptionalities.

3.2. Beginning special education professionals understand and use general and specialized content knowledge of teaching across curricular content areas to individualize learning for individuals with exceptionalities.

CEC Initial Preparation Standard #5: Instructional Planning and Strategies (partial)

Beginning special education professionals select, adapt, and use a repertoire of evidence-based instructional strategies to advance learning of individuals with exceptionalities.

5.1. Beginning special education professionals consider an individual's abilities, interests, learning environments, and cultural and linguistic factors in the selection, development, and adaptation of learning experiences for individuals with exceptionalities.

5.5. Beginning special education professionals develop and implement a variety of education and transition plans for individuals with exceptionalities across a wide range of settings and different learning experiences in collaboration with individuals, families, and teams.

5.7. Beginning special education professionals teach cross-disciplinary knowledge and skills such as critical thinking and problem-solving to individuals with exceptionalities.

CEC Initial Preparation Standard #6: Professional Learning and Ethical Practice (partial)

Beginning special education professionals use foundational knowledge of the field and their professional Ethnical Principles and Practice Standards to inform special education practice, to engage in lifelong learning, and to advance the profession.

6.3. Beginning special education professionals understand that diversity is a part of families, cultures, and schools, and that complex human issues can interact with the delivery of special education services.

REFERENCES

Asselin, S. B. (2014). Learning and assistive technologies for college transition. *Journal of Vocational Rehabilitation*, *40*, 223–230.

Banks, J. (2014). Barriers and supports to postsecondary transition: Case studies of African American students with disabilities. *Remedial and Special Education*, *35*(1), 28–39.

Bartholomew, A., Papay, C., McConnell, A., & Cease-Cook, J. (2015). Embedding secondary transition in the common core state standards. *TEACHING Exceptional Children, 47*(6), 329–335.

Black, J. (2010). Digital transition portfolios for secondary students with disabilities. *Intervention in School and Clinic, 46*(2), 118–124.

Bobroff, S., & Sax, C. L. (2010). The effects of peer tutoring interview skills training with transition-age youth with disabilities. *Journal of Vocational Rehabilitation, 33*, 143–157.

Boyle, M. (2012). Federal financial aid for students with intellectual disabilities. *Insight, Issue 16.* Thinkcollege.net

Brault, M. W. (2012). *Americans with disabilities: 2010.* U.S. Department of Commerce, U.S. Census Bureau. Retrieved from census.gov/prod/2012pubs/p70-131.pdf

Cease-Cook, J., Fowler, C., & Test, D. W. (2015). Strategies for creating work-based learning experiences in schools for secondary students with disabilities. *TEACHING Exceptional Children, 47*(6), 352–358.

Connor, D. J. (2012). Helping students with disabilities transition to college. *TEACHING Exceptional Children, 44*(5), 16–25.

Cuenca-Carlino, Y., & Mustian, A. P. (2013). Self-regulated strategy development: Connecting persuasive writing to self-advocacy for students with emotional and behavioral disorders. *Behavioral Disorders, 39*(1), 3–15.

Duncan, A., & Ali, R. (2011a). *Students with disabilities preparing for postsecondary education: Know your rights and responsibilities.* Washington, DC: U.S. Department of Education. Retrieved from http://www 2.ed.gov/about/offices/list/ocr/transition.html

Duncan, A., & Ali, R. (2011b). *Transition of students with disabilities to postsecondary education: A guide for high school educators.* Washington, DC: U.S. Department of Education. Retrieved from www2.ed.gov/about/offices/list/ocr/transitionguide.html#keys

Durodoye, B. A., Combes, B. H., & Bryant, R. M. (2004). Counselor intervention in the post-secondary planning of African American students with learning disabilities. *Professional School Counseling, 7*, 133–140.

Dymond, S. K., Chun, E. J., Kim, R. K., & Renzaglia, A. (2013). A validation of elements, methods, and barriers to inclusive high school service-learning programs. *Remedial and Special Education, 34*(5), 293–304.

Flexer, R. W., Baer, R. M., Luft, P., & Simmons, T. J. (2013). *Transition planning for secondary students with disabilities* (4th ed.). Boston, MA: Pearson.

Greene, G. (2011). *Transition planning for culturally and linguistically diverse youth.* Baltimore, MD: Paul H. Brookes.

Greene, G. (2014). Transition of culturally and linguistically diverse youth with disabilities: Challenges and opportunities. *Journal of Vocational Rehabilitation, 40*, 239–245.

Hammer, M. R. (2004). Using the self-advocacy strategy to increase student participation in IEP conferences. *Intervention in School and Clinic, 39*(5), 295–300.

Kellems, R. O., & Morningstar, M. E. (2010). Tips for transition. *TEACHING Exceptional Children, 43*(2), 60–68.

Kleinert, H. L., Jones, M. M., Sheppard-Jones, K., Harp, B., & Harrison, E. M. (2012). Students with intellectual disabilities going to college? Absolutely! *TEACHING Exceptional Children, 44*(5), 26–35.

Larson, S., Lakin, C., Anderson, L., & Kwak, N. (2001). *Demographic characteristics of persons with MR/DD living in their own homes or with family members.* Minneapolis, MN: University of Minnesota. https://ici. umn.edu/index.php?products/view/116

Lee, G. K., & Carter, E. W. (2012). Preparing transition-age students with high-functioning autism spectrum disorders for meaningful work. *Psychology in the Schools, 49*(10), 988–1000.

Lee, S. S. (2009). Overview of the Federal Higher Education Opportunity Act Reauthorization. Retrieved from http://www.thinkcollege.net/images/stories/HEAC_Overview(1).pdf

Lehmann, J. P., Davies, T. G., & Laurin, K. M. (2000). Listening to student voices about postsecondary education. *TEACHING Exceptional Children, 32*(5), 60–65.

Martin, J. E., Marshall, L. H., & Sale, P. (2004). A 3-year study of middle, junior high, and high school IEP meetings. *Exceptional Children, 70,* 285–297.

Morgan, R. L., & Riesen, T. (2016). *Promoting successful transition to adulthood for students with disabilities.* New York, NY: Guilford Press.

National Organization on Disability. (2010). *Kessler Foundation/NOD Survey of Americans with Disabilities.* Retrieved from http://www.2010disabilitysurveys.org/

Newman, L., Wagner, M., Cameto, R., & Knokey, A. M. (2009). *The post-high school outcomes of youth with disabilities up to 4 years after high school: A report of findings from the National Longitudinal Transition Study-2 (NLTS2)* (NCSER Report No. 2009-3017). Menlo Park, CA: SRI International. Retrieved from nlts2.org/reports/2009_04/nlts2_report_2009_04_complete.pdf

Nochajski, S. M., & Schweitzer, J. A. (2014). Promoting school to work transition for students with emotional/behavioral disorders. *Work, 48,* 413–422.

O'Brien, J. W., Pearpoint, J. C., & Kahn, L. D. (2015). *The PATH and MAPS handbook.* Toronto, ON, Canada: Inclusion Press.

Papay, C., Unger, D. D., Williams-Diehm, K., & Mitchell, V. (2015). Begin with the end in mind: Infusing transition planning and instruction into elementary classrooms. *TEACHING Exceptional Children, 47*(6), 310–318.

Pellegrino, A. M., Sermons, B. M., & Shaver, G. W. (2011). Disproportionality among postsecondary students seeking evaluation to document disabilities. *Disability Studies Quarterly, 31*(2). Retrieved from dsq-sds.org/article/view/1588/1556

Reinschmiedt, H. J., Buono, F. D., Sprong, M. E., Upton, T. D., & Dallas, B. (2013). Post-secondary students with disabilities receiving accommodations: A survey of satisfaction and subjective well-being. *Journal of Rehabilitation, 79*(3), 3–10.

Riesen, T., Morgan, R., Schultz, J., & Kupferman, S. (2014). School-to-work barriers as identified by special educators, vocational rehabilitation counselors, and community rehabilitation professionals. *Journal of Rehabilitation, 80*(1), 33–44.

Shany, M., Wiener, J., & Assido, M. (2012). Friendship predictors of global self-worth and domain-specific self-concepts in university students with and without learning disabilities. *Journal of Learning Disabilities, 46*(5), 444–452.

Shattuck, P. T., Orsmond, G. I., Wagner, M., & Cooper, B. P. (2011). Participation in social activities among adolescents with an autism spectrum disorder. *PLOS One, 6,* 1–9. doi: 10.1371/journal.pone.0027176

Shaw, S. F., Dukes, L. L., & Madaus, J. W. (2012). Beyond compliance: Using the summary of performance to enhance transition planning. *TEACHING Exceptional Children, 44*(3), 6–12.

Sitlington, P. L., Neubert, D. A., & Clark, G. M. (2010). *Transition education and services for students with disabilities* (5th Ed.). Upper Saddle River, MA: Pearson.

Skouge, J. R., Kelly, M. L., Roberts, K. D., Leake, D. W., & Stodden, R. A. (2007). Technologies for self-determination for youth with developmental disabilities. *Education and Training in Developmental Disabilities, 42*(4), 475–482.

Smith, F. A., Grigal, M., & Sulewski, J. S. (2012). *Postsecondary education and employment outcomes for transition-age youth with and without disabilities: A secondary analysis of American community survey data.* Retrieved from http://www.thinkcollege.net/administrator/components/com_resdb/files/Insight_15_D2.pdf

Test, D. W., Fowler, C. H., & Kohler, P. (2013). *Evidence-based practices and predictors in secondary transition: What we know and what we still need to know.*

U.S. Department of Education, National Secondary Transition Technical Assistance Center. Retrieved from transitionta.org/sites/default/files/effectivepractices/Execsummary_PPs_2013.pdf

Test, D. W., Fowler, C. H., Richter, S. M., White, J., Mazzotti, V., Walker, A. R., Kohler, P., & Kortering, L. (2009). Evidence-based practices in secondary transition. *Career Development for Exceptional Individuals, 32*(2), 115–128.

Test, D. W., Mazzotti, V. L., Mustian, A. L., Fowler, C. H., Kortering, L., & Kohler, P. (2009). Evidence-based secondary transition predictors for improving postschool outcomes for students with disabilities. *Career Development for Exceptional Individuals, 32*(3), 160–181.

Thomas, S. B., & Dykes, F. (2011). Promoting successful transitions: What can we learn from RTI to enhance outcomes for all students? *Preventing School Failure, 55*(1), 1–9.

Trainor, A. A. (2002). Self-determination for students with learning disabilities: Is it a universal value? *Qualitative Studies in Education, 13*, 711–725.

Trainor, A. A. (2005). Self-determination perceptions and behaviors of diverse students with LD during the transition planning process. *Journal of Learning Disabilities, 38*(3), 233–249.

Trainor, A. A., Murray, A., & Kim, H.-J. (2016). English learners with disabilities in high school: Population characteristics, transition programs, and postschool outcomes. *Remedial and Special Education, 37*(3), 146–158.

U.S. Census Bureau. (2015). *25th anniversary of Americans with Disabilities Act.* Retrieved from census.gov/newsroom/facts-for-features/2015/cb15-ff10.html

U.S. Department of Education (2006). *Building the legacy: IDEA 2004—Transition services.* Retrieved from idea.ed.gov/explore/view/p/%2Croot%2Cregs%2C300%2CA%2C300%252E43%2C

U.S. Department of Education. (2015). *Thirty-seventh annual report to Congress on the implementation of the Individuals with Disabilities Education Act.* Washington, DC: Author.

VanBergeijk, E. O., & Cavanagh, P. K. (2012). Brief report: New legislation supports students with intellectual disabilities in post-secondary funding. *Journal of Autism and Developmental Disorders, 42*, 2471–2475.

Webster, D. D., & Queen, R. M. (2008). Transition to postsecondary education. In R.W. Flexer, R. M. Baer, P. Luft, & T. J. Simmons (Eds.), *Transition planning for secondary students with disabilities* (3rd ed., pp. 258–289). Upper Saddle River, NJ: Pearson.

Wehman, P. (2001). *Life beyond the classroom: Transition strategies for young people with disabilities* (3rd ed.). Baltimore: Paul H. Brookes.

Wehmeyer, M., & Shogren, K. A. (2013). Self-determination: Getting students involved in leadership. In P. Wehman (Ed.), *Life beyond the classroom: Transition strategies for young people with disabilities* (5th ed., pp. 41–68). Baltimore, MD: Paul H. Brookes.

Wells, J. C., & Sheehey, P. H. (2012). Person-centered planning: Strategies to encourage participation and facilitate communication. *TEACHING Exceptional Children, 44*(3), 32–39.

Zionch, A. (2011). Digital simulations: Facilitating transition for students with disabilities. *Intervention in School and Clinic, 46*(4), 246–250.

⑤SAGE edge™ • ●

Review → Practice → Improve

Get the tools you need to sharpen your study skills. Access videos, practice quizzes, eFlashcards and more at **edge.sagepub.com/prater.**

APPENDIXES

APPENDIX A: SAMPLE SCRIPTED WRITING LESSON PLAN

Topic	Writing Informative Texts
Common Core Standards	7.W.2. Write informative/explanatory texts to examine a topic and convey ideas, concepts, and information through the selection, organization, and analysis of relevant content. 7.W.2.C. Use appropriate transitions to create cohesion and clarify the relationships among ideas and concepts.
IEP Objective	Given a topic, students will write a well-organized two-page informative paper about the topic including relevant content from three additional sources and no more than two grammar or spelling mistakes.
Unit Objective	Given a choice of topic, students will write a well-organized one-page informative paper about the subject including appropriate transitions between ideas and having no more than two grammar or spelling mistakes.
Lesson Objective	Given eight pairs of sentences and the transition chart, students will select and write an appropriate transition word or phrase between the sentences to "clarify the relationships among ideas and concepts" in the sentences with 7/8 correct.
Materials	Guided and Independent Practice Worksheet Transitions Chart: 1. Read the sentences 2. Look at the relationship between the sentences 3. Pick a transition 4. Write the transition

Comparing	Contrasting	Explaining
Similarly	However	For example
Likewise	On the other hand	Therefore
In addition	In contrast	In other words

Lesson Component	Teacher's Instruction, Questions, Feedback, and Sample Error Correction	Anticipated Student Responses
Attending Cue	SAY: "Everyone get out a pencil. It's time to start our writing lesson! Remember to raise your hand if you have a question or comment."	Students look at teacher.
Review & Prerequisite Check	SAY: "Yesterday we worked on putting our ideas in an order that makes sense so that when we write, the reader can understand what we're talking about." ASK: "Give me a thumbs-up if you remember working on ordering your ideas."	 Students give a thumbs-up.

(Continued)

(Continued)

Lesson Component	Teacher's Instruction, Questions, Feedback, and Sample Error Correction	Anticipated Student Responses
	FEEDBACK: "I'm glad you all remember doing that."	
	SAY: "I am going to give you all a worksheet that looks like the one we did yesterday. I want you to number the ideas in the order that makes the most sense. Remember to read carefully."	
	Teacher monitors student work. If students accurately complete the review sheet, the teacher continues with the lesson. If students do not demonstrate mastery, teacher reteaches concept from the previous lesson.	Students complete review worksheet.
	SAY: "I'm glad you all remember how to order your ideas."	
	SAY: "Today we're going to use some words that I want to make certain you understand. They are compare, contrast, and explain. Turn to your partner and decide on your best definition and use each in a sentence."	Students work in groups.
	Call on individual pairs to provide their definition and sentences. Remediate if there are misunderstandings.	Students state their definitions and sentences.
Anticipatory Set & Purpose Statement	ASK: "How many of you have ever listened to the radio?"	Students raise their hands.
	SAY: "I love listening to the radio when I'm in the car. Something I've noticed when I listen to the radio is that the songs usually blend together."	
	ASK: "How many of you have noticed that one song doesn't stop completely before the next one starts?"	Students raise their hands.
	FEEDBACK: "I'm glad you have all noticed that too."	
	ASK: "Why do you think they do that?"	Possible responses: "It's awkward if there's a pause." "They don't want you to stop listening." "The end of songs is boring."
	FEEDBACK: "Those are all good answers."	
	SAY: "One of the main reasons they don't end is so that you don't stop listening. It also makes it so there isn't an awkward pause between songs. The blend between the songs is called a *transition*."	
	ASK: "What is the blend between songs called?"	"A transition."
	FEEDBACK: "Very good!"	
	SAY: "We also use transitions in writing so that our sentences blend together in a way that makes sense. Transitions also make it so there are no awkward pauses in our writing, just like there are no pauses between songs on the radio. Today we are going to learn how to add transitions to our writing. Using transitions make it easier for readers to understand what we write. Learning to use transition words will help you with the papers you write."	

Lesson Component	Teacher's Instruction, Questions, Feedback, and Sample Error Correction	Anticipated Student Responses
	ASK: "What are we going to learn and why?" FEEDBACK: "Good job! Let's get started."	"How to add transitions to our writing. It will help us write papers and make them easier to understand."
Instruction	SAY: "Transition words have two purposes. The first is to make two ideas flow together. The second purpose is to clarify the relationship between two ideas." ASK: "What is the first purpose of transition words?" FEEDBACK: "Excellent! Transition words make two ideas flow together." SAY: "When ideas flow together, it makes it so the reader will keep reading what we wrote." ASK: "What is the second purpose of transition words?" FEEDBACK: "Very good! Transition words clarify the relationship between two ideas." SAY: "Transitions are so important so that our writing blends together and makes sense, kind of like the radio! When I add a transition, I usually put it at the beginning of the second sentence." ASK: "Where do we put the transition?" FEEDBACK: "Very good! We will put transitions at the beginning of the second sentence." SAY: "There are over 100 words that can be used as transitions, but we are going to focus on only nine of them. We will use comparing transitions, contrasting transitions, and explaining transitions." ASK: "What are the three categories of transitions we'll use?" FEEDBACK: "Fantastic! We have comparing, contrasting, and explaining transitions." SAY: "I am going to pass out this sheet of paper that has our nine transition words and phrases on it." Teacher passes out chart [included at end of lesson plan]. SAY: "Read with me down the lists of transition words. *Similarly, likewise, in addition, however, on the other hand, in contrast, therefore, for example, in other words*." FEEDBACK: "Good job reading all together!" SAY: "These are the transitions we are going to work with."	"To make two ideas flow together." "To clarify the relationship between two ideas." "At the beginning of the second sentence." "Comparing, contrasting, explaining." Students read with teacher.

(Continued)

Lesson Component	Teacher's Instruction, Questions, Feedback, and Sample Error Correction	Anticipated Student Responses
Modeling	SAY: "I am going to show you how to add a transition to a pair of sentences. When I do this, my first step is to read the sentences." Point to the step on the chart. ASK: "What is my first step?" FEEDBACK: "Very good! I have to read the sentences." SAY: "Listen to me read these sentences. *People from Spain were the first to settle in Mexico. The primary language in Mexico is Spanish.*"	"Read the sentences."
	SAY: "Now that I have read the sentences, my second step is to look at the relationship between the sentences." ASK: "What is my second step?" Point to the step on the chart. FEEDBACK: "Super!" SAY: "When I look at the relationship between the sentences I ask myself if the second sentence is comparing, contrasting, or explaining the first one." ASK: "What do I ask myself?" FEEDBACK: "Very good!" SAY: "In asking myself if the second sentence compares, contrasts, or explains the first sentence, I think the second sentence is explaining the first one. It isn't comparing Mexico or the Spanish language with another country and it isn't contrasting Mexico with anywhere else either. So I know that it is explaining something we learned in the first sentence." ASK: "What is my second sentence doing?" FEEDBACK: "Nice job!" SAY: "My third step now is to pick a transition." ASK: "What is my third step?" Point to the step on the chart. FEEDBACK: "Very good, I need to pick a transition." SAY: "When I pick a transition, I look at my chart." ASK: "What do I do when I pick a transition?" FEEDBACK: "Good work! I look at the chart." SAY: "I know that I need an explaining transition because that's what I decided in the second step. So I look at the explaining transitions on my chart and I read the sentences with each explaining transition word." SAY: "Now I will read the sentences with each of the explaining transitions. While I read them, give me a thumbs-up if you think it is a good transition that makes the sentences flow together and a thumbs-down if it's not a good transition.	"Look at the relationship between the sentences." "If the second sentence is comparing, contrasting, or explaining the first one." "Explaining the first one." "Pick a transition." "Look at the chart."

Lesson Component	Teacher's Instruction, Questions, Feedback, and Sample Error Correction	Anticipated Student Responses
	SAY: "People from Spain were the first to settle in Mexico. *For example*, the primary language in Mexico is Spanish.	Thumbs-down
	People from Spain were the first to settle in Mexico. *Therefore*, the primary language in Mexico is Spanish.	Thumbs-up
	People from Spain were the first to settle in Mexico. *In other words*, the primary language in Mexico is Spanish."	Thumbs-down
	SAY: "When I read those, the transition *therefore* made the most sense."	
	ASK: "Which of the transitions made the most sense?"	"*Therefore*"
	FEEDBACK: "Very good!"	
	SAY: "My last step, now, is to write the transition."	
	ASK: "What's my last step?"	"Write the transition."
	FEEDBACK: "Yes, I am going to write the transition."	
	SAY: "I know I write it at the beginning of the second sentence where I put it when I read it, so I will insert it here in the blank that our sentences read: *People from Spain were the first to settle in Mexico. Therefore, the primary language in Mexico is Spanish*."	
	SAY: "And that's how I add a transition to my sentences. Watch me do another one."	
	Follow the script to go through another one or two examples. Possible additional examples are	
	• "In basketball, a player gets 2 points for every shot within the three-point line. [*However or In contrast*], free throws are only worth 1 point."	
	• "To play the piano, you have to know when to push the pedals down. [*Similarly or Likewise*], you have to know when to push the pedals down when you play the organ."	
Guided Practice	SAY: "We are going to do one together now. (Teacher passes out guided and independent practice worksheet.) Look at number 1."	
	ASK: "What is our first step?"	"Read the sentences."
	FEEDBACK: "Very good! We have to read the sentences."	
	SAY: "Let's read these sentences together. *One part of the brain controls your breathing and your heart rate. Another part of the brain controls your memory*."	Students read sentence with teacher.
	FEEDBACK: "Good work reading together, everyone!"	
	ASK: "Now what is our second step?"	"Look at the relationship between the sentences."

(Continued)

(Continued)

Lesson Component	Teacher's Instruction, Questions, Feedback, and Sample Error Correction	Anticipated Student Responses
	FEEDBACK: "Very good! We have to look at the relationship between the sentences."	
	SAY: "When we look at the relationship between the sentences, what do we ask ourselves?"	**"I don't know."**
	SAMPLE ERROR CORRECTION	
	SAY: "Look at your worksheet with the label at the top of the table. Find the words comparing, contrasting, and explaining. We are going to ask ourselves if the second sentence is comparing, contrasting, or explaining the first one."	
	ASK: "When we look at the relationship between the sentences, what do we ask ourselves?" (Repeat if necessary.)	**"If the second sentence is comparing, contrasting, or explaining the first one".**
	FEEDBACK: "Excellent response!"	
	SAY: "I want you all to take a minute and think of what relationship these sentences have."	
	ASK: "What is the relationship of the sentences?"	"Comparing."
	FEEDBACK: "Very good! Our second sentence is comparing one part of the brain to another part of the brain."	
	ASK: "Now we know the relationship, so what is our third step?"	"Pick a transition."
	FEEDBACK: "Very good, we need to pick a transition."	
	ASK: "What do we use to pick a transition?"	"The chart!"
	FEEDBACK: "Fantastic! We use the chart."	
	ASK: "What kind of transitions on the chart are we picking from?"	"The comparing ones!"
	FEEDBACK: "Yes, let's read the sentences together trying each of the comparing transitions.	
	SAY: "One part of the brain controls your breathing and your heart rate. *Similarly*, another part of the brain controls your memory.	Students read sentences with teacher.
	One part of the brain controls your breathing and your heart rate. *Likewise* another part of the brain controls your memory.	
	One part of the brain controls your breathing and your heart rate. *In addition*, another part of the brain controls your memory."	
	ASK: "Which of the transitions made the most sense?"	"*Likewise*" or "*Similarly*"
	FEEDBACK: "That's a good choice!"	
	ASK: "What's our last step?"	"Write the transition."
	FEEDBACK: "Yes, we will write the transition."	
	SAY: "I want you all to write the transition in the blank on number 1."	Students write "*likewise*" or "*similarly*" in the blank.

Lesson Component	Teacher's Instruction, Questions, Feedback, and Sample Error Correction	Anticipated Student Responses
	ASK: "Will you read with me the sentences now that we added a transition?"	"One part of the brain controls your breathing and your heart rate. Similarly, another part of the brain controls your memory."
	FEEDBACK: "Good job everyone!"	
	SAY: "Let's do the second one on your worksheet."	
	ASK: "What is our first step, [student name]?"	"Read the sentences."
	FEEDBACK: "Very good!"	
	ASK: "Will you read the sentences for me, [student name]?"	"Families all over the world are different. Families in China can only have one child and families in Africa have lots of kids."
	FEEDBACK: "Good job reading!"	
	ASK: "Now what is our second step, [student name]?"	"Look at the relationship between the sentences."
	FEEDBACK: "Great job! We have to look at the relationship between the sentences."	
	SAY: "When we look at the relationship between the sentences, what do we ask ourselves, [student name]?"	"If the second one compares, contrasts, or explains the first."
	FEEDBACK: "Very good remembering!"	
	SAY: "I want you all to take a minute and think of what relationship these sentences have."	
	ASK: "What is the relationship of the sentences, [student name]?"	"Comparing."
	SAMPLE ERROR CORRECTION	
	SAY: "Let's look at these sentences again. [student name] please read the sentences aloud. And then add the comparing words from the worksheet between the sentences.	**Student reads sentences.**
	ASK: "Do they make sense?"	**"No."**
	SAY: "[student name] read the contrast words between the sentences.	**Student reads sentences.**
	ASK: Do they make sense?	**"No."**
	SAY: "Now let's all read the sentences with the explanation transition words."	**Students read sentences.**
	ASK: Do they make sense?	**"Yes."**
	ASK: So, what is the relationship of the sentences [student name]?	**"Transition"**

(Continued)

(Continued)

Lesson Component	Teacher's Instruction, Questions, Feedback, and Sample Error Correction	Anticipated Student Responses
	FEEDBACK: "Very good! Our second sentence is explaining what two different types of families in the world look like." ASK: "Now what is our third step, [student name]?" FEEDBACK: "Very good, we need to pick a transition." SAY: "Everyone take a minute to read through the sentences with the different transitions in your head." ASK: "Which of the transitions makes the most sense, [student name]?" FEEDBACK: "That's a good choice!" ASK: "What's our last step, [student name]?" FEEDBACK: "Yes, we will write the transition." SAY: "I want you all to write the transition on your worksheet." ASK: "Will you read the sentences now that we added a transition, [student name]?" FEEDBACK: "Good job everyone!" Follow the script until students no longer need teacher assistance. Then move to independent practice. Add more sentences to ensure students do eight on their own.	"Pick a transition." *"For example"* "Write the transition." Student reads sentences inserting "for example."
Independent Practice	SAY: "Now you're ready to write transitions on your own. Remember to follow all four steps and work carefully. Raise your hand when you finish the first two so I can come check." Teacher walks around to monitor students while they work.	
Closing	SAY: "Today you learned how to add transitions between two sentences to make them flow together and to clarify the relationship between them. This is going to help you write better papers." SAY: "Tomorrow we will practice this again by adding transitions to our rough drafts of our informative papers."	

Guided and Independent Practice Worksheet:

Comparing	Contrasting	Explaining
Similarly	However	For example
Likewise	On the other hand	Therefore
In addition	In contrast	In other words

1. One part of the brain controls your breathing and your heart rate. _____, another part of the brain controls your memory.

2. Families all over the world are different. _____, families in China can only have one child and families in Africa have lots of kids.

3. The leaves of aspen trees turn yellow in the fall. _____, the leaves of maple trees turn red in the fall.

4. All baked goods have a leavening ingredient. _____, bread has yeast in it and cookies have baking soda.

5. You cannot have two pet betta fish live in the same bowl. _____, you can have two cats or two dogs in the same house.

6. The trumpet only has three buttons to push down. _____, a clarinet has at least 18 keys to push down.

7. To be good at tennis you have to know how to serve. _____, to beat someone at ping pong you have to know how to serve.

8. There are 12 months on a calendar used today. _____, the calendar used in Ancient Rome only had 10 months.

9. To calculate the area of a shape, you have to know length and width. _____, you have to know length, width, and height to calculate volume.

10. Tetris used to be the most popular video game. _____, Minecraft is the most popular video game these days.

APPENDIX B: *SAMPLE TEST-TAKING SKILLS SCRIPTED LESSON PLAN*

Topic	Test-Taking Skills
IEP Objective	When given a year-end achievement assessment with multiple choice questions, students will read each question, read all of the possible answers, and mark the best choice for each question with 90% accuracy.
Lesson Objective	When given three sample tests, students will follow the five steps of the DETER strategy with 5/5 correct.
Materials	DETER poster: D—read the **D**irections E—**E**xamine the test T—check the **T**ime E—**E**asy ones first R—**R**eview my work Sample tests worksheets

Lesson Component	Teacher's Questions, Instructions, Feedback, and Sample Error Correction	Anticipated Student Responses
Attending Cue	Teacher rings a bell. SAY: "It's time to put away your math and get ready for our study skills lesson. Let's count to ten to see if everyone can be ready by the time we reach ten." Count to ten with students. FEEDBACK: "Great job!"	Students put away math materials. Count to ten with teacher.
Review & Prerequisite Check	SAY: "We are going to learn a strategy today to help us while we are taking a test. But first, I need to make sure you remember how to prepare for tests." ASK: "How many days should we take to prepare for a test?" FEEDBACK: "Excellent!" SAY: "I want you all to pull out a piece of paper and number it 5, 4, 3, 2, 1. Next to each number write what you do on that day before the test." Teacher collects papers. If students do not remember the 5-day test preparation steps, review those instead of continuing on. SAY: "Thank you for doing that! It looks like you all remember how to prepare for a test."	"5 days!" Students write responses.
Anticipatory Set & Purpose Statement	SAY: "Sometimes we do all of those things you just wrote down to prepare for a test. But when the teacher hands it out, we get stressed and don't do as well on the test as we know we can." ASK: "How many of you have had that happen to you?" FEEDBACK: "It's happened to me too!"	Students raise hands.

Lesson Component	Teacher's Questions, Instructions, Feedback, and Sample Error Correction	Anticipated Student Responses
	SAY: "Today we are going to learn a strategy to help us when we take tests. Students who apply this strategy do better on their tests. This is called the DETER strategy."	
	ASK: "What are we going to learn today?" "What will it help us do?"	"The DETER strategy" "Better on our tests"
	FEEDBACK: "Very good! Let's get started."	
Modeling	SAY: "The DETER strategy is an acronym, which means each of the letters stands for something we will do when we take a test."	
	ASK: "What is the word *DETER*?"	"An acronym."
	FEEDBACK: "Very good!"	
	Teacher displays DETER poster on board.	
	SAY: "This poster has all the letters and what they stand for. When I take a test, I follow the steps on the poster. The first letter is *D*, which stands for directions. The first step is *read the Directions*."	
	ASK: "What is the step I do for the letter *D*?"	"Read the directions."
	FEEDBACK: "Very good! I read the directions."	
	SAY: "On this test, my directions say *Read each question and decide which option best answers the question*. These directions are easy to understand. But sometimes, the directions are hard to understand. When they are, I ask the teacher to explain them."	
	ASK: "What do I do if I don't understand part of the directions?"	"Ask the teacher."
	FEEDBACK: "Excellent!"	
	SAY: "After I read the directions, my next letter is *E*, which stands for *Examine the test*."	
	ASK: "What does the *E* stand for?"	"Examine the test."
	FEEDBACK: "Very good!"	
	SAY: "When I examine the test, I look at the whole test to see how much I have to do. I also look at what types of questions are on the test."	
	ASK: "What do I look at when I examine the test?"	"What types and number of questions on the test."
	FEEDBACK: "Yes, I look at what types and number of questions on the test."	
	SAY: "This test has 15 multiple choice questions."	
	ASK: "What does this test have?"	"15 multiple choice questions."
	FEEDBACK: "Very good!"	
	SAY: "I will write *15 multiple choice* at the top of my paper so I remember there are 15 multiple choice questions. Now that I examined the test, the next letter is *T*. The *T* stands for *check the Time*."	

(Continued)

Lesson Component	Teacher's Questions, Instructions, Feedback, and Sample Error Correction	Anticipated Student Responses
	ASK: "What does the *T* stand for?"	"Check the time."
	FEEDBACK: "Very good responding!"	
	SAY: "I need to determine how much time I should spend answering each question. For this test, it says at the top that I have 30 minutes to complete the test."	
	ASK: "How many minutes do I have to complete this test?"	"30 minutes."
	FEEDBACK: "Yes, this is a test that I have 30 minutes to take!"	
	SAY: "I have 15 questions and 30 minutes, so I divide 30 (number of minutes) by 15 (number of questions), which gives me 2 minutes per question."	
	ASK: "How much time do I have to answer each question?"	"2 minutes."
	FEEDBACK: "Yes!"	
	SAY: "I will write 2 minutes at the top of my paper so I remember how much time I have for each question. My next letter now is the second *E*. This stands for *Easy ones first*."	
	ASK: "What does the second *E* stand for?"	"Easy ones first."
	FEEDBACK: "Very nice! I do the easy ones first."	
	SAY: "To do the easy ones first, I skim through the test and circle the numbers of the questions that will be easy for me to answer."	
	ASK: "What do I do to the ones that will be easy for me to answer?"	"Circle the number."
	FEEDBACK: "Very good!"	
	SAY: "On this test, it looks like questions 1, 2, 5, 7, 10, 11, and 14 will be easy. I circle those numbers, and then I go back and answer the ones I circled first. After I finish the easy ones first, then I answer the rest of the questions."	
	ASK: "Which questions do I answer first?"	"The easy ones!"
	SAY: "My last letter is *R*, which stands for *Review my work*."	
	ASK: "What does the *R* stand for?"	"Review my work."
	FEEDBACK: "Yes, I review my work!"	
	SAY: "I review my work after I finish answering all the questions. If I have time left over, I go back and review my work by checking my answers."	
	ASK: "How do I review my work?"	"Check your answers."
	FEEDBACK: "Excellent! I check my answers."	
	SAY: "Because we don't have time right now, I'll pretend I answered all the questions. I'll check number 1 and 2. When I check the answer, I read the question and my answer and I make sure I chose the best answer. I got number 1 and number 2 right, so I put a check mark next to the number."	
	ASK: "What do I do when I check an answer?"	"Put a check mark next to the number."
	FEEDBACK: "Great! Let's try one together now."	

Lesson Component	Teacher's Questions, Instructions, Feedback, and Sample Error Correction	Anticipated Student Responses
Guided Practice	Teacher passes out worksheet of sample tests.	
	SAY: "We are going to look at sample test 1."	
	ASK: "What is our first step?"	"Read the directions."
	FEEDBACK: "Very good!"	
	SAY: "Let's read the directions all together. *Carefully read each question. Each of the questions is a short answer question. Answer each question with a complete sentence.*"	Students read with teacher.
	FEEDBACK: "Excellent reading everyone!"	
	ASK: "What is our second step?"	"Examine the test."
	FEEDBACK: "Nice job!"	
	ASK: "What do we look at when we examine the test?"	"How hard the test is."
	SAMPLE ERROR CORRECTION	
	SAY: "One of our steps is to look for the easiest questions to answer, but that isn't this step. Examine the test means we look at the types and number of questions."	
	ASK: "What do we look at when we examine the test?"	**"The types and number of questions."**
	FEEDBACK: "Correct! We look at the types and number of questions."	
	ASK: "What types and number of questions are on this test?"	"5 short answer"
	FEEDBACK: "Very good! We have five short-answer questions."	
	SAY: "Let's write that on the top of our test."	Students write *5 short-answer* on the test.
	ASK: "Now what is our third step?"	"Check the time."
	FEEDBACK: "Excellent!"	
	ASK: "How much time do we have for this test?"	"15 minutes."
	FEEDBACK: "Very good!"	
	ASK: "If we have 15 minutes for the test, and 5 questions on the test, how many minutes do we have for each question?"	**"5 minutes."**
	SAMPLE ERROR CORRECTION	
	SAY: "Remember we need to divide the number of minutes by the number of questions on the test."	
	ASK: "So, what do we do on this step?"	**"Divide the number of minutes by the number of questions."**
	FEEDBACK: "Correct!"	
	ASK: "Fifteen (for the number of minutes) divided by five (for the number of questions) equals what?"	**"Three"**
	FEEDBACK: "Yes."	
	ASK: "So how many minutes can we spend on each question?"	**"Three minutes."**

(Continued)

(Continued)

Lesson Component	Teacher's Questions, Instructions, Feedback, and Sample Error Correction	Anticipated Student Responses
	FEEDBACK: "Right! We have 3 minutes per question. Let's write that at the top of the test too."	Write 3 minutes at top of test.
	ASK: "What is our fourth step?"	"Easy ones first."
	FEEDBACK: "Good job! We will do the easy ones first."	
	ASK: "How do we know which ones are the easy ones?"	"We circle the questions."
	FEEDBACK: "That's right. We skim the questions and circle the numbers of the ones that will be easy."	
	SAY: "Everyone take a minute to skim the questions and circle the easy ones."	
	ASK: "What ones did you circle, [student name]?"	"1, 2, and 5."
	FEEDBACK: "Great!"	
	ASK: "Did you circle any different ones, [student name]?"	"I circled 1 and 3."
	FEEDBACK: "Those work too! Because we all know different things, we all have different ones we think are easy."	
	SAY: "Everyone take a minute to answer the first question only. We will pretend we answered all the questions."	
	ASK: "What's our last step?"	"Review my work."
	FEEDBACK: "Very good!"	
	ASK: "And how do we review our work?"	"Check our answers."
	FEEDBACK: "Nice job!"	
	SAY: "I want you all to check your answer to number 1. Make sure you followed the directions to answer in a complete sentence."	
	ASK: "What do you do if it's right?"	"Put a check mark next to it."
	FEEDBACK: "Very good! And if it's not right, change it and check it again."	
	SAY: "That was great using the DETER strategy everyone!"	
	Repeat script as needed with additional practice tests until students no longer need teacher assistance.	
Independent Practice	SAY: "Now you're ready to practice using the DETER strategy on your own. Please read the directions out loud, but quietly. Remember to do all five steps and work carefully."	Practice the DETER strategy on practice tests.
	Teacher walks around to monitor students while the work.	
Closing	SAY: "Today you learned how to use the DETER strategy when we take tests. It will help you do better on your tests. Tomorrow we will practice this strategy even more and try to memorize all the steps."	

Guided and Independent Practice Worksheet:

Sample Test 1:

Name: _____   Date: _____

Time to complete test: 5 minutes

Directions: Carefully read each question. Each of the questions is a short-answer question. Answer each question with a complete sentence.

1. Who was the first president of the United States?

2. During which war did the United States declare independence from Great Britain?

3. Who was the commander of the U.S. Army during this war?

4. Why did the United States declare its independence from Great Britain?

5. Who won the war?

APPENDIX C: *SAMPLE SCRIPTED READING LESSON PLAN*

Topic	Reading Comprehension: Setting
Common Core Standard	2.RL.1. Ask and answer such questions as *who, what, where, when, why*, and *how* to demonstrate understanding of key details in a text.
IEP Objective	Given a second-grade level reading passage, students will identify the main idea and key details of a story, including *who, what, when, where, why,* and *how*, with 100% accuracy.
Unit Objective	Given a second-grade level narrative reading passage, students will identify the main idea and key details with 100% accuracy.
Lesson Objective	Given five second-grade level narrative passages, students will read a passage and write where and when the passage happened with 100% accuracy.
Materials	Finding the Setting chart 1. Read the passage. 2. Find where the event happened. 3. Write where the event happened. 4. Find when the event happened. 5. Write when the event happened.

Lesson Component	Teacher's Instructions, Questions, Feedback, and Sample Error Correction	Anticipated Student Responses
Attending Cue	SAY: "1, 2, 3, eyes on me!" FEEDBACK: "Thank you for looking at me!" SAY: "We're ready to start our lesson. Remember our class rules." (Review the posted rules, as needed).	Students look at teacher.
Review & Prerequisite Check	SAY: "Yesterday we learned how to answer a question when we read a story." ASK: "What question did we learn how to answer?" FEEDBACK: "Very good!" SAY: "I'm going to read 2 very short stories and I want you to tell me the 'who' is in the story." Read 2 short stories and ask students.	"Who?" Students tell who is in the story.
Anticipatory Set & Purpose	ASK: "How many of you like telling stories to your friends?" SAY: "I like telling stories too! Turn to the person next to you and tell them a short story about what you did yesterday after school." ASK: "How many of you told your partner where you were when the story happened?"	Students raise hands. Students tell story to partner. Some students raise their hands.

Lesson Component	Teacher's Instructions, Questions, Feedback, and Sample Error Correction	Anticipated Student Responses
	SAY: "I want you to all tell the story one more time and include where you were when the story happened."	Students retell the stories.
	SAY: "It's important to include where and when the story happened. It helps readers better understand the story and it helps writers better communicate their story to others."	
Instruction	SAY: "An important detail in stories is what we call the *setting*."	
	ASK: "Can you all say that word with me? *Setting*."	"Setting."
	FEEDBACK: "Very good!"	
	SAY: "The setting is where and when the story happens."	
	ASK: "What is the setting?"	"Where and when the story happens."
	FEEDBACK: "Excellent!"	
	SAY: "We want to know the setting because it helps us understand the story better when we know where and when the story happens."	
	SAY: "Tell me one more time what the setting is?"	"Where and when the story happens."
	FEEDBACK: "Fantastic!"	
	SAY: "Today we are going to learn how to identify the setting."	
	ASK: "What are we going to do?"	"Identify the setting."
	FEEDBACK: "Very good! Let's get started."	
Modeling	SAY: "When I identify the setting, my first step is read the passage." [Point to the chart.]	
	ASK: "What's my first step?"	"Read the passage."
	FEEDBACK: "Good job, I read the passage!"	
	SAY: "Listen while I read this passage from *Stuart Little*:	
	One fine morning in the month of May when Stuart was three years old, he arose early as was his custom, washed and dressed himself, took his hat and cane, and went downstairs into the living room to see what was doing. Nobody was around but Snowbell, the white cat belonging to Mrs. Little.	
	(From *Stuart Little* by E. B. White, p. 17)	
	SAY: "After I read the passage, my second step is to find where the event happened." [Point to the chart.]	
	ASK: "What is my second step?"	"Find where the event happened."
	FEEDBACK: "Excellent!"	

(Continued)

(Continued)

Lesson Component	Teacher's Instructions, Questions, Feedback, and Sample Error Correction	Anticipated Student Responses
	SAY: "To find where the event happened, I skim over the passage again. I need to see if it talks about where the event happened. I see here that it talks about the living room, but that's where he went after he woke up. So I'm going to guess that he woke up in his bedroom. And all these are part of their house. So this takes place in the house."	
	ASK: "Where does this take place?"	"The house"
	FEEDBACK: "Nice!"	
	SAY: "My third step is to write where the event happened." [Point to the chart.]	
	ASK: "What is my third step?"	"Write where the event happened."
	FEEDBACK: "Excellent!"	
	SAY: "Since I decided it took place in the house, I will write *house* on the line."	
	ASK: "What will I write on the line?"	"House"
	FEEDBACK: "Very good!"	
	SAY: "My fourth step, now, is to find when the event happened." [Point to the chart.]	
	ASK: "What is my fourth step?"	"Find when the event happened."
	FEEDBACK: "Great job!"	
	SAY: "I look back at the passage and see that it says, 'One fine morning in the month of May when Stuart was three years old . . .' I think that describes when the event happened."	
	SAY: "Now my last step is to write when the event happened." [Point to the chart.]	
	ASK: "What is my last step?"	"Write when the event happened."
	FEEDBACK: "Very good responding!"	
	SAY: "I will write *morning*, *May*, and *when Stuart was 3* on the line because those are the three things I know about when the event happened."	
	ASK: "What did I write on the line?"	
	FEEDBACK: "Fantastic!"	"Morning, May, and when Stuart was 3."
	SAY: "And that is how I identify the setting in a passage."	
	Provide one to three more examples depending on student responses.	
Guided Practice	SAY: "Let's do one together now."	
	ASK: "What is our first step?"	"Read the passage."
	FEEDBACK: "Very good!"	
	SAY: "Let's read the passage all together. *It was an afternoon in late September. In the pleasant little city of Stillwater, Mr. Popper, the house painter, was going home from work. He was carrying his buckets, his ladders, and his boards so that he had rather a hard time moving along* (From *Mr. Popper's Penguins* by Richard and Florence Atwater, p. 1)."	Students read with teacher.

Lesson Component	Teacher's Instructions, Questions, Feedback, and Sample Error Correction	Anticipated Student Responses
	ASK: "What is our second step?"	"Find where the event happened."
	FEEDBACK: "Good work everyone!"	
	SAY: "I want you all to think about where the event happened."	
	ASK: "Where did the event happen?"	"In Stillwater"
	FEEDBACK: "Excellent! It says it happened "In the little city of Stillwater."	
	ASK: "What is our third step?"	"Write where the event happened."
	FEEDBACK: "Awesome! We write where the event happened."	
	ASK: "What are we going to write?"	"Stillwater."
	FEEDBACK: "Great work everyone!"	
	SAY: "Take a minute to write that on your line."	
	ASK: "What is our next step?"	"Find when the event happened."
	FEEDBACK: "Very good!"	
	SAY: "Take a minute to look for when the event happened."	
	ASK: "When did the event happen?"	**"In the afternoon."**
	SAMPLE ERROR CORRECTION	
	SAY: "You're right. It happened in the afternoon. Let's read the passage again to see if there is even more information about when it happened."	**Reread the passage with the teacher.**
	Read the passage with students.	
	ASK: "Does the author tell us something else about when it happened?"	"In late September."
	SAY: "Right! In late September. We can't stop at the first answer we find about when the event happened. We read the passage carefully to make certain we get all the information about when it happened."	
	ASK: "When did the event happen?"	**"An afternoon in late September."**
	FEEDBACK: "Very good!"	
	ASK: "And what is our last step?"	"Write when the event happened."
	FEEDBACK: "Good job!"	
	SAY: "I want you all to write when the event happened."	Students write.
	ASK: "What did you write down, [student name]?"	"An afternoon in late September."
	FEEDBACK: "Fantastic work everyone!"	
	SAY: "Let's do one more together."	
	ASK: "What is our first step, [student name]?"	"Read the passage."
	FEEDBACK: "Great job!"	
	SAY: "Read the passage to yourself. Give me a thumbs-up when you're done." *Momma was the only one who wasn't born in Flint so the cold was coldest to her. All you could see were her eyes too, and they were shooting bad looks at Dad. She always blamed him for bringing her all the way from Alabama to Michigan, a state she called a giant icebox.*	

(Continued)

Appendix C   599

(Continued)

Lesson Component	Teacher's Instructions, Questions, Feedback, and Sample Error Correction	Anticipated Student Responses
	(From *The Watsons Go to Birmingham*, by Christopher Paul Curtis, p. 2) ASK: "What is our second step, [student name]?" FEEDBACK: "Great!" SAY: "Everyone find where it happened." ASK: "Where did the event happen, [student name]?" FEEDBACK: "Super!" ASK: "What is our third step, [student name]?" FEEDBACK: "Awesome!" SAY: "I want you all to write where the event happened." ASK: "What is our fourth step, [student name]?" FEEDBACK: "Good job!" SAY: "Think hard about when the event happened. You may have to use your context clues to figure this one out." ASK: "When did the event happen, [student name]?" FEEDBACK: "Nice! That's good use of your context clues." ASK: "And what is our last step, [student name]?" FEEDBACK: "Great job!" SAY: "Everyone do the last step." SAY: "Now you're ready to find and write down the setting on your own. Remember to follow all five steps and work carefully. Raise your hand when you finish the first one so I can come check." [Worksheet should have five passages.] Teacher walks around to monitor students while they work.	"Find where the event happened." "Flint, Michigan." "Write where the event happened." "Find when the event happened." "Winter" "Write when the event happened." Students write. Students complete worksheet.
Closing	SAY: "Today you learned how to identify when and where a story takes place." ASK: "What do we call the when and where of a story?" FEEDBACK: "Yes, the setting!" ASK: "And what was the other part of a story we learned about yesterday?" FEEDBACK: "You are correct, we learned to identify who in the story." SAY: "Tomorrow we will practice some more identifying the who and the setting with other stories."	"The setting" "Who"

APPENDIX D: *SCRIPTED MATH LESSON PLAN*

Topic	Fractions
Common Core Standard	4.NF.B.3.a. Understand addition and subtraction of fractions as joining and separating parts referring to the same whole.
IEP Objective	Given a worksheet of 20 addition problems involving proper fractions with like denominators, students will solve and write the sum as a proper fraction or mixed number with at least 90% accuracy on 3/3 trials.
Unit Objective	Given 20 addition problems with addends that are proper fractions with like denominators and sums that are less than one whole, students will solve and write the sum with at least 90% accuracy.
Lesson Objective	Given 15 pictures representing proper fractions with denominators less than or equal to 12, students will write the fraction the picture represents with 13/15 correct.
Materials	Graham cracker

Independent practice worksheet

Write the steps on the board:

1. Count all the parts in the whole.

2. Write the denominator.

3. Count the parts.

4. Write the numerator. |

Lesson Component	Teacher's Instructions, Questions, Feedback, and Sample Error Correction	Anticipated Student Responses
Attending Cue	SAY: "Eyes on me, everyone. We're ready to start our math lesson. Remember to sit in learning position and answer on my cue."	Students look at teacher.
Review & Prerequisite Check	SAY: "Yesterday we learned about denominators." ASK: "Where does the denominator go in a fraction, everyone?" FEEDBACK: "That's right! The denominator is the bottom number of a fraction." ASK: "What does the denominator tell us?" FEEDBACK: "That's absolutely correct. The denominator tells us how many parts are in the whole thing." SAY: "I'd like to see how much you remember about denominators. Here's a review sheet that looks just like the one we did yesterday. Next to each circle, write the denominator of the fraction the picture shows." ASK: "Where do you write the denominator?" FEEDBACK: "Very good!" Teacher hands out review sheet.	"On the bottom!" "How many parts are in the whole." "On the bottom."

(Continued)

Lesson Component	Teacher's Instructions, Questions, Feedback, and Sample Error Correction	Anticipated Student Responses
	SAY: "Here is the worksheet. Work quickly and quietly. Do your best. When you finish, raise your hand and I will check your work."	Students complete review sheet.
	Teacher monitors student work. If students accurately complete the review sheet, the teacher continues with the lesson. If students do not demonstrate mastery, teacher reteaches concept from the previous lesson.	Raise hands when review sheet is complete.
	SAY: "Thanks for completing the review sheet. You did a great job remembering what you learned about denominators! Knowing about denominators is really important for our lesson today."	
Anticipatory Set & Purpose	SAY: "Look what I found in the teacher's lounge this morning. It's a graham cracker. I'm so glad I found it because I'm really hungry." (Teacher eats ¼ of the graham cracker.)	
	ASK: "Do I still have a whole cracker?"	"No."
	SAY: "You're right; I don't have a whole cracker anymore. But, I do have some of the parts of the graham cracker left. A fraction will tell us what part of the whole cracker I have left."	
	ASK: "What will tell me what part I have left?"	"A fraction!"
	FEEDBACK: "Very good!	
	SAY: "Today we're going to learn more about fractions which are important to understand because many things we use in our lives involves fractions, like money, time, and cooking."	
Instruction	SAY: "Fractions have two numbers. (Teacher points to the bottom box.) You've already learned about the bottom number."	
	ASK: "What is the bottom number called?"	"The denominator."
	FEEDBACK: "Yes, the bottom number is called the *denominator*."	
	SAY: (Teacher points to the top box.) "The number that goes on the top is called the numerator. Everyone say numerator with me. *Numerator*. The numerator is the top number of the fraction."	"Numerator."
	ASK: "Where is the numerator?"	"On top."
	FEEDBACK: "Good job!"	
	SAY: "And what is the top number called?"	"Numerator."
	SAY: "Yes, the top number is called the numerator. Say numerator one more time."	"Numerator."

Lesson Component	Teacher's Instructions, Questions, Feedback, and Sample Error Correction	Anticipated Student Responses
	Teacher continues until students correctly identify the top number as the numerator. Practice discriminating between the numerator and denominator. SAY: "Today you will learn how to write complete fractions with a numerator and a denominator." ASK: "What will you learn?" FEEDBACK: "Nice! Let's get started."	"How to write complete fractions with a numerator and a denominator."
Instruction	SAY: "The numerator tells us the number of parts we have out of the whole." ASK: "What does the numerator tell us?" FEEDBACK: "Excellent. The numerator tells us how many parts we have out of the whole." SAY: "The numerator is different from the denominator. The denominator tells us how many parts are in the whole thing. The numerator tells us how many parts of those parts we actually have." ASK: "What does the denominator tell us?" FEEDBACK: "Super! The denominator tells us how many parts are in the whole thing." ASK: "And what does the numerator tell us?" FEEDBACK: "Yes, the numerator tells us the number of parts we have out of the whole."	"The number of parts we have out of the whole." "How many parts are in the whole thing." "How many parts we have."
Modeling	SAY: "Let's look at an example that looks just like my graham cracker. Here is a picture of a rectangle that looks like my cracker. (Display a rectangle divided into fourths with three shaded.) I am going to show you how we write the complete fraction that this picture represents." SAY: "Let's look at the picture. My first step is to count all the parts in the whole." ASK: "What do I do first?" FEEDBACK: "Very good! First, I count all the parts in the whole." SAY: "Count the parts with me—1, 2, 3, 4." FEEDBACK: "Great counting! There are four parts in the whole." SAY: "My second step is to write the denominator."	"Count all the parts in the whole." "1, 2, 3, 4."

(Continued)

Lesson Component	Teacher's Instructions, Questions, Feedback, and Sample Error Correction	Anticipated Student Responses
	ASK: "What's my second step?"	"Write the denominator."
	FEEDBACK: "Very good! My second step is to write the denominator."	
	SAY: "Remember that my denominator is on the bottom of the fraction. My denominator is 4 because there are four parts in the whole."	
	ASK: "What's my denominator?"	"4."
	FEEDBACK: "Yes, my denominator is 4."	
	SAY: "I will write a 4 right here. Now my third step is to count the parts I have."	
	ASK: "What's my third step?"	"Count the parts I have."
	FEEDBACK: "Yes, I count the parts I have."	
	SAY: "If you think back to my cracker, the shaded parts represent what I have and the white represents the part that is gone because I ate it. Since we want to count the parts I have, count the shaded parts with me—1, 2, 3."	"1, 2, 3."
	FEEDBACK: "Thank you for counting out loud with me!"	
	SAY: "I have three parts. My last step, now, is to write the numerator."	
	ASK: "What's my last step?"	"Write the numerator."
	FEEDBACK: "Great job! My last step is to write the numerator."	
	SAY: "The numerator tells me how many parts I have. Since I have three parts, my numerator is 3."	
	ASK: "What's my numerator?"	"3."
	FEEDBACK: "Very good! My numerator is three because I have three shaded parts."	
	SAY: "I will write my numerator above the fraction line because the numerator goes on top of the fraction."	
	ASK: "Where does my numerator go?"	"On top of the fraction."
	FEEDBACK: "Very nice everyone!"	
	SAY: "We now have a complete fraction with both a numerator and a denominator! This fraction is 3/4."	
	ASK: "What is this fraction?"	"3/4."
	SAY: "I'm going to show you how to do another one."	
	Teacher follows same script to model one to four more examples, depending on student responses. Possible examples: 4/7, 3/8, 2/5, 8/11.	

Lesson Component	Teacher's Instructions, Questions, Feedback, and Sample Error Correction	Anticipated Student Responses
Guided Practice	SAY: "Now let's do some examples together. Please pull out a sheet of paper. Now look at this picture on the board."	
	ASK: "What is our first step, everyone?"	"Count all the parts in the whole."
	FEEDBACK: "Perfect! Yes, we count all the parts in the whole."	
	SAY: "Let's count the parts together. Point to each part as we count out loud. Ready, 1, 2, 3, 4, 5, 6, 7, 8."	"1, 2, 3, 4, 5, 6, 7, 8."
	FEEDBACK: "Good job counting together everyone. There are eight parts in the whole picture."	
	ASK: "What is our second step?"	"Write the denominator."
	FEEDBACK: "Yes, we write the denominator."	
	ASK: "What is our denominator everyone?"	"8."
	FEEDBACK: "Very good! Our denominator is 8."	
	ASK: "Where do we write the denominator?"	"On the bottom."
	FEEDBACK: "Yes, everyone draw a fraction bar and write an 8 on the bottom for our denominator."	
	ASK: "What's our third step everyone?"	"Count the parts we have."
	FEEDBACK: "Yes, our third step is to count how many parts we have."	
	SAY: "Let's count how many parts we have together—1, 2, 3, 4, 5."	"1, 2, 3, 4, 5."
	FEEDBACK: "Thank you for counting together. We have five parts."	
	ASK: "What's our last step?"	"Write the numerator."
	FEEDBACK: "Good job, we write the numerator."	
	ASK: "What's my numerator everyone?"	"5."
	FEEDBACK: "Yes, our numerator is 5 because we have five parts."	
	ASK: "And where does the numerator go?"	"On the top."
	FEEDBACK: "Very good!"	
	SAY: "Let's write our numerator of 5 on the top of the fraction."	
	SAY: "And now we have a fraction! This fraction is 5/8."	
	ASK: "What is our fraction?"	"5/8."
	SAY: "Now let's do one more out loud. Look at next picture on the board."	

(Continued)

(Continued)

Lesson Component	Teacher's Instructions, Questions, Feedback, and Sample Error Correction	Anticipated Student Responses
	ASK: "What is our first step, [student name]?"	"Count all the parts in the whole."
	FEEDBACK: "Perfect!"	
	SAY: "Everyone count the parts in your head."	
	ASK: "What is our second step, [student name]?"	"Write the denominator."
	FEEDBACK: "Nice job!"	
	ASK: "Will you all write down the denominator on your paper?"	Students write the denominator.
	FEEDBACK: "Very nice!"	
	ASK: "What's our third step [student name]?"	"Count the parts I have."
	FEEDBACK: "Very good!"	
	SAY: "Everyone take a minute to count how many we have."	
	ASK: "What's our last step [student name]?"	"Write the numerator."
	FEEDBACK: "Great work."	
	SAY: "Everyone write down our numerator. And now we have another complete fraction!"	**Student writes 8/5.**
	SAMPLE ERROR CORRECTION	
	SAY: "I see that we could use a review on where we write the numbers."	
	ASK: "Does the numerator or denominator go on the bottom?"	**"Denominator."**
	FEEDBACK: "You're correct. The denominator goes on the bottom."	
	ASK: "In this problem, which number is the denominator?"	**"8."**
	FEEDBACK: "Yes, 8 is the denominator because the denominator represents how many parts there are in the whole."	
	SAY: "Where do we write the number 8?"	**"On the bottom."**
	FEEBACK: "That's right. The denominator always goes on the bottom."	
	ASK: "Does the numerator or denominator go on the bottom?"	**"Denominator."**
	FEEDBACK: "Right!"	
	Repeat script as needed with additional examples until students need little teacher assistance.	
Independent Practice	SAY: "Now you're ready to write fractions on your own. Remember to follow all four steps and work carefully. Raise your hand when you finish the second line so I can come and check."	
	Teacher walks around to monitor students while they work.	

Lesson Component	Teacher's Instructions, Questions, Feedback, and Sample Error Correction	Anticipated Student Responses
Closing	SAY: "Today you learned how to write a complete fraction with both a numerator and denominator. Thank you for working hard and following our class rules. Tomorrow we will practice this some more and then we will learn about mixed numbers."	

Independent Practice Worksheet

1.

2.

3.

4.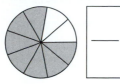

5.

6.

7.

8.

9.

10.

11.

12.

13.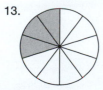

14.

15.

APPENDIX E: *SAMPLE SCRIPTED SOCIAL STUDIES LESSON PLAN*

Topic	Analyzing Primary Sources
Utah State Core Standard	5.SS.4.3. Evaluate the course of events of the Civil War and its impact both immediate and long term.
	5.SS.4.3.a. Identify the key ideas, events, and leaders of the Civil War using primary sources (e.g., Gettysburg Address, Emancipation Proclamation, news accounts, photographic records, diaries).
IEP Objective	Given an oral prompt, students will orally explain the immediate and long-term effects of the Civil War on slavery in America including at least five important people and events.
Lesson Objective	Given six primary sources related to the Civil War, students will identify and write who the source is from, the main idea of the source, and its effect on the Civil War with 15/18 parts correct.
Materials	Write the definition of primary sources and the following instructions on the board. 1. Read the source. 2. Write who the source is from. 3. Write the main idea of the source. 4. Write how the source affected the Civil War.

Lesson Component	Teacher's Instructions, Questions, Feedback, and Sample Error Correction	Anticipated Student Responses
Attending Cue	SAY: "Hello my fellow American citizens! Let's get ready for our U.S. history lesson."	Students attend to teacher.
Review & Prerequisite Check	SAY: "Before we start today's lesson, I need to make sure that you remember some of the important people in the Civil War."	
	ASK: "Who was president of the United States during the war?"	"Abraham Lincoln."
	FEEDBACK: "Very good!"	
	ASK: "Who was the leader or president of the Confederate States of America?"	"Robert E. Lee."
	FEEDBACK: "Not quite. Jefferson Davis was the leader or president of the Confederate States of America."	
	ASK: "Who was the leader or president of the Confederate States of America?"	"Jefferson Davis."
	FEEDBACK: "Exactly!"	
	ASK: "Who was the general for the Union during the Civil War?"	"Ulysses S. Grant."
	FEEDBACK: "Excellent remembering!"	
	ASK: "And who was the general for the Confederacy during the war?"	"Robert E. Lee."
	FEEDBACK: "Great job!"	
	SAY: "I have one more bonus question. I'll give you 10 seconds to think about it."	"Appomattox Courthouse."
	ASK: "Where did the Civil War end?"	

Lesson Component	Teacher's Instructions, Questions, Feedback, and Sample Error Correction	Anticipated Student Responses
	FEEDBACK: "Excellent!!" SAY: "It is very important for us to remember Abraham Lincoln, Jefferson Davis, Ulysses S. Grant, Robert E. Lee, and the Appomattox Courthouse for our lesson today."	
Anticipatory Set	SAY: "Today we are going to learn how to look at and understand primary sources about the Civil War." ASK: "What are we going to learn?"	"How to look at and understand primary sources."
Instruction & Purpose Statement	SAY: "Primary sources are original documents, pictures, or objects created during the time period we are studying." ASK: "What are primary sources?" [If students don't respond with the correct definition, repeat the definition and ask once again.] FEEDBACK: "Very good!" SAY: "We probably think that primary sources look like really old pieces of paper. That is true, but I don't have access to the pieces of paper that Abraham Lincoln touched because those are in museums. It's still considered a primary source if it's the same words that are on those original documents." ASK: "Do primary sources have to be really old pieces of paper?" FEEDBACK: "Right!" SAY: "Primary sources are important to us because they help us learn about history from the people that were there. In secondary sources someone else has interpreted the primary source and they may be right or wrong in their interpretation." ASK: "Why are primary sources important?" FEEDBACK: "Very good! The people that were there know more about history than we do." SAY: "Let's get started with looking at Civil War primary sources."	"Original documents, pictures, or objects created during the time period we are studying." "No!" "They help us learn history from people that were there."

Modeling	SAY: "When I look at a primary source, my first step is to read the source."
	
	ASK: "What is my first step?"
	
	FEEDBACK: "Very good! I read the source."
	
	SAY: "I am going to read the source including the information at the top that tells us what the source is. This source says
	
	    Gettysburg Address
	
	    Abraham Lincoln
	
	    November 19, 1863."
	
	ASK: "What do you remember about the Gettysburg Address? We talked about it last week."
		"Read the source."
		
		"Abraham Lincoln wrote it quickly and delivered it on a battlefield."

(Continued)

(Continued)

Lesson Component	Teacher's Instructions, Questions, Feedback, and Sample Error Correction	Anticipated Student Responses
	SAY: "That's correct. Well, now we are actually going to get to read the Gettysburg Address! This is considered a primary source because it's an original document from the Civil War time period. Let's read this primary source."	
	[Read the Gettysburg Address as a class using group oral reading.]	Read the Gettysburg Address.
	FEEDBACK: "Excellent reading everyone!"	
	SAY: "Now that I've read the source, my next step is to write who the source is from."	
	ASK: "What is my second step?"	"Write who the source is from."
	FEEDBACK: "Yes, I write who the source is from."	
	SAY: "I know that at the top it says Abraham Lincoln. I also remember that last week we talked about how Abraham Lincoln gave the Gettysburg Address, so I know my source is from Abraham Lincoln."	
	ASK: "Who is my source from?"	"Abraham Lincoln!"
	FEEDBACK: "Very nice! I will write Abraham Lincoln."	
	SAY: "My third step is to write the main idea of the source."	
	ASK: "What is my third step?"	"Write the main idea of the source."
	FEEDBACK: "Excellent work."	
	SAY: "When I try to say what the main idea is, I have to look back at the source and ask myself what the source was about. I can also use my background knowledge to help me."	
	ASK: "What can I use to help me find the main idea?"	"The source and your background knowledge."
	FEEDBACK: "Yes!"	
	SAY: "I see that Abraham Lincoln said, 'We here highly resolve these dead shall not have died in vain.' I also see that a little bit earlier he talks about how the battlefield is the 'final resting place for those who died here, that the nation might live.' He's talking a lot about remembering those who died. Then, using my background knowledge, I remember that the Gettysburg Address was given after the Battle of Gettysburg where there were over 50,000 casualties. So knowing those things, I would say that the main idea of the Gettysburg Address is to remember all the people that died fighting for America during the Civil War."	
	ASK: "What is the main idea of the Gettysburg Address?"	"To remember all the people that died fighting for America during the war."
	FEEDBACK: "Very good! I will write that on my paper as the main idea."	
	Teacher writes the sentence on the board.	
	SAY: "My last step in looking at the primary source is to write how the source affected the Civil War."	
	ASK: "What is my last step?"	"Write how the source affected the Civil War."
	FEEDBACK: "Perfect!"	

Lesson Component	Teacher's Instructions, Questions, Feedback, and Sample Error Correction	Anticipated Student Responses
	SAY: "So I need to ask myself how the Gettysburg Address affected the Civil War. This was in the middle of the war and I remember that it inspired the Union to fight harder against slavery."	
	ASK: "What did the Gettysburg Address inspire the Union to do?"	"Fight harder against slavery."
	FEEDBACK: "Very good!"	
	SAY: "I will write here that *It inspired the Union to fight harder against slavery.* And that is the process I go through to look at primary sources from the Civil War."	
Guided Practice	SAY: "Let's look at another primary source together now."	
	ASK: "What is our first step, everyone?"	"Read the source."
	FEEDBACK: "Very good! Let's read the source together."	
	[Read the excerpt from Jefferson Davis's Speech to the Senate as a class, using a classroom strategy such as teacher reading, group oral reading, or partner reading.]	
	SAY: "Excellent reading everyone."	
	ASK: "What is our second step?"	"Write who the source is from."
	FEEDBACK: "Very good!"	
	ASK: "Who is this source from?"	"Jefferson Davis!"
	FEEDBACK: "Very good! It's from Jefferson Davis, just like it says at the top."	
	SAY: "I want you all to write that down."	Write Jefferson Davis.
	ASK: "Now what is our third step, everyone?"	"Write the main idea of the source."
	FEEDBACK: "Excellent! We need to write the main idea of the source."	
	SAY: "I want you all to take a minute and think about what you think the main idea of the speech is. Remember that you can use your background knowledge about Jefferson Davis to help you." [After a minute or two . . .] "Now turn to the person next to you and talk about what you think the main idea is."	
	ASK: "What did you decide is the main idea of the passage?"	**"We don't know."**
	SAMPLE ERROR CORRECTION	
	SAY: "Let's go back and look at the reading passage together and use what we've already learned about identifying the main idea."	
	[Read several different passages as a class while asking students if they think that could be a main idea and why or why not. Assist students in narrowing down to several possible main ideas and then the overarching main idea.]	
	ASK: "So what did we decide is the main idea?"	"Jefferson Davis supports Mississippi in leaving the Union. Mississippi seceded from the Union."
	[Write the answer on the board.]	

(Continued)

(Continued)

Lesson Component	Teacher's Instructions, Questions, Feedback, and Sample Error Correction	Anticipated Student Responses
	SAY: "I want you all to write on your paper what the main idea is." ASK: "What is our last step?" FEEDBACK: "Excellent!" SAY: "Take a minute to think about how this speech affected the Civil War."	"Write how the source affected the Civil War."
	ASK: "What are some ways that this affected the Civil War?" FEEDBACK: "Very good responses!" SAY: "There are a lot of ways that the secession of states from the Union affected the Civil War. Take a few minutes and write down how you think the source affected the Civil War." FEEDBACK: "Good job everyone!"	Possible answers: "Jefferson Davis led the Confederacy after he left." "Mississippi was one of the states that left."
	SAY: "Let's do one more together. Look at the next one, which is the excerpt from Abraham Lincoln's A House Divided speech." ASK: "What is our first step, [student name]?" FEEDBACK: "Very good!"	"Read the source."
	SAY: "Everyone take a minute to read the source silently. Give me a thumbs-up when you're done." ASK: "What is our second step, [student name]?" FEEDBACK: "Perfect!"	"Write who the source is from."
	SAY: "Everyone write who the source is from." ASK: "What did you write, [student name]?" FEEDBACK: "That is correct!"	"Abraham Lincoln."
	ASK: "What is our third step, [student name]?" FEEDBACK: "Excellent!"	"Write the main idea of the source."
	SAY: "Everyone, look at the source and use your background knowledge to decide on the main idea and write it down." ASK: "What is our last step, [student name]?" FEEDBACK: "Perfect!"	"Write how the source affected the Civil War."
	SAY: "I want you all to write down how this affected the Civil War." FEEDBACK: "Very good looking at primary source everyone!" Continue the steps if needed based on student responses.	
Independent Practice	SAY: "I think you're ready to do them on your own. Remember to do all four steps that are written on the board to help you remember."	Students complete independent practice worksheet.
Closing	SAY: "Thank you for your hard work. We learned how to look at and understand primary sources from the Civil War. Tomorrow we will look at other types of primary sources like pictures and letters."	

Sample Practice Worksheet

Excerpt from *Emancipation Proclamation*
Abraham Lincoln
September 22, 1862

"That on the first day of January, in the year of our Lord one thousand eight hundred and sixty-three, all persons held as slaves within any State or designated part of a State, the people whereof shall then be in rebellion against the United States, shall be then, thenceforward, and forever free; and the Executive Government of the United States, including the military and naval authority thereof, will recognize and maintain the freedom of such persons, and will do no act or acts to repress such persons, or any of them, in any efforts they may make for their actual freedom."

Who: _____

What: _____

_____

How affected the Civil War: _____

_____

Possible additional primary sources:

- South Carolina Secession Act

- Robert E. Lee's farewell to the Army of North Virginia

- Thirteenth Amendment of the Constitution

- Letter from Ulysses S. Grant to his father, April 1861

- General Order No. 66, 28 June 1863

Topic	Making Requests
IEP Objective	Given a prompt to make a request, greet someone, get the teacher's attention, and accept feedback, students will perform each step of the social skill as listed on a checklist with 100% accuracy on 5/5 trials.
Lesson Objective	Given a prompt to make a request of the teacher or another student, students will look at the person, get their attention, make the request, and say "thank you" after the request is granted on 3/3 trials.
Materials	Write on the board: 1. Look at the person. 2. Get their attention. 3. Make the request. 4. Say thank you. Bowl of candy

Lesson Component	Teacher's Instructions, Questions, Feedback, and Sample Error Correction	Anticipated Student Responses
Attending	SAY: "Let's do three jumping jacks together. 1, 2, 3. Ok, time to sit back down in ready position!"	Students do jumping jacks and sit down.
Review	SAY: "Last week we learned how to get the teacher's attention appropriately. I'd like to see if you remember how to get my attention appropriately. I'm going to ask some questions. If you have an answer, get my attention appropriately, and I will call on you." ASK: "Are you all ready for my questions?" FEEDBACK: "Very good responding all together!" ASK: "What is your favorite color?" [Call on one student and have them answer.] FEEDBACK: "Good job raising your hand and waiting until I called on you to answer." Ask additional questions until each student has had the chance to answer at least one question after getting the teacher's attention appropriately. SAY: "Very good job with getting my attention everyone!"	"Yes!" Students raise hands.
Anticipatory Set & Purpose Statement	SAY: "I have this bowl of wrapped candy here. They look pretty delicious." ASK: "How many of you would like one of these?" SAY: "I would love to give them all to you, but only after you ask for one. Today we are going to learn how to make a request." ASK: "What are we going to learn?"	Students raise hands. "How to make a request."

Lesson Component	Teacher's Instructions, Questions, Feedback, and Sample Error Correction	Anticipated Student Responses
	SAY: "It's important for us to know how to make requests so that we can nicely ask for what we want. We make requests all the time. For example, when you order a hamburger at McDonald's, you are making a request. Or when you ask your friend to borrow a pencil, you are making a request!"	
Modeling	SAY: "When I make a request, my first step is to look at the person."	
	ASK: "What is my first step?"	"Look at the person."
	FEEDBACK: "Very good! I look at a person when I make a request."	
	SAY: "I am going to make a request for a candy from [student name], so I will look at him."	
	SAY: "My second step is to get their attention."	
	ASK: "What is my second step?"	"Get their attention."
	FEEDBACK: "Excellent! I get their attention."	
	SAY: "Since I am making a request of [student name], I get his attention. When I am making a request of the teacher, I raise my hand and follow the steps we learned to get the teacher's attention. When I am making a request of another student, I say their name."	
	ASK: "How do I get the teacher's attention?"	"Raise your hand."
	FEEDBACK: "Very good!"	
	ASK: "And how do I get the attention of another student?"	"Say their name."
	FEEDBACK: "Good job!"	
	SAY: "I am getting the attention of another student so I will say his name. My third step is to make the request."	
	ASK: "What's my third step?"	"Make the request."
	FEEDBACK: "Very good!"	
	SAY: "To make the request is another way to say that I ask them my question. My request right now is to ask [student name] for a candy. So I say '[student name], can I please have one of your candies?' When I make a request I have to ask politely."	
	ASK: "How do I have to ask?"	"Politely."
	FEEDBACK: "Very good! We must ask politely."	
	SAY: "My last step is to say 'thank you' after my request is granted."	
	ASK: "What is my last step?"	"Say thank you!"
	FEEDBACK: "Excellent!"	
	SAY: "[Student name] gave me a candy and granted my request, so I will say 'Thank you [student name]!' And that is how I make a request."	
	Demonstrate with two or three more examples, depending on student responses.	

(Continued)

Lesson Component	Teacher's Instructions, Questions, Feedback, and Sample Error Correction	Anticipated Student Responses
Guided Practice	SAY: "Let's practice saying the steps together so that we can memorize them. Say each step as I point to it."	"Look at the person.
		Get their attention.
	FEEDBACK: "Fantastic responding all together!"	Make the request.
	Practice orally three or four more times, erasing a step each time, until students can say all four steps without visual prompts.	Say thank you!"
	SAY: "Remember my bowl of candy? We are going to practice making a request for candy. The good news is that you get to have one if you can appropriately make the request all together."	
	ASK: "What is our first step?"	"Look at the person."
	FEEDBACK: "Very good! Looks like you're all looking at me!"	
	ASK: "What is our second step?"	"Get their attention."
	FEEDBACK: "Excellent remembering!"	
	SAY: "Show me how you will all get my attention."	Students raise hands.
	ASK: "What is our third step?"	"Make the request."
	FEEDBACK: "Nice job!"	
	SAY: "To ask me for a candy, I want you all to politely ask me by saying 'May I please have a candy?'"	"May I please have a candy?"
	FEEDBACK: "Thank you for saying that all together!"	
	SAY: "You all said that so politely after getting my attention appropriately, so I will give you all a candy to enjoy."	
	ASK: "Now what's our last step?"	"Say thank you!"
	FEEDBACK: "Very good! We say thank you after the request is granted."	
	SAY: "I want to hear a chorus of thank yous!"	"Thank you!"
	FEEDBACK: "Excellent everyone!"	
	SAY: "Now I want each of you to practice asking another student for a new pencil. Get in pairs."	
	ASK: "What is our first step, [student name]?"	"Look at the person."
	FEEDBACK: "Very good!"	
	SAY: "Everyone show me what that looks like with your partner."	
	ASK: "What is our second step, [student name]?"	"Get their attention."
	FEEDBACK: "Excellent!"	
	SAY: "Show me how you will get the attention of another student."	**"Raise my hand."**
	SAMPLE ERROR CORRECTION	
	SAY: "When we want to get the attention of the teacher we raise our hand. When we want to get the attention of another student we say their name."	

Lesson Component	Teacher's Instructions, Questions, Feedback, and Sample Error Correction	Anticipated Student Responses
	ASK: "How do we get the attention of another student?"	**"Say their name."**
	FEEDBACK: "Yes!"	
	ASK: "How do we get the attention of the teacher?"	**"Raise my hand."**
	FEEDBACK: "You are so smart."	
	SAY: "Show me how you will get the attention of another student."	Students say name of partner.
	FEEDBACK: "Great job!"	
	ASK: "What is our third step, [student name]?"	"Make the request."
	FEEDBACK: "Superb!"	
	ASK: "Will you show me how you will ask for a new pencil, [student name]?"	"May I have a new pencil?"
	FEEDBACK: "Very good!"	
	SAY: "Everyone take turns asking your partner for a new pencil."	Practice asking for a new pencil.
	ASK: "What is our last step, [student name]?"	"Say thank you."
	FEEDBACK: "Great work!"	
	SAY: "Show me that step everyone!"	Students say "thank you" to partner.
	FEEDBACK: "Very good everyone!"	
Independent Practice	SAY: "Now I am going to have you practice by yourselves. When I come to you, I will ask you to make three requests. While you are waiting, turn to a partner and practice making requests for a piece of paper, a drink of water, or something out of their lunchbox."	
Closing	SAY: "Excellent job today! Today we learned how to make a request. Tomorrow morning we will review and practice how to make requests again. Then I will be watching to see how many of you make requests the way we've learned when you want or need something."	

Checklist:

Name: _____

	Look at the person.
	Get their attention.
	Make the request.
	Say thank you.

	Look at the person.
	Get their attention.
	Make the request.
	Say thank you.

	Look at the person.
	Get their attention.
	Make the request.
	Say thank you.

APPENDIX G: *SAMPLE SCRIPTED LIFE SKILLS LESSON PLAN*

Topic	Restaurant Skills
IEP Objective	Given the opportunity, students will enter a restaurant, verbally order from the menu, calculate the tip, write a tip amount, total the bill, and pay for the meal with 100% accuracy on 3/3 trials.
Lesson Objective	Given 12 sample restaurant bills with the subtotal of the meal, students will calculate and write the tip amount with 10/12 correct.
Materials	Timer Review and independent practice worksheets Calculators for each student Write steps on the board: 1. Look at the receipt. 2. Find the subtotal. 3. Multiply the subtotal by .15. 4. Write the tip amount.

Lesson Component	Teacher's Instruction, Questions, Feedback, and Sample Error Correction	Anticipated Student Responses
Attending Cue	SAY: "I'm going to turn on the timer to 3 minutes to see if we can beat the timer in putting away our materials and prepare for our next lesson. You will need your calculators and a pencil." [Turn on timer. Praise students if they beat the timer.]	Students clean up and get out their calculator and pencils.
Review	SAY: "Yesterday we practiced multiplying amounts of money by decimals with our calculators. I am going to give you a review sheet with problems just like the ones we did yesterday. You can use your calculators. Do your very best!" Teacher passes out review sheet and monitors students as they work. SAY: "Great job everyone! Please hand in your review sheets."	Students complete review sheet.
Anticipatory Set	ASK: "Who has a favorite restaurant?" SAY: "I have a favorite restaurant too. Turn to your neighbor and tell them your favorite restaurant and why it's your favorite."	Students raise hands. Students share their favorite restaurant.
Prerequisite Check. Instruction and Purpose Statement	SAY: "When we eat at restaurants, we have to pay for the food. But we also need to pay the waiter or waitress for helping us." ASK: "Who do we pay for helping us?" FEEDBACK: "Very good!" SAY: "The money we pay a waiter or waitress is called the *tip*." ASK: "What do we call the money we pay a waiter or waitress?" FEEDBACK: "Excellent!"	"The waiter or waitress." "The tip."

(Continued)

(Continued)

Lesson Component	Teacher's Instruction, Questions, Feedback, and Sample Error Correction	Anticipated Student Responses
	SAY: "The cool thing about a tip is that we get to figure out how much we pay for the tip by ourselves."	
	ASK: "What do we get to figure out?"	"How much we pay for a tip."
	FEEDBACK: "Very good!"	
	SAY: "The normal amount for us to pay for a tip is 15% of the price of our meal."	
	ASK: "What's the normal amount for us to pay for a tip?"	"15%"
	SAY: "Yes, it is 15% of the price of our meal."	
	ASK: "We need 15% of what?"	"The price of our meal."
	FEEDBACK: "Perfect!"	
	ASK: "Why do you think it's important to learn to pay the right amount of a tip?"	Possible answers: "So the waiter isn't mad." "To impress our date."
	FEEDBACK: "Those are all very good reasons to learn how to pay the tip."	
	SAY: "Today we are going to learn how to calculate the amount of money we will pay for our tip."	
	ASK: "What will we learn?"	"How to calculate the amount of money we will pay for our tip."
	FEEDBACK: "Very good! Let's get started."	
Instruction	SAY: "We just learned that the normal amount for a tip is 15% of the price of our meal."	
	ASK: "What's the normal amount for a tip?"	"15% of the price of our meal."
	FEEDBACK: "Very good!"	
	SAY: "We need to find 15% of the price of the meal. But there is no percent sign on our calculator. This is why we have to know how to multiply by decimals. When we find 15% of a dollar amount, we multiply the dollar amount by .15 [point one-five]."	
	ASK: "What do we multiply the dollar amount by?"	".15"
	FEEDBACK: "Excellent! We multiply by .15."	
	SAY: "The reason we multiply by .15 is because 15% written as a decimal is .15."	
	ASK: "What is 15% as a decimal?"	".15"
	FEEDBACK: "Good job! This is important for us to know when calculating the amount of money we will pay for a tip."	
Modeling	SAY: "When I calculate the amount of money I will pay for a tip, my first step is to look at the receipt."	
	ASK: "What is my first step?"	"Look at the receipt."
	FEEDBACK: "Yes, I look at the receipt."	

Lesson Component	Teacher's Instruction, Questions, Feedback, and Sample Error Correction	Anticipated Student Responses
	SAY: "My second step is to find the subtotal."	
	ASK: "What is my second step?"	"Find the subtotal."
	FEEDBACK: "Very good! I find the subtotal."	
	SAY: "To find the subtotal, I look for the word *subtotal* and look at the amount of money listed next to the subtotal. On this receipt, my subtotal is $26.04."	
	ASK: "What is my subtotal on this receipt?"	"$26.04"
	FEEDBACK: "Nice job!"	
	SAY: "My third step is to multiply the subtotal by .15."	
	ASK: "What is my third step?"	"Multiply the subtotal by .15."
	FEEDBACK: "Very good! I will multiply the subtotal by .15."	
	SAY: "Because my subtotal was $26.04, I will multiply that by .15. So I take my calculator and I type in 26.04 x 0.15 =. And then the calculator gives me an answer."	
	SAY: "My last step is to write the tip amount."	
	ASK: "What is my last step?"	"Write the tip amount."
	FEEDBACK: "Excellent everyone! I need to write the tip amount."	
	SAY: "When I hit the equal button on my calculator, it gave me my tip amount, or 15% of the price of my meal. Because that is my tip amount, I will write it on the line on the receipt."	
	ASK: "Where do I write the tip amount?"	"On the line on the receipt."
	FEEDBACK: "Very good! I write the tip amount on the line on the receipt."	
	SAY: "My tip amount for this one is 3.90. The calculator shows 3.906, but when we use money, we only go to two decimal places."	
	ASK: "How many decimal places do we go to?"	"Two places."
	FEEDBACK: "Excellent!"	
	SAY: "Now I will write my tip amount on the line, which is $3.90. And that is how I calculate the amount of money I will pay for my tip."	
	[Teacher follows same script to model one to three more examples, depending on student responses. Possible subtotals: $18.01, $22.94, and $11.25.]	
Guided Practice	SAY: "Let's do one together now. Please get out a piece of paper to use."	
	ASK: "What is our first step everyone?"	"Look at the receipt."
	FEEDBACK: "Great, let's look at this receipt on the board."	
	ASK: "What is our second step?"	"Find the subtotal."

(Continued)

(Continued)

Lesson Component	Teacher's Instruction, Questions, Feedback, and Sample Error Correction	Anticipated Student Responses
	FEEDBACK: "Yes, we need to find the subtotal."	
	ASK: "Will you come up to the board, [student name], and point to the subtotal?"	Points correctly to $18.98.
	FEEDBACK: "That's correct."	
	ASK: "What is our third step, everyone?"	"Multiply the subtotal by .15."
	FEEDBACK: "Good job! We multiply the subtotal by .15."	
	SAY: "I want you all to use your calculators and multiply the subtotal by .15."	
	ASK: "What do all of your calculators say?"	"2.847"
	FEEDBACK: "Very good everyone!"	
	ASK: "What is our last step?"	"Write the tip amount."
	FEEDBACK: "Very good! We need to write the tip amount."	
	ASK: "How many decimal points do we go to for our tip amount?"	"Two"
	FEEDBACK: "Nice job!"	
	SAY: "Write the tip amount on your paper."	**Student writes 28.47**
	SAMPLE ERROR CORRECTION	
	SAY: "We don't move the decimal for the tip. We just use two decimal places." [Point to the decimal point and review how $2.84 means 2 dollars and 84 cents. And that we can't go any lower than that so we ignore the 7.]	
	ASK: "If we calculated a tip to be $3.832, what would be the actual tip?"	**"3.82"**
	FEEDBACK: "That's correct." [Practice with additional examples if needed.]	
	ASK: "Back to our original problem, what amount did we write on our paper?"	"$2.84"
	FEEDBACK: "Very good! That is our tip amount!"	
	SAY: "We are going to do one more together."	
	ASK: "What is our first step, [student name]?"	"Look at the receipt."
	FEEDBACK: "Very good! Look at this receipt on the board."	
	ASK: "What is our second step, [student name]?"	"Find the subtotal."
	FEEDBACK: "Excellent. Everyone find the subtotal."	
	ASK: "What is our third step, [student name]?"	"Multiply the subtotal by .15."
	FEEDBACK: "Very good!"	

Lesson Component	Teacher's Instruction, Questions, Feedback, and Sample Error Correction	Anticipated Student Responses
	SAY: "Give me a thumbs-up when you finish that step." ASK: "What is our last step, [student name]?" FEEDBACK: "Excellent job!" ASK: "Will you all write the tip amount on your piece of paper?" FEEDBACK: "Great job everyone!" [Repeat script as needed, depending on student responses.]	"Write the tip amount." Students write tip amount on piece of paper.
Independent Practice	SAY: "Now you're ready to calculate the tip on your own. "[Hand out independent practice worksheet.]" Remember to follow all four steps and work carefully. Raise your hand when you finish the first row so I can come check." Teacher walks around to monitor students while they work.	Work on independent practice worksheet.
Closing	SAY: "Today you learned how to calculate the amount of money we will pay for a tip. Tomorrow we will use what we learned today to figure out how much total money we will pay when we go to a restaurant." FEEDBACK: "You did an amazing job today!"	

Independent Practice Worksheet

Receipt 1:

Items	$3.50
	$4.99
	$6.32
Subtotal:	$14.81
Tip:	_____

Receipt 2:

Items	$5.75
	$8.31
	$11.25
	$10.68
Subtotal:	$35.99
Tip:	_____

Receipt 3:

Items	$7.81
	$6.13
	$7.48
Subtotal:	$21.42
Tip:	_____

Receipt 4:

Items	$9.99
	$5.60
	$9.38
	$12.15
	$8.63
Subtotal:	$45.75
Tip:	_____

Receipt 5:

Items	$5.75
	$12.14
	$12.73
Subtotal:	$30.62
Tip:	_____

Receipt 6:

Items	$8.25
	$6.99
	$4.26
	$5.00
Subtotal:	$24.50
Tip:	_____

(Continued)

(Continued)

Receipt 7:		Receipt 8:		Receipt 9:	
Items	$7.31	Items	$2.25	Items	$9.50
	$4.05		$3.01		$3.49
	$7.88		$4.21		$2.15
Subtotal:	$19.24	Subtotal:	$9.47		$7.04
Tip:	_____	Tip:	_____	Subtotal:	$22.18
				Tip:	_____

Receipt 10:		Receipt 11:		Receipt 12:	
Items	$8.11	Items	$8.31	Items	$7.00
	$11.42		$4.97		$6.26
	$6.24	Subtotal:	$13.28		$4.08
	$10.13	Tip:	_____		$9.83
	$6.60			Subtotal:	$27.17
Subtotal:	$42.50			Tip:	_____
Tip:	_____				

GLOSSARY

ABC recording: method in which the observer records anecdotally all of the events (antecedents, behaviors, and consequences) that occur within the setting over several observation periods

Abstract instruction (in mathematics): the use of symbols, including numeric, algebraic, statistical, and geometric

Academic difficulties: students with high-incidence disabilities all demonstrate academic difficulties but cannot receive special education services unless their difficulties hamper their educational experience

Accommodation: an adaptation that makes the general curriculum or assessment accessible to the student without changing the curriculum or learning standard

Achievement tests: tests that measure student performance on knowledge and skills typically taught in school such as reading and math

Acquisition: first stage of learning in which students acquire the knowledge or skill being taught

Acronyms: a mnemonic strategy; the first letter of each piece of information is used to create another word or words to facilitate recall

Acrostics: a mnemonic strategy; the first letter of words in a list are used to create new words to represent a phrase or sentence to facilitate recall

Active engagement: the amount of time students are actively engaged in learning tasks that are instructionally appropriate

Activities-based instruction: instruction based on concrete, hand-on experiences

Adaptation: an overarching term that encompasses both modifications and accommodations in differentiated instruction

Advance organizer: verbal or written technique used to activate prior knowledge about a topic and provide a general description of the entire lesson

Allocated time: amount of time in the school day allocated, or set aside, for instruction

Alternative teaching: co-teaching in which one teacher selects a small group of students to be instructed in a way that is different from the larger group

Americans with Disabilities Act (ADA): a U.S. law signed in 1990 and amended in 2008 that prohibits discrimination and ensures equal opportunity for persons with disabilities in employment, State and local government services, public accommodations, commercial facilities, and transportation; also mandates the establishment of TDD/telephone relay services

Antecedent: a stimulus or event that precedes a behavior

Anticipatory set: part of a lesson introduction intended to entice students in learning the content of the lesson

Applied Behavior Analysis (ABA): application of the principles of behavior and verification of those principles through systematic record keeping and decision-making procedures

Assessment: process of using any tool or technique to measure student performance and behavior to make educational decisions

Assistive technology (AT) devices: any item, piece of equipment, or product system that is used to increase, maintain, or improve the functional capabilities of a student with a disability

Assistive technology service: any service that directly assists a student with a disability in the selection, acquisition, or use of an assistive technology device

Attention: the ability to concentrate on a particular stimulus

Attention–deficit/hyperactivity disorder (ADHD): persistent pattern of inattention and/or hyperactivity-impulsivity that interferes with functioning or development; considered a disability although not covered as a disability in IDEA.

Attribution: how an individual explains the causes of his or her successes and failures

Autism: a developmental disability significantly affecting verbal and nonverbal communication and social interaction, usually evident before age 3, which adversely affects a child's educational performance

Aversive stimulus: a stimulus that typically results in pain or discomfort and may produce escape or avoidance behavior

Baseline data: data collected prior to the implementation of an intervention

Behavioral modeling: demonstration of a skill in a direct instruction lesson

Bibliotherapy: the use of literature as a catalyst to help facilitate changes in students' thoughts, feelings, and behaviors

Big ideas: the major ideas, concepts, or principles that are taught and that serve as anchors for additional or more information

Blended learning: instruction is delivered in a mix of in-person and online; the most common is the flipped classroom model

Cardinality: knowing the number of objects in a set

Categorical approach: grouping students by their disabling condition for instruction and other services

Classroom ambiance: the atmosphere of the classroom

Classwide Peer Tutoring (CWPT): a reciprocal peer tutoring program designed to be used classwide; competition and reinforcement are part of the implementation

Cognition: conscience mental activities, such as thinking, learning, and remembering

Cognitive modeling: self-talk that assists students in understanding the thought processes of the person modeling

Collaboration: an interactive style between at least two coequal individuals who share decision-making responsibility while working on a common goal

Common Core State Standards (CCSS): define what students should be able to know and do at certain benchmarks of their schooling experience

Competitive employment: work that takes place in community-integrated settings where the employee receives at least minimum wage, interacts with coworkers without disabilities, produces valued goods or services, and has opportunities for increased earnings and responsibilities

Computer-assisted instruction (CAI): instructional materials that are delivered by the means of computer technology; includes presenting new knowledge in a tutoring-like session, providing drill-and-practice opportunities, or simulation activities

Concepts: the fundamental structure for thoughts and ideas

Concrete instruction (in mathematics): manipulating objects to represent numerals and operations

Consequences: events that follow the occurrence of a behavior

Conspicuous strategies: learning strategies made explicit by the teacher or the curriculum materials (e.g., textbook)

Consultation: one professional, the consultant, helps another professional in addressing a problem related to a third party, usually a student

Content (in differentiated instruction): what students should know, understand, and do as a result of instruction

Content Enhancement Routines (CERs): instructional routines designed to support student comprehension of content by linking effective instruction with a visual device or organizer (e.g., graphic organizers, mnemonic devices, advanced organizers)

Content-specific vocabulary: words for discussing, reading, or writing specific expository information

Contingency contract: written document indicating the contingencies for reinforcement

Continuous schedule of reinforcement: reinforcement is delivered for every occurrence of the behavior

Continuum of services: the range of services or placements available for students with disabilities from least to most restrictive

Cooperative learning: a set of instructional strategies that facilitate student-to-student interactions in small groups to accomplish shared goals while maintaining individual accountability

Co-teaching: two credentialed professionals teaching the same group of students together; can take place with two teachers, or a teacher with another school professional (e.g., speech therapy can take place with two teachers, or a teacher with another school professional e.g., speech therapist)

Creative comprehension: creatively extending the author's message (e.g., putting oneself in the story line, predicting what may happen after the story has ended)

Criterion-referenced assessment: indicates student's performance relative to a specified criterion level or standard

Critical comprehension: critiquing the author's writing to determine if it is fact or opinion, fiction or nonfiction, possible or not possible

Cross-categorical approach: grouping students in an educational setting based on instructional needs of students, not disability category

Culturally and/or linguistically diverse (CLD): students from backgrounds of other languages or cultures

Culturally responsive teaching: methods that support CLD students' cultural and linguistic backgrounds integrated with evidence-based instructional practices

Curriculum: the content being taught, but may also include state- or district-wide standards students are expected to achieve and goals and objectives identified on student IEPs

Curriculum-based assessment (CBA): formal or informal teacher-made assessments based on the curriculum taught in the classroom

Curriculum-based measurement (CBM): a formal CBA that uses standard procedures and includes timed tests and charting of student performance

Curriculum integration: combining objectives, activities, and outcomes across disciplines instead of teaching isolated content

Data-based decision-making: the use of student performance data to evaluate current progress and to recommend necessary changes in instruction and interventions

DIBELS (Dynamic Indicators of Basic Early Literacy Skills): set of procedures and measures for assessing the acquisition of early literacy skills from kindergarten through sixth grade

Differential reinforcement of other behavior: procedure in which problem behavior is put on extinction while another incompatible desirable behavior is reinforced

Differentiated instruction: proactively planning and implementing strategies that match instructional content, process, and product to a student's differences in readiness, interest, and learning needs

Direct Instruction: commercially-produced instructional programs based on effective evidence-based teaching principles

Direct instruction: generic effective evidence-based teaching principles

Distance learning: delivery of instruction to an individual student who is not present in a traditional classroom

Domain-referenced tests: representative questions or performances are selected from a larger domain of skills or knowledge

Duration: length of time in which the student engages in the behavior

Duration recording: method in which the observer measures the duration of a behavior with a stopwatch

Education for All Handicapped Children Act (EAHCA): original special education law that was signed in November 1975 and required states to provide services to all children and adolescents regardless of their disabilities; title changed and now is referred to as the Individuals with Disabilities Education Act (IDEA)

Elementary and Secondary Education Act (ESEA): original law that provided federal support to elementary and secondary education; in 2001 became the No Child Left Behind Act (NCLB); and in 2015 the Every Student Succeed Act (ESSA).

Emotional/behavioral disabilities (EBD): characterized by behavior or emotional responses in school so different from appropriate age, cultural, or ethnic norms that they adversely affect educational performance (i.e., academic, social, vocational, and personal skills)

Emotional disturbance: the label used in IDEA to identify students with EBD characteristics

Emotional regulation: the ability to identify and label emotional states and then decide if and how to act on the emotions

Engaged learning time: the time during which students are attending to relevant instructional activities with a high rate of success

English Learner (EL): a student whose first language is not English and who has limited English proficiency such that he or she needs additional support to benefit from general education instruction; also called English language learner (ELL)

Entrepreneurship: a form of competitive employment where the student (often with help of family members or adult-service agencies) creates his or her own small business

Ethnicity: affiliation of a group of people who have the same sociological or cultural factors, such as nationality, religion, socioeconomic class or linguistic origin

Event recording: method used to record the frequency of a behavior within a specified period of time

Every Student Succeeds Act (ESSA): the new name of Elementary and Secondary Education Act (ESEA); changed to this during the 2015 revisions

Evidence-based interventions or practices: instructional methods and interventions that have demonstrated effectiveness through research and are based on strong theoretical principles

Expository text: writing that conveys information, such as textbooks and nonfiction books

Externalizing behaviors: observable behaviors that include aggressive, noncompliant, argumentative, hyperactive, impulsive, and disruptive behaviors

Extinction: when a behavior that was previously reinforced is no longer reinforced and the behavior decreases in the future

Fixed ratio (FR) schedule of reinforcement: reinforcement is delivered after a specified number of correct responses

Flipped classroom: students receive teacher-directed instruction online as homework and then engage in practice and application during class time

Fluency: the skill of reading accurately, at an appropriate rate, and with expression

Formal assessment: assessment involving pre-identified test items and/or observation procedures that must be administered using standardized procedures

Formative assessment: assessments frequently administered throughout learning to guide the teaching and learning process

Free and appropriate public education (FAPE): all children must be afforded the opportunity to attend school and that schooling must be provided at public expense

Frequency: number of times the behavior occurs

Function of student behavior: reason why the student engages in the behavior

Functional behavior assessments (FBA): assessment method in which data are gathered about the antecedent conditions and consequences related to a behavior in an attempt to determine the function of the behavior

Generalization: ability to use learned knowledge or skills in a setting outside of where the skill was learned

General vocabulary: commonly used words for everyday speaking, reading, and writing

Good Behavior Game (GBG): a form of token economy where groups of students earn and lose points based on how well they follow classroom rules

Graphic organizer: visual representation of knowledge that arranges facts and concepts in an associative organization

Group homes: a residential home in which several individuals with disabilities live together with at least one trained caregiver who is available 24 hours a day

Group processing (in cooperative learning): involves the group deconstructing and reflecting on the members' actions that helped or hindered goal attainment and making decisions about what actions to continue or change

Guided notes: outlines and/or graphic organizers with blank spaces in which students can write main ideas, vocabulary, concepts, and/or relationships

Guided practice: portion of direct-instruction lesson when students perform the task along with the teacher who provides prompts throughout

High-functioning autism (HFA): individuals with autism who demonstrate significant social interaction difficulties and unusual patterns of behavior or interests but have average or above-average intellectual ability

High-incidence disabilities (HID): disabilities that occur in more than 100,000 people in the United States: learning disabilities (LD), emotional/behavioral disorders (EBD), mild to moderate intellectual disabilities (ID), high-functioning autism (HFA), and attention–deficit/hyperactivity disorder (ADHD)

High-stakes assessments: assessments used to establish whether or not students have met district or state standards and sometimes used to determine if students graduate or are advanced to the next grade level

IEP process: set of procedures outlined in IDEA that governs how school districts provide special education and related services

IEP team: develops the IEP and evaluates student's progress; members consist of school professionals as well as student's parents

Implementation fidelity: a measure of whether the intervention was delivered as it was designed to be implemented; also referred to as treatment fidelity

Inclusion: integration of students with disabilities into general education classrooms

Independent living: living with minimal reliance on others in making decisions and performing everyday activities

Independent practice: end of a direct-instruction lesson when students are expected to perform the task independent of the teacher or with no prompts

Individual accountability (in cooperative learning): requiring that all students be held responsible for learning the material, as well as for contributing to the group

Individualized Education Program (IEP): written document developed by parents and school personnel that details services and goals related specifically to the student's educational needs

Individuals with Disabilities Education Act (IDEA): Legislation passed in 1975 to ensure that children and adolescents with disabilities have the same opportunity to receive a free appropriate public education as other students through special education and related services

Inferential comprehension: understanding the inference the author is communicating

Informal assessment: assessments included in daily and weekly instructional routines

Intellectual disabilities (ID): significantly subaverage general intellectual functioning, existing concurrently with deficits in adaptive behavior and manifested during the developmental period that adversely affects a child's educational performance

Intelligence tests: standardized tests used to assess a student's general intelligence

Interdependence: individuals are linked with each other, and in order for the individual to succeed, the group needs to succeed and vice versa

Interdependent living: the concept that all individuals depend on others for various aspects of living such as tax preparation, medical and health care, household maintenance, and so forth. All individuals have some degree of interdependence

Intermittent schedules of reinforcement: reinforcement is delivered following some, but not all, occurrences of the behavior

Internalizing behaviors: behaviors that are covert, inwardly directed; manifestations may include acting fearful or sad, not participating or interacting with others, and low activity level

Interval recording: method in which the observation period is divided into equal intervals during which the observer records whether the behavior did or did not occur at any time during the interval

Interval schedule of reinforcement: reinforcement is delivered if the behavior occurs during a specified interval of time

Intrinsic motivation: learner acts, participates, or behaves because of curiosity or desire to succeed, contribute, or participate

Jigsaw: a cooperative learning structure in which team members read their assigned section of the material, then meet with members of different teams who have been assigned the same material; students then return to their original teams and teach their teammates about their section

Judicious review: structured opportunities for the student to recall or apply previously taught information, which is distributed over time, cumulative, and varied

Keyword: a word that sounds similar to a piece of information to be recalled that can be easily visualized (e.g., pen for Pennsylvania)

Latency: length of time between when instructions or directions are given to perform and the occurrence of the behavior

Latency recording: method in which the observer measures the latency of a behavior such as using a stopwatch

Learned helplessness: students with a history of failure believe they are incapable of learning

Learning disabilities (LD): a disorder in one or more of the basic psychological processes involved in understanding or in using language, spoken or written, which disorder may manifest itself in the imperfect ability to listen, think, speak, read, write, spell, or do mathematical calculations

Least restrictive environment (LRE): students with disabilities are to be educated with students without disabilities to the maximum extent possible

Literal comprehension: understanding directly what the author is communicating

Living support: periodical visits are made by an adult-services worker to help the resident with tasks such as shopping, paying bills, making appointments, or other areas in which the resident may need assistance

Local Education Agency (LEA): usually the equivalent of the school district; a representative from which must be present at the IEP meetings

Maintenance: ability to retain the knowledge or skill over time without reteaching

Mediated scaffolding: instructional guidance provided by teachers, peers, curriculum materials, or task given to students as they acquire new information

Memory: the ability to recall information or experiences

Mentoring: an experienced and skilled teacher provides new teachers with the technical and emotional support needed to successfully begin and continue their careers

Metacognition: broad general awareness and knowledge of cognition (what we know) and cognitive processes (how we know)

Mnemonic: technique or device for improving or strengthening memory, for example, acronyms, acrostics, rhymes, keywords, and pegwords

Modeling: part of instruction where the teacher models the lesson objective through behavioral demonstration and/or self-talk

Modification: an adaptation that involves changes in the curriculum or learning standard

Morpheme: smallest unit of language that has meaning

Motivation: the need or desire that causes someone to act or behave

Multidisciplinary team: group of professionals and student's parents who determine whether a student qualifies for special education or related services and the student's educational needs; usually the same as the IEP team

Multitiered interventions: varying and increasing levels of instructional or behavioral supports that are provided in usually three tiers; students who are not successful in Tier 1, for example, receive more intensive services in Tier 2 and so forth

Multitiered systems of supports (MTSS): an umbrella term that describes an implementation framework for schools to ensure all students are provided high quality core instruction and the necessary supports when students are not succeeding

Narrative text: writing that tells a story, whether real or imaginary, with characters, a plot, and setting

Negative reinforcement: an aversive stimulus is removed from the environment following the occurrence of a behavior, which increases the future likelihood of the behavior

No Child Left Behind Act (NCLB): law that was originally the ESSA and is now ESEA; required that all students learn to grade level standards

Nondiscriminatory assessment: using evaluation methods that are nonbiased and multifaceted when diagnosing the student's disability and providing appropriate program plans and educational placements

Nonreciprocal peer tutoring: peer tutoring in which tutors and tutees do not exchange roles

Norm-referenced assessment: identifies an individual's performance relative to a group of individuals

Number sense: the ability to understand numbers, numeric relationships, and how to use numeric information to solve mathematic problems

Numbered Heads Together: a cooperative learning structure in which groups of about four work together to answer questions, and then one member of the group is randomly called on to answer for the group

Numerically powerful students: use procedural strategies accurately and know how to make sense of numerical and quantitative situations

Online learning: delivering instruction through computer networks

Other Health Impaired (OHI): IDEA disability category that renders students eligible for special education services if they have limited strength, vitality, or alertness that is due to chronic or acute health problems and adversely affects a child's education performance

Overcorrection: student is taught the correct behavior through an "exaggeration of experience" (two forms of overcorrection: restitutional and positive-practice

Paraeducators: school employees who, following appropriate training, perform tasks as prescribed and supervised by the teacher or other licensed school professional

Parallel teaching: co-teachers jointly plan, but they deliver instruction separately to one-half of the classroom

Parental participation: one of the six guiding principles of IDEA

Peer-Assisted Learning Strategies (PALS): a peer-tutoring program that uses highly structured activities, high rates of responses between tutor and tutee, and reciprocity of roles

Peer coaching: process through which two or more professional colleagues work together reflecting on current practice, building or refining new skills, sharing ideas, conducting action research, teaching one another, and/or problem-solving

Peer tutoring: a student of the same chronological age or grade level tutors another student

Pegword: words that sound like numbers and can be easily visualized are paired with keywords to facilitate recall (e.g., one = bun)

Person-first language: referring to individuals with disabilities by defining the individual first and the disability second, thus focusing on the person rather than the disability

Phoneme: smallest unit of sound in a language

Phonemic awareness: recognition that spoken language can be broken down into phonemes

Phonics: the ability to match sounds to letters in order to read and write

Portfolio assessment: assessment measure in which students create a portfolio of work to display their best work, show growth or progress, or demonstrate the completion of a goal or benchmark

Positive Behavioral Interventions and Supports (PBIS): framework that incorporates multitiered interventions and supports by focusing on preventing student behavior difficulties, as well as intervening quickly when problems do occur

Positive reinforcement: a consequence that maintains or increases a behavior when it is delivered contingent upon the occurrence of that behavior; can increase or maintain both desired and undesired behaviors

Positive-practice overcorrection: following an occurrence of a problem behavior, the student must exhibit an exaggerated practice of the appropriate behavior

Postsecondary education: includes any program whose emphasis is further education or institutional-based vocational and technical training and includes 2- and 4-year colleges and universities, private vocational schools, apprenticeship programs, and trade or adult education programs

Premack principle: a behavior that has a high probability of occurring may be used as a reinforcer of an activity that has a low frequency of occurrence

Present Levels of Academic Achievement and Functional Performance (PLAAFP): statement at the beginning of an IEP that refers to the student's current academic and functional strengths and limitations and the skills to be improved

Primary reinforcers: reinforcers that are biologically important to an individual (i.e., food and water)

Primed background knowledge: exists when the curricular materials take advantage of students' previous knowledge

Procedural due process: protects the rights of parents and the school district when disagreements arise related to identification and placement decisions for students with disabilities

Process (in differentiated instruction): how the content will be taught and learned

Product: the manner in which the student will be evaluated, usually in the form of tests, projects, written work, or oral presentations

Prompts: assistance provided to increase the likelihood of the student responding correctly

Pull-out programs: students with disabilities remain in the general education classroom except for a portion of the day in which they are pulled out to a resource classroom

Punishment: a change in a stimulus or event after the occurrence of a behavior that decreases the future probability of that behavior

Race: a human characteristic based on biological factors.

Rate: ratio of frequency over time

Ratio schedule of reinforcement: reinforcement is delivered after a behavior is exhibited a specific number of times

Reciprocal peer tutoring: a pair of students switch roles between being the tutor and the tutee

Reinforcement: a change in a stimulus or event after the occurrence of a behavior that increases the future probability of that behavior

Reinforcer: a consequence that increases or maintains the previous response or behavior

Related services: developmental, corrective, and other supportive services needed to assist a student with a disability to benefit from special education (i.e., speech-language pathology, physical therapy, counseling services)

Reliability: the degree of accuracy and consistency of test scores or other assessment measures

Representational instruction (in mathematics): teacher uses visual representations such as tally marks, dots, picture, and so forth

Response cost: the removal of specific amounts of positive reinforcement contingent upon the occurrence of a particular behavior

Response-duration schedule of reinforcement: reinforcement is delivered if the behavior is exhibited for the duration of a specified interval of time

Response to Intervention (RTI): a multitier system of support in which at-risk students with academic problems receive increasingly intensive support

Restitutional overcorrection: following an occurrence of a problem behavior, the student must restore the disturbance caused in the environment and improve upon it

Reward accountability (in cooperative learning): refers to group members receiving rewards based on a total of individual contributions

Rubric: assessment scoring method that provides scoring criteria with a rating scale or checklist to evaluate the student product or performance on forms of work that are difficult to grade

Scaffolding: providing high levels of teacher support as students learn a new skill then gradually fading to independent student work

Schedule of reinforcement: the frequency with which reinforcement is delivered

Screening: a systematic way of identifying students who may need additional support in academics or social-emotional learning

Secondary reinforcers: reinforcers that have acquired reinforcing effects by being paired with primary reinforcers

Section 504 of the Rehabilitation Act: a law passed in 1974 that banned all federally funded programs from discrimination against persons with disabilities

Selective attention: ability to select the appropriate stimuli, focus on those stimuli, and ignore all other irrelevant stimuli

Self-management: encompasses many procedures in which students participate actively and take responsibility for their own behavior and learning (e.g., self-assessing, self-recording, self-regulating)

Semantics: meaning of words

Service learning: an instructional strategy that integrates meaningful community service with instruction and reflection with the goals to enrich the learning experience, teach civic responsibility, and provide community service

SETT Framework: framework to use during assistive technology consideration that focuses the IEP team on the *s*tudent, *e*nvironment, *t*asks, and *t*ools

Sheltered employment: usually entails working in a segregated center like a sheltered workshop or adult day program; employees receive subminimum wage, and have little, if any, contact with coworkers without disabilities

Social and emotional learning (SEL): the way individuals manage emotions and appropriately identify and respond to the feelings of others

Social competence: the interpersonal skills necessary to be accepted and fulfilled socially.

Social skills: the personal skills needed for successful social interactions and relationships (e.g., beginning a conversation, negotiating, and coping with being left out)

Socioeconomic status: a measure of a person or family's social and economic status in relation to others

Special education: specially designed instruction that meets the unique needs of a student with a disability; most commonly includes academic, social-emotional, and/or life skills instruction

Speech-to-text recognition: technology that synchronously transcribes text from speech input and displays the text on a whiteboard or computer screen

Standardized tests: tests with structured materials and systematic procedures for the administration, scoring, and interpretation of results

Station teaching: co-teachers divide the instructional content and take responsibility for teaching it simultaneously to smaller, rotating groups within the larger classroom

Strategies: how students think and act when planning, executing, and evaluating their performance while completing an academic task or solving a problem

Summative assessment: administered at the end of instruction to demonstrate how much a student has learned

Supervised apartments: apartments in which support staff is available close by but are only present in the resident's home a few hours a day for support and training in daily living skills and for interpersonal and recreational skills training

Supported employment: work that is performed in an integrated setting at least 20 hours a week, wages are paid, and on-going training and support (e.g. job training, interpersonal skills) is provided on-site

Supported eText: electronic text that is modified or enhanced to increase reading comprehension or enhancing students' ability to learn from text

Supported self-employment: training and support provided in an integrated paid work environment

Syntax: sentence structure and the arrangement of words in sentences

Systematic phonics teaching: teachers use explicit sequential instruction to model and teach sound-spelling relationships, and then carefully monitor associated student application to reading and writing

Task accountability (in cooperative learning): refers to each student being accountable to the team for her portion of a team project

Task analysis: breaking a task into smaller manageable parts or steps, teaching steps as separate objectives, and then combining all steps to complete the entire task

Team teaching: co-teachers share planning for and instruction of all students

Testing: administration of a predetermined set of questions or tasks for which predetermined responses are sought

Text comprehension: ability to understand and use information that is read

Text-based instruction: instruction is based on text materials, usually a textbook that students are expected to read independently to gain information

Textbook enhancements: teacher practices that help the organization of content information to facilitate students' comprehending and recalling information from the textbook

Think-Pair-Share: a cooperative learning structure in which each student thinks about the answer, then shares it in pairs, and then shares it with the group of about four

Tier 1 (in MTSS): the universal or primary tier; all students are involved in Tier 1 interventions and support

Tier 2 (in MTSS): secondary or targeted academic or behavior interventions for at-risk students who did not respond to Tier 1 strategies

Tier 3 (in MTSS): tertiary, prevention or intensive intervention for at-risk students who did not respond to Tier 2 strategies

Time-out: denying a student access to the opportunity for reinforcement for a fixed short amount of time contingent upon the occurrence of a particular behavior

Time sampling: method in which the observation period is divided into equal intervals in which the observer records whether or not the student engaged in the behavior at the end of the interval

Token: object or symbol that has little to no reinforcing value alone, but takes on value when paired with a positive reinforcer

Token economy: behavior-management system in which students earn tokens for exhibiting certain behaviors, which can later be exchanged for back-up reinforcers

Transition services: a coordinated set of activities for students with disabilities focused on improving their academic and functional achievement to facilitate moving from school to post-school activities, which can include postsecondary education, employment, independent living, and community participation

Unit: a learning experience that takes place over several days or weeks, is broader in scope than daily lessons, and incorporates multiple learning objectives

Unit Organizer: a way in which a unit of study can be structured; includes elements such as a unit map, unit questions, and unit schedule, among others

Universal Design for Learning (UDL): designing and using instructional materials that allow the instruction goals to be achieved by a wide range of students regardless of their abilities

Universal screening: collecting data on all students to assess risk status, which can help determine which level of tiered supports a student needs

Validity: the degree to which the assessment instrument measures what it was designed to measure

Variable interval (VI) schedule of reinforcement: reinforcement is delivered if the behavior occurs during an interval of time that varies around a specified average interval

Variable ratio (VR) schedule of reinforcement: reinforcement is delivered after a number of responses that varies around a specified average number

Video modeling (VM): instruction delivered through video clips in which an adult, a peer, or self as model demonstrates a behavior being taught

Video self-modeling (VSM): instruction delivered through video clips in which self as model demonstrates a behavior being taught

Visual perception: ability to perceive and understand accurately what you see

Vocabulary: knowledge and use of words that make up a language

Zero Reject: no child may be excluded from public education because all children can learn and can be taught, regardless of the severity or nature of their disability; included in IDEA

INDEX